CRISIS:
IN THE THIRD WORLD

"For beginners: You haven't missed much yet . . .
The world crisis is only just beginning".

"I've worked myself up from nothing
to a state of extreme poverty."

GROUCHO MARX

CRISIS:
IN
THE THIRD WORLD

Andre Gunder Frank

Holmes & Meier Publishers

New York • London

First published in the United States of America 1981 by
Holmes & Meier Publishers, Inc.
30 Irving Place
New York, N.Y. 10003

Library of Congress Cataloging in Publication Data

Frank, Andre Gunder, 1929–
   Crisis: In the Third World.

   Bibliography: p.
   Includes index.
   1.   Underdeveloped areas. 2.   Economic history—
1945–   3.   International economic relations.
I. Title.
HC59.7.F685   1980   330.9172'4   80–23944
ISBN 0–8419–0584–3
ISBN 0–8419–0597–5 (pbk.)

Manufactured in the United States of America

Contents

Preface

This book, as well as its companion volume, *Crisis: In the World Economy* (abbreviated as WE), examines the development of the new economic and political crisis in the world. According to my dictionary, a crisis is a decisive turning point, filled with danger and anxiety, possibly meaning life or death for a diseased person, social system, or historical process. The outcome need not necessarily be death, but could be new life, if—in our case—the economic, social, and political body is able to adapt and to undergo a regenerative transformation during its time of crisis.

Both books are part of a global study of the contemporary development of a deep and widespead economic, social, and political crisis in the world, which seems to be centered on a new crisis of overaccumulation of capital in the capitalist West, and on the consequent transformation of its relations with the socialist East and the underdeveloped South. This book examines the position of the Third World South in the global crisis, and the more general companion volume (WE) traces the crisis's development in the West, East, and South. Each book can be read separately, if the importance of the interrelations in the global economic system, whose initiating force remains in the West, is kept in mind. Although the problems dealt with in both books are very serious, it has been my intention to employ an analysis and to write in a language that any interested reader can understand.

Crisis: In the Third World distinguishes between the principal kinds of Third World economies and the different modifications of their participation in the world economy under the impact of the crisis. These are principally the intermediate development in the seven major semiperipheral economies of Brazil, Mexico, Argentina, India, Iran, Israel, and South Africa (which are examined individually in Chapter 1); the economies in which agricultural export, especially through agribusiness, is important (Chapter 2); and the economies promoting other exports of manufactures, oil, and minerals, as well as the expendable regions with very few exports (Chapter 3). The analysis then turns to some features and processes that are more or less common to all of these Third World countries despite their differences: the increase in foreign debt (Chapter 4) and its burden, paid through the greater exploitation of the local population; the increasing superexploitation of many members of the labor force in the Third World (Chapter 5); political economic repression (extensively documented in Chapter 6), which is necessary to sustain this exploitation and superexploitation; the transformation of the state (Chapter 7) as one of the principal instruments of the adoption of the Third World and its population to its new world roles, as well

as the militarization of society and other emerging forms of institutionalization; and, finally, the growing arms economy and military conflict in the
Third World (Chapter 8). A concluding Chapter 9 (similar to the conclusion
in WE) summarizes the above argument in the context of the development of
the crisis also in the West and East and poses some questions about
socialism and nationalism in a single world system, which only the future can
answer.

The research for this book (as well as for WE) and the preparation of the
material took several years. Therefore, one, two and sometimes three years
lapsed between writing and/or revising different parts of this book. Chapter 1
was written in 1977 and 1978, but because its country surveys are time-
bound, they have been updated to the beginning of 1980. The data on Third
World exports, debt, and military activities were updated in 1980 (often with
a two-year or more lag in the data available from official sources) although
the bulk of these chapters was originally written in 1976 and 1977. The
analyses of the structural evolution of the economy, society, and states of the
Third World have been left substantially as they were written in 1976 to
1978. Only minor amendments in the presentation of new facts were made,
since most of the argument can stand on the earlier material. Thus, most of
the empirical material in this book refers to the mid 1970s, but new data have
been added where possible if recent events have warranted updating. In short,
this book examines some of the major economic transformations that the
Third World is undergoing both today and possibly in the future under the
impact of the world economic crisis. The book tries not only to document and
analyze the political processes and institutions involved, but to take account
of the differential social costs and benefits of these transformations as well.

Crisis: In the World Economy (WE) examines the development of the
effects of, and the responses to, the world economic and political crisis in the
industrial capitalist countries of the West, including "Western" Japan in the
"socialist" countries of the East, and in the Third World capitalist underdeveloped countries of the South. The book begins (WE: Chapter 1) with a
review of the expansive boom years of the two decades following World War
II. WE: Chapter 2 traces the cyclical development of the new crisis of capital
accumulation in the industrial capitalist West since 1967. WE: Chapter 3
reviews and in part tries to preview the corresponding political economic
responses of capital, labor, and the state in recent and coming years. This
chapter places particular emphasis on the policies of economic austerity and
the deliberate creation of unemployment by social democratic governments,
as well as on the growth of political repression and the apparently (accelerating) political and ideological shift to the right nearly everywhere in the
West. In the presentation of this development in WE: Chapter 2 and 3, I
have chosen to alternate successively between the recording of a particular
historical event, such as the recession of 1970, and the analysis of a
particular major problem, such as the recession of 1970, and the analysis of a
particular major problem, such as unemployment. Each problem is discussed

in connection with the period during which it first arose, even though it may have already existed or become more serious later, as in the case of unemployment both during and after the recession of 1973–1975. After analyzing such a problem, I go on to record what happened during the next historical period of the crisis's development, before turning again to the analysis of another problem that is particularly associated with the later period and so on throughout the book. WE: Chapter 4 examines the accelerating integration of the socialist economies of the Soviet Union, Eastern Europe, China, Korea, and Vietnam in the capitalist international division of labor in part as a response to the crisis of the capitalist system, which affects these economies and societies as well. WE: Chapter 5 examines the demands by spokesmen for the Third World for a "new international economic order" (NIEO) and considers the somewhat unfavorable prospects for its realization. A sixth and summary chapter reviews and previews the entire development of the crisis in the West, East and South. Though substantially written earlier, the text of WE is updated through the end of 1979 and the concluding chapter takes account of some development in early 1980. Thus, *Crisis: In the World Economy* offers a review of some of the important contemporary economic, social, and political developments that the new world crisis is generating in all three parts of the world—the West, East, and South.

Both books are the outgrowth of my work on the history—including the present as history, to borrow the felicitous phrase of Paul Sweezy (1953)—of capital accumulation on a world scale (as Samir Amin [1970] calls it) and of dependent accumulation in the so-called Third World. Already in 1965 I wrote in the preface to my *Capitalism and Underdevelopment in Latin America* that there is "the need . . . for the development of a theory and analysis adequate to encompass the structure and development of the capitalist system on an integrated world scale and to explain its contradictory development which generates at once economic development and underdevelopment" (Frank 1967: xv). My own attempt to contribute to this theory and analysis did not begin until 1970 in Chile, when I started to write the book now published as *World Accumulation 1492–1789* (Frank 1978a). The coup in Chile and other considerations interrupted this historical account of world accumulation at the beginning of the industrial revolution. At the same time, my conviction grew that the capitalist world had entered another major crisis of capital accumulation. I had expressed this opinion publicly in 1972 (see Frank 1977c, Chapter 1). This conviction also persuaded me that the analysis of current events is now increasingly urgent. I therefore decided to embark on a study of the two centuries since the industrial revolution in order to write a second volume to complement the one mentioned above by beginning at the end, that is, today, and working backward. This work on "today" began in 1973, and it has continued on the contemporary and just-past events ever since. However, I became so engaged in, and absorbed by, the contemporary crisis, that most of the historical work came to be relegated to some time in the future, although I did brush up on part of the historical study of the underdeveloped countries within the world economy until the present, which was published under the title *Dependent Accumulation and Underdevelopment* (Frank 1978b).

Thus, my intention to analyze two centuries of world capital accumulation, became, under the increasing influence of the new world economic and political crisis, a study spanning some two decades past, present, and future of that crisis itself. However, although I tried to analyze the crisis in the world or at least in the capitalist world, process of capital accumulation as a whole *in theory*, in practice my study seemed increasingly to dwell on the industrial West, the socialist East, and the underdeveloped South each taken individually, albeit in relation to each other. In the case of the "socialist" countries, I did not try to study the internal structures of their societies as much as their economic relations with the West and South and the political implications of these relations, particularly for the Third World. My study of the effects of the world economic crisis on the South and the corresponding modifications of the economic participation and political response of the Third World became so extensive (though by no means complete) that it is now published separately as this book. To a significant extent, this separate treatment of the Third World thus violates in practice the fundamental theoretical guideline of this study, which is to analyze the world economic or at least capitalist system as a whole. Of course, the recent developments in the Third World and its parts are herein analyzed as part of a historical process in the world as a whole; but often these developments are presented separately as though they were analyzed in and of themselves. This procedure constitutes an important practical and theoretical limitation, which I believe it is my duty to stress.

Since the parts of the world system are presented separately in each of these books, it is perhaps appropriate to stress here how much of what goes on in each part of the world should be regarded as the various parts of a single process. The overaccumulation crisis of world capitalism manifests itself for capital through a decline in the rate of profit. Like the previous crises through which capitalism passed in the past two centuries, this one can only be resolved through far-reaching and basic modifications in the international capitalist division of labor. For capital this exigency presents itself as the need to reduce costs of production in order to raise profits again. Therefore, capital tries to administer several remedial economic measures simultaneously to the world economic body. Some of these are the austerity policies, rationalization of production processes, and reorganization of work processes in the industrialized West. Others involve the accelerated incorporation of the East through increased trade, but even more significantly by producing in the socialist countries with technically qualified but cheap labor for the capitalist world market. Other economic measures include the "runaway" transfer of some manufacturing industries to the Third World and the increased superexploitation of many parts of the labor force in the South, which are directly and indirectly engaged in the production of manufactures and primary goods as well as services for the world market of capital. All these are complementary and mutually reinforcing measures to confront the same crisis of capital. The corresponding political policies of increasingly conservative social democratic governments and authoritarian tendencies in the West, of uneasy détente and negotiated collaboration between the West and the East, and of military and other authoritarian states and more acute armed conflict in the Third World are the necessary political instruments and manifestations of the aforementioned economic crisis responses by capital and its states. The social, political, and ideological response of labor and other sectors of society to this challenge by capital to restructure capitalism will determine whether, how, and to what extent capitalism will overcome its present crisis and go on to another later period of expansion.

If labor and the population at large are not willing to accept and bear the costs of the new capitalist order that capital is trying to impose on the world, and if these people successfully rebel against this order, then this crisis of capitalism would be its undoing and a really new noncapitalist order would emerge from the crisis. The reading of reality in the pages that follow suggests that, though the measure of social conflict within and between some states is likely to increase, the prospects of such a change are not very large for the forseeable future. (They are perhaps best in the "socialist" countries of Eastern Europe, which are least examined in these books.) For this reason also, without fundamental political change within the participating countries, the "new" international economic order that some Third World spokesmen demand among nation states is at best likely to turn out to be the same old order in some new emperor's clothes. Their design and measure, however, may well be the result of strategic and military disputes between the East and West that unfortunately remain unexamined in this book except partially insofar as they are carried over into the South.

Some readers may think that the superexploitation and repression in the Third World during the present crisis contradicts the thesis of the "development and underdevelopment" (Frank 1966, 1969), according to which underdeveloped satellite economies fare less badly during a crisis in the center. But on the one hand that thesis was not meant to suggest that every part of the periphery develops more during a crisis in the center, and some semiperipheries are shown (Chapter 1) to experience a new development—or underdevelopment—today. On the other hand, Chapters 7 and 8 and WE: Chapter 5 suggest that other parts of the periphery may still come to fare less badly during the present crisis, if this economic crisis or its political and military manifestations get so serious as to lead to a substantial breakdown of the international division of labor.

The scope, method, and sources of this study may seem to some readers like an unholy mixture of a superficially worldwide sweep with very selective local detail, of scientific (at least pretendedly so) objectivity with (certainly intentional) political engagement, and of standard official statistics with a wide variety of stray newspaper clippings. In part these combinations may be explained, if perhaps not justified, by my work substantially as a "loner" in physical isolation from a library that could offer permanent access to standard reference and research materials and maybe in intellectual isolation from the pressing or fashionable concerns of some institutions and currents of thought. I have sometimes tried to break through this isolation through occasional quick flights to talk with, and collect documentary material from, people at the UN Economic Commission for Europe (UNECE) and UNCTAD in Geneva, the OECD in Paris, the EEC Common Market Commission in Brussels and other institutions (whose abbreviations, like all others used here, are listed under Abbreviations at the end of the book), and to engage in longer political discussions with friends and comrades around the world from Bombay to Belgrade, Lisbon to London, Mexico to Montreal, and Tokyo to Tananarive, as well as the many who passed through Frankfurt and stopped to visit.

In part my scope, method, and sources are, however, also the deliberate (and I hope justified) attempt of a single concerned person to confront some, though certainly not all, of the pressing issues of the day with the objective scientific *and* common-sense regard guided by conscious political concern. The examination in historical perspective of these contemporary events and processes, some of which are evident to the naked eye and others less so, is meant to be expository—and sometimes denunciatory—but not prescriptive. I am trying to "tell it as it is" and not as we might or might not like it to be. I am not trying to say—at least not in these pages—what we should, or would have to, do to change things so as to make them the way we want them to be. Of course, I am also partial; but my—or our—partiality should not blind us, as it unfortunately and often even deliberately does, to reality as it is.

For this reason also I have relied very heavily on the daily press for my sources of information (the list of abbreviations identifies over one hundred periodical publications and their respective abbreviations. Some of them I have cited only a few times in the text and others hundreds of times, like the *International Herald Tribune*, which is abbreviated IHT and is published in Paris by the *New York Times* and the *Washington Post*). This does not mean that I regard the press as entirely truthful or infallible. On the contrary, more often than not it has a political and ideological ax to grind; and I have tried to put that ax to good use. Thus, I have sought to rely on spokesmen of business, like *Fortune* (FOR), *Business Week* (BW), *The Financial Times* (FT), *The Economist* (ECO), and *Business International* (BI) or its various regional newsletters (BA, BE, BLA) and other sources, such as official government documents or declarations, as sources that are relatively "unimpeachable" spokesmen or reflections of business and government action or opinion. For instance, the extensive documentation of political repression for economic reasons, recorded in Chapter 6 for some thirty countries all around the Third World, is almost entirely provided—and deliberately selected—from the business, "bourgeois," and local press as well as from official government documents or declarations, such as that which begins, "Now, therefore, I, Ferdinand E. Marcos, President of the Philippines . . . decree. . . ." On the other hand, though I have had much less access to documentation from the socialist countries themselves, the analysis of their willing and anxious participation in the capitalist international division of labor is based on the evidence supplied by responsible official and other sources and is accompanied by at least a selection of quotations to that effect by their most authorized spokesmen, such as Leonid Brezhnev and Hua Guofeng and others.

Similarly, the analysis—and, if you will, denunciation—in WE: Chapter 3 of the deliberate deflationary policy of austerity and unemployment in one Western country after another is not only documented by, but verily distilled from, the reports and declarations of the most authorized officials and political representatives and spokesmen of these Western governments, such as the Organisation for Economic Cooperation and Development (OECD), President Carter and his Cabinet members and Prime Ministers Callaghan and Thatcher of Britain, Schmidt of West Germany, and Barre of France, as well as news coverage and editorial opinion about their policies by the *New York Times* (NYT), the London *Financial Times* (FT), and many other organs of the press. When I have needed statistical series over a longer timespan, I have taken them from United Nations, OECD, U.S. government, and other similar official sources insofar as they were available to me (without direct access to a library); or sometimes, if necessary, and especially for data on the most recent times, I have again relied on the press for reports or summaries of such information provided by these agencies and others such as the European "Common Market" Economic Commission (EEC) in Brussels. I have mined these sources for statistical data and other information, but this book is not intended to be a compendium of such sources or to compete with them and other texts as a complete catalogue of statistical data, other information, and their exhaustive analysis about the world or any of its parts or processes. Moreover, the cutoff date for the use of current material necessarily varied from one book and chapter to another, although I have updated them as explained above.

Finally, I believe there is some further method in this madness of so laboriously—and it is that unless one can rely on an institutional clipping service—reading through, discarding the chaff and selecting the grain, of clipping, filing, evaluating, and using this information from the press. It shows that, despite all of the many indisputable limitations and failures of the press, it is possible to mine it for hidden golden information, if one is mad enough to work out—and systematically work through—a method to smelt and refine these bits and pieces of golden information out of masses of ore and to compare and cross-check them before combining them as in a jigsaw puzzle, until a picture emerges that more or less objectively reflects reality. In short, much of what is recorded in the following pages is the result of an often maddening but hopefully useful exercise in methodical newspaper reading.

For the historian—be it of the past or of the present, or for that matter of the future—reading "yesterday's newspaper," contrary to the old adage, need not be "out of date."

It is a pleasure and an honor to be able to acknowledge gratefully the institutional and financial support of several organizations and the personal help and encouragement of friends associated with the same. When this work began in Chile, I was at the Centro de Estudios Socio-Economicos (CESO) of the University of Chile; several of my then colleagues and political compañeros have continued to encourage me although they are themselves now in exile all around the world. For the winter semester 1973–1974 I was at the Lateinamerikainstitut of the Freie Universität Berlin, where my interest in the crisis continued to grow. Between May 1974 and July 1975 I had the privilege of being a Visiting Research Fellow (Freier Wissenschaftlicher Mitarbeiter) at the Max-Planck-Institut in Starnberg, West Germany, although I was only physically present there until August 1975. The Institute's administrative and scientific councils and particularly its director, Professor Carl-Friedrich von Weizsäcker, extended continuing generous support to me and my research, including full financial support for a year, without asking for—or receiving—any tangible or visible return. The staff of the Institute library, like Ms. Mundorf and others, especially Ms. Karen Friedman and Ms. Ulla Enders, were of incalculable help in supplying me with research materials; particularly since they have tried to bridge the 450-kilometer distance that has physically separated me from the Institute since mid 1975. Folker Fröbel, Jürgen Heinrichs, and Otto Kreye, to whose project at the Institute I was formally attached, have extended me their completest personal friendship and scientific and practical help as well as their indispensable moral support, to work on "the crisis," even though in their own book (Fröbel et al., 1977) from which I have copied so much, they started out denying that there is any crisis at all.

From May 1975 to April 1978, while still formally a guest at the same Institute in Starnberg, I received generous full-time financial support for my research from the Deutsche Gesellschaft für Friedens-und Konfliktforschung (DGFK), for my proposed research project on "Capital Accumulation, Economic Crisis, Social Conflict and International Relations." At the DGFK I had the friendly support of the chairman of its Research Commission, Dr. Karlheinz Koppe, as well as that of other members like Dr. Dieter Senghaas and Mr. Kreye, who were burdened with reading my interminable "progress" reports. Dr. Humberta Wienholz, Mr. Norbert Ropers, and Ms. Ursula Semin-Panzer of the DGFK administrative staff good-naturedly put up with my frequent appeals to straighten something out for me (that I had usually twisted myself). I am most grateful to all of them for their support and confidence, as well as this long financial support, particularly since they were still extended when it already became apparent that I would not be able to fulfill all of the perhaps unrealistic promises that I had held out in my original research proposal. For the three months from May to

July 1978, I gratefully acknowledge the supplementary financial support of the Berghof-Stiftung and its scientific director, Dr. Senghaas, and board member, Dr. Heinrichs, which permitted me to complete the original draft of this study after I should already have finished it, and particularly to write the chapters on the economic and political crisis in the industrial West. For editorial help (to eliminate some of my many errors, confusions, and inconsistencies) and for typing I am particularly grateful to Ms. Yolanda Broyles, Ms. Barbara Wraight and Mr. Matthias Fienbork.

Since August 1978 as professor at the University of East Anglia in England, I have enjoyed the institutional support of my School of Development Studies (DEV) and the financial support of its Consolidated Research Fund. I have taken advantage of both to use the invaluable services of Ms. Jill Hodges and Ms. Leyla Strutt for the copy editing and reproduction, respectively, of individual chapters on these books as DEV discussion papers, of Ms. Jackie Spray and again Ms. Barbara Wraight for retyping them, and of Ms. Corinna Chute and most especially Ms. Sheila Pelizzon in managing the extremely laborious tasks of clipping, filing, and retrieving the innumerable press clippings and other current sources that I have drawn on to update these books in 1979 and 1980. At Holmes & Meier, I am grateful to my publisher, Max Holmes, for his extraordinary confidence in me and his interest in my project; to my editor, Nathan Laks, for his very intelligent and useful editing and general supervision of these books under the pressure of time; and to the copy editor, Carole Freddo, for the responsible but vast improvement once again of the style and readability of this book, which merits the thankfulness of both the author and the readers.

Last but certainly not least I am grateful for the personal, moral, and political support of my wife, Marta Fuentes, whom I superexploited to do bibliographies, clip newspapers (and then find them again) and varied other dirty work on this book, as well as in our home where I worked, and my sons Paulo and Miguel, whose personal and political appreciation of my "work on the crisis" have helped me maintain the hope, which may be an illusion, that there may be some sense to the work it has cost me and the very great sacrifices it has cost them. Though in one or another fit of temper I have now and then been tempted to blame one or another of the above named for some minor shortcoming in my work, deep down I realize and gladly acknowledge publicly that the major shortcomings in this book, of which I am overly aware, are my own or the results of my own crisis. And for the latter I can only offer the partial explanation—and plead for partial dispensation—that it is *the* crisis that engulfs us all.

A.G.F.
Frankfurt, 17 July 1978
Norwich, 6 March 1980

Chapter 1

Unequal Accumulation: Intermediate, Semiperipheral and Subimperialist Economies

Capitalist development and capital accumulation are always spatially unequal and temporally uneven. Each major crisis of accumulation forces major structural readjustments in the international division of labor. The major Third World economies, which differentiated themselves from others in the Third World in the interwar economic crisis and seem to be reacting in important new ways during the present crisis, are examined individually. Recent and prospective developments in the intermediate, semiperipheral, or subimperialist economies of Brazil, Mexico, Argentina, India, Iran, Israel, and South Africa are each examined in turn.

Saudi Arabia, Iran, Brazil and Mexico, as "major new powers," should be brought into the "inner circles" of international decision making on economic affairs.

Trilateral Commission (IHT 19 August 1976)

Unequal Accumulation in the Third World

Capital accumulation and capitalist development are and always have been spatially/sectorally unequal and temporally uneven. Moreover, it is one of our principal hypotheses that the qualitatively major differentiations or radical shifts in spatial/sectoral development tend to occur during, and are accelerated by, the periodic crises in the temporally uneven development. Our hypothesis is that the contemporary crisis of world capitalist capital accumulation will also be marked by noteworthy departures in unequal spatial/sectoral development. An important feature of this unequal development will likely be the further division of the world capitalist economy into old and new metropolitan centers of powers, differentiated intermediary economies, colonial and neocolonial economies and client states, and economically expendable populations, regions, or whole countries.

The "major new powers" selected by the Trilateral Commission for inclusion in the inner circle of economically and politically intermediate powers are Saudi Arabia, Iran, Brazil, and Mexico. South Africa and Israel are potential candidates for inclusion, and India and Argentina are heavily potential candidates. In a different way, so is the Soviet Union (and perhaps some other socialist economies; see Chapter 4).

According to a Trilateral Commission paper:

> The so-called "Third World" has become at least three worlds—the oil-producing countries . . . the relatively well-off developing countries with other valuable resources or a growing industrial base (i.e. Brazil, Malaysia, Mexico, Zaire), and the "have-not" developing countries such as those in the Indian Subcontinent. . . (cited in FER 25 March 1977: 40).

The world capitalist economy has always been characterized by the unequal development of declining old and rising new leading economies or metropolitan centers, new developing and old underdeveloping intermediate economies, peripheral economies, and, for a long time, by various societies that were effectively outside the world economy. Leadership in world capitalist development passed from northern Italy in the fifteenth and sixteenth centuries (perhaps briefly via parts of the Iberian peninsula) to England in the eighteenth and nineteenth centuries and to the United States in the twentieth century. Leadership and power passed from the old center to the new one principally during periods of crisis to which the old center was unable to adjust. Thus Mediterranean Europe was replaced by Britain—which outcompeted Holland and then France for power—in the seventeeth-century crisis, and Britain, was, in turn, replaced by the United States, which won the competition with Germany in the crisis after 1873 and this century's long crisis between 1914 and 1945. First Britain and then the United States were able to adjust to, and eventually to profit from, the economic and political crisis that affected the capitalist system as a whole.

Capital accumulation and capitalist development have since their beginnings also included intermediate as well as "peripheral" economies. Wallerstein (1974) calls these formations "semiperipheral" and Marini (1974) has termed some of the contemporary ones "subimperialist." These semiperipheral and/or subimperialist economic centers do more than occupy an intermediate place between the center and periphery of the capitalist international division of labor. According to both Wallerstein and Marini and his followers, these intermediate powers act as political intermediaries—in a role analogous to that played by the "middle classes" between capital and labor—in the unequal bargaining between the metropolitan center and its periphery. Wallerstein suggests this intermediary role is both useful and necessary if the metropolitan center is not to pay too high a political or military price for its effective domination of the periphery. The

"Nixon Doctrine" of inducing geopolitical and military powers to police their respective regions by having "Asians fight Asians," and the Trilateral Commission's proposal to include some major new intermediary powers in the inner circle of world capitalist governmental decision making (at least formally), are two contemporary examples of the central economic powers' reliance on intermediate states to maintain the dependence of the periphery.

The development of intermediate, semiperipheral economies and powers, both through the "rise" from the periphery and more rarely through the "decline" at the center, seems historically to have accelerated during periods of crisis in world capital accumulation. Sometimes this development has been extended during subsequent periods of economic expansion. For instance, Eastern Europe (east of the Elbe) and the Iberian peninsular powers may be termed economies that declined to intermediate and intermediary semiperipheral positions in the seventeenth century (Wallerstein 1974; Frank 1978a). Thus the intermediary role played in the eighteenth century by the rising semiperipheral Northeast and Middle Atlantic American colonies in the "triangular" trade between Europe, the slave plantations of the Caribbean and the U.S. South, and the sources of slaves in Africa was crucial for the capital accumulation and capitalist development of the United States in the nineteenth century (Frank 1978a,b).

The passage of the United States from the status of semiperipheral economy to leading central power was unique. The United States not only replaced British leadership, which declined relatively after 1873 and absolutely after 1914, but also outpaced the rival economies of Germany, Japan, and semiperipheral Russia. These three countries simultaneously accelerated their growth in the last three decades of the nineteenth century, and Germany and Japan unsuccessfully challenged the U.S. bid for leadership during the crisis period of the two world wars and the interwar depression of the twentieth century.

It has been argued that during the contemporary crisis period these same three economic and political powers are again challenging U.S. economic and political power, whose dominance appears to be declining, at least relatively, just as British dominance declined during the crisis a century ago. The British economy is now threatened by an absolute decline to semiperipheral or even underdeveloping near-peripheral status. In return for an International Monetary Fund (IMF) $3.9 billion loan to "support the pound sterling," Britain has had to accept conditions usually meted out only to "banana republics" and other underdeveloped peripheral countries.

During the last major crisis of capital accumulation and capitalist development of the interwar period, but particularly during the Great Depression of the 1930s and the wartime 1940s, unequal capitalist development generated the growth of "import substitution" in parts of Brazil, Argentina, Mexico, India, and (with special conditions) in South Africa, and after the war (under very particular circumstances) in Israel. These economic and political units, and to a much lesser extent some others elsewhere in the

Third World, came to occupy an intermediate place and to play a semi-peripheral role. In South Africa and to a lesser extent in Rhodesia and Israel this development was complicated by the special oppressive relation between the European settlers and the local population and the political and military roles of the former in their respective regions. For these regions, and because of the peculiarity of their economic dependence on the metropolitan powers and the apparent structural similarity of their economies to those of the center, South Africa and Israel are often classified as "remote" metropolitan central economies (for South Africa, see, for instance, Amin 1977a).

During the period when depression reduced metropolitan demand for primary raw material exports (and in India and Brazil during the period of war-induced foreign demand for some of their industrial commodities) these economies turned to the partial substitution of imported industrial goods by nationally produced ones. Though concentrated in consumer goods (particularly textiles), this industrial growth through "import substitution" included the production of (e.g. textile) machinery and some capital goods, especially steel. The decision to produce industrial consumer goods for the internal market made it imperative to provide a part of the population with purchasing power sufficient to buy these goods. Accordingly, there was a good economic reason to distribute income somewhat more equally so that textile workers, for instance, could afford some of the textiles they produced. For this reason, import substitution provided the economic rationale for a political alliance between the "national" bourgeoisies and petite bourgeoisies and organized labor in the progressive/nationalist "populist" movements associated with Getulio Vargas in Brazil, Cardenas in Mexico, Peron in Argentina, and Gandhi and his successor Nehru in India.

"Import substitution" of consumer goods did not, however, replace all imports with independent local production. This policy really meant substituting some imports for others, since it was still necessary to import the intermediate goods needed to make these consumer goods. Thus when raw material prices and export earnings declined after the Korean War it became increasingly difficult to maintain the "import-substituting" industries, which were dependent on foreign inputs, without recourse to additional sources of foreign exchange.

Accordingly, the mid-1950s witnessed a series of devaluations followed by a renewed push to export primary goods in order to earn foreign exchange. These actions were accompanied by invitations to foreign investors to produce locally for the internal market. In some cases, changes of government and a realignment of class alliances had to precede these modifications in policy. The realignment was based on a greater share of power by local producer-exporters of raw materials and, increasingly, foreign capital, along with the national capital that became the latter's junior partner.

Moreover, as the possibilities for the simplest import substitution became exhausted in the limited internal market, the economic basis for the populist alliance with labor was eroded and replaced by an increasingly regressive distribution or concentration of income. This measure and the reduction of real wages were necessary to create a high-income upper-middle-class and state market, as well as an incipient export market, for the durable consumer and capital goods now produced by national capital in alliance with foreign capital and local primary goods producers-exporters.

This crisis in import substitution and its resolution since the 1960s (which

differed from one country to another according to internal and external political circumstances) has been exhaustively analyzed, especially for the Latin American countries, in the voluminous literature on dependence and new dependence.

Those intermediate economies that through the "import substitution" policy advanced in productive capacity to a stage of capital accumulation based on the production of machinery and other capital goods, are now among the principal candidates for semiperipheral participation in the international division of labor.

Most advanced in this direction is Brazil, whose development since 1968 received the baptism of "subimperialism" by Ruy Mauro Marini (1974) and "associated development" by Fernando Henrique Cardoso (n.d.) and others. To a lesser degree, both terms may be applied to Mexico as well; and these two countries are among the four that the Trilateral Commission study recommended for inclusion in its inner circle. Israel and South Africa are, in effect, already members of this charmed circle, the first for political and strategic reasons, the second for economic and strategic reasons, though it may not be politic to say so in black and white. Argentina has been unable to keep pace in this competition because of the bourgeoisie's inability so far to discipline the working class sufficiently, though the military regime that took control on April 23, 1976, has been making a renewed effort to do so. The Indian bourgeoisie opted for economic and political engagement with the Soviet Union to counterbalance Western capitalist ties (which may explain India's absence from the Trilateral list even though its state of development is comparable to that of Brazil and Mexico). But the Indian option for Soviet-supported state capitalism has thus far failed to resolve the crisis of capital accumulation that India, like Argentina, has suffered since the mid 1960s.

The other candidates for intermediate, semiperipheral, and subimperialist status are the new petroleum-producing economies and their reactionary political regimes. Iran and Saudi Arabia are at the head of this list, where the Trilateral Commission report put them.

Brazil, Mexico, Argentina, India, Iran, Israel, and South Africa are each discussed in detail below. The place of the socialist economies in the capitalist international division of labor merits a chapter apart (WE: Chapter 4).

Brazil

The most spectacular and widely heralded intermediate or semiperipheral and so-called associated or subimperialist country in the Third World is Brazil. The "economic miracle" of the "Brazilian model" has been recommended by Nobel laureate Milton Friedman (among many others) as a guide to other Third World countries on all continents and even to "Great" Britain. During his 1975 official visit to Brazil Henry Kissinger proclaimed Brazil an "emerging power" and singled it out among Latin American countries as meriting the privilege of "prior consultation" by the United States in matters of common concern. (By the time of Kissinger's visit the "miracle" was already over, and for his own reasons President Carter rescinded Brazil's privileged status.)

The Brazilian response to the problems created by declining prices for raw materials in the mid-1950s was, under the presidency of Juscelino Kubitıchek, to encourage the massive entry of foreign capital. This made it possible for Brazil to enter the age of automobile production while concomitantly expanding its steel industry. Between 1956 and 1962 GNP rose at an annual rate of nearly 8 percent and a per capita rate of 4 percent. Real wages, however, declined every year after 1958 (except in 1961, the first year of the Goulart government). Then the boom turned into a recession; between 1962 and 1967 GNP grew at only 3.7 percent annually or 1.3 percent per capita. Goulart's timid policy of seeking an end to the crisis by progressive expansion of the internal market through land reform and other populist measures as well as export promotion was reversed by the military coup of March 31, 1964. The economic recession continued through 1967. Income was concentrated to restructure the market and production for the "economic miracle" that began in 1968. Census data show that between 1960 and 1970 the highest 5 percent of income recipients saw their annual income increase from $1645 to $2940 and their share of national income rise from 27 percent to 36 percent; the lower 80 percent of income recipients saw their share decline from 45 percent to 37 percent, and the poorest 40 percent of the population endured a reduction in share of national income from 22 percent to 9 percent, or to $90 per capita. Since 1970 this concentration of income has been aggravated still further. By 1975 real minimum wages had been cut to 29 percent of the 1958 level and 45 percent of the 1964 level. (BD n.d.: 4,19; see also Cardoso n.d.; Oliveira 1973; Arroio 1976.)

The "economic miracle" began in 1968 and lasted through 1973, after which Brazil found itself in a crisis related to the world recession. The boom was "led" by the automobile industry and other durable consumer goods destined for the domestic high-income market concentrated among five million consumers (5 percent of the population). It was accompanied by an expansion of the capital and intermediate goods industry and new or newly developed production of some agricultural and livestock products, and it was supported by massive state (including military) demand, which had been particularly vital during the years of continued recession through 1967, as well as by growing exports. These developments were orchestrated by multinational capital, to which the Brazilian economy became more subservient than ever.

From 1968 to 1974 Brazilian GNP grew at a sustained annual rate of 10 percent and industrial production at 11 percent. Between 1969 and 1972 the output of clothing and footwear grew only 1 percent, and that of textiles declined by 4 percent; much of this production was diverted from the domestic to the export market. Exports sextupled between 1964 and 1975, rising from $1430 million to $8200 million. The share of the traditional coffee exports, however, declined from over one-half to less than one-quarter of total exports, while the export of other primary products, such as iron ore, its derivatives, and particularly meat (from 1 percent to 5 percent of total exports) and soy beans and sugar, increased both absolutely and relatively. The most spectacular increase was registered by manufactures or industrial products, which rose from 7–10 percent to 15–20 percent (depending on the definition) of total exports that themselves sextupled. While the relatively more sophisticated industrial exports have found a market within Latin America, the simpler consumer goods are destined primarily for the United States and Western Europe. These exports include machinery and automotive vehicles and parts (including Volkswagen engines for assembly into finished cars in the United States), and semiprocessed industrial raw materials and chemical products, but the majority of manufactured exports are the labor-intensive textile, clothing, and footwear products, "processed" instant coffee, and other simpler goods. There is some dispute about what share the multinationals and their affiliates have of these "Brazilian" exports. Marini (1974), Córdova (1975), and others argue that it is high—well over 50 percent for many products—and Cardoso (n.d.) says that it is low, and that much of the export is by smaller Brazilian firms that cannot compete adequately on the domestic market. What is beyond dispute is that the multi- or transnational monopolies control a very substantial part of Brazilian industry through mixed enterprises with national and state capital—90 percent in motor vehicles, 80 percent in rubber, 70 percent in machinery, 60 percent in electrical and communications equipment, and 50 percent in food, textile, and nonmetallic minerals industries—and that international agribusiness is rapidly entering Brazilian agricultural production. This integration of the Brazilian economy into the international division of labor through transnational, state, and national capital production of technologically advanced industrial products for the domestic market and state demand as well as for export is only one side of the coin.

The other side is the concomitant increase in the import of technology, equipment, and intermediary inputs and "services" for transnational and other industry. These imports have risen even faster than export earnings and have been financed by foreign credits and a growing foreign debt, which has risen very much faster still. For despite—or really because of—the dependent nature of the advanced technology and sophisticated industrial production, the country still imports over 50 percent of the equipment needed for industrial production. For this and other reasons, while exports increased from $1.43 billion to $8.2 billion between 1964 and 1975, as observed above, imports increased from $1.25 billion to $12.2 billion. The balance-of-trade deficit thus reached $3.3 billion in 1975. Note this was only the *trade* deficit. On top of that there was a *financial* deficit of $3.2 billion on service account for the remission of profits, foreign debt service, and so forth. So the balance-of-*payments* deficit on current account was about $6.7 billion for 1974,

1975, and 1976. In 1977 Brazil enjoyed a small trade surplus, but in 1978 the trade deficit was about $1 billion, which grew to nearly $2.5 billion in 1979, largely because of increased imports of agricultural products in a bad crop year. On financial (profit remittance and debt service) account, the balance was increasingly negative, so that each year's balance-of-payments deficit was added to that of the preceding year.

Deficits on this order of magnitude can only be covered by a massive influx of foreign capital and loans. This explains why the foreign debt of Brazil rose from $4 billion in 1968 to $10 billion in 1972, to $22 billion in 1975, to an estimated nearly $30 billion—or three to four years' total export earnings—in 1976, and to $50 billion—or $40 billion of net foreign debt in excess of $10 billion of foreign reserves—by the end of 1979. The service costs of amortizing and paying the interest on this debt alone eat up about two-thirds of Brazil's entire earnings of foreign exchange from exports, compared to the about half of export earnings spent on imported oil at the new 1979 prices. (FT 16 October and 6 December 1979). No wonder that Brazil spends more than it earns and runs up ever more debts.

The narrow limits of the "economic miracle" and the fragility of the "Brazilian model" have become universally apparent since 1974 (indeed since the end of 1973), when several factors combined to bring the miracle to an abrupt end: the end of the expansive phase of a domestic cycle of capital accumulation begun in 1968; the rise in import costs due to increases in the price of imported petroleum on which Brazil is dependent (but which accounted for less than half the 1974 deficit) and world inflation, which affected the price of other imports; the reduced demand for Brazil's exports of manufactures and other products due to the world recession; the greater transnational hesitancy to expand investment during a period of recession; and the stringent conditions on which the necessary additional credits have been granted to Brazil. After the end of 1973 the annual growth rate of GNP declined by more than one-half to less than 4 percent in the mid-1970s and 5 percent in 1977 and 1978. To counteract the decline in the rate of profit, inflation doubled from the earlier yearly rate of about 15 percent to 30 percent in the mid-1970s and to 70 percent by 1979. Brazilian business circles agreed on "the need to review the model" (*Gazeta Mercantil* December 1975), but they disagreed on what political-economic remedy to impose: a more equitable and progressive distribution of income to expand the internal market for popular consumer goods again; or even stronger export promotion, with perhaps greater emphasis on processed and semi-processed agricultural and mineral raw materials and greater specialization in particular categories of industrial products. Since 1974 the main emphasis seems to have been on an uneasy compromise of import substitution, but increasingly of capital rather than consumer goods. And to pay for these imports and the increased costs of oil and debt servicing, the promotion of exports, including new agricultural products such as soya beans, has received the highest priority. Neither part of this combined strategy contributes significantly to a more equal distribution of income or a wider internal market. Instead, credit restrictions on installment purchases imposed in 1979 have been putting a damper on internal consumer demand.

Looking into a clouded crystal ball, the possibility of more progressive economic policies seems dim in a national economy that has long since passed through the stage of capital accumulation based on the production of consumer goods, and in a world economy in which the tendency in the international division of labor is clearly toward greater specialization in the production for export. Export promotion thus seems a more plausible policy and is likely to continue and even accelerate Brazil's development as an intermediary, semiperipheral, and subimperialist economy and power. The cost may be renewed political repression.

President Geisel introduced a *dictablanda* ("soft" instead of hard dictatorship), but he had to suspend proposed democratic reforms during the last part of his presidency as interbourgeois conflict about the choice of economic strategy to replace the worn-out "economic miracle" continued. To succeed him in the presidency, Geisel chose the head of military intelligence, General Joao Baptista de Oliveira Figueiredo, one of the most right-wing of the presidential candidates. Growing political opposition obliged President Figueiredo to allow a political thaw and even to declare an amnesty, which permitted the return of the most important political figures exiled since 1964. However, "the main objective of the Amnesty Bill [was] to split the Opposition as exiles return" (GUA 29 June 1979). The renewed economic crisis in 1979 and the fear of much worse to come—of "a slide back to 'banana economy' " (GUA 25 November 1979)—places a dark cloud over these modest democratic gains. The reappointment to the economic planning ministry of the wizard of the economic miracle, Antonio Delfim Neto, and his elevation to czar of the Brazilian economy while more progressive ministers were forced to resign suggest a renewal of the hard line.

The "Brazilian model" has had internal structural limitations that depend not only on its cyclical fortunes or misfortunes but also on the structure of the international division of labor. Since these are examined in greater detail in Chapter 3 they will be only summarized here. Briefly, the limitations of the Brazilian model are that its dependence on enterprise, state, high-income, and especially external demand does not promote the increase of the wage rate and the expansion of the internal market (as import substitution did) but instead requires the depression of the wage rate to make profitable production and competitive exports possible. The whole development is limited to between 5 percent and perhaps 20 percent of the population, while the other 80 percent (perhaps up to 95 percent) of the people are excluded by economic, political, and military force from all benefit and often from any participation. Fifty-six percent of Brazilians are "absolutely marginalized" and limited to basic food consumption; 75 percent of the population is "relatively marginalized" and confined to primary necessities only (*Gazeta Mercantil* December 1975). Roberto Campos, the Brazilian Minister of

Planning who laid the foundation for the Brazilian model after the 1964 military coup, observed that "the wage discipline of Brazil seems socially cruel, but it was the price that had to be paid to re-establish [its industry] to investment capacity in the public as well as the private sector" (ESP 1 December 1971, cited in Oliveira 1973: 462). Accordingly, assessments like the following have been made by numerous observers of the Brazilian model and its economic miracle:

Brazil: The Contradictions in the Economic Model
The Claws of the Multis Do Not Let Loose

The "model," moreover, shows three contradictions that have political explosive power: firstly, the de-Brazilianization of the economy is increasingly getting the upper hand, so that the power of decision is being transferred to the centers of international capital; secondly, the need for imported goods, foreign technology and foreign capital increases all the more the stronger the presence of the multinational becomes, which leads to an alarming increase in the Brazilian external debt; thirdly, the economic growth, which is oriented toward the needs of the minority, continually accentuates the social polarization: the poor remain poor and become more numerous all the time, the middle class remains thin, and the upper class enriches itself at a breathtaking speed (DAS 26 December 1976).

The government saw to it that, through the concentration of the growing wealth in the hands of only 20 percent of the population, an internal market for high income goods was increased. The tax and wage policy . . . increased the share of the 20 per cent in the national income from 54 to 62 per cent. The remaining 90 million Brazilians, on the other hand, don't even have enough means to cover their food needs. The Minister of Health himself called 40 million citizens "undernourished." A further 15 million people are unable to work as victims of epidemic diseases like chagas, leprosy and tuberculosis. Also infant mortality rises from year to year . . . (SZ 4–6 January 1976).

The most significant characteristic of the Brazilian model is its structural tendency to exclude the mass of the population from the benefits of accumulation and technical progress. Therefore, the durability of the system is in great measure based on the capacity of the governing groups to suppress all the forms of social opposition that its anti-social character tends to stimulate.

The model of Brazilian development is inseparable from a repressive policy: in order to guarantee the reproduction of the social inequalities on which the chosen kind of accumulation feeds, the regime is obliged to silence all those that would rise to protest (cited in CE August 1976: 921–23).

Dr. Hans Günther Sohl, President of the Federal Association of German Industry, particularly emphasized the excellent working climate [in Brazil], which is not limited by any strike, and the low wages in comparison to the Federal Republic [of Germany] (HB 17–18 August 1974).

The following scattered indices suggest some of the dimensions of the "social cost" of the Brazilian model. The number of hours of work necessary to buy a subsistence diet for a worker and his family (of five members, including himself) at the minimum wage was five and three-quarters hours in 1960, seven hours in 1965, and eight and one-half hours in 1970 (Arroio 1976: 38). According to another estimate, to buy a specific basket of basic consumption goods at the minimum wage, it was necessary to work 87 hours in 1965, 113 hours in 1971, 132 hours in 1972, and 155 hours in July 1974 (Souza 1975: 63). No wonder 15 to 30 percent of the people employed in various industries worked more than fifty hours a week according to the 1970 census (Arroio 1976: 40). Overtime work is obligatory on pain of losing one's job (a major threat with unemployment rates above 10 percent); it is a device used by employers to save on social security payments for additional workers. In São Paulo, the biggest industrial city in Brazil and indeed all Latin America, twelve hours of work seven days a week is not uncommon (Souza 1975), and according to the *Estado de São Paulo* (12 May 1976) in the Pernambuco sugar mills sixteen hours of work a day is usual to "compensate" for the low wages. When the regional delegate of labor ordered that working hours be held to a maximum of twelve hours a day, the president of the union "promised to close his eyes to noncompliance, because the decision will otherwise make workers suffer from hunger." This superexploitation explains why the accident rate at work rose from 18 percent in 1971 to 20 percent in 1973—that is, 1.6 million accidents, of which 13,000 were fatal and 50,000 were permanently disabling, for an economically active population of 8 million. In industry the average accident rate in 1973 was 30 percent, and in some branches it was even higher—for petroleum products, for example, it was 45 percent (Souza 1975: 66; Arroio 1976: 41). According to a technical report on road tunnel construction per kilometer, four dead is "ideal," six dead is considered medium risk, and eight dead represents high risk, while ten dead per kilometer implies that there are "no conditions for work" (Souza 1975: 71). This kind of superexploitation is not limited to male workers but extends to women and frequently to child workers. Disease, including tuberculosis, blindness from *chaga* bites, and other ailments, affects tens of millions of Brazilians and has risen over the years of the "miracle." The rate of infant mortality per 1000 live births was 105 for Brazil as a whole and 180 in the poor northwest in 1970, compared to 13–20 in various European countries. In the most "developed" state, São Paulo, infant mortality fell from 90 in 1950 to 63 in 1960, but then rose again to 69 in 1964, 93 in 1970 and 101 in 1972 (data from Gazeta Mércantil 1975; Arroio 1976; dos Santos

1977b). According to the Secretary of Health of the State of São Paulo, Walter Leser, in an address before the 1974 meeting of the Brazilian Society for the Advancement of Science, there is a "depressing parallel between the fall in the real minimum wage in the municipal area of São Paulo and the rates of infant mortality" (cited in *Gazeta Mercantil* December 1975; 2). In the northeast of Brazil

> About 56 per cent of infants less than 10 years of age are estimated to suffer from malnutrition. In one fifth of the cases . . . malnutrition has been prolonged and severe enough to cause permanent brain damage. With only a minority of homes possessing sewerage facilities and running water, infections and parasitic diseases are rampant, accounting for almost half of the deaths among children less than 5 years of age. . . . Infant mortality has remained steady at about 10 per cent of live births in the last five years. In the more remote rural zones, it reaches higher than 25 percent (IHT 26 January 1977).

The longer Brazil pursues this intermediate, semiperipheral, subimperialist development, the farther along the road to the oblivion of living death will it lead the vast majority of its people.

President Geisel once said that "the economy is doing fine, but the people are not." His successor, President Figueiredo, was asked by a ten-year-old boy at a children's ceremony, "Mr. President, how would you feel if you were a child and your father earned the minimum wage?" The President's quick answer, which was broadcast on national television that night, was "I would put a bullet through my head" (GUA 25 November 1979).

Mexico

Mexico is another intermediate Third World country selected by the Trilateral Commission report for inclusion in the inner circle of world economic policy making. The steady growth of Mexico's economy for over three decades was widely regarded as a "permanent miracle"—at least until August 31, 1976, when Mexico devalued the peso, which had been pegged to the dollar since 1954, and thereby announced to all the world that the growing pains of the permanent miracle had led to a crack in the economy.

A popular saying in Mexico, which harks from the time before the Mexican Revolution in 1910, is "poor Mexico, so far away from God and so close to the United States." The common border with the United States has always distinguished Mexico's economic (and other) development in important ways. In the first half of the nineteenth century Mexico lost half its territory to its northern neighbor as the border was pushed south to the Rio Grande. In the second half of that century part of Mexico's agricultural economy and all of its mining economy were put at the service of the American westward and industrial expansion. The political organization of this economic integration into the American economy under Porfirio Diaz generated, particularly after the economic crisis of 1907 in the United States, the political conflict that produced the Revolution of 1910 and the subsequent land reform carried out by President Cárdenas during the Great Depression between 1934 and 1940. The subsequent counterreform (and the growth of "nylon," that is, synthetic latifundia) and the "import-substituting" industrial growth of the 1940s were strongly induced by American demand for Mexican exports, generated by scarcities during and after World War II. The devaluations of the Mexican peso in 1948–1949 and again in 1954 were automatic responses to the American postwar recessions, as well as to the end of the export boom that was simultaneously felt elsewhere.

The relatively sustained growth of the Mexican economy and its healthy outward appearance compared to many economies in the Third World (e.g. the maintenance of the same fixed exchange rate for twenty-two years after 1954) has also been significantly influenced by Mexico's common border with the United States. The entrance into the economy of American industry and the resulting distortions of the structure of production and consumption, the outflow of service payments and the consequent permanent need for credits, mark similar underdeveloped economies, and could have occurred without the common border. But the common border with the United States has afforded Mexico several unique opportunities to prolong its "permanent miracle" while postponing the consequences (particularly on its balance of payments) that are otherwise inevitable with this kind of intermediate, semiperipheral growth. One of these opportunities was to earn substantial foreign exchange on service account through massive American tourism from across the border. The lowering of tourist class and charter air fares to other shores, however, gradually removed much of Mexico's comparative cost advantage; and the severe 1974–1975 recession reduced the absolute amount of American tourism. The shallow Rio Grande has facilitated the illegal border crossing of "wetback" or *bracero* Mexican agricultural workers, who have entered the American labor market in such numbers that the illegally resident "Chicano" community in the United States is now estimated to exceed five million persons. Many of them remit earnings home, while others bring money home on their return from temporary work across the border; and all of them have reduced the nonetheless very high rate of unemployment and therefore social and political tension in Mexico itself. The closing of the border to further legal immigration and the tightened control against illegal crossings, occasioned by the recession and unemployment in the United States, have significantly reduced this outflow of labor and inflow of dollars, however. The "border transactions" goods, services, and labor have always left Mexico with a net inflow of foreign exchange. Hundreds of thousands of acres of Mexico's best irrigated land on "nylon" and other latifundia have specialized in agribusiness production of tomatoes, lettuce, strawberries, and other vegetable products as well as cotton for the American market. Finally, particularly during the last decade, American industry has lined the Mexican side of the border with labor-intensive *maquillaje* assembly plants to take advantage of cheap labor—sometimes with a twin installation on the American side to receive and finish the manufacture if only by stamping "Made in U.S.A." on the products to avoid import duties. These tension-reducing circumstances may also have made it easier for the Mexican bourgeoisie to discipline the Mexican labor force through bureaucratized and state-controlled "yellow dog" labor unions led by *charro* labor leaders who, with isolated exceptions, are as coopted by the establishment as those in a corporative fascist state.

Thus proximity to the United States afforded Mexico several exceptional sources of foreign exchange, employment, and safety valves that permitted the prolongation of the "permanent miracle"—until the crisis, which was highlighted by the sudden and sharp devaluation of the Mexican peso in August 1976 from 12.50 to the dollar and its subsequent "stabilization" at 23 to the dollar.

The crisis in the "external sector" of the Mexican economy had been building up for some time and was visible to some observers through the growth of foreign debt. Long-term (over one year) public sector debt alone reached US $13,000m or more than two years' total export earnings, in June 1976 (CE August 1976: 880).

> Mexico's debt is nearer to US $30,000m than the official figure of US $26,000m, according to the economic consultant to the Mexican confederation of chambers of commerce, Julio Millán. He estimates that the private sector foreign debt is US $10,000m rather than the US $6,000m quoted by the government (LAER 13 May 1977).

The balance-of-trade and current-account deficits both doubled in proportion to GNP between the early 1960s and the early 1970s and had to be supported by increasing recourse to foreign credits. The interest and amortization payments—as well as the growing remission of profits, etc.—put an increasing strain on the balance of payments at a time when foreign exchange earnings from both goods and services were growing more slowly. The crisis became acute when the current-account balance-of-payments deficit rose from $700 million in 1971 and 1972 to $1.2 billion in 1973, $2.4 billion in 1974, and $3.6 billion in 1975, or half of foreign exchange earnings for that year (CE June 1976: 652). Then the deficit fell to $2.6 billion in 1976 and $1.4 billion in 1977. However, in 1978 the deficit rose to over $2 billion again, and probably reached $3 billion in 1979 despite the spectacular increase in export earnings from petroleum, reviewed below (FT 11 January 1980 and other sources). The GNP growth rate fell after 1975. Public and particularly private investment fell off drastically, while prices (which had long been exceptionally stable in Mexico) increased sharply and then skyrocketed after the devaluation from 15 percent in 1975 and 1976 to 29 percent in 1977 before returning to 17 percent in 1978 and 1979. This inflation drastically reduced the purchasing power of Mexicans. The President observed that the "organized labor movement has responded with great historical responsibility by accepting an increase in salaries of only 9 or 10 percent" (IHT 2 February 1977) while prices rose over 30 percent. From 1977 to 1979 Mexican workers again lost 20 percent of their purchasing power (FT 30 October 1979). Finally the relative rise in the prices of Mexican manufactures stemmed their export to the United States and other countries where inflation was lower.

Manufacturing barely increased and total industrial output actually decreased during part of 1976 and 1977 (automobile production declined by about 10 percent in each of these years), while gross domestic product (GDP) rose only 1.7 percent (1976) and 3.2 percent (1977). However, in 1978 manufacturing again increased by 8.5 percent, industrial output by 9.6 percent, and GDP by 6.6 percent (Banco de Mexico in CE March 1979). In 1979 industrial output seems to have grown at similar rates, but agricultural production declined 9.4 percent while yields per hectare dropped 2.6 percent. The prospects for 1980 are no better. The 1979 output of the major consumer staples, maize and beans, fell by 18 and 32 percent, respectively; and the price of tortillas, Mexico's maize-flour staple bread, nearly doubled (FT 11 and 24 January 1980). In response to this economic crisis and its legacy, President José Lopez Portillo says he is "carrying forward a program of economic restructuring" (IHT 2 February 1977). Since 1976 expansion of production, especially of exports, has been planned in petroleum, fertilizers, steel, chemicals, and forest products (CE June 1976: 655). But all of these are highly capital-intensive rather than labor-absorbing industries. The most important is undoubtedly petroleum and its derivatives.

The world oil crisis has transformed Mexico's fortunes. Very much higher prices have resulted in increases in gas exports from an average of $22 million a year between 1970 and 1973 to $117 million in 1974, $460 million in 1975, $555 million in 1976, $916 million in 1977, $1,725 million in 1978, and $4,270 million in 1979 (CEE October 1979). With the construction of a pipeline from Mexico's east coast fields to the industrial north and the United States, Mexico is now—after drawn-out negotiations and mutual recriminations about the sale price—beginning to supply significant amounts of gas to the United States. More importantly, intensified exploration has led to the discovery of at least three major new oil fields, which are perhaps as rich as those off Alaska and in the North Sea. With these discoveries, Mexico's proven reserves rose from five billion barrels in 1968 to sixteen billion in 1977 and forty-six billion in September 1979. Probable reserves are an additional forty-five billion barrels and total potential (including proven and probable) reserves are perhaps two hundred billion (CEE October 1979: 407; FT 11 January 1980). So Mexico is now in a league with major oil suppliers in the Middle East. The "problem is no longer to get oil and gas production up . . . but to keep it down in the face of insistent demands for more supplies from U.S. and other eager buyers" (FT 11 January 1980). The 1979 exports were 585,000 barrels a day or 213 million a year. The current target is to produce 2.25 million barrels a day and to export half of them. At $30 a barrel, these 400 million barrels a year would bring in $12 billion from the export of crude oil alone. Exports of gas should bring in more than $2 billion by 1982 (CEE October 1979: 406).

Besides offering a solution to the recent crisis in Mexico's external balance of payments, this oil and gas bonanza alters the prospects for Mexico's development. The government's Department of Planning is very optimistic:

Prospects for 1979–1982

Over the next few years, hydrocarbons exports [of oil and gas] will be responsible for fundamental changes in the Mexican economy. It is estimated that their value will increase from 4.27 billion dollars in 1979 to 14.67 billion in 1982, with their share of total goods exports rising from 49 to 71 percent. Thus, if these expectations are borne out, the significance of such exports as a generator of foreign exchange will be extraordinary and will finance the purchase of goods essential for the country's economic growth and for improved exploitation of the factors of production. Of particular importance in all this will be the number of new jobs generated. Indeed, these exports are expected to finance 39% of the country's total goods imports in 1979, and 76% of such imports in 1982. If this contribution is limited to imported production goods, these same percentages are 47 and 80 percent, respectively.

If the prognostications are fulfilled, the potential wealth which lies below the ground will be turned into real productive wealth, in the form of goods and services. Thus, it is possible that the coming years will see growth rates of between 7 and 10 percent in the gross domestic product. . . .

If productive use is made of the increased internal income generated by the expansion of hydrocarbon exports, it may be predicted that it will not have a serious inflationary effect (CEE October 1979: 401–7).

Neither the Department of Planning or anyone else has clarified just how an increase in oil-financed imports, especially of capital-intensive producer goods, is supposed to generate enough new jobs to make productive use of the vast army of unemployed. One government ministry has put forward a ten-year industrial development plan to diversify exports from more high-technology industry and to increase the domestic production of basic foodstuffs in more labor-intensive agriculture. The plan "is the most powerful public sector exponent of the domestic market strategy, although even it does not envisage income redistribution" (LAER I June 1979: 165). But "private sector reaction to the plan has been muted . . . [and] one important weakness of the plan's optimistic design for Mexico's future is that the inflationary effects of the extra expenditures are unlikely to be as low as it predicts" (LAER 4 May 1979: 130). "The weakest link in Mexico's industrial growth remains its limited ability to generate employment, which is actually decreasing per unit of capital invested" (LAER 1 June 1979: 164).

Until now, regional and sectoral imbalances in Mexican economic growth, and above all the massive unemployment and underemployment, which have recently been made more difficult to bear by restrictions on emigration abroad and inflation at home, have generated what Mexican President Lopez Portillo has called "the incredible distance between rich and poor" (IHT 2 February 1977). Despite—indeed because of—Mexico's rapid industrial growth, this distance between rich and poor has certainly grown; the income of the poor has declined not only relatively but also absolutely. According to the English language edition of *Comercio Exterior*, the official publication of the Mexican government's foreign trade bank:

> Over the course of the 25 years from 1950 to 1975, 40% of the population at the poorest end suffered a 38% drop in real income. 12 million inhabitants in the rural zones are seen as living in conditions of extreme poverty.... More than 20 million inhabitants in rural areas lack any health service; in 1973, almost 14 million had no running water; only 55% of children between the ages of 6 and 14 enjoyed access to basic education.... Malnutrition is virtually the general condition in the countryside, but it is above all the children that are most affected: 96% of the pre-school population suffers from malnutrition. By grades of malnutrition, 46% are in the first category, almost 28% in the second, and 3.4% in the third on the very limits of starvation (CEE July 1979: 244).

The economic crisis of the mid-1970s aggravated this situation, not only in rural areas but also in urban ones:

> "The first indicator is when we see infant mortality rising again," said Dr. Adolfo Chavez of the National Nutrition Institute. "In some really depressed rural communities, few children born since 1974 have survived. We have what we call generational holes. But infant mortality is also growing in slum areas of the cities." ...
>
> Unemployment and underemployment have expanded to include more than half the workforce and prices have rushed ahead of wages. For millions, it has meant less to eat (IHT 9 March 1978).

The question naturally arises whether Mexico's oil bonanza and the new industrialization program based on it are likely to eliminate or at least alleviate these problems of economic poverty and social tension, or whether these problems are likely to be intensified.

> The new opportunities that the petroleum surplus offers can only be used to real advantage if simultaneously there are structural changes that permit an increase in production and social justice in the countryside, that increase the efficiency and diversification of the excessively

protected industrial apparatus and that permit its linkage with other activities . . . (CE April 1978: 455).

Euphoria over Mexico's recent oil discovery is beginning to give way to uneasy recognition that the new wealth will not solve—and may even aggravate—many of the country's deep social problems. . . . Some leftist analysts have argued that no rate of oil exploitation would release funds for more labor-intensive economic activities involving agriculture, small- and medium-sized industry and commerce. Only through a broader employment base, they assert, can the government resolve current educational, health and housing problems without creating an oil-financed welfare state. . . . "The real issue is whether oil allows the government to postpone necessary social and economic reforms," one leading economist said. "What's needed is an entirely new strategy of development, but so far it has not been forthcoming" (IHT 4 January 1978).

It is altogether possible that the main material benefits derived from the export of petroleum will go to the national and foreign groups who have the most economic and political power, and along with them to the urban high income social strata. Both groups have the necessary capacity to use the facilities . . . and to influence the direction of public investment. . . . On the other hand, the rural social strata, the marginal and low income people, whose political economic power is miniscule, could be mere spectators of an increase in welfare in which they do not participate, and the intermediary sectors could receive only some marginal benefits (CE April 1978: 428)

This is exactly what has happened in Mexican development so far; and it is what happened in concentrated and accelerated form during the oil boom in Iran, where it led to a social earthquake.

A 1980 *Financial Times Survey* of Mexico entitled "Oil Heralds Brighter Future" foresees "every likelihood that Mexico will hit its targeted growth rate of 10 percent in the course of the next two or three years." Nonetheless, the same analysis continues more prudently:

Sr. Rolando Cordera, one of the most acute economists in Government service, commented a few weeks ago: "After more than 40 years' more or less rapid industrial development, I think that we can conclude that Mexican capitalism has been unable to resolve the fundamental imbalance (between town and country) by means of urban industrial development. It is difficult to expect that through more rapid industrial development, implying on one hand the massive absorption of the workforces of the town and countryside, and, on the other, the industrialisation of farm production these problems can be resolved." The question for Mexico in the 1980s is therefore whether any government will have the will and ability to change a 40-year-old pattern. . . . The odds stacked against those setting out to effect such changes are clearly immense. The lobby of private industry is very strong and the organised urban workforce is powerful too. The massed battalions of the rural sector look puny in comparison (FT 11 January 1980).

Argentina

The last intermediate industrial economy in South America to be considered here is that of Argentina. For over a century Argentina's fortunes in an imperialist economy dominated first by Britain and then by the United States have been determined by the conflict between the producers of wheat and meat, who generate the bulk of export income, and the industrial labor force, which holds the key to industrial development. The industrial bourgeoisie, allied more strongly than elsewhere to the landed export interests, and the substantial petite bourgeoisie, allied more often than elsewhere to the working class, have shifted political alliances and therefore economic policy back and forth between the opposing poles of the agricultural export interests and the industrial working class. At the risk of exaggerating through excessive schematicism, it may be suggested that this constant tug of war between agricultural capital and industrial labor has made Argentina miss the political-economic boat at least twice during the last century: Between 1880 and the First World War the relative weakness of the working class and labor movement relative to the export interests led to excessive agricultural export orientation instead of industrial protectionism. Thus Argentina never realized the "Australian model" of development (for which it had certain advantages over Australia) and missed the boat in its direct competition with Australia. (In Australia the relative strength of the working class imposed a much more protective infant industrial policy on the agricultural export interests.) The result was that the development of Australia, with only half the population of Argentina, has far outpaced that of Argentina since then. Paradoxically, after the Second World War the strength of the Argentinian working class, which had in the meantime grown both absolutely and relative to the other major political economic interests, prevented the introduction of measures that superexploit labor—the measures necessary for a smooth functioning of the "Brazilian model." Argentina was therefore unable to adopt the "Brazilian model" of development, and missed the subimperialist boat taken by rival Brazil in Latin America.

The increase in the strength of the Argentinian working class had to do with the onset of the Great Depression of the 1930s and the consequent substantial loss of the European export markets for Argentinian wheat and meat. The agricultural exporting bourgeoisie itself then promoted a policy of industrial growth through import substitution, which produced an important industrial bourgeoisie and working class and petite bourgeoisie by the end of World War II. Allied under the leadership of General Peron after 1943, these political-economic interest groups continued to pursue import-sub-stituting industrialization for another decade with the powerful labor unions gaining influence and benefits. The decline in raw materials prices after the Korean War in 1952–1953 undermined this growth model. It no longer worked satisfactorily because there was a decline in the foreign exchange necessary to keep industry going—at least at the level of wages it was then paying. After he spent nearly two years of temporizing but cutting wages, Peron was overthrown by the armed forces and replaced by a regime that, with the support of the landed export interests, sought to turn the clock back to the agricultural and livestock export economy of the period before 1930. Indeed, this has been a constant aim of some political-economic sectors in Argentina, and it is being attempted with greater force than ever before by the new military regime installed by the coup of March 24, 1976. But the new economic interests created by the previous growth of industry cannot be overlooked and the political force of the industrial labor movement cannot be easily destroyed.

The past two decades in Argentina have been marked by growing economic crisis and a permanent political emergency in which the agro-export interests, in alliance with sectors of the big industrial bourgeoisie (now increasingly allied with American and Continental European instead of the traditional British capital), have sought to discipline the industrial labor force sufficiently to impose an Argentinian version of the Brazilian or at least the Mexican model. This so far unsuccessful effort was particularly harsh under the military regime of General Ongania and his successors after 1966, when the Argentinian economy entered a period of deep economic crisis; it is being pursued with even greater violence today.

Ongania and his successors, Generals Livingston and Lanusse, were unable to break the back of the Peronist labor unions, though they alternately tried to suppress them (Brazilian style) and to coopt them bureaucratically (Mexican style). They were therefore unable to impose the model of renewed capital accumulation that has been "successful" in Brazil. Of course, the Brazilian bourgeoisie did not have to face the insurmountable obstacle of a working class as militantly organized as that in Argentina, and since it enjoyed the position of favored U.S. ally, it could exercise subimperialist power over other parts of the southern cone of South America such as neighboring Paraguay, Bolivia, and Uruguay, where Argentina had been Brazil's traditional rival for influence. Here again, Argentina seems to have missed the boat. Though the real wage rate was severely depressed, the Argentine working class rallied time and again in various political offensives, such as that of the "Cordobazo" in 1969. International capital preferred to bestow its "favors" on the more "stable" Brazil. Finally, the economic failures of the Argentinian military regime and the political strength of the Peronist movement obliged President Lanusse to step aside in 1972, at a time when the progressive Allende governed in neighboring Chile, and to permit the return of a civilian government. The election was won by a Peronist stand-in, Campora, and General Peron himself returned from nearly twenty years exile.

Now it was Peron's turn to try his hand at disciplining the unions and the movement that bore his name. The effort was tragically but symbolically begun by the right-wing Peronists, who shot several members of the more militant left wing while both were waiting at the airport for Peron's plane to land. (In another symbolic action the plane was diverted to a small, isolated field.) Just as thirty years earlier, the economic spirits seemed to favor Peron's mandate—wheat and meat prices rose sky high on the world market and the Argentine balance of payments was most favorable. So at first Peron was able to placate labor and to disarm its militant wing partially with wage rises. Nonetheless, Peron's bid for leadership in the Third World and through the backing of European and then Arab capital failed. So did his health. And so did his political economic program when in the ensuing world recession the European Economic Community closed its borders to Argentinian beef. The Peronist honeymoon ended quickly when the general died and was replaced by his wife Isabella, and the brief export boom was replaced by a return to the permanent crisis of the Argentinian economy. The right wing of the Peronist movement dominated the counsel of the widow President, first under the fascist hand of "Welfare" Minister Lopez Rega and then under the economic austerity program of Economic Minister Celestino Rodrigo. The militant working class, however, was able to force the resignation of both; but within the limitations of its reformist framework, it was unable to offer or to impose an alternative. The economy stagnated once more—GNP declined 1.4 percent in 1975 and 3.5 percent again in 1976, (IPC 17 March 1977: 10) and domestic fixed investment declined by annual percentages ranging from 10 to 20 percent during parts of 1975 and 1976 (CEE December 1977: 490). Inflation flourished—it was 80 percent in the year preceding April 1976—and real wages declined sharply throughout 1975 and the beginning of 1976. All the while the military waited in the wings, debating when to take over the government again.

The inevitable coup took place on March 24, 1976, under the leadership of the "moderate" General Videla, who sought to keep the right wing of the military in check. One of its representatives had announced before the coup:

> We know this war and we have decided to win it on the terrain they have chosen. In the mountains of Tucuman, in the streets of our cities, in the factories where one tries to sabotage our capacity to produce, in the universities where our youth is poisoned with foreign doctrines, in the mass communication media which deform our country, in the Church which pretends to change our God become man by man become God, in the judiciary apparatus which is venal and complacent, in the political organizations which feed subversion, or in any other organization where subversives are infiltrated. We will give them no respite. We will wipe them out. We know exactly what our mission is and we are going to accomplish it (LM 9 December 1975).

On the first anniversary of the coup Amnesty International reported there were twenty thousand political prisoners (twenty-five thousand according to an advertisement in LM 24–25 October 1976) who were enduring worse treatment even than Chilean prisoners under General Pinochet. Three years later there were still ten thousand political prisoners according to accounts at a press conference held in Geneva by the Argentinian Commission for Human Rights (EPA 9 March 1979). A confidential report attributed to the U.S. State Department and the U.S. Armed Forces Intelligence Service estimated there were between twelve thousand and seventeen thousand political prisoners and six thousand "presumably assassinated" persons in early 1978 (*Excelsior* [Mexico] 14 February 1978; *Cambio 16* [Madrid] 19 February 1978, cited in CEE January 1979:21).

Having learned a lesson from the bad publicity that attended the Pinochet government's inhuman treatment of prisoners, the Argentinian military regime has perfected the technique of making people disappear without a trace (there are no witnesses when arrests are made on the street instead of at home) and then torturing them to death with impunity. "Daily reports in the press of 40–50 terrorists killed (none captured or wounded) are expected to continue to be commonplace" (EIU 1st Quarter 1977: 2). By 1979 the number of those who have so disappeared was between twenty thousand and thirty thousand, although the junta acknowledges only four thousand, according to the Argentinian Human Rights Commission (EPA 9 March 1979). There was no visible political reaction to these measures on the part of the labor unions. This repression, which is exercised particularly against the leadership of the working class, is the political correlate of the new regime's economic policy under Economics Minister Martinez de Hoz, which is to impose the Friedman/Chicago–Pinochet/Chile model on the Argentinian economy.

In 1979 the junta dissolved the once powerful General Federation of Labor Unions (CGT) and prohibited the unions from taking political action or controlling their own finances. The right to strike is not included in the new law (EPA 17 November 1979). The *New York Times* summarizes the situation:

> There is no other place [like Argentina] where the ideology of the "National Security State" so threatens the ordinary citizen with arbitrary government terror. . . . The guerrillas were defeated some time ago, but the campaign against "subversion" goes on and on, now claiming among its victims those whose only crime has been to show an interest in politics. The country's foreign trade has once again shown a surplus, but at the cost of depression, drastically reduced real wages and the extinction of workers' union rights (quoted in CEE July 1979: 261).

The real wage of an industrial worker, using January 1973 as an index of 100, had fallen to 80 by December 1975. By March 1976 it was 70; and in the first four months after the coup the real wage was instantly depressed to 50 (Chossudovsky 1977: Table 3). Employees' salaries fell even more, to 40 and even 30. An estimate of the work required to purchase a particular basket of consumer goods suggests that what could be bought for five hours' work in December 1974 cost seven and one-half hours in December 1975, ten hours two months later, and fourteen hours by July 1976 (FR 23 July 1976). Even the Central Bank of Argentina allowed that by July 1976 real wages had declined 43 percent from December 1975 and 51 percent from 1974 (CE September 1976: 1050, citing *La Nacion* [Buenos Aires] 5 August 1976). Since then, "wages continue to decline in real terms." The wage increases decreed in January 1977 were only 20 percent of what workers would have required to achieve the same purchasing power they had in December 1975 (when real wages had already been deflated) (EIU 1st Quarter 1977: 8). Real wages declined 40 percent *after* the coup and wage earners' share of national income was reduced to 34 percent (IPC 17 March 1977: 11). In September 1977 the real value of minimum wages, based on information from the National Statistical and Census Institute (INDEC), was 41 percent of their average during 1974 and their precoup level in January 1976 (CEE December 1977: 491). Indeed, according to the Association of Banks of the Argentine Republic, the average real wage of industrial workers in 1977 was but 42 percent of the average over the past ten years. Thus only 10 percent of the workforce could afford to buy the shopping basket of basic goods as defined by the government itself (LAER 7 April 1978: 104). In June 1978 real wages still were 43 percent below their January 1976 level. *Comercio Exterior* commented that "the fall in wage costs has been so great that it would seem impossible for companies to obtain further benefits under this head" (CEE January 1979: 17).

While wage declines, albeit not such drastic ones, have occurred before, Economics Minister Martinez de Hoz has made it clear that "this is not just one more of the many economic changes the country has experienced in the past years; but [this change] means really turning a page in the political, economic and social history of the country, which means the beginning of a new era" (CE September 1976: 1049). Indeed, besides applying the Chilean/Chicago school boycott treatment to the Argentinian economy through the reduction of public employment and middle-class employee income and the depression of the wage rate and the economy generally, the "new" economic policy seems to consist of a truly radical shift from the internal market to export promotion and from industrial to agricultural production. This is indeed an attempt to turn a page of history—back to the era from 1880 to 1930 when agricultural and livestock products exports were the "master wheel" of the Argentinian economy.

The present economic policy constitutes the most serious and integral attempt to return to the social equilibrium of the thirties, while passing over forty years of history. To pursue this policy it was necessary not only to foment the inevitable disqualification of the Peronist political apparatus and to aid in its dismantling, but also to liquidate the presence of unionism: only that way is it possible to try to keep wages exceptionally low in order to put the agricultural and livestock economy back in the privileged place it had in the *belle epoque*. . . . Now the economic policy of the military consist in returning to the traditional development model based on agricultural and livestock exports. . . .The military government seems to be pursuing an exclusivist policy of promoting the agricultural and livestock sector at any price. . . . (CE September 1976: 1051, 1053).

This policy involves the depression of wages and salaries and the simultaneous elevation of the (traditionally low) internal price of export commodities in order to (in the Chicago school's language) "reallocate resources" and transfer demand from the internal market to export and from industry to agriculture. In addition to favoring the agro-export interests to a degree beyond memory, this policy seems to have at least two more far-reaching intentions: to join the accelerated worldwide race to accumulate capital, and to specialize in the export of commodities in which Argentina has a "comparative advantage,"— wheat and meat—at a time when these products are in such demand that multinational agribusiness is intent on producing them around the globe. Of course, the new regime (like that in Chile) is also interested in promoting the export of industrial commodities to take advantage of the already large industrial capacity and highly skilled labor force. For this reason, the junta is again throwing open the doors to foreign multinational enterprise (BLA 23 March, 7 April 1976; Reuters 15 August 1976). But there are two problems: the Argentinian industry is geared to a wide internal market, not to specialization for export; and no one, not even the Videla regime, has so far been able to cage the Peronist tiger and to discipline the labor force. So despite its "comparative advantage" in industrial equipment and skill, Argentina is at a fatal political and economic disadvantage for industrial export—to say nothing of creating new industrial lines. The development of new industries for export would require international capital, and so far foreign capital has not shown any visible signs of interest in Argentina. The IMF and eleven·Western countries did offer the junta $1 billion in credits within three months of the coup (AP 30 July 1976—or $1.3 billion according to another source (FR 9 August 1976)–and the foreign debt rose by 20 percent to $12 billion within a year of the coup (IPC 17 March 1977: 11).

The second intention of the "new" economic policy is to discipline the industrial labor force and to prepare for the restructuring of industry by *inducing* "a recession in manufacturing industry of a depth previously unequalled in Argentina" (CE September 1976: 1051). This has meant 30 percent excess capacity and declines of 8 percent in industrial production, 20 percent in manufacturing for the internal market, and 16 percent in fixed capital investment compared with the already depressive year of 1975 (IPC 17 March 1977: 10–11). Since it has never been possible to adequately discipline the labor force in Argentina through "yellow dog" unionism, simple terror, or even the refined terror of the present junta; perhaps this historic task can be accomplished by pulling the industrial rug out from under the workers by depressing industrial production and increasing the (traditionally low) rate of unemployment (which has remained low even under the military government). A thoroughgoing industrial depression can also be used to weed out enterprises that are only suited to supplying the internal market and to concentrate capital into domestic and foreign hands that can dedicate it to the promotion of exports, agricultural and industrial—after the depression has run its course and a substantial number of workers and white-collar employees have been obliterated.

In 1977 earnings from meat exports rose substantially and even exceeded those of the 1973 boom year. Industry, however, went into recession in 1977 and 1978. By the first half of 1978 gross industrial output had fallen back to its 1971 level and was nearly 8 percent below its 1973 level. Its share of gross domestic product dropped to 30 percent compared to the average of 34 percent and peak of 37 percent during the five previous years (CEE January 1979: 16). By mid-1979 "the Argentine economy has emerged from last year's recession, but at the price of renewed inflation" (IHT 5 June 1979).

Comercio Exterior commented:

> Naturally, industrial re-conversion, which has led to a considerable reduction in the sector's gross product, is not an anti-industry policy on a global scale. Although the economic strategy, as will be seen, rests undeniably on the promotion of the agrarian sector on the basis of its comparative advantages, it does not seek to discourage industry as a whole, but—fundamentally—to concentrate it on a smaller and more select market and toward exporting. Though not all companies will succeed in achieving the latter goal, those which manage to survive the present stage of contraction will later be able to take advantage of a market in which there will be fewer competitors. . . . Industrial re-conversion is characterized, then, by the displacement of some entre-preneurs by others. Furthermore, in contrast to what is generally believed, it is not the transnational corporations which will most gain in this industrial re-conversion but, rather, a group of companies fi-nanced by Argentine capital. . . .The capitalist development model introduced by the military government implies a far-reaching mod-ification of the country's social structure, to the detriment of the great mass of wage-earners and a large part of the industrial bourgeoisie with ties to the domestic market. . . . The new organization of the economy, implying the disappearance of part of the industrial bourgeoisie, the plummeting of real wages to a level almost 50% below that of five years ago, and the weakening of the public sector, [has] only been brought about amid the most violent repression. Thus, the new organization of

the economy presupposes a new political order. . . . The repression is a reflection of [the] extent of the reorganization being undertaken, the potential resistance this might give rise to, and the very character of Argentine political life over the past few years (CEE January 1979: 17–19).

India*

India, like Argentina, is an economy in a chronic and ever-deepening economic crisis of accumulation. Attempts at salvation through subimperialism à la Brazil have failed thus far. Despite Indira Gandhi's recourse to Emergency Rule from June 26, 1975, until her electoral defeat in March 1977, the Janata government of Moraji Desai, the caretaker government of Charan Singh, and the reelection of Indira Gandhi in January 1980, still no end of this crisis is in sight. India is commonly regarded as an agricultural village society. About 80 percent of the people live in rural areas and 72 percent depend for their living on agriculture, which, however, accounts for less than 50 percent of the national product and income. Although fluctuations in the harvest vitally affect popular consumption and government fortunes, it must be emphasized that industry, particulary heavy industry, is also decisive in the determination of the political-economic fortunes of India as a capitalist economy. Along with South Africa, and the three major countries of Latin America, India has the largest and most highly developed industrial sector in the Third World, one comparable to those in parts of Southern Europe—a case in point is India's development of the atomic bomb and manufacture of jet fighters. India also has perhaps the most sophisticated and independent bourgeoisie in the Third World. Since Independence, investment, much of it by the state, has preferentially gone into industry, particularly into very capital intensive heavy industry. Despite the public attention and private effort devoted to industry—or rather perhaps because of the overinvestment in industry and underinvestment in concomitant inputs and underdevelopment of market demand in the agricultural sector—Indian industry and the Indian economy have endured a chronic crisis marked by stagnating production, widespread underutilization of installed productive capacity, and low or purely speculative investment since the mid-1950s. These conditions brought about the institutionalization of economic, political, and military repression under Emergency Rule, which was designed to further favor Indian and foreign monopoly capital without solving the economy's structural problems.

The chronic crisis of Indian industry was foreshadowed by declining growth rates beginning in 1963. However, the definitive arrival of the crisis of the economy was the absolute decline of industrial production in 1966 and

---

*This section is a substantially shortened and updated version of an article on the Emergency (Frank 1977b).

the less than 1 percent growth in 1967. These developments were coincidental with the economic crisis and Ongania military coup in Argentina, the economic recession in Western Europe, and the onset of the contemporary world crisis of capital accumulation in the mid-1960s.

The growth of industrial production and economic growth generally have been much slower and much farther below planned targets since the end of the Third Five Year Plan in 1965–1966. For the First Five Year Plan in (1951/52–1955/56) the planned growth in large-scale manufacturing output was 7 percent and the realized rate was 6 percent. For the Second Plan (1956–1960/61) the planned rate was 10.5 percent and the realized one 7.2 percent; and for the Third Plan (1961–1965/66) the rates were 10.7 percent and 8 percent respectively. The Fourth Five Year Plan, orginally published in 1966, aimed for a rate of 10.7 percent as well; but with the onset of the crisis it was replaced by three annual plans during the "plan holiday" until 1968. The final version of the Fourth Plan, published in 1969, raised this target to 12 percent; but the Draft Outline of the Fifth Five Year Plan, published in 1973, "realistically" lowered it to 8 percent again. Still, the realized annual growth rates were only 3.5 percent between 1965 and 1970 and 2.7 percent from 1970 to 1974, or only one-third to less than one-half the targeted ones. The compounded annual growth rate of industrial production in factory enterprises was 7.4 percent in 1951–1956, 6.8 percent in 1956–1961, and 8.9 percent in 1961–1965. It then fell to 3.3 percent in 1965–1970 and 2.8 percent in 1970–1974 (Raj 1976: 223, 225). Industrial investment as measured by annual rates of growth of installed capacity dropped from 6.2 percent between 1960 and 1967 to 4.5 percent from 1967 to 1970 (Paul 1974: 2027). Percentages of utilization of installed capacity declined by 10 or more points according to differing estimates since the mid-1960s: from about 90 percent to about 80 percent (Raj 1976: 226), or from about 80 percent to 70 percent on the basis of official Reserve Bank calculations (Mishra 1974: 2064). Other estimates do not show such an overall decline, but put the utilization rate at only about 55 percent for the whole period since 1960 and find that capacity utilization rates fell from 58 percent to 42 percent in the capital goods industries (Paul 1974: 2029). The *Eastern Economist* reported capacity utilization at less than 50 percent in thirty-six out of sixty-one industries in 1970 (Frank 1973: 123).

The "problem" industries have been, first, heavy industries, particularly steel and electric power, which are largely state financed (not incidentally with substantial Soviet technology and inputs) and hence subsidize the private capitalist industries that use these products in their own manufacturing; and second, consumer goods industries, particularly coarse cotton textiles, that use high-priced agricultural inputs (which favors agricultural producers) but face an increasingly restricted market for lack of popular purchasing power. With wages declining both absolutely and as a share of national income (Shetty 1973; Sau 1973,1977) and real income falling in the poorest segments of rural India, manufacturers of coarse textile goods have seen their profits squeezed and/or been forced to switch to finer cotton or synthetic goods for the higher-income and export markets. While in the first three Plan periods per capita income increased at the modest annual compound rates of 1.8 percent, 2.9 percent and 2.3 percent (first four years), respectively, the increase slowed to 0.3 percent per year for the whole decade 1965/65–1973/74 (EPW 22 November 1975: 1793). The distribution of this income has become increasingly unequal. For the poorest rural and urban populations, income actually declined, as documented in the now classic study by Dandekar and Rath (1971).

In mid-1974, after the balance-of-payments and general economic crisis in India had been *aggravated* (but not caused) by the steep rise in the prices of the oil and wheat that India is obliged to import in large quantities, politicians and the domestic and foreign press cried that India was suffering the worst economic crisis since Independence in 1947 (NZZ 18 October 1974). Capital increased its complaints about excessive wages and demanded that "labour indiscipline . . . be curbed with a heavy hand" (quoted in Frank 1973: 124). That this prospect was in the offing through "pre-fascism, semi-fascism or neo-fascism" was noted by many observers, including the present writer (Frank 1973). The central government had already crushed the rural Naxalite and allied movements in Bengal and elsewhere in 1971–1972. Then came the railway strike of April 1974. "The Government was itching for the strike so that it could crush it" (MR 1974), and it did so brutally with fifty thousand arrests and fifteen thousand dismissals. The political writer Mohan Ram would observe (EPW June 8 1974: 892) that "the Government's massive repression of the strike has sinister implications for the working class movement as a whole. It might even be a prelude to a total moratorium on all strikes and lock-outs." Another commentator suggested that "after the Government's success in crushing the railwaymen's strike, the Prime Minister evidently feels confident about the feasibility of an unqualified wage freeze and seems even to believe that this is called for. . . . But this is not all. The logic of populism turning towards authoritarianism has been relentlessly unfolding on a wide and ever-expanding front" (BM, EPW 15 June 1974). Indeed, a journalist would later recall that "in Bombay, I met with J.R.D. Tata, the board chairman of the Tata group of industries, the largest industrial giant of the land. . . . Tata told me why he supported the Emergency: 'Things had gone too far. You can't imagine what we have been through here—strikes, boycotts, demonstrations. Why there were days I couldn't walk out of my office onto the street. The parliamentary system is not suited to our needs.' " The implication is that labor was not only threatening capital's profits but was challenging its untrammeled political power as well.

On 26 June 1976 Prime Minister Indira Gandhi declared a state of Emergency on the pretext of a threat to her government from the right, which had been trying to disqualify her from office through the courts on charges of violating the election laws. The Maintenance of Internal Security Act

(MISA) was amended through executive ordinance to permit detention without grounds for one year (TI 1 July 1975). Leaders of the right-wing opposition—J. P. Narain, Piloo Mody, Moraji Desai, and others—were jailed immediately, a move that perhaps confused a large part of the population and a small part of the left (but not those the author talked with during his visit at that time) about the real thrust and meaning of Mrs. Gandhi's coup. Soon, however, politicians, cadres, and particularly labor leaders on the left were detained also. They, however, have remained in prison while most of the rightist detainees were released. A member of the Indian Parliament, S. Swamy, estimated that 175,000 people were detained and held without charges or trial during the first year of Emergency Rule (HOL 25 July 1976). Others have put the number at 200,000 or more (NIB 5 May–June 1976). The government maintained strict censorship of the press and other media, further amended the laws, restricted the action of the courts, and changed the constitution to extend the time and scope of its Emergency Rule.

Not unexpectedly, the declaration of Emergency was accompanied by populist demagogy reminiscent of Mrs. Gandhi's ill-fated 'Garibi Hatao' (eliminate poverty) program of a few years earlier. A Twenty Point (initially twenty-one) Program of Development was proclaimed. Only one of these points—increased credit for the rural bourgeoisie—was implemented with any concrete economic effects.

Also not unexpectedly, Mrs. Gandhi's acceleration and sharpening of bourgeois crisis management through Emergency Rule bore its most immediate economic fruits on the labor front:

> Within a month of the proclamation of emergency and the decision not to have strikes and lock-outs, nearly 20,000 employees have been either retrenched or laid off by various multi-national business houses (*Business Standard* 29 August 1975, cited in EPW 6 September 1975).

A half year later "the visible improvement of labour discipline in the course of the state of emergency" was hailed (NZZ 18 March 1976). "Workers toe the line" (FER 20 February 1976) became the most notable economic comment of the foreign press. The U.S. big-business newsletter *Business Asia,* a subsidiary of *Business International,* informed its readers:

> Progress under emergency rule is claimed to include better labor discipline, increased productivity, and a revival of the stock market. . . . Much of the recent improvement—in fields such as for example, industrial relations—is simply due to fear (BA 12 March 1976).

The head of a West German pharmaceutical company in India remarked that "for the first time in 17 years we were no longer on the defensive in collective bargaining" (HP 25 September 1976). A member of the Oberoi family told a journalist after the imposition of Emergency Rule on June 26, 1975, "Oh, it's just wonderful. We used to have terrible problems with the unions. Now when they give us any troubles the Government just puts them in jail" (*NYTM* 4 April 1976).

Man-days lost through strikes had roughly doubled from 1973 to 1974 (in the first half of the latter year the railway strike took place). In the first half of 1975 they remained high—seventeen million—but after the imposition of Emergency Rule in June there was a drastic decline to two to four million. A lower strike rate—that is, better "labor discipline"—was maintained through 1976, when the number of man-days lost was 12.8 million, although a higher share was due to lockouts. After the end of Emergency Rule in 1977 the loss of man-days rose to 21.2 million (FER 28 October 1978). In public-sector enterprises, which employ twice as many workers as large private-sector ones, the improvement in labor discipline thanks to the Emergency was even more dramatic: In all of 1975 only 1.4 million man-days were lost out of a total of 17.9 million (FER 20 February 1976). The trend for lockouts and layoffs was in the opposite direction:

> The Union labour minister had to admit that the incidence of lay-offs and lock-outs had been on the increase in recent months. . . . After the declaration of the Emergency, while there had been "a significant fall in man-days lost due to strikes," there had been "many cases of large-scale lay-offs, particularly by big companies including a number of multinationals." . . . According to the government's own figures, lock-outs had accounted for 57 per cent of the total number of man-days lost due to industrial disputes in January 1976. However, in July, as many as 96 per cent of all man-days lost were on account of lock-outs (EPW 30 October 1976: 1709).

According to the Reserve Bank of India, profit ratios rose during 1976–1977, while the share of salaries, wages, and bonuses in the value of production fell (EPW 18 November 1978: 1870). The number of small enterprises shut down after June 1975 was greater than at any time in the preceding decade (Swamy n.d.: 20). The number of workers laid off during the first year following the declaration of Emergency Rule was reported as 475,000 (HO 25 July 1976) and 479,000 (HO 27 June 1976), and these statistics do not include figures for several important states; layoffs for India as a whole were estimated as 700,000 (EPW 8 January 1976). Registered unemployment was 2.6 million in 1966 and 8.2 million in 1973 (NIB 3 May–June 1976: 9), 8.4 million in 1974, and in excess of 10 million in 1976 (EPW 3 July 1976). One estimate, based on employment exchange data, indicated a 28 percent rise in unemployment (Swamy n.d.: 20). (Estimated unemployment was already 18.7 million in 1971 according to official sources reported in NIB 3.) Even though real wages had already declined before the declaration of Emergency, money wages were frozen or even reduced in some cases (HO 8 August 1976; B3W August 1976), and annual bonuses were cut from 8 percent to 4 percent (FER 20 February 1976) despite inflation, so that real wages declined still further. No wonder that Mrs. Gandhi's labor minister

Reddy was able to remark with satisfaction that the climate of industrial relations had changed beyond recognition (HO 8 August 1976).

The improvement of industrial relations from the point of view of capital was, however, only one aspect of the marked improvement in the political-economic climate for business generally as a result of the "remarkable volte face" (as FER 22 August 1975 called it) of Mrs. Gandhi's government since the "progressive" program adopted by the All-India Congress Committee in 1967, and particularly since the declaration of Emergency Rule in June 1975. Only two months after this declaration, FER (22 August 1975) noted:

> Certainly Mrs. Gandhi would seem to have won the first round in her efforts to ensure the support of the big industrialists. . . . Industrialists and investors have welcomed her initiatives. . . . Under India's new slogan of "Produce more," the big family companies such as Tatas, Birlas, Maratlal and Thapar will be allowed to resume their expansion.

On December 20, 1975, EPW reported under the title "Corporate Sector: Never Had It So Good":

> One conclusion that straightaway strikes one is that the private corporate sector did very well during this period even though in terms of achieving some of the key Plan objectives, the performance of the Fourth Plan was the poorest of all Plans so far. . . . There occurred serious shortfalls in every major industrial sector. . . . Despite such poor performance . . . the number of companies with operating profits . . . increased. . . . Profit margins and profitability ratios too improved quite notably. . . . Profit margins and profitability ratios have since equalled and even surpassed the highest levels achieved in the past.

This was a "Time for Rejoicing," not only for Indian big business, but also for international capital interested in India:

> The budget for the current year and a series of other initiatives towards unshackling industrial enterprise have been widely appreciated and welcomed not only by Indian business and industry but also by foreign investors (EPW 11 September 1976).

Mrs. Gandhi's Emergency Rule offered a "New Deal for Foreign Capital":

> Such measures as the investment allowance scheme, reduction in capital gains tax, reductions in the rates of taxation at the upper income and wealth brackets, rationalization of taxation on foreign companies, norms for non-resident Indian investment in India and liberalization of trade policies were listed as being most encouraging for profitable business, both Indian and foreign. Also specially noted were changes in the operating conditions for foreign business in India, such as reduction in the tax on royalties earned by foreign companies and easing of the tax burden on dividends received by foreign companies, including exemption from surtax in some cases (EPW 4 December 1976, 1884).

Conditions were not only eased in "priority" high-technology and high-export industries, but their application was in effect made discretionary, permitting retention of 51 percent and up to 74 percent foreign equity ownership in Indian industry.

> These changes were also spelt out in the agenda papers for the Indo-US Joint Business Council meeting. . . . A striking feature in this context has been the unanimity among visiting business interests that vast and positive changes have already taken place in the government of India's attitude towards them (FER 4 December 1976).

Furthermore:

> The import policy for 1976–77 . . . carries the country another giant step in the free market direction and away from planning. As with industrial licensing, it is now difficult to say what remains of import control (EPW 17 April 1976: 579).

And on the other hand, "export incentives too have risen phenomenally since 1969–70."

After annual export growth rates of 1 percent, 2 percent, and 4 percent during the First, Second, and Third Plan periods, respectively, the rate jumped to 13.6 percent during the Fourth Plan years. After 1972–1973 annual growth rates of exports rose to 22.5 percent, 28 percent, 31 percent, and 16 percent in value terms, and 12.1 percent, 4.2 percent, 6.4 percent, and 7 percent in volume (EPW 15 May 1976: 713). Thus, long before India's increased import bill because of the rise in oil and wheat prices, India had joined the 1970s rush to "export substitution," "export promotion," and "export-led growth." The further liberalization of foreign trade and incentives to export industries under Emergency Rule only accelerated this trend.

Exports (in rupees unadjusted for inflation) increased from Rs 80 million in 1965–1966 to Rs 330 million in 1974–1975, and by 19 percent to Rs 394 million in 1975–1976. From April–October 1975 to April–October 1976 alone, exports increased 34 percent (advertisement in EPW 29 January 1977: 128). But "there has been a threefold increase in the flow of export credits from the scheduled commercial banks" (FEX 5 October 1976, cited in EPW). "The beginnings at export of machinery and equipment made recently, howsoever encouraging, they might be, have hitherto been the result primarily of inadequate domestic demand . . ." (EE Annual Number 1977: 1377).

> The key sector is engineering, now the most important of India's export industries and one particularly depressed in 1974 and 1975. . . . 1975 had been the worst year for industry since 1969, especially in West Bengal. But by March 1976 there were signs of improvement in demand, output, capacity utilization balance between costs of production and selling price, and inventory control. Most of this demand had come from the export sector where some large and prestigious

jumbo projects orders have been won in the Middle East. . . . From
being an importer India has now moved to be a substantial *steel* exporter (EIU 4th Quarter 1976: 18–9, 22).

The [engineering] industry has undertaken a major export drive. . . .
The Fifth Five Year Plan document has stated that by the end of the
Plan engineering exports would emerge as the single most important
group of items of exports (EE Annual Number 1977: 1365).

And though hundreds of millions of Indians may be undernourished and
millions literally dying from starvation, this capitalist export drive has
extended to foodstuffs. In 1976–1977 the "increased export earnings of other
food items, estimated by the Ministry of Commerce at Rs 2.7 bn. rising to a
level of Rs 9.5 bn. Amongst products with good prospects are animal feeds
based on groundnut extraction, vegetable oils (linseed and castor), fish, fresh
vegetables and fruits" (EIU 4th Quarter 1976: 22). Moreover:

the Government may have to arrange for the export of some crops
which have been purchased largely as a price support measure. This
was indicated here today by the Union Agriculture Minister (TI 4
September 1976, cited in EPW).

India will be in a position to export rice in the next three or four years,
the Union Minister of State for Agriculture . . . said here today (FEX 9
September 1976, cited in EPW).

EPW's correspondent rightly observes:

Food Surplus for Export!
The principles governing commercial agriculture which is being
promoted with so much diligence for the last ten years under the banner
of the new agriculture strategy are at last beginning to assert themselves. The approach is all of a piece with that towards other sectors of
economic activity. If steel, coal, cement and similar industrial goods
can find profitable export outlets when effective demand in the domestic market is not enough to absorb the current level of production, there
is no reason why foodgrains cannot emerge as yet another export
commodity on a similar basis!

The features of the Indian economy that underlie this development are
superficially clear, but the essential causes remain the subject of debate.
"There is a large measure of consensus that the limits to the growth of the
Indian economy are now set primarily by the insufficiency of domestic
demand caused by abject poverty of the overwhelming majority of the
country's population. It is also conceded that this has been the outcome of the
type of development we have had so far" (EPW 29 April 1978: 709). This
view is echoed by foreign observers, such as the *Financial Times* (5
February 1979), which notes that "the high level of surplus domestic
resources stems basically from depressed levels of demand and consumption

in the rural areas because of the large numbers of people living at subsistence level." Indeed, the Indian Planning Commission itself notes that "the pattern of industrial development that has emerged obviously reflects the structure of effective demand, which is determined by the distribution of incomes. An unduly large share of . . . demand of this relatively small class [of higher-income groups] . . . sustains a large part of the existing industrial structure" (Planning Commission, Draft Five Year Plan 1978–1983, cited in Roy 1980: 32–33). According to the Planning Commission, in 1977–1978, 48 percent of the population in rural areas and 41 percent in urban areas—a total of 290 million people—were living below the poverty line. Between 1971 and 1978, of a growth of thirty-five million people in the labor force, only nine million were absorbed by nonagricultural activities (cited in Roy 1980: 30–31). Other estimates indicate an absolute and relative *increase* in the number of rural Indians living below the poverty line: from 38 or 52 percent in 1960–1961 to over 70 percent in 1978–1979 (*India Today* 16–31 March 1980: 30–31). As a result, despite the increased exports, there has been an *absolute decline* in the consumption and production of mass consumer goods such as cotton textiles (from 4.6 million meters in 1960 to 3.9 million in 1976) and footwear. There has been a concomitant shift away from labor-intensive and employment-generating agro-based industries to capital-intensive mineral- and chemical-based industries that employ fewer people. In the organized manufacturing sector, which absorbs only 10 percent of the annual increase in the labor force according to the Planning Commission, the annual rate of employment increase fell from 6 percent in 1960–1965 to 1.5 percent in 1965–1976, and in the informal unorganized sector, which is generally regarded as providing increasing employment, the decline in employment growth was even sharper (Khanna n.d.).

At the same time, the concentration of landownership and the productivity and output of the bigger farms has increased with the green revolution, and the concentration and centralization of big industry as well as its share of production have grown rapidly. A chicken-or-egg debate ensued as to which is cause and which effect. Most observers emphasize underconsumption and low investment as reflections of the level and structure of demand and the inequality in the distribution of property and income. Others, like Ranjit Sau (1977, 1979) and Ajit Roy (1980), argue that these are only the manifestations of the crisis, and that its cause is to be found in the process of concentration of landownership and centralization of capital, which are proceeding apace (see, for example, the ongoing debate in *Economic and Political Weekly* begun by Sau 1979 and Menon 1979).

The Indian bourgeoisie's bid for a "Brazilian model"—i.e., a capital-intensive and export-oriented subimperialist—solution to its crisis of capital accumulation also takes other forms, Indian foreign investment ventures and military production not the least among them. Both, moreover, are related to India's rivalry with Pakistan and its pretensions in Bangladesh and South and Southeast Asia generally. The Indian bourgeoisie and government, which, of course, materially supported the independence of Bangladesh, entertained considerable expansionist economic, political, and military hopes in that country after the Indo-Pakistani War and the secession of Bangladesh from Pakistan in 1971. Many of these hopes have, however, been substantially frustrated by circumstances, including major-power rivalry. On the other hand, Indian capital has launched a modest program of foreign investment since 1970, much of it in Southeast Asia. By 1 January 1976, there were sixty-five recorded foreign investment ventures by Indian capital in forty-three countries, forty-nine of them begun since 1970 and twenty-three in 1975 alone. Sixty-three further ventures were in various stages of implementation in 1975–1976. Fifty-one percent of the existing ventures involving 56 percent of the capital were in Southeast Asia, most importantly in Malaysia; and 59 percent of the proposed ventures involving 71 percent of the capital were in this same area. Africa is the next most heavily represented region for existing ventures, and the Middle East for newly proposed ventures. A not insignificant 15 percent of existing and proposed Indian foreign investment is in the developed countries. Surprisingly, the lowest number of Indian foreign ventures, Latin America, are elsewhere in South Asia. Many of Indian capital's foreign ventures are designed to promote or assure export markets abroad. However, 105 ventures with a higher combined Indian equity than those in operation have been abandoned either after approval or after initiation, indicating the obstacles that Indian capital encounters in the realization of its subimperialist ambitions abroad. (All data on foreign ventures are from Balakrishnan 1976.)

The unanswered question is whether and to what extent India can successfully follow the Brazilian model of capital-intensive, internationally open, subimperialist growth. The emasculation of the labor movement and of the left before and after the declaration of Emergency Rule and their poor performance during the Janata government, as well as the return of Indira Gandhi, suggest that labor opposition can be overcome in India just as it has been in Brazil. (Moreover, the Moscow-aligned Communist Party of India supported Indira Gandhi and her emergency rule, and the "independent" Communist Party of India-Marxist supported the Janata government.) In the meantime, the Indian bourgeoisie found a powerful rival—but also a collaborator—in subimperialism in Iran, which used its oil to set itself up as the subimperialist economic, political, and military powerhouse of the Indian Ocean and Persian Gulf region under the leadership of the Shah. Iran called the shots there, even to the extent of obliging India to accept her traditional rival Pakistan in a sort of "Greater South-West Asian Co-prosperity Sphere" based on the Regional Cooperation for Development and led by Iran (FER 16 July 1976). It is too early to tell whether or to what extent the fall of the Shah and new economic policies in Iran will increase the limited chances for success of an Indian version of the Brazilian subimperialist policy in the region.

The fall of the Gandhi government in the March 1977 elections, its replacement by the Janata coalition led by Moraji Desai, and that coalition's succession in 1979 by the caretaker government of Charan Singh, and finally the return to power of Indira Gandhi as Prime Minister in January 1980 have changed the underlying structure and process of the Indian economy remarkably little. By far the most important economic development since 1977 has been the unusual succession of three excellent harvest years, which increased the supply of food rather than food prices and even permitted the accumulation of food stocks to weather the bad harvest of 1979–1980. Additionally, invisible (service) export earnings and especially remittances from Indian workers in the Middle East and elsewhere produced a favorable balance of payments and led to an increase in India's foreign exchange reserves (which means that, in effect, India became a foreign lender of capital!). These strokes of economic good fortune provided a margin of political maneuverability to the Desai and Singh governments, whose political demise might otherwise have been even quicker. Similarly, the accumulated stock of domestic good grains and of foreign exchange should help Mrs. Gandhi's political resurrection get off to a good start. But this temporary economic good fortune will not alter anything fundamental in India's structural economic crisis or in its government's political-economic policies of crisis management.

The assessment of government political-economic policy by the *Economic and Political Weekly* for the beginning of 1978 may be said to hold for the entire period of the Janata and Charan Singh governments: "industrial policy: confused goals, ineffective trends" (EPW 28 January–4 February 1978) and "the confusion is total" (EPW Annual Number February 1978). The *International Herald Tribune* (27 March 1978) proclaimed, "Desai Finds Change Comes Slow in India, Maybe Never." The government budget was to "little purpose" (EPW 4 March 1978) and "breaks no new ground and conforms to the pattern set by previous budgets . . . [and] has once again not been able to break free of traditional shackles" (EPW 9 July 1977). Although, predictably, there was a policy shift from large to small industry and from industry in general to agriculture, this change was more rhetorical than real.

> Mr. George Fernandes, the Socialist Minister for Industry, has not been able to get his way on further nationalisation, no more than Mr. Charan Singh was able to put into practice his nostalgic dreams of restoring India to a pastoral economy. . . . The Janatas opposition to the further growth of large industrial houses has been turned on its head. . . . A policy of withdrawing assistance from exporters in last year's budget is now being reversed under the shock of finding that export receipts have dropped this year. There is a growing list, as well, of companies being allowed to bring in foreign technology. All this points to . . . realism gaining the upper hand over political rhetoric (FT 5 February 1979).

At the same time, under the post-Emergency governments, in which rich farmers, represented particularly by Charan Singh, had relatively greater influence, the degree of exploitation and oppression of small peasants and landless laborers (70 percent of rural householders own no land) became even greater. Reported violence against and assassinations of outcast Harijans increased during the Janata rule.

> There are as many as 2.7m bonded workers in India. As many as 52% of these workers have become bonded in the past three years, a devastating comment on the growing pauperisation of the rural masses. The small farmer has been mortgaging his land and losing it, becoming a landless labourer, borrowing money which he cannot repay, and ending up as a debt slave. There are cases where unborn children have been mortgaged by their parents. Entire castes in some villages are tied to perpetual serfdom to their masters. Girls are sometimes sold to brothels. ... The fact is that many landless labourers are actually worse off than bonded workers, who at least are free from the fear of imminent starvation (ECO 7 April 1979).

In part because of the consequent growth in rural violence, the Janata government was extremely slow to meet its promises to repeal MISA and preventive detention and very quick to replace them at the federal level by other provisions that were very much their functional equivalents and to pass "little MISAs" in several Janata-governed states.

Even so, according to *Business Week* (18 September 1978), the "Desai policy of giving top priority to agriculture and of encouraging the growth of small industry is taking its toll of business confidence. ... Many businessmen would be happy to see Desai's authoritarian predecessor, Indira Gandhi, back in the driver's seat." After the sharp post-Emergency increase in strikes during 1977 and 1978, the Federation of Indian Chambers of Commerce and Industry called upon the caretaker government to make the enforcement of discipline on workers its foremost task (EPW 8 September 1979). As for the real hope of Indian big business, "neither she nor her party has expressed regret for the Emergency" (FER 18 January 1980) and "many Delhi intellectuals believe that, after a brief honeymoon, the state of emergency effectively will be reimposed" (GUA 13 January 1980). In the northeastern state of Assam, where a strong nationalist movement has disturbed business and industry and threatens central state authority, the degree of political and police repression, including a ban on strikes in all major industries, was already "worse than [in the] Emergency days" (EPW 19 April 1980).

At what pace and to what extent political repression is likely to spread elsewhere in India again depends on economic developments and political, including regional nationalist, mobililizations. Most of India's economic growth since 1977 has been due to agricultural output favored by the weather and not to industrial investment or production. For fiscal year April 1979–

March 1980 industrial output probably declined by 3 or 4 percent. As a result of the worst drought in twenty-five years, food production fell about 7 to 10 percent, and this agricultural failure will exercise a depressive influence on industrial production and profits. For 1980 no increase in real investment is forecast. Despite the cushion provided by carry-over food stocks and foreign exchange reserves, these developments immediately exerted an upward pressure on prices, which rose 21 percent in 1979 and accelerated to an annual rate of 23 percent by April 1980 (data from ECO 20 October 1979; FER 4 January 1980; FT 5, February 1980; EPW Review of Management February 1980; FT 23 April 1980). Another consequence is likely to be renewed pressure on the balance of payments and foreign exchange reserves. There are insistent rumors that the new government is courting the multinationals again and intends to revise the Foreign Exchange Regulation Act in their favor (IT 16–31 March 1980).

Happy Days Are Here Again

Industry circles are delighted, even jubilant, over the "constructive dialogue," as their leaders put it, that the leaders of the government have entered into with them, with the Prime Minister herself actively participating in it. Their latest meeting with the Prime Minister, with the Finance, Commerce, Industry and Labour Ministers in attendance, seems to have been especially gratifying for them. If so far only the Finance Minister had been forthcoming and directing come-hither looks at them, the Prime Minister has now lent the full weight of her authority behind the overtures to industrialists to take advantage of the government's responsive mood towards their needs and aspirations in order to help them step up production and investment.

What is most interesting to watch in this context is the forthright manner in which business leaders feel free to state their demands and stake their claims to concessions and incentives and the warmth with which the government side responds to these demands. The Prime Minister herself told them face to face that the government would be willing to grant them all that they were asking for, to remove alleged constraints on their activity, give them more incentives for gainful production, and further relax licensing restrictions and irksome controls on prices and distribution (EPW September 6, 1980).

One thing seems certain: the Indian bourgeoisie is again united behind Mrs. Gandhi, and the political opposition has fallen into complete disarray. Mrs. Gandhi has already pushed her advantage to intervene in and change the governments in nine Janata-ruled states; if she is successful, as is likely, she will probably go after the three CPI(M) governments in Kerala, West Bengal, and Tripura. Industrial labor will probably be unable to withstand another assault from business and the state, if the further deterioration and/or concentration of the economy moves them to launch one. Rural India may again be visited by severe instability and violence, however. The green revolution has left many big farmers and medium peasants with costly investments in agricultural equipment and techniques, which the rise in fuel costs and the prices of petroleum-based inputs such as pesticides have rendered unprofitable. One or more bad growing seasons could exacerbate their profit situation and make them politically more active toward government and more oppressive toward small peasants and landless laborers, driving many of the latter to desperation. Therefore, Ranjan Sen (1980: 6) predicts that "bigger flare-ups are in the offing in rural India," especially in regions where the green revolution was important. Where it was not, and not only in the unstable Northeast, further regional nationalist rumblings and perhaps explosions are in the offing.

Iran

The most serious new candidate for intermediate economy, semiperipheral status, and subimperialist state role has been Iran. Indeed, the Shah of Iran claimed that "in 25 years we will be one of the Big Five" countries in the world (NW interview 14 October 1974). With its millennarian Persian tradition—whose twenty-five-hundredth birthday was ostentatiously celebrated by the Shah with worldwide publicity in 1974—its strategic location between the West and the Orient (and since 1917 on the border of the socialist East), and in recent decades its petroleum, Iran has long had an important role in the play of world economic and political forces. It has suffered from these forces throughout its unique history as a buffer state, but its ruling groups have also sought to take advantage of Iran's intermediate position.

After the Soviet Revolution of 1917 a short-lived "socialist" state was set up in part of Iran. During World War II the country was occupied by Allied forces in their war against Germany. In 1951 Prime Minister Mossadegh nationalized the Anglo-Iranian Oil Company and, with the support of organized and other urban supporters, forced the Shah into exile. Mossadegh was first opposed by Britain, which organized a boycott of Iranian oil, and then overthrown by a CIA-organized coup in 1953, which brought the Shah back and put him into indisputed power. To consolidate this power, the Shah opened doors to foreign and particularly American capital, and built up his American-backed armed and police forces to counter the Soviet Union abroad and to repress the population at home. After a brief respite between 1960 and 1963, the repression was resumed, now accompanied by a new social and economic program.

In 1963 the Shah launched a "Great White Revolution" in a land reform that transferred about 10 percent of the land from large to small owners, built up a middle and bureaucratic class based on the service sector and financed out of oil revenues, and promoted modest industrial growth based on import substitution for the newly generated internal market. Teheran's 1963 population of 1.5 million more than doubled in less than a decade. Industrial production was organized through a combination of large, substantially foreign-owned producers and inefficient, small local producers. But the production and export of petroleum continued to be the backbone of the economy. The secret police, SAVAK, and the army increasingly became the arbiters of domestic and foreign political policy. By the early 1970s Iran was a most active agent in the strengthening of OPEC, and then in the raising of petroleum prices in 1973 and 1974. At the same time, because of the progress of the import substitution policy and the spectacular change in the availability of resources derived from the huge oil revenues, and also because of modifications in the world economy, Iran switched from import substitution of light industry to export promotion and the development of heavy industry.

> The fifth five year plan [1973–1978] lays the basis for the Iranian industrialization policy. If, since the beginning of the "revolution of the Shah and the People," the development of heavy industry and the import-substitution of consumers and simple investment goods was the priority, today the main trend is the broadening and diversification of industrial production and export orientation. With an investment volume of 12 billion US $ for industry, substantial attention is devoted to the development of chemical, petrochemical and steel industry, the establishment of agro-industrial centers as well as the production of foodstuffs and the forecasted development of agriculture. . . . The already mentioned export orientation of the Iranian economic policy finds its programmatic expression in calling the 1970s the decade of export promotion. . . . Because in the meantime the domestic market for many products remains narrow, the development of optimal sizes of production units with mass production is dissolubly linked to getting export markets for the newly to be developed industries. . . . One of the principal determinants of the Iranian economic policy is the maintenance of a good investment climate. . . . The stable domestic political and foreign policy situation of the country and the therewith related continuity of the economic policy have led many enterprises of the Federal Republic of Germany to invest. The preferred branches for joint ventures are the electro industry, shoe manufacture, pharmaceuticals, motor building and the fabrication of buses. Under discussion are a number of major capital projects, such as a shipyard . . . two nuclear power plants . . . a thermal power plant, a steel plant, as well as social housing and hospitals (Kaiserliche Iranische Botschaft 1976: 16–17, 21, 23).

Government policy on industrialization is based on the overall target of Iran being an important industrial power by the 1990's, by which time oil production will be declining and the country must be a major exporter of industrial goods. The overall objective is to establish a balanced

industrial sector, utilising the country's natural resources where possible, but not based on indigenous raw materials. The time of establishing local industries merely to substitute imports has long passed.
Today Iran is looking for industries which will be competitive in world
terms, industries which in addition to meeting the country's increasing
need for particular products will be capable of competing in export
markets. Such industries should, within a predetermined period of time,
make a positive contribution to the country's balance of payments in
overall terms. ... [Through] the system of manufacturing licenses
... the Government can limit the number of manufacturing units in any
particular sector, thus avoiding a proliferation of small, inefficient, high
cost plants. ... If the Government feels that an outside company will be
better able to execute a certain project they will very often select the
outside company rather than the local company (Metra Consulting
n.d.: 126–30).

Iran appeared to be launched on an industrialization drive fired by
petroleum. The object was to convert the country into a Brazilian-model
intermediate economy and subimperialist power—if not the world's fifth
industrial power, as the Shah used to insist. But not everybody was
persuaded by these grandiose schemes. For instance, the director of the
European branch of the futurologist Hudson Institute argued in early 1975:

Iran hasn't got a chance of becoming a superpower, or even a major
economic power within the period of time—20 years—during which its
estimated oil reserves will last. ... Iran's economy by 1985, even on
the best projections, remains not much beyond what India's will be by
then, and possibly equal to or just behind Mexico's (IHT 4 March
1975).

The projections seemed to depend on the uncertainties of the world
economy. After the quadrupling of oil prices in 1973–1974 most targets of
the 1973–78 fifth five-year plan were immediately doubled and Iran became
an instant paradise for multinational enterprise and every kind of business
and personal profiteer. Indeed, many corporate balance sheets and several
countries' balance of payments were saved by sales to Iran during the 1974–
1975 recession, when sales faltered elsewhere. Iranian ports were clogged,
Balkan and Turkish roads were filled with European (including East European) trucks carrying Western merchandise to Teheran, and disorganization,
corruption, and speculation spread havoc all over the country. Yet, the world
recession reduced the demand for oil—and the price differential between
Iranian and Saudi Arabian oil reduced the demand particularly for Iranian
oil—so that Iranian foreign exchange receipts were cut drastically in 1975–
1976. Only shortly after the targets of the five-year plan were doubled, the
Iranian regime was forced to put many major projects on the back burner or
take them off the fire altogether for lack of funds. After October 1973 it was

feared that the Shah and the Arab oil barons, would destroy the world financial system with their balance-of-payments surpluses. Then in 1974–1975, in an interesting reversal, they were courted as foreign investors by the US and Germany and as lenders who would recycle their oil money to the major imperialist financial institutions and industrial enterprises. But in 1976 Iran returned to the international money market again as a borrower (albeit with an improved credit rating) to finance its balance-of-payments deficit. Its export receipts had grown by 2 percent but its import expenditures had jumped by nearly 50 percent in the year ending March 21, 1976. Like some other intermediate economies, Iran had experienced an instant boom that was quickly deflated by the recession. Being a more unstable, dependent economy than some, Iran had received a ruder shock from the cyclical recession.

Plans were made for the development of a petrochemical industry based on local petroleum, for the exploitation of the world's second-largest known reserves of natural gas, for a steel industry with the most modern gas reduction of iron ore, for copper mining and processing, for an automotive and other machine-building industry, for nuclear power plants. But the realization of the projected economic policy of export promotion faced various barriers:

> . . . the tremendous surge in domestic consumption, greater than forecast in nearly every sector, means that production will be absorbed by local demand, leaving little if any export capacity. . . . So the message is very much that Iranian industry's main concern over the next five to seven years is to keep pace or catch up with domestic demand. This is a change of emphasis even from two years back when both Iranians and prospective foreign partners were envisaging a substantial proportion of production being earmarked for export (FT 21 June 1976: Survey 19).

> The problem of productivity and wage costs touches the heart of Iran's ambitions. . . . Iran is acquiring an impressive industrial base, but it is highly questionable where competitive non-oil exports will come from except the capital intensive sectors of steel and petrochemicals. . . . From a position of virtual agricultural self-sufficiency in the late 1960's Iran is now one of the larger importers in the world . . . [which] may well hit the $2 bn. mark during the current year. . . . Several major studies have recently concluded that food imports are likely to increase rapidly over the next decade no matter what . . . (FT 21 June 1976: Survey 19, 12, 16).

These analysts and others found a combination of bottlenecks in industrial and agricultural production, and increased domestic demand and costs of production due to excessively high wages, particularly for scarce skilled labor, and too many inefficient small farms. From this observation they concluded that export promotion was not a realistic policy, except in capital-intensive industries associated with local raw materials.

But these findings suggested another conclusion: it would be expedient to relieve the supply bottlenecks and some of the "excessive" domestic demand by a forced reduction in wages, a forced increase in the efficiency—that is, first of all the size—of agricultural units, and a forced reduction of internal demand from labor and the peasantry as well as from some parts of the service-sector middle classes. This conclusion necessarily implied further economic and political repression. And this is the conclusion the Shah endorsed in order to ride the wave of export promotion. His government imposed wage ceilings, recruited large inflows of skilled workers from abroad (Pakistan, India, Korea, the Philippines) to keep down wages; initiated an agrarian counterreform to merge peasant holdings into units of not less than twenty hectares and to farm these through agribusiness; and took measures to restrict some imports and to promote exports. The already "accelerating gap between rich and poor" (FT 21 June 1976: Survey 11) grew even faster, which was inevitable with this "Brazilian model" process of capital accumulation based on capital-intensive production and export promotion in the international division of labor. As usual, the masses in Iran were excluded from the benefits of this process, which were reserved for privileged local groups that operated in junior partnership with the multinationals. The only way these groups could defend their privilege was through armed repression.

The Shah had assumed an ostentatious subimperialist economic and military-political role in the Persian Gulf and Indian Ocean region. The strategy was associated with his domestic development policy, and like it ran into trouble:

> The Shah of Iran's ambitious plans to create a new economic community, with Pakistan, Turkey, Iran, Afghanistan and India as its first members, has run into difficulties ... [and] has foundered on the continuing hostility between several of the member nations. Building on the 12-year-old Regional Cooperation for development (RCD) with Iran, Pakistan and Turkey as members, the Iranian leader hoped the organization would develop a political bite useful to his Indian Ocean and Persian Gulf strategy. His apparent success in selling the idea to the first six potential members fuelled hopes of a further expansion, taking in countries like Saudi Arabia, Egypt, Jordan, Bangladesh and Indonesia (FER 16 July 1976: 31).

Iran seemed to be trying to establish a sort of latter-day "West Asian Greater Co-Prosperity Sphere" in which it would use its oil, oil money, and military strength to bargain for economic "cooperation" with Iranian economic interests and to maintain political "stability"—both internationally and domestically—by preventing "subversion" in the Gulf states and an internal split-up on regional-ethnic bases in Pakistan. This strategy required overcoming Indo-Pakistani rivalries and Soviet influence in Afghanistan, as well as confronting Soviet military power in the Indian Ocean and on Iran's borders—

not an easy task since the Soviet Union was Iran's principal market for non-oil exports. It also required confronting the ambitions and suspicions of rival Saudi Arabia.

Iran had a very small industrial base (much smaller and less sophisticated than India's, for instance) to sustain these subimperial ambitions. Instead Iran the Shah had chosen to build up the Third World's most formidable military machine, with an annual budget of $8–$10 billion. This represented 27 percent of the total budget, taking identifiable military expenditures, and perhaps 12–15 percent of GNP if hidden military expenditures were counted (FT 21 June 1976). Since the military equipment was preponderantly imported from the United States, Iran was almost entirely dependent on the U.S. for its maintenance and use:

> Iran is now this country's biggest customer for arms, buying inordinate amounts of the most advanced and complex weaponry. Iran, as a nation and a people, does not have the technological base for this kind of armoury. Keeping it in operation requires Americans, in large and conscious numbers, on the airfield and in the maintenance shops. . . . The United States has sold Iran weapons that include the new F-14 Tomcat fighter and the Spruance class destroyer. "The F-14 system is so complicated that the U.S. Navy is having trouble keeping it operational; Iran's Spruance class detroyer will be even more sophisti-cated than those being procured by the U.S. Navy. . . . There is general agreement among U.S. personnel involved with Iranian programs that it is unlikely that Iran could go to war in the next 5 to 10 years with its current and prospective inventory . . . without U.S. support on a day-to-day basis. Can Iran count on that support? (*Washington Post* editorial, in IHT 6 August 1976; see also IHT 14–15 September 1976).

(For further discussion of the military, see Chapter 8).

The partial disintegration of the Iranian army during the revolution led by the Ayatollah Khomeini in 1978–1979 answered this question.

The overthrow of the Shah in February 1979 and subsequent political developments in Iran were hardly anticipated by anyone in the world, despite the increasing political turbulence throughout 1978. For instance, in August-September 1978 Metra Consulting Group concluded its ten-page assessment of the "present political environment" in *Iran: A Business Opportunity for the 1980s* as follows:

> In summary it can be said that whilst in mid-1978 the political situation is to an extent in a state of flux it is by no means unstable. . . . It must be remembered that a relatively volatile political climate has existed in Iran for many years. . . . So why did the situation suddenly change? In all probability it has not suddenly changed but is again showing a continuing swing of the pendulum. . . . Furthermore, taking a longer

term perspective, whilst the Shah's popularity and power have exhibited a somewhat cyclical pattern the long term trend of his popularity is upward. . . . There is no reason to suppose that today the basic religious problem poses any greater threat than it did in the past . . . whilst there is a significant amount of political unrest in Iran this is unlikely to be other than a relatively short-term factor. . . . It is the fact that there are so many conflicting interest groups in Iran which is itself likely to ensure moderation in the future. . . . In brief, by the end of 1979 there may well have been important political changes in Iran but, in our view, they are not likely to be of a sort or on a scale to reverse or even significantly hinder the country's economic future (Metra Consulting 1978: 21–24, 7).*

Nonetheless, the religious groups, the bourgeois "elite," the intelligentsia, the educated middle and lower-middle classes, the peasants, and especially the militant workers did topple the Shah and his army. As a result:

Littered across the Iranian countryside are hulks of hundreds of unfinished or unusable development projects. As one Western ambassador commented bleakly, surveying his country's wrecked hopes, "Iran has become an industrial cemetery." . . . [However], the failure of the Shah's hopes for industrial take-off through massive injections of capital and foreign technology is also, in part, the failure of Western multinationals to restrain themselves or their eager clients from indulging in inappropriate schemes. . . . In the case of Iran the consequence has also been a level of losses unprecedented in business experience world-wide, short of a major natural disaster or a global war. On conservative estimates, the likely loss of business for foreign concerns, only of major civilian projects in Iran will be nearly $38bn (£18, 6bn). Less readily identifiable defense contracts and smaller scale industrial and infrastructure work would probably double that figure (FT 4 June 1979).

Despite this gloomy assessment of the losses of the multinationals in the aftermath of the Iranian revolution, an earlier "BI survey of a dozen manufacturing firms suggests that most MNCs have done a good job protecting themselves against actual losses. These companies stand to forfeit potential sales rather than lose income from current contracts or investments" (BI 16 February 1979). Moreover, after the temporary shutdown of the oil wells, production was again raised and then leveled off at about 3 million barrels a day.

*The Metra author, in giving permission to quote, writes in part in a letter dated 26 September 1980: "The sentence 'Furthermore, taking a longer term perspective . . .' upward should either be quoted in its true context (from a low in the early 1940s to a high in 1946, to a low in 1953) or deleted. With the above reservations, I will accept the other editing, acknowledge that I got it wrong and just add that the story is not over yet (which you can also quote if you wish). Yours faithfully, [signed] Melvyn J. Else"

As of this writing in the spring of 1980, there is an ongoing internal political struggle between the followers of the Ayatollah Khomeini—with support from that part of the revolutionary left that has survived decimation at the hands of the Ayatollah's party—who oppose "Western" capitalism, and the more conciliatory and "reasonable" forces, backed by business and the West, who want to work out a "realistic" *modus vivendi* with capitalism and the West. The first President, Bani-Sadr, who was elected with 70 percent of the vote, mediates between the two but seems to lean toward the latter forces. These forces also favor the renewal of foreign investment in Iran, albeit on a less extravagant scale than before the revolution; and there are occasional reports of renewed or new contracts with major foreign and especially Japanese firms in Iran. As this struggle continues, Iran remains dependent on imports for nearly 25 percent of its food, and unemployment has grown past 4 million or over one-third of the workforce (FT 14 February 1979; IHT 7 April 1979). Despite all the fire and brimstone, the distribution of property and income has not changed substantially, and the level of living of the masses has not improved but rather declined since February 1979. There is an even greater sense of deprivation and militancy among the minority nationalities in the Kurdish, Turkish, Baluchi, and Arab-speaking regions of Iran, and in many cases the new regime in Teheran has exacerbated their repression. All of these problems plus the geopolitical strategic pressures created by the Soviet-American conflict over Afghanistan are exerting pressure on the West to promote and achieve a renewed accommodation with Iran. But the Shah's dream of making Iran the world's fifth economic and military power has been shattered. However, as we suggested above, this dream was never more than a delusion of grandeur.

Israel

Israel is a European settler state in the Middle East. Like South Africa, it includes a substantial non-European population that bears the brunt of exploitation and oppression: these are the Jews of Middle Eastern origin and Arabs who lived in Israel before 1947 (one-seventh of the population), the population in the territories occupied since the 1967 war, and over a million Palestinian refugees. Israel has a most outspoken subimperialist role in the oil-rich Arab world, a role that has been bolstered by substantial inflows of capital and military and political support from the West, particularly the United States.

> Within the Zionist movement the "subimperial" idea has existed from the beginning (Theodore Herzl, in the 1890's, habitually spoke of a Jewish state in Palestine as a potential "rampart of Europe against Asia") and there is plenty of evidence that it has increasingly been realized in recent years (Lockwood 1973: 57).

European Jewish immigration to Palestine came in several waves starting in the 1880s, which relied on outside financial support (beginning with the Rothschilds) and local Arab labor. The most profitable businesses and the best paid jobs were reserved for the Jews. During the world crisis of the 1930s and early 1940s the British interest in suppressing Arab nationalism in the Middle East largely coincided with Jewish interests in the British Mandate over Palestine. The British—often for strategic reasons—undertook substantial infrastructural road construction and port development of Jewish, but not Arab, manufacturing industry in Palestine, and permitted the inflow of petit bourgeois Jewish migrants fleeing with their capital from Nazi Germany.

> The tremendous increase in manufacturing activity was the result of two factors. First, the great wartime demand, much of it resulting from the activity of the Middle East Supply Centre; second, Palestinian industry had virtually total protection . . . (Yago 1976–1977: 124, citing Kleinov-Malul and Halevi).

After the establishment of the Israeli state in Palestine in 1948 the inflow of migration and capital accelerated and a substantial number of Palestinians became refugees. Those who remained constituted the bulk of the labor force, along with the Middle Eastern Jews. The Israeli economy was supported by an extraordinary capital inflow (in excess of exports) of over $7 billion until 1968, or $2650 per person living in the pre-1967 borders. About 70 percent of this inflow was in the form of gratuitous remittances (Yago 1976–77: 135, citing Grass and Machover). During the "fat years" between the 1967 and 1973 wars the inflow of capital accelerated: $4.3 billion came into the country during the years 1967–1970 alone (Yago 1976–1977: 136). Of course, this capital did not benefit the Palestinian refugees or the population in the occupied territories.

> The 1967 war and its aftermath pulled the Israeli economy out of its worst recession since 1950. The post-war economic boom was the result of the following factors: (1) the new markets and cheap labor available in the occupied territories; (2) the qualitative increase in the flow of capital imports and unilateral transfers from abroad which more than doubled the pre-1967 yearly average; (3) the new increase of immigration; and (4) last but far from least, large-scale demand generated by the war economy, which resulted in a partial structural shift in the economy and in the appearance of a significant military-industrial complex (Yago 1976–1977: 142 citing Bober).

Since 1973 the internationally highly open and dependent Israeli economy has suffered severely from the world crisis in capital accumulation, and particularly from the 1974–1975 recession. The results have been devaluations, severe austerity programs, the replacement of the (fairly reactionary) labor government by the "right" in the 1977 elections, and last but far from least the further development both absolutely and relatively of Israel's arms economy and subimperialist stance.

From 1974 to 1977 domestic investment dropped by more than 30 percent and GNP growth declined to nearly zero. Inflation exceeded 42 percent in 1977, and the Israeli pound was devalued several times, from 4.2 to the dollar at the end of 1973 to 15.4 to the dollar in 1977, after the pound was allowed to float. Then

> in October 1977, after consulting with Chicago economist Milton Friedman, the government announced its *mahapach*: the abolition of multiple exchange rates and the institution of a float to foster exports, as well as the phased reduction in domestic food subsidies. The cut in food subsidies would push prices up, controlling consumer demand (IHT 3 April 1978).

> The policy was designed to move Israel away from a planned economy toward a free market system, and to get the gross national product growing again after the shock of the 1973 war. By removing currency controls, cumbersome government export incentives and domestic food subsidies and by floating the Israeli pound, the government—coached by University of Chicago economist Milton Friedman—hoped that the value of the Israeli pound would plunge, the prices of Israeli-produced food would jump and domestic demand would drop. Manufacturers would thus gear production for export. The program partly succeeded (IHT n.d. May 1979).

In the first four months of 1977 prices rose 16 percent "and businessmen complained that exports had not been favored." In 1978, however, GNP recovered and grew at the highest rate since 1972, 5.2 percent, while inflation rose by over 50 percent (IHT 3 April 1978 and May 1979). Paradoxically, the peace treaty concluded with Egypt increased the demand for military expenditures, which already accounted for more than 30 percent of the government budget, as Israel began to replace its existing military installations in the Sinai peninsula—which it had agreed to return to Egypt—with new ones in the Negev desert. Military expenditures increased to over 40 percent of the budget and "for months the Cabinet has been wrangling over allocating the necessary budget cuts . . . [to reduce the relatively] heavy overspending in the civilian sector" (IHT 29 May 1979).

> The new finance minister, Yigael Hurvitz, last Monday made Israelis a lot poorer by abolishing nearly all subsidies on basic foods and services, freezing wages, cutting government services and imposing a series of fiscal restrictions. But he simultaneously upheld the decision of a cabinet committee, chaired by [Prime Minister] Begin, to settle up to 15,000 Jewish families annually in the West Bank. The estimated yearly cost is about £2,300 million, almost half of this year's national budget (STM 25 November 1979).

Domestic prices rose rapidly and the value of the Israeli pound fell faster still. The government announced the conversion of ten old pounds for one new shekel in February 1980.

> Few, if any currencies in the world, can have been devalued to the extent that the Israeli pound has. Over the last decade it has depreciated something like 10 times against the U.S. dollar. In the past year its value has fallen even faster as a result of inflation that was officially calculated at 115 percent in 1979 and was running at an annual rate of nearly 170 percent in the last quarter.

> In line with its promises of a more liberal economic policy Mr. Menahem Begin's Likud Government decided in October, 1977, to allow the Israeli pound to float. Since then the erosion in the value of the currency has been even more rapid than it was before. But there has not been a corresponding improvement in the competitiveness of Israel's exports, and last year the deficit in the country's balance of payments widened by $700m to a record $4.14bn (FT 27 February 1980).

The policy of maintaining Israel as a Western (especially American) subimperialist outpost in the Middle East and of arming it to the teeth to promote "stability" in the region continues.

> The idea that Israel might become the "watchdog" for the West was by no means novel. . . . A forced settlement along the lines of Resolution 242 would enable Egypt and Saudi Arabia to revert to their preferred role as American client states and Israel would remain the major military force in the region, with substantial arms production and advanced industrial development. As such, it would remain a valued ally for the United States, which will continue to rely on Israel and Iranian power to offset Russian influence and disruptive Arab forces. An Iranian diplomatic source explains that "without Israeli power in the Middle East the Shah feels that the Arabs would be difficult to control and the Russians would very much gain an upper hand in the entire area. . . ." Value judgements aside, there is plausibility to [U.S.] Senator Henry Jackson's observations that Iran, Israel and Saudi Arabia "have served to inhibit and contain those irresponsible and radical elements in certain Arab states . . . who, were they free to do so, would pose a grave threat indeed to our principal sources of petroleum," and that "the Saudis understand . . . that Israel and Iran play a vital stabilizing role." Like the United States, Saudi Arabia fears Russian influence, revolutionary movements in the peninsula (where Iran is already engaged in counterinsurgency), the leftist regime in South Yemen, and future Qaddafis. It is likely to accept a powerful Israel, with more limited ambitions,within an American-based alliance. The same is true of Egypt. . . . (Chomsky 1974: 29).

Russia requires Western currencies if it is to pursue its policies of détente, and can therefore be expected to try to maintain a major role in providing armaments to the Arab states, as will the European powers. The gradual conversion of Israel into a military arsenal can be expected to continue under such an arrangement. About one-quarter of the Israeli work force is reported to be employed in armaments production, which already constitutes a major export industry and may soon become the major source of foreign exchange. The interests of ruling groups and the imperial powers converge on the creation of a network of hostile states, jointly committed to repression of radical nationalism. Not a pretty picture, but a plausible projection, I am afraid. One might add that a system of Balkanization under the American aegis, while perhaps fairly stable, nevertheless contains explosive forces that might erupt into a major war.

If the emerging system includes a Palestinian state, there is every likelihood that it will be under the domination of Israel and Jordan, which will continue to pursue parallel policies as American allies. Since 1967, Israel has come to rely heavily on an Arab proletariat imported by day from occupied territories. ... The Palestinian state is likely to be a kind of Bantustan, a reservoir of cheap labor . . . while perpetuating conditions of economic dependence. ... One can expect the Palestinian state, if it comes into being, to develop on the same model. The Palestinian movement is sometimes described in the West as a movement of revolutionary socialists, but this is far from an accurate characterization. Radical and libertarian elements in the movement will not have a bright future in a Palestinian state dominated by its neighbors, with discriminatory structures that may even be exaggerated in reaction to hopelessness and subordination (Chomsky 1974: 30–33).

The Israeli government has so far steadfastly refused to consider the establishment of a Palestinian state. Prime Minister Begin remains totally opposed to the idea and defends his position with the claim that it is the problems of the Arab world in general, and not those of the Palestinians, that constitute the real threat to stability in the Middle East. However, "the opposition Labour Party, while officially favouring splitting the West Bank with Jordan, is privately toying with the idea of an Israeli-Palestinian-Jordanian economic federation on the lines of Benelux" (FT 25 February 1980). Moreover, President Carter has already publicly called for a "home" for the Palestinians; and former U.S. Undersecretary of State George Ball, who has often been a weathervane of American foreign policy, especially toward the Middle East, seems to favor the establishment of a Palestinian state to resolve the issue and has written under the title of "Palestinians and th Fate of Western Civilization":

We can no longer doltishly ignore the prime political reality of the Palestinian issue. So far we have persistently approached the Middle

Eastern problem from the wrong side. . . . So long as the United States delays a frontal attack on the Palestinian issue, it is alienating the whole Moslem world, as shattered U.S. embassies have demonstrated (GAW 3 January 1980: 15, citing WP).

The governments of important West European countries individually and collectively are also offering "increasing support . . . for the Palestinian cause" (FT 22 February 1980). Thus, the pressures for the beginnings of some kind of Palestinian settlement may become irresistible.

About one-quarter of Israeli industrial employment and production is in the armaments sector (Chomsky 1974: 30, citing Sheldon Krishner in *New Outlook* September 1973 for employment; Albrecht et al. 1976: 48, citing *Israels Aussenhandel* No. 7, 1975: 6–8).

> Israel has established the most sophisticated and probably in terms of turnover the largest arms production of all developing countries. Due to its unique situation with immigration of highly qualified personnel from industrialized countries as well as technical and large financial assistance, primarily from the United States, Israeli companies started the development and production of a wide range of weapon systems. The economic crisis of the country and the limited absorption capacity of its own armed forces have driven Israel to start an unprecedented export drive to keep its existing capacities occupied. Despite some success in exporting arms indiscriminately to any country willing to pay, these efforts are limited in scope since Israel's biggest technology supplier, the United States, reserves the right to control the end use of supplies. . . . The intrinsic pattern of arms production has put Israel today in a situation where the whole industry is tailored according to the requirements of arms manufacture while the economy's survival depends increasingly on the large scale export of arms at almost any price (Lock and Wulf 1977: xiii–xiv, xix).

According to recent estimates of the Israeli Defense Ministry, this outflow [of arms] will amount to at least $80 million in 1972. By 1975 it is expected to reach $150 million. (Lockwood 1973: 58).

Israeli Arms Sales Up Fivefold Since 1973 War
Aim Is $400 Million This Year

Israel's arms industry, which has grown rapidly since the Yom Kippur war of 1973, has vastly increased its exports of armaments to foreign countries, with total sales last year of $320 million compared with prewar sales averaging $60 million a year. . . . For a small country, with a staggering balance of payments deficit, the burgeoning arms industry represents both a means of trying to close the trade gap as well as a commitment toward providing much of its own weaponry while vigorously competing in the world arms market to sell its surpluses. . . . Israel is identified as a primary arms supplier to Bolivia, Ecuador, El Salvador, Mexico and Nicaragua (NYT 16 January 1976).

Israel's arms exports amounted to 500 million US $ in 1976. US sources predict a 100 percent increase for 1977, namely 1 billion US $ (*Aviation Week and Space Technology* 13 December 1976: 14, cited by Lock and Wulf 1977: xix fn.).

Israel has also decided to produce a fighter plane of its own at an estimated deployment cost of between $750 million and $2 billion (FT 26 February 1980). And numerous reports attributed to the CIA claim that Israel has already produced nuclear bombs, both independently and in collaboration with South Africa, which supplied the uranium.

It is no accident that weapons are presently [1973] one of Israel's principal industries. In terms of Israel's role as one of the protectors of imperialism in the Middle East, it is logical that such firms as Motorola or General Telephone would seek to establish local branches in order to profit from the demands of the Israeli armed forces. At the same time, Israel's political and military role in certain Third World nations has laid the foundation for profitable military exports. For more than a decade, Israeli "foreign assistance" programs, which are largely financed by American sources, have included such components as training of paratroopers . . . or counterinsurgency training for the police and armed forces. . . .

One of the basic factors behind expanding weapons production is private investment, particularly by American companies. Their goal is to develop Israeli subsidiaries that can supply both the domestic arms market and foreign markets. This ambition was bluntly stated by an American businessman:

We have a number of objectives here in Israel. The first is to begin supplying the local air force . . . and the third aim is to turn Israel into our base of international operations for the supply of our expanding export business. The latter now encompasses some 20 countries (Lockwood 1973: 63, 59, citing interview with N. M. Zelazo, president of Astronautics Corporation of America, *Israel Export and Trade Journal* December 1971).

South Africa

South Africa is often regarded as an economic, social, and political system so unique as to defy classification or comparison. Sometimes South Africa, or at least its four million white population, is regarded as part of the "metropolitan" industrialized world or as one of its white settler dominions, analogous to Canada and Australia. The more than twenty million black inhabitants of South Africa and its recently formed "independent" Bantustan republics (as well as its two million "coloreds") are left out of this classification or are simply counted as part of the rest of Africa, although economically, socially and politically they are effectively part of the Republic of South Africa. The policies of segregation, then apartheid, and other aspects of race relations in South Africa, Namibia/South West Africa, and so far in Zimbabwe/Rhodesia are generally regarded in the West as aberrations of a racist ideology founded on the numerical relation between the white minority and the black majority. In Africa, however, there is consciousness that racism and apartheid in South Africa and Rhodesia are really the political instruments of the economic exploitation of the black by the white population and its bourgeoisie at home and abroad. This relationship has been persuasively analyzed by Legassick (1974), Wolpe (1972), and others.

> Apartheid is the attempt of the capitalist class to meet the expanding demand for cheap African labor in the era of industrial manufacturing capital; at the same time it is the realisation of the demand of White workers for protection against the resulting competition from Black workers (Wolpe 1972: 427).

> Apartheid has meant an extension to the manufacturing economy of the structure of the goldmining industry (Legassick 1974: 47).

The function of the reserves in which the labor supply is produced, maintained in part, and reproduced for supply as superexploited cheap migrant workers to the mining and agricultural economy of South Africa is examined in the discussion of superexploitation (Chapter 5). Apartheid and the "pass laws," which restrict the residence and movement of black workers in South African urban areas and the employment of black labor in certain occupations or occupational and supervisory grades, are but an extension of the racist segregation essential to the industrial economy. In South Africa superexploitation is enforced through political oppression by the military and police force.

Industrial production, including heavy industry, machine building, and major armanents production, has indeed grown rapidly in South Africa during the last decades, as it has in India and Brazil. Military expenditures increased tenfold during the decade of the 1960s. South African industrial development has been marked by far-reaching and deep-going penetration by imperialist—British, U.S., German, French, and other foreign—capital on the one hand, and by low wages in the agricultural, mining, and much of the industrial sector on the other. The basis of this "progress" has been the superexploitation of black workers and the exclusion of the vast majority of the population from all benefits of accumulation and development through apartheid. For instance, by orthodox reckoning, the seven million people or over 30 percent of the population in the Bantustans account for a 2 percent share in the South African GNP (Turok and Maxey 1976: 247, citing U.N. data). Thus, as an imperialist junior partner, South African capital and its state superexploit the "peripheral" African population.

South Africa may also be regarded as an intermediate, semiperipheral economy, and by virtue of its role and ambitions on the continent, as a subimperialist power. In this regard Ehrensaft writes:

Until recently, the hybrid South African form of semi-industrial capitalism appeared to be the product of a unique historical experience. Looking at the Brazilian "economic miracle," however, one is struck by a number of parallels with the South African political economy. The two societies seem to share the following characteristics: (1) the national market for durables (which have higher capital-output rations than non-durables) is increased by squeezing the real income of the masses and redistributing an already skewed income even more in favor of the upper and middle classes; (2) squeezing the masses requires an organizationally and technologically proficient military and police apparatus which has the support or acquiescence of the upper—and middle—income groups (roughly a fifth of the population) which pursues a policy of crushing all opposition to the state; (3) the state is strongly linked with metropolitan capital, largely in the form of direct investment by multinational corporations; these corporations dominate the durable and capital goods sector; (4) the state is an active organizer of the accumulation of capital and operates with a long-term perspective toward strengthening the relative power and autonomy of the national economy in the world system; in particular, the state operates in conjunction with capital to increase the proportion of manufactured goods in total exports. These four characteristics together define a mode of semi-industrial capitalism which is termed "polarized accumulation." There is a fifth characteristic present for Brazil and South Africa, which, however, may not be an essential element of polarized accumulation: subimperialism, one aspect of which is the opening up of export outlets in weaker surrounding societies and gaining concessions from the metropole with respect to market openings in return for services rendered. . . .(Ehrensaft 1976: 65).

It seems unlikely that income redistribution will serve as a principal vehicle for maintaining South Africa's rate of industrial expansion. Low wages and tight control of labor make South Africa attractive to multinational capital as a regional export center for manufactured goods, as in the case of Brazil. . . . (Ehrensaft 1976: 84).

Ehrenshaft suggests the following alternatives to widening the internal market and exporting manufactures to other peripheral countries that might demand more than symbolic reductions of apartheid as political concessions for their purchase of South African exports:

First, the state might develop high-technology exports for selected sectors which will be internationally competitive in and of themselves, such as military equipment, mining equipment, or nuclear energy processes. Second, the regime may use its scarce mineral resources to extract concessions from metropolitan governments concerning entry of South African manufactures, such as textiles, leather goods, or agricultural products. Third, export revenues could be used to support export industries until optimal scales are reached, at which point the low wages of non-whites would yield competitive advantages and elimination of the need for subsidies. Trade flows from all three categories would be largely to the central countries of the world system, where there is far less resistance to South African goods than in the periphery. Finally, there is another strategy which could cut dependence on exports of wasting assets—namely, investment of capital gained from these exports to the central economies, capital, which would eventually bring an inflow of capital returns. Anglo-Americans have already experienced the impulsion to expand ... investments beyond South Africa or stagnate.... (Ehrensaft 1976: 84–85).

Despite South Africa's alleged pariah status in the world and countless resolutions by the United Nations and the Organization of African States intended to isolate South Africa, the country has a fundamental economic, political, and strategic position in the imperialist system, a position that has seemed to grow on all three counts during the contemporary crisis. For one thing, South Africa produces 80 percent of the capitalist world's gold, whose price has multiplied and whose financial importance seems destined to grow during the crisis despite American "efforts" to demonetize it. Thus, although South Africa has suffered the strains of the world economic crisis like other economies, increases in the price of gold—which skyrocketed in late 1979 and early 1980—have given the South African economy a big shot in the arm. South Africa is also one of the most important producers and exporters of uranium, platinum, antimony, copper, lead, zinc, manganese, chrome, vermalite, fluorspar, asbestos, vanadium, vermiculite, and sillimanite in the imperialist world. South Africa's strategic location between the Atlantic and Indian oceans on the petroleum transport route from the Middle East to Europe and America is evident. Evident also are the economic dependence of Zimbabwe/Rhodesia; Mozambique, which following independence *and* the decline in the gold value of wages reduced the export of migrant laborers to the South African mines from one hundred thousand a year to thirty thousand, but still offers its port facilities to South African trade and intends to export electricity from its Cabora Bassa Dam to South Africa under the revolutionary Freilimo; and Zambia, whose President Kaunda has had to turn economically and politically to South Africa to help his country out of its economic crisis. Furthermore, the crucial political role of South Africa in any political "solution" in the whole southern African region is evident from the daily press.

Because of the advanced development of the South African mining and industrial economy combined with the low wages enforced through apartheid and repression, as in Soweto, South Africa is a paradise for foreign investment, which earns higher rates of profit there than almost anywhere else. An advertisement placed in British newspapers by the South African Embassy reads in part:

> In South Africa, new business opportunities are developing as fast as our industry. Nowadays South Africa offers more than just a vast market for the British businessman. Our industry has grown at an ever increasing rate, founded not only on gold and diamonds, but soundly based on many manufacturing of all types. As these industries continue to develop, so does our need for finance and know-how. . . . "South Africa is on the eve of a new era of economic developments and achievements." Not the words of an optimistic politician, but a hard-headed financier. . . . Our policy is to create a nucleus in Southern Africa of independent states, . . . a stable economic bloc in which individual economy may grow unhindered by artificial restraints. . . . Already British enterprise has played a major role in our development. It's estimated that of all direct investment in South Africa by foreign companies UK capital and technical know-how represents 60 percent of the total. With our lack of restrictions on the export of profits and dividends, this directly helps the British economy. Hence the sight of a booming South African economy is good news to any British business-man. . . . Equally we feel that Britain will welcome many manufactured products that South Africa produces. This is already borne out by the dramatic increase over the past three years in our exports of man-ufactured goods to your country. . . . And in many cases, the goods we send you have been manufactured by companies in which British enterprise has a substantial stake. . . . What is needed is further in-vestment by your companies in this rich field. . . .

Some of the major development projects and investment opportunities specifically mentioned in the advertisement are hydroelectric schemes, a nuclear power station, enriched uranium "from our own unique process," a 500-mile rail link to mining areas, mining expansion, coal mining for export, new harbor complexes, extension of the three national steel works, and smelters for other metals.

The narrowness of the South African market, which could only be expanded through economically and politically unacceptable relaxations of the apartheid policy, drives South Africa to develop export markets else-where in Africa. The result is the sometimes secret, sometimes not "dia-logue" with at least a dozen black African states. "The background of the dialogue is economic reasons; South Africa needs the African market" (FAZ 25 September 1974). The African states—as well as some South African and imperialist business interests, such as the Anglo-American Oppenheimer, who fear declining supplies of skilled and other workers as Mozambique and

Malawi restrict the flow of migrant labor—press for some relaxation of apartheid. Consequently, there has been a fundamental change in the thinking of high officials in the South African governments on apartheid. It is now recognized that South Africa's racist ideology will have to be modified to accomodate the economic facts of life. The proposed response was outlined in the Wiehahn and Riekert commissions on labor laws (FT 2 October 1979).

The Wiehahn Commission recommended that black workers be permitted to unionize, and the Rickert Commission recommended that the pass laws be relaxed to permit greater freedom of movement for the black population. If implemented, both proposals would open the door for black workers to skilled jobs, for which white South African and international capital is finding an increasing shortage of white workers. However, the bills to reform the labor law that were subsequently introduced into Parliament by Labor Minister Fanie Botha were only "a pale shadow of the Wiehahn proposals— a 'cynical exercise' " (IHT 12 June 1979). Black migrants and commuters, that is about 80 percent of black workers, were excluded from the proposed reforms, and racial segregation in the unions was to all intents and purposes maintained. In fact, the control over and expulsion of Africans who are living in the cities "illegally" has been strengthened by increasing fines on their employers and threats against their landlords.

The political-economic objective of the South African regime seems to be to foster a relatively more privileged skilled working class and middle class among urban blacks in an attempt to divide and rule all the blacks better. This policy has nothing to offer rural blacks, who are considered less of a political threat in South Africa.

> For urban blacks the Riekert Commission on labour mobility and Wiehahn Commission on black labour rights have given an impression of change. But the practical results of their recommendations have been few, with the main novelty being that the government of Mr. P. W. Botha has replaced a few legal obstructions by other more subtle ones—a move in line with his general tendency to make administrative rather than political changes. His visit to Soweto and talk of amending the marriage laws received publicity, but achieved little (FT 3 March 1980).

Even so, "Botha faces [a] right-wing backlash at [the] party congress . . . against the cautiously reformist approach of his administration. . . . The key issue at the congress will be the proposed changes in labour laws . . . [as] the extreme right-wing Herstige Nasionale party" steps up the counterattack under the leadership of the disgraced former Minister of Information Connie Mulder (FT 17 September 1979). For Prime Minister Botha, the mild domestic reforms are part of a "total strategy" that is relatively dovish on internal economic reforms and extremely hawkish on political and foreign "security" issues.

> The concept of the total strategy is that the onslaught on South Africa is only 20 per cent military, and 80 per cent political and psychological.

The conclusion is that the Government must launch a gigantic hearts-and-minds campaign to win the domestic population's support—especially that of the black majority. . . . The strategy is already being implemented, and has resulted in Gen. Malan and his fellow military commanders rising rapidly to prominence. . . . The key organisations in the new structure are the State Security Council and the Prime Minister's Office. The State Security Council . . . has now been promoted to being a full Cabinet Committee . . . and is regarded by many as a sort of inner Cabinet (FT 29 February 1980).

The Botha strategy is the "total strategy" of his military advisers who still are closest to him as he wears the two hats of Prime Minister and Minister of Defense. It is the strategy against what is seen as a total onslaught on the "Christian western values" which he believes his Government represents. "It is a struggle of the Christian western civilisation against the powers of darkness and Marxism," he said in a characteristic passage to the Congress, "not just a black-white struggle." It therefore covers the whole spectrum, socio-political, economic, and international. Much of it has been left deliberately vague, at least in part not to frighten the deeply conservative majority of Mr. Botha's own party. But enough has been spelt out to give a clear indication of the intended direction (FT 2 October 1979).

"It does indicate a totalitarian drift," Dr. Frederick van Zyl Slabbert, leader of the opposition Progressive Federal Party says (FT 29 February 1980).

According to the *Financial Times* (29 February 1980), "Pretoria prepares for total war." The similarity between this "total strategy" in South Africa and the "national security doctrine" espoused in Brazil, Argentina, Chile, and other countries in Latin America and elsewhere (examined in Chapter 7) is all too painfully evident. So is "Mr. Botha's strategy . . . for a 'constellation of states' in Southern Africa. At times the constellation appears to be a planned anti-communist military alliance covering all those countries south of the equator in Africa which might be persuaded to be sympathetic" (FT 2 October 1979)

It is hard to tell how realistic this South African strategy is. Domestically, it is possible that the policy of further differentiating the black population may backfire by first encouraging and then frustrating the economic and social ambitions of "favored" blacks, some of whom may react by offering more militant political leadership to the black population as a whole. Unless and until these and other developments lead to visibly sharpened conflict between the races within South Africa, internationally the South African strategy is bearing fruits. For some years now, and despite their protestations against apartheid, both south and north of the equator:

scores of countries trade with South Africa, including 19 black African states . . . Angola, Botswana, Central African Republic, Chad, Congo,

Gabbon, Ghana, Ivory Coast, Lesotho, Liberia, Malagasy Republic, Malawi, Mauritius, Mozambique, Nigeria, Senegal, Swaziland, Zaire, Zambia. Their economic dealings with South Africa are flourishing and growing: large-scale imports and exports of raw materials, building equipment, pharmaceuticals and foods, airline passenger and freight connections; railway projects; shipping lines; construction of office buildings, hotels and housing; tourism; technical aid in disease control; construction, engineering and metallurgical equipment for copper and diamond mines; financial investments, development loads and long-term credit arrangements. . . . Such principled friends of African liberation as Saudi Arabia, Kuwait, Jordan, Egypt, Dubai and Abu Dhabi traffic with South Africa (IHT 13–14 November 1976).

South Africa's strongest economic, political, and military ties outside the West, however, are with other subimperialist states and bastions of the imperialist West: codevelopment of weapons with and exports of uranium to Israel, uranium-oil exchange and naval base facilities with Iran, secret police cooperation with Taiwan against Chinese "penetration" in Africa, military relations with Australia, and increasing economic ties with all of these nations. South Africa's armaments production is examined elsewhere (Chapter 8). Here we can note that, according to some reports, South Africa has been developing the atomic bomb with the help of West Germany and, particularly, France in a trilateral arrangement with Iran (FAZ 29 June 1974). According to other reports, South Africa has already built a nuclear bomb in cooperation with Israel and exploded one at sea in 1979.

Conclusion

The current world economic crisis is generating pressures and opportunites for a limited number of Third World economies to participate in the international division of labor in new ways and on the basis of a further development of their own productive forces. We have examined some aspects of this economic adaptation in Brazil, Mexico, Argentina, India, Iran, Israel, and South Africa. In most of these countries economic growth and the associated political power have been manifested through "subimperialist" policies. Nonetheless, this intermediate semiperipheral development in the Third World is limited in several important ways. The world crisis generates new obstacles as well as new opportunites for these economies to participate in a new international division of labor. Like others in the Third World, they—even petroleum-exporting Iran—suffer from balance-of-payments problems that threaten their development. Domestic and foreign investment is restricted by generally low rates of profit for the metropolitan countries and more onerous terms for the debtor countries. Exports are inhibited by limited market demand and/or protectionist restrictions in the importing countries. The "model" of capital accumulation and economic development in these intermediate economies is very much based on and limited by production for export, for public demand of capital goods from the private sector, and for luxury demand by a small group of high-income earners. In none of these economies is there any prospect that the masses of the population will in the forseeable future share the benefits of this growth model to any substantial extent. On the contrary, in several of these countries the relative and absolute population that is excluded from any benefits of economic growth is rising as increasing numbers of people are either superexploited or bypassed by the productive process. (This holds for Israel if the Palestinians are counted as part of the population.) For the same reason, the prospects for political liberalization remain dim indeed.

None of these countries is likely to become a metropolitan economy in the forseeable future. For any country to do so, it would have to reverse the internal disarticulation of the economy, which excludes a majority of the population from benefits, and successfully outcompete countries in Southern and Eastern Europe, including the Soviet Union, and perhaps China, whose opportunities for emergence from semiperipheral status to a central role in the world economy are very much greater.

Chapter 2
Third World Agriculture and Agribusiness

World agriculture is undergoing rapid and important changes in the course of the economic crisis. Agricultural prices and investment were maintained at low levels during the postwar industrial expansion, but the crisis in industry has rendered the raw materials sector relatively more important. The economic crisis is dampening aggregate income and demand and at the same time making the distribution of income increasingly unequal in the North and especially in the South. As a result, there are significant shifts in consumer demand for agricultural products, including a shift to low-quality meat for hamburgers in the North and to certain high-income foods in both the North and the South. Guided by transnational agribusiness, agricultural production in the Third World is adapting to meet this new export and internal high-income demand. In its rapid spread through many parts of the Third World, agribusiness is managing to make local agriculture and its peasants or laborers bear the major investment costs and risks of the agricultural enterprise and to exclude them from most of the benefits of agribusiness and even from much of their land. Consequently, more and more people in or from rural areas in the Third World can't afford to live.

Agribusiness has rapidly become recognized as the most important economic enterprise in the world, employing over 60 per cent of the world's economically active population.
Ray Goldberg, Harvard Business School, inventor of the term agribusiness

Instead of there being an offshore business and a domestic business, there is a world market.
Chairman, Coca-Cola Company

With strong demand, negligible stocks, and high

prices it is not now advantageous to U.S. agriculture to move significant amounts of food under PL 480 [Food for Peace]. . . . Neither we nor other rich countries are willing to forego substantial foreign exchange earnings in the interest of feeding the poor.

Lyle P. Schertz, Foreign Affairs

To give food aid to countries just because people are starving is a pretty weak reason.

Dan Ellerman, U.S. National Security Council

Our primary concern is commercial exports. . . . We can't subordinate our commercial exports to needy people.

Richard Bell, U.S. Assistant Secretary of Agriculture

Food is a weapon. It is now one of the˙principal tools in our negotiating kit.

Earl Butz, U.S. Secretary of Agriculture

Food is power. In a very real sense it is our extra measure of power.

U.S. Senator Hubert Humphrey

In a cooler and therefore hungrier world, the U.S. near-monopoly as a food exporter . . . could give the U.S. a measure of power it never had before— possibly an economic and political dominance greater than that of the immediate post-World War II years. . . . Washington would acquire vital life and death power over the fate of multitudes of the needy.

U.S. Central Intelligence Agency,
Office of Political Research

People Who Can't Afford to Live
Let Them Eat Promises
Headlines in the London Observer *and* Guardian

Food Is Power

These eminently realistic statements of fact and highly objective predictions from authoritative sources were all made in or about 1974. In that year, and the preceding one, a cyclical world food shortage manifested itself both in exceptionally high prices for agricultural commodities—which benefited principally producers in the industrially developed countries (see WE: Chapters 2 and 5)—and in widespread deaths from famine in several parts of the Third World. These circumstances, and the 1974 World Food Conference in Rome, where agribusiness contributed the largest delegation by far, briefly focused public attention on food power and the associated chronic hunger and starvation in the Third World.

At the end of World War II food power became an important foreign policy tool of the U.S. government. The United States supplied war-ravaged hungry countries with food through, successively, Lend-Lease, UNRRA, and bilateral programs—at a rising political price. Later, in the 1950s and 1960s, "surplus" U.S. food, generated by a price support program designed to protect big American farmers (while sacrificing millions of small family farmers to progress), was taken off the domestic market through the Public Law 480 "Food for Peace" program. Through this program U.S. producers penetrated Third World markets and competed with local producers. The sales of U.S. food in Third World countries generated "counterpart" funds in foreign currencies, which the United States used to further its imperialistic economic, political, and military programs (this program has been frequently analyzed, e.g. Gustafsson 1977; NACLA 1975a; George 1976: Chapter 8, Wallenstein 1976).

In the 1970s the United States abandoned much of its domestic agricultural price support program and replaced the associated Food for Peace grants with a massive commercial agricultural export drive to boost profits at home and to help fill the gaping hole in its balance of trade and payments. Since the beginning of the U.S. New Economic Policy on August 15, 1971, and the devaluation of the dollar (aimed in part at boosting agricultural exports) the two principal items in the U.S. export drive have been agricultural commodities and weapons, whose commercial sale also replaced the earlier grants (see Chapter 8). The U.S. Department of Agriculture and the Central Intelligence Agency have predicted increasing market shortages of food, particularly of the grains whose most efficient producer and major exporter is the United States. If these predictions are borne out, American food power will increase even without a subsidized Food for Peace program and even taking into consideration the twenty-year cycle of drought in the U.S. wheat belt (1910s, 1930s dust bowl, 1950s, and right on schedule again in the mid 1970s). From 1977 grains were again in surplus, and in 1978 American farmers organized a march on Washington coupled with an attempted strike (reminiscent of earlier ones that failed) to demand the reintroduction of "parity" price supports. The U.S. Secretary of Agriculture, Bob Bergland, tried to organize Canada and other grain exporters into a United States–led world cartel to support the world wheat market price (IHT 5 July 1977). The United States exports over half its production of wheat, wheat flour, and rice, and its exports account for about half of the world's trade in these products (OECD 1976b: 135–6). For the foreseeable future the United States and, to a lesser extent, Canada, Australia, France, and Argentina will remain the major exporters of wheat and wheat flour, which is the most important agricultural product in world trade, and of grains in general. The United States is also the world's largest exporter of soybeans (a fourth of its output and half of world exports) as well as animal fodder and feedstuffs.

The European Common Market countries are also major efficient producers of agricultural products. France in particular, but also Germany and other countries, support and protect farmers and domestic markets with consumer- and state-subsidized prices and with import restrictions on food produced outside the Common Market through their Common Agricultural Policy. The European Economic Community, with the partial exception of Great Britain, has increasingly reduced its dependence on agricultural imports, particularly from the Third World, since 1960 and is entirely or almost self-sufficient in the production of sugar beet, potatoes, wine, milk, butter, cheese, beef, pork, poultry and eggs, all grains (91 percent), and fresh vegetables (94 percent) (Bergmann 1977: 412). The European Economic Community still imports "tropical dessert" crops and fruits from the Third World, with preference given to the African, Caribbean, and Pacific countries that subscribe to the Lomé Convention, and also imports over three quarters of its vegetable fats and oils and protein concentrates for animal feed, which it buys principally from the United States. France has traditionally exported wheat (outside the Common Market) and some other commodities, such as butter at subsidized prices. There are several reasons to believe that Western Europe will soon follow in the footsteps of the United States and use or modify its protectionist agricultural policy to promote a commercial export drive.

> Since European economies will not be able to cope with their employment problem, one of their aims will be to keep as many people as possible on the land. Since they will tend to be fairly productive there, outlets will have to be found for their production. Another component of the intrinsic output-oriented tendencies is the export value of agricultural surpluses. For obvious reasons connected with lack of raw materials—particularly oil—the trade balances of most European countries will show chronic tendencies toward deficits. Exporting grain and even meat may be one of the few ways of alleviating foreign trade difficulties. . . . The conclusions of the OECD . . . therefore seem unassailable; the EEC will, in coming years, be more and more present as an exporter on world markets . . . [which] will certainly not be welcomed by the United States (Bergmann 1977: 412–13).

Yet there is another aspect to the export drive, which is perhaps politically and economically more important than keeping people down on the farm to control urban employment. If European capital and its states feel constrained to keep real wages down in order to become more competitive on the world market, in addition to the deliberate unemployment policy that is already being pursued (Frank 1978d) they will have to hold down the cost of wage goods such as food by eliminating some artificial price supports and compensating farmers through increased (perhaps subsidized) exports of agricultural commodities.

But both of these alternatives (more and cheaper agricultural products either for export or for the home market) or variants of a single policy (bigger and more profitable agricultural production) would involve the sacrifice of inefficient small farmers on the altar of national or West European policies designed to increase agricultural exports and/or to increase or maintain industrial exports produced at competitive wage rates. The latter policy might even involve increased imports (instead of or in addition to exports) of food to hold down the prices of food and thereby the cost of wage goods. The other alternative is to continue to (over) protect inefficient small farmers at the cost of consumers and taxpayers. In essence, several West European countries, and particularly France, face a difficult political choice. One policy, favored by big internationally oriented capital (represented in France by President Giscard and his Prime Minister Barre) and perhaps labor (represented by the parties that formed the Union de Gauche) if it is placated with lower food prices, would sacrifice many small farmers and merchants for greater efficiency, lower costs, and higher profits. The other policy (represented by the Gaullist Jacques Chirac) would protect farmers and capital oriented to the domestic market, but would generate labor unrest and perhaps alarm internationally oriented capital. This intraclass policy difference between the "internationalists" on the one hand and the "nationalists" and farmers on the other poses a difficult political problem in the context of the sharpening class struggle between labor and capital over wages and profits and the growing competition between national or European capital for protection and European and American multinational and Japanese exports for a "free market." Both of these struggles are being intensified by the world economic crisis. (This intrabourgeois policy conflict was presented in another context for France by Gilbert Mathieu in *Le Monde,* 22 March 1978.) The resolution of this unsettled political policy conflict between the right and far right parties in Europe—which, of course, differ also on other aspects of their political "model solutions" for the current crisis—will affect the prospects for agricultural supply and demand on the European market, and therefore Third World agricultural exports.

Japan, on the other hand, is and may be expected to remain the world's largest importer of agricultural commodities (ten percent of the world total), especially from the United States (OECD 1976b: 153, 164) but for some products increasingly from the Third World.

Eastern Europe and the Soviet Union are both exporters and importers of agricultural commodities, but on balance they are importers and they can be expected to become increasingly important ones. The Soviet Union exports grain to some grain-deficit countries in Eastern Europe, and these in turn export higher-value agricultural commodities, such as meat and vegetables, to Western Europe. The Soviet Union, Poland, Czechoslovakia, and the German Democratic Republic are significant importers of grain, the first two particularly from the principal Western exporters, especially the United States. Much of this imported grain, like the protein concentrates that Western Europe imports from the United States, is used to support livestock and growing meat consumption (and some export) in Eastern Europe and the Soviet Union. The Soviet Union also imports meat from Argentina; in fact, the U.S.S.R. is the principal importer from Argentina, particularly since 1974, when Argentina and other meat-exporting countries were excluded from the Common Market. The long-term grain purchase agreements concluded between the U.S.S.R. and the United States, as well as analyses of Soviet and East European economic, social, and political developments, suggest that these countries are becoming increasingly important importers of agricultural commodities, especially high-value products like meat, fruit, and dessert crops, as well as industrial crops, such as cotton, that may increasingly be supplied by Third World countries.

Long-term and middle-range projections of supply and demand, surpluses and shortages at world and regional levels, and import requirements and export availabilities of agricultural commodities have become a common exercise for business and research organizations. Notable among these projections are those of the United Nations Food and Agricultural Organization (FAO) and its allied institutions such as the World Food Council (WEC), the U.S. Department of Agriculture (USDA), and the Organization for Economic Co-operation and Development (OECD) of the industrial capitalist countries. But these projections are not very reliable or useful either for the Third World or for the world as a whole (if they are made for the latter at all).

> Projections of domestic demand and supply . . . at best represent a statistical exercise. Both because of the limitations of the methodology and the data available such exercises cannot be more than broad approximations. As is well-known, because of the difficulties in assessing likely political and social situations and future price trends, most demand projections take into account mainly population and income growth. In simple projection exercises these two are sometimes treated as exogenously determined and independent of each other. Similarly, on the supply side, it is only quantifiable variables that are taken into consideration. No attempt is made to include political or sociological variables in a model, even though one would accept, particularly after the Chinese example, that sociological variables do have a significant influence on agricultural production. All this suggests that demand and supply projections have to be used with a great deal of caution essentially as broad indications of likely trends (Aziz 1977: 652).

Looking at . . . the projections for 1980, one finds that FAO projects a huge surplus in the world while USDA projects a much smaller surplus—USDA III virtually nil. FAO projects a very large surplus for developed countries and a small deficit for developing countries. USDA, by comparison, projects a much smaller surplus and much larger deficit. . . . For 1985, USDA projects just about equilibrium for the world. . . . FAO projects a very large deficit for the developing countries in general and more so in particular for the developing market economies. USDA projections, in this respect, are just the opposite. If one were to formulate policy measures on the basis of these projections . . . FAO projects a large surplus for 1980 so that one can argue for a policy to reduce production; USDA projections, on the other hand, would imply a policy to encourage production. A policy-maker can be, and is, genuinely confused. Whom should he/she believe? (Diwan 1977: 499).

Future trends in supply, demand, and trade of food and other agricultural commodities in the world, particularly the Third World, can only be speculated about because of the unreliability of projections and the limitations of averages among surplus, self-sufficient, small- and large-deficit countries, and between those who consume too much and those who consume hardly at all within these countries. In general,

> there clearly are two completely contrasting tendencies; production is growing much faster than population in developed countries, whereas the reverse is true in developing countries, . . . [but] the high rate of production growth (relative to population) extrapolated for the developed market economies and the still higher rate for the developed centrally planned economies (3.5 per cent) will materialize, in fact, only if a demand for massive exports from these countries occurs (FAO 1974: 121).

Annual growth rates of food production per capita are summarized in Table 2.1.

TABLE 2.1
World Food Production
(Annual percentage rates of growth)

	1962–1970		1971–1975	
	Total	Per Capita	Total	Per Capita
World	2.9	0.9	2.2	0.3
Developed capitalist countries	2.3	1.3	1.9	1.0
Eastern Europe and U.S.S.R.	4.3	3.3	2.3	1.5
Developing socialist countries	2.7	0.9	2.4	0.7
Underdeveloped capitalist countries	2.8	0.2	2.5	−0.2

Source: Aziz 1977: 657.

World food production increased at about 3 percent a year and 1 percent per capita during the 1960s; but this growth slowed down markedly during the first half of the 1970s—particularly from 1972 to 1974—so that production growth barely exceeded population growth. The years 1976 and 1977 were, on balance, good growth seasons, though not in China and Southeast Asia. In the developed countries, particularly in Eastern Europe and the Soviet Union, production exceeded population growth substantially; and in the developing Asian socialist countries per capita food production rose by nearly 1 percent throughout the period. But in the underdeveloped countries of the capitalist Third World per capita food production rose by only 0.2 percent during the 1960s and *declined* at an equal rate during the first half of the 1970s. The decline was most marked in Africa (−2 percent) and in Latin America (−0.3 percent, which it must be remembered includes food-exporting Argentina). Only the Near East had a significant increase of 0.8 percent a year (Aziz 1977: 657). These regional figures are for production and not consumption, which also depends on exports and imports. Throughout this period the Third World exported a substantial share of its own food production and had to depend increasingly on imports of grains from the developed countries to feed its population.

Looking into the future, the supply and demand of food and feed in the developed countries is projected to increase more or less as in the past, at an annual rate of roughly 2 percent total and 1 percent per capita, with 80 percent of the increase in the demand for grains attributable to animal feed (Aziz 1977: 652), which is expected to rise from 60 percent of these countries' total cereal demand in 1970 to 66 percent in 1985 (FAO 1974: 118). The accuracy of these projections, however, depends very much on the development and fluctuation of relative prices and the demand for meat, which after growing rapidly in the postwar period has slowed markedly since 1974 (Buxedas 1977). The use of grains for livestock feed is likely to increase still faster in the Third World (FAO 1974: 118) and will be examined later in this chapter.

The most widely quoted and used demand and supply projections for the Third World are those prepared by FAO. These suggest annual growth trends of food demand at 3.6 percent and of food production at 2.6 percent, leaving an average deficit of 1 percent a year, which is greater in Africa and lesser in Latin America, with only the Middle East producing a surplus. However, this projection does not seem to take into account the increased food demand in the Middle East since the oil boom (FAO 1974: 121). For cereals, world demand is projected to increase from 1,207 million metric tons in 1970 (1969–1971 average) to 1,725 million tons in 1985, of which 422 million and 650 million tons, respectively, are attributable to animal feed. Of this total the developed countries account for 617 million tons (372 million tons or 60 percent for feed) in 1970 and 796 million tons (523 million tons or 66 percent for feed) in 1985. Third World capitalist countries (on the FAO assumption that they will remain capitalist) would increase their demand for cereals from 386 million tons (36 million tons for feed) in 1970 to 629 million tons (79 million for feed) in 1985. But Third World production is expected to increase only from 370 million tons in 1970 to 544 million tons in 1985 (TNI 1974: 119, from FAO data). The Third World deficit and import demand, therefore, would rise from 16 million tons in 1969–1971 and 27 million tons during the 1972–1974 food crisis to 85 million tons in 1985. But the FAO observes that if cereal-exporting Argentina (wheat) and Thailand (rice) are excluded, the projected Third World *deficit* for the mid-1980s rises to 100 million tons per year, and in a bad crop year to 120 million tons or more, compared with *total* production of 386 million tons in 1970 (FAO 1974: 122). The cost of importing 85 million tons of cereal would at 1973–1974 prices of $200 per ton reach $17 billion a year, which would place a well nigh unmanageable strain on Third World countries, balance of payments. They will be further burdened by an import demand for other foods, as well as ever increasing imports of industrial commodities and "services" from the industrialized countries (FAO 1974: 124).

These estimates of market and import demand do not envision significant changes in the distribution of income—such as the growing inequality now taking place—that could lead to significant shifts in the structure of market demand for grains and other foods. Moreover, "the market viewpoint, which is only concerned with effective demand . . . in fact conceals the real problem of the physical needs of individuals" (OECD 1976: 22). Thus market demand today in no way covers the minimum nutritional requirements of the 460 million people in the Third World who were suffering from malnutrition in the early 1970s according to the estimates of various U.N. agencies (e.g. ILO 1976: 3). And the market demand projected for 1985 would not cover nutritional requirements either. According to these same estimates, food consumption in thirty-four Third World countries with a combined population of 800 million people would still be below the average minimum nutritional requirements in 1985 (FAO 1974: 119); even where the minimum *average* is met, its unequal distribution would leave many undernourished. "Bearing in mind that a proportion of this production must feed the increasing urban population, it seems unlikely that the quantity of food *per rural inhabitant* and *available* for rural consumption will be greater in 1985 than it is today" (FAO 1974: 126, emphasis in original). The provision of even a modest increase of 250 calories per capita per day would raise these estimates of cereal consumption and imports by an additional 20 million tons in 1985 (FAO 1974: 124). "Deficiencies in data do not permit an estimate of the additional quantities of food which would be required to assure nutritionally adequate diets to all, or virtually all, people" (FAO 1974: 124). Such an estimate would be merely an academic exercise anyway, since these projections, which "make no attempt to include sociological or political variables," and the contemporary and foreseeable political reality of political repression and economic super-exploitation (see Chapters 5 and 6) suggest that by 1985 many hundreds of millions more people will be deprived of a nutritionally adequate diet.

The whole discussion of demand and supply projections in relation to nutritional requirements is little more than academic speculation and philosophical moralization. Under the capitalist system of private property, privileged income, and their unequal distribution between the haves and the have-nots, nutritional and other physical human needs are largely irrelevant. Determination of supply and demand for food and other agricultural commodities is profit motivated. The physical capacity of the earth (including the seas and the air) and the technical capacity of men and women to provide more than adequate supplies of food and other necessities beyond the year 2000, even with rapid population growth, has been demonstrated on paper over and over again—the Club of Rome's early alarmism notwithstanding (Baade 1960; Leontief 1977; for a review of studies see Buringh 1977)—and is now substantially accepted by the Club of Rome itself (Tinbergen, RIO 1976). Large areas of the world, particularly in Latin America and Africa, are still underpopulated and underused for agricultural production; and cropping as well as livestock raising is being increasingly extended into these areas, sometimes with, but mostly without, irrigation. Besides the technological advances in agricultural machinery and its use, the production and application of chemical fertilizers and pesticides, the development and planting of hybrid and other high-yield varieties (HYV), the use of high-protein animal-feed concentrates for livestock and vegetable-protein meat extenders for human consumption (hamburger), and other recent developments that agribusiness and the green revolution have spread around the globe, several other new food-producing processes are in the investment and production pipeline or on the horizon. "Agricultural biology could well be on the threshold of a major revolution, based on new techniques of recombinant [DNA] genetics, in which genes of diverse species are hybridized, and of somatic-cell genetics in which single cells are manipulated in special cultures" (Revelle 1976: 173). The use of petroleum to feed single-cell organisms and the widespread farming of algae, not to mention the already incipient harvesting of krill (miniature shrimplike animals) in the sea, are in the offing. Other single-cell or simple multicellular organisms like bacteria, yeast, and fungi are also under the microscope for development into major new sources of food. Plowless planting with the massive application of herbicides to kill off weeds and other unwanted growth (Triplett 1977), pesticides and other measures to control animal pests, improvements in animal productivity, and innovations in food processing and packaging are all in the process of development—but by and for agribusiness (for the interest and participation of agribusiness see BCC 1975). Instead of being pursued to eliminate hunger and raise the nutritional level of the poor, however, under capitalism these technological developments will only take place on a widespread commercial basis if there is some assurance that they will reduce production costs and/or satisfy market demand. If this major agricultural revolution on whose threshold we are does take place, it will wipe out small farmers, peasants, and landless agricultural laborers much more efficiently than the green revolution did. To many small suppliers of agricultural commodities in the Third World, this revolution in agribusiness spells their doom as producers and their consequent growing misery as nonconsumers. It will leave them less able to provide for themselves through their own production and too impoverished to participate in the envisioned new market demand.

Where, then, is the market demand for increases in agricultural production through traditional or modern, even revolutionary, agricultural methods? There are two contradictory trends. On the one hand, alarm over prospective world food shortages, particularly in the Third World—shortages in both nutritional requirements, which is a moral and perhaps a political issue, and shortages on the market, which is of real economic concern—seems to be generating research, investment, and other measures to increase food production. On the other hand, important tendencies that seem to restrict market demand for certain foods make some of these production increases irrational from the strictly economic point of view, which is, unfortunately, the prevalent view. We have, then, contradictory predictions of market shortages and restricted market demand.

Market shortages can be traced back to the postwar decades of economic boom, which were characterized by preferential overinvestment in industry and underinvestment in agriculture and mineral raw materials, which led to inadequate productive capacity in agriculture and mineral extraction (most visible in energy sources). Additional investment in these fields now seems to be the order of the day.

> For some agricultural products . . . the 1960s and early 1970s constituted a long period during which prices were relatively low, and certain indicators suggest that since the urge to invest was weak, the long-term production cycles passed to the bottom of their curves (GATT, cited in Udry 1975: 58).

In the United States, for instance, wheat and other grain lands were taken out of production, leading to the 1972–74 wheat deficit. United Nations Secretary General Waldheim emphasized at the 1974 World Food Conference that industrial development policy in both the developed and the underdeveloped countries, and the pricing policies in the latter to keep urban food prices down (that is, to provide cheap wage goods to permit industrial growth through low real wages), had discouraged investment and production in agriculture (FAZ 6 November 1974). In general, industrial growth was privileged since it was more profitable than agriculture. This is reflected in the growth rates of production and trade in manufactures, which were more than twice as high as those for foodstuffs and other raw materials. (This disparity is also reflected in the differences in postwar growth rates and participation in world trade between industrial countries and those that produce raw materials, which is examined in WE: Chapter 1.) This postwar overdevelopment of industry relative to agriculture was almost worldwide; it characterized the developed and underdeveloped as well as the socialist economies, excepting perhaps China. Since the recession of the mid-1970s the developed and underdeveloped capitalist economies have found themselves with excess un- or underutilized industrial capacity. Because of the consequent fall in the rate of profit, industrial investment in the OECD countries declined after 1973 and did not regain its previous level until 1978. Industrial production only barely recovered its 1973 level in 1976, while agricultural production increased in the industrial countries (EO 1976, 1977; GATT 1976, 1977).

With industry-wide prospects for profits dim during the contemporary world crisis of capital accumulation, the time has perhaps come for a relative shift of investments into the energy, mineral, and agricultural sectors that were neglected during the previous boom. Something like that seems to have happened a century ago when a long (1850–1873) boom was replaced by a crisis of accumulation (1873–1896), which was resolved, in part, through the imperialistic development of new sources of agricultural and mineral production around the world. This pattern, however, did not repeat itself— except for the development of petroleum—during the interwar depression of the twentieth century, when agricultural prices and production declined steeply. Thus the contemporary prospects for development of these sectors remain unclear and in dispute.

Industrial crops such as cotton and minerals are, of course, dependent on the demand that industry generates for them and their substitutes. But their market prospects can also be affected by revolutionary reductions in the cost of production, such as through the "mining" of manganese nodules in the sea, or significant changes in the production of competing products. Thus the recent rise in the price of petroleum has given coal, and also cotton and natural rubber as "substitutes" for petroleum-based synthetic fibers and rubber, a new lease on life. The profit prospects for food production, of course, depend directly on consumer demand.

Consumer demand for food, in turn, depends largely on the number of consumers (population), the level of income, and the distribution of income among the potential consumers, as well as on the prices of food relative to other consumer goods. The number of potential consumers continues to increase through population growth, but as long as hundreds of millions of people earn no or an insufficient income, they cannot exercise any effective demand for food on the market. Nigel Harris correctly pointed out in the London *Observer* (8 November 1974), "in many parts of the world the immediate problem is not a simple lack of food, but the inability to buy it at today's prices. . . .[Here quoting Leonard Joy] We are seeing today the growth in the number of people who simply can't afford to live." In the developed countries, where income is already at high levels, increases in income do not mean corresponding increases in the demand for staple foods (whose income elasticity of demand is low according to Engels' law) and may even reduce demand as consumers replace cheap grains with expensive meat in their diets. Indeed, throughout the postwar period the consumption of meat and other high-priced "quality" foods rose rapidly (but since livestock consumes seven to ten times its own caloric value in grains, the demand for grain as livestock feed rose until it accounted for 60 percent of grain use). In the poor underdeveloped countries, however, where a much larger share of the family budget is spent on food and thus the income elasticity of demand for food is higher, rising incomes generate rapid increases in the demand for food. (Thus the sudden increase in income that a large part of the population, especially the poor, received under the Allende government in Chile after 1970 led to spectacular rises in the demand for food, which had to be imported because the country was unable to increase its production correspondingly overnight.)

This raises the question of what changes in the level and distribution of income are in progress or will be in the foreseeable future in various parts of the world. Besides the "economic" variables incorporated into the major institutional projections and other economic consequences of the contemporary world crisis of capital accumulation, the answer to this question depends substantially on the "sociological and political variables" that many institutional analysts are reluctant or unable to consider. The growth of income in the developed capitalist countries markedly slowed or declined since 1973. The OECD foresees a progressive (that is, regressive) shift in income from labor to capital (EO December 1976; WE: Chapter 3, and Frank 1978d). This development is not likely to have much effect on the demand for staples in the developed countries because of the low responsiveness (elasticity) of demand to changes in income. But income changes may affect the demand for higher-priced quality foods. The demand for meat, which grew rapidly until 1973, ceased to do so after that (Buxedas 1977), no doubt in part because middle- and low-income groups no longer had sufficient (increases in) income to buy additional meat, particularly at the higher prices resulting from increased feed costs, and thus switched to lower-quality meat substitutes. In the United States the consumption of hamburger meat, fried chicken, and the like at "fast food" chains increased enormously in recent years, but the content of hamburger "meat" and other protein products there and elsewhere is changing rapidly. Sales of vegetable protein meat substitutes or "meat stretchers" or "extenders" (soybean meal and other additives) in the United States rose from $82 million in 1972 to over $300 million in 1976, and were expected to explode to $1.5 billion by 1980 (or 10 to 20 percent of processed meat according to OECD 1976b: 134). Sales of dairy substitutes rose from about $850 million to $2,300 million over the same period (BCC 1975: 39). North America and Western Europe protect their domestic meat producers through import restrictions, are self-sufficient in high-quality meat production for direct consumption (steaks), and only import low-quality processed (canned) meat products or meat for processing (hamburgers, sausages, TV dinners) in significant quantities. Indeed, as already suggested, these countries may soon be in a position to export meat (they already export their even more protected dairy products). On the other hand, the regressive redistribution of income toward the high-income portion of the population may increase demand in the developed countries for certain kinds of luxury fruits and vegetables, as well as for flowers imported from the Third World. In the Soviet Union and Eastern Europe relatively sustained increases in income (albeit at lower growth rates than in the past) and growing social and political pressures will probably generate an increased demand for higher-quality foods, especially for meat and fruit and dessert crops produced in the Third World.

So there are some present and potential sources of demand for relatively high-quality vegetable, fruit, flower, and meat exports from the Third World to the developed capitalist and socialist countries. But it is difficult to see how this demand will justify extensive expansion of cropping, grazing, and production in the Third World and large investments in agriculture, especially by multinational agribusiness, unless there is a clear prospect of significant cost reduction with a substantial shift of investment costs and risks to Third World producers themselves without substantial risk and/or significance profits from sales to markets in the Third World itself.

Future demand for food and other agricultural commodities in Third World domestic markets (or in export markets elsewhere are difficult to analyze and predict.

> As regards these countries, it is first necessary to stress that the available economic indicators are unsuitable for an analysis of their food demand prospects and nutritional situation. . . . The size and direction of the future expansion of food demand in Third World countries is therefore determined by income distribution just as much as by growth in average incomes (OECD 1976: 42–43).

The projections of market demand for cereals in the Third World do not guarantee that these countries will use their income or foreign exchange to import them from the developed country producers. Indeed, those who make and use these projections believe that Third World countries must sharply increase their own production of food to meet domestic market demands, not to mention the nutritional needs of their people (FAO 1974: 126; ILO 1976; TNI 1975). But political-economic trends in the Third World suggest that rather the opposite is happening. Instead, changes in the distribution of income may become even more determinant.

The world crisis of capital accumulation and the political economic responses to it in the Third World (examined in Chapters 6 and 7 and WE: Chapter 2) are producing a sharply increased polarization in the distribution of income in the Third World, both between and within countries. The post-1973 increase in the price of oil was transferring $15–$30 billion from the oil-importing to the oil-exporting Third World countries annually, even before the renewed price increases since 1979. The increased income of the exporting nations, particularly in the Middle East, is generating a growing import demand for all kinds of investment and consumer goods, including food. The import demand for staple foods to feed the local and migrant or immigrant labor force has risen spectacularly in some Arab countries and in Venezuela. The beneficiaries of the oil income bonanza generate demands for meat, vegetables, fruit and luxury foods, and other goods, including cotton textiles, imported from other Third World countries or elsewhere. Because of the relatively small size of the total population and the tiny class of rich in these oil-exporting countries, however, the impact of their import demand on aggregate world trade in foodstuffs is necessarily limited.

Much more significant is the polarization of income *within* the Third World countries. As the rich get spectacularly richer, the poor are deprived of their meager incomes through the implementation of the "austerity" policies of superexploitation and repression demanded by international capital through the International Monetary Fund (IMF) and the banks, and imposed by one military or military-backed regime after another (see Chapters 6 and 7). Thus the Pinochet military junta in Chile cut real wages by more than two-thirds and changed the distribution of income between labor and capital from 60 percent: 40 percent to 30 percent: 70 percent (Frank 1976). Similarly, the military junta in Argentina under General Videla reduced real wages by 40 percent within one year of the 1976 military coup and forced an analogous, if lesser, shift in the distribution of income between the laboring majority and other sectors of the population (see Chapters 1, 5, and 6). Similar policies in other Third World countries have in recent years sharply accelerated the negative and regressive redistribution of income from the poor to the upper-middle and upper class that was already under way in the previous decades. These changes in the level and distribution of income have been accompanied by organized domestic measures and foreign exchange or trade policies designed to reduce imports, particularly those of staple foods (as in Chile, cf. Frank 1976a), as well as policies dedicated to increasing "nontraditional" exports of agricultural and industrial commodities (see chapter 3; for Chile see Frank 1976a). Other domestic pricing policies discriminate against the production of mass-consumed staples and encourage the production of quality and luxury food and other agricultural exports. The result is necessarily—and intentionally—relative and (as in Chile) often absolute declines in the domestic consumption of mass-market staple foods. These declines are accompanied by "progressive" increases in the demand for higher-quality vegetables, fruits, and particularly meat and processed dairy foods on the domestic market and the diversion of some of these luxury foods into the export market.

> As in many developing countries, agricultural priorities [in Mexico] are, first, food for export, second, food for industrial processing and, third, food for the population at large. While winter vegetables, strawberries, tomatoes and coffee are being produced for export, for

example, the government must import corn and beans. Similarly, more basic grains are consumed for animal forage than by 20 million peasants. . . . Over five years, the prices of corn and beans have increased, but more slowly than those of the seed and fertilizer that small farmers need to increase their yields (IHT 9 March 1978).

This process has been deliberately accelerated in Chile by the following four policies of the "National Economic and Social Development Strategy": (1) reinstitution of a free market for the sale and purchase of agricultural land to natural and legal "persons," eliminating the acreage and other limitations that had been imposed by ten years of land reform; (2) elimination of preferential tax treatment for agriculture and peasants; (3) encouragement of free market prices for agricultural products and inputs to bring them into line with world market prices and to promote a reallocation of agricultural resources and choice of crops and techniques that will command the highest prices; and (4) displacement of public credit and assistance to agriculture by the private commercial credit market (MRC 24 February 1978 editorial entitled "Toward a Market Agriculture"). Clearly, this "market agriculture" is simply the promotion of big capitalist farming at the expense of small farmers, peasants, and domestic mass-market consumers.

Accordingly, in one Third World country after another small-scale production of staple foods for the producer and his family and for local rural, small-town, and mass-urban consumption is being displaced. Local producers are being replaced by others who increasingly produce meat (on extensive grazing lands with little labor), soybeans as well as other oil seeds, cotton, vegetables, and fruit on larger, more "efficient" farms and orchards with modernized techniques—for the high-income urban and export markets. Multinational agribusinesses and other transnational enterprises are penetrating and taking over Third World agriculture to produce for the high-income domestic and export markets. Agribusiness (realistically) regards almost the entire globe as both its market and a suitable locus for its agricultural production. The result throughout the Third World is increasing landlessness, rural un- and underemployment, poverty and hunger on the land, and unemployment and misery in the mushrooming urban slums, as the rural population migrates to megalopolises that cannot accommodate or employ them.

To put it mildly,

these countries are faced with a difficult choice: Either [they can] satisfy the demand of the rapidly growing urban population, concentrating on the most modern sector of agriculture. In this case, the mass of the peasant population would be neglected; its diet would remain at the same inadequate level. . . .Or [they can] try to raise productivity in subsistence agriculture, to improve the food situation for the great mass of the rural population. The food needs of the urban centers would then have to be met by mounting imports; yet the slender foreign exchange resources are insufficient . . . (OECD 1976b: 16–17).

Of course, there is a third choice, and that is to satisfy neither the mass urban market nor the mass peasant need, but rather to exploit the producers in both sectors to get them to produce the products that will generate the foreign exchange necessary to satisfy the high-income market at home and the export market abroad. With this choice the political economic leadership can oblige the rural and the urban poor to bear all the costs and disadvantages of "market agriculture"—if they will do so. The role of agribusiness and export agriculture in the resolution of this choice in the Third World is examined in the next section.

There's No Business Like Agribusiness

Implicit in WFC [1974 World Food Conference in Rome] conclusions is the assumption, and rightly so, that private industry will take the initiative and efficiently implement measures to cope with the world food problem. . . . For example, who is better suited than the private sector to build required additional fertilizer capacities, to promote expansion of irrigation capacities, to facilitate the supply . . . of necessary pesticides, to extend storage and transport facilities, or to meet nutrient deficiencies through fortification of staples or other widely consumed foods (BCC 24).

So wrote Martin J. Forman, director of the Office of Nutrition, U.S. Agency for International Development (AID), under the title "Helping the Underdeveloped Countries Feed Themselves." His answer to the world food problem was not the individual peasant, and still less cooperative farming or state agriculture, but private industry—in a word, agribusiness.

The word *agribusiness* was invented by Ray Goldberg at the Harvard Business School, who wrote:

Agribusiness has rapidly become recognized as the most important economic enterprise in the world employing over 60 per cent of the world's economically active population. As we have defined it at the Harvard Business School, it consists of all the participants in a vertical food system from input supplier to farmer to processor to distributor to ultimate consumer. . . . Agribusiness involves those individuals and organizations engaged in the production, processing, transport, storage, financing, regulation and marketing of the world's food and fibre supplies. In effect, agribusiness is a seed-to-consumer system composed of a series of closely related activities that together enable agricultural produce to flow from the farm to the market place. . . . Action and decisions taken at one point in the system impinge on other segments. . . . The interactive nature of the system and the need for close co-ordination is largely a result of the unique agronomic characteristics of agribusiness (cited in Feder 1976a: 1066).

Ernest Feder distinguishes three kinds of agribusiness concerns: firms manufacturing inputs for worldwide agricultural production, firms engaged in agricultural production and/or marketing, and firms engaged in ancillary activities and services such as advertising, technical assistance, feasibility studies, legal advice, and technology transfers (Feder 1977a: 59).

It must be emphasized here that agribusiness is not limited to firms that do their entire or even major business in agriculture or in its inputs or products. Firms whose major business is in apparently quite unrelated sectors also have important investments and operations in agribusiness. For instance, Volkswagen in Brazil owns vast stretches of land on which it grazes cattle, and Renault sells machinery to make soluble (instant) coffee in Morocco and exports agricultural products from Colombia in an arrangement to remit profits from its automobile production there. The major international banks also finance agribusiness around the world, and for the conglomerates, which have grown so rapidly in recent years, agribusiness is just another business. Though in the words of Erich Jacoby, "there is no business like agribusiness," truly agribusiness—no less than show business—is also a business like any other.

According to Gonzalo Arroyo (1976: 164, citing J. L. Rastoin), of the one hundred largest agribusiness firms in the world in 1974, forty-seven were American, twenty-three British, nine French, seven Japanese, five Canadian, three Dutch, two Swedish, and one each German, Austrian, Spanish, and Swiss, of which the largest were the well-known Swiss Nestlé and the Dutch-British Unilever. Arroyo (1976: 170–71) suggests the following typology for the operations of these firms and their integration of Third World agriculture into agribusiness: (1) direct integration of agricultural production through traditional investments in land to assure the direct production of agricultural commodities, as in plantations; (2) direct integration of agricultural production through the purchase and opening of virgin lands. The first kind of investment seemed to have neared its end in the 1960s when, for example, the United Fruit Company (now United Brands) sold off many of its holdings in land and banana production in Central America to concentrate on the more profitable commercialization and processing of agricultural commodities. But this trend seems to have been reversed since the late 1960s and agribusiness again began buying up vast amounts of virgin and grazing lands in the Third World. Thus U.S. agribusiness firms bought 32 to 35 million hectares of Brazilian land—over 10 percent of the total agricultural land reported in the 1960 census—in the new Amazon and Matto Grosso regions and also in the more settled southern part of Brazil in lots averaging 400,000 hectares. Since the buyers made purchases through straw men as well as directly, the average size of these holdings is still higher (Feder 1977a: 563, 1974: 73). This renewed surge in the purchase and direct operation of land by foreign agribusiness and other enterprises (the largest purchaser of cattle grazing land in Brazil is Volkswagen) is evident throughout Latin America as well as in Africa and Asia.

Where open purchase is legally impossible or impolitic, agribusiness resorts to what Arroyo calls (3) quasi-integration through purchase by straw men or other intermediaries and/or through the rental of agricultural land and (4) more frequently through contracts with local producers, who receive credit for the purchase of machinery, seeds, fertilizers, pesticides, and other inputs from the agribusiness and agree to deliver all or part of their harvest to the latter for processing and/or commercialization. Ernest Feder (n.d.b.) has analyzed one example of this contract agriculture in his *Strawberry Impe rialism*. A variation is the concept of satellite farms proposed by Orville Freeman, a former U.S. Secretary of Agriculture and then president of Business Asia and of the U.S.-India Council. Satellite farms combine categories 1 and 2 and sometimes even 3 in the form of a nucleus estate surrounded by private farms that supply it on a contract basis (BCC 11). This arrangement was widespread in prerevolutionary Cuban sugar production through the *colonos*, and is an agricultural version of the putting out system or the production of automotive parts by numerous satellite firms for sale to a nucleus automobile production and assembly plant. Ernest Feder comments:

> In the production contract system, now widely used and bound to cover ever more commodity systems, the situation is complex. Agribusiness likes the system for economic and political reasons. Economically, it makes the contracted growers dependent upon the buyer as he furnishes them with the needed inputs and "assistance"; he makes additional profits and secures additional profit repatriations from input sales; and the system makes his supply operations flexible in that he is for all practical purposes free to accept or reject growers' (particularly the small growers') output without any cost to him, in accordance with market conditions. Politically agribusiness can and does argue that it is a "less extreme form of vertical integration," politically more acceptable . . . (Feder 1977a: 565).

Moreover, if profits decline because of a fall in demand and/or productivity, agribusiness can simply pull up stakes and move on to another region or country, leaving the local producers holding the bag.

Finally, Arroyo distinguishes another arrangement (5) that is coming into increasing favor; triangulation between Third World states that undertake large-scale infrastructural development through irrigation projects and the like, local agricultural producers, and foreign agribusiness, which provides the financing and undertakes processing and distribution of produce it receives under contract from the other two partners.

Walter W. Simons, deputy executive secretary of the Industry Cooperative Program (ICP) of the Food and Agriculture Organization, summarized the "Role for Agro-Industry in Implementing World Food Conference Decisions":

The question of how best to do business in developing countries was discussed at Toronto and analyzed again in our survey. Depending on specific situations, management contracts and long term operating arrangements with LDC [Less Developed Countries] producers, co-operatives and governments seemed attractive options for production-oriented projects. Minority equity and consulting contracts were also popular; but most respondents shied away from majority ownership. Large scale farming in developing countries is again attracting foreign entrepreneurs. The concept of "satellite farms" was proposed by Orville Freeman at Toronto and seems increasingly acceptable to LDC governments. . . . There are other indications that the small farmer and the foreign multinational may be more natural allies than many thought possible. One major US firm is contracting directly with LDC small holders for a major commodity; and we have discussed how this system might be valid for rice or other basic crops. The input companies are also innovating ways to serve the small farmer market, now that rural credit is becoming more available. . . . Several—particularly US and British firms—have taken on management contracts to manage large rice, sugar and other commodity production for governments. . . . Such experience and the increased attention which WFC [World Food Conference] has brought to developing country agriculture has stimulated more and more interest in what is commonly called "triangulation"—the linking of industry management and technical resources with developing country partners and third party finance. Last month our membership at their annual meeting supported a proposal for expanding IPC's role as "honest broker" in such triangulation efforts. . . . In the US, the Agribusiness Council, the Export-Import Bank and perhaps other organizations are also expanding such functions. The third member of our partnership—the international organizations—are already reacting to the impact of WFC, FAO and other UN agencies and are adjusting work programmes to support WFC priorities and the World Bank is planning large increases in lending both for agriculture and rural development. The regional banks are also seeking new agricultural projects, OPEC funds are increasingly being channeled into development and may yet be the major building block for the proposed new International Fund for Agricultural Development.

The specific dynamics of partnership between government, industry and international organizations will become clearer in the months ahead. . . . Several of these new efforts as I believe . . . illustrate some of the new opportunity areas for international agro-industry and imply some of the varieties of partnership we will be dealing with. . . . Ambassador Martin's Consultative Group on Investment has already begun work. It is headquartered at the World Bank in Washington. . . . The group will encourage large flows of external resources into LDC agriculture; improve coordination of investment and technical assistance programmes; and seek more effective use of available resources. This

means focusing on three major areas—investment policies and programmes; production inputs; and institutional development. Investment
needs in fertilizer, pesticides, seeds, equipment and other agro-industries
will probably be among the initial priorities taken up by the Group. . . .
The animal health products industry will also receive a boost from
WFC. . . . Industry experts will help FAO determine the needs for
farm machinery. . . . The WFC resolution on nutrition stresses the need
for expanding mass feeding programmes—another area involving
industry's expertise—as well as new efforts to produce foodstuffs that
counteract protein, calorie, vitamin and other deficiencies. . . . At our
Annual Meeting a consortium was proposed to pool the expertise of
FAO, NASA [U.S. National Aeronautics and Space Administration],
and industry to apply remote sensing data to the identification of new
agricultural production projects, and to help train LDC personnel in the
interpretation of such data. Although remote sensing is a highly politically sensitive subject, the eventual possibilities are great for accelerating the coordination of investment resources. Agricultural research
is slated for major expansion, especially through the Consultative
Group set up a few years ago by the World Bank, FAO, UNDP and
outside interests like the Rockefeller Foundation. We will look for
linkages between this Group's international research centres and company efforts in priority areas.

   We are optimistic that the international agro-industry will also
respond to the challenge of the partnership in the development process;
and that the long term results will be a matter of both pride and profit to
executives who, like you, guide industry (BCC 1976: 11–13).

Mr. Simons also introduced the Industry Cooperative Programme, of which
he became deputy executive secretary:

   ICP is a "joint venture" between FAO and international industry,
   and is headquartered in Rome. It is unique in the UN system. On the
   one hand it is an official FAO programme, meaning it is officially
   supported by the nations belonging to FAO. But the programme is
   financed by membership fees making it self-supporting. Today our
   membership numbers 102 international agro-industrial firms worldwide, each represented by at least one senior executive. . . . Operating
   within the neutral UN system greatly facilitates our primary task of
   stimulating agro-industrial expansion in developing countries by linking
   the decision makers of international industry and Third World governments (BCC 1976: 8).

Further background on ICP was offered by J. F. P. Tate, executive director
of the British agribusiness firm Tate and Lyle and chairman of the ICP
subcommittee on finance:

   The need for a direct link between FAO and major companies

working in agro-industry was first recognized some 10 years ago by the director general of the FAO at that time, Dr. B. R. Sen. He knew certain industrialists who were interested in this concept and 18 of them gathered together with him in 1968, when it was decided to form a privately financed programme within FAO. From these 18 initial companies the membership has expanded to the present figure of 104. . . . The membership fee is the same for all companies and stands at $6,500. Certain companies have contributed more than this to assist specific projects. . . . The activities which are supported by membership funds therefore include industry working groups and joint task forces on dairy and meat development, animal health, feed resources, plastics, pesticides, forestry, fisheries, farm mechanization, and protein food development.

The organization of the Bankers Programme is similar to that of ICP; there is a membership fee and a secretariat and, of vital importance, the members are not only the commercial banks world wide but the major national development banks as well. There are now almost 50 banks in membership. The programme is highly project-oriented. . . . While the ICP and the bankers may sometimes be working jointly from the start on a particular project it is more probable that they will come together when one or the other has reached the final stages in deciding on a project (LT 8 April 1976, Nations in Need, a special report to mark 10 years of work of the Industry Cooperative Programme, p. II).

More critical interpretations of how agribusiness has used the "neutrality" of the United Nations and its financial and technical resources as well as its links to Third World governments to further its own pride and profits through the "honest brokerage" of the ICP Investment Programme and Bankers Programme may be found in the writings of independent observers like Erich Jacoby (1975) and Susan George (1976: Chapter 9). The FAO subsequently severed its connection with the ICP, apparently in response to excessive criticism of UN sponsorship of such activities.

The testimony just quoted suggests that a major component of agribusiness strategy in the Third World, especially in its use of triangulation, is the World Bank (IBRD) and the associated International Finance Corporation (IFC) and International Development Agency (IDA). This suggestion has been amply confirmed by official declarations and lending programs by the World Bank and by the independent analyses of Ernest Feder and others. The president of the World Bank, Robert S. McNamara, devoted over half of his Address to the Board of Governors at the 1973 meeting in Nairobi to the Bank's new emphasis on agriculture.

Let me begin by outlining the scope of the problem in the developing countries which are members of the Bank. It is immense: there are well over 100 million families involved—more than 700 million individuals.

The size of the average holding is small and often fragmented. . . . And it is, of course, output per hectare which is the relevant measure of agricultural productivity in land-scarce, labor-surplus economies; not output per worker. . . . I suggest that the goal be to increase production on small farms so that by 1985 their output will be growing at 5 per cent per year . . . [so] they can double their annual output between 1985 and the end of the century. Clearly this is an ambitious objective. A 5 per cent rate of growth has never been achieved on a sustained basis among smallholders in any extensive areas of the developing world. . . .

What can the Bank do to assist this effort? First of all, we expect to lend $4.4 billion in agriculture during the next five-year program (1974–1978), as compared to $3.1 billion in the first five-year program (1969–1973), and $872 million in the 1964–1968 period [representing an increase from 15 percent to 23 percent and 20 percent, respectively, in the relative share of World Bank loans going to agriculture]. . . . In the next five years we expect that about 70 percent of our agricultural loans will contain a component for the smallholder. . . . Is it a realistic goal? The answer is yes, *if* governments in the developing countries are prepared to exercise the requisite political will to make it realistic. It is they who must decide. . . . But if the governments of the developing world—who must measure the risks of reform against the risk of revolution—are prepared to exercise the requisite political will to assault the problem of poverty in the countryside, then the governments of the wealthy nations must display equal courage (McNamara 1973: 15, 16, 25, 28).

Mr. McNamara returned to the same theme in his report to the 1974 meeting in Washington. He proposed even greater acceleration of financial support for agriculture, and by way of illustration of his program he reviewed some of the Bank's recent projects, the first five of which were approved within a single two-week period: a $10.7 million credit for agricultural development in the southern region of the Sudan for food crops, cash crops, and disease-free livestock; an $8 million credit for Upper Volta; a $21.5 million credit for livestock development in Kenya; an $8 million credit for Mali; a $30 million credit for dairy development in India; a $10 million credit for Tanzania; a project for farm-to-market roads, new marketing and credit services, and small irrigation works in northern Nigeria; a project to improve extension, credit, and marketing in northeastern Brazil; a project for drought-prone areas in India with a population of 66 million; and "perhaps [the] most comprehensive project," an investment of $1.2 billion over a four-year period in Mexico, especially for fruit and vegetable growing (McNamara 1974: 4–6). However, by 1976, certainly by 1977, it became apparent that McNamara was shifting the emphasis of his yearly Address to the Board of Governors from agriculture to other sectors (McNamara 1977). This shift perhaps reflects the uncertain profitability of investment in agriculture discussed above.

McNamara's own words, the stated purposes of the projects, and an analysis of the whole World Bank program for agriculture shows that the Bank's objective is not the elimination of poverty among the 700 million rural poor in the Third World; indeed, the Bank programs are likely to increase poverty for hundreds of millions. The World Bank's objective, rather, is to be another "honest broker" in furthering the "natural alliance" of agribusiness and the rural rich. Thus McNamara states that his goal is to increase productivity per hectare, *not* productivity (still less consumption) per *worker*. Indeed, the growing number of landless agricultural workers and their families—the poorest of the poor—are not even contemplated in McNamara's program for "smallholders." Merely a "component" of 70 percent of the World Bank loans is destined for the smallholders. And the productivity of the smallholders' *land* is to increase at the heretofore unknown rate of 5 percent a year, at the cost of forcing some of these same smallholders out of business and landownership. For instance, in the World Bank's Guatemala project over 50 percent of the Bank funds are allocated to only 18 percent of the beneficiaries whom the Bank itself defines as large or medium farms. The Bank defines "small" farms in Guatemala as those of less than 45 hectares (112 acres), which includes 97 percent of all Guatemalan farms—some of which are quite large by anybody else's definition. The 82 percent of the beneficiaries receiving the other half of the funds are quite large holdings at the upper end of the spectrum of the 97 percent of farms designated as "small." Therefore, the program gives the real smallholders nothing at all (Collins 1977: 17–18).

Even if we take McNamara at his word, according to the estimates of Ernest Feder (1976b) it would take sixty years at recent rates, and thirty years at accelerated rates, of Bank lending to "benefit" 100 million "smallholders." In the meantime, as Mr. McNamara himself clarified in the review of his projects, the Bank is furthering commercial agriculture, especially for export, through cash crops, disease-free livestock suitable for meat export, dairy development, farm-to-market roads, credit and marketing services in the drought areas of the Sahel in Africa (Upper Volta, Mali, northern Nigeria), India, and elsewhere. The more than $1 billion allotted for fruit and vegetables grown in Mexico will presumably benefit projects similar to the already existing vast projects on contract for or operated by agribusiness for export to the United States. Far from benefiting the peasants, these programs, as Ernest Feder shows in his *Strawberry Imperialism*, result in landlessness, rural unemployment, and subproletarianization (see also Susan George 1976: Chapter 10).

After examining McNamara's statements and analyzing the World Bank's recent agricultural projects on the basis of its own publications, Ernest Feder drew the following conclusions:

(a) only a small fraction of the estimated 1.7 million families were actually poor benefiting smallholders; (b) the loan funds allocated to the poor are a fraction of my previous estimate of $480–557 million;

(c) . . . the major portion of agricultural loans continue to go to the non-poor in agriculture, in accordance with long-established Bank tradition. In this context it is noteworthy that . . . the average credit per beneficiary in projects serving medium and large producers (beneficiaries) is about 14 times higher than in other projects; (d) under these circumstances there is no telling how many generations it would take the Bank to reach its "target population" of 100 million smallholder families. If these conclusions are correct, then notwithstanding the big apparatus which the Bank appears to set up on behalf of the rural poor, its real aim is not to help 100 million poor families within our lifetime, even if it were to redouble its lending activities. In fact, the programme could be directed at best to a privileged class of smallholders as I intimated already earlier on other grounds. . . .

In conclusion, if we strip McNamara's scheme of its pretenses—including his claim that development assistance is a moral issue, that he is out to help the rural poor, and all the false arguments behind the "logic" of his reoriented "development" strategy—we discover that the real aim is to increase and strengthen the private large landholding sector and agribusiness and that his "socially oriented" (i.e. oriented towards the poor) programme is nothing but a facade. I cannot help but think that there is a truly machiavellic component to McNamara's plan. . . whose result is to magnify the polarization of the rural classes under our very noses: the unconcentrated poor and the landless. Their numbers are large and increasing. Nothing will be done on their behalf because in the process of capitalist expansion they are not needed. They do not have land to contribute to the process of growth controlled by the multinationals and their World Bank. Thus McNamara's strategy implicitly includes the calculated risk that hundreds of millions of these forgotten most absolutely poor will be led to death from absolute poverty and starvation. Could this be the World Bank's revenge on the poor for creating the problems it admittedly does not know exactly how to solve? (Feder 1976b: 537, 539).

Feder (n.d.a: 29) estimates that these World Bank programs will generate an additional $10 billion in sales by multinational corporations over a ten-year period. In his analysis of the World Bank's agricultural lending program and Mr. McNamara's speeches, Jean-Jacques Devron (1976: 28–29) similarly concludes that "the selected, superincorporated small farms that are [to be] integrated into the market are at the heart of the agricultural project of the World Bank" and that "at the level of the international market, such a policy promotes the enlargement of the market of the agro-industrial firms."

Erich Jacoby summarized the situation:

The World Bank, the capitalistic arm within the UN system, which is now allied with more than one hundred transnational giants and seventeen international commercial banks, has gradually imposed its rule upon the policy of FAO and other UN agencies. It is getting more and more difficult indeed to draw a dividing line between the transnational corporations and the World Bank (Jacoby n.d.: 6).

A concrete examination of agribusiness projects illustrates the devastating effects for the region. The two sides of the agribusiness coin—increased profits for the controlling multinationals and their banks, and widespread poverty and starvation for the masses—characterize those Third World regions submitted to "development" under agribusiness. Some of the major Third World regions that have been widely discussed, surveyed, analyzed, and in some cases transformed into such large-scale agribusiness projects are the Amazon Basin, Matto Grosso, and other regions in Brazil, and contiguous Brazilian colonized areas in Paraguay and Bolivia; the belt between 10 and 15 degrees north of the equator and south of the Sahara in Africa from Senegal in the west to the southern Sudan in the east and perhaps into the Arabian peninsula as well; the 40 million hectares of the Indus-Ganges-Brahmaputra plain of Pakistan, India, and Bangladesh; and "smaller" regions in Southeast Asia and elsewhere. In Brazil vast virgin lands, many of them recently purchased by foreign capital, are already being dedicated to extensive cattle grazing for meat production for the high-income domestic and export markets. Other agricultural land has been converted to the massive production of soybeans, of which Brazil has become the world's second largest exporter after the United States.

The Sahel region south of the Sahara receives and deserves particular attention. This region suffers from ten-year minor and thirty-year major drought cycles (the latter have occurred after 1913, in the first half of the 1940s, during the mid-1970s, and presumably will recur after the year 2000). Because of the advance of the desert and persistent drought, famine resulted in the deaths of several hundred thousand nomads and other inhabitants of the Sahel—over 100,000 by 1975 according to the (OECD 1976) and perhaps up to 250,000 (IHT 9 September 1977)—as grazing and croplands dried up and 30 to 40 percent of the cattle died from thirst. These shocking figures were not due to a drought more severe than usual but rather to commercial farming and overgrazing, deforestation and diversion of water for cash crops—primarily for export. These activities over the previous decades of "development" had seriously disturbed the ecological balance of the region. For the Sahel as well as for drought regions in Ethiopia and elsewhere, "the dominant theme here at the United Nations Conference on Desertification . . . now is that man's activities, not nature's, are the main cause of desert creation and enlargement" (IHT 5 September 1977).

Like the 1975 floods in India and Bangladesh, the drought in the Sahel not only brought immediate suffering to great numbers of the region's inhabitants but also laid the socioeconomic and political basis for still greater suffering in the future, as the poor were obliged to sell off their land and animals, which represented their economic security over the long term, in order to buy food for the here and now. Thus landownership became increasingly concentrated in fewer hands, which are devoting land not to production for subsistence or local consumption but increasingly to cash crops for sale to the cities and for export.

Ostensibly "to combat drought and famine," agribusiness and the international organizations are beginning to transform the Sahel with irrigation projects, cash crops, livestock raising, and export agriculture. For instance, two dams in the Senegal delta are to irrigate 355,000 hectares in Senegal, Mauritania, and Mali. Other irrigation projects were planned for Upper Volta, Ghana, Niger, and northern Nigeria (FAZ 17 September 1974). The real purpose and the devastating consequences of these and other agribusiness projects are suggested by projects already in operation:

> Out of the drought regions comes a steady stream of trucks with fruit and vegetables going to the airports of the capital cities. The bellies of jumbo-jets are filled with delicious goods that are brought to the European market in nightly nonstop flights. Agriculture cannot feed the local population any longer—but the export of agricultural products increases steeply. . . . In Dakar-Yoff arrive the trucks with eggplant, green beans, tomatoes, melons and paprika that are produced on the nearby model farm of the Dutch-American agribusiness Bud-Senegal. These products are destined for Paris, Amsterdam, Stockholm and other European metropolises. Production began in 1972, that is in the fourth year of the great drought. It has grown rapidly since then, while in the country itself hunger increased steadily. The "success" of Bud-Senegal is closely connected with the surrounding hunger. This is indicated by the very low wages. . . . The director of the enterprise, Bud Antle, of German ancestry, assured himself of the support of the Senegalese government and the World Bank from the very beginning. In practice, this means that the government of Senegal and the international financial institutions made money available for some other production that might serve the sustenance of the local population. (FR 31 December 1977).

There have also been other reports of "many glaring examples of high-yielding plantations in 'dry' deserts and in the midst of starvation in 1973 (vegetable farms in Senegal—for export to Europe; cattle ranches in Niger—for export of meat; cotton yields increase of 20–25 per cent surrounded by famine in northeastern Ethiopia)" (Bondestram 1976: 1973).

Another region of substantial existing and major potential agribusiness investment and development is in the Sudan. "The southern half of the Sudan is potentially one of the richest farming regions in the world, with soil, sunlight and water resources to produce enormous quantities of food—as much, perhaps, as the entire world now produces" (Hopper 1976: 201). The Lonhro Company, the World Bank, West Germany, Kuwait, France, and Norway have already made significant investments in the Sudan (Bondestam 1976: 190). Plans are under way to turn the southern Sudan into the bread basket of the Arab world. These plans are being financed by OPEC, particularly Saudi Arabia, and Western agribusiness. Cotton, sugar, wheat, and other crops will be produced on a super-large scale—for export, of course. "Moreover, the combination of conservative Arab wealth and Western know-how [in the Sudan] could prove an irresistible force capable of swinging a number of African states back toward the West" (IHT 3 February 1977). Indeed, the holy political alliance of Saudi Arabia, Egypt, Sudan, and Somalia is already in operation, with U.S. support, in the Horn of Africa. Agribusiness in the Sudan is part of the payoff.

A study of the installation and operation of the King Ranch (one of the largest and most famous of those based in Texas) in Morocco, where it produces meat both for export to Europe and for the national market observes:

> The King Ranch has produced its own environment to the detriment of the poor peasants and pastoralists. . . . The elaboration of contracts of association with Moroccan cattle ranchers is an attempt to integrate the rich or medium ranchers. This is made possible *through the very effects of the installation of the Ranch itself* which engenders the speculation and concentration of landed property, and the pauperization and proletarianization of a large part of the peasantry in the regions where [the Ranch] is implanted (Benaim 1976: 5).

After working with FAO, the World Bank, the Asian Development Bank, as well as the Ford Foundation, someone like W. David Hopper, now president of the International Development Research Centre in Ottawa, can express the hope that

> the development of watering places, improved ranges, disease-control centers, meat-packing establishments and other facilities could dramatically enlarge Africa's ability to add to world food supplies, particularly to the supply of protein (Hopper 1976: 203).

But with such projects

> there is therefore nothing surprising in the combination of poverty, hunger and even starvation on the one hand and food exports on the other—a reality in many African countries. It shows once again that within the capitalist system food is grown for profit, not to feed people—especially hungry ones. . . .
>
> Cash crop producing countries buy food for some of their export earnings but one may ask how much of this food reaches those who really need it and deserve it, i.e. those who have been transferred from subsistence agriculture into production for export in order to serve the rich of the world. It is not a coincidence that half of those African countries, whose food imports exceeded one-third of national consumption, faced the most severe famine in 1972–73 (Bondestam 1976: 207,210).

What are the foreseeable consequences of this massive penetration of agribusiness in Third World? Susan George suggests that

> the kind of penetration of UDC agriculture we are currently witnessing—and which is bound to increase—could make the green of the Green Revolution seem a very pale olive colour by comparison. If the Green Revolution has been a social disaster, the effects we can legitimately expect from direct Western agribusiness intrusion into traditional rural societies may be nothing short of catastrophic. There is already plenty of evidence to suggest that agribusiness is capable of destroying everything it touches: local employment patterns, local food-crop production, consumer tastes, even village and traditional family structures (George 1976: 159).

The green revolution, it may be recalled, was designed in the late 1950s and 1960s to halt the red one, to food supply for the cities, to create a thriving business for large landowners, merchants, and national and foreign suppliers of inputs. All of these goals were to be achieved through the "transformation of traditional agriculture" with high-yield variety (HYV) "miracle seeds," fertilizers, farm machinery, irrigation, and other methods in Mexico, the Philippines, India, and elsewhere in the Third World. Although local agricultural productivity and national agricultural production did increase, the green revolution's politically most sophisticated and influential proponents, like Wolf Ladejinsky (1973: A-135), accept the fact that in Asia primarily, and particularly in India, "even many of those who grant the green revolution's widespread beneficial effects which flow from increased productivity are, nevertheless, concerned by rising income disparities between regions and within regions, the inequitable flow of credit and inputs, the accentuated undermining of the position of tenantry and sharecroppers." In a major study by the United Nations Research Institute for Social Development (UNRISD), the author "demonstrates how biased technical change and market imperfections combine to ensure that the benefits of the 'green revolution' accrue largely to the more prosperous regions and the more prosperous landowners. In other words, he suggests that technical change in agriculture is resulting in greater income inequality and a polarization of social classes" (Griffin 1972: 1). (For an UNRISD analysis that comes to similar conclusions about the green revolution's birthplace, Mexico, see Hewitt de Alcantara 1976.) Nonetheless, the inventor of the green revolution, Norman Borlaug, received the Nobel Peace Prize.

If we make analogies between the development of agriculture and that of industry, then the green revolution was analogous to local manufacturing with some foreign industrial inputs; and agribusiness is equivalent to the giant multinational that increasingly dominate national economic structures and political processes with foreign-state financial, political, and military support. Indeed, agribusiness is not merely comparable to giant multinational enterprise, but is in fact a new facet or extension of it. If the medium stage agriculture of the green revolution had such disastrous consequences for the local and national market in the 1960s, what literally catastrophic results will follow from multinational agribusiness operations in the Third World in the 1980s?

Erich Jacoby summarizes:

> The present process of economic, social and political disintegration in underdeveloped countries is indeed unique. It is promoted by a network of transnational corporations and their daughter-companies which enjoy a status of extra-territoriality with regard to both capital and management. Contrary to the large colonial enterprises of the past transnational corporations are not interested in the actual ownership of resources but rather in gaining complete control of operations. They penetrate the agriculture of underdeveloped countries by the vertical integration of the entire production process. They combine the cultivation of food with processing and marketing and gradually expand their activities to the fields of retail trade and tourism by the establishment of chain stores, hotels and restaurants. The real basis for their powerful position, however, is the "ownership" of the techno-logical process and of the knowhow of efficient management. Through their commercial manipulations the transnational corporations have established a firm hold on underdeveloped countries which is difficult to attack by normal procedures of expropriation and nationalisation. Their excessive monopoly prices for ready-made equipment and licenses further strengthen their control of the economy and society as a whole since they limit the acquisition of technological progress to those groups who have the necessary economic resources. The activities of transnational corporations thus increase inequality and establish an economic and political alliance with the élite against the people.
>
> But this is not all. In large parts of the underdeveloped world transnational corporations are changing the land utilisation pattern by introducing the cultivation of industrial crops and luxury foods for export to the rich countries, thereby detracting land and labour from the production of food for home consumption. This was the case in Ethiopia where, in the Awash Valley, cotton and coffee plantations were expanded into the traditional pasture areas of the nomadic tribes or in the Sahel region of West Africa, where transnational corporations profitably use thousands of hectares for truck farming, cotton growing and cattle ranching at the expense of domestic grain production. The reduction of the area originally under food crops for local consumption and the simultaneous diversion of the often scarce water resources for capital intensive farming inevitably worsen the effects of drought. In many underdeveloped countries today a close relation has become apparent between the agricultural operations of the transnational corporations and the imminent danger of famine. . . .

This whole development seems to indicate the "alienation" of Third World agriculture. To an increasing extent traditional farming is being replaced by capitalist agriculture which is directly or indirectly associated with transnational corporations. This is a still more destructive policy than that of the former colonial administrations who were satisfied after all to pursue their exploitative praxes within a plural economy and leave the indigenous community intact to fend for itself, as was the case in Indonesia and Malaya. The activities of the transnational corporations, on the other hand, gradually uproot the rural people in underdeveloped countries and thus destroy their social and economic pattern in utter disregard for the human factor. The uncontrolled introduction of advanced technologies reduces employment in agriculture and accelerates the exodus of peasants.... The most fatal aspect of the operations of the transnational corporations is the transfer of a large part of the employment potential in Third World agriculture to the industries of the developed countries which produce fertilizers, chemicals, tractors and other goods needed for agricultural production. In other words, the workers of industrialised countries actually manufacture the very equipment which substantially reduces the employment possibilities of agricultural labour in underdeveloped countries. The focal point of Third World agriculture is gradually being transferred to the industrialised countries where the transnational corporations exercise the control of trade relations and finance sophisticated technical research whose application will only further disintegrate the rural community (Jacoby 1975: 92–95).

While export agriculture is an important element of agribusiness, it is by no means the only one. Moreover, agribusiness production for export does not necessarily replace but may complement production for the national market in Third World countries. But agribusiness, like all large business, does transform both market supply and market demand. It transforms the supply conditions through both its direct production and delivery contracts with local medium and small growers, who have to produce predetermined kinds and qualities of crops with specified inputs. Similarly, agribusiness, like all big multinational business, contributes to the redistribution of income in Third World countries—making it more unequal—and thus modifies the patterns of consumption and the structure of demand. The "value added" through processing and distribution operations, not to mention seed, fertilizer, and machinery inputs, from which agribusiness derives relatively more profit than local growers, rises relative to the simple crop value.

Investment in Third World agriculture is attractive to multinational agribusiness not only because it increases export and national demand for food and other agricultural commodities, but also because it changes market and demand structure, a process agribusiness and other multinational businesses help to generate. These changes come at the expense of the nutritional satisfaction and real income of large masses of small producers and poor consumers who are forced or left out of this process of capital accumulation. Moreover, "investment" in Third World agriculture more often than not requires very little real investment by the agribusiness firm, and the firm can realize what little investment it makes exceptionally rapidly. Much of the real investment, even more so than in industry, is provided by the state, which finances much of the irrigation, transportation, and other infrastructure facilities, and by the direct producers who supply much of the working capital and labor. Again, even more so than in industry, the direct and indirect cost of agricultural labor in the Third World is far lower than it is in the metropolitan countries. Moreover, the production cycle in agriculture is short (a growing season or a year); and the distribution cycle is even shorter. Thus agribusiness capital loaned to direct producers and/or invested in agricultural processing and distribution yields high absolute profits even at relatively low rates of interest or profit per year or turnover period. But all these advantages and profits for multinational agribusiness are not matched by benefits to small peasants and landless agricultural producers and the poor consumers in these countries. On the contrary.

The disadvantages and costs of agribusiness to the bulk of the rural population and the people generally in Third World countries have been detailed by Ernest Feder (n.d. a 1976, 1977):

1. Governments, local entrepreneurs, peasants, organized and unorganized labor, as well as consumers—in descending order—lack adequate bargaining power. They are unable to get favorable terms and conditions from multinational agribusiness in the short run with regard to quality, suitability, and prices of inputs sold by monopolistic agribusiness suppliers. The same holds true for purchase prices of agricultural produce and labor power bought by monopolistic agribusiness buyers and employers. In the medium run local agricultural suppliers can be obliged to absorb the costs of cyclical declines in market demand and prices for the produce they supply to agribusiness on contract. Furthermore, local agriculture bears a substantial part of the investment in a particular line of production in "alliance" with the multinational firm. Therefore local agriculture is completely at the mercy of the multinational firm if it decides to pull up stakes and move to greener pastures elsewhere because of a decline in soil productivity or for other reasons.

2. The local and national distribution of the benefits of agribusiness is highly concentrated in the hands of a few landowners, producers, and merchants, and secondarily among those immediately employed in the production and processing of the agricultural output for agribusiness. Competing small producers, peasants, tenants, sharecroppers, and agricultural laborers are displaced; land is taken out of production for local and national consumption needs, while water and financial resources are diverted and allocated to production for export; the local and national food supply becomes increasingly inadequate, to the particular detriment of the poorest of the poor, who cannot pay shortage prices. The state is obliged to use its

scarce foreign exchange to import food for those who can pay for it and to subsidize those who cannot. In Latin America, where agribusiness has made the greatest advances so far, per capita agricultural production of export crops increased by 27 percent but per capita production of subsistence crops decreased by 10 percent in the decade 1964–1974 (NACLA 1978a: 5, which cites statistics of the U.S. Department of Agriculture). In the meantime, agribusiness in the Third World ravages and depletes the soils, groundwater levels, forest, and other vegetation covers and may destroy the local ecological balance. Hence it renders whole regions less able to provide for their inhabitants after agribusiness moves on.

3. Like foreign investment and transnational enterprises in industry, multinational agribusiness drains capital and economic surplus from Third World countries and places an additional burden on their balance of payments by obliging them to import foreign inputs for local agriculture. The balance of payments is also burdened by the ever rising payments for the associated "services" of licenses, know-how, etc., and the interest on the loans from the World Bank and other international agencies and foreign banks to pay for all this.

4. There is increasing polarization of rural inhabitants, and indeed the entire society, as peasants are proletarianized. Agricultural laborers are displaced by "technologically advanced modern agricultural methods," rural unemployment and underemployment increases, and rural migration into the city slums is accelerated. Feder (1977b: 27) concludes "that the entire evidence available with respect to capitalist development in agriculture demonstrates beyond the shadow of a doubt that the same or much higher output can be produced with a constantly and sharply declining labour force and that a capitalist agriculture can function splendidly practically without many people altogether." This labor displacement is all the more serious when agricultural lands are converted to grazing lands for extensive meat production.

> Thus, the almost incredible phenomenon will occur—and occurs under our very noses—that a programme destined to feed the peoples of the world will cause large unemployment, greater poverty and more hunger in the rural sector. It is most unlikely that surplus foods, which will be produced with the new high-yielding varieties, will be fed to the hungry nationals of the developing countries. Instead, they will be exported and sold to those who can pay for [them]. If increased food production is to assist the peasants, it will have to take place under an entirely different institutional structure in which the distribution of power, wealth, income and opportunities is more equal (Feder 1973–1974: 16).

5. The political consequences of the "natural" alliance of the Third World with multinational agribusiness is that some favored middle peasants, the rural bourgeoisie, the agro-industrial-financial bourgeoisie at the national

level, the state in the Third World countries, the international organizations, and the metropolitan imperialist governments all line up behind agribusiness against the lowly peasants, agricultural laborers, and poor consumers. This alliance is also seen—to a lesser extent—in those countries with national export agriculture, for instance Argentina and, increasingly, Chile.

> The implications for the rural proletariat are much more serious; the old class struggle between peasants or the landless and the local elite has increasingly broadened international connotations. Rural labour is not facing just a powerful national class enemy anymore, but trans-national investors and corporations whose political and economic power is infinitely greater than that of the former since they are backed by the economic, political and military machines of the industrial nations which they actually represent. . . . It becomes increasingly unrealistic to speak, as many still do, of national agricultural or agrarian problems. . . . The rural population cannot even count any more on the modest and marginal support with which Latin American governments furnished them from time to time. . . . The influence of agribusiness and their allies has become so pervasive that it excludes the possibility of adopting even the mildest plans and programmes for redistribution of wealth and income. National agricultural programmes and institutions are now shaped so as to support exclusively inter-national agribusiness ventures overseas (Feder 1977a: 561–62).

> [Agribusiness] expansion of capitalism is a counter-reform and coun-ter-revolutionary strategy, centered around economic social and po-litical strengthening of the large landowners. . . . This conscious strat-egy, supported by a multitude of agencies, is clearly politically inspired. It is bound to increase the contradictions inherent in underdeveloped agricultures . . . (Feder 1976a: 1077).

> It has therefore become the *political* aim of the industrial nations and their multinational agribusiness clients to make *any* redistributive programmes—even mild ones—unthinkable. Today, international agri-business is a more powerful force aligned against reform than the traditional landed oligarchies ever were in the Third World (Feder 1977b: 58, emphasis in original).

Agribusiness is a business like any other with worldwide multinational operations. Former U.S. Secretary of Agriculture Earl Butz, the late Senator Hubert Humphrey, and the CIA are certainly right in proclaiming that food is a weapon with the power of life and death over multitudes of the needy who, as the London *Observer* aptly puts it, can't afford to live.

Chapter 3
Third World Export Promotion

Export promotion seems to be replacing import sub-stitution as the dominant development policy in Third World manufacturing. This export-led growth policy, with special emphasis on manufacturing, is in line with the emerging international division of labor through which capital in the West seeks to reduce labor costs of production by shifting some industrial processes to the East and South. Labor-intensive industries particularly, including textiles, garments, footwear, and electronics manufacturing, but also certain former leading industries that are now in crisis, such as the automotive, steel, and petrochemical industries, are being increasingly located in the Third World and in the socialist countries, but with much of their production destined for export to the world market. As a development strategy for the Third World, export promotion does not, in fact, seem to fulfill any of the supposed benefits its promoters invoke, which are an improved balance of payments, reduced unemployment, technological development, and general economic devel-opment. Export promotion also extends to the petroleum- and minerals-exporting Third World economies that are examined below, but the terms of production and com-mercialization have been changing under the impact of the crisis. Some densely populated regions in South Asia, Central Africa, and South America appear to be in-capable of contributing much to the international division of labor. Their populations are therefore not economi-cally useful to capital, and are considered expendable.

Manufacturing Export Production

The colonial, then neocolonial, satellite, or client peripheral countries—first called "undeveloped," then "underdeveloped," and now developing"— long participated in the international division of labor primarily through the export of primary products and the import of industrial ones. Many of them still do export primary products, and all of them import industrial ones, though the nature of these imports has changed. However, in consonance with the changing international division of labor, an increasing number of these peripheral regions and states are now also exporting some industrial products. They import the raw materials, semiprocessed goods, and equipment necessary to produce these exports, and often the foodstuffs to feed part of the labor force as well. To some extent, this manufacturing export is simply the extension of industrial production originally developed for import substitution. Yet more often the promotion of industrial exports starts from what is literally a *tabula rasa*. A flat piece of land is supplied with the necessary infrastructure (factory buildings and productive equipment) and the materials that are to be processed are brought in from afar (often the other side of the globe). The labor to process these materials is supplied from the surrounding rural or urban areas. The archetype of this "new industrial development" is the "free production" or "export promotion" zone, which specializes in producing textile and electronics components for export to the "world market."

Third World manufacturing exports (excluding foodstuffs) multiplied nearly tenfold in little more than a decade: they were $3 billion in 1962, $10 billion in 1971, and $30 billion in 1974 (see Table 3.1). The 1974–1975 recession slowed this exponential increase, but since 1976 it has taken off again. Metropolitan imports of Third World manufactures increased at the rate of 15 percent a year from 1962 to 1972, 54 percent in 1973, and 39 percent in 1974 when they obtained an 8 percent share of the developed

TABLE 3.1

Exports of Manufactures (SITC* 5 to 8 less 68)
from Less Developed Countries by Regions
(in $ million at current prices)

Year	Latin America	Africa	Middle East	Other Asia	All LDCs
1962					3104
1966	688	653	487	2862	4912
1967	750	683	558	3468	5710
1968	905	774	623	4224	6844
1969	1080	910	752	5150	8380
1970	1855	903	800	4943	8626
1971	2140	917	1053	6110	10,326
1972	2820	986	840	9920	14,610
1973	4530	1318	1255	15,790	22,990
1974	6610	1750	1925	20,050	30,460

*Standard Industrial Trade Classification

SOURCE: For 1966–1971, UNCTAD, *Trade in Manufactures of Developing Countries,* various annual reviews; for 1972–1974, U.N. *Monthly Bulletin of Statistics,* Aug. 1976, pp. xxxvii–xliii (from Nayyar 1976a: 6; 1962 from Nayyar 1975: 44).

countries' total imports of manufactures (UNCTAD 1975 i: 11), but still only 1 percent of these countries' consumption of manufactures (UNIDO 1979:155).

Nayyar warns us "to keep these magnitudes in perspective," arguing that import-substituting local sales in 1966 accounted for 92 percent and in 1974 for 89 percent of all sales of foreign manufacturing affiliates of U.S. companies in Third World countries (Nayyar 1976a: 21). Moreover, the Third World share of total world manufacturing output increased from 6.9 percent in 1960 to 9.0 percent in 1977. At its 1975 conference in Lima, UNIDO established a 25 percent target for the Third World share in world manufacturing output for the year 2000. But extrapolation of recent trends in manufacturing output would still leave the Third World with only 14 percent of the total manufacturing (with 71 percent of the world's population) by the target year (UNIDO 1979: 2, 33, 56).

While manufacturing output increased at about 6 percent a year in the capitalist and socialist countries, it rose at 7.4 percent a year in the Third World between 1960 and 1975. The increase in Third World manufacturing output was, however, concentrated in a relatively few countries. Seventy-three percent of the growth of value added in manufacturing in the Third World between 1966 and 1975 was in ten countries. This increase in Third World manufacturing was concentrated in Brazil (24 percent), Mexico (11 percent), Argentina (9 percent), South Korea (8 percent), India (6 percent), Turkey (5 percent) and Iran, Indonesia, Hong Kong, and Thailand (2 to 3 percent each) (UNIDO 1979: 42, 53).

Third World manufacturing exports, however, grew more than twice as fast between 1966 and 1976 (15.3 percent as against 7.4 percent) than domestic manufacturing output, and their share of total Third World exports, excluding fuels, increased dramatically from 19 percent in 1960 to 45 percent in 1976 (UNIDO 1979: 142).

However, until recently, very few Third World countries also accounted for most of these manufactures exports. Fourteen countries provided 74 percent of the total in 1962 and 70 percent in 1972. India alone accounted for nearly 20 percent in 1962, though only 7 percent in 1972. The principal Third World manufacturing exporters other than India have been Hong Kong (18 percent of the total), Yugoslavia (10 percent), South Korea (less than 1 percent in 1962 but 9 percent in 1972), Singapore (6 percent), Brazil (5 percent), Mexico (4 percent), Argentina, Pakistan, Egypt, and Colombia (1–3 percent each), and Thailand, Malaysia, and the Philippines (0.5–0.8 percent each) (Nayyar 1975: 44). Hong Kong, South Korea, Mexico, Singapore, and Brazil supplied 54 percent of the Third World manufacturing exports to the industrialized countries in 1972. The first three countries alone accounted for 44 percent of the total in 1972 and about 50 percent in 1974. The importation of these Third World manufactures is similarly concentrated: the US, West Germany, Britain, and France take about 75 percent of these imports (Nayyar 1975a: 48; UNCTAD 1975 i: 8).

Third World manufacturing exports are classified into five groups by Nayyar: (1) traditional labor-intensive manufactures, especially textiles, clothing, footwear, leather goods, and simple metal manufactures (these have been the most significant Third World manufacturing exports, with textiles and clothing accounting for 35 percent and leather and footwear for another 6 percent of the total in 1972); (2) new labor-intensive products, such as sporting goods, toys, furniture, wigs, and plastic goods; (3) new manufacture and assembly of components, particularly for the electronics industry, which had a spectacular expansion first in the Far Eastern client states specializing in manufacturing exports and in the border region of Mexico, and recently in free production or export promotion zones around the world; (4) processing of domestic food, wood, mineral, and metal resources (together with about 15 percent of the total in 1972) which is to some extent "traditional" in some Third World countries but is now increasingly promoted to raise the share of value added and employment at home and the foreign exchange earned thereby; and (5) heavier industrial and engineering manufactures in the chemical, steel, transport equipment, and machine-building industries. The industries in this last category often began as "import substitution" industries and then became dedicated to "export substitution." Increasingly, however, especially in the case of petrochemical industries and steel production through gas reduction of iron ore, these heavy industries are being built up especially for export. In 1972 engineering and metal products and chemical, iron, and steel between them accounted for about 25 percent of the manufacturing exports of Third World countries to developed capitalist ones; in 1962 the share had been only 15 percent (Nayyar 1975a: 31).

Nayyar has summarized the changes in the composition of Third World manufacturing exports during the period 1962–1973:

> First, processed goods (e.g. products made from foodstuffs, tobacco and wood) and traditional manufactured exports (e.g. textiles and leather), most of which originated in domestic-resource-based industries, accounted for two-thirds of manufactured exports from LDCs in the early 1960s. This share dropped to about 40 percent by the early 1970s. Second, the importance of product groups such as clothing, engineering goods and miscellaneous light manufactures grew steadily and, over the same period, their share in the total rose from 18 percent to 45 percent (Nayyar 1976a: 25).

It is difficult to establish definitively how much of this Third World export is controlled by local capital and how much is in the hands of foreign capital, either through purchasing organizations or through full or part equity ownership by multinationals of the manufacturing facilities. In the late 1960s multinational corporations accounted for some 30 percent of the Third World countries' manufacturing exports, ranging from about 10 percent in India and Pakistan to 50 percent in Singapore. There were, however, important variations depending upon the type of industry and the continent.

Multinational participation was (and is) particularly strong in the new electronics components manufacture in Asia and Mexico (category 3 above) and in heavy industrial and engineering products (category 5), whose Third World production for export has so far been concentrated in some Latin American countries (and in India, which, however, has exported these products preferentially to the Soviet Union). Multinational participation has also been strong in the processing for export of raw materials, whose production the multinationals also control, especially in Latin America. Textile production for export has been predominantly in the hands of local capital in the Asian countries, but much of the export-import of these products is controlled by transnational buying organizations, which also contract for a substantial part of the production in their Third World client countries (Nayyar 1976a; Fröbel et al. 1977).

The "models" for the development of "export-led growth" were South Korea, Taiwan, and the city-states of Hong Kong and Singapore in the 1960s. In each of these cases political support of existing regimes (in the first three instances as bulwarks against socialism) would seem to have played a part in creating a growth model that would be economically "viable" and politically "stable." A major similar development was the construction on the Mexican side of the U.S. border of factories for the *maquillaje* (makeup) of textile, clothing, and electronics products for the American market. The perhaps initially unforeseen change in the international division of labor since the mid-sixties involving the transfer, and indeed the rapid development of, labor-intensive productive processes in the electronics industry made the South Korea–Taiwan–Hong Kong and Mexican border model economically viable and therefore the object of emulation and refinement elsewhere. The result is the recent mushrooming of "free production zones" and "world market factories" around the globe.

Otto Kreye found such zones, or similar industrial production for the world market without such zones, in operation or under construction in 1975 in 51 of the 103 underdeveloped countries he examined (Fröbel, Heinrichs, and Kreye 1977). There were free production zones in eleven out of thirty-three Asian countries: Bahrain, Hong Kong, India, Jordan, South Korea, Lebanon, Malaysia, the Philippines, Singapore, Syria, and Taiwan. In four of these countries (India, Malaysia, the Philippines, and Taiwan) there was also significant production for the world market outside such zones; and four other countries (Indonesia, Iran, Thailand, and Turkey) also produced manufactures for the world market without free production zones. Free production zones were being constructed by four countries that did not yet have such zones—Indonesia, the Democratic Popular Republic of Yemen, Thailand, and West-Samoa (the last two produced for the world market outside such zones)—as well as by seven that already did.

In Africa there were "world market factories" (Kreye's term) in eight countries in 1975: Ivory Coast, Morocco, Swaziland, Egypt, Mauritius, Senegal, Togo, and Tunisia; the last five of these countries also had free production zones, and Tunisia had additional facilities producing for the export market. In four other countries world market factories were under construction—Botswana, Ghana, Lesotho, and South Africa—and a free production zone was being created in Liberia. In Latin America sixteen out of twenty-six countries produce for the world market: Brazil, Dominican Republic, El Salvador, Guatemala, Haiti, Colombia, Mexico, Panama, and Puerto Rice in free production zones; and Barbados, Costa Rica, Jamaica, Nicaragua, the Netherlands Antillies, Santa Lucia, and Trinidad and Tobago outside such zones. Among the countries with free export zones, Brazil, Mexico, Haiti, and Puerto Rico also had substantial production for the world market elsewhere. Free production zones were under construction in Chile, Honduras, Jamaica, Nicaragua, Uruguay, and Venezuela; but in Ecuador export production outside such a zone was in planning. According to Kreye's estimates, countries that produce for the world market already employ 750,000 workers, of whom over 500,000 work in free production zones (Fröbel et al. 1977: 496). These countries are concentrated primarily in East and Southeast Asia and secondarily and more recently in the Caribbean.

Kreye thus identified fifty-three underdeveloped countries in which industrial production for the world market was either going on or was in the planning stage in 1975. Some of these—for example, Hong Kong because of its specialization, Mexico because of its location, and India and Brazil because of their size—are many times more important than several of the others combined. To this list of important Third World industrial producers for the world market we may add Argentina and Pakistan. Though they are not usually designated "Third World" countries, Yugoslavia and Israel may also be included in this category. They do substantial manufacturing for export to the West, as do several of the "Second World" socialist economies. A few of these countries—Brazil, Argentina, Mexico, India, South Africa, and Israel—have economies that can be termed "intermediate" (see Chapter 1). Others, though they do export some manufactures, specialize in the export of primary commodities from mineral or agricultural sources (see Chapter 2 and below in this chapter).

Because of their specialization in manufacturing production for export, or because of the increasingly significant concentration of such production on their shores, many of these peripheral underdeveloped countries may now be called "secondary client" states (in come cases, regions). Chief among them are South Korea, Taiwan, Hong Kong, Singapore, increasingly Malaysia, and incipiently the Philippines and Thailand in East Asia, and lastly Pakistan. Also important, or potentially important, are Mauritius, Tunisia, and Morocco in Africa, as well as the Suez Canal Zone in Egypt if plans for its conversion into one, or three, huge free production zones materialize as part of a political "settlement" in the Middle East; and the border zone of of Mexico, Puerto Rico (which because of its "associated" or "commonwealth" status has long since been inside the U.S. tariff zone), perhaps

Panama if a free production zone is made part of the final political settlement of the Canal question, and some Caribbean islands, countries, or
regions (e.g. the east of Venezuela) in Latin America. Because labor costs
have increased in the "older" of these industrial export countries, particularly
the city-states of Singapore and Hong Kong and secondarily in South Korea,
Taiwan, Puerto Rico, and northern Mexico, labor-intensive industry has
begun to move to some of the "newer" areas in search of a cheaper work
force. In line with this change, the governments of the "older" export regions,
particularly Singapore and Hong Kong, are making efforts to "upgrade" their
export industry to more capital-intensive and technologically complex
productive processes.

The United Nations Industrial Development Organization (UNIDO),
which has been particularly active in preparing and promoting feasibility
studies of free production zones, advances the following as supposed
advantages of these zones:

> The creation of an Industrial Free Zone is commonly considered by a
> combination of several reasons, such as:
>
> (a) a part of an overall industrial development programme of the
>   country or of a certain region of the country;
> (b) a measure for solving the employment problem by the creation of
>   new labour opportunities;
> (c) stimulation of development of export-oriented industries, to in-
>   crease export volume and foreign exchange receipts;
> (d) acquirement of modern industrial techniques from abroad through
>   which the level-up of the domestic industrial standard may be
>   achieved;
> (e) encouragement of new industrial investments from domestic, as
>   well as foreign capital markets;
> (f) means of a concentrated and rational development of infrastruc-
>   ture with the industrial free zone acting as an industrial pole
>   (UNIDO, n.d.: 7).

Most of these declared reasons for promoting manufacturing exports in
general, and free production zones or other world market factories in
particular, for the Third World are mentioned again and again in official
declarations and propaganda statements (as surveyed by Fröbel et al. 1977:
552–54; AMPO 1977: 63; Helleiner 1976). To facilitate the evaluation of
these declared reasons, we may classify them into the following four
categories: (1) the achievement of a healthy balance of payments in particular, and external balance in general, through substantial increases in
exports and foreign exchange earnings; (2) the advancement of the technical
training of the labor force and the technological development of the economy;
(3) increased employment and the elimination, or at least amelioration, of
unemployment; and (4) the promotion of "self-reliance," "independence,"

and economic development. An examination of this type of manufacturing "export-led growth" shows that under present and foreseeable conditions it does not fulfill any of these promises.

1. Not external balance, but foreign debts are promoted, because foreign exchange earnings are limited while import expenditures and indebtedness to finance them seems to grow without limit. The import components of this export manufacturing activity and its foreign exchange costs are high, particularly when undertaken by foreign firms. To begin with, the investment in the infrastructure essential to export manufacturing often has a high import component. Then, production itself is highly dependent on imported equipment, raw materials, components for processing or assembly, patents, trademarks, technology or other know-how, and high-salaried foreign technicians and businessmen who are often paid in dollars. The average import component for foreign firms is two or more times as high as for national firms. Moreover, these transnational firms that are active in manufacturing for export from Third World countries buy components and sell products among their own branches spread around the world at "transfer prices" set within the firm. These internally determined prices do not reflect market prices but rather the desire to maximize the global profit of the firm at the cost of particular host countries. These firms typically overprice their imports and underprice their exports in order to avoid local taxes, to get around foreign exchange regulations—in general, to escape the host countries' efforts to appropriate a fair share of the profits. The result is that the host countries are forced to spend increasing amounts of their foreign exchange for imports at the same time that they are suffering a reduction in foreign exchange earnings from exports. A large amount of foreign exchange earnings escapes transfer to the local central bank through such devices as "bonded" and duty-free imports and exports.

When export manufacturing is in the hands of foreign or transnational firms, the principal source of foreign exchange is the inflow for the payment of local wages and salaries. In the Mexican border zone, for instance, this type of inflow accounts for 75 percent of the foreign exchange spent by the firms and earned by the country for its foreign-controlled manufacturing export production (Bitran and König 1977: 792). Foreign exchange earnings are, in turn, limited by this dependence on wage payments in two ways. In the first place, though the production may be "labor intensive" from the point of view of the developed countries, it is relatively capital intensive for a Third World country. Therefore wage costs are limited, and consequently so is the inflow of foreign exchange earnings needed to pay them. On the other hand, the imported technology and equipment cost the country a considerable part of its foreign exchange. In the second place, since the principal reason for installing this manufacturing in the Third World is the low cost of labor, the whole operation has a built-in bias against higher wages. So, Third World export manufacturing actually works against achieving a healthy balance of payments and external balance by holding down both the quantity of labor and the wage it receives, and therefore the inflow of foreign exchange to pay local labor.

This kind of development has the added disadvantage of increasing import costs, and foreign exchange expenditures, through its negative influence on the structure of production, the distribution of income, and the pattern of demand. Resources are "reallocated" from production—often important agricultural production—for the internal market to production for the external one. This kind of reallocation often increases the need for imports, including foodstuffs, to supply domestic needs. Another effect is an increasingly unequal distribution of income that makes the rich richer and the poor poorer and more numerous (see WE: Chapter 5). The change in the distribution of income also changes the pattern of demand from cheap local products for the mass-consumer market to expensive imported goods and services (including tourism abroad) for the high-income market that consume foreign exchange. Therefore "export promotion" actually promotes imports.

Conclusive evidence that export promotion promotes imports, balance-of-payments deficits, and foreign debts is to be found in the major Third World economies that have promoted exports for the longest time and to the greatest extent: Brazil, Mexico, and South Korea. All three of these countries are plagued by continual and increasing balance-of-payments deficits. Brazil and Mexico have run up foreign debts of about $50 billion each, and by themselves account for over half the total foreign debt of all Third World countries. Brazil, Mexico, and South Korea ($7 billion debt in 1976, FER 20.8.5.77; slightly less than $10 billion according to Union Bank of Switzerland Report, March 1977) account for about 60 percent of the privately held foreign debt of the 130-odd Third World countries. In Taiwan the official figures of $3.8 billion of government-guaranteed debt would seem to understate the real foreign debt by nearly half (FER 17 June 1977: 89). These figures give a realistic measure of the "success" of manufacturing export promotion in these star "miracle" performers.

2. The promise that manufacturing for export will result in technical training of the labor force and technological development of the economy is belied by the logic of and extensive experience with such manufacturing throughout the Third World. Export manufacturing in Mexico and Asia relies on unskilled workers for 90 percent or more of its labor (Bitran and König 1977: 792; Fröbel et al. 1977), and many of these manufacturing operations employ women aged fifteen to twenty-five in 90 percent of the jobs (Fröbel et al. 1977: 529–30). The "training" for these jobs often takes no more than three weeks (Fröbel et al. 1977: 560), and annual turnover rates are 50 to 100 percent. To the extent that handicrafts and small industry in the Third World are replaced by large industry, export manufacturing actually promotes a "deskilling" of labor on the global level. The "deskilling" is also implicit in the production process itself, which is broken down into partially mechanized operations and partially simple, repetitive manual operations. Moreover, some export production is divided so that one operation is

performed in one part of the world, while others are undertaken elsewhere, and the final product is assembled in still another part of the world. No one country, therefore, achieves the technological capacity to produce the end product or—since the multinationals control both the procurement of necessary inputs and marketing throughout the world—the ability to run the productive process or sell the outputs of any factory or firm they might foolishly decide to nationalize. The technical training and technological development promised by export manufacturing is obviously limited, then, by the inherent economic and political logic of the capitalist international division of labor.

The technological development of the Third World is further impeded by the refusal of the multinational firms to transfer (or the local firms to import) any technology besides that which is embodied in the imported equipment and the partial productive processes. These, of course, are effectively controlled from abroad in the interests of the profitability of the multinational and not the integral development of the local economy. Research and development for new products, equipment, and productive processes are largely withheld from the Third World countries, while their most trained technical personnel are drawn out of the country (the famous "brain drain").

International horizontal integration impedes domestic horizontal and vertical integration through the development of backward linkages into raw materials processing and equipment manufacture and forward linkages into further product development. The recent development of shipbuilding and construction for export in South Korea and machine building in Brazil have taken place despite rather than because of multinational-directed export promotion.

The effects of manufacturing export promotion, particularly when done by transnational firms or for foreign-buyer syndicates, are evaluated in the following summaries:

> In a study of Motorola Korea Limited (MKL) it was found that "the skills learned in production are not readily transferred into other types of operations. . . . Techniques learned in MKL are not applicable in general to life outside the plant. . . . (Behrman and Wallender 1976, cited in Münster 1977:III 85).

> South Koreans do not learn *the technology* which is linked to the production system itself, but rather *the techniques* necessary to run the production process (AMPO 1977: 73).

> The technology transfer through offshore activities by foreign firms has not been effective until now [in South Korea] (Chung, cited in Fröbel et al. 1977: 562).

> On the whole, however, product- and process-embodied technology transfer does not appear to have been of great significance in United

States operations [in Southeast Asia] (Allen, cited in Fröbel et al. 1977: 561).

The evaluations of Helleiner (1976) and Nayyar (1975, 1976), as well as of Sabolo (1976), Trajtenberg (1976), Michalet (1976), Vaitsos (1976), and others who took part in the ILO Multinationals and Employment in the Third World project are similarly negative.

3. The promise of increased employment and the elimination or amelioration of unemployment through export or even all industry is an illusion at best, and more likely a delusion. Consider the present unemployment picture in the Third World (discussed in WE: Chapter 1). Since manufacturing employment for export employs people, it may eliminate (at least temporarily) unemployment in *some* city-states such as Hong-Kong and Singapore. But it has not done so in Puerto Rico after three decades of "pulling itself up by its bootstraps" (and sending a third of its population to New York City where much of it is on relief); or in Mexico, where a third of the population is still unemployed despite the border industry program, and over 5 million Mexicans have crossed the border into the United States, or in South Korea. What hope, then, is there that manufacture for export will improve the lot of the 600 million people of India? To put the matter in perspective, we may recall that total Third World employment in manufacturing for export has been estimated at 725,000 (Fröbel et al. 1977: 496) and total Third World employment by multinational firms has been estimated at 3 million, while the number of unemployed and underemployed in the Third World today is estimated at 300 million (ILO 1976: 3). No conceivable increase in Third World employment in export manufacturing or any other kind of industry or related activity could possibly absorb a significant portion of this unemployment under capitalism in the forseeable future. There is no hope for such full employment in any of the larger countries, let alone in the Third World as a whole.

> Larger countries which pursued similar [industrial] strategies, like Brazil and Mexico or even Yugoslavia and the Philippines, or which became interested in the export drive in certain specific cases, like India and, more recently, Egypt, found out that the direct and indirect employment effects of manufactured exports represented a very small share of their employable population. Rough, yet indicative, studies on this issue, through use of input-output analysis and labor co-efficients, have concluded that there are not many developing countries which can alleviate their unemployment problems through manufacturing exports (Vaitsos 1976: 48).

Does the promotion of manufacturing for export on balance make *any* contribution to reducing unemployment in the Third World or any larger part or country thereof? Or does it, on the contrary, directly and indirectly generate unemployment and a real or potential industrial labor reserve army?

It may be argued that in theory, if not in fact, export manufacture promotes unemployment because the "pull" of export manufacturing and other industry creates a labor force larger than it can employ. And since the duration of employment in the Third World is short and the turnover high, this *un*employment-generating effect is all the more marked. Furthermore, the deformations of the productive, income, and demand structure in Third World economies caused or abetted and accelerated by both export promotion and the actions of the multinationals render these economies increasingly unable to provide employment to the population and convert an ever greater part of that population into an immediate or potential reserve army of industrial labor. A study in the ILO World Employment Programme concludes:

> To the extent that foreign investment has failed to satisfy the job expectations of the rural population it drew to the firm's productive centers ... it has contributed indirectly to growing social distress, tensions and mounting unemployment in the towns, brought about by an absence of adequate job opportunities (Vaitsos 1976, citing Long: 48).

> Such outcomes create an *employment illusion* which consists of the following: foreign firms appear as contributing to high employment absorption as suggested by the statistics referred to above. Yet, displacement of appropriate national activities and the over-all distorted industrialisation effects lead to continuously narrowing scopes for employment in the whole economy and generate conditions which aggravate certain employment problems particularly those concerning poverty in the host countries (Vaitsos 1976: 31, emphasis in orginal).

4. The summary claim that "export substitution" and "export promotion" of manufacture lead to "export-led growth and economic development" is belied by many of our findings with regard to the more specific claims about export earnings, technical and technological development, and employment. But manufacturing export promotion has many other drawbacks, some of which are specifically examined elsewhere (WE: Chapter 5).

Much of this manufacturing development is directly financed by the state and private capital in the Third World country itself through multiple concessions to and ties with the more resourceful and stronger multinational firms and foreign buying agencies. The latter's greater bargaining power, which is enhanced by the competition among Third World countries, assures foreign capital the lion's share of the profit. This unequal exchange and distribution of gains is augmented by —and in a vicious circle augments—the denationalization and monopolization of the Third World (and other) economies. The process of monopolization, in turn, is accelerated by cyclical recessions, in which capital is concentrated into fewer (often foreign) hands, while smaller national industry and the workers whose employment and wages decline are left holding the bag when foreign and national demand declines. In periods of recession, and particularly in the current world economic crisis, the increase in economic superexploitation, political repression, and the development of authoritarian state forms, social institutions, and ideologies (discussed at length in Chapters 6 and 7) are further costs of this "export-led development."

Some of the "many potential sources of difficulty for the less developed countries in the new manufacturing for export" have been listed by Helleiner (1976: 247):

1. A substantial degree of control by transnational enterprises.
2. Highly imperfect markets for the relevant technologies.
3. A large number of low-income countries all seeking to develop exports of a similar type, and therefore competing.
4. High tariff and nontariff barriers against their manufactured exports in their major prospective markets.
5. The absence of international conventions or rules that might protect the less developed countries against discriminatory treatment.
6. The frequent practice of transnational enterprises controlling the right to export on the part of subsidiaries or technology purchasers.
7. The weak administrative capacity and political power of the typical government in the less developed countries, which renders difficult the process of effective bargaining, monitoring, and control with respect to foreign agreements and transnational enterprises.

In Mark Selden's evaluation

> free export zones contribute to rising Gross National Product curves but bring in relatively little capital to the nations involved. Moreover, only a small portion of the capital which is generated is channelled into effective development. The bulk of the financing for foreign enterprises is provided by locally generated capital and their products go virtually untaxed; they rarely raise significantly either the local pool of technical or entrepreneurial skills; they provide relatively few jobs when compared to the immense unemployed labor pool in most Third World countries, and these jobs remain contingent on the vagaries of a market 12,000 miles away. Above all, with production exclusively for export, their contribution to co-ordinated national development is virtually nil (Selden, cited in Utrecht 1976b: 61–62).

This "new international division of labor," as Fröbel et al. call it, may be regarded from different perspectives. One perspective is that of Nelson Rockefeller, whose name speaks for itself:

> In essence, what we the people of the Western Hemisphere really need is a more efficient division of labor among us. The division of labor is one of the tried and true economic principles that will be as valid in 1976 as it was in 1776 when it was first spelled out by Adam Smith. . . .

What is needed now is a broadening division of labor among the nations of the Western Hemisphere. At present, the United States is producing, at high cost behind tariff walls and quotas, goods which could be produced more economically by other hemisphere nations. The U.S. is short of skilled labor and, if anything, this shortage promises to get worse. The shortage of skilled labor is intensified when the U.S. continues to keep workers in lines which are, by definition, inefficient since production can only be carried on here behind tariff or quota barriers. National productivity would be enhanced by shifting workers and capital out of protected industries into industries where advanced technology and intensive capital investment permit the U.S. to pay high wages and still remain competitive in world markets. The goods the United States is now producing inefficiently would be imported, mainly from less developed countries. Consumers would gain through lower prices, workers would receive higher wages, and the return on capital would be higher.

The less-developed countries would also gain. With abundant supplies of labor and wage levels well below those in the United States, they could export processed food, textiles, apparel, footwear, and other light manufactures, as well as meat and other farm products. This would provide increased employment at higher wages than are now available. Workers could move off farms into higher paid industrial jobs. The increase in income would raise living standards generally, contributing to the improvement of the quality of life. Such nations would become better customers for the high-technology products of the United States.

In a real sense, the failure to develop a full division of labor in the Western Hemisphere can be termed inhumane (Rockefeller 1969: 102–3).

But the "old" division of labor inaugurated by the industrial revolution was not exactly "humane" for the peoples of the Third World (or generations of workers in the First World, for that matter); if it had been, there would now be no "need" for Mr. Rockefeller's new division of labor. And there is no guarantee that the new will be any more humane. On the contrary, as an ILO report notes:

The new type, on the contrary, means a rediscovery of labour manpower that can be used in a way that the modern evolution of capitalism has made impossible at the centre. Thus the approach will be from the opposite direction, i.e. by isolating highly labour-intensive processes and transferring these to areas where labour can be used with equal intensity. The effect is equivalent to what would happen in the central country if hours and speed of work could be increased and particularly wages reduced. There is some analogy with the conditions prevailing in the early decades of the Industrial Revolution, when intensive accumulation coincided with extensive pauperisation. . . .

In short, the penetration of certain peripheral economies by transnationals in search of low-cost labour has features similar to those of a
substantial surrender of sovereignty over part or the whole of the
nation's territory, with effects reminiscent of the traditional enclaves of
extractive industry. There is a subtle difference between them. The
traditional form produces something approaching a transfer of land
along with the labour living there. The more recent trend is towards a
transfer of the *labour* along with the land underneath them. The
combination of circumstances that we have mentioned make it unlikely
that this model of worldwide expanson by transnationals will turn into a
process of sustained accumulation for the receiving countries (Trajtenberg 1976: 2,36).

Or in the perspective of another ILO report:

Now this trend coincides with—or may even be caused by—the
abandonment by most developing countries of development models
based on import substitution. The best stimulus to growth is now seen
in greater export trade. Thus, a new complementarity between the
centre and the periphery is taking form. Its main characteristic is that it
is no longer based exclusively on the exchange of goods, but on an
internationalisation of the production cycle, in which the first signs of a
new integration between unequally developed economies are now
appearing. This trend makes it possible to start thinking of the movement of goods, services, technology, capital and labour between different
nations or regions taking place within a single system. But the singleness
of the emerging system does not mean that unequal development will
disappear. On the contrary, it is the actual establishment of the system
that makes it easier for a hierarchical structure to spread (Michalet 1976:
43).

What remains to be questioned about all this is what, if anything, is
really so new about this capitalist international division of labor and
whether the modern evolution of capitalism has really made such
exploitation of labor and underdevelopment of regions impossible at the
center and therefore possible or necessary only in the periphery. The
development of the world capitalist accumulation crisis gives reason to
doubt this relatively "optimistic" view. In brief, there is no short-run
poverty-alleviating or distributional magic in manufacturing for export
(Helleiner 1976: 255).

If the practical results of Third World export manufacturing are so useless
in terms of declared objectives and so disastrous in terms of general welfare, it
may be asked why it is undertaken at all. For the transnational corporations,
the answer is relatively simple: lower costs of production. The evidence as
reported in studies by the ILO, the U.S. Tariff Commission, UNIDO, and

individual researchers such as Nayyar, Helleiner, and Fröbel and colleagues is overwhelming that the two essential factors are low wages and "good" political conditions or "investment climate." According to Fröbel et al., the reasons for promoting export manufacture in the Third World are threefold: the practically inexhaustible availability of cheap labor; the recent development of cheap and efficient means of transport and communications that facilitate the international division of labor; and the ability to divide the productive process into part operations that can be performed by unskilled labor. Without disparaging these economic and technical factors, it can be argued that they have become crucial at this point in history only because the world capitalist accumulation crisis is obliging capital to seek to reduce costs of production to a minimum. This need to reduce costs dictates the transference of labor-intensive operations to areas of cheap labor. But in order to accomplish this transfer certain economic and political measures have to be taken first. Thus the structural crisis evokes a structural adjustment through an accelerated change in the international (and other) division of labor.

The question remains: why do capital, labor, and the state in the Third World participate in this process? The answer is they mostly have no alternative. As profit-maximizing participants in the world capitalist system, local capitalists in the Third World have to play by the rules of the game imposed by dominant capital at the center of the system. The most profitable course for them now is association as junior partners with multinational capital in the production and sale of commodities determined by the latter for the local and world market. Or course, not all local capital can achieve this association and integration with multinational capital; much of that which cannot is absorbed or forced out of business by that which can. The state in the Third World becomes the instrument of this alliance between international capital and its local junior partners, which (barring partial alternatives offered by petroleum or special political-strategic considerations) use it not only to promote their own advantage and the disadvantage of sectors of local capital that are "noncompetitive" or limited to supplying the local market, but also to force the working class, the peasantry, and the petit bourgeoisie to bear the costs of this "new international division of labor." The political repession, the military-technocratic state, and the ideology adopted to implement this process are examined in Chapters 6 and 7.

OPEC—The Organization of Petroleum Exporting Countries

The oil-exporting and OPEC countries of the Third World have certainly received sufficient attention since the price of petroleum began to rise in 1973. Much of this attention has erroneously suggested that this price increase has automatically propelled these countries out of the Third World into some other one. Therefore, we shall consider here a few sobering facts. Of the Third World oil-exporting countries, only Mexico (which has refrained from joining OPEC for political reasons connected with its relations with the United States) and for a time apparently Iran could realistically aspire to even an intermediary place in the world economy (See chapter I).

The other OPEC states may be divided into those that have large oil reserves and few people, and those that have large populations and relatively little oil. In the first category are Saudi Arabia (in a class by itself), Libya, and Kuwait, Qatar, Bahrain, Oman, and the United Arab Emirates on the Arabian Gulf. In the second are Indonesia, Nigeria, Angola, Algeria, and Ecuador. Gabon, Iraq, and especially Venezuela are in a more intermediate position. The cumulative balance-of-payments surplus from oil-export earnings has been vastly overestimated for the OPEC countries as a whole; only the first-category "countries" of the Arabian Gulf have huge surpluses (see Chapter 4). The other OPEC oil-exporting countries never, or only very briefly, achieved such a surplus and, with the exception of Venezuela, share the usual problems of Third World countries elsewhere.

The OPEC countries with the largest populations are faring the least well. Indonesia (130 million people) has hardly benefited from the oil boom at all. Japanese demand for Indonesian petroleum has been limited since 1975, and the state oil company, Petromina, has been in a deep crisis. "Indonesia may cease to be a significant oil exporter far sooner than had been expected. . . . Indonesia's questionable prospects are also depressing hope for a revival of the Southeast Asian oil boom which collapsed in 1975–1976" (IHT 8–9 Apr. 1978). The country with the next largest population (80 million), Nigeria, "is being out-priced on the sluggish market and is facing sharp competition from the North Sea and Alaska. Nigeria's once prized low-sulfur oil is no longer in such demand and production has dropped. . . . Estimates of the resulting drop in government revenue vary between 20 and 40 per cent. . . . The Nigerian chief of state. . . . announced a 10 per cent cut in government expenditures and new hardships for individual Nigerians. . . . Economists suddenly realized that commitments for capital projects were more than three times the money available" (IHT 21 Apr. 1978). Perhaps that is just as well, to the extent that these projects were planned like the cement imports that clogged Nigeria's harbors with ships in 1975–1976. In Ecuador the oil boom vanished when both internal supplies and external demand turned out to be lower than expected. Algeria, despite its increasing reliance on the export of liquified natural gas to the United States, never enjoyed an oil boom and has suffered the usual Third World problems of balance-of-payments deficit, budget and investment restrictions, unemployment, and growing poverty. The construction of a petrochemical complex and the innovation of ultra-modern gas reduction steel plants in Algeria indicate an export-oriented development strategy.

Venezuela did experience an oil boom after the price rise and it launched a large-scale investment program, particularly to exploit its rich iron ore resources through the development of a steel industry. It also expanded its petrochemical industry and import substitution of automobiles and other industrial products. Incomes have risen, spectacularly for the rich and moderately for the poor. Up to a million workers have entered Venezuela from neighboring Colombia (many of them illegally) and these immigrants account for perhaps 15 percent of the labor force, taking on most of the low-paid work in the Western frontier region. Venezuela initiated some significant financial investments in Central America and other parts of Latin America. Nonetheless, since 1976 Venezuela has had to cut back its petroleum production more than 30 percent below the 1973 output; and because of this cutback, as well as the decline in real oil prices, the country has begun to suffer from lack of funds for its investment program. An austerity program of sorts has been imposed.

Far and away the greatest beneficiary of the increase in oil prices has been Saudi Arabia. It has only 4–8 million native inhabitants (estimates vary widely) but accounts for perhaps half of all OPEC oil reserves and a third of its exports. The state and the economy, including the oil business, are tightly controlled by the ruling Saudi family, which has become by far the richest in the world. This family amassed reserves estimated at $100 billion in financial assets, besides the real reserves of the oil below ground (IHT February 1978). Despite a massive building boom and plans for a high-cost petro-chemical industry, development in Saudi Arabia remains superficial. The Saudis have been able to invest and spend only a small part of their earnings at home. What is not spent on luxury consumption abroad is invested chiefly in metropolitan banks, bonds, stocks, real estate, and so forth in the United States and Western Europe. Only a very small portion of earnings is spent on "aid" and investments in the Third World.

These circumstances have led the Saudis to pursue two major strategies with far-reaching economic and political consequences for their neighbors, other OPEC countries, and the world in general. One strategy is to keep as much of their oil underground for as long as possible, because that is the best possible "investment" from the Saudi point of view. The other is to invest in the world capitalist economy so as to earn the maximum secure income. Both strategies have led the Saudis to insist on maintaining the price of oil lower than most other OPEC countries desire. With one-third of the exports, and even more of the reserves—as well as the support of other Gulf states in similar circumstances, which gives them effective control over 50 percent of exports—Saudi Arabia has an effective veto power on any OPEC decisions that go against its interests. Indeed, by maintaining the price of oil below that which other OPEC states and especially Venezuela desire or require to expand their own oil production, Saudi Arabia has managed to exclude some of its rivals from power or influence within OPEC.

Still more significantly, the Saudis, with major investments in the world capitalist economy, have a strong interest in maintaining the health of the world capitalist economy. They reason that higher oil prices would earn them less on their oil exports than it would lose them on their financial investments in the West—because higher oil prices would have a depressive effect on the already faltering world economy. For this reason, the Saudis have opposed attempts to recover the effective price of oil which had been eroded by world inflation, the devaluation of the dollar (for which most oil is sold), and discounts that some OPEC suppliers have had to give to avoid losing too many sales in a weak market. From 1976 through much of 1978 oil was in *over*supply and inflation deroded the nominal 1978 price of $12 a barrel back to an equivalent real value of $7 in terms of 1974 dollars (which is the floor price Kissinger asked for). The temporary oil shortage in 1979 permitted OPEC countries again to raise the price of oil to and then beyond its previous real price. Some new oil production and the 1980 recession again created an oil surplus, and oil market analysts have been debating how long this renewed excess supply of oil is likely to last. The answer depends first of all on the course of the world economic crisis, and secondly on whether supplies of oil and other sources of energy will be found and exploited. The latter, in turn, depends partly on the price of oil, which determines whether or not it is profitable to increase investments to increase the supply of oil. And this factor is subject to the influence of the Saudis, who have a veto on questions of price, who alone can significantly affect the oil supply (in concert with the oil companies) by increasing or decreasing their own production, and who have a measure of influence on the health of the world economy. Indeed, by shifting but a small part of their liquid financial assets, or even threatening to do so, the Saudis can significantly affect the value of the dollar and other currencies, and stabilize or destabilize the world capitalist financial system in general and some stock prices in particular. This vast financial influence of the Saudis gives them a strong stake in maintaining the stability and prosperity of the world capitalist economic system and its institutions. No wonder the Trilateral Commission and other institutions in the centers of world capitalist economic and political power offer Saudi Arabia formal participation.

The Saudis also have a large stake in the economic and political stability of their own region, the Middle East. Of course, they are most intent on maintaining themselves in power. Therefore, the Saudis translate their oil money into political—and military—influence in an attempt to nip in the bud all progressive or other social movements that might destabilize any part of the Middle East and eventually Saudi Arabia itself (the rebel occupation of the sacred mosque in Mecca shocked the Saudis and the world into the realization that instability in Saudi Arabia itself may not be far off). The Saudis have exercised economic and political influence on other Arab countries, especially on Egypt, which has been dependent on Saudi Arabian aid, to "moderate" their policies with respect to the Palestinian-Israeli conflict and other issues. The Saudis are increasing their economic "aid" and political influence in Africa, especially in the Sudan and Eritrea. In all these arenas the Saudis' foreign economic and political policy plays an important reactionary role in consonance with their antiquated domestic social system and policy and their status as a major regional ally of the United States.

The Saudis have imported large numbers of foreigners to provide the "needed" work force on construction sites and in some service industries. These second-class citizens—or more precisely, noncitizens—include about a million workers from North and South Yemen and many others from Pakistan and elsewhere, as well as part of the contingent of over 40,000 South Koreans who work for Korean companies on construction sites throughout the Middle East. Foreign workers are now probably more than one-third of the labor force in Saudi Arabia.

The importation of unskilled and skilled labor from other Arab countries (including Palestine), Pakistan, Afghanistan, India, the Philippines, and elsewhere, and those on special contract from South Korea—to say nothing of the technical and managerial civilian and military personnel from the United States and Europe—has become an important feature of the entire Persian-Arabian Gulf region, where their number may now exceed 3 million. In some of the United Arab Emirates the proportion of foreign workers may be reaching 90 percent. In other Gulf states immigrants exceed 75 percent of the work force and 50 percent of the population (MERIP 1977; ILO WER 8–19 May 1976; FR 4 November 1977). Many workers enter illegally and thus are especially prey to exploitation and discrimination through low pay and the denial of civil and political rights (as in classical Athens, which distinguished between its own "citizens" and "barbarians").

The other small-population Arab states on the Gulf—Kuwait, Quatar, Oman, and the United Arab Emirates—import proportionately (and perhaps absolutely) more labor than Saudi Arabia. In part for that reason "development" in these "countries" threatens to be even more ephemeral than in Saudi Arabia. The oil industry employs little more than 2 percent of the labor force, and "oil-based" development . . . disproportionately encourages the growth of occupations that are either transient or unproductive. In particular it fosters growth in three sectors: state employment, services and construction. . . . Industrial production grows slowly and the longer-term productive capacities of the society, independent of oil, are not expanded, and a reduced industrial proletariat is coming into existence" (MERIP 1977: 6–7). Bahrain is an exception. Oil production began in the 1930s, immigration is small, and the local population is increasingly engaged in manufacturing for itself and other Gulf states. Kuwait is a partial exception. It produces oil to only about a third of its capacity; it has undertaken some industrial investment, including the design and manufacture of equipment to desalinate seawater, which it needs for itself and intends to export as well; and it has introduced a relatively benign welfare state with popular participation—at least by native Kuwaitis. But since the restrictions in oil production and the effective decline in oil prices since 1976, this measure of economic, social, and political democracy has been reduced in Kuwait.

In short, the oil bonanza has been relatively short lived and very localized in a few OPEC countries. Only in the desert city-states of the Arabian Gulf can it be said to have transformed the economy and society, and that transformation has been accomplished with immigrant labor, most of which will eventually be sent home. Saudi Arabia's internal development is likely to remain limited at least under its present regime, while the Saudi family and other beneficiaries of the oil wealth invest their fortunes and throw their economic and political weight around the world. In the other OPEC economies the economic influence of oil and of the earnings derived from it is limited in breadth and depth, except in Venezuela and, to a degree, in Algeria and Iraq, as well as in the small circle of *nouveaux riches* in the Persian-Arabian Gulf area, Nigeria, and Ecuador. The development of petrochemical industries in the oil-producing Third World countries is good business of the metropolitan countries, and to a much smaller extent for Brazil, Mexico, and South Korea, which sell and install these complexes; but it may not be such good busines for present and future producers of petrochemicals, which for the time being are in oversupply.

The shockwave that went around the capitalist world after the 1973 and 1974 oil price increases soon abated. Until the renewed price increases of 1979 the United States and West Germany achieved a balance-of-trade surplus with the OPEC countries, which became some of their best customers for industrial—and military—equipment. The few OPEC countries that have had a balance-of-payments surplus recycled their money to and through the Western banks and financial markets. The deficit counterpart of the first post 1974 "OPEC surplus" was shifted to the nonoil-producing Third World countries, where the state and the bourgeoisie obliged the masses to bear the burden of the higher costs of the world's oil (see Chapter 4). The oil price increase of 1979 and the recession of 1980(-81?), coupled with the increasing instability of world financial markets, raise serious questions, however, to what extent such shifting of the burden and recycling to the Third World are again possible in this round.

Not only Iran (see WE: Chapter 1) and Saudi Arabia but also lesser oil states have been delegated to a subimperialist role, albeit with uncertain success. For instance:

Let Nigeria Do It

It's a good sign that Nigeria is trying to use diplomacy to ease the Angola-Zaire tension that led the United States to start shipping emergency military supplies to Zaire last week. . . .

One should recognize that Nigeria, by acting in its own interest, can sometimes serve goals shared by the United States (*Washington Post* editorial IHT 26–27 March 1977).

Mineral-Exporting Economies and Attempts at Their "OPECization"

Another category of peripheral underdeveloped countries in the Third World are those that seem destined to specialize in the production and export of raw materials (other than 'petroleum) as their principal participation in the international division of labor. Among these countries we may distinguish between those that specialize primarily in minerals, and those that export vegetable or agricultural raw materials (some countries export both and even some petroleum and manufactures).

Among the minerals-exporting countries (excluding the intermediate economies) we may distinguish the traditional Third World producers of iron ore like Liberia, Guinea, Mauritania; of tin like Bolivia, Malaysia (though it also exports rubber and more recently manufactures), Thailand, and Indonesia; of copper like Chile, Peru, Zambia, Zaire, and more recently Papua New Guinea and to some extent the Philippines; of bauxite like Jamaica, Surinam, Guiana, and Guinea; of manganese like Gabon; of phosphates like Morocco (though it also exports agricultural products and manufactures); and of other minerals such as lead, zinc, molybdenum, tungsten, nickel, and uranium (which is exported by some of the Third World countries named above, as well as other countries).

The dependence of these countries on mining, and to an increasing extent on the partial processing and exporting of these minerals, is nothing new. But several "new" circumstances vitally affect the conditions of dependence under which these countries will produce and export these minerals in the foreseeable future. One is the trend, begun some years ago, to nationalization of the mines. Of some 1000 cases of nationalization between 1960 and 1974, about a third were in primary commodity industries and 7 percent in mining. However, nationalization in general has been concentrated in about a dozen countries, and in mining in still fewer countries (Hveem 1975: 31; 1976: 10).

The advantages of nationalization have been limited and counteracted by certain tendencies. For one thing, nationalization has been concentrated at the upstream mining end, while the downstream semiprocessing, processing, and fabrication end has largely remained under foreign and multinational ownership and control. Indeed, the greater the share of value added (and profit derived) in downstream processes, the more these processes are retained by the metropolitan countries. Thus only the upstream processes (in which value added and profits are low) are left to the primary producing underdeveloped countries (Hveem 1976: 30). In addition, when Third World countries nationalize mines or otherwise demand a greater share of the profits derived from mining in their countries, the multinationals use their technological, price-setting, financial, and marketing control to shift greater shares of the whole stream's profits to the processes they own and manipulate. The costlier, and especially the most risk-absorbing, processes are left to the Third World countries: "Profit where profit is due" (Moran 1971–1972: 124–26). At the same time, the multinationals increasingly vertically integrate all the processes from upstream to downstream in one global operation that may also be horizontally integrated in many places. Thus the mining industry house organ *Mining Annual Review* speaks frankly about "the emergence of large international mining groups coupled with the trend towards even greater mining units . . . the internationalism in outlook of these

20 or 30 groupings and the sophistication of both their financial and technical operations" (MAR 1970: 5,4); it also speaks of "joint ventures" and the fact that "it is no longer practical to think of metal markets in a Free World context. These markets have become truly global" (MAR 1972: 9). Thus, on the one hand, Theodore Moran (1973) can entitle an article "Transnational Strategies of Protection and Defense by Multinational Corporations: Spreading the Risk and Raising the Cost for Nationalization in Natural Resources"; and on the other hand, Helge Hveem can state that there is

> continuous centralization of control over these processes which the corporations, due to their monopoly in technological innovation and information handling, their organizational skill and financial power and thier access to the support of their home governments, exercise and still may be able to exercise. The present structure of many of the world's primary commodity industries thus is a mirror-image of the firm (Hveem 1976: 1).

Nationalization, which places the mines under state ownership, makes the state more interested in the profitability of the mines than it was before. Even such progressive governments as those of Allende in Chile and Velasquez Alavrado in Peru were intent on keeping miners' wages down, not only because they wanted to control the cost of mining, but also because wage concessions in this state-owned sector set a pattern for other sectors, both public and private. Then, too, it takes a certain amount of money to operate a mine, and even more to expand or discover new mines. Investment costs particularly have soared in recent years and have had to be increasingly covered by multinational mining companies or underdeveloped states, or by joint ventures between them, with loans raised on the international financial markets. The *Mining Annual Review* notes:

> There have been two major changes; the capital cost of new, lower-grade mines, dependent upon the economies of scale for success, has escalated in real terms—and by staggering proportions. . . . Secondly . . . [there] has been a marked increase in long-term debt (MAR 1975: 13).

> Funds borrowed from private sources will account for about 30 per cent of the capital requirements for independently owned projects and for about 70 per cent in cases of joint venture. . . . Of six large joint ventures undertaken in recent years 83 per cent of the investment requirements were financed through debt of which 73 per cent was by way of funds borrowed from private sources (MAR 1974: 25).

Under the circumstances, and especially when Third World states assume much of the debt (as even Allende's constitutional amendment nationalizing the copper companies provided for in Chile) and/or the guarantees for the debt, it is not surprising that the multinational mining companies (and their governments) do not object to nationalization—so long as "just" compensation is paid. The companies are glad to invest these funds elsewhere. The *Mining Annual Review* comments:

> This direct government involvement must be welcomed in many situations (MAR June 1971: 11).

> There is of course no inherent reason why free mining enterprise should only be motivated in circumstances where management and ownership are indivisible. At bottom, free-enterprise is not dictated to any particular form of ownership. It is dedicated to making profits, and, provided the terms are right, it should be no more difficult (and quite a lot less risky) to make profits from the sale of mining skills and management services than from the discovery and exploitation of mineral deposits (MAR 1974).

> Developing nation governments have moved to fill the vacuum created temporarily by mining companies unwilling to commit themselves to major development schemes. . . . Partnership with [such] government can, in fact, be an assistance in fund raising for prospective lenders can observe that government itself is committed to the success of the project and will not burden the operation with high taxes—at least until the loans are repaid! . . . Peru is an example. . . .(MAR 1973: 13).

Thus nationalization and joint ventures in minerals development in Third World countries, far from making these countries less dependent, tie the economy and also the state even more firmly to the circumstances and vagaries of the international division of labor and finance—and this must have political consequences in state action of the countries concerned (see Chapter 7).

Other recent and foreseeable circumstances of minerals production also affect—mostly adversely—the Third World exporters. The capital accumulation crisis seems to be inducing a relative shift in investment away from secondary industry and toward primary products, including minerals—although each new recession reduces absolute demand for both primary and secondary products. Much of this new minerals development seems to be destined to take place outside the Third World—in the industrialized capitalist countries themselves, in the socialist countries, and under the control of both in the ocean or sea bottom and in Antarctica. Indeed, the turn to the exploitation of low-grade ores in operations with large economies of scale (to which the quote from *Mining Annual Review* refers) involves primarily highly capital intensive mining in the developed capitalist and socialist countries, such as iron ore in Canada, Australia, and the Soviet Union, and copper in the United States the Soviet Union. Similarly, the mining of the sea bottom for manganese modules—which contain copper and nickel as well—and the possible processing of seawater for its mineral content as well as the possible exploitation of iron ore and other minerals in Antarctica are also highly capital intensive operations favored by enterprises in the developed capitalist and socialist countries.

For example, a study of the threshold at which exploitation of the ocean floor would begin indicated that an increase of only 6% in the price of nickel (compared to the 1973 price) and of only 21% for copper would make it profitable to develop extensive seabed exploitation of four products simultaneously: copper, cobalt, nickel, and manganese (Kyklos 1976:292–309). This sort of project also accounts for the confrontations over the question of control of the ocean floor (Udry 1976:47).

The efforts of the Third World at the U.N. Law of the Sea Conferences to exercise some control over ocean mining—both to secure some of the profits from it for themselves and to protect their share of the world market against this new source of minerals—show little promise of being crowned with success. Roughly two-thirds of world minerals production and export is now in the developed capitalist and socialist countries. These new trends make the underdeveloped countries' position in the world minerals market increasingly insecure.

"OPECization" of mineral production has not materialized for many reasons. For iron ore, for instance, it has been effectively blocked by the refusal of Canada and Australia to join the Third World countries. Capital-intensive minerals development outside the Third World countries' control will oblige them either to try to participate in the competition for investment funds—in the developed countries and the financial market under their control—or to attempt to compete with lower-cost or state-subsidized production. Such competition will mean labor-intensive exploitation of the mineworkers and/or of workers in general to maintain competitiveness on the world market, or direct or indirect state subsidy through the service of the external debt incurred to finance mining enterprises (Chapter 4).

All of these circumstances are exerting strong pressures on their states in the peripheral underdeveloped countries, to maintain or depress wages in the mining and processing industries. Holding down wages involves the imposition of economically repressive policies of devaluation, containment of government expenditures, consumption subsidies, welfare programs, and other policies disadvantageous to Third World societies. The IMF and other international and metropolitan financial institutions generally demand the implementation of these policies as the price for providing financing for minerals production and balance-of-payments deficits (see Chapter 4). Repressive economic policies necessitate repressive political policies and reactionary political alliances—witness the many military governments and right-wing coalitions throughout the Third World. Peru, not to mention Chile, is an example of this too. (See Chapters 6 and 7.)

Since the success of OPEC, and as part of the Third World call for a "New International Economic Order" (NIEO) at innumerable conferences of United Nations agencies and Nonaligned countries, Third World proposals to strengthen or form similar producer-exporter associations for other raw materials have grown. These have been coupled with increasingly insistent demands for agreements between producer and consumer countries to stabilize prices and production of particular commodities. Also being demanded is an Integrated Commodity Program that would allocate production quotas, control prices, stockpile commodities for eighteen mineral and vegetable raw materials simultaneously, and finance the whole operation out of a Common Fund. Ten of these commodities—sugar, coffee, cocoa, tea, cotton, jute and allied fibers, hard fibers, rubber, copper, and tin—are exported primarily by Third World countries and their acquisition would cost 44 percent of the proposed fund's outlay. Five commodities—wool, lead, zinc, iron ore, and aluminum—are exported by both Third World and industrial countries and would account for 12 percent of the fund. But the remaining 44 percent of the fund would be devoted to the acquisition of the three major grains—wheat, maize, and rice—which are exported mainly by developed countries and imported by both developed and underdeveloped countries (UNCTAD 1975g: 4). The proposal for this Common Fund was made by UNCTAD and discussed at its Fourth Conference in Nairobi in 1976; then it was taken up at the North-South Dialogue in Paris in 1976–1977 and at several subsequent conferences. The seventy-seven so-called LDCs (less-developed countries) have supported the program and have taken some initial steps to implement it, although some important LDCs such as India, which import many more of these commodities than they export, have been distinctly less than enthusiastic about the Integrated Program. The major industrial countries—led by West Germany and the United States and joined by the Soviet Union—offered substantial resistance to the establishment of such a program. They also object to any Common Fund that would be dominated by the Third World countries. Moved less by Third World pressure than by their interest in assuring stable raw material supplies, the industrial countries have grudgingly accepted the principle of some intervention in raw materials production and prices on a piecemeal basis, with funds largely controlled by themselves. Thus Henry Kissinger proposed an International Resources Bank that "could be associated with the World Bank Group" at UNCTAD IV. A fund has been set up with capital subscriptions of $700 million to intervene in some commodities markets, but it is not even a pale reflection of the Common Fund and Integrated Commodities Program that was originally proposed with a capital of about ten times that amount. Of course, without the cooperation of the industrial countries and the OPEC surplus countries which would have to provide some of the financing for these proposals, it will be impossible to implement them. So far the dominant industrial countries have used their bargaining and veto power to block real progress in this regard.

Some producer-consumer country agreements have been continued or renewed for individual commodities such as wheat, coffee, and tin. Producer-exporter country associations have been formed by Third World countries for copper (CIPEC by Chile, Peru, Zambia, and Zaire, with Papua New Guinea and Indonesia associated); bauxite (IBA by Australia, Jamaica, Surinam, Guyana, Guinea, Yugoslavia, and Sierra Leone); bananas (UBEC); and other commodities. But their success has been limited and their advantages for participating countries have been small. This was inevitable in view of the economic, political, and military power of the industrial interests and countries, and the conflict of interest among the Third World countries themselves. Helge Hveem comments that

> if contradicting economic and political interests among members still put a brake on OPEC's transformation into a full-fledged efficient association (and according to its own recently adopted program of principle), this seems even more true in the case of the other associations created or about to be created (Hveem 1976: 121).

In recent years successful concerted action has been limited to phosphates, sisal and to some extent bauxite (Hveem 1975: 29).

Hveem lists the factors favoring producer alliance action in raw materials among underdeveloped countries (UDCs):

1. UDCs are not highly penetrated and controlled by DCs.
2. Branch is not vertically integrated by DC agencies (multinational corporations).
3. Consumer side (DCs) is not cartel-like structured, i.e. there is a high degree of inter-DC competition (for the product and/or for the country).
4. Producer side is founded on ideological, culturo-ethnical, and political homogeneity.
5. "Monopoly" of production is located in UDCs and—more importantly— UDCs have a "monopoly" on world exports.
6. Number of producing countries is small.
7. Producing countries command a relatively equal (and stable) share of the production/export of the product.
8. National income of producers (UDCs) is not highly dependent on export of product.
9. Employment is not highly dependent on the production and/or export of product.
10. Demand is (a) established on a relatively high level; (b) characterized by low price elasticity (and high income elasticity).
11. Production in UDCs is (and will continue to be) economically advantageous (comparatively).
12. Product is not easily substitutable.
13. Product is not easily recycled (by DCs holding great amounts of scrap).
14. Extraction of alternative sources is time-consuming and demands the development of costly technology.
15. UDCs have a relatively highly developed, relatively independent industrial-technological basis.
16. The product is a nonrenewable resource.
17. There are few (known) reserve sources of the product in DC territory.
18. The extraction/production of the product is highly pollutive and subject to restriction in the DCs (Hveem 1975: 28).

Since the relatively successful actions of OPEC there has been worldwide debate about the extent to which these factors would permit similar successful concerted action by other producer-exporter associations in the short, medium, or long run. Helge Hveem (1976) discussed the pros and cons at length and compared his evaluations with those of two other major studies (See Table 3.2 for a summation of Hveem's analysis.)

The commodities on which there is substantial agreement on high feasibility for successful producer-exporter associations are few and far between—essentially only phosphate rock (in which Morocco is dominant, and will be even more so if it succeeds in absorbing Western Sahara) and bauxite (in which the developing countries would have to reach an agreement with Western-allied Australia). The feasibility of producer associations for diamonds and manganese requires the collaboration of the Soviet Union and South Africa, which presents political obstacles that the OECD may not have evaluated adequately (or has it?). A larger number of commodities offer medium-high feasibility for successful associations; however, the success of associations for the minerals among them, especially iron ore, would depend on prosperous recovery from the present economic crisis that is depressing the steel- and copper-using industries. Moreover, the developed capitalist and socialist countries dominate the production of these minerals. In sum, the prospects for successful Third World producer-exporter associations are dim or nonexistent for the majority of commodities because the conditions are unfavorable to the exercise of any significant monopoly power by these countries.

Thus, the vaunted "dependence" of the industrial countries on raw materials imports—the United States imports over 90 percent of its strontium, columbium, mica, cobalt, manganese, titanium, chromium graphite, natural rubber, and coffee; over 80 percent of its tantalum, aluminum, asbestos, platinum, tin, flourine, mercury, and bismuth; and between 50 and 80 percent of half a dozen other important raw materials (U.S. Bureau of Mines and USN 4 February 1974)—does not mean the producer countries in the Third World are in a good bargaining position. For one thing, many of these materials are supplied by other developed countries. But more importantly, as the Brookings Institution in the United States has noted with satisfaction:

> When oil and food are set aside, commodity questions take on an entirely different dimension. Trade in all other primary commodities taken together is comparatively small, fits no clearly defined pattern, and makes fears that raw materials cartels will spread and become a growing source of economic disruption unrealistic. . . . No item in this other group is overwhelmingly large. In 1973 combined exports of the seven largest—copper, cotton, iron ore, wool, rubber, tin and phosphate rock—accounted for about half of the total group. The other half was spread over twenty-five to thirty additional commodities for most of which exports were under $500 million a year. Possibilities for substituting among these raw materials are considerable and shifts

TABLE 3.2

Comparisons of Some Evaluations of the Feasibility of Producer Associations on a Commodity-by-Commodity Basis

Feasibility	Economist Intelligence Unit	OECD Secretary General	Hveem's Study
High	Bauxite	Tin Diamond Phosphate rock Antimony Manganese	Bauxite Phosphate rock
Medium (to high)	Bananas Iron Ore Natural rubber Pepper Sugar Tin	Silver Chromite Bauxite	Rubber Tungsten Bananas Iron ore Copper Tea Spices (pepper) Cocoa
Medium (to low)	Cocoa Tea	Cobalt Mercury Uranium Zinc Copper	Jute Hard fibers Coffee Sugar Manganese Tin Lead Zinc
Low	Coffee Copper Wool	Lead Tungsten Iron Ore	Cotton Wool Oilseeds Groundnuts Timber Nickel Fruits
Other	Phosphate rock and Cloves: short run (medium) potential only		Uranium

*Evaluated industrial minerals and metals only.

SOURCES: Anthony Edwards, *The Potential for New Commodity Cartels*, The Economist Intelligence Unit Ltd., QER Special No. 37 (1975), and The Secretary General, *Industrial Raw Materials*, Paris 23 April 1975; in Helge Hveem, *The Political Economy of Producer Associations*, 1976, mimeo, p. 118.

occur between primary and secondary sources according to price. . . . Mineral ores (copper, bauxite, tin and phosphate rock, for example), which are often cited as materials that lend themselves to cartelization and market manipulation, account for a comparatively small proportion of the commodity trade of these countries. . . . When it is further recalled that the developing countries concerned usually have small financial reserves and are not drawn together by shared political aims, the outlook for more OPECs can be seen in proper perspective. Cartel experiments among the primary commodity exporters will be few and most of these attempted will be short-lived (Owen and Schultz 1976: 201–2, cited in Roberts 1977: 23).

The Third World as a whole accounts for only about one-third of world production of raw materials, and in many cases a not much larger share of world exports. The ability of Third World countries to form cartels and exercise monopoly power is further limited by the developed countries' policy of divide and rule. For this reason, many official Third World spokesmen and others like Helge Hveem propose the establishment of producer-exporter associations that would cover several commodities—or substitutable commodities (e.g. copper and bauxite). But in the face of multinational mining consortia and agribusiness, and the constant threat of political and/or military intervention in the Third World by metropolitan governments, there doesn't seem to be much hope for this proposal. However, insofar as the Third World countries do not hang together, they will assuredly hang separately.

Nonexporting, Uneconomic, and Expendable Regions

A number of countries—even whole regions with very large populations—are considered by world capital to be economically, and apparently politically, expendable. The archetype of the expendable country is Bangladesh, the world's most densely populated nation with 76 million people, of whom 70 million are living below the poverty line (HO 2 January 1977) and of whose rural work force 7 million to 10 million are unemployed (HO 24 October 1976). Large, thickly populated areas of neighboring India probably fall into the same category, as do some populous areas in the northeast of Brazil, the Andean regions, and the south of Mexico. Also considered expendable are some of the smaller land-bound "least developed countries" in Africa and Latin America, notably Chad, Niger, Central African Republic, and Paraguay.

There is another type of society in Africa, which I call the non-economies, like Niger, the Central African Republic, Chad etc. . . . These are states that have no viable resource base at all. . . . [In this situation] I am worried because I see rather the foundations of genocide; we have arrived at a new era in Africa in which we begin to solve the problems by eliminating the men. In such a situation even a socialist revolution would not solve the problems. At best a socialist revolution would permit a revolutionary party to take advantage of the states to stimulate the integration of the neighboring socialist states if they exist (Resnick 1975: 140).

Ernest Feder writes of the expendable populations in Latin America:

The combined effect of the various factors which adversely affect employment and income of the peasant masses tends to increase the proportion of the rural labour force which, with practically no employment whatever or with seasonal or occasional jobs at best, live entirely at the margin of society and perhaps even entirely outside of it. It would seem that the day is not far off when Latin America will see poverty as abject as, say, India, as Edmundo Flores also foresaw not long ago. The simple truth is that a growing proportion of the rural labour force is not absorbed by a growing agriculture and a growing economy. Under prevailing conditions the agricultural and the other sectors can continue to produce, and produce more, without having to incorporate them in productive employment. *A superfluous labour force would be one which with the prevailing socio-economic and political system is not needed in any sense by the system for its functioning, survival and growth.* This was described very plausibly by Professor Rafael Baraona with respect to the displacement of workers in Ecuador's Sierra, but applies to much of the remainder of the hemisphere. . . . The point I wish to stress [here] is that there may be a *tendency* (which already exists or which may be in the offing) *for a growing portion of the labour force which is already beyond the stage of a reserve army, a totally superfluous body of too poor, too outcast, too miserable, too dispairing, too short-lived, to contribute in any significant or meaningful sense, or perhaps in no sense whatever, to even keep the wage bills low (as there are already so many others in the "labour force" to fulfill this function) or to contribute to a process of capital accumulation* [i.e. "economic growth" in a capitalist economy] *or participate in any local, communal or national activities.* Certainly nothing could condemn the existing system more severely than the fact that one might even consider that such a process could emerge or exist (Feder 1973: 42–43; emphasis in original).

What "distinguishes" these regions and populations is that they do not seem to be destined to participate in the international division of labor either as suppliers of labor or of its products—still less as demanders of products on the international or national market. Yet these populations have not remained untouched by the economic, social, and political process of world capitalist development. On the contrary, particularly in East Bengal (Bangladesh) and northeastern Brazil, past development has weighed heavily on them. For this reason, and also because of the political-economic organization in these regions, which international and national capitalism is intent on preserving, these peoples are unable to support themselves at even a subsistence level, and will be still less able to in the foreseeable future. Since they make no essential contribution to the international division of labor, and there seems to be little likelihood of their mounting a credible political threat to the capitalist system, the ideological and political representatives of capital seem inclined to abandon them on grounds of what they like to call "triage" or the "lifeboat" principle.

George W. Ball, former U.S. Undersecretary of State and longtime member of the inner circle of U.S. policymakers (he was on the final list of those considered for Secretary of State by Jimmy Carter), summarizes this principle in his recent book *Diplomacy for a Growing World*:

> In World War I, triage was the system for separating the wounded into three groups—those likely to die no matter what was done, those who would probably recover even if untreated and those who could survive only if cared for immediately. Because of limitations on supplies and manpower, attention was given to the third group alone. It was the Paddocks' proposal [in a book published in 1967 entitled *Famine— 1975*] that, where the population growth has already passed the agricultural potential, it would be "throwing sand in the ocean" to try to provide food. The country they foresaw most likely to suffer this tragic crisis was India. . . .
>
> Dr. [Garrett] Hardin, in subsequent writings, devised another figure of speech to illuminate the "triage" dilemma. He spoke of "lifeboat ethics." The rich nations, as he saw it, are adrift in lifeboats, while those with high [population] growth rates are swimming outside. To take everyone aboard would sink the lifeboats. Thus, Dr. Hardin argued, since we may already have exceeded the carrying capacity of our land, we should apply the realistic "ethics of a lifeboat." In other words, we should, as someone has put it, be cruelly kind instead of kindly cruel (Ball 1976: 240–41).

The principle of triage is also taken seriously by important scientists, influential journalists, and other ideologues of capital. Consider the following column by Anthony Lewis on the editorial page of the *International Herald Tribune* in 1974, reporting on the recommendations of the president of the U.S. National Academy of Sciences, Dr. Philip Handler:

> The problem is most acute, by far, in South Asia. Resources there are scarce, the population huge and growing, the prospect of multiplying food production dim. Dr. Handler raises the possibility that the developed world may simply decide to "forget" the countries of South Asia—"to give them up as hopeless."
>
> He says, as a scientist, it would be better to do nothing—because a lesser effort [that is, less than a massive program of aid and development]

would be "counterproductive." It would encourage continued population growth—and more deaths later. . . . "Cruel as it may sound," Dr. Handler says, ". . . it may be wiser to let nature take its course as Aristotle described it: 'From time to time it is necessary that pestilence, famine and war prune the luxuriant growth of the human race.' Then, he said, "the adjustments required by the rest of the world . . . will still be severe but can be feasible. . . ."

It will be difficult to dismiss Philip Handler as a crank crier of doom. He is a respected biochemist, an eminent advisor to governments, a man of wide experience and common sense. His voice is not so much gloomy as uncompromisingly realistic. How good it would be if some political leaders heard his voice and understood.

At least one political leader did hear Handler's voice and understood, though it is not clear to what extent he agrees: George Ball (1976:244) who quotes Handler to the same effect.

Under the title "The World's Poorest Relation" the *International Herald Tribune* reports about Bangladesh:

"I'm very pessimistic about the medium-term outlook," says a Western diplomat. . . . Foreign officials think out loud about cutting or stopping the aid. Many foreigners say Bangladesh will not help itself—and they always cite the need for increasing food production—unless it has no other choice. "How cruel do you have to be to be kind?" is how one economist describes the dilemma (IHT 1 September 1976).

Under the title "Third-World Poverty: 2 Solutions" Jonathan Power writes (IHT 4 February 1977):

Zbigniew Brzezinski, President Carter's national security adviser, is a compassionate intellectual. . . . Yet last year he put his name to an astonishing advertisement printed in the *Wall Street Journal*. Its argument was crude and simple: the poor of Africa, Asia and Latin America are poor because they have too many children; they have done little or nothing to remedy this situation; and they have depended on the United States to bail them out. It ends up with this warning: "At some point, we in the United States are going to find that we cannot provide for the world any more than we can police it." The implication of this kind of latter-day Ricardian thinking is worrying. It suggests that the West has been over-generous to no avail and that in the end we might have to abandon some of the developing countries to choke on their own mess.

The triage or lifeboat policy has advanced beyond the speculative stage; it has actually been applied. During the famine in Bangladesh and parts of India after the 1974 floods, and in the Sahel region of North Africa and in Ethiopia after the drought, the developed countries refused to make an effective effort to rescue the hundreds of thousands of people who starved to death. Let famine prune the human race, as Aristotle—and Dr. Handler—proposed . . . and pestilence as well! Disease continues to ravage hundreds of millions of people in the underdeveloped world, as the World Health Organization (WHO) data testify, and certain diseases are on the increase after having been all but eradicated in some areas. A notable example is malaria, which had been brought under control in India in the postwar decades but is now spreading again (Sinha 1976).

Experts Fear Malaria Cases to Rise on India Subcontinent

By 1965, an intensive malaria eradication program using DDT insecticide and quinine drugs had greatly reduced the incidence of malaria on the Asian subcontinent and had confined malaria deaths to the remotest areas of the country where drugs were not readily available.

Since then, however, malaria incidence has steadily increased. The 1973 oil embargo which quadrupled the price of insecticide further hampered the eradication programs.

According to international malaria authorities, India recorded about 6 million cases of malaria last year. Authorities estimate that about the same number of cases went undetected, meaning there were about 10 million to 12 million malaria cases altogether.

This year there have been at least 90,000 cases of malaria officially recorded among the 5 million residents of New Delhi, compared to 18,000 cases reported for the same period last year.

"There is no question that malaria has made extensive inroads in India and in the region," said an official of the World Health Organization.

"Given the resources of the local governments, we are no longer talking about eradicating malaria, only controlling malaria," he said (IHT 1 September 1977).

Malaria seems to be on the increase in most of the Third World:

The major areas of recent upsurge of malaria have been in South and Southeast Asia. By far, the most dramatic increases have occurred in India and Pakistan. In India the incidence of the disease rose steadily between 1962 (62,000 cases) and 1969 (349,000 cases) and thereafter expanded explosively to a dismaying 4,200,000 in 1975. The number is predicted to rise to 10 million by 1978. In neighboring Pakistan, the United States Agency for International Development (USAID) reports that the number of malaria cases had already risen to 10 million by 1974 from only 9,500 in 1968 and 108,000 in 1971. The World Health Organization, Farid and Brown et al. also report serious increases of malaria in the 1970's in Afghanistan, Sri Lanka, Nepal, Bangladesh, Burma, Thailand, and Indonesia. Several countries in Central America (Honduras, El Salvador, Costa Rica) and one in the Caribbean (Haiti) have also experienced serious increases in the disease. In the most malarious area of the world—Africa south of the Sahara—the incidence has been rising more slowly but was already at a very high level in the 1960's. In other areas, however, such as the Middle East and South America, many countries either remained free of the disease or made progress in its eradication.

When we look at these developments historically, we see that they constitute a reversal of earlier trends established by the success of the control and eradication programs of the 1950s and 1960s (Cleaver 1977: 559).

This renewed increase of malaria can be attributed only in part to new, DDT-resistant strains of malaria-carrying mosquitoes. There are also economic, social, and political reasons for the renewed spread of malaria. The trend offers Cleaver (1977: 559) "the basis for hypothesizing that malaria decontrol is not a blunder, but perhaps a policy of repression." He writes under the title "Political Economy of Malaria De-Control":

By 1969–70 it was obvious that increasing numbers of Third World governments were already backing out of their commitments to malaria eradication and shifting back to an emphasis on control. In 1972 this movement gave birth to a WHO conference with the politically as well as linguistically awkward title "WHO Interregional Conference on Malaria Control in Countries where Time-Limited Malaria Eradication Is Impracticable at Present." This, of course, is the polite way of saying that in the current conjuncture the resources necessary for the peoples of these countries to be freed from malaria will not be forthcoming either locally or internationally. . . . We must be frank and state that in our time *malaria is a political disease* (Cleaver 1976: 1469, 1471; emphasis in original).

The political nature of the disease seems to be authoritatively confirmed by the following news item:

Alarming Increase in Malaria

Resistance of mosquitoes to insecticides and the disintegration of control programmes in developing countries has led to a rampant increase in malaria around the world, according to the National Center for Disease Control.

"In recent years, there has been a serious resurgence of malaria in the tropics and an alarming increase in imported malaria in temperate-zone countries," said Mr. Myron G. Schultz, Director of the Parasitic Diseases Division at the CDC. "It is running out of control in Central America, India and South America" he said on Friday in an interview.

"Problems of resistance of mosquitoes to insecticides, resistance of parasites to drugs, administrative difficulties and radical changes in the world's economy have all contributed to the present resurgence of malaria," Mr. Schultz said.

Malaria exists in more than 100 countries, and it is estimated that one quarter of the world's population currently lives in areas where malaria is transmitted.

"There used to be control programs in developing countries but most of these have disintegrated," Mr. Schultz said (IE 25 March 1980).

This "political disease," as Cleaver's title implies, derives from considerations of political economy during the present crisis of capital accumulation. The effects of the crisis can be seen on the national level—for example, in India the 1976 draft version of the Fifth Five Year Plan showed a reduction in social welfare expenditures by 25 percent and in health programs by 14 percent from the 1973 draft version (EPW 16 October 1976, 1641–42; more extensively cited in Chapter 7)—and on the international level, where the triage policy is being put into practice. And Aristotle's third remedy, war, may yet arrive to make its contribution (see Chapter 8).

Chapter 4
Third World Debt
Bondage and Exploitation*

The most immediate impact of the Western economic crisis on Third World economies is the deterioration of their balance of payments and the consequent surge in their foreign debt. Since 1973 Third World debt has multiplied and has been lodged increasingly with private Western banks. These banks loan money at higher rates of interest and at lower terms of maturity than public and international agencies do, as they seek to recycle Western and Arab OPEC surplus funds to the debtor Third World countries. The greatest debts have been run up by the Third World countries, such as Brazil, Mexico, and South Korea, that have participated most actively in export promotion and the new international division of labor. The desparate need of Third World countries to borrow from Peter to pay Paul exposes them to pressures so intense they amount to blackmail by the International Monetary Fund and the big Western banks to adopt policies that further export promotion. These policies are the standard IMF package: currency devaluation, reductions in public spending and in subsidies for social purposes and reduced wages, all of which increase the exploitation of the poor and often lead to "IMF riots." Therefore, the imposition of these measures usually requires an increase in political repression, which the IMF sometimes calls for by demanding the replacement of one economies minister or even a whole government by another.

The I.M.F.'s rigorous conditions have sometimes driven finance ministers and even governments from office. A Washington wit once said that the monetary fund had toppled more governments than Marx and Lenin combined.

—*New York Times,* 5 February 1980

*This chapter was written in early 1978, but some of the first part on the growth of the debt and its burden was updated in 1980.

'Senor, Has Your Left Hand Met Your Right Hand?'

By permission of Bill Mauldin and WIL-JO ASSOCIATES, INC.

Debt through Exploitation

Third World foreign debt has risen to an enormous size in recent years, but nobody seems to know exactly how high it is. The mystery is due in part to the rapid increase, and in part to the fact that much of it is held by private banks and the Eurocurrency market, whose operations are often secret. The growth, size, and concentration of the debt in certain countries, and the enormous strain servicing this debt is placing on Third World economies, have led, on the one hand, to Third World demands for organized multilateral cancellation or rescheduling of some of the debt, and on the other, to recurrent fears of unilateral moratoriums or defaults by Third World countries. It is feared that the inability of some Third World countries to pay back interest or capital will cause bank crashes and consequent chain reactions in the imperialist countries.

> Overall, the level of debt outstanding at the end of last year [1976] increased fourfold since 1967 and has doubled in the years 1973–1976. Measuring the exact size of the debt is difficult, as countries themselves do not make public much data and the international organizations and banks which attempt to keep such scores do not all use the same yardsticks. But however it is measured, the same countries show up as the biggest debtors, Brazil and Mexico together accounting for 20 per cent of the outstanding and undisbursed debt of 75 non-oil LDCs as measured by the World Bank. According to the Bank of International Settlements, Brazil and Mexico account for 48 per cent of the LDC debt held by the banks. These two, together with Argentina, Peru, South Korea, Spain and Taiwan, account for 75 per cent of the debt, the BIS statistics show (IHT, Euromarket, December 1977: 5S).

> The question . . . that ran through the U.S. Senate hearings on "International Debt, the Banks and U.S. Foreign Policy": Is the mounting burden of debt arising from the five-fold increase in oil prices likely to throw the capitalist world into another crash like 1929? (IHT Euromarket, December 1977: 1S).

> Ever since the Arab oil embargo, the international financial system has lent itself to a doomsday scenario, which goes something like this: Less-developed countries pile up debts to pay for oil. Commercial banks— mainly American—lend them the money, but the oil-short nations cannot repay on time. One or two countries default. The lending capacity of the banks is impaired. A few fail. The American economy lurches. And, finally, the delicately balanced structure of international finance begins to come apart.

> Like all good scenarios, this one has its roots in reality (NYT Editorial, IHT 1 August 1977).

While the Chase Manhattan Bank's David Rockefeller "hits scare stories" (IHT 17 March 1977), other bankers from Morgan Guaranty Trust and Manufacturers Hanover Bank "say loans abroad are less risk than U.S. credits" (IHT 18 March 1977), and officials from the U.S. Office of the Controller and elsewhere call loans "sound" (IHT 4 May 1977), and the International Finance Corporation of the World Bank says "lending to developing states can go on" (IHT 15 September 1977). Other representatives of capital have made so many similar reassuring statements over the past few years that one is reminded of the old adage: where there is smoke there is fire.

Third World foreign debt is a mystery wrapped in an enigma. Consolidated statistics on these debts are published by the World Bank (WDT), the Bank for International Settlements, the OECD, the Morgan Guaranty Trust Company, and other sources. Their coverage and estimates display confusing differences, however. The number of LDCs covered varies widely. They include 144, 96, 86, 84, 80, 75, 70, and other numbers of "less developed countries" (LDCs), "non-oil-exporting less developed countries" (NOLDCs), and OPEC countries. Sometimes they refer to "total" foreign debt and sometimes only to that part of it that has already been "disbursed." Sometimes they include (though usually they exclude) short-term debts of one year or less and commercial credits. Often they distinguish between "official" loans granted by foreign governments and international institutions on the one hand, and those extended—at shorter terms of maturity and higher rates of interest—by private banks, particularly in Eurocurrency market. The latter, which are increasingly important, are not subject to national or supranational control, or even record. Some of these loans carry government guarantees and others do not.

> The annual publication of the World Bank *World Debt Tables* (and their occasional supplements) constitute the most important source of statistical information about the situation of the external debt of the LDCs and of the less developed advanced countries. . . . Unfortunately, these figures cannot be considered either complete or definitive for various reasons. Nor should it be thought that they adequately reflect the net real private debt of each of the LDC borrowers (Wionczek 1977: 1331).

Wionczek (1977: 1330), for instance, believes that the World Bank estimates of $169 billion total debt (of which $89 billion is private debt) for eighty LDCs in 1976 should be raised by $50 billion to include short-term debt, but not withdrawals from the IMF. Nobody knows how much money is really lent out on the Eurocurrency market or to whom, and some analysts suggest that real Euromarket (or Asia dollar market in Singapore) loans to the Third World are double the haphazardly reported ones (Payer 1976a: 5, citing Levine).

Eurocurrency credits to Third World countries are reported to have increased by 31 percent in 1975 and by another 34 percent in 1976 (IHT Euromarket 1977: 8S). According to an IMF study, total international lending increased 40 percent in 1976 to $95 billion from $68 billion in 1975. For 1977 the IMF expected lending to increase at about the same rate. But lending to Third World countries in 1977 was variously reported to have grown at the slower rates of 8 percent and 13 percent for the first eleven months (IHT Euromarket 1977: 5,8s).

The uncertainty about the total of Third World debts is illustrated by the

large number and wide range of estimates for particular years. For instance, for 1972–1973 estimates ranged from $70 billion and $93 billion (IMF 1977: 1344) to $100 billion (UNCTAD 1975c) and $125 billion (*Times*, 23 October 1974). By 1976 this debt had risen to $169 billion (World Bank, in Wionczek 1977), $171 billion (World Bank, in IMF 1977: 1344), $200 billion (Wionczek 1977: 1330) for seventy-five LDCs; to $212 billion (World Bank, in IMF 1977: 1344) for eighty-four LDCs; and to $150–$200 billion (U.S. Senate 1977: 1379) and "more than $260 billion" (IHT Euromarket 1977: p.1). There were many other estimates for unspecified Third World countries. The annual growth rates of this debt were variously cited as 20–25 percent (Bein 1977: 717), 16–17 percent (UNCTAD 1975c), 15 percent (Cleveland and Brittain 1977: 734), and intermediate rates.

Engellau and Nygren have made a valiant effort to create clarity out of the welter of confusing statistics, and we summarize some of their composite data in Table 4.1. These authors themselves emphasize, however, that "unfortunately there are no statistics which fully elucidate the indebtedness of developing countries." Therefore, their statistics, reproduced in Table 4.1, are "not fully comparable," "less exhaustive," "particularly uncertain" and "the actual total figure is probably much larger." In particular these figures do not include LDC short-term debts estimated at $70–$73 billion for 1978, or about 20 percent in addition to those registered in the table (Engellau and Nygren 1979 passim).

These figures (and some not included in the table) reveal a number of important developments since the early 1970s. Compared to the growth of

TABLE 4.1
World Financial and Third World Debt Figures
(in billions of U.S. dollars and percentages)

	1971	1972	1973	1974	1975	1976	1977	1978
World trade	351	416	576	838	878	991	1122	1300
Eurocurrency deposits	85	110	160	215	250	310	380	475
International lending	37	41	69	81	79	114	134	164
Eurocredits and bonds	28	36	60	67	58	94	105	131
Export credits	6	2	4	8	14	12	19	24
Development aid	3	3	5	6	7	8	10	9
LDC gross borrowing			9	9	13	20	27	45
as % of exports			7	4	5	7	9	14
LDC gross debt	87	98	119	146	179	217	264	321
as % of GNP			17	14	17	17	20	
LDC debt service	11	13	17	22	26	32	41	52
as % of exports	16	17	14	9	12	12	13	16

SOURCE: Engellau and Nygren 1979: passim.

world trade (3.7 times in current values) between 1971 and 1978, Euro-currency credits (5.5 times) and international lending (4.4 times) increased even faster. Development aid declined from 8 percent to 5 percent of international lending, as Euroloans and export credits grew rapidly, especially in the most recent years. Third World borrowing increased by five times between 1973 and 1978 and doubled as a proportion of Third World exports. As a result, the cumulative Third World debt quadrupled since 1971 and increased faster than GNP in recent years. Debt service (amortization and interest payments) increased even faster and nearly doubled their share of export earnings since 1974, although in so doing they only reattained their share in 1971. However, Third World (and other) debt service was kept down during much of the late 1970s by interest rates that, though hardly keeping pace with inflation, grew from 30 percent of debt service in 1971 to 38 percent in 1978. The very sharp rise of interest rates in world financial markets since 1979 bodes very much greater ill for the level and burden of debt service in the near future (see below). Moreover, the burden of Third World debt is also rising because of the marked shift of Third World borrowing from public and international agencies, which charge relatively low rates of interest, to high-cost private creditors whose share of Third World debt increased from 17 percent in 1970 to 39 percent in 1978, according to Engellau and Nygren (1979: 47) and from 47 percent in 1970 to 60 percent in 1977, according to the World Bank (WDR 1979: 29). Total debt of the non-oil-exporting Third World countries was $329 billion in 1979 and is estimated by UNCTAD to reach $384 billion in 1980 and $440 billion in 1981 (FT 24 February 1980).

Not surprisingly, these credits have been very unequally distributed. Most of the poorest countries were left to be taken care of—if at all—by institutional lenders, whose funds have become increasingly scarce. Indeed, "many of the poorest countries are lenders. This group includes, for example, Afghanistan, Bangladesh, Ethiopia and Sri Lanka. . . . It seems as if the developing countries that save are often among the very poorest ones. Insofar as this is true, one could argue that the banks channel savings from poor to wealthy developing countries" (Engellau and Nygren 1979: 27). The distribution of debt among Third World countries classified by income appears in Table 4.2.

Engellau and Nygren comment that the low-income countries with about 60 percent of the Third World population have received only 24 percent of the credits. Since these countries are very poor, their debt is the highest (26 percent) relative to their GNP, but they receive credits on the most favorable terms from institutional lenders (that is, not much from private ones) so that they have the lowest ratio of debt service to debt outstanding. But

> that the need to borrow should be less for low-income countries than for high-income countries does not seem credible. What the table gives a hint of is that the opportunities for borrowing increase with rising

TABLE 4.2

LDC Debt of Countries Grouped by Income, 1977

Countries	Share of debts in percent	Debt per capita in US dollars	Debt as % of GNP	Debt service as % of debt
Low-income	24	48	26	8
Lower middle-income	20	137	23	14
Higher middle-income	35	288	21	19
High income	9	442	14	15
OPEC	12	334	13	24
All developing countries	100	122	20	16

SOURCE: Engellau and Nygren 1979:48–49.

income. The higher the income, the greater the ability of the countries to service their debt and the higher their creditworthiness (Engellau and Nygren 1979: 48), especially from the point of view of private bankers.

Thus, Eurocurrency loans were preferentially concentrated in the countries that were the best business proposition, either because as oil producers they offered markets and security of repayment, or because as major Third World exporters of industrial goods they attracted investments and loans. In order to continue to do so, these countries, like Brazil and Mexico, have been in the forefront of the Third World debtor countries that *oppose* all Third World and Nonaligned discussion and negotiation of debt moratoriums.

During the period 1971–1975 the five largest loan recipients in the Euromarket (Mexico, Brazil, Indonesia, Algeria and Iran) took 17,578 million, almost 60% of the total of 29,600 million; the ten largest (the "five big ones" plus Peru, Philippines, Argentina, South Korea and Hong Kong) negotiated 23,168 million, more than 78%, and the fifteen largest (the aforementioned plus Venezuela, Malaysia, Zaire, Panama and North Korea) received 25,978 million, 87.8% of the total (Wionczek 1977: 1333).

Table 4.3 summarizes some official data on the size of the foreign debt and the burden of servicing it for some major debtor countries in the Third World in 1977. As usual, estimates vary; generally, World Bank estimates are the lowest, OECD estimates intermediate, and UNCTAD estimates the highest. For some countries other, sometimes unofficial, estimates are much higher than those in the table. Moreover, the debt outstanding and the cost of servicing it has risen steeply since 1978. For instance, for Brazil, the country with the largest debt, Table 4.3 shows debt totals of $23 and $32 billion, but estimates of the Brazilian foreign debt at the end of 1979 are $50 billion (FT 16 October 1979). For the Philippines ($6 billion debt and debt service at 6

TABLE 4.3

Foreign Debt of Selected Countries, 1977 (in billions of dollars and percentages)

	1	2	3	4	5	6	7	8	9
		Debt Outstanding					Total As % of Export Earnings	Debt Service	
	Total	By Public Institutions	To Private Banks	As % of World Bank	GNP OECD	Total Bank	As IMF	OECD	UNCTAD
Brazil	32	23	21	17	20	6	18	47	53
Mexico	25	21	20	26	36	5	48	66	45
Argentina		7	3	10			15		23
Peru		6	3	38			30		28
South Korea		13	4	29	31	1	9		13
Philippines		6	3	14	14		6		
Indonesia	12	16			30	1	12	13	
India	15	19		15	16	1	11		
Egypt	8	12		69	67	1	23	23	
Algeria	10	14		42	53	1	16	24	

Sources: Columns 1, 5, and 6: OECD in Engellau and Nygren 1979:52.
Columns 2, 4, and 7: World Bank, in World Bank 1979 Annual Report, Tables 4 and 5, and World Development Report 1979, Table 15.
Column 3: IHT Euromarket 1977:6S
Column 8: OECD and IMF in Engellau and Nygren 1979:53.
Column 9: UNCTAD from IHT Euromarket 1977:5S.

Note: Totals and percentages vary between sources of estimates and their inclusion especially of undisbursed loans.

percent of exports in our table), the Philippine Central Bank claimed $8.74 billion of debts or about one-third of GNP in 1979, and a debt service below the 20 percent of export earnings "danger level" set by the World Bank. But the *Far Eastern Economic Review* interviewed bankers in the Philippines who said that "the statistics released by the government understated the seriousness of the country's plight . . . [and] if the total foreign debt were included, we estimate the ratio [of debt service to exports] would be nearer 40% than 20%" (FER 14 September 1979). Peru's foreign debt ($6 billion and debt service as 28–30 percent of exports in 1977 according to Table 4.3) had grown to $9 billion by 1978 and $9.4 billion in 1979, or 70 percent of GNP in this latter year; and the debt service of over $1 billion in 1978 used up 56 percent of Peru's merchandise export earnings (calculated from Peruvian Central Reserve Bank data in AEP, April 1980). Refinancing of Peru's debt has reduced this burden again, but at the cost of borrowing from Peter to pay Paul—and having to pay Peter later—which is one of the two ways the deeply indebted Third World countries are able to manage their foreign debts. The other—and ultimately *real* way to finance these debts—is to squeeze more out of the working population, a process we shall examine below.

Huge increases in foreign debt have by no means been limited to oil-*importing* Third World countries, as already noted. Much of the so-called OPEC surplus turns out to be illusory under close examination. The spectacular increase in oil prices in 1973 and 1974 and the concomitant increases in the earnings of oil-exporting countries (and companies!) gave rise to fantastic estimates of the "OPEC surplus." The World Bank, for instance, projected this surplus as $624 billion for 1980 (McNamara 1974: 21) and $1,206 billion for 1985 (Terzian 1977: 21). These countries have enjoyed real surpluses since 1973, though it is difficult to know just how big they have been. Various authoritative sources differ by as much as $103 billion in their predictions of the 1980 surplus. More mystifying is the fact that these authorities also differ on the figures for annual surpluses in past years. Thus the estimates of OPEC current account surpluses range from $55 billion to $70 billion for 1974, and from $26 billion to $52 billion for 1975. IMF estimates of the OPEC surplus are: 1973, $6 billion; 1974, $68 billion; 1975, $35 billion; 1976, $40 billion; 1977, $32 billion; 1978, $6 billion; 1979, $60 billion (GATT Press Release 15 February 1980). Estimates of surpluses accumulated over the past several years differ by hundreds of billions of dollars from one banking source to another (Terzian 1977: 21). This uncertainty about OPEC surpluses—and, as we shall see, about deficits and debts—must be kept in mind when evaluating the interpretation of the figures by banking and official sources.

Two facts, however, are fairly certain. One is that

what has become clear is that both oil-producing and consuming governments are devoting almost as much time and energy to the staging of the energy crisis as they are to trying to solve it. . . . The United States does not really want oil prices lowered. Sheik Ahmed Saki Yamani, the Saudi Petroleum minister . . . is also known to have said recently that high-level U.S. officials, including Mr. Kissinger, who visit Saudi Arabia have never seriously discussed lowering prices with him (IHT 30 September 1975).

The high price of oil forced upon the world by the Organization of Petroleum Exporting Countries [OPEC] has actually been good for the United States. The country is stronger today than it was five years ago . . . while competitors and friends in Western Europe and Japan have suffered. . . . The U.S.–OPEC relationship more closely resembles a partnership, an intricate symbiosis . . . (IHT 12 July 1977).

Indeed,

the OPEC price rise has done more good to the West German economy than harm. No domestic policy, they maintain, could have as effectively channeled purchasing power away from the consumer to the capital-goods sector (IHT 17 November 1977).

The second fact is that "OPEC surplus" is a misnomer because eight of the thirteen OPEC countries have debts or even deficits (Iran became a major borrower on international capital markets) and account for some 25 percent of Third World private debt. The startling reality is that Saudi Arabia and Kuwait together account for 82 percent of the "OPEC surplus," and Abu Dhabi, Qatar, and Libya share another 13 percent among them. This circumstance and the related preponderance of Saudi Arabia's reserves and exports of petroleum explain the sudden admission of her "desert sheiks" to the highest financial and political councils of the capitalist world.

Estimates also vary concerning how these OPEC surplus petrodollars have been "recycled" or used. The U.S. Senate Foreign Relations Committee has suggested that of $133 billion accumulated surplus dollars, $102 billion, or 77 percent, have been "invested in public bonds, stocks, real estate and bank deposits in the industrialized countries of the West," and $16 billion, or 12 percent, have gone directly to the non–oil-producing underdeveloped countries (U.S. Senate 1977: 1378). According to the Bank of England, the industrial countries received 60 percent of OPEC surpluses accumulated between 1974 and 1976 (Terzian 1977: 24). For 1974 and the first half of 1975, respectively, the United States and Britain received 57 percent and 29 percent of these surpluses; other Western countries got 37 percent and 62 percent and the International Organizations received 4 percent and 9 percent (Bank of England QB, September 1975). According to the *Financial Times* (10 December 1974), in 1974, 36 percent of the funds went to the United States and Britain, 7 percent to other European countries, 46 percent to the Eurocurrency market, and 11 percent to the

Third World. Another source gave a more detailed breakdown of the re-cycling: Eurodollars 35 percent; direct investments in Europe and Japan 15 percent, bank and government deposits in Britain 12 percent; U.S. government bonds 10 percent; loans to developed countries other than the United States and Britain 9 percent; bank deposits in the United States 7 percent; direct investment in the United States 2 percent; loans to Third World countries 4 percent; and contributions to international financial institutions like the IMF and the World Bank 6 percent (Mandel, citing *Newsweek* 10 February 1975). It has been estimated that certainly less than 28 percent and probably less than 16 percent of the 1973–1976 OPEC surplus was channeled into long-term productive investment (LAER 6 January 1978, citing an estimate by Ronald Mueller et al. at American University). Whatever the exact figures, it is clear that the bulk of "the placement of funds by the OPEC countries [is] in the financial centers of the industrial countries. As financial centers the industrial countries re-lent these funds (supplementing them with aid) to the net deficit areas, thereby financing a portion of their exports to them" (GATT 1976: 11–12).

These developments in world trade, balance of payments, and foreign debt were summarized by the *Report on International Trade 1975/76* of the General Agreement on Tariffs and Trade (GATT), which is generally known in the underdeveloped countries as the rich man's club:

Trade Accounts

The trade surplus (f.o.b.–c.i.f.) of the *oil-exporting developing countries* was reduced from $85 billion in 1974 to $57 billion in 1975 as the area's imports continued to grow while its exports declined. . . . The aggregate trade deficit (f.o.b.–c.i.f.) of *industrial countries*, excluding Southern Europe, was sharply reduced from $43 billion in 1974 to $12 billion in 1975. The largest shift occurred in the United States, where a trade deficit of $9.5 billion in 1974 turned into a surplus of $4.2 billion in 1975. . . . The combined trade deficit of *Southern Europe*, which had almost doubled in 1974, rose further to nearly $20.5 billion in 1975, the largest deficit being recorded in Spain ($8.6 billion). The combined trade deficit of the *oil-importing developing countries* (f.o.b.–c.i.f.), following the upsurge from $13 billion in 1973 to $34 billion in 1974, rose further to $45 billion in 1975. Whereas in 1974 the largest part of the increase in the deficit occurred in trade with the oil-exporting countries, the 1975 increase stemmed from the growing deficit with industrial areas. As in the preceding year, there were wide discrepancies between individual developing countries, the largest deficits being recorded in Brazil (nearly $5 billion), Mexico ($3.7 billion), Singapore ($2.8 billion), Egypt ($2.3 billion), the Republic of Korea ($2.2 billion) and India ($1.8 billion). The *Eastern trading area's* overall trade deficit widened still further to $10 billion (f.o.b.–c.i.f.) in 1975, as compared with $4 billion in 1974 and $1½ billion in

1973. For the area as a whole the deterioration of the overall trade balance reflected primarily the further rise in the trade deficit with industrial countries, from $7.6 billion in 1974 to $13 billion in 1975. Most of the increase in the deficit with industrial countries was accounted for by the Soviet Union, which turned a slight surplus ($0.3 billion) in 1974 into a deficit of nearly $5 billion in 1975. . . .

There is no indication of sharp changes in the main trends of general economic activity in the second half of 1976. . . . The events described in the previous section reflect the operation of more basic developments which will continue to affect the world economy for at least the remainder of the decade. . . .

Current Account Imbalances

Since the beginning of 1974 the oil price increase and the worst recession of the post-war period have combined to aggravate already existing account imbalances. From the data . . . which indicate the evolution of the flow of current payments in a five-area division of the world economy, the following general pattern emerges. In 1975 the OPEC countries and the industrial countries had current account surpluses (excluding government transfers) of $34.6 billion and $21.2 billion, respectively. These surpluses had their counterpart in the deficits of Southern Europe ($8 billion), the oil-importing developing countries ($37.5 billion) and the Eastern trading area ($10 billion). What the table does not show is that the industrial countries ran a large bilateral deficit with the oil-exporting countries (their imports of oil account for some four-fifths of the latter's total export earnings), which was more than offset by the placement of funds by the OPEC countries in the financial markets of the industrial countries. As financial centres the industrial countries re-lent these funds (supplementing them with aid) to the net deficit areas, thereby financing a portion of their exports to them. The three deficit areas together purchase a quarter of the combined exports of the United States, Japan, and the EEC (if intra-EEC trade is excluded, the proportion rises to 42 per cent). Their relatively strong import demand during 1974–75—made possible primarily by the financing available from the industrial countries—benefited the industrial countries by allowing them to generate an export surplus and by providing a welcome addition to aggregate demand during a period of serious unemployment. . . .

Looking at each of the deficit areas in more detail, in the *oil-importing developing countries* the large deficits were possible because the necessary financing was available, in the form of aid, direct investment, and public and private credits. The availability of the additional finance . . . allowed the oil-importing countries to avoid the alternative of massive reductions in imports and reserves. . . . But avoidance of this alternative was not costless. In 1974–75, the credit elements of the financial inflows became relatively much more important than in previous years, and the external debt of the oil-importing developing countries increased substantially (GATT 1976: 7–13).

GATT estimated the related balances of payments on current account through 1979 (see Table 4-4. Their measure also differs appreciably from one source to another, depending on whether official transfers, the treatment of unrepatriated earnings, etc., are included or not, but we may use the data published by GATT as an example).

TABLE 4.4

Current Account Balances[a] by Region, 1973–1979
(billion dollars)

	Cumulative 1971–73	1973	1974	1975	1976	1977	1978	1979
Industrial areas	17	19	−13	14	−3	−7	20	−15
OPEC	4	6	68	35	40	32	6	60
Other developing countries	−10	−11	−30	−38	−26	−21	−31	−50
Eastern trading area[b]	½	1	−4	−10	−7	−3	−7	−3

[a]Excluding official transfers.
[b]Trade balance (f.o.b.-f.o.b.).
Data for 1979 are preliminary.

SOURCE: From IMF, *Annual Report* and secretariat estimates for the Eastern trading area. In GATT Press Release 15 February 1980:19.

The OPEC countries' surplus jumped twentyfold between 1971–1973 and 1974, declined in 1975 as their imports increased and oil exports decreased because of the world recession, and then "stabilized" at $30 to $40 billion in 1976–77, fell drastically in 1978, and jumped again in 1979. In 1974 all the oil-importing countries suffered a corresponding deficit, although the bulk of it was immediately shifted to the non–oil-exporting Third World countries, whose deficit tripled in one year from about $10 billion to $30 billion. But "the industrial countries ran a large bilateral deficit with the oil-exporting countries . . . which was more than offset by the placement of funds by the OPEC countries in the financial markets of the industrial countries" (GATT 1976: 11–12)—that is, for 1975–1978 as a whole the industrial countries showed a surplus again. For the Third World countries, however, the deficit grew by nearly another $10 billion, if the deficitary oil-exporting countries are included (in Table 4.4 they are not). Thus the oil-importing countries of the Third World and those of Southern Europe carried the entire deficit and more than the OPEC countries, or more precisely Saudi

Arabia and Kuwait, received in surplus. In 1975 the Third World deficit exceeded the OPEC surplus; in 1976 and 1977 the Third World deficit was equivalent to about two thirds of the OPEC surplus. In 1978 the Third World deficit was 5 times greater than the reduced OPEC surplus; and in 1979, when the OPEC surplus jumped, so did the Third World deficit, which was almost the same. For 1975 it was estimated that the Third World countries "financed" this deficit through the receipt of $12 billion in grants, $18 billion in loans from developed countries through the Euromarket and other agencies, and $6 billion in loans directly from countries themselves, leaving a gap of $2–$4 billion unfinanced or unaccounted for (IHT 11 and 13 December 1975). The $18 billion in loans, give or take a few billions, are the surplus petrodollars that were recycled from Saudi Arabia and the other rich OPEC states through the Euromarket and other agencies to the debt-ridden oil-importing Third World countries. OPEC imports of capital goods and other industrial exports from the recession-ridden industrial countries have been lifesavers for these countries' balance of payments, exports, production, employment, and, of course, profits. Direct OPEC loans, let alone "aid," to the poor Third World countries were very modest before the late 1970s; and imports from Third World countries have consisted mostly of cheap labor from Yemen, Pakistan, and some other Asian countries, and construction contracts (complete with contract labor) from South Korea. With these hardly significant exceptions, the non–oil-exporting Third World countries were left to bear the brunt of the oil price rise and the recycling of the misnamed OPEC surplus.

All these developments have most frequently been blamed entirely or substantially on the rise in oil prices. But more important factors have been the recession in the industrial countries and increased exploitation in the underdeveloped ones. The increase in oil prices did affect the non–oil-producing Third World countries' balance of payments adversely, forcing them to borrow heavily at a time when the "international banking system" was flooded with petrodollars seeking profitable use. But the 1973–1975 world recession and the halting recovery thereafter, as well as the accelerated world inflation, also affected Third World countries' balance of payments adversely through declining terms of trade and restrictions on their exports. The recession and slow recovery of investment inhibited profitable use of recycled petrodollars in the industrial countries and made it expedient for the international banks to lend money to the underdeveloped countries at high rates of interest.

After the short-lived (eighteen months) raw materials price boom in 1972–1974, which brought an increase in export earnings that was three times greater for the developed countries like the United States that export wheat and other grains than for the underdeveloped countries that export other primary goods (UNCTAD 1974), the prices of primary commodities fell again. Since 1974 these prices decreased sometimes absolutely and certainly relative to the prices of industrial commodities and foodstuffs the underdeveloped countries must import. By the first quarter of 1975 Third World country import prices had increased more than twice as much as the prices of their exports (192 percent as against 84 percent since 1970–1972). Developing countries' food and beverage export prices rose 100 percent over the same period, while their food and beverage import prices rose 250 percent (UNCTAD 1975h). Indeed, the rise in the cost of food imports was greater than that for oil imports. Grain (and some other food) prices have fallen since then, but world inflation has driven up the prices of industrial imports. UNCTAD data suggest that for 1975, *only 15 percent* of the increased import costs of the non–oil-exporting Third World countries was attributable to oil; 85 percent was due to inflation in the prices of manufactures (Mato 1977:130). At the same time, the world recession depressed some Third World exports. In Brazil, for instance, which is heavily dependent on oil imports, less than half the 1974 balance-of-payments deficit was attributable to increased petroleum prices (*Gazeta Mercantil* December 1975). Thus we may agree with the conclusion of the vice presidents of Citibank (and disciples of the monetarist economist Milton Friedman) that

> in sum, our analysis suggests that the preponderant cause of the non-oil LDC's large current account deficits and heavy foreign borrowing during the last three years was the recession, while the price of oil also made an important contribution at the beginning of the period. . . . The recession explains over 55 percent of the deterioration from 1973 to 1974 and nearly 75 percent of the deterioration from 1973 to 1975 (Cleveland and Brittain 1977: 744–45).

But we cannot agree with them that the third factor is "the overly expansive domestic policies followed by some LDC's" (p. 739), which, perhaps not accidentally, they do not bother to measure. On the contrary, following the recommendations of these Citibank vice presidents (among others), as well as of their mentor Milton Friedman (who has advised the governments of Chile and Israel) some LDCs have been pursuing excessively depressive policies in order to make themselves eligible for deficit-financing loans and to pay off previous ones. So, the contention that "recycled OPEC surpluses" have been "financing" LDC deficits draws the veil of a "money illusion" over what is really a rakeoff by capital through the superexploitation of the working masses in the Third World.

The growing financial burden on Third World states has been quickly translated into an increasingly exploitative burden on their peoples. We have seen that Third World borrowing, especially from private banks, has increased rapidly since 1973. Service payments on Third World external debt (amortization and interest on the debt, but not profit remittances on foreign investments and other financial service payments) rose at an average annual rate of 14 percent between 1950 and 1969. In 1969 these service payments represented 0–15 percent of export earnings in sixty countries, 15–25 percent in fifteen countries, and 20–25 percent in the four big countries, India,

Pakistan, Argentina, and Mexico, plus little Uruguay. Between 1971 and 1973 the debt service of eighty LDCs rose from 9.4 percent to 13.3 percent of total export earnings; if profit remittances are included, the increase was from 16 percent to 24.8 percent of export earnings (UNCTAD 1975c). Default became imminent for several countries, and some, e.g. Zaire and Argentina, did actually default on their payments (Payer 1976a: 4–5). More widespread debt crises were averted—or perhaps merely postponed—by the 1972–1974 increase in raw materials prices and by subsequent massive Eurocredit and other private bank loans. For the developing countries as a whole, debt service consumed 11 percent of export earnings in 1977 and was estimated to increase to 18 percent by 1985 *before* the 1979 oil price increases, which have again raised their borrowing requirements (WDR 1979). The debt service of non-oil-exporting Third World countries alone for 1979 is estimated at $40 billion (IHT 25 May 1979).

The average term, or length until maturity, of (mostly) official loans to Third World countries declined from 14.1 years in 1967 to 12.8 years in 1974 (Mato 1977: 1310). But according to American Express International, during the surge of private lending to Third World countries in 1975 and 1976, 88 percent of the loans had terms of less than eight years; and it has been estimated that 95 percent of the non–oil-exporting Third World countries' outstanding debt in the Euromarket will come due by 1983. In 1980 more than half of new Euromarket loans to the Third World will be used simply to finance already existing debts; it is estimated that by 1985 this share will be two-thirds (Wionczek 1977: 1332).

> The next four years will be a period of huge debt repayments as the grace periods end on loans taken out in 1974 and 1975. The ballooning of amortisation and interest payments is expected to push non-oil debt repayments to US $20,000–$25,000 million a year through 1981. This compares with just US $8,000 million in 1973, US $10,500 in 1974, US $12,000 million in 1975 and US $15,000 million last year. Hence while the current accounts deficits of these countries may drop to US $25,000 million by 1980, their gross capital needs will rise to US $55,000 million from US $49,000 million (FER 8 April 1977: 35).

> There is no way private loans can be increased at rates exceeding 30 per cent a year, as in the recent past, in the absence of sharply increased LDC export revenues. The banks themselves . . . say that the recent pace of lending has to be slowed, as indeed it has this year [1977], to around an 8-per-cent annual increase. This is the view that Arthur Burns, chairman of the Federal Reserve Board, has communicated to bankers in what he describes as "strident tones." . . . But what has only barely been perceived is that the debt is really a deadly boomerang. To pay it off, the borrowers must increase their exports which already are a major threat to basic industries in the industrialized countries. And failure to export more means an inability or unwillingness to pay off the

debt. . . . The LDCs, however, have concentrated their new industrial capacity in a narrow band of labor-intensive industries: textiles, clothing, steel, shipbuilding and other transportation equipment building products. . . . It is precisely these depressed, distressed industries of Western Europe and the United States which are screaming for protection from low-cost imports which they cannot compete against (IHT Euromarket 1977: 1,5).

This is the vicious circle of contradictions. How long can it continue? Where will it be broken?

An official of the Chase Manhattan Bank, one of the biggest lenders to Third World countries, states the problem in the magazine *Euromoney*:

On the one hand, a purely technical analysis of the [non–oil-exporting developing countries'] current financial condition would suggest that defaults are inevitable; yet on the other hand, many experts feel that this is not likely to happen. The World Bank, the IMF, and the governments of major industrialized nations, they argue, would step in rather than watch any default seriously disrupt the entire Euromarket apparatus with possible secondary damage to their own domestic banking systems, which in many cases are already straining under their own credit problems (quoted in Payer 1976b: 59).

Exploitation through Debt

The inevitable questions are: How would they step in? What would be the consequences? What preparations are being made to face the problem?

The first step was to sound the alarm, which is in itself a form of intervention and pressure:

Now a crescendo of warnings about bank over-exposure to risky NOLDC debt is pouring forth. The most important voice to be heard to date is that of Arthur Burns—Chairman of the US Federal Reserve. Testifying to the Senate Banking Committee recently, Burns said that US banks "must not and cannot continue lending" to LDCs at the fast pace of recent years. . . . The statement by the Chairman, buttressed by similar words from Gordon Richardson, Governor of the Bank of England, is quickly leading to a reversal of lending policy by US banks (FER 9 April 1977, 34–35).

But since simple reduction of lending would reduce the debtors' ability to pay back past loans and therefore boomerang on the banks, simultaneous measures are necessary to generate an alternative source of ability to pay and to protect the "Euromarket apparatus . . . and our own domestic banking systems." Arthur Burns had concrete proposals to these ends:

I plan to comment tonight on the need for order in international finance. My choice of topic does not require lengthy justification. . . . Many countries will be forced to borrow heavily, and lending institutions may well be tempted to extend credit more generously than is prudent. A major risk in all this is that it would render the international credit structure especially vulnerable in the event that the world economy were again to experience recession on the scale of the one from which we are now emerging. To minimize the risks that face us, there is a clear need for a strong effort involving all major parties at interest. . . . The ability of the Fund to act forcefully in speeding the adjustment process will be strengthened in still another way once the five-year effort of amending the IMF's Articles of Agreement is completed. . . . Under the revised Articles, the Fund could take the initiative in determining whether individual countries are complying with formally prescribed obligations to foster orderly economic growth and price stability. This authority, once available, will enable the IMF to broaden progressively its oversight role even when a country is not an applicant for a loan . . . because an IMF "certificate of good standing" becomes essential to further borrowing from private lenders. . . . If the rule of law in international monetary affairs is ultimately to prevail, all countries— there can be no exceptions—must fully respect the IMF's integrity. . . .

A number of actions . . . either need to be taken or avoided to achieve a new sense of order in international finance. . . . First, in order to contribute to a more stable international system, the IMF must act with new assertiveness in monitoring the economic policies of its members. To give the Fund added leverage for such a role, its resources must be enlarged. But those resources must be used sparingly and dispensed only when applicant countries agree to pursue effective stabilization policies. [There is a] clear need for better financial discipline around the world. . . .

Second, governments need to resist the temptation to circumvent the Fund by seeking bilateral official loans or to embarrass the Fund by exerting political pressure on Fund officials. Commercial and investment bankers must also need to recognize that their actions must not undercut IMF efforts to speed adjustment. . . . Third, a better framework of knowledge for evaluating the creditworthiness of individual countries is badly needed. Among other things, central banks could work together through the BIS [Bank of International Settlements] and establish a common list of informational items that borrowing countries will be expected to supply to lenders.

Fourth, commercial and investment bankers need to monitor their foreign lending with greater care. . . . Fifth, protectionist policies need to be shunned by all countries. Sixth, countries with persistent deficits need to adopt effective domestic stabilization policies. Seventh, non-OPEC countries experiencing large and persistent payments surpluses also need . . . some appreciation of their exchange rates. . . . Eighth, all countries . . . need stringent oil conservation policies. . . . Ninth, the members of OPEC must avoid a new round of oil price increases (Burns 1977: 5–12).

In short, Arthur Burns and others in high places have been proposing the conversion of the IMF into a superimperialist political-economic central intelligence and executive agency.

Other proposals have gone a step further:

> Manufacturers Hanover Trust has asked the International Monetary Fund to study the possibility of establishing a formal system under which private banks and the IMF would co-finance international balance-of-payments loans. Gabriel Hauge, chairman of the bank . . . noted that "the IMF can get information from" national borrowers that individual commercial banks simply cannot. In addition, the executive noted, the IMF has the power to attach conditions to its loans . . . [to] require the nation to bring its domestic spending into line with its receipts (IHT 9 June 1977).

This proposal goes beyond using the IMF's information and leverage which Arthur Burns had suggested. Like analogous ventures of public-private cooperation, it seeks to privatize the profits from such cofinancing ventures and to socialize any losses (through the IMF). As the official from the Chase Manhattan Bank argued, the World Bank, the IMF, and the industrialized nations' governments are to step in to prevent disruption of the financial system. But as others have argued, such an arrangement is not possible if "the IMF does not want to lose the trust of the governments with which it deals by making privileged information about their countries available to commercial banks" (IHT 7 October 1977).

Mr. Burns' proposals have already been put into practice, though perhaps not yet on the widespread and organized scale that he demanded. In recent years, the financial press has published unending reports of increasing IMF pressure on Third World debtor countries and most especially on Peru, where these pressures have involved changing the Minister of Economics or the Central Bank president five times in as many years; Turkey, where Prime Minister Ecevit fell victim to his inability adequately to resist or otherwise handle IMF pressure until he was replaced again by the Conservative Demirel as Prime Minister, who hastened to make the deal that the IMF demanded; Zaire, where the economic ministries and public financial institutions have been taken over, lock, stock, and barrel, to be directly administered by foreign "experts"; Jamaica, where Prime Minister Manley is almost certain to experience the fate of Mr. Ecevit in Turkey—that is, conceding too much to the IMF while his economic and political position was relatively strong and then trying to resist IMF demands too much after having lost the necessary economic and political room for maneuver, until the conservative opposition makes political capital out of the Premier's accumulated weakness; and Tanzania, where President Nyerere is still trying valiantly to resist the IMF, but with an increasingly uncertain future. Some press accounts may be cited here by way of example (others are reproduced in Chapter 6; for a detailed account of the IMF and Turkey, Peru, and Zaire, see Caballero et al. 1980).

Banks Tell Peru, Others to Improve Credit Rating

Citibank senior vice-president, Irving Friedman, told the Senate Foreign Relations Subcommittee on Foreign Economic Policy that new loans to Peru and Zaire, both of which are in dire straits, will be withheld pending proof of their "creditworthiness." ... In July, the [Peruvian] cabinet turned down a new credit arrangement with the IMF, bringing the resignation of the country's finance minister and the governor of the central bank. ... Peru is now negotiating with the IMF and Mr. Friedman indicated that Citibank might reconsider giving private loans if Peru comes to terms with the IMF (IHT 12 October 1977).

International bankers holding most of Peru's $6 billion in foreign debt sighed with relief in November when the International Monetary Fund approved a $106 million standby credit, and the government began implementing a strict new austerity plan to pull the economy back from disaster. But the brutal fact is that Peru's foreign exchange coffers are again virtually empty, and the government of General Francisco Morales-Bermúdez will have to turn to the banks for at least an additional $300 million in 1978.

Viewed from Citibank's New York headquarters, however, the prospect is far from hopeless. Says Irving S. Friedman, senior vice-president of Citibank, Peru's leading foreign banker: "We are impressed with Peru's efforts to gain control over its economic situation. The sol is reaching realistic levels, and the austerity program is in train. There are many factors, and we are not naive, but our view is a positive one" (BW 23 January 1978).

Devaluation Hits Jamaican Hopes of Resurgence

Kingston—Last weekend's 10% devaluation of the Jamaican dollar is a damaging setback to whatever hopes the government entertained for an early start to the reconstruction of the island's economy.

According to prime minister Michael Manley and finance minister David Coore, the devaluation, demanded by the IMF as a condition for further financial assistance, was much higher than the government thought necessary. But the fact that the government was forced to go along with the IMF demand indicates the crucial importance it attaches to receiving aid, not only from the IMF, but also from international commercial bank consortia willing to lend if the IMF makes the first move.

The impression created by the government is that it was forced into taking this move because it had failed one of the tests set by the fund for further tranches from a US $74m package agreed last year (LAER 20 January 1978).

Soares Gives Austerity Plan
to Parliament, Calls for Unity

Lisbon, Feb. 2 (AP)—Premier Mario Soares, appealing for national reconciliation, gave parliament today a 300-page legislative program based on the austerity that he said is needed to save democracy.

The program, if approved in a vote by the Assembly of the Republic scheduled for Feb. 11, would open the way for resumed negotiations on economic controls with the International Monetary Fund. Agreement with the IMF, in turn, would unlock $800 million in Western emergency loans to help cover last year's payments deficit of $1.3 billion.

Legislative endorsement of the program was predicted, since the Socialist-Conservative government sworn in Monday controls 143 votes in the 263-seat parliament. Mr. Soares's previous Socialist minority cabinet fell Dec. 8 when rightist and Communist opponents refused to accept his austerity proposals.

Mr. Soares said that he was offering "austerity, of which so much has been discussed, and so little practiced," to solve "the economic problem hanging over our heads like a sword" (IHT 3 February 1978).

Obviously international capital is using the IMF to oblige the governments of countries in the Third World, and increasingly elsewhere, to implement the "austerity" measures that the U.S. Federal Reserve and the Manufacturers Hanover Trust call "effective domestic stabilization policies ... to bring domestic spending into line with receipts." In truth, these are the policies of economic superexploitation and political repression (documented in detail in Chapters 5 and 6). Some of their consequences and implications are summarized in a report prepared by a staff member of the U.S. Senate Foreign Relations Committee:

Through close cooperation between the private banks and the IMF, pressure is exerted on the countries who have debts because of deficits to balance their external accounts through internal austerity measures. The $10 billion special Fund which the IMF is building through contributions of the industrial and petroleum countries is not designed to replace private bank credit but to give the Fund more elements of financial pressure to convince the deficit countries to adopt austerity measures.

The measures that the IMF and the private banks stimulate the deficit countries to adopt usually include limitations to the growth of the money supply, reductions in public spending and devaluation. These measures are destined to maintain the level of domestic consumption low and to reduce the demand for imports. The growth of export industries is regarded as very important to help equilibrate the balance of trade and to assure that the country receives enough foreign exchange to service its foreign debt. Countries may also be stimulated to create a favorable climate for foreign investment and for the private sector in general.

The problem with these measures is that, although they may be the most effective way quickly to compensate the balance of payments deficit of a country, they can also lead to greater unemployment, to the reduction in social welfare, and to a lower standard of living for the people, at least in the short run. In the poorest countries, in which the majority of the population barely reaches a minimum level of subsistence, the government decision to impose a program of strict economic austerity can create social and political disturbances. The demand to reduce government spending and to expand the private sector can also contradict the long term economic and social goals of the governmant or of some political sectors of the country.

If the IMF and other creditors do not take adequate account of these internal limitations, they can push a government into such a position as to oblige it to chose between accepting some of the terms imposed by the external creditors—or maybe to use political repression in order to be able to impose them—or repudiate the IMF, the banks and possibly its debts, recurring instead to economic protectionism and to an isolationist policy. . . . Finally, and as we have shown, in many countries there seems to be a direct correlation between economic difficulties and political repression. The Carter Government, therefore, may see itself obliged to choose between continuing its efforts in favor of human rights or to support the creditor demands to implant drastic economic austerity programs that could only be imposed at the expense of civil liberties in the countries that adopt them (U.S. Senate Foreign Relations Committee, August 1977, reproduced in CE November 1977:1379–80, and retranslated from the Spanish).

Little wonder that, as Cheryl Payer (1976a: 13) has observed, "the list of countries under attack for human-rights violations is nearly identical with the list of those with imminent debt problems: Brazil, Chile, Argentina, Indonesia, Philippines, South Korea," to name a few. And yet the *Washington Post* could defend international capital and the IMF in a holier-than-thou editorial entitled "When Human Rights Are Wrong" in which it opposed an amendment proposed in the U.S. House of Representatives that would have barred the use of U.S. funds for IMF loans to countries that violate human rights.

The newspaper claimed that such a limitation would turn the IMF, that "large gray institution whose operations rarely draw much notice," into a "political weapon" that others might use against "more vulnerable targets" (IHT 21 February 1977). What is the IMF now, one may ask, if not a political weapon against vulnerable targets?

How efficacious, ultimately, are IMF prescriptions for ailing economies?

> Felix Dias Bandaranaike, Finance Minister of Sri Lanka . . . has one question which he persistently puts to the "examiners" of the fund when they lay down restrictive guidelines to countries seeking loans. "Name me one country whose economy has recovered as a result of following your policies," he asks visiting IMF officials. "I never get an answer to that question," Felix triumphantly points out to the press (FER 5 November 1976).

Since Mr. Bandaranaike and his own country failed the IMF examination and were forced to swallow the IMF medicine, which evidently is not prescribed to make any Third World country's economy recover, it is difficult to understand why he felt triumphant.

After observing that "increasingly, private banks turned to the IMF as allies in lending to oil-importing LDCs . . . [who] will probably have to follow IMF restrictions when they go to commercial banks as well," the *Far Eastern Economic Review* comments:

> All this is designed to protect the banks' exposure overseas and to take some of the risk out of lending to oil-importing LDCs. . . .Nation after nation began to run up against the country lending limits of the major comercial banks. . . .The essential link in this logic is expansion of the IMF to pick up the financial burden where the banks are now leaving off. . . .That, at least, is the strategy in New York and Washington. . . .
>
> With recovery choking in most of Europe, with Germany steadfastly refusing to reflate its economy further and with leftist advances in France and Italy imperilling NATO, all the self-righteous verbiage has gone down the drain. The rebirth of the IMF, as main agent for the transfer of money from the surplus nations to the deficit countries, has nothing to do with the real needs of the oil-importing LDCs but dates from the realisation that the imbalance in the world's economy is here to stay—and Europe must somehow be saved. . . .Despite the huge infusion of additional cash, the IMF will first look after its own brood— the industrialised countries of the West (FER 8 April 1977, 34–38).

More specifically, the IMF will look after the inner circle of its own brood in international banking and industrial capital. As the U.S. Senate Foreign Relations Committee pointed out, the IMF has not been above pressuring Britain and Italy to apply "austerity measures"—and these are *Western* countries. But "probably the most undiscussed issue regarding LDC debt is the embarrassing fact that, had the LDCs not maintained a steady level of imports, the 1974–75 recession in the North—the South's main supplier—would have become more severe" (FER 8 April 1977, 42–43. For further evidence see WE: Chapters 2 and 5). But would not the austerity measures on the people in the North have had to be even more severe if it had not been for the superexploitation of the people in the South?

Thus we may agree with Wionczek's conclusion that

> since mid 1977 and for the first time in the last ten years the growth of the credit activities in the Euromarket is insufficient to satisfy the demand for financial resources of the LDCs; this is not due to a lack of funds, but because some big financial intermediaries as well as some of their governments—like that of the United States—consider that the risk of lending to some LDCs at least may have grown excessively. . . . [This] could indicate the beginning of a new tendency, which reflects the often forgotten paradox of the private loans: they are conceded only to the "acceptable risks," not to those who need them most. If this is so, not even the recuperation of the world economy would guarantee the automatic access of the LDCs to the private international capital markets during the coming years.
>
> The situation appears even worse if that recuperation does not happen, which cannot be rejected. . . . It is very difficult to see who could cover the gap in the financial resources of the LDCs in a situation of prolonged world economic recession. In summary, it appears that never, since the end of the last war, does the future of the LDCs depend as much on the international economic cycle as it does today (Wionczek 1977: 1338).

Indeed, as the *Far Eastern Economic Review* suggests, "after the debt crisis . . . the credit crunch" is likely to follow.

> Just when the non-oil-producing developing countries are facing a debt crunch, two major sources of commercial lending are tightening up. Japan's Ministry of Finance, worried about the country's mounting current account deficit, is restricting capital outflows through yen loans by banks, while the US is extracting itself from the role of intermediary. . . . US banks are backing out of their role of recycling petrodollars. . . . They will not be able to repeat [the post-1974] performance in the wake of the latest oil price rises. . . . The second recycling in six years will not be nearly as easy (FER 9 November 1979).

Therefore, as the *Far Eastern Economic Review* suggests and the evidence confirms, the IMF and the World Bank—and perhaps a new capital fund such as the one proposed by the Brandt Commission Report at the end of 1979—increasingly have to lend a hand again. But that also means that the Third World debtor countries will have even less chance "to escape the heavy-handed conditions imposed by the IMF in return for access to balance-of-payments loans" (FER 29 November 1979)—and that the heavy hand of the IMF may become a balled fist. The only other hope is that the Arab banks will recycle more OPEC surplus themselves, though that too will be at a price.

The essential mechanisms—the provision of "financial resources" to the "acceptable risks"—that link LDCs to the international economic cycle is the superexploitation of the masses and the political and military repression to enforce it. Only these measures have succeeded in establishing the economic "discipline" and political "stability" demanded by the imperialist lenders.

This link appears vividly in the quotations from official sources and the press that are documented in the following chapters on superexploitation and political economic repression in the Third World.

Chapter 5
Superexploitation in the Third World

Superexploitation is the appropriation by capital of so many of the fruits of the workers' labor that the workers cannot maintain themselves or reproduce their labor power. In each major crisis of accumulation, capital has resorted to increased exploitation and superexploitation somewhere in the world. In the present crisis exploitation and superexploitation are spreading through the Third World as industry and agriculture are extending the daily and weekly working hours, intensifying the work pace—with a resultant increase in industrial accidents—and lowering the rates of pay. In some Third World export-promoting countries, most notably South Korea, weekly working hours are twice as long as in the industrial countries of the West, and annual working time is 50 percent higher. Capital's literal exhaustion of workers, particularly young women, is rendered possible by rapid rotation: workers whose productivity declines are rapidly replaced by a new supply of virgin workers. Wage rates in the South are as low as one-tenth those in the West, although labor productivity if often nearly equal and sometimes higher in equivalent productive activities in the Third World. These cost differentials help to stem the decline of profits during the world economic crisis.

The contemporary world economic crisis is exerting far-reaching pressures for an accelerated modification of the international division of labor to reduce costs of production and to raise rates of profit. Far from leading to the New International Economic Order demanded by Third World leaders, in which their peoples would be less exploited, the new modalities of the process of capital accumulation involve the accelerated superexploitation of growing masses of workers already engaged in or newly drawn into production for export.

Export promotion, as we have seen, is the order of the day, not only in "traditional" raw materials–exporting economies, but also in those economies that already have an intermediate industrial base (originally built up primarily to supply the internal market), as well as in those that are now developing one for export. Moreover, in the raw materials–exporting economies, the present crisis generates "new" conditions that limit and even reduce the economic, social, and political distribution of the benefits from the production and export of these primary commodities.

An essential feature of the new export promotion distinguishes it from import substitution and even from raw materials exports—both of which in the past resulted in the distribution of benefits to the middle classes, which in turn provided an internal market for manufactures. The market for import substitution is internal and must be supported through the progressive provision or extension of purchasing power at home. This economic need provides the basis for a nationalist and populist progressive political alliance between national capital, the petite bourgeoisie, and some sectors of the working class. In contrast, the market for export promotion is external, and there is no reason to support or widen it through progressive extension of income and purchasing power at home. On the contrary, the most essential criterion of profitable success in export promotion is the maximum reduction of the costs of production in order to be able to compete most advantageously with others who pursue the same policy. Moreover, the technological, financial, and marketing conditions of export promotion imply a dependent association of local capital, and more often than not of the state as well, as junior partners with transnational capital. This enables international capital to play one underdeveloped country off against another, and gives it substantial bargaining power to call the economic and political shots. Consequently, export promotion implies the lowest possible real wage rate and the effective prohibition of strikes to raise wages or otherwise to interfere with profitable production. Export promotion further implies limitations to the distribution of income through state employment, welfare, and other expenditures; exclusivist development that "marginalizes" substantial populations economically and socially through unemployment and poverty; state subsidization of infrastructure and utilities (transportation, energy, water, etc.) and sometimes of inputs such as steel; maximum freedom for capital to come and go because of minimal local taxes and customs duties; and a suitable exchange rate, which in practice usually means successive devaluations. Moreover, as the huge concentrations of foreign debt in Brazil, Mexico, and South Korea demonstrate, export promotion, far from promoting a favorable balance of payments, as one might naively suppose, generates a chronic and ever-growing deficit that provides additional reasons for the imposition of an "austerity" program. All these conditions require the imposition and institutionalization of a repressive political apparatus. These, then, are the economic, social, and political features of the intermediate or semiperipheral Third World countries that are pursuing export promotion as a major policy today.

This chapter analyzes the superexploitation of increasingly large parts of the labor force associated with this policy in the Third World. The consequent political repression, the militarization of societies, the new monopoly and technocratic state forms, and the corresponding ideology of "national security" are examined in Chapters 6 and 7.

Superexploitation

Capitalism has always involved exploitation. What distinguishes the contemporary process of capital accumulation is its increasing superexploitation of labor in the Third World. In other words, capital is now appropriating more than the surplus value produced by labor beyond the wages received for the sustenance and reproduction of labor power; it is appropriating also part of the consumption fund workers need to survive, that is to sustain and reproduce labor power (see Marx, *Capital*, Vol. I: 599–602). The "forcible reduction of wages below this value . . . [which] transforms, within certain limits, the labourer's necessary consumption fund into a fund for the accumulation of capital" (ibid.: 599) we may call "superexploitation." This superexploitation is often related to, if not based on, the capitalist accumulation through (capitalist) wage labor that is produced, sustained, and/or reproduced at least in part through nonwage "precapitalist" or "noncapitalist" relations of production, especially in some rural sectors of the Third World and in the "household"—that is, primarily women's—sector of capitalism generally. The most far-reaching recent analysis of this process of accumulation is that of Claude Meillassoux (1975) in his *Femmes, Greniers et Capitaux*. Meillassoux defines primitive accumulation as "the accumulation [that] comes from a transfer of value from one mode of production to another" (145n). To distinguish this contemporary primitive accumulation from the "so-called primitive accumulation" of precapitalist times discussed by Marx, the terms *continuing* or *permanent primitive accumulation* (Bartra 1974a, b) and *primary accumulation* (Frank 1977a, 1978a) have been proposed. Common to these and other recent analyses (Fröbel et al. 1977; Amin 1973; Senghaas-Knobloch 1976a, b; Wolpe 1972; Marini 1973; Osorio 1975) of superexploitation in contemporary capital accumulation is the thesis that it is possible to pay wage laborers wages that are inadequate for their sustenance because these wages are subsidized by the contribution of unpaid labor by the workers' families and others, who are thereby exploited indirectly (and sometimes directly as well).

Three important categories of this primitive or primary accumulation through superexploitation of the wage earner are: (1) wage earners who are "reproduced" by their children and subsidized by the unpaid domestic labor of their wives; (2) migrant workers in southern Africa, Western Europe, and southwestern United States who are "reproduced" by their home countries and communities and sustained by them during part of their lives; and (3) industrial workers in many underdeveloped countries who do not earn enough to support themselves and their families. (Analogous examples, perhaps, are the "brain drain" from the underdeveloped countries, where the brains are produced and educated, to the developed ones, where they produce and leave the fruits of their education; and the appropriation of the value produced by socialist labor in the East for accumulation in the capitalist West, which is discussed in WE: Chapter 4.)

We have argued elsewhere (Frank 1977a, 1978a) that superexploitation through continuing primary accumulation seems to increase in (at least one) part of the periphery during each crisis of accumulation at the center, as capital in the center seeks to protect or restore its profit position. This seems to have been the case in the accumulation crises of 1762–1790 (the "Rape of Bengal" in India and increased exploitation of slaves in the French Antilles), 1816–1849 (the cotton regions of the U.S. South and Egypt), 1873–1895 (the transformation of "natural economy," as Rosa Luxemburg called it, through imperialism in many parts of the periphery), and 1914/29–1945 (Nazi exploitation of Eastern Europe and concentration camp labor, Japanese "Greater East Asian Co-Prosperity Sphere," and elsewhere). And such an increase in superexploitation and primitive or primary accumulation is going on today. The vehicles of this policy are export promotion in the Third World (the "new international division of labor") and the incorporation or reincorporation of the socialist economies into the capitalist international division of labor (see WE: Chapter 4). Perhaps the recent upsurge of interest in the analysis of superexploitation and primary accumulation through noncapitalist modes of production is an outgrowth of the increase in the phenomenon itself, which is generated by the contemporary crisis. Meillassoux distinguishes

> three components of the value of labor power: sustenance of the worker during his time of employment (or *reconstitution* of the immediate labor power); *maintenance* of the worker during periods of non-employment (unemployment, sickness, etc.); replacement of the worker by the support of his off-spring (which we will, following convention, call *reproduction*) (Meillassoux 1975: 152).

The worker is superexploited when the wage he receives from capital is insufficient to cover his needs for any one or more of these literally vital processes that are necessary for the continued supply of labor power to capital. We will use the terms *primitive* or *primary accumulation* of capital to denote a situation in which the value of at least one of these vital processes is not compensated through the wage payment to the worker, but is received by the capitalist for free, or through the subsidy by "noncapitalist" work of family members or others who help support the wage earner and through him subsidize the capitalist's maintenance or reproduction of labor power.

Reproduction of Labor Power

When capitalist exploitation takes on characteristics which involve the disregard for the exchange value of labor power, we are talking about a capitalist exploitation that takes on a superexploitative character. The concept of super-exploitation, therefore, does not [simply] mean higher rates of exploitation, in the sense of beginning to talk about super-exploitation after exploitation reaches a certain level. Rather, super-exploitation involves exploitation when the latter violates the value of labor power. . . . To pay labor power for its value signifies for the producer finding the whole of the conditions necessary to produce and reproduce his labor power, among which the wage plays an important, but not the only, part. . . . The forms of super-exploitation that capitalist exploitation can assume are fundamentally three: increase in the intensity of work, extension of the working day, payment of labor power below its value (Osorio 1975: 6–7).

The question arises how, in view of such low wages, the reproduction of labor power is possible. The answer is, roughly speaking, that in countries such as South Korea the wages are always sufficient for the daily reconstitution of labor power, but that they are insufficient either to permit the rearing of a new generation or to permit the adequate old-age or invalid care of the workforce that has left the productive process. These "additional costs" must, for better or for worse, be borne by a sector of the economy of these countries which is not capitalist in the narrow sense of the word (Fröbel et al. 1977: 160).

The labor force itself and/or its means of subsistence are produced in "non-capitalist," "traditional," etc., sectors, which, moreover, often have to provide for the "old" age of the exhausted labourers. The cost of the labour force is, therefore, to a high degree externalized as viewed from the capitalist sector proper (Fröbel et al. 1976: 160).

(1) . . . The wages (including fringe benefits) that are really paid by capital are roughly 10 to 20 per cent of those in the traditional industrialized capitalist countries. . . . (2) The working day (work week, work year) is significantly longer than in the traditional industrial countries. . . . (3) For comparable productive processes, productivity generally corresponds to that of the industry of the traditional industrial countries. (4) The labor force can be hired and again fired almost at will. This means, among other things, that higher work intensity can be squeezed out of a more rapid exhaustion of the labor force; the exhausted labor force can be replaced by a virgin one almost at will. (5) The size of the available industrial reserve army permits an "optimal" selection of particularly suitable workers (for instance young women) (Fröbel et al. 1977: 52).

The superexploitation of labor by capital and the capitalist reliance on so called noncapitalist economies or economic sectors for the production or reproduction of labor power—and in large part for its support or maintenance during the workers' periods of inactivity—has been practiced for a long time and has been studied widely. In effect, the Spaniards had recourse to this practice when, in the sixteenth century, they obliged the Indian communities in Mexico and Peru to supply the silver mines with migrant laborers who were sent for certain periods in rotation through the *catequil* or *mita* labor *repartimientos*, just as they are supplied from the reservations and Bantustans in South Africa in the twentieth century. This system has been widely analyzed (Woddis 1960; Arrighi 1973; Wolpe 1972; Legassick 1974), and was defined long ago by the colonialists themselves, such as Lord Haley in 1938:

> The reserves are used as "shock absorbers" in the sense that they satisfy the needs of the unemployed, the sick, the old without any cost to the state. . . . There is no other alternative except that of a permanent labor force installed in the cities around the mines and factories and completely separated from the land; but such a labor force would need higher wages, adequate housing, schools, entertainment and social security (cited in Meillassoux 1975: 176, retranslated from the French translation).

That is, the nature of the value produced by the reserves not only assures the reproduction of the labor force without any charge on capital, but it also contributes substantially to the maintenance of the labor force: by maintaining those sick, disabled, or exhausted workers who would otherwise have to be maintained by capital during the periods when they cannot work because of unemployment, sickness, disability through accidents, exhaustion, or simply aging. If capital were forced to cover the maintenance and reproduction of the labor force in its mines and factories, it would not only have to pay higher wages but also more indirect labor costs. A significant indication of the importance of this superexploitation to capital is the extremely high turnover rate of labor. Capital rapidly exhausts the working capacity of the migrants, and then deliberately sends them home to the reserves and Bantustans to be replaced by vigorous new workers.

This reliance of capital on the subsidy of labor reserves is by no means limited to South Africa, though that country, with its racist apartheid and pass laws, is the archetype of capitalist superexploitation (whose purest form in recent times was perhaps Hitler's concentration camps). Amin, and particularly Jaffe, warn that South Africa may be the forerunner of a capitalist 1984 toward which part or all of the capitalist world is moving (Amin, Frank, Jaffe 1975). This model of the capitalist future is perhaps already visible in the underdeveloped economies that promote exports through free production zones.

In these free production zones—as well as in other sectors of industry, particularly the export-promoting industry—the process of capital accumulation seems to be organizing a sort of "functional equivalent" of the South Africa migratory labor and reserve system. Here the "reserves" are the increasing masses of unemployed (see WE: Chapter 1) in the urban slums and the rural hinterlands, as well as sometimes in neighboring countries (e.g.

Malaysia vis-à-vis Singapore) or even distant countries (e.g. Pakistan's supply of labor to the Middle East). (The "guest workers" from Southern Europe who supplied northern Europe with necessary labor during boom times and their increasing expulsion since the onset of the 1974–1975 recession and the Mexican "wetbacks" who work in the United States are other functional equivalents.) In these underdeveloped countries capital is displaying an increasing tendency to hire very selectively, that is, to employ only those workers whom it considers most "efficient"—which in practice means most exploitable. After literally exhausting their labor power, capital finds it easy to replace them with new workers. Thus, Kreye found the "distinguishable characteristics of the occupational structure in free production zones and world market factories" to be preponderant employment of women (70–90 percent) at 20–50 percent lower wages than men; preponderant employment of fourteen- to twenty-four-years-olds; and preponderant employment of unskilled or apprentice labor. This occupational structure prevailed in both new factories and in those that had been operating for years. The maintenance of this occupational structure is, of course, made possible by extremely high turnover rates: 5–7 percent a month and 50–100 percent a year, as recorded by Kreye (Fröbel et al. 1977: 529–30). This high turnover rate seems to be programmed into the employment and production process by both employees and employers. Employers systematically "lay off" apprentices, who are paid less than other workers because the employer is "training" them and often they are not covered by minimum-wage legislation, and immediately replace them with new ones. Similarly, workers are fired after they suffer disabling accidents, debilitating illness, or become worn out from the pace and pressure of the work. These tactics are widespread:

> The workers of both sectors [metallurgical, and mechanical and electrical in São Paulo, Brazil] total 366,093, so that there are only about 25 thousand with more than 20 years in the industry. The other 341,093 were thrown out on the street, and today all of them are new workers (*Boletim da Oposiçaõ Sindical de São Paulo*, June 1972, cited in Souza 1975:67).

> In this picture, a 30 year old man is already considered old for employment. The use of the work of minors and of women (with lower wages) is not only already common in all the sectors of economic activity of the country [Brazil], but additionally is increasing. It is not accidental that Brazil decided not to ratify the ILO convention last year in which the minimum age for the work of minors was fixed at 15 years. The government of Brazil stated in its explanation of its reasons "the convention is extremely limited, in that it does not consider the suitability for a developing country like Brazil, which has to adopt special solutions to solve its problems" (Souza 1975: 67–68).

Child labor, at wages even lower than women's, is *increasing* around the Third World:

The number of children under 14 years of age who regularly have to contribute to the support of their families and who are "economically active" is estimated at more than 54 million, among which most are in Asia, according to UNICEF and ILO (*Hannoversche Allgemeine Zeitung*, 26 February 1977).

For the electronics firms, the newness of the work force they are creating is an advantage. Not only are the young women more tractable than older women or men might be, but since they are not believed to be supporting families, their wages can be kept low and they can be laid off with relatively few repercussions. Thus employers give first preference to women with no work experience and generally refuse to hire married women, although they do not necessarily fire them if they marry after being hired. The ability to lay off their workers at will is essential to the electronics firms, because the work is almost by definition temporary. After three or four years of peering through a microscope, a worker's vision begins to blur, so that she can no longer meet the production quota. The unspoken expectation of the company is that she will marry and "retire" by the time she becomes unfit for work, but she will be laid off in any case (SAC No. 66, January–February 1979:10).

This rotational employment—with continuous replacement by virgin labor from a seemingly inexhaustible supply in the geographical or economic hinterlands—and the concomitant creation of an industrial reserve army of unemployed constitute the functional equivalent of the African migrant-labor-reserve system. And not only labor but capital also migrates—and has the same effect of depressing the wage rate. The transfer of industry from the center of capitalism to the periphery is, of course, the principal contemporary mechanism of this migration. When for geographical, political, or economic reasons the rotating supply of labor begins to dry up and labor threatens to become scarce and/or more costly in one Third World location, capital simply moves to another one next door or halfway round the globe. See these reports in the *Wall Street Journal* and the *Financial Times* (London):

Electronics Firms Rush to Malaysia as Labor Gets Costly and Scarce Elsewhere in Asia . . .

The first big wave of electronics companies hit Asia about a decade ago, but these companies settled in such places as Hong Kong, South Korea, Taiwan and Singapore. At the time those spots had hordes of unemployed, easily trainable workers. But that is no longer the situation—labor is becoming scarce and costly in these locales—so the companies now are looking elsewhere, mostly southward, mostly to Malaysia and occasionally to Indonesia. . . . And here in Malaysia is where the cheapest labor can be found (WSJ 20 September 1973, cited in Fröbel et al. 1977: III, 38–39).

Malaysia, which by 1974 had replaced Singapore as the most favoured offshore location and the world's largest source of integrated circuits, experienced only minor retrenchment by some companies [during the 1974–1975 recession] and even expansion in employment by others, some of which were relocating their labour-intensive processes from sister plants in Singapore. (FT 8 October 1976, cited in Fröbel et al. 1977: III, 83).

The Third World governments compete among themselves to offer international—and national—capital the most "favorable" conditions of exploitation. Thus, for instance, the *Investor's Guide* published by the Zona Franca Industrial y Commercial de Cartagena (Z.F.I.C.) in Colombia states:

Low Cost Labour: this is without doubt the chief incentive offered by the Z.F.I.C. as the salaries are more or less the same as those that prevail in the industrial zones of the Far East. . . . Male and female workers are easily obtained due to high rate of unemployment, rapid increase of population and the emigration from rural zones to the cities (cited in Fröbel et al. 1977: III, 58).

Business Week (23 February 1976) observes:

The Mexicans are competing with Taiwan, El Salvador and Haiti for assembly business. So, to make things more attractive for in-bond operators, new rulings were effected last month . . . (cited in Fröbel et al. 1977: III, 5, 544).

A Japanese manager reports:

It was the end of 1972 as I visited South Korea, Taiwan, Hong Kong, the Philippines, Thailand, Indonesia and finally Malaysia in order to find the best location for this project (*Investment Opportunities in Malaysia*, cited in Fröbel et al. 1977: 588).

A Malaysian labor leader reports:

The firms have also let us know that, in case of labor trouble or wage demands, they can stop production within a month and transfer to another neighboring country with a cheaper labor force in the Asian area (Electrical Industry Workers' Union, Malaysia, Country Report, p. 14, cited in Fröbel et al. 1977: 595).

Maintenance of Labor Power

One consequence of this superexploitation, through which capital fails not only to pay for the reproduction but even for the maintenance of labor power, is the deplorable standard of "living" in the Third World. It has been argued persuasively many times that this is not simply a carryover from "pre-capitalist" times but is in large measure the result of past capitalist exploitation. In that context it is significant that high mortality, malnutrition, disease, mental illness, violence, and so forth are not limited to the agricultural countryside, but exist also in the industrial cities. And it can be demonstrated that the present process of capital accumulation is extending and intensifying these deplorable "living" conditions for vast portions of the population in these urban areas.

A study of the "living" conditions in Greater São Paulo is instructive. This city of over 8 million inhabitants is the principal site of the "economic miracle" of the "Brazilian model"; most of the 50 percent of Brazilian industry of São Paulo State (17 million inhabitants) is concentrated here.

Some figures: In the Capital there are 4.5 sq. meters of green land per inhabitant, whereas the desired minimum is 9 sq. meters. In the metropolitan area, out of 8,000 km. of roads used by traffic, only 40 per cent are paved; 870,000 inhabitants live in houses with no electric light; only about 30 per cent of homes are connected to the drainage system. Result: "the people in general use blind cesspools, dry privies, and septic tanks . . . and water from shallow wells, usually contaminated from their proximity to the blind cesspools." In the "periphery" of the Capital the situation is even worse: only 20 per cent of the houses are connected to the drainage system, and 46 per cent to the water supply. To have some idea of the environmental pollution, it is sufficient to say that three quarters of the dwellings in the "peripheries" empty their drains into simple blind sewers, if that. Even in the Capital itself there are large areas, mainly in the Southeast, Northeast and East, where more than two-thirds of the roads are unpaved and 70–80 per cent of extensive areas have no electric light. . . . The water supply of the city of São Paulo served 61 per cent of the population in 1950 and only 56 per cent in 1973. . . . In 1971, 35 per cent of the population were reached by this [sewage] service, while four years later the ratio fell to 30 per cent. . . . 52 per cent of the population in the city of São Paulo, and 73 per cent in the other [surrounding] municipalities suffer from undernourishment . . . (Kowarick n.d.).

Infant mortality in Greater São Paulo (excepting the inner city) declined during the 1950's but it has risen again during the economic "miracle" of the military regime:

1950	148
1960	73
1961	65
1962–1965	67–69
1966	74
1967	77
1968	74
1969	88
1970	99

(Kowarick n.d.)

In urban transportation, the number of daily trips has risen from 7 million in 1968 to 14 million in 1974. The average time spent in intraurban home-to-work travel has risen 30 percent, and workers who live on the city outskirts now travel three to four hours a day in buses that carry an average of 130 passengers, though they were designed to carry half that number.

The important point to emphasize is that each area, as it expands, creates its own periphery, either within or beyond the municipal confines. . . . The settlement of new areas, far from following a planned programme, is based on the withholding of land for speculative reasons. This is a common phenomenon in the city of São Paulo, where vacant lots abound. . . . The method used was as follows: a built-up area was never continuously developed alongside a previously developed area where public utility services were already provided. On the contrary . . . an empty space was purposely left undeveloped. As soon as building was completed in the new area of development, the bus routes to serve it would, of necessity, have to be extended from the last service point. Such an extension of the bus route [and other public services] means that it passes through the area which has been left undeveloped, and therefore the land in that area increases in value. . . . In this way, a public transport system which should be organized to serve the needs of the working population tends to become, owing to the speculative alchemy of the property/building sector . . . a service geared to the needs of the more privileged social strata. The process of "expulsion" is, in fact, intense in areas of rapid land valorization in the metropolitan area. There are many and flagrant examples of the "cleaning up" process which takes place in certain zones when the rise in property prices becomes incompatible with the continued presence of low income groups. . . . In fact all the slum-dwellers are turned out of their shacks as soon as the price of the land for private housing rises, or some public utility service provides the land on which the shanty-town is sited with the requirements of a new urban zone.

There are, as has been said, 130,000 people living in shanty-towns in the city of São Paulo. There are 615,000 people living in slum tenements, and 280,000 people who are forced to share a dwelling house. There are, furthermore, and this is an important point, 1.8 million people who live in "precarious housing" of the periphery. These figures refer only to the city of São Paulo itself [and not to the surrounding municipalities of Greater São Paulo where conditions are even worse].

It is important to note that more than half of the private homes in Greater São Paulo are owner-occupied or in the process of being bought. . . . The working classes have been settled in the peripheral areas, building their own houses in their spare time, with the unpaid help of family, relations and neighbours. The building of one's own home is a practice which fits in admirably with the logic of the exploitation of labour, for it reduces the cost to the worker for his own reproduction, of which housing is an important element, and in the final analysis, allows for the fixing of wages at low levels (Kowarick n.d.).

The "Brazilian model" for intermediate economies and the University of Chicago–inspired "Chilean model" for other underdeveloped economies, including Argentina, have involved a drastic reduction in social and welfare expenditures as part of a calculated "reallocation of resources" from "improductive" uses to "productive" investment (Frank 1976a; Chossudow-sky 1975, 1976). In fact, the imposition of crisis "austerity" plans has meant first and foremost the sacrifice of the social, welfare, and consumption-subsidy state expenditures that had to a small extent been ameliorating the effects of superexploitation on the masses. Since this reduction of public welfare expenditures has come at the same time as cuts in direct real wages, it has aggravated the crisis for labor and the poor. The result is increasing direct and indirect superexploitation and pauperization of ever larger groups and numbers of the population.

To meet the exigencies of accumulation during the present crisis, capital is increasing superexploitation, as well as "normal" exploitation, at the work-place. An important feature of superexploitation is the intensity of work that capital demands and receives from labor in the underdeveloped countries, especially in the export-promoting economies. The "intensity" of work consists of the "extension" of the amount of time worked and of the intensity of effort expended, and the amount of the product produced per unit of time worked, other things (e.g. equipment) being equal. There is reason to believe that the work intensity is increasing in many underdeveloped countries, especially under the pressure to produce more for export. The extension of work time can be measured in the number of hours worked per day, week, and year. However, the usefulness of this measure is limited because most data refer to averages for the work force and reflect cyclically induced shutdowns or expansions of the productive enterprises. The intensity of work per amount of time worked is difficult to establish, except as an inference from data on labor productivity, which are designed to reflect the "pro-ductivity" and not the "exploitation" of labor.

A very rough indication of the difference in the extension of work time between developed and underdeveloped countries is supplied by comparative data on "hours of work" in the ILO *Yearbook of Labour Statistics*. For the years 1965–1975, hours of work in nonagricultural sectors and manufac-turing industry in the United States and the Soviet Union were 40–41 per week. In West Germany, which depends on substantial migrant labor from the less-developed Mediterranean countries, the corresponding time was 40–44 hours. By comparison, the weekly number of hours worked in underde-veloped countries were as follows: Mexico 45–46, South Africa 46–48, Thailand 47–51, Singapore 47–49, Philippines 45–50, Egypt 50–55, and South Korea 50–58 (ILO Yearbook 1975: 489–93). Since these data reflect cyclical fluctuations in employment more than anything else, they are unfortunately not suitable for establishing trends in work hours per worker over this period. They do, however, suggest a clear pattern of longer than average work hours (45–58) in the underdeveloped countries than in the developed ones (40–44 hours). Nonetheless, because they are economy-wide averages based on officially reported legal work times, it can be assumed that these data fail to reflect the real extension of the work time for many workers in underdeveloped countries.

For an indication of the real extension of the work time, particularly in export-promoting underdeveloped economies, we must look at more specific, albeit scattered, data and testimony. In Hong Kong work weeks of over sixty hours are common. Indeed the Hong Kong Trade Development Council itself advertises that "there is no legal restriction on the hours of work for men over the age of 18 years. Consequently many men work ten hours a day, with a rest period of one or two hours, although three-shift working, enabling machinery to be used 24 hours a day, is common" (cited in Fröbel et al. 1977: 538). Indeed, in 1968, 52 percent of Hong Kong workers worked ten hours or more a day and 58 percent of them worked seven days a week. According to the 1971 census, 174,439 workers worked 75 hours a week or more, including 13,792 who worked 105 hours and more a week. Thirty-six thousand children worked illegally (the economically active population was 1.9 million and the manufacturing work force 700,000 in 1976) (Hong Kong Research Program 1974: 25–28). Work time would seem to have increased during the 1970s.

In Singapore "in a number of textile and electronics factories young women worked 12 hours a day, because there are only two shifts instead of three" (Utrecht 1976a: 91). Among the printing workers in Calcutta "working hours are supposed to be 8 hours a day but are actually 10 to 12 hours" (EPW 9 April 1977: 595). In Brazil, according to the 1970 census, 15–30 percent of the workers in various industries, and 24–29 percent in the food and beverages, construction, and mechanical industries, worked over fifty hours a week. Eleven to twelve hours a day in some industries, and sixty-six hours a week in the metallurgical industry of São Paulo, are considered normal (Arroio 1976: 40–41); twelve-hour days, seven days a week—or eighty-four hours a week—are "not uncommon" in São Paulo (Souza 1975); and people work sixteen hours a day in the sugar mills of Pernamubuco to "compensate" for the low wages. Although the regional delegate of labor recently issued an order to keep working hours to a maximum of twelve hours a day, the president of the labor union "promised to close his eyes to non-compliance, because the decision will otherwise make workers suffer from hunger" (ESP 12 May 1976).

As the ILO work-week averages suggest, the greatest extension of the economy-wide work week is in South Korea, which is a "model" of export promotion. There seven-day, eighty-four-hour work weeks are not uncommon (IHT 13 February 1976, cited in Fröbel et al. 1977: 538), and sixty-hour work weeks are normal. The *Guide to Investment in Korea*, published by the Economic Planning Board, states that "Working hours may be extended to 60 hours a week by mutual agreement. An extended work week has become common practice in manufacturing and export industries" (cited in Fröbel et al. 1977: II, 73).

> The Labor Law stipulates that workers cannot claim payment of labor of less than one hour. In Masan Free Export Zone, many companies require workers to arrive 30–45 minutes earlier and let them off 30–45 minutes late. In this way, the companies rip off up to one-and-a-half hours unpaid labor. . . . The machine never stops. . . . The workers take "pep-pills" (known as "Timing"). . . . Most bus conductors in Seoul work 18 hours a day. . . . We work from five in the morning to one or two o'clock at night. . . . I fall asleep in the galloping bus. . . . At the garment factories in the Peace Market . . . workers start at 8–9 o'clock and only finish when the workload, arbitrarily imposed by shop owners, is completed. Usually they work for 14–16 hours a day. In peak demand periods, they are frequently asked to work two or three days without any sleep. . . . Another means of exploitation is the system of probational employment. . . . At the Hyundai Shipyard in Ulsan, workers on probation are fired and immediately re-employed by the company on probation again. In this way many workers remain on probation several years. During probation, the company is not required to pay regular wages, bonuses and other allowances (Kim 1977: 33–35).

Not only the number of hours worked per day and the number of days worked per week, but the number of weeks worked per year (fifty or more) with little or no vacation are much longer in these economies. The total number of hours worked per year is as follows in some of these countries compared with West Germany:

Germany	1760–1860 hours
Ecuador	2152
Tunisia	2226
Malaysia	2288
South Korea	2800

Thus in South Korea the extension of the work time per year is 55 percent, and in Malaysia and Tunisia 25 percent, higher than in West Germany (data from Fröbel et al. 1977: 538–39). The German government Office for Economic Cooperation (DEG) reports in a comparative study of shoe production that for the same amount of work "100 workers are necessary in Germany and in Tunisia—despite lower productivity—only 93, because of the significantly higher effective number of hours per year that are delivered" in Tunisia (cited by Fröbel et al 1977: III, 65).

Workers in these underdeveloped economies also spend an inordinate amount of unpaid time getting to and from the job. This travel time—a cost to the worker but not to his employer—has been continually increasing because of the socially irrational but capitalistically rational checkerboard design of metropolitan areas (described for the case of São Paulo above), and the equally irrational development of private rather than public transportation. "The average worker," said a labor leader in São Paulo, "the *average* worker in this city spends six hours a day travelling between his home and his job" (IHT 29 April 1977). In Chile wages became so depressed that workers could no longer afford buses and found themselves obliged to *walk* to work and back, sometimes over enormous distances. The number of bus fares sold accordingly declined (Frank 1976a).

Work intensity in the other, narrower sense is the amount of work delivered per unit of time worked. Normally this is measured as labor "productivity" of output per man-hour. The question arises: Do lower wages and longer hours in these underdeveloped economics result in lower labor productivity compared to the developed economies, so that the advantages of cheap labor for capital are canceled out? Or are the differences in productivity less than those between wages and work extension, so that production in the underdeveloped countries is advantageous to capital? If productivity is even higher in the underdeveloped countries than in the developed ones, of course, capital gains a double advantage: low wages and long hours, and greater "intensity" of work per hour. The following analysis of scattered data on productivity is an attempt to examine productivity as a function of work intensity rather than productivity per se.

According to the conventional wisdom, productivity in the underdeveloped countries is much lower than in developed ones because of the lesser complement of capital equipment, the lower skill of the workers, worse management and organization, and/or the "stupidity" or "laziness" of the workers. But all of these charges have been challenged. Amin (1970), for example, has argued that in many industries, particularly in those that are capital intensive, capital equipment and labor productivity are substantially the same in developed and underdeveloped economies. Reliance on foreign management, training of local personnel, and the transfer of industrial organization (often incorporated into the equipment of the assembly-line manufacturing process) often make the organization of the productive process in the underdeveloped countries a copy of the same in the developed ones. And the fact that multinational firms are able to train workers in two weeks to two months in free production zones and other underdeveloped export economies suggests that these workers' intelligence and skills, at least for many industries, are comparable to those of workers in the developed countries (for comparisons see Fröbel et al. 1977; Utrecht 1976b). The charge of "laziness" can be countered by citing the much longer working hours and the high incidence of child labor. So it may be argued that in many industries, particularly those that compete on the world market, the productively relevant industrial skills, organization, and capital inputs are roughly comparable for the developed and underdeveloped economies. The main differences are that in the latter there is less productive equipment and it tends to be technologically less advanced and older in years of usage (sometimes it is secondhand equipment imported from the developed countries). Also, in the underdeveloped economies labor-intensive manual productive processes sometimes do what more mechanized, capital-intensive ones do in the developed economies. For instance, younger "underdeveloped" women perform with the naked eye electronic assembly operations for which older "developed" workers in the United States have to be supplied with microscopes (Baerresen, cited in Fröbel et al. 1977). Only in exceptional cases do underdeveloped countries use more, or more advanced, capital equipment for the same industry or product. Therefore, if we find comparable levels of "labor productivity" in the two economies—or more precisely in the two sectors of the world economy—we may suppose that the intensity of work per hour is greater in the underdeveloped economies.

The U.S. Tariff Commission has prepared comparative studies of productivity to support the protectionist argument for tariffs against imports from low-wage countries with comparable productivity. The commission states in its report on economic factors:

> Productivity of workers in foreign establishments assembling or processing products of U.S. original generally approximates that of workers in the same job classifications in the United States. . . . On the average (based on 30 reported instances in 9 foreign countries) foreign labor required 8 per cent more man-hours than the man-hours required by U.S. workers to assemble such articles as radios, phonographs, television receivers and sub-assemblies and semi-conductors. . . . On the average (based on 12 reported instances in 6 foreign countries) foreign labor required three per cent *less* man-hours than was required by U.S. workers to assemble such diverse articles as luggage, baseballs, toys, footwear, gloves, photographic equipment and scientific instruments (U.S. Tariff Commission, 171–73, cited in Fröbel et al. 1977: III,75; emphasis added).

Presumably, the figure of 3 percent less man-hours in "traditional" industries outside the United States is not the result of more or better equipment, and the figure of 8 percent more man-hours in the newer industries may well be the result of more than 8 percent less equipment (or less productive equipment). Therefore, the conclusion that productivity elsewhere "generally approximates" that in the United States implies that the intensity of work during the same number of working hours was higher in the other economies than it was in the United States.

Other studies suggest that in some cases—notably in export industries of export-promoting economies—productivity in underdeveloped countries is substantially *higher* than that in the United States. In his study of *The Border*

Industrialization Programme of Mexico Baerresen (1971) reports that productivity was 40 percent higher in metal products, 10–25 percent higher in electronic products, and 30 percent higher in sewing work than in the United States. He also reports that in the judgment of American managers who have run factories in both countries, productivity in South Korean factories is 20–40 percent higher than in Mexican ones (cited in Fröbel et al. 1977: 540, 534).

An American manager, who in the United States was accustomed to hiring applicants with an average manual dexterity score of 14–16, hired 90 of the 280 workers with scores of 20 after having tested 300 applicants out of the 2000 who applied within a day of a newspaper advertisement in Ciudad Juárez, Mexico. Other comparative studies have found similar results (Baerresen 1971: 32–33, cited in Fröbel et al. 1977: 534).

Approximately comparable—and sometimes higher—labor productivity in the same industry with sometimes less advanced or mechanized productive processes in these underdeveloped economies implies that, in addition to *much lower wages* and *substantially longer working hours,* workers in the underdeveloped economies also suffer from a *significantly higher intensity of work per hour.* In other words, they are triply exploited. Additionally, the working conditions—temperature, noise, light, crowding, clothing and other protective measures, and so on—are worse in the underdeveloped countries, which adds a fourth dimension to the exploitation. For a vivid illustration of these facets of exploitation, picture a barefoot, ill-clothed man—or indeed, a woman or child—carrying heavy loads on unsafe scaffolding on a noisy, dusty, hot construction site for ten to twelve hours (plus two to four hours back and forth from home to work by bus or foot) for the pay of $1 a day. Analogous conditions of work are common in sweatshop factories around the underdeveloped world. The data are perhaps inadequate to prove that this exploitation and superexploitation are increasing in the underdeveloped world. But it is reasonable to suppose that both are increasing in quantity and intensity in the export-production industries generated by the world capitalist crisis of accumulation.

Industrial Accidents

Superexploitation, particularly through the extension and intensification of the working day and week, also manifests itself through industrial accidents, from which workers suffer not only directly (life and limb) but also indirectly (dismissal with little or no accident insurance payments, and lesser—or no—possibilities of reemployment). Unfortunately, comparative and time-series data on "industrial" accidents are extremely fragmentary and unreliable. During the 1975 recession in West Germany, for instance, the registered rate of accidents and hospital as well as *kurort* (sanitarium) visits declined, not because work became safer or life healthier—on the contrary—but because the threat of unemployment induced workers to reduce their reporting of minor accidents and consumption of health services for fear of employer reprisal.

Because of international differences in coverage and reporting, the ILO *Yearbook of Labor Statistics* does not report nonfatal accidents, and from its list of fatalities it excludes occupational diseases and accidents suffered in home-to-work transport. Moreover, the *Yearbook* covers only a few selected countries and the measures of incidence differ from one industrial category to another. Nonetheless, despite these severe limitations, the *Yearbook* is useful because it shows the patterns of fatal accidents in socialist, industrial capitalist, and most underdeveloped and underdeveloped export-promoting economies. In mining and quarrying, for instance, South Korea has a fatal accident rate five and ten times higher than other underdeveloped countries, and in manufacturing it is consistently exceeded only by Sri Lanka.

Brazil has an active population of 33 million, of whom 18 million work in agriculture. Of the remaining 15 million only 8 million are registered under the social security system, and it is for this part of the working population that accident statistics are available. The registered accident rate has risen as follows:

Year	No.	%
1971	1.4 million	18
1972	1.5 million	19
1973	1.6 million	20
1974	1.8 million	
1975	1.9 million	
1976	1.9 million	

SOURCE: 1971–73, Souza 1975: 66; 1974, ESP 22 July 1975; 1975–1976, DB 1978, No. 1:34.

In 1973, 13,000 of these (1.6 per thousand) were fatal and 50,000 (3.1 per thousand) were permanently disabling. In industry the accident rate was higher: 30 percent higher overall and up to 45 percent higher in the petroleum products industry. In São Paulo State there were 712,000 accidents registered in 1973 and 780,000 in 1974. These numbers indicate that nearly 25 percent of the work force (including low-accident white-collar employees) suffered accidents—a rate that is three times higher than that in France—and that the growth rate for accidents is 10 percent a year. Research on a sample of 4000 industrial accidents revealed that 23 percent were attributable to human error, 40 percent to lack of safety measures primarily, and the remainder to lack of safety measures associated with other causes (Souza 1975; Arroio 1976: 41).

Workers' testimonials reveal that the *reasons* for the accidents are excessive fatigue and insufficient care attributable to long hours at work and in travel resulting in insufficient sleep, low food consumption resulting in weakness, speed-up of the assembly line or other productive process, and reasons such as the following:

> More than half the accidents which occur affect the upper part of the body; and the use of gloves, according to experts from the Ministry of Labour, would reduce accidents in 22% of cases. . . . A minimum production rate is laid down, based on the performance of the more able worker. The more skilled are able to carry out this operation while wearing gloves. The others are not. They work without gloves. When they hurt themselves they are dismissed. Sometimes they lose a part of, or the entire, nail or hand. This happens in the modern dynamic factory of a multinational company in São Paulo (Kowarick n.d.).

In South Korea:

> Industrial disabilities increased 2.7 times between 1970 and 1976 to a level which is reportedly 3–5 times higher than the ILO standard. In 1973, 840 workers died of industrial accidents and in 1976 the number was 887. At the Kyunghee Medical Center in Seoul alone, 25 workers were hospitalized for amputation last year (Kim 1977: 35).

In the Masan Free Export Zone of South Korea accidents occur at the rate of 4500 a year for 24,000 employees—or 19 percent in a workforce that is 75 percent female. "Such a high rate of industrial accidents is a direct result of the pressures for high intensity work exerted by companies which enter Korea to exploit cheap labor-intensive production" (AMPO April–September 1976: 58, 65). Industrial accidents in Algeria have risen as follows: 1970: 39,860 (250 mortal); 1971:41,913 (253); 1872:43,121 (295): 1973: 46,283 (324). (The number of people in the workforce was not given in the source [ELJ No. 18. December 1976: 9].)

In Hong Kong the number of workers in manufacturing establishments known to the Labor Department was about 700,000 in March 1976.

> The Labor Department's last annual report put the figure for known work injuries in 1975 at 54,506 of which 212 were fatal and 16,956 involved possible permanent disability. Furthermore, statistics for the first nine months of 1976 indicate that last year's accident record is likely to be possibly 20 per cent or 30 per cent worse. The human cost is therefore tremendous, with the fatal accident rate two to three times higher than the much more publicised homicide rate. With an ill-developed system for even basic state welfare measures and antiquated legal machinery for accident compensation, the consequences of injury or serious illness are disastrous (FER 18 March 1977:49).

We may suppose that the "antiquated legal machinery" also fails to register very many accidents, so the real rate is no doubt much higher than the 8 percent noted above. This supposition is strengthened by the registered 31 percent rate of permanently disabling accidents, which is excessively high compared to elsewhere.

Industrial accidents in five industries (construction, plywood, quarry, chemical, and shipyard) in Singapore increased as shown in Table 5.1.

TABLE 5.1

Industrial Accidents in Singapore

	1970	1971	1972	1973	1974
All 7 industries	888 (32)	1,322 (41)	1,759 (48)	1,791 (66)	
of which shipyard	328 (1)	458 (5)	679 (12)	724 (19)	870 (38)

SOURCE: Utrecht, 1976a: 92.

Note: Fatal accidents in parentheses.

Wage Rates

The most obvious exploitation is the underpayment of wages and salaries. The testimony of business managers, the business and financial press, and even the prospectuses and advertisements of the governments in the "host" underdeveloped countries all testify that "cheap labor" is the principal magnet drawing transnational industry from the center to the periphery and to the socialist countries. (For a sampling of this testimony see Fröbel et al. 1977: 508ff.) Compared to the developed countries, the distribution of income between high- and low-income receivers and between capital and labor is much more unequal in the underdeveloped countries, and the absolute wage rates there are lower (and profit rates higher). Moreover, the evidence is mounting that the distribution of income is becoming increasingly unequal between the developed and underdeveloped countries as well as within the underdeveloped countries, and that the wages and income of the lowest-income recipients are falling absolutely.

A recent OECD study observes:

> We have no more than elementary notions about existing unem-
> ployment levels, less than this for income distributions, and practically
> nothing quantitative about trends for either income distribution or
> unemployment. . . .
> [Nonetheless] the general consensus of opinion would seem to be
> that income distribution has probably become more unequal in most
> important [developing] countries and that the income situation of the
> poorest groups in both rural and urban areas has changed very little in
> real terms. . . .
> [Yet] we would argue that the most likely general consequence of an
> intensifying employment problem [which this study and all others

predict] will be a further twist in the already highly skewed income distribution with possibly some absolute deterioration in the standard of living among the poorest groups and certainly not much prospect for improvement (Turnham 1971: 115, 78, 20).

The director general of the International Labour Office summarizes the situation in a diplomatically guarded statement:

> There is no doubt that the number of poor have increased, in spite of the rapid economic growth in most developing countries. There is also considerable evidence, although often fragmentary or circumstantial, that the material conditions of life for large numbers of people are worse today than they were one or two decades ago. In a very few countries average levels of living have fallen. . . . Whether in addition income distribution has in fact worsened in most developing countries is difficult to determine. There are very few studies of changes in income distribution in individual developing countries over time. The limited available studies indicate that income distribution has become more equal in recent years in some developing countries but has worsened in a number of others (ILO 1976: 23).

Nonetheless, other United Nations publications inform us about Latin America:

> Data for 1960 and for 1970 for three of the largest countries (Brazil, Colombia and Mexico) indicate that the upper-middle income receivers improved their relative position while the position of the poor deteriorated. . . . In all three countries, the 20 per cent of income receivers just below the top decile . . . gained from 2 to 3 percentage points. . . . The 50 per cent below the median lost ground in two countries and gained slightly in the third. The poorest 20 per cent dropped sharply in share of income in two countries and held its own in the third. . . . Data . . . reinforce the conclusion that for many countries the growth rate of income of the lowest or poorest 40 per cent of the population was below the growth rate of gross national product, and that inequality increased during the period. . . . It is also possible that in some countries with lower income levels and slow growth rates the poorest group lost ground absolutely. Such distribution trends, as far as the evidence goes, might be expected to reinforce the existing style of development and provide for a degree of political stability. The groups that have gained something—in absolute, if not relative, terms—greatly outnumber those that have not, and the largest gains went to the better educated and better organized upper-middle groups whose support is particularly important. . . . While consumption has diversified and patterns have changed, there is no widespread evidence of significant improvement for the lower-income majority in the two most basic components of the level of living—food and shelter (UNDESA, 1974: 46–48).

More bluntly stated:

> In the 1950s and 1960s so-called economic development meant that
> the lowest 60 per cent [of income receivers] suffered a loss in their
> relative participation [in the distribution of income] in our sample of
> five countries [Argentina, Brazil, Colombia, Mexico and Peru], which
> have about two thirds of the population of Latin America. The only
> question that remains to be answered is simply what part of the upper
> third benefited by the loss of the majority: the upper middle class or the
> upper class? (Weisskoff y Figueroa 1977: 904).

The answer, by and large, is the upper middle class.

Studies of changes in income distribution in Africa are less available, but
the U.N. report cited above suggests:

> The income level of almost 30 per cent of the African population is
> below $50 a year. Income inequalities persist between urban and rural
> areas and among the regions and ethnic groups. . . . It is suggested that,
> all other things being equal, the gap between the top and bottom levels
> of income distribution may widen as growth proceeds up to a level of
> some $500 per capita (UNDESA 1974: 64).

Concerning eastern Asia and the Pacific, the same report says that there is
little evidence about country-wide changes in the distribution of income, but
that the green revolution, which was introduced in several Asian countries,
particularly India and Philippines, has—and all other studies confirm this—
increased the inequality of income distribution (UNDESA 1974: 80–83).

The growth patterns generated by the accumulation crisis of the 1970s can
only aggravate these tendencies toward inequality and the superexploitation
of the poorest groups.

Beyond the certainty that wages are generally—but not uniformly—low in
Third World countries, it is difficult to evaluate and compare the data for
wages (skilled, unskilled, semiskilled, and average) for different work periods
(hour, day, week, month, year), different and changing prices (and their
structures, indices), and consumption patterns among countries and over
time for different and changing exchange rates (fixed and floating, real and
unreal). For these and other reasons, the data on wages and salaries in the
ILO Statistical Yearbook do not offer a reliable overview of comparative
wages, still less of their changes over time. With the proviso that all attempts
to construct comparative wage tables must be used with caution, Table 5.2
and Figure 5.1 are offered as summaries of some wage data.

Acording to the Union Bank of Switzerland (1976) survey of *Prices and
Earnings around the Globe*, wages and purchasing power in Tokyo are only
a little over half what they are in Zurich. (The same survey found that in four
U.S. cities purchasing power is 119–139 percent what it is in Zurich.) But in
the underdeveloped countries wages of unskilled construction workers range

TABLE 5.2
Gross Annual Earnings and Purchasing Power in Selected Cities

	Construction Industry (Unskilled Worker)		Textile Industry (Un- or Semiskilled Female Worker)		Toolmaking (Skilled Lathe Operator)		Purchasing Power in Relation to Price levels)
	$ million	*Index*	*$ million*	*Index*	*$ million*	*Index*	*Index*
Zurich	10,771	100	8,400	100	15,152	100	100
Tokyo	6,372	59	4,872	58	8,219	54	57
Bogota	704	7	880	10	1,525	10	32
Buenos Aires	961	9	1,082	13	3,017	20	19
Hong Kong	1,815	17	2,096	25	5,201	34	42
Manila	420	4	672	8	1,400	9	26
Mexico	2,390	22	3,087	37	3,412	23	45
Rio de Janeiro	876	8	1,026	12	3,695	24	50
Singapore	1,664	15	1,161	14	2,841	19	35
Teheran	1,865	17	3,228	38	4,161	27	44
Johannesburg	1,711[a]	16	1,296[b]	15	8,239[c]	54	72

SOURCE: Union Bank of Switzerland, *Prices and Earnings around the Globe, 1976*, pp. 28, 6–7.

Note: Index based on Zurich = 100. a + b= black workers, c= white workers.

from 4 percent in Manila to 22 percent in Mexico of the Zurich level; wages of female textile workers range from 8 percent in Manila to 38 percent in Teheran; and of skilled toolmakers from 9 percent in Manila to 34 percent in Hong Kong (according to the same source Caracas wages are relatively higher, and in São Paulo the wages of toolmakers are nearly twice as high as in neighboring Rio de Janeiro). The range in purchasing power compared to Zurich, which includes that of higher-salaried categories, is narrower: from 19 percent in Buenos Aires to 50 percent in Rio (63 percent in São Paulo). (The extremely low index for Buenos Aires probably reflects the price explosion and sharp decline in real wages before and after the 1976 military coup, since wages in Argentina are "normally" higher than in most other underdeveloped countries.) Unmistakably, the wages of unskilled workers and their purchasing power (which is certainly much lower than the overall wage and salary averages given in Table 5.2) are only a small fraction of what they are in the developed countries.

Otto Kreye has constructed a table of comparative hourly wage rates (converted into U.S. cents) in the Third World based in part on his canvass of the economic and technical literature and in part on his own observations. Table 5.3 reproduces Kreye's findings on wage rates in some of the Third World countries that are most involved in export promotion of manufactures.

Figure 5-1 Comparative Purchasing Power
Hourly Pay Compared with Prices in 41 Major Cities
(Source: U.S. NEWS & WORLD REPORT, December 13, 1976.)
100=Purchasing Power in Zurich

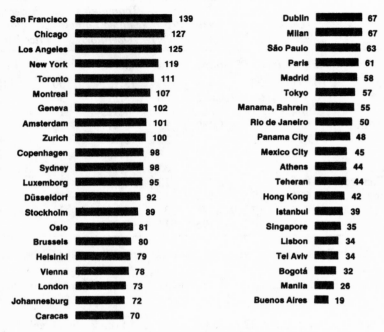

San Francisco	139	Dublin	67
Chicago	127	Milan	67
Los Angeles	125	São Paulo	63
New York	119	Paris	61
Toronto	111	Madrid	58
Montreal	107	Tokyo	57
Geneva	102	Manama, Bahrein	55
Amsterdam	101	Rio de Janeiro	50
Zurich	100	Panama City	48
Copenhagen	98	Mexico City	45
Sydney	98	Athens	44
Luxemborg	95	Teheran	44
Düsseldorf	92	Hong Kong	42
Stockholm	89	Istanbul	39
Oslo	81	Singapore	35
Brussels	80	Lisbon	34
Helsinki	79	Tel Aviv	34
Vienna	78	Bogotá	32
London	73	Manila	26
Johannesburg	72	Buenos Aires	19
Caracas	70		

Note: Based on currency exchange rates in Zurich in May 1976.
Purchasing power based on pay before deductions.

Where Kreye gave a range of wage rates, Table 5.3 presents the average (mean), which is certainly higher than what the "average" worker earns, and often significantly higher than the lowest wage rate in that category.

For unskilled workers in manufacturing, thus, the hourly rate ranges from 9 cents in Mauritius to 70 cents in Mexico, with a whole series of countries in the 15-to-20-cent range. These wage rates are confirmed by those certified by an accounting firm, which for 1975 reported *daily* wages for unskilled labor of $1.90 in South Korea, $1.45 in Indonesia, and $1.75 in the Philippines (FER 20 August 1976: 38). There are frequent reports of $1 *per day* wages. In Calcutta there have been reports of $28 for skilled labor, $25 for semiskilled, and $18 for unskilled printers *per month,* which amounts to a little more than 50 cents to less than $1 a day. Where minimum wages are not enforced, wage rates are as low as $10 a month, which is about 33 cents a day for ten to twelve hours of work (EPW March 1976). See Table 5.4 for a comparison made by the West German government's Office for Economic Cooperation (DEG) of hourly wages for seamstresses in the textile industry.

TABLE 5.3

Hourly Wage Rates in Manufacturing in Selected Underdeveloped Countries
(1974 or 1975 in U.S. cents)

Country	Unskilled	Semiskilled	Skilled	Average
		Asia		
South Korea				
Male				43
Female				21
Hong Kong	43	61		
Singapore	38	41	72	
Malaysia	17	20	39	
Philippines	15	21	25	
India	15	21	31	
Taiwan				
Male	25	34		
Female	23	25		
Thailand	15	31	61	
		Africa		
Mauritius				
Male	20	24	38	
Female	9	11	13	
Tunisia	29	43	65	
Morocco	34	56	112	
		Latin America		
Brazil	30	70	128	
Mexico	70			
Colombia	20	32	50	
Haiti	16	45	75	
Costa Rica	39	42	54	

SOURCE: Fröbel et al. 1977: 633–34.

TABLE 5.4

Comparative Wages in the Textile Industry
(in German marks of mid-1975)

Germany	10.00	Greece	3.25
United States	9.00	Portugal	3.20
France	8.20	Iran	2.10
Switzerland	5.80	Tunisia	1.80
Italy	5.70	Brazil	1.15
England	5.00	Malaysia	1.00
Austria	4.75	Taiwan	1.00
Japan	4.60	South Korea	0.90

SOURCE: FAZ 10 June 1976, cited in Fröbel et al. 1977: 158–59.

Comparative wage rates in Asian free export zones in 1973 are shown in Table 5.5.

TABLE 5.5
Wage Rates in Asian Free Export Zones
(in 1973 in U.S. dollar equivalents)

Country	Location	Principal Area Serviced	Approximate Minimum Hourly Labor Costs (in $)
Taiwan	Kaohsiung	Far East, Southeast Asia, North America	0.22–0.30 (unskilled) 0.80–1.63 (skilled)
Hong Kong	Hong Kong	Far East, Western Europe, North America	0.32–0.40 (unskilled) 0.98–1.63 (skilled)
India	Kandla	Southeast Asia	0.15–0.40 (unskilled) 0.20–1.39 (skilled)
Malaysia	Penang Island	Southeast Asia	0.15–0.24 (unskilled) 0.70–1.16 (skilled)
Singapore	Port of Singapore	Southeast Asia, North America	0.15–0.23 (unskilled) 0.30–0.75 (skilled)
Thailand	Bangkok	Southeast Asia, North America	0.25–0.40 (unskilled) 0.80–1.20 (skilled)
South Korea	Masan	Far East, Southeast Asia, North America	0.30–0.50 (unskilled) 0.80–1.50 (skilled)

SOURCE: Mark Selden, "American Global Agreement on Enterprise," cited in Utrecht 1976b: 61.

In a survey of "international subcontracting" Henrik Plaschke (1975: 92) gives the following comparative wages (in dollar equivalents for 1972):

United States	2.50
Puerto Rico	2.00
Japan	0.90
Dominican Republic	0.60
Mexico	0.51
Hong Kong	0.40
Singapore	0.35
South Korea	0.31
Colombia	0.30
Taiwan	0.16
Indonesia	0.10

To an export oriented industrialization based on cheap labor power, corresponds a repressive policy towards the working class. . . .

The political conditions in different countries are of a decisive importance in the selection of subcontracting countries. Potential candidates must have "stable" political conditions, and they must pursue policies favourable to private business. In practice this means that countries with well-established right-wing governments are preferred as subcontracting countries, as they usually pursue such policies. . . . (Plaschke 1975: 94,92).

Studies of comparative costs of production in developed and underdeveloped capitalist countries suggest that the difference in operating costs is attributable almost entirely to differences in wages. A comparative cost study for shoe production in West Germany and Tunisia, published by the German Office for Economic Cooperation (DEG), makes the following cost estimates for production of 220,000 pairs of shoes per year (in German marks): total costs in Germany DM 2,683,134, in Tunisia DM 909,488, difference DM 1,773,646; wage costs in Germany DM 2,125,200, in Tunisia DM 329,870, difference DM 1,795,330. Salaries, depreciation, other operating costs, and financial costs are almost the same in both countries. Virtually the entire difference in total costs lies in the difference in wage costs (moderate transport costs must be added for production in Tunisia [DEG, *Schuhproduktion Tunisian*, Köln, January 1975, cited in Fröbel et al. 1977:572]). A comparative cost study for the production of electronic components in Western Europe and in Southeast Asia of 3 million units for the European market estimates a difference of $451 per thousand units (between $1,164 and $713) in total costs, and of $482 (between $670 and $188) in costs of production. Extra freight costs add $30 to production costs in Southeast Asia. Other costs are the same. Again, the significant difference appears to be the wage element in production costs (UNCTAD, *International Subcontracting Arrangements in Electronics*, p. 40, cited in Fröbel et al. 1977: 572–73). Investment costs are also lower in the Third World countries.

A study of the cost structure of industrial production in Bangkok revealed the distribution of sales revenue among cost of materials, depreciation, wages, and profits (that is, earnings of capital including rent and interest) in productive units of various sizes (see Table 5.6). For the total of 18,340 firms surveyed, wages accounted for only 9 percent of the distribution of the proceeds from sales, while profits (including interest and rent) absorbed 24 percent. The other 67 percent was spent on materials inputs or reserved for depreciation. Wages accounted for 12 percent of total costs, excluding profits. Profits were 35 percent of fixed assets. But the cost structure, especially the distribution between wages and profits, differs significantly from one size category to another. The larger the enterprise, the lower the share of revenue paid out in wages and the higher the profit share. Thus in the smallest firms, which account for 87 percent of all firms but produce only 11 percent of all output, wages and profits absorb 20 percent each. In the next smallest category of enterprises (accounting together with the smallest for over 98 percent of the firms and 35 percent of the production in categories I and II in Table 5.6) profits are 18 percent, but wages fall to 13 percent—to 9 percent if category II is considered alone. In the larger enterprises (category III—1.4 percent of the firms with 36 percent of the output), and the largest (category IV—41 firms, or only 0.2 percent of the enterprises, with 28 percent of the output, or two and a half times the total of the 15,895 smaller firms) wages fall to 7 percent, but profits rise to 25 percent and 31 percent, respectively, of total sales revenue. The largest firms, not surprisingly, are the foreign firms. Although foreign firms are reputed to pay higher wages (a contention that is disputed by Fröbel et al. 1977), in Bangkok they pay out to all their wage earners only 9 percent of what they take in as registered profits (590 million baht versus 2,466 million baht out of total sales proceeds of 7,853 million bahts). Recall that the smallest firms, on the average, distribute wages and profits evenly at 20 percent each. No wonder large firms can afford to pay higher wages, for at 7 percent of receipts, or 9 percent of total costs, it would take a 12 percent raise in wages to increase total costs by 1 percent. The share of wages in value added varies from 11 percent in beverages to 98 percent in the labor-intensive tobacco industries in Bangkok, but more significantly it falls from 50 percent in the small enterprises of category I to 20 percent in the large ones of categories III and IV. After noting this inverse relationship between size and wages and the direct relationship between size and profits, the author of this study of industrial structure in Bangkok comments:

> The profits earned by the large firms being 1,535 times higher than [those] of the small firms, this rapid rise in the net aggregate profit accounts for the inexorable pressure for the industrial firms to increase their scale of operation and the huge surplus that they themselves produce to provide out of their own accumulated funds for the expansion. It is this very high growth potential of industries that make the developing countries so eager for industrialization and not for false prestige or ignorance as it is so often asserted by Western economists. . . . As the size of the factory increases, the surplus generated rises not only in absolute quantity but relatively also. The problem of inequitable distribution arises because this surplus accrues to the owners of the factory. It is rarely realized that the question of industrialization cannot be separated from the question of growing disparity in income under a system of private enterprise. The technical conditions of production (as differentiated from the market conditions) is such that the growth of industry will inevitably lead to the growth of inequality of income as long as industrialization takes place under private enterprise. While private enterprise may generate efficiency in production its effect on distribution thus is always negative (Sarkar 1974: 72, 78).

TABLE 5.6
Cost Structure of Industrial Production in Bangkok

Firm size category	I	II	I & II	III	IV	I to IV
% of all firms in category	87	12	98	1.4	0.2	100
% share of all sales revenue	11	24	35	36	28	100
% of firm proceeds spent on materials	50	68	62	64	52	60
% of firm proceeds res. for depreciation	10*	5	7	5	9	7
% of firm proceeds spent on wages	20	9	13	7	7.5	9
Profits as % of proceeds	20	18	18	25	31	24

SOURCE: N. K. Sarkar 1974, *Industrial Structure of Greater Bangkok,* pp. 70–71.
   *Includes residential dwelling, inflating depreciation to unknown degree.

Low wage rates are only minimally affected by minimum wage legislation, which is rarely enforced. An article in the ILO *International Labour Review* states:

> The impression that the impact of minimum wage adjustments has been rather marginal is in conformity with the consensus to that effect among government, union and business officials. . . . Many countries have been confronted by growing unemployment and underemployment. This has caused a shift from high-wage to a low-wage policy, in some countries, e.g. in East Africa. In some other countries, e.g. Brazil, anti-inflationary considerations have resulted in a similar change. In order to avoid triggering off a round of wage increases, governments tend to fix new minimum rates below what most eligible workers are already earning in enterprises that are responsive to the legislation. . . . But a far more important reason may be the lack of enforcement of the legal provisions. Enforcement of minimum wage legislation is limited mainly to the unionised sector . . . and large numbers of workers in unorganized sectors continue to earn less than minimum rates. . . . In Mexico, for example . . . a large proportion of workers (65 per cent in the case of the construction industry) earn less than the minimum. . . . Minimum wage legislation in developing countries . . . appears to have failed so far to attain even the more modest objective of similar legislation in developed countries, i.e. protection of the marginal

portions of exceptionally low-paid unorganised workers (Watanabe 1976: 354–57).

Though minimum wage legislation does not do much to protect workers, it sometimes affords an indication of changes in real wages over time.

> It appears that in 15 out of 29 [Asian, Latin American and mostly African] countries the minimum wage in real terms declined by more than 10 per cent over the period [1963–1974] shown in the table. In three other countries it rose by less than 10 per cent, which might be considered insignificant in view of the quality of the price statistics. In only 11 of these countries has the real minimum wage risen by more than 10 per cent, including three countries . . . which would not have figured in the group but for their large increases in 1974 (Watanabe 1976: 352).

One of the reasons for the bad "quality" of the price statistics is that governments deliberately calculate the consumer price indices to understate the real rate of inflation, not just for vague "political" reasons, but because minimum and other wages are often legally or politically linked to the price indices. Therefore, underestimating and understating price increases is a way of reducing real wages. Moreover, the "basket" of goods whose prices are indexed contains more goods, or a different relative weighting of goods, than the few basic goods consumed by low-wage and -income receivers, and the prices of these basic goods rise faster than those on the index. Therefore, we would not be far amiss in supposing that between 1963 and 1974 in eighteen of these twenty-nine countries the minimum wage fell (that is, it fell in all but the eleven countries in which it rose more than 10 percent) and in a few at best remained the same, and that between 1963 and 1973, in twenty-one out of the twenty-nine countries the *real* minimum wage declined. As for the "large proportion of workers" who earn less than the minimum wage, the presumption is that their real wage fell even more. Minimum wages may have risen in three of these sample countries (Congo, Morocco, and Tunisia) in 1974. But by and large, in the years of world recession since 1973 inflation, unemployment, and often political repression have certainly brought real (and real minimum) wages down in many if not most underdeveloped countries. The decline in real wages is documentable probably in most, and certainly in the most important, countries of Latin America, and in South and Southeast Asia—at least in 1974 and 1975—outside of Indochina. In the oil-boom countries of the Middle East wages have probably increased since 1973, and in Africa the movement seems to have been uneven.

Clearly both the amount of exploitation and the rate of superexploitation increased in most Third World countries during and after the recession of the mid-1970s. The poorest countries and populations have been made to bear the brunt of increased prices for petroleum, food, and manufacturing imports. Superexploitation is probably most massively prevalent in the agricultural sector (which is examined in Chapter 2). Real wages, and often the extension and the intensity of work, are generally worse on the land in the Third World than in the cities. The real income of self-employed small peasant owners and tenants is also generally lower than income in most other occupations. By conventional measure, productivity is usually also lower in agriculture. But this measure reflects the relative prices of industrial products (including inputs into agriculture) and of agricultural commodities, as well as investment and technological bias in favor of industry. Industrial production and profits have been systematically supported by the provision of cheap agricultural raw materials for industrial production, and even more importantly by cheap agricultural wage goods as food for industrial workers. (The exception to this rule is the protection and price support of agriculture in North America, Western Europe, and Japan.) The counterparts of high-priced manufactures and low-priced agricultural commodities in the Third World countries are the low earnings, exploitation, and superexploitation of agricultural workers and peasants. These people have been forced to support urban (and foreign) consumers of agricultural products and urban producers and consumers (as well as foreign importers) of industrial commodities through their very poorly remunerated work on the land. The measure of the superexploitation of workers and peasants in agriculture in the Third World is that it is virtually immeasurable.

Chapter 6.
Political-Economic Repression in the Third World

The imposition of greater exploitation and superexploitation in the Third World as instruments of export promotion and participation in the international division of labor during the world economic crisis must be enforced through political repression. In one country after another during the 1970s martial law, states of emergency, and military governments have suppressed labor movements and union organizations and repressed large sectors of the population through systematic violations of their political, civil, and human rights. This repression is not accidental or merely ideologically motivated. Rather it is a necessary concomitant of economic exploitation, as is demonstrated by the evidence reviewed below from each of several dozen countries around the Third World. This evidence is incontrovertible, for it comes in the form of direct quotations from the most unimpeachable sources, in the international and financial press, which generally supports these regimes, from authorized spokesmen and political leaders of these repressive Third World governments, from Amnesty International, and even from the U.S. Department of State and the U.S. Senate.

The state is the principal instrument used by capital to create, maintain, extend, and intensify the political conditions necessary for superexploitation, particularly at the service of "export promotion" around the Third World. The state functions as the watchdog of superexploitation by repressing first and foremost labor and its organizations, and then by imposing "austerity" measures on the general population through "emergency" rule, constitutional "reform," and martial "law." These austerity measures are oftentimes enforced through repressive military regimes and then institutionalized through military and civilian authoritarian states.

This chapter documents this process through the extensive citation of the most authoritative business, financial, political, official, and independent press sources and reports at both the local and the international level.* It is a tedious chore to construct (and read) an argument based on so many quotations, but it is preferable to asking the reader to take the author's word for what might appear to be unfounded charges. With this method, the reader gets the evidence right from the horse's mouth, so to speak (e.g. "I Ferdinand E. Marcos, President of the Philippines . . . "), as well as from sources whose independence or support of the economic and political interests that exercise repression is unquestioned. This chapter reviews political repression for economic reasons in a wide-ranging sample of countries selected from each of the major regions of the Third World: Northeast and Southeast Asia, South Asia, the Middle East and North Africa, sub-Saharan Africa, South America, and the Caribbean. The same pattern of political-economic repression is evident in other Third World countries not reviewed here because the author has decided to exclude countries that have recently received very substantial coverage in the world press, such as Iran, Chile, and the Central American countries, and also those reviewed individually in Chapter 1, such as Brazil. Documentation of political-economic repression in these and dozens of other Third World countries is included in the reports by Amnesty International and by the United States Department of State cited at the end of this chapter. The institutionalization of political-economic repression by the state through its transformation into an apparatus at the service of international and national capital accumulation in this time of world economic crisis is analyzed in Chapter 7.

The situation in the Third World is summarized by Kreye:

> It is therefore not surprising that the list of countries in which free production zones are in operation or under construction is in large measure the same as that in which labor unions are either prohibited or strongly restricted and in which strikes and other means of organized labor struggle are widely repressed. Unions or union activity is either prohibited, as in Bahrain, Iran or Thailand; or politically split or restricted, as for instance in Hong Kong, India, Malaysia, Philippines and South Korea; or politically corrupted or neutralized, as for instance in Indonesia, Singapore and Egypt. Strikes are prohibited and repressed in most of the countries in which free production zones and world market factories are in operation, among them in India, Indonesia, Malaysia, Philippines, Singapore, South Korea, Egypt, Tunisia, Brazil and Haiti (Fröbel et al. 1977: 546).

Unfortunately, Kreye's list is incomplete. To it must be added Latin American countries with industrial production and raw materials (RM)

---

*Although most of the sources cited in this chapter were published before mid-1978, the situation, unfortunately, is unchanged, and similar news items continue in a seemingly unending flow.

production and processing, which Kreye did not consider in the context of his analysis, for export: Chile, Argentina, Uruguay (RM), Bolivia (RM), Peru (RM), Venezuela (RM), and Mexico (which is a model of the corruption and neutralization of labor unions), among others.

We shall document this political-economic repression country by country, going around the Third World from East to West.

COUNTRY STUDIES

South Korea

The average wage of Korean workers is reportedly one fifth that of their Japanese counterparts and one fifteenth that of U.S. workers. . . .As of March 1977, 78.8 per cent of workers were receiving less than 45,000 won a month and over 85 per cent fell below the recommended "minimum" living standard . . . . The downward trend in the workers' living standard is also manifested by the fact that the percentage of food expenses to total expenditures rose from 37.8 per cent in 1970 to 42.9 per cent in 1974. The percentage of food expenditure for the lowest income class is of course much higher. . . .

The history of the labor movement in Korea is short: in that time, there have been few labor disputes. . . . Strikes, sabotages, lockouts, and other forms of labor violence are very few in Korea because when labor disputes arise, such agencies as the [state] Office of Labor and the Central and Local Labor Committees mediate. . . . The Law prohibits the use of violence and destructive acts in labor disputes. . . . In a foreign-invested enterprise . . . the [Labor] Office will take arbitration measures for a fast and just conciliation. Thus, the Government takes direct responsibility and control of matters pertaining to labor union activities and disputes in the foreign investment enterprises: it is therefore hoped that labor union problems will be minimized and whenever possible, eliminated (Fine Instruments Center, *Guide to Electronics Industry Investment in Korea*, pp. 26–27, cited in Fröbel et al. 1977: 546–47).

Strikes are prohibited by law and the trade unions are a shadow of their western counterparts. . . . The strict labour laws permit the government to break up any union which it considers has become a threat to the safeguarding of public order. . . . On December 27, 1971, the government introduced a series of emergency measures including the outlawing of strikes. Since that date the penalty for striking has been a prison sentence for up to seven years (*The Times* 26 September 1975, cited in Fröbel et al. 1977: 547)

Backed by Park's Authority
Low Wages Help Boost S. Korean Exports

[Exports have increased by] about 7 per cent a year since 1963, but at the moment low wages are crucial to export goals and government officials admit it.

What they will admit only indirectly is that President Park's authoritarian power has been used to make sure that wages stay low and that the labor force remains devoted to converting South Korea into an advanced nation.

For the average South Korean, this means labor law and order: no strikes, no minimum wage, no unemployment compensation, no meaningful industrial safety regulations.

"Influence" on Wages

Even the World Bank survey referred to "the extraordinary influence that government agencies can exert on wage settlements."

South Korea's few significant labor unions are reliably reported to have been infiltrated by the Korean Central Intelligence Agency. The few labor riots that have erupted have been quickly suppressed and news of them has been censored out of the mass media. The harshest prison terms for political dissenters have been those given to critics of working conditions, among them Kim Chi Ha, the poet, and Kim Dae Jung, a former candidate for president (IHT 30 May 1977).

... A politically stable country. Viewed politically, the DEG [Deutsche Entwicklungs Gesellschaft] has no reservations against private investments.... Institutions like the World Bank, ADB [Asian Development Bank], IFC [International Finance Corporation], PICA and American Banks evaluate the investment climate as positive and promote the continued development of the country (Deutsche Gesellschaft für wirtschaftliche Zusammenarbeit [West German Governmental Development Corporation Office], Reisebericht Korea 23 March 1976: 1, 3, cited in Fröbel et al. 1977: 506).

Testimony before the U.S. Congress summarizes the relation between economic policy and political repression:

At the heart of Korea's human rights problems is the economic growth strategy of the country, a strategy which requires the repression and manipulation of labor (through government-controlled "trade unions" and a ban on strikes) and the tight control of free political expression.... The absence of full human rights is neither arbitrary nor coincidental; it is the product of the choice to have an export-oriented economy which leaves internal needs unmet (*Congressional Record,* 5 April 1978: H 2517, cited in Siegel 1980:19).

Philippines

Since President Marcos imposed martial law and initiated the New Society in Sept. 1972, the Philippine investment climate has shown daily improvement. Indeed the turnabout has been . . . remarkable. . . . A new political, economic and social environment has come into being in which corporations can invest with confidence, secure in their future status in a new context of Filipino pride and national consciousness, and abundant natural resources and a vast and underutilized labor force offer added attraction (Orville L. Freeman, former U.S. Secretary of Agriculture, now publisher of *Business International Asia/Pacific,* quote from issue of 27 November 1974).

Now, THEREFORE, I, FERDINAND E. MARCOS, President of the Philippines, by virtue of the power invested in me by the Constitution do hereby order and decree as follows:

Section 1. It is the policy of the State to encourage trade unionism and free collective bargaining within the framework of compulsory and voluntary arbitration and therefore all forms of strike, picketing and lockouts are hereby strictly prohibited. . . .

Section 8. No person, organization or entity, whether foreign or national, may give any donations, grants or other forms of assistance, in cash or in kind, directly or indirectly, to any labor organization, group of workers or any auxiliary thereof, such as cooperatives, credit unions and institutions engaged in research, education or communications without prior written permission by the Secretary of Labor.

The disturbing thing about [the above decree] is the statement of the Philippine National Trade Union Coordinating Center supporting and in fact, endorsing [it]. . . . Now we know the leaders of the Federation of Labor Union are really useless, or in fact are tools of the administration to further their aims. I think that is very clear to us now (cited in AMPO October–December 1975, p. 52; excerpts also in FER 14 November 1975: 47).

In terms of real wages, using 1965 as the base, wages have declined for skilled and unskilled workers by 35 per cent and 29 per cent respectively, according to Central Bank statistics (FER 14 May 1976).

The State Department, in a report prepared for Congress, has criticised the government of President Marcos in the Philippines for the use of torture and "severe intrusions on individual rights." Despite this, government officials said the Carter administration plans to maintain existing levels of military aid to the Philippines next year (IHT 7 February 1978).

Martial Law Is Expected to Remain in Philippines (IHT 17 April 1978). Philippines to keep martial law (FT 11 September 1979).

> Mr. Marcos himself has predicted that serious social unrest may result from the nature of the political economies of southeast Asian countries, including the Philippines. . . .[Recently] he identified the trends which, unless halted, would subject these countries to more "economic colonisation." They are: "Highly attractive treatment for foreign investments, particularly transnational corporations. . . . A low wage policy. . . . Reliance on the free enterprise model. . . . Relative to the concentration of wealth in the hands of the elite, the material conditions of life of the broad ranks of our people will deteriorate, giving way to explosive political repercussions rooted in the social conditions as . . . people become conscious of the need for social justice and economic democracy.". . . Ironically, the policies he criticised are those that guide his own martial law Government (GUA 15 April 1980).

Papua New Guinea

A strike in the Bougainville copper mines was put down with the help of police forces flown over from the main island.

> Foreign investors will be guaranteed that, except in unusual circumstances, there will be no nationalisation or exploitation and that earnings on capital can be remitted overseas . . . the level judged a "reasonable rate of return" on investment exceeds 25 per cent (FER 14 May 1976).

Singapore

Singapore: A Lid on Wages

> The justification for the clampdown on wages was that "if these practices continue, Singapore labour will be the most expensive in East and Southeast Asia, outside Japan" (FER 19 March 1976).

Investors can expect that the lid will be kept on wages for some time. The Singapore Government and the organized labour movement under its firm control are making a special effort to restore the island's attractiveness as a low-wage centre instead of allowing wages to continue to rise above those paid in competitive manufacturing centres such as Taiwan, Hongkong and South Korea (FER 14 May 1976).

Malaysia

The Government's policy regarding industrial relations is aimed at maintaining industrial peace and harmony with justice so as to create a favourable climate for investment, industrial expansion and growth in employment opportunities. Some of the main features of the Industrial Relations Act [of] 1967, which are designed to achieve this objective are: Prohibition of strikes and lockouts for causes connected with negotiation of Trade Unions, or on matters connected with management functions. . . . Power for the Minister of Labour to intervene and to refer disputes to the Industrial Court established under the Act. Awards by the Industrial Court are legally binding (Federal Industrial Development Authority [Malaysia], Labour and Wage Rates, pp. 13–14, cited in Fröbel et al.: III-85).

The effect of the amendment [to the Employment Ordinance] is to abolish the legal right and entitlement of a worker to retrenchment benefit—even where he has worked for more than three years. Under the new law, it is left to the Minister, where he chooses, to "prescribe entitlement to and payment of retrenchment benefit." [Labour Minister] Le San Choon's explanation for the power of the Minister to exempt or exclude employers from all or any of the provisions of the Employment Ordinance is also unacceptable. . . . The antiworker amendments to the Employment Ordinance were clearly designed to try to attract back foreign investors who, in the past 18 months, because of internal and regional development, have shied away from Malaysia. . . . Stability cannot be built on further exploitation of the workers and drastic denial of their basic rights to a decent and human life (Lim Kit Siang, opposition leader, Malaysian Parliament, Letter to the Editor of FER 22 October 1976).

Thailand

The gap between rich and poor widened ceaselessly even though the economic situation had improved visibly after the slump of 1975. . . . For the first time more than a million unemployed were officially registered (LM 13 November 1976).

Incapable under these conditions of putting an end to the social struggles that had been endemic since October 1973, the governments of Kukrit and Seni Pramoj lost the confidence of investors, both foreign and domestic. . . . In 1975 the United States cancelled sixty-seven investment projects in Thailand. As for national capital, it began to "flee" at growing speed to Hong Kong. One of the major objectives of the military junta now in power is thus to reestablish investor confidence. Although the trade-union movement has not formally been declared illegal, strikes are now forbidden and a purge of unions has begun (IPC 63, 25 November 1976: 17).

Power holders in Thailand propose democracy in 16 years. "An

Election in the Near Future Would Lead to Nothing." "Our economy is bankrupt. We are all sinking in overpowering debts. We have to tackle the problem even if we have to tighten the belt. Give me four years time to bring the economy into shape," said [the new Prime Minister] Thanin (FR 15 October 1976).

"At last we have a government that's capable of taking decisions. . . . At last we should get those long-delayed decisions that allow business to move," commented one prominent businessman, brimming with cheer over Thailand's new government. With one significant exception, no such decisions have been taken [within a month of the October 6, 1976, military coup]. . . . The one area in which the new regime has acted—labour relations—has contributed to the buoyant mood. The first announcement by the National Administrative Reform Council (NARC) was to ban strikes and lockouts for the period of martial law. This was followed by raids on union offices and arrests of a number of labour activists under martial law Order 22 against "persons dangerous to society" (FER 12 November 1976).

. . . 27 workers' leaders [were] arrested and charged with "endangering society" and violating the ban on strikes imposed when the military seized power four months ago. . . . [The] Director of Maintenance of Internal Peace and Order announced on national radio that such industrial action was detrimental to national security. He threatened violators with imprisonment. Observers here interpreted the Government's reaction as being designed partly to impress foreign investors, partly to flex its muscles in the face of criticism that it is weak and indecisive, and partly to pre-empt any further labour unrest. Meanwhile reports are mounting of flagrant breaches of collective agreements by both the private sector and State-enterprise employers since the coup. Managements have apparently been reneging on a wide variety of pledges covering wages, overtime pay, holidays, sick leave and maternity leave. . . . Despite all this the unions are powerless to act . . . and there are growing indications that their very existence may soon be in jeopardy (FER 4 February 1977).

Thai Investment Drive

The *tour de force* of the four-month-old Thanin Kraivichien Administration has been an investment promotion campaign to help both foreign and domestic private capital recover from the combined shock of Thailand's democratic politics and the world recession. . . . Thanin's *pièce de resistance,* however, is a new investment promotion bill that has been greeted at each stage of its progress into law as a major step in the drive "to return the nation to full stability, confidence and growth." The bill is reputedly a new package of incentives that will increase Thailand's attractiveness to foreign investors. But it is viewed by some foreign businessmen as something more: "It's a gesture to business as a whole that the Government is sensitive to their needs and the neglect of the past will be undone." ...Tax exemption. ... Tariff exemption. ... A guarantee against nationalisation. ... (FER 22 February 1977).

The October coup put an end to the politics of reform. The Thanin Administration is reversing the pro-labour and farm policies of the democratic period and turning squarely towards business and manufacturing. Investment has become the top priority, in the hope that industrial growth will solve the country's long-term unemployment and trade deficits. Nothing has been heard of land reform. ... (FER 4 February 1977: 39).

India

In South Asia "emergency" repression has been similarly rampant and increasingly institutionalized. After—indeed because of—a decade of growing economic crisis and the railway strike of 1974 (Frank 1977b; Sau 1977), Prime Minister Indira Gandhi declared "emergency" rule on June 26, 1975.

Within a month of the proclamation of Emergency and the decision not to have strikes and lockouts, nearly 20,000 employees have been either retrenched or laid off [in West Bengal] by various multi-national business houses (*Business Standard* 29 August 1975).

Progress under Emergency Rule is claimed to include better labour discipline, increased productivity, and the revival of the stock market. ... Much of the recent improvement—in fields such as for example industrial relations—is simply due to fear (*Business Asia* 12 March 1976).

Oh, it's just wonderful. We used to have terrible problems with the unions. Now when they give us any trouble the Government just puts them in jail (a member of the Oberoi family quoted in *New York Times Magazine* 4 April 1976).

The number of man-days lost through strikes rose significantly in 1974 and in the first half of 1975 before the declaration of Emergency Rule. After the declaration of Emergency, the number of man-days lost through strikes declined by 83 percent from January–April 1975 to January–April 1976. For foreign and Indian big business, this repression of labor and the concomitant concessions to business were "a time for rejoicing" (Frank 1977b).

M. Desai's Janata Party won the March 1977 parliamentary elections largely on the strength of its opposition to the political repression of Indira Gandhi's Emergency Rule and its promise to repeal the hated Maintenance of Internal Security Act (MISA)—which incorporated into one act earlier laws, including those providing for preventive detention. However, for a year?

quite deliberately, and in blatant betrayal of its own promises, the Janata government has done nothing to dismantle the basic structure of authoritarianism that Indira Gandhi had erected and whose purpose was clearly to provide strength and hope to the ruling classes. In fact, the Janata party has made its own modest contribution to further extension of that structure, in the shape of preventive detention laws in the states— . . . mini-MISA[s]. . . .When the next crisis overtakes the ruling classes, the kind of repression that will be let loose will be far more severe than that experienced till now. . . . (EPW Annual Number, February 1978: 175).

MISA was eventually repealed after lengthy wrangling about how to replace it with acceptable substitutes. However, it was then decided that

detention without trial is to be reintroduced in India after only six months. It had been an almost permanent feature of the Indian legal system from Independence until the overthrow of Mrs. Indira Gandhi 18 months ago. In March, this year, it was abolished by the Janata Government amid cheers in both Houses of Parliament.

But the ruling Janata Party says it is bringing back preventive detention, not because its commitment to democracy, or the rule of law is weakening, but because in recent months crime, labour unrest, student indiscipline, and violent political protest have increased alarmingly. Faced with these problems the Government has reluctantly decided that normal laws will not cope.

The gloomy conclusion was reached last week at a private meeting of chief Ministers of the country's 22 states. Chief Ministers owing allegiance to Mrs. Gandhi or belonging to parties other than Janata agreed to the move at the New Delhi meeting (GUA 5 October 1978).

Subsequently, the "caretaker" government headed by Charan Singh passed a Prevention of Blackmarketing and Maintenance of Supplies of Essential Commodities Ordinance. *Economic and Political Weekly* reported fears that the measure would be used less against black marketeers—who were rarely prosecuted in the past despite adequate legislation and preventive detention provisions—and more against the working class, especially railway and other transport workers, who could fall within the ordinance terminology of "acting in any manner prejudicial to the maintenance of supplies of commodities essential to the consumer." EPW commented:

In a sense, such a measure was inevitable; the wonder is that for more than a year now, there has been no law providing for detention without trial on the statute books. . . . The Indian political system has never been able to, and probably cannot, function without recourse to such provisions. The Janata began to regret its promises to undo MISA almost as soon as it was in office; and Charan Singh has only restored to the government its historic heritage. There is yet another and more important compulsion for the bringing back of preventive detention. The Indian ruling classes are increasingly in a bind, since the objective crisis is fast overtaking them. The Emergency demonstrated that the functioning of Indian polity without recourse to measures even more extraordinary than those already familiar to large sections of the working people and national minorities was not possible. . . . It was only a matter of time before the same "solutions" tried by the earlier factions would be once again tried (EPW 6 October 1979: 1657–58).

When Indira Gandhi returned as Prime Minister, "neither she nor her party . . . expressed regret for the Emergency" (FER 18 January 1980) and "many Delhi intellectuals believe that, after a brief honeymoon, the state of emergency will be reimposed" (GAW 13 January 1980).

Outcry over Gandhi's new powers

Fears that Mrs. Indira Gandhi, India's Prime Minister, would again unleash the repressive measures used during her Emergency Rule from 1975 to 1977 were voiced by Opposition leaders yesterday, following promulgation of an ordinance to legalise preventive detention without trial. . . .

The new ordinance, which has been called "draconian" by the opposition, permits detention without trial for a maximum of 12 months for a person thought to be acting against national security and endangering public order, or maintenance of essential supplies and services. . . .

The opposition fears Mrs. Gandhi will misuse powers to act against her political opponents if they threaten her position. At the moment, this is unlikely because of opposition disunity.

But conditions could change within a year or two, especially if Mrs. Gandhi is not able to check inflation and the social tensions that economic backwardness and the country's structural weaknesses are causing.

In that case, the opposition groups contend, the powers conferred on the Federal and State Governments by Monday's ordinance could be liable to misuse (FT 24 September 1980).

Sri Lanka

The parallels between Indira Gandhi, emergency laws and Sirimavo Bandaranaike [in Sri Lanka] are too well known to need elaboration (EPW 10 April 1977: 622).

Sri Lanka has been under a State of Emergency since April 4, 1971, following the youth uprising. . . . The Emergency regulations in Sri Lanka have been declared invalid (FER 24 September 1976).

An embattled Mrs. Sirimavo Bandaranaike, the Sri Lankan Prime Minister, has introduced a string of tough Emergency laws to counter a two-pronged political assault against her as well as to stabilize the rocketing prices of essential goods (FER 4 June 1976).

Unrest and Discontent Spreading on Sri Lanka (NYT/IHT 27 December 1976).

Pakistan

Enforcing State of Emergency
Pakistan Limits Independence of Courts

A Constitutional amendment passed and signed into law in September [1976] prohibits any court challenge to laws implementing Pakistan's five-year-old national state of emergency. It restricts the courts' jurisdiction to guarantee civil liberties in political cases, permits judges to be transferred without their consent and abolishes the life terms of chief justices. . . . Under the emergency rule, the government can jail persons who allegedly threaten the nation's "security" or "integrity." It is estimated that there are several hundreds or thousands of political prisoners here. . . .

In the last two years, the government has cracked down on its political opposition. The courts responded by enforcing constitutional guarantees. Mr. Bhutto then cracked down on the courts (IHT 5 November 1976).

Characteristically, the military was called out not to control the agitation when the orthodox [right wing] parties were heading it but to clamp down upon the mobilization of the working class as it stepped up strike actions in Karachi and elsewhere. Throughout the crisis, Bhutto had sought to negotiate and compromise with the orthodox Right . . . but he proclaimed martial law as soon as the trade unions . . . began to capture the initiative and thus posed the possibility of a viable challenge from the Left. Thus, the new militarisation serves . . . the more profound aim of striking at the very heart of the mass movement itself. . . . Meanwhile, the orthodox parties had been preparing conspiratorially to take advantage of a social crisis and make a coup d'état from the extreme Right, ousting the Bhutto regime (EPW 4 June 1977: 907).

Suppression of Trade Unions under Martial Law

Within a few days of the imposition of Martial Law in Pakistan on July 5, 1977, specific orders and regulations relating to the activities of the working class were issued. As a result of these orders and regulations, many of the rights and privileges gained by the working class through trade union struggles and strikes have been severely undermined. . . .

On July 10 the Chief Martial Law Administrator General Zia ul

Haq issued Martial Law Regulation No. 12 stating that "all kinds of activity relating or pertaining to, or connected in any manner whatsoever with, trade unions, labour associations or any other body of similar nature [are] prohibited" (EPW 17 December 1977).

Pakistanis Relieved by Coup, Skeptical about Vote Pledge
Will the Military Step Down as Promised?
(IHT 9 July 1977).

Pakistan Cancels Oct. 18 Election
Zia Extends Martial Law Rule Indefinitely
"I have come to the conclusion that to hold elections on Oct. 18 will only be an invitation to a new crisis," said the general, who ousted Prime Minister Zulfikar Ali Bhutto in a coup d'état three months ago. "I have great respect for the institution of elections, but I cannot allow the country to face disaster for their sake," he said (IHT 3 October 1977).

Pakistan's ruling junta is now using the noose and the lash against a wider section of society in the continuing stepped-up martial law clamp down launched on October 16 [1979]. Apparently realising that troublesome political parties were merely a symptom and not the cause of the country's malaise, the government moved against others apart from politicians and journalists to demonstrate its strength in a bid to halt if not reverse the drift to an uncertain future. . . . Although cooperation remains the foremost requirement of the regime for perpetuating its rule, its draconian face—deliberately made more ferocious recently—seems designed more for unquestioning obedience. One more problem the regime faces is the economists' latest estimate that general prices are poised for a 20–25% jump within about six to eight weeks. Additional social complications could arise from proposed changes in labour laws, permitting employers to sack unwanted workers, as also from the proposed denationalisation of several overstaffed public-sector industries.

The points immediately in favour of the junta are the current silencing of all domestic criticism, its absolute power to do what it pleases with anyone in the country and solid, unflinching support from ultra-right political forces in the country—and from China (FER 9 November 1979).

There are six branches of police, four of them brand new and devised by the Bhutto regime. . . . This 3,000 per cent increase in budget allocations for police and intelligence services covered only the first two years of the Bhutto regime. Further increases occurred during the past three years as well. . . . This expansion of domestic repressive forces of course . . . kept the civilian population in a state of perpetual terror (EPW 1 April 1978: 575).

Bangladesh

A highly significant event has emerged on Bangladesh's foreign investment front which has been almost totally ignored. . . . Now American investors are contemplating what will be their largest foreign investment in the entire South Asia sub-continent. In asset value it will be greater than all American investments in India and Pakistan combined. It is no drop in the bucket and its political and military implications within Bangladesh are enormous. . . . International Systems and Control Corporation of Houston, Texas (USA), was negotiating an 800 million dollar investment deal to exploit Bangladesh's extensive natural gas reserves. . . . The correspondent of the *Financial Times* travelling with [British Prime Minister] Callaghan reported from Dacca [on January 6, 1978]: "The prospect of a major U.K. involvement in the exploitation of the rich natural gas fields of Bangladesh appears to be much closer following talks between Mr. James Callaghan and President Zia. Talks involving the British Gas Corporation and a major private company are well advanced. . . . An ambitious proposal will be developed which would entail the ordering from British yards of around six tankers to export the natural gas to the West Coast of the US and to Japan. . . . The value of the vessels . . . could easily be in the 450m [million pound] area—four times the value of the recent Polish order." . . .

The main obstacle to a final go-ahead on the ambitious investment scheme is the American investors' uncertainty of the internal security and political situation. They want to be confident that no radical regime will come to power and nationalise what will be one of the largest and most profitable investments in Asia. Some observers in Bangladesh are talking of the possibility of an Indonesian style "crackdown solution" to the dilemma. The most recent executions are seen as only a prelude to what might develop. The arrival of the British Military Advisory Team . . . [is] seen . . . as not unrelated to securing a confident "stable" environment agreeable to foreign investing interests. The British are deeply involved along with the Americans in the proposed investment schemes. . . .

Ziaur Rahman has opened an ugly breach. Mass executions of the imprisoned ordered by the central authority of the state is something repugnantly new. . . . [These are] the first official mass executions that have been known in this century in South Asia. . . . The *Washington Post* [10 February 1978] wrote . . . "the State Department quoted the regime in Dacca as having executed 37 rebels. . . . Our best estimate, drawn from sources available to the embassy as a whole, is that 217 military personnel were executed. . . . President Ziau Rahman had slain large numbers of suspected rebels without bringing them before courts-martial!" . . . On March 5, 1978, *The Sunday Times* of London reported: "About 600 servicemen have been executed in Bangladesh since October in a bloodbath." Amnesty [International] estimates that as of April 1977 there were between 10,000 and 15,000 political prisoners in Bangladesh. . . . Many observers of the Bangladesh situation consider Amnesty's figures highly conservative. . . .

But the crucial developments on which all three ambitious investment schemes ultimately rely is the internal political situation and the man concerned is Major General Ziaur Rahman. The issue now for the West is whether he can become Bangladesh's General Suharto, the Indonesian military figure whose American-backed countercoup ended in the massacre of the Indonesian Communist Party (PKI), and securely opened the country to the Petramina oil export boom of the next decade. A number of Western observers see an Indonesian style solution as the only answer to Bangladesh's radical traditions. Whether Ziaur Rahman is the man for the job is the question (EPW 25 March 1978: 551, 557).

Egypt

Egypt's new orientation since the October war is beginning to pay off. . . the economic liberalization [has] made capital aid for the urgently needed foreign exchange possible again and [has] awakened the interest of private investors (FAZ 9 September 1974).

In February 1974 three decrees were issued creating various bodies to channel investment, guarantee private investment and prevent nationalization; "free zones" were established along the Suez Canal wherein all companies would be exempt from taxes and duties; corporations newly investing in Egypt were granted five-to-eight-year exemptions from taxes throughout the country and investment banks were exempted from currency controls. In June 1974 an investment law opened industry, metallurgy, banking and insurance (all previously nationalized) to foreign investment. In addition, Egyptian citizens were granted permission to become representatives of foreign firms (IPC 1977).

Recognizing the benefits that foreign investment can bring to the country, the Arab Republic of Egypt, the most populous country of the Arab world, is now welcoming foreign capital in a wide range of fields. . . . Foreign investment is allowed in a range of industrial, mining, energy, tourism, land reclamation, animal husbandry, and banking activities, and for Arab investors, in housing construction and rehabilitation. . . . Recognizing that Egypt's past record makes investors wary, the new foreign investment law provides guarantees against unlawful nationalization or expropriation of investments. . . . Egypt has a surplus of employable labour. In these inflationary times, Egypt retains its significant wage-cost advantage over many other developing countries. . . . With favourable prospects for political stability, with a renewed faith in a significant role for the private sector, and with plans for rapid economic growth, Egypt with its new incentives should be an appealing place for foreign investment (Egyptian Government multi-page announcement published in *African Development*, cited in IPC 1977).

Why Peace Doesn't Buy Prosperity for Egypt

President Sadat needs an "economic revolution"—but that's easier said than done. . . . The Government's difficulties are staggering. In 1976 alone, Egypt must import 1 billion dollars' worth of food for its people, a population of 38 million that is increasing by a million a year. . . . Most foreign firms have been unwilling to invest or pay import duties and taxes at the unrealistic official rate. They want the Egyptian currency to be floated so that profits and costs can be calculated at the same rate of exchange. The International Monetary Fund has recommended basic economic and monetary reforms to get President Anwar Sadat's so-called open-door policy toward foreign investment moving into gear. The rich Arab nations say that's exactly what they, too, want Egypt to do. Yet such reforms would almost certainly lead to higher prices, austerity and hardship, which would combine to undermine Sadat's political opposition (USN 23 August 1976).

The Prime Minister Announces an Austerity Plan
(LM 29 January 1977)

Egypt's Masses Do Not Want To Follow Their Leader Anymore

Only the new-rich commercial caste was able to profit from Anwar el-Sadat's New Economic Policy (FR 28 January 1977).

The decree raising the prices was announced on Monday [17 January 1977]. The first public reaction came about midnight Tuesday, when crowds began gathering in Tahrir (Liberation) Square in the center of Cairo, chanting, "With life and blood we shall bring down prices." . . . Mr. Sadat called out army troops, the first time they had been used against the civilian population in 25 years, and flew back to Cairo for crisis talks with his ministers. The final toll from the two days of rioting was 79 dead, 566 injured and damage that ran into hundreds of millions of dollars (IHT 24 January 1977).

In his statement, he [Mr. Sadat] denied the existence of the deep-seated social discontent that even the friendliest foreign diplomats find obvious. He has attributed the riots to Moscow, the Communists and other leftist radicals and has vowed to "finish them off." . . .

The regime, it seems, is . . . readying the tolls by which any political challenge to the President could be repressed. . . . Egyptians voted today to approve or reject a decree of repressive law-and-order measures signed by President Anwar Sadat in the aftermath of the bloody and destructive bread riots last month. . . . The measures include hard labor for life for strikes, sit-ins, demonstrations, obstruction to government activities and "causing damage to public or private property." Membership in "organizations that are opposed to the regime" also is subject to hard labor for life (NYT 10 February 1977).

Offensive Against the Left in Egypt

More than 3,000 persons, among them 94 communists, have recently been detained in Egypt and accused of "subversive activities against the regime and national unity," according to yesterday's report in the Egyptian newspaper *Al Ahram*. . . . What the press does not say is that anti-Sadat manifestations are multiplying and intensifying against the "corrupting modernization" and the "pro-Americanism" of the regime. Students and religious leaders and Muslim integralists have been involved in these protests in recent days in Cairo, Alexandria and Assuan (EPA 15 January 1980).

Not much imagination is necessary to connect the news item above with the following one, published three weeks later:

Egyptians Seek Seal of Good House-keeping
Roger Matthews, in Cairo, Previews Forthcoming Efforts to
Secure an IMF Aid Package

The Egyptian Government hopes to clinch a $1bn agreement with the International Monetary Fund during the next six weeks which according to some officials would be the largest-ever three-year facility granted by the Fund to a developing country. . . . But with public unease over prices becoming more evident and Mr. Sadat still having little to show in material terms for his peace treaty, it is going to be the Minister of the Interior who has the dominant voice on that aspect of policy. The IMF will be well aware of this, just as it is of strong Western political pressure to reach an agreement (FT 2 February 1980).

Tunisia

Oasis for Investments
Tunisia Attracts Foreign Capital

Tunisia became an investment oasis for German textile and clothing industry during the course of only the last three years. Lately the producers of electronic products also discovered the advantages that the country offers them. Above all the 1972 Law for Export Promotion offers great attraction. . . . At present for experienced seamstresses one has to pay an average wage of DM 1,30 [plus] about 40 per cent social security costs. . . . The lowest wage scales lie about 20 to 30 pfennig under those of the seamstresses; for mechanics and foremen it is necessary to pay up to 50 pfennig more. Work is 48 hours a week. . . . (FR 27 April 1977).

Certain electronic components can be manufactured much more cheaply in Tunisia than in the Federal Republic of Germany. This is the opinion of representatives of the Association of Electronic Components. . . . Tunisian wages, inclusive of fringe benefits, are up to 83 per cent lower, but labor productivity is about as high as in the Federal Republic. Additionally, the Tunisian government offers various advantages, for instance, tax holidays for 10 years (SZ 15 November 1974).

Tunisia Luring Export-Based Cos.
Critics See Little Lasting Benefit

But Tunisia stoutly defends its program. . . . Slaheddine Bacha, general director of the official investment promotion agency, . . . said . . . in the last four years the agency has approved 404 projects for export industries, with a planned investment of $322 million and the creation of 43,692 jobs. Of those approved, 160 projects are now in operation providing 16,000 jobs. The export industry has created an average of 4,000 jobs yearly or one quarter of the 16,000 jobs annually, according to Mr. Bacha. . . .

One such operation, Marsa Modes, set up in 1972 by a unit of Borden Inc., produces 4,000 garments a day that go to the Common Market. . . . Above all there is labor peace, Marsa's general manager Henry Gerson emphasizes: virtually no strikes, lower absenteeism than in France or Italy and "reasonable" wages. The average sewing machine operator was [paid] 50 cents an hour until it was raised recently to 60 cents under a national wage increase (IHT 9–10 April 1977).

Since 1970, reintroduction of liberalism in the economy with growing opposition and systematic repression of the political opponents of the regime. . . . This stability could only be reached at the cost of political repression (Amnesty International, Tunisian Hintergrundbericht, May 1976: pp. 5–7).

Tunisia Hit by Rioting
Emergency Rule Set

The disorders grew from a 24-hour general strike called against the economic policies of Premier Hedi Nouira and, by extension, against Mr. Bourguiba.

The firing a month ago of Interior Minister Tahar Belkhoja, a veteran regarded as a moderate, was interpreted as a sign of high-level dissent within the government and suggested that Mr. Bourguiba had decided to crack down on the strikers.

He was replaced temporarily by Defense Minister Abdallah Farhat, who has frequently called for tougher action against the anti-government agitators. Later Dhaoui Hanablia, a newcomer to the government, was named interior minister (IHT 27 January 1978).

Labor Leader Held in Tunisia after Anti-Regime Riots

Tunis, Jan. 29 (AP)—President Habib Bourguiba's government has arrested union leader Habib Achour in connection with anti-government rioting on Thursday that left at least 40 persons dead, Tunisia's official news agency said today (IHT 30 January 1978).

The government called the armed forces to quell a general strike [and] left a heavy toll estimated at 130 dead and 450 injured (IHT 16 February 1978).

The riots that recently swept Tunisia typified many disturbances in the Third World and in the developed world as well: Thousands of unemployed youths took advantage of a planned national strike to vent their rage against a society that cannot provide them with jobs. But the brutal way the riots were put down spotlighted a fearful regime, embroiled in a succession struggle and aloof from the concerns of the bulk of Tunisia's six million people. The United States has influence on that regime. It should use it to ease the increasing repression. . . .

Until recently, Tunisia has been a profoundly "civilian" state, with small, poorly equipped military forces—an encouraging contrast to its neighbors. But Prime Minister Hedi Noira, evidently Bourguiba's chosen successor, has begun a program of military "modernization" and expansion supported by credits from the United States. . . . Many of the weapons Tunisia has bought from the United States, such as helicopters and armored personnel carriers, are useful against internal as well as foreign opponents (NYT editorial, cited in IHT 14 February 1978).

Nigeria

Nigerian Unionists Condemn Antilabor Decree

As part of its ongoing effort to hamstring the Nigerian trade-union movement, the military junta of Lt. Gen. Olusegun Obasanjo has enacted another repressive industrial law.

The Trade Disputes (Essential Services) Decree 1977 provides fines of up to 10,000 naira (about $14,500) for anyone found guilty of "disrupting" the economy or impeding the functioning of "essential services." Formally, the decree applies to both workers and employers, but in the context of the regime's overall antilabor policy it is obviously directed primarily at the workers' right to strike. . . .

The right to strike had already been seriously curtailed the year before, when Obasanjo banned virtually all strikes in what were described as "essential services," meaning government departments, communications, transportation, airports and harbors, electricity, water, fuel and hospitals.

In addition, the whole trade-union movement is being restructured under government dominance. The 1,870 previously existing unions are being reorganized into seventy authorized unions, with the regime having the power to appoint their general secretaries. By the beginning of 1978, sixty-four of these new unions had been established, and hundreds that did not qualify were outlawed (IPC 30 January 1978).

Ghana

First, it was Gen. Achcampong who brought political tensions to an intolerable level by foisting "Union Government"—a form of civilian-military power-sharing—on an unwilling population.

When he fell, the Akuffo Government backed away slowly from Union Government and towards a U.S.-style Presidential contest.

But there have been endless rows over the form of the constitution, the banning of many former politicians from elective office, and the number of parties allowed to run.

Amid the general confusion, most of Ghana's parties recently asked Gen. Akuffo to delay the handover date from July 1 to January 1 next year. He refused, but the new rulers might be more responsive to the idea.

Enthusiasm for the whole electoral process had been dampened by the country's grave economic difficulties, which mean that the average Ghanaian is no better off now than in 1957.

At the heart of the problem lies falling production of cocoa, Ghana's main foreign exchange earner, and failure to diversify into other crops (FT 6 June 1979).

. . . Gen. Frederick Akuffo turned to a consortium of international bankers for advice and initiated belt-tightening measures. He cut government spending, devalued the cedi by 58 percent and came up with the leanest budget Ghana had seen in years. In January, the International Monetary Fund approved a $90-million loan to Ghana.

But as inflation continued to climb, at a rate of about 50 percent, it became obvious that even more stringent measures were required. The currency conversion is not expected to be the last of these measures (IHT 18 April 1979).

Zambia

Zambia Austerity Plan Meets IMF Terms
Clears Way for $390-Million Loan

Zambia, which devalued its currency by 10 percent and announced a series of austerity moves last week, has apparently met the stringent terms set by the International Monetary Fund as conditions for a $390-million loan to shore up this country's badly buffeted and sagging economy. . . .

The new austerity program is being imposed on top of a spartan budget adopted earlier this year that has cut social services and raised taxes. Transport problems on the only railroad in the country that still is operating have intensified, further snarling imports and exports.

Furthermore, under the impact of the worsening economy and increasing unemployment, the crime rate has risen sharply. The police recently have made sweeps aimed at marauding bands whose violence has touched off a small but ominous emigration of technicians from the copper belt.

Finally, there are chronic shortages. These have gone beyond luxury items and now include such items as meat, medicine and fertilizer.

Although these difficulties are connected, the measures announced in Parliament by John Mwanakatwe, the minister of finance, focused largely on improving the position of the copper mines. The mines, which are the economic heart of the nation, have suffered greatly as world copper prices have hit the lowest point in 25 years.

In his presentation, the minister sought to depict the austerity package in its best possible light. "The devaluation of our currency," he said, "will allow an increase in revenue to the mining industry of some $37 million."

This amount is approximately half the loss sustained by the mines in the last year, losses that have been supported by heavy government borrowing. The minister also disclosed that other measures that he did not describe would further reduce the operating deficit of the mines, 51 per cent of which are owned by the government

Unspecified Measures

Some diplomatic and banking sources here were speculating that the unspecified measures might include dismissals of workers, a recommendation thought to be among those urged by an IMF team that visited here last month. Dismissals would be difficult for the government to swallow, particularly since this is a presidential election year.

The minister also reported that there would be wage controls, including a yearlong freeze on all salaries in the public sector.

Despite the distaste with which many Zambian politicians regard the IMF proposals, they were reportedly won over by the recognition that in the absence of the loan the country might be forced to default on its debt-service payments, further damaging investor confidence and perhaps affecting other aid (IHT 21 March 1978).

Uruguay

Political-economic repression in Chile has received so much publicity worldwide (and has been analyzed by the author [Frank 1976a] in two open letters to Milton Friedman and Arnold Harberger, republished under the title *Economic Genocide in Chile*) that documentation here is unnecessary. Unfortunately, the similar experience of Uruguay, which used to be regarded as "the Switzerland of Latin America," has received far less attention than it deserves. Therefore, it may be appropriate to examine the Uruguayan experience in some detail.

In February 1978, *Business Latin America* assured its readers that "the profitability of foreign branches operating in Uruguay in 1976 recovered in comparison with previous years. The fiscal balance 1976 for the 50 largest companies shows profits of over 106%, while the inflation rate for the same year was around 40 percent."

The Social and Political Price of the New Model

The regime proclaims that the country has enjoyed "uninterrupted economic growth" over the past five years, and that exports have been notably diversified. The explanation of these apparent economic achievements lies in the drastic reduction in the people's standard of living. Real wages have dropped 44% in comparison with 1971 (30% in the last four years) (*Excelsior,* July 7, 1978). Wilson Ferreira Aldunate declared last year to a Madrid daily that, if the results of the last census are extrapolated, Uruguay should have a population of between 3,300,000 and 3,500,000 inhabitants. According to recent figures, the actual total is only 2,700,000. That is to say, 600,000 to 800,000 persons are missing. "This is the worst case of population drain in modern history. The emigration is moreover, eminently selective: intellectuals, artists, specialized workers, half cadres" (*El Dia,* Mexico City, June 27, 1978). This means that the new economic model, inspired in the monetarist projections of the Chicago school, provides a lower income for a much reduced population. Meanwhile, for all the high levels of emigration, a 13% unemployment rate subsists.

The surplus produced by the growing exploitation of the workers has not been equitably distributed among the dominant classes. The cattlemen still enjoy a relatively privileged position, but the industrial bourgeoisie producing for the domestic market has been impoverished and decimated and many establishments have closed their doors. The new rich of this regime, the privileged of the moment, are the industrialists who produce for export.

The new Uruguayan model is seeking to insinuate itself into a place in the scheme of international division of labor promoted by the transnationals. The technological competence to sweep the world markets demands heavy investment, which can only be recovered by paying low wages. This is the secret of the so-called *stabilization* plans: to create markets of cheap labor that will enable the transnational corporations to compete on the industrialized markets. When the breakdown of the old regime became apparent, the cattlemen became the second-class partners of the privileged, among whom must be counted the foreign investors.

According the figures of the Faculty of Economic Sciences and Administration (controlled by the military government, as are the country's other educational establishments, since 1973), the cost of living rose 992% between January 1, 1973 and December 31, 1977 (*El Dia,* Montevideo, February 5, 1978). During the course of 1978, popular consumption of items of primary necessity was reduced 20%; consumption of bread fell 18.7% and that of meat 37%. According to official figures, in the first five months of the year, the cost of living rose 15.4%. The most striking increases occurred in food, particularly meat, milk and derived products, though other important categories, such as clothing and housing, also suffered sharp increases.

The proscribed National Workers' Convention denounced the fact that "the figures for the real income of Uruguayan workers continue to show constant falls." Based on 1971, "the drop in wages and salaries had reached 54% by May this year (1978)." What has been taken away from the workers between May 1977 and April 1978 amounts to more than 500 million dollars, a sum almost equal to Uruguay's annual exports. "The exploitation of the workers through reducing real wages has been further reinforced by stepping up the rhythm of work and increasing the length of the working day."

An internal report of the National Party agrees with the assertions of the workers' central and comments that "the most painful aspect of the economic process that the Republic has lived through since 1973 has been the constant and unrelieved drop in the real wages of those who work by the week or by the day. This fall has been brought about by using the system of ministerially fixing such wages, which systematically in every readjustment are kept below the prior increase in the cost of living, without the workers having any recourse, even criticism, for their own defense" (*El Dia,* Mexico City, December 28, 1977).

The application of the new economic model has demanded the total destruction of union organizations and freedoms, as well as the paralysis of political activity and the crushing of opposition in any form. The rights of meeting, association and free expression, individual guarantees, the inviolability of the home and of correspondence, the right of habeas corpus, etc. have all been completely abolished. Just a few press organs remain, essentially supportive of the government, and even so tightly muzzled. An all-embracing Executive Branch governs with the collaboration of the Council of State, whose members are appointed "by pointing a finger"; the Judicial Branch lacks autonomy and is subordinated to the will of the Executive. Following the dissolution of Parliament, 15,000 citizens who had appeared in the lists of candidates in earlier years were deprived of their political rights for fifteen years.

All opposition sources agree in estimating the number of political prisoners at almost 7,000, a figure which is proportionally higher than those for Chile and Argentina (*Excelsior,* March 2, 1978). Since 1972, a system of "exceptional justice" has been in operation, according to which anyone accused of subversive activities is tried by a military court. On June 20, 1978, the Supreme Military Court revealed that 4,420 persons have been tried on accusations of undermining the security of the State (*Excelsior,* June 21, 1978). This number does not include those detained under the "immediate security measures," which have been in continuous force since that same year. Among the trials, one which had a special echo culminated in a sentence of 14 years imposed on General Líber Seregni, presidential candidate of the Broad Front in the 1971 elections. Four accusations gave rise to this sentence: having usurped public functions, because young members of the FA carried out a campaign of cleaning up and decorating public places during the 1971 electoral campaign; having been subject to the anarquist [sic] ideological influence of his father, during his youth; having taken part in a political coalition that included the Communist Party, and having attended a meeting of 30 young people, one of whom belonged to the National Liberation Movement (Tupamaros) (*El Día,* Mexico City, May 7, 1978).

The Uruguayan regime has been the object of severe criticism because of the systematic torture of political prisoners. "Uruguay is the torture-chamber of Latin America," said American Congressman Edward Koch. European social democrats and German Christian democrats have confirmed the accusation. In 1978, the Uruguayan communist leader Rodney Arismendi reported that more than 50 members of his party have died under torture. This figure does not include victims belonging to other trends within the opposition, such as the militants in the guerrilla organizations. The Government of Uruguay has also been accused of practicing terrorism outside its frontiers, particularly as a result of the assassination of Senator Zelmar Michelini and of the former president of the Chamber of Deputies, Héctor Gutiérrez Ruiz, which were perpetrated in Buenos Aires in May 1976. To the foregoing must be added the disappearance of dozens of Uruguayan exiles in Argentina and, more recently, the kidnapping of a Uruguayan couple in Porto Alegre, with the complicity of Brazilian police agents (CEE March 1979: 109–110).

Argentina

Coup in Argentina Sets the Stage for Reconstruction

This week's coup against the administration of Isabel Peron marks a decisive turning point for Argentina. Corporate planners must now put away alternative scenarios and assess the country's business outlook and its impact on their operations in light of the new government. [Here are examined] what the military's economic policy stance is likely to be and what it means for companies. The new regime, led by Army Commander General Jorge Videla moved quickly to bring the country under military control. Congress, provincial legislatures and municipal assemblies were abolished, members of the Supreme Court dismissed and an all-military cabinet named. . . . Foreign investment will be encouraged. . . .

Labor. The military is cracking down on labor leaders in a move to break their stranglehold on the formation of economic policy. Unions have been suspended and most key Peronist labor leaders jailed. . . . The brunt of the anti-inflation drive will probably be born by wage earners. . . . Following an initial devaluation, the authorities will try to maintain an exchange rate adequate for exports (BLA 24 March 1976: 89).

Argentina Plans Sweeping Changes to Revive Economy

As expected, Jose Martinez de Hoz, who reportedly submitted an economic program that won the approval of the military before it actually took power, has been made Minister of Economy. . . . The new economic plan is reportedly rooted in classic free-market economic principles that represent a sharp shift from the Peronist administration's populist policies. . . . Foreign investment will clearly be made welcome. . . . [T]he policy of encouraging "Argentinization" of companies [will be reversed]. . . . [F]oreign firms [will become] eligible for incentives . . . [and] also have access to credit for working capital on the same basis as local companies. . . . Union political activity will be prohibited and strict control maintained over union finances. The right to strike will be regulated, and in the case of public services, prohibited. All wage negotiations between companies and unions are likely to be suspended, with raises granted only by government decree. There will be no automatic linkage of wage increases to the cost of living index. . . . [P]rice controls will be completely eliminated. . . . The long-term goal is to eliminate exchange controls. As an immediate step, the government is expected to unify the exchange rates and devalue the peso (BLA 31 March 1976: 97–8).

Argentina Frees Prices, Moves Toward Unified Exchange Rate

This is an effective 26.7 per cent devaluation. . . . Stock prices shot up four-fold in heavy trading (BLA 7 April 1976: 105).

Real wages declined 40 per cent *after* the coup and wage earners' share of national income was reduced to 34 per cent (PC 17 March 1977: 11).

The military regime in Argentina has put thirteen important labor union organizations under state control (NZZ 3 April 1976).

Argentina's Junta Tames the Workers
Eight-hour Day, Claims to Vacations and the Right
to Strike are Practically Eliminated

The purchasing power of [the average worker's] wage has thus fallen to a third of what it was at the end of 1974. . . . The right to strike has been annulled in principle through government decree. Those who use this instrument of pressure anyway can be dismissed immediately and in addition commit a "subversive act," which can lead to imprisonment for an indefinite period (FR 23 July 1976).

Argentina: French Jurists Denounce the Aggravation of Repression

The state of law in Argentina has been degraded much faster than in Chile after the military coup d'état. The entire judiciary has been booted out, which the Chilean military had not dared to do. The Supreme Court judges have been replaced. The new judges took a loyalty oath to the new regime before taking up their functions. Military court martials take place in several parts of the country but in the greatest of secrecy. . . . No similar [to the albeit incomplete Chilean] list of prisoners can be obtained in Argentina. . . . (2) The situation in the prisons is grave. Torture . . . is common practice (LM 30 July 1976).

In Argentina there are now 25,000 political prisoners. . . . Nonetheless the names and the reasons and places of their detention is unknown (advertisement, LM 24–25 October 1976).

If required, in Argentina, all persons necessary so as to achieve the security of the country will have to die (Press Conference in Montevideo, Uruguay, during the XI Congress of Latin American Armed Forces, cited in Chossudovsky EPW 16 April 1977: 633).

Poised to claim power now is a group of extreme right-wing generals whose goals and methods are well expressed by their leader, Gen. Iberico Saint-Jean:

"First we will kill all the subversives; then we will kill their collaborators; then . . . their sympathizers; then . . . those who remain indifferent; and finally, we will kill those who are timid" (IHT 26 May 1977).

An active policy to reduce government involvement in the economy will have numerous and favorable implications . . . and more intense bargaining between labor and management to establish realistic and fair wage levels. . . . Another highlight of the Argentine economic situation is the new Foreign Investment Law, promulgated Aug. 13 [1976]. One of the most liberal laws of its kind in Latin America . . . it provides guarantees and incentives to attract foreign investors. . . . International organizations like the IMF, the World Bank, and the Inter-American Development Bank, as well as commercial banks in the United States, Western Europe and Japan, have carefully studied and evaluated the combination of economic policies of the new government. Organizations in both categories have praised the policies and their results in the most practical of ways, by granting loan guarantees to support the national plans (U.S. Department of Commerce, *Commerciel America* 31 January 1977: 8–9).

The economic and political program of the Argentine military government is examined in greater detail in Chapter 1.

Bolivia

Wages have never recovered from the 1972 devaluation, when most wage earners lost about 40 per cent of their purchasing power and have never made it up. The *campsino* sector was equally badly hit by the devaluation (LAPR February 1978: 34).

Investors Content as Military Imposes Stability in Bolivia
Vast Potential in Minerals

La Paz, March 15 (WP)—A U.S. banker here, asked if he thought Bolivia's military government would keep its promise to call elections in 1980, replied: "I hope to God not." For the first time since independence [in 1823], he said, Bolivia has stability and a favorable business climate that it never achieved while political parties were operating. Businessmen are happy in Bolivia, there is no question about it.

President Hugo Banzer Suarez, a tough army general who took power in a coup in 1971, now holds this century's record for permanence in office here. . . . Stability has been achieved at the cost of repressive police tactics, widespread arrest and torture and the exile of at least 5,000 persons, according to sources in the Roman Catholic

Church. Unions and political parties are silenced.... But there has been an undeniable change in attitude on the part of financiers since Mr. Banzer came to power. A total of $1.2 billion in foreign loans has entered Bolivia since 1971 from the International Development Bank, the World Bank, the U.S. Export-Import Bank, private consortia and individual governments (IHT 16 March 1977).

Bright Prospects

Bolivia's chances of obtaining the foreign capital necessary for its 5-year plan are good. Thanks to the political stability that has prevailed since 1971, the country received for the first time in a long while more financing offers in 1976 than it needed. Early in 1977 the World Bank's consultative group of industrial natioins recommended to its members that they participate in financing Bolivia's development projects to-talling $3.1 billion (Union Bank of Switzerland, *Business Cycle and Industry Studies,* October 1977).

Both the government and the United States ambassador in La Paz are worried about effects of democracy on the economy.... [U.S. Ambassador] Boeker and the government are in full agreement, however, on the threat posed by the reorganization of the labour movement, and the demand for general and considerable wage rises. Boeker foresaw a drastic reduction in private investment, perhaps even down to zero within two years, largely in response to the resurgence of the unions. David Balnco, the economy minister, returned from a recent trip to Washington with a similar message. He reported that IMF officials had told him that a general increase in wages of the levels being suggested would be "suicidal." ... The retention of the law of state security and a mass of other decrees is keeping the labour movement in check to some extent (LAPR 17 March 1978: 84–5).

Peru

Several sources revealed that U.S. Secretary of State Henry Kissinger during his February visit here had expressed sympathy with Peru's financial straits but indicated that aid would hinge on friendlier relations. "He said the time had come to stand up and be counted on one side or the other of the two-power world," according to an influential former official. ... There is a foreign debt of $3.7 billion, a balance-of-trade deficit of $1.2 billion. ... An all-out effort [is being made] to get foreign loans for the annual debt service payment. ... (IHT 4–5 September 1976).

Banks in U.S. Tie Loan to Peru to Economic Reforms

A group of U.S. commercial banks are on the verge of approving a new loan of $150 million to $200 million to the hardpressed government of Peru. The loan was contingent on the adoption of a drastic economic stabilization program.... Two weeks ago ... President Francisco Morales Bermudez dismissed the prominent leftists in his military government. While this was happening the president of the Peruvian central bank returned to New York to resume discussions on the loan. Last week the banks indicated they would grant credits from $150 million to $200 million. In addition private banks in Canada, Japan and Western Europe were expected to provide Peru with $100 million in credits (NYT 26 July 1976).

Revolution Derailed

Peru's revolution generated admiration beyond the Americas, even among those who in other circumstances would have deplored the harshness with which the generals silenced opposition or the slipshod manner in which many of the reforms were carried out. Peru replaced Castro's Cuba as a model for developing nations, and the generals relished their role as Third World leaders who had defied Uncle Sam. Those heady days are over.... Last month ... Gen. Francisco Morales Bermudez fired most of the remaining radicals in the Cabinet, including the Premier, Gen. Jorge Fernandez Maldonado.... To obtain new credits for more than $200 million, desperately needed to make repayments on a $3.7-billion foreign debt, Peru has accepted a surveillance over its economy by a group of private U.S. banks that would have been unthinkable in the chauvinistic phase of the revolution. Morales is having to pay the economic—and political—price for Velasco's excesses and for the failures of many reform programs. Only those immune to the ideals that inspired the revolution will rejoice at its derailment (*New York Times* editorial, IHT 5 August 1976).

Peru's New Regime Is Ending Era of Socialist Experiment

[The regime] is restoring private enterprise in much of the economy.... These liberalizing tendencies by the military dictatorship are taking shape under the stress of an economic crisis.... Repressive measures by security forces against leftist activities have been severe.... Private employers, as well as some state enterprises, such as the naval shipyards in Callao, have been dropping union delegate and labor representatives from company management boards (IHT 27 December 1976).

Choosing the annual executives' conference in Arequipa last week, President Francisco Morales Bermudez spelt out the changes the government is planning to make in labour legislation, in order to attract more private investment. The principal modification, in response to insistent demands from the Sociedad de Industrias (SI) and other business groups, involves the reduction in workers' shareholdings in their companies.... The President said that decision-making will remain in the hands of management, "where it belongs." . . . Further labour legislation changes, including the removal of job stability guarantees, are expected before the end of the year (LAER 3 December 1976: 185).

Under Martial Law Peru Shifted to the Right

Emergency and curfew, as well as a wave of arrests especially among labour unionists, peasant leaders, students, critical journalists and Latin American refugees, followed one day after the announcement of austerity measures and a 44 per cent devaluation of the Sol [Peruvian currency] relative to the dollar. The simultaneous announcement of price increases for all state controlled basic foodstuffs of 15 to 55 per cent, for gasoline of 115 per cent, for local public transport of 30 per cent, after there had already been a state decreed price increase of about 20 per cent in January, touched off general mobilization (FR 2 August 1976).

Revolution in Reverse Gear
The Peruvian Reform Course Is Over

The population has been made to feel in the past months that the "chilenization" of the economic policy—an austerity program, which makes the unemployment rate shoot up still higher and which cannot halt the increasing inflation—does not remain without internal political consequences. Leading representatives or followers of the "Peruvian revolution" were deported or escaped imprisonment through exile. . . . [Many are on] the black lists that are the guidelines of the nightly razzias. . . . (FR 5 January 1977).

The International Federation of the Rights of Man is worried about the repression against Labor Unionists (LM 11–12 April 1976).

Though the military government of General Morales Bermudes systematically reversed most of the reforms and dismantled the institutions of the previous government, it has not escaped foreign economic and political pressure. On the contrary, since 1976 Peru has passed through several external debt, balance-of-payment, internal austerity, and political crises. Perhaps more accurately, Peru is suffering from one continuing crisis, whose frequent high points are reported in the press. Some recent press headlines and reports about the development of the latest crisis are revealing:

Banks Tell Peru and Others to Improve Credit Ratings

Citibank might reconsider giving private loans if Peru comes to terms with the IMF (IHT 12 October 1977).

More emergency measures in Peru.

The economy minister announced the government's latest package of emergency measures on 13 January in an attempt to give some credibility to the 1978 budget. . . . Last year the International Monetary Fund (IMF) war demanding a reduction in the budgetary deficit (LAER 20 January 1978).

Peru and IMF [are] still at odds over austerity measures (LAER 10 March 1978).

Peru Misses IMF-Set Goals, Risks Defaulting on Its Debts

Without IMF approval, Peru's commercial creditors, including banks in the United States, Canada, Europe and Japan, have refused to refinance the more than $300 million they are owed this year. . . . Failure to resolve the situation could mean a cutoff of international financing. . . . More immediately, informed sources here said, it could result in the fall of the military government of Gen. Morales-Bermudez, and his replacement as President with a more hard-line military faction (IHT 14 March 1978).

Government under Fire as Peru Fails to Secure Loan

A top-secret memorandum to President Morales Bermudes from the navy high command . . . criticised the [central] bank for its inability to carry out the austerity programme and, by implication, the President himself for tolerating such incompetence. . . . The navy's recommendation was that the full austerity programme should be implemented without delay . . . overriding the objections within the cabinet (LAER 17 March 1978).

The IMF Plan contains the following demands: devaluation by 50 per cent, increase of gasoline prices, limitation of this year's wage increase to ten percent [while inflation is several times higher], sacrifice of most state subsidies, re-privatization of certain public enterprises, reduction of the public budget deficit, tax reform and friendly disposition towards foreign capital. The Junta has already acceded to some of these demands (FR 12 April 1978).

Peru Announces Austerity Plan (IHT 16 May 1978).

Peruvians Riot as Prices Rise (IHT 18 May 1978).

Regime Declares Martial Law in Peru
Price Increases Led to Violence

At least 12 persons died last week. . . . Police jailed hundreds of leftist labor leaders and cancelled television and radio broadcasts of political parties campaigning for next month's constitutional assembly elections, the first in 10 years. . . . There were rumors of a move to oust Mr. Morales (IHT 22 May 1978).

The elections were . . . postponed (FR 22 May 1978).

Sporadic street clashes between strikers and riot police, the occupation of several embassies and a hunger strike by more than 50 Left-wing leaders continued in the Peruvian capital this week. The Government of Gen. Francisco Morales Bermudez is also locked in battle with the main teachers' union, which has been on strike since June 4.

The stoppage, the biggest political challenge to Gen. Morales Bermudez this year, is in protest against the Government austerity programme and inflation, which has cut the real wage levels of some workers by two-thirds since 1975. General retail sales in Peru were down 21.7 per cent in the first half of this year and food sales dropped 22.9 per cent. . . .

The strike, by one of the largest unions in the country, has been collapsing, particularly in the capital, but tens of thousands of provincial teachers are still out. Rioting connected with the strike has already claimed three lives.

The stoppage has led to a momentary show of unity by the splintered Left, Sr. Jorte del Prado, leader of the Moscow line Peruvian Communist Party, is among several dozen leaders on hunger strike in the San Marcos university, while Sr. Hugo Blanco, the Trotskyite leader, is fasting at the Catholic university.

Supporters are worried about the health of Sr. Del Prado, who is 69.

Despite widespread popular sympathy for the strikers, the Government seems set on a fight to the finish. The Maoist Sutep leadership is not relaxing its wage claims, and demands for a closed shop in the state school sector.

Meanwhile, the Government has hailed the signature in New York on Wednesday of a $388.6m loan to the state oil company Petro Peru, led by Chase Manhattan, as signifying a new confidence by foreign bankers in the country. The loan is for five years at 1⅝ per cent over London inter-bank offered rate. Petro Peru, whose output has risen steeply this year, has been selling oil at up to $33 a barrel (FT 14 September 1979).

Ecuador

Ecuadorean Unions Suffer under the Military Boot

One of the least attractive aspects of the military government now drawing to a close has been its attitude to organised labour. It has imprisoned and persecuted union leaders, limited the right to strike, and carried out occasional acts of ferocious repression, the most notable of which was the massacre of sugar workers at Aztra last October. It has also encouraged divisions in the labour movement by lending its support to the most conservative elements in Ecuador's three young, labyrinthine and politically confused union confederations.

These policies have been highly successful. A spell in jail for José Chávez, the president of the Confederación Ecuatoriana de Organizaciones Sindicales Libres (CEOSL) for example, seems to have helped his conversion from militant supporter of labour unity to leader of a new breakaway party, the Partido Ecuatoriano del Pueblo (PEP) and electoral supporter of Liberal candidate Raúl Clemente Huerta.

The repression following last year's general strike has broken the spirit of Ecuador's workers. The prolonged detention of a few leaders, such as Manuel Antón Vélez, of the Unión Nacional de Educadores (UNE) has been enough to weaken the entire movement, while leaving the field open to the sectarianism and internal dissension that has always been a feature of Ecuadorean labour politics. The efforts to achieve unity that characterised the activities of the three *centrales* in recent years has now all but gone by the board (LAER 4 August 1978: 240).

Colombia

A "state of economic emergency" was decreed [in 1974] (CE November 1977).

Colombia Imposes Martial Law Rule (IHT 9 October 1976).

Violence in Bogotá Subsides; 15 Are Dead, 4,000 Arrested

Strike spurred riots. . . . President Alfonso Lopez Michelsen refused to yield to union demands for 50-per-cent pay increases to offset inflation running at 48 per cent a year. . . . Mr. Lopez Michelsen mobilized 100,000 police and army troops across Colombia (IHT 17–18 September 1977).

A repressive campaign by the Colombian armed forces against the principal urban guerrilla organization has produced widespread charges of violations of human rights and concern over the military's role in the country's democracy. . . . Many of those arrested have charged that they were tortured under questioning by military officers (IHT 21 March 1979).

Colombia Gives Military Wide Anti-Rebel Powers (IHT 23 May 1979).

Jamaica

"Democratic Socialist" Manley Cracks Down on the Workers

Prices rose and workers' living standards plummeted. Unemployment jumped to 30 per cent as thousands were laid off, including dock, construction, and tobacco workers. . . . The government created a special new post for supervising protest activity—minister of mobilization. . . . (ICP 13 March 1978: 306).

Jamaica's prime minister Mr. Michael Manley and his socialist government have so far withstood the hurricane of public protests which followed last week's increases of up to 30% in petrol and oil-product prices. Mr. Manley believes the riots are politically inspired, others that the higher oil prices were the last straw for a nation forced to live with horrendous inflation (35% a year according to the government but put at 50% by outsiders) and unemployment of 25% among the adult workforce.

The government claims it is hamstrung by the terms of the package agreed with the IMF last year. Jamaica was given a US$240m loan on condition that it cut consumption's share of gdp by an eighth in order to release resources for much-needed investment and increase production. Mr. Manley also agreed to devalue the Jamaican dollar progressively over 12 months by 43.6% and to hold wage increases within a 15% limit.

Bitter pills for a socialist prime minister to swallow (ECO 20 January 1979).

In January the net foreign debt over reserves of the government and private banking system stood at Jamaican $658m (£170.4m), a deficit that has tripled in two years. Unemployment is around 30 per cent of the population of working age and it is thought that only perhaps two school leavers out of five have a chance of finding a job today.

Wage rates are only about 55 per cent in real terms of what they were a year ago. In 1978 the national income per head fell 18.6 per cent to US$981. It probably fell by the same amount last year, when inflation was around the 20 per cent mark.

Until Tuesday of last week the International Monetary Fund, with which the government of Mr. Michael Manley had been negotiating since 1977, was pressing for further deflation and devaluation to cure the situation. But on that day Mr. Manley, bowing to pressure from his People's National Party (PNP), decided to halt negotiations for US$180m on the argument that the country could hardly do worse without the IMF than it could with it (FT 3 April 1980).

Mr. Edward Seaga, leader of the Opposition, has warned that the economic squeeze, and the prospect of even a temporary cessation of IMF assistance will lead to shortages of food and raw material, and widespread economic dislocation. The hope is that the IMF will agree to the waiver and spare the economy further hardship. A senior Central Bank official feels the fund will be lenient. . . .

Political scope for dealing with Jamaica's economic situation is limited. Mr. Michael Manley, the Prime Minister, recently reshuffled his Cabinet, dropping six Ministers in the hope that the smaller team could handle the crisis better. In spite of his decision to take on the important agriculture portfolio, detractors are sceptical about the value of the move and label it as the beginning of plans to campaign for the general election due next year (FT 3 January 1980).

The IMF was not so lenient, however, and Mr. Manley's government is almost certain to fall as a result of his inability to manage the crisis. The opposition leader, Mr. Seaga, has already declared that once in government, he will pursue the required political economic policy. One assessment of the Jamaican experience, with possible lessons for other countries, is the following:

> Pictures of Manley hugging Fidel Castro did not help and things became really bad when a spate of highly publicised violence deterred tourists for a couple of seasons. When Jamaica could no longer rate loans on the open market there was nothing for it but to call in the hard men from the IMF. Manley's hair shirt has been in place for five months now and the rhetoric has certainly cooled, but there is still no sign of investors returning. Left-wing members of the ruling People's National Party, and radicals such as Trevor Munroe of the Workers Liberation League, believe the IMF in terms are part of an American-inspired plot to discredit and bring down the Manley Government. . . .
>
> The real lesson of this sad state of affairs is that no country whose economic health relies on outside investment can afford to take off in a leftish direction or even to talk about doing so (NS 17 November 1978).

AMNESTY INTERNATIONAL REPORTS

The violations of human rights that result from the political-economic repression reviewed here are systematically investigated, catalogued, and reported by Amnesty International (AI) in its yearly general reports and in its occasional reports on specific countries and problems, such as torture. The organization has branches in many countries and seeks the release of and/or defends particular "prisoners of conscience," as it calls them. The preface to each report states that "Amnesty International acts on the basis of the Universal Declaration of Human Rights (adopted by the United Nations) and other international instruments. Amnesty International is a worldwide movement which is independent of any government, political grouping, ideology, economic interest or religious creed." In 1978 Amnesty International was awarded the Nobel Peace Prize for its work. To safeguard its independence, which it regards as necessary for its work, AI deliberately avoids direct references to the political and economic factors that precipitate violations of human rights, and concentrates instead on the violations themselves. The following excerpts from the *Amnesty International Report 1976* for the period 1 June 1975 to 31 May 1976 discuss conditions throughout *Asia*:

There are more political prisoners in Asia than in the rest of the world. . . . Far too many people are arrested to meet the supposed needs of governments to maintain national security. Far too many prisoners remain in detention because they are consigned to an administrative limbo from which it is difficult for them to be extricated. The massive need for a detention and interrogation apparatus induces governments to make use of military personnel and chains of command. These military men are prone to regard prisoners less as suspects and more as "enemy" with the result that there is dreadful violence in the treatment of prisoners. . . . It is not uncommon to find patterns of governmental and administrative laxity which lead to arrests of tens of thousands of people following some political incident. Many of those arrested are merely victims of circumstance. . . . The beating up of such "suspects" during interrogation is commonplace in most Asian countries. Increasingly, there is employment of "sophisticated" torture techniques, including application of electric shock and heating designed to leave no visible scars. . . .

The most unhappy example is *Indonesia,* where more than 55,000 prisoners, and perhaps as many as 100,000, are now in their 11th year of imprisonment. Denial of justice of this kind is common throughout Asia. . . . [Since] the imposition of a national state of emergency in *India* in June 1975 . . . at least 40,000 people are estimated to be detained without trial for political reasons under the emergency regulations. [Other estimates are as high as 180,000—A.G.F.]. . . . Presidential decrees in the *Republic of Korea* and in *The Philippines* actually removed constitutional safe-guards. Emergency regulations, preventative detention laws, special ordinances relating to international security, constitute serious erosions of human rights in *India, Pakistan, Malaysia* and*Singapore*. . . . In soe Asian countries, especially in the *Republic of Korea,* torture can be said to be employed systematically in order to intimidate. . . . Where prisoners are tried—and these form a minute proportion of the total prisoner population—[it is] before special tribunals, often consisting of military officers, as in *The Philippines* and the *Republic of Korea*. . . . The procedures in military courts in *The Philippines* are those of court martial, even though the military courts administering martial law are not supposed to be trying military men. . . .(Amnesty International 1976: 117–119).

On the *Middle East,* the same report has this to say:

The greatest obstacle . . . is still the lack of reliable and detailed information. This is particularly true for those countries, such as *Iran* and *Iraq*, where the human rights situation gives the greatest cause for concern, and to a somewhat lesser extent, for *Oman, Syria* and *Libya*. . . . Repressive systems have intimidated the population. . . . There has been an identifiable increase in repression of opposition within Iran and an extension of the activities of SAVAK (Iranian National Intelligence and Security Organization) to countries in which Iranians are living abroad, in an attempt to prevent criticism of the Iranian regime. The exact number of political prisoners in Iran is not known, but AI believes it to be several thousands. Other sources have given approximate numbers which range from 25,000 to 100,000. . . . The torture of political prisoners . . . appears to be routine practice (Amnesty International 1976: 179–83).

Amnesty International has repeatedly documented the repression by racist regimes in South Africa, Namibia (South-West Africa), and Zimbabwe (Rhodesia before independence) and noted repressive consequences of war in Angola and the Western Sahara, as well as conditions in Mozambique after its liberation. The organization observed that in *Africa* "the level of political violence in some independent states seems to be increasing" (Amnesty International 1976: 53). In its general review of the continent AI recorded violations of human rights grouped under the following categories:

1. Attempted or successful coups and assassinations.
2. Detention/imprisonment for political reasons.
3. Political trials.
4. Execution, deaths of people in detention, atrocities, mistreatment, often including torture.

It noted the existence of these four categories of violations throughout the African continent:

Algeria	3,4	Morocco	4
Benin	1,2,3,4	Niger	1,3
Central African Republic	1,2,3,4	Nigeria	1,4
Chad	4	Senegal	3
Congo	2	Sierra Leone	4
Ethiopia	2,3,4	Sudan	1,3,4
Equatorial Guinea	4	Tanzania	2
Ghana	1,4	Tunisia	2,3,4
Guinea	4	Uganda	4
Kenya	4	Zaire	1,3,4
Malawi	2,4	Zambia	2,4

(Amnesty International 1976: 53–54)

The report observed, for instance, that "faced with mounting economic and political difficulties . . . Zambia invoked full emergency powers on 28 January 1976. It was widely regarded as an attempt to stifle internal criticism. . . . The situation in Tunisia during the period 1975–76 has been marked by new student unrest and, an increasing repressive attitude by the authorities towards young leftwing dissidents" (Amnesty International 1976: 82, 80).

In its consideration of Latin America, the AI report declared:

> Throughout 1975–76 there has been a slight but unmistakable deterioration in the overall human rights' situation in the Americas, particularly in the *cono sur* (southern cone) countries of Latin America. . . . *Chile, Argentina, Brazil* and *Uruguay* . . . contain the heaviest concentration of political prisoners in Latin America. Approximately 30,000 political prisoners are believed held in these four countries alone. . . .
>
> In *Uruguay*, with a population of only 2½ million, one out of every 500 persons is a political prisoner—the highest ratio in the Americas. . . . Furthermore, all four countries have the highest socio-economic and cultural standard in Latin America. Whereas less developed countries such as *Paraguay, Nicaragua* and *Haiti*, with stable autocratic regimes, had the highest number of political prisoners more than 10 years ago, today the reverse is true. It is notable that in the richer countries, repression is characterized by a systematic and well organized apparatus which has at its disposal advanced technology and highly sophisticated equipment. . . .
>
> Figures for the number of political prisoners are misleading if they fail to take into consideration political assassinations. This particularly Latin American pattern of political repression is especially prevalent in *Guatemala* and *Argentina*. . . . In *Brazil* at least, death squads extend their work to executing petty criminals and tramps: statistics for those killed in this category are understandably incomplete. An important secondary motive for political assassinations is the creation of a climate of fear and uncertainty to discourage any form of opposition to the ruling élite. Therefore, the methods of assassination are deliberately shocking: often the victim has been tortured first. . . . There is strong evidence to suggest that in some countries these activities are condoned if not encouraged by the authorities. . . . Throughout 1975, the number of abductions and assassinations attributable to groups like the AAA (*Alianza Anti-Comunista Argentina*—Argentinian Anti-Communist Alliance) dramatically increased, and in August 1975 Amnesty International prepared a survey of 461 murders that occurred in the period between July 1974 and June 1975. In all cases some political motive could be identified. . . . A new and disturbing feature of the retaliatory activities of the AAA had been the extermination of whole families. . . . There is strong evidence to suggest that highly placed officials have condoned or actively supported rightwing acts of terrorism. . . . Torture is allegedly a routine practice in many local police and military headquarters throughout the country (Amnesty International 1976: 83–86).

One year later the preface of the Amnesty International Report for 1977 noted:

> As many as 116 countries are mentioned in this publication. In most of them serious violations of human rights have been reported. And yet this survey is far from complete.
>
> It is not only the number of countries where violations have occurred which is alarming. The positive elements in this report are few: there have been substantial releases of political prisoners in certain countries but these are outweighed by deteriorating situations in other parts of the world.
>
> In some Latin American countries security forces and para-military groups have been used as instruments for a policy of political murder. There, and in other parts of the world, the system of justice no longer functions in practice. Emergency laws have been misused to legalize brutal repression—even when by objective standards there are no emergencies.
>
> Government-sanctioned torture is still practised in a horrifying number of states, in spite of the newly adopted United Nations declaration against all forms of torture. Several regimes have introduced the death penalty for new crimes and the rate of execution is still high, especially in Africa and Asia. Some governments still retain corporal punishment such as flogging or cutting off hands.
>
> In many countries, especially in Asia, a system of long-term detention has been developing. Prisoners are kept in poor prison conditions year after year and the authorities do not grant them the basic right to a trial. Strictly speaking, this means that innocent people are deprived of their freedom for five years, 10 years or even more. In other countries where political trials have taken place the defendants have been denied the opportunity for a proper defence. The laws themselves have in some cases constituted appalling violations of the Universal Declaration of Human Rights, making a mockery of justice. The trial procedures have been such that they could only serve the interest of the rulers. . . .
>
> The techniques of repression and the impact of these techniques vary. There are differences not only in number of victims, but also in methodology, objectives, duration and both short-term and long-term consequences. In some countries regimes allow para-military groups to kidnap, torture and assassinate political activists; in others prisoners are kept in detention for years without trial. In some police stations torture is carried out with electric shocks; in others with psychological methods. In some prisons the inmates are refused all communication with their families; in others they are starved. There is absolutely no point in trying to judge which measures are categorically "better" or "worse" than others (Amnesty International 1977: 9–10).

Amnesty International Reports 1978 mentions no less than 111 countries. . . . The Report does give a depressing picture of systematic violation of basic human rights in most countries of the world. People are imprisoned because of their opinions, prisoners are tortured and even executed. . . . [T]here are new trends in repression. . . . In some Latin American and African countries terrorist acts have been given authorization by governments. Kidnapping, torture and killing have been developed into a systematic method of wiping out the opposition. Para-military groups or security forces have acted as death squads in Argentina, Chile and Guatemala. . . . In several Asian countries the rulers make use of emergency laws to "legalize" the preventive detention of political opponents: by this technique, governments detain people without trial for long periods. Other régimes make arrests and take years to prepare a trial, if they ever do so. Examples are Singapore, Malaysia, Brunei, Indonesia and the Philippines. Besides these new tendencies, old-type violations continue in many countries. . . . This *Report* gives a horrifying account of how the leaders of too many nations condone or instigate terrorist methods against their own citizens (Amnesty International 1978: 3–4).

U.S. GOVERNMENT REPORTS

The United States Department of State has reviewed the violation of human rights around the world, though it omits to mention the political-economic reasons for these violations, which frequently occur under governments supported by the United States:

Human Rights Abuses around World Cited in U.S. Report

The State Department has told Congress in reports on human rights in 105 countries that, despite some improvements in 1977, repression and abuse of individual liberties are still widespread in most parts of the world. The reports, made public yesterday, accuse governments of several nations closely allied to the United States—among them Iran, South Korea, the Philippines and Morocco—of allegedly violating the rights of their citizens.

The Middle East and South Asia: Israel's tactics in the occupied lands are found to include "the use of extreme physical and psychological pressures during interrogation," using excessive force to quell demonstrations, searching the homes of Arabs without warrants and occasionally expelling Arabs suspected of terrorist involvement. Elsewhere in the region, the reports cite evidence of repression and allegations of mistreatment in Morocco, Iran, Syria, Pakistan, and Bangladesh. . . .

East Asia and the Pacific: The Philippines . . . is charged with torturing political prisoners and of engaging in extensive corruption. Similarly South Korea . . . Indonesia, Malaysia, and Singapore. Conditions in Thailand are described as improved despite the continuing authoritarian nature of the military regime there.

Africa: The report finds a general pattern throughout the continent of one-party states or military dictatorships where severe restrictions are placed on political activity and expression. This, the report finds, leads to frequent abuses. . . .

Latin America: Allegations of widespread abuse, sometimes involving murder and torture, continue against such military dictatorships as Bolivia, Paraguay, Nicaragua, El Salvador, Guatemala, Uruguay and Haiti. . . .

Several countries that have figured prominently in rights controversies . . . are not described because they do not receive U.S. aid (IHT 11–12 February 1978).

Despite a 1976 law requiring that the government here [in Washington] consider such abuses as damaging a country's qualifications for receiving U.S. military aid, only Nicaragua has been marked for a major cutback in military assistance under the Carter administration's 1979 foreign-aid budget (IHT 8 February 1978).

The correlation between repressive "socio-political measures and investment climate" in the Third World is documented from a Japanese point of view in a "risk table" (Table 6.1) published in *Nikkei Business,* Japan's leading business magazine. The table was analyzed as follows:

The first variable, market size, is derived from per capita national income and population size; the second, economic environment, is a composite index of such statistics as gross national product growth, inflation rate, trade balance, foreign reserves and external debt burden.

The last index, socio-political and investment climate, is derived from an assessment for each country of political stability, policies towards foreign capital and the exchange rate, foreign policy lines and feelings towards the Japanese.

When the variables are measured for each country, the three figures are added for risk evaluation (FER 18 March 1977).

Finally, to substantiate some of the economic reasons for repression again, we may refer to a document prepared by the staff of the Senate Foreign Relations Committee. This document is cited more extensively in another context in Chapter 4, but a part of it may be quoted here:

Through close cooperation between the private banks and the IMF, pressure is exerted on countries who have debts because of deficits to balance their external accounts through internal austerity measures. . . . Countries may also be stimulated to create a favorable climate for foreign investment and for the private sector in general. The problem

TABLE 6.1
Overseas Investment: Assessing the Risks

	Market Size	Economic Environment	Socio-political and Investment Climate	Risk Rating
West Germany	58	71	94	AAA
United States	74	49	95	AAA
Canada	50	45	91	AA
Australia	48	50	83	AA
Sweden	35	53	90	AA
Netherlands	38	50	90	AA
Saudi Arabia	18	71	83	AA
Belgium	28	46	94	A
Iran	15	61	82	A
Spain	21	40	83	A
Britain	30	24	87	A
New Zealand	13	42	83	A
Italy	24	34	78	A
Singapore	7	41	80	BBB
Portugal	8	41	79	BBB
Brazil	13	30	77	BBB
Mexico	11	31	76	BBB
Malaysia	6	37	64	BBB
Indonesia	2	39	65	BBB
Philippines	3	33	68	BBB
Argentina	17	12	70	BB
Chile	5	11	79	BB
Kenya	1	22	72	BB
Pakistan	2	29	63	BB
South Korea	5	33	54	BB
Peru	4	27	60	BB
Thailand	3	34	54	BB
Egypt	2	39	30	BB
India	2	24	23	B

with these measures is that . . . they can also lead to greater unemployment, to the reduction of social welfare, and to a lower standard of living for the people. . . . The government decision to impose a program of strict economic austerity can create social and political disturbances. . . . Finally, as we have shown, in many countries there seems to be a direct correlation between economic difficulties and political repression. . . . Creditor demands to implant drastic economic austerity programs . . . could only be imposed at the expense of civil liberties in the countries that adopt them (U.S. Senate 1977: 1379–80).

Chapter 7
Economic Crisis and the State in the Third World

The present worldwide economic crisis requires the reorganization of the state in the Third World to serve as the political nexus of its economy's changing role in the international division of labor. This reorganization of the Third World state was foreshadowed by studies such as the Rockefeller Commission's *Report on the Americas*. It involves the reorientation of state expenditures in the present interest of national and international capital, the institutionalization of political repression, and often the militarization of society. These measures have been widely defended in the name of a doctrine of national security. The recent liberalization of some regimes is not necessarily a sign of reversion to parliamentary democracy. More likely this liberalization and the return to elections in some countries of the Third World represent an attempt to forge what the United States government has called "viable democracies": that is, governments capable of institutionalizing the new model of export-led growth while at the same time preventing popular discontent from interfering unduly with domestic political stability and the international economic role of the Third World.

Engels' and Lenin's thesis that the bourgeois state is first and foremost an instrument of the bourgeoisie to provide and assure the conditions for its exploitation of labor is particularly observable in the Third World. There the state intervenes more directly and visibly in the organization of the economic, social, cultural—in a word, political—process than in the developed capitalist countries. Moreover, as in the latter, the state is an essential and active nexus between the national and the world economy. However, in the dependent economies of the Third World the dependent state is also an essential instrument for the administration of the dependent role of the Third World economies in the international division of labor and the capitalist world process of capital accumulation. Increasingly also, the Third World state mediates between its national capital—and labor—and international capital; and as a dependent state it does so substantially to the benefit of international capital at the relative cost to national capital and at the absolute sacrifice of local labor. The exigencies of the process of capital accumulation and the international division of labor, worldwide and in the underdeveloped countries themselves, thus become the principal determinants of the role and the form of the state in the Third World (as well as elsewhere in the capitalist world).

The Dependent Third World State

Progressive and Marxist empirical and theoretical studies of the state have revived only recently. C. Wright Mills (1956) and William Domhoff (1967) gave them an impulse with their analysis of *The Power Elite* and *Who Rules America?* in the United States. In Europe Ralph Miliband (1969, 1973) made an institutional analysis of *The State in Capitalist Society* and Nicos Póulantzas (1968, 1973) countered with an instrumentalist study of the state as the instrument of the bourgeoisie under the title *Political Power and Social Classes.* Each criticized the limitations of the other in a long debate in the pages of *New Left Review* (1969–1973). Both, in turn, have been criticized by Holloway and Picciotto (1977), Laclau (1977), and others: the approach of Miliband is too general, and that of Poulantzas, who followed his mentor Louis Althusser, is too abstract to permit ready application to the concrete analysis of particular states at particular places and times in the class struggle. Many of their critics, however, have also failed in their efforts to steer a suitable course between the Scylla of heroic theoretical assumptions about the instrumentality or autonomy of the state with regard to a class or its sectors, and the Charybdis of rank descriptive empiricism.

Robin Murray apparently tries to combine both approaches when he writes under the title "The Structural Role of the State as an Economic Instrument in Capitalism":

> I will distinguish six economic *res publica,* or state functions. 1. The guaranteeing of property rights . . . backed by the forces of law: the police and armed forces. . . . 2. Economic liberalisation . . . the abolition of restrictions on the movement of goods, money or people within the territorial area and the standardisation of currency, economic law, weights and measures and so on. . . . 3. Economic orchestration . . . includes the regulation of business cycles and economic planning. . . . 4. Input provision. . . . Labour . . . the existence of a proletariat . . . training the proletariat . . . control of wages of a proletariat. . . . Land. A market for land has been required. . . . Capital . . . [and its] supply of finance to industry. . . . Technology . . . to finance over half of all R + D. . . . Economic infrastructure, particularly energy and communications . . . [and] cheap, secure supplies of these services. . . . General

manufacturing inputs.... 5. Intervention for social consensus... to
mollify the most manifest disruptive effects on and exploitation of noncapitalist classes.... 6. The management of the external relations...
[including the] aggressive... support of the state's own capitalists...
defending quasi-monopolistic positions established by domestic capitalists.... The instruments used in the performance of these functions are: (i) military power... (ii) aid... (iii) commercial sanctions
... (iv) financial sanctions... (v) government controls... co-ordinat-
ing or orchestrating domestic/foreign economic relations in the form of
supervising the Balance of Payments.

Five further functions suggest themselves... securing demand in
the form of mass purchases from the private sector... the state as a
taxation authority... as enforcer and protector of particular monopolies... of first aid to ailing sectors and firms... the state as absorber of
surplus (Murray 1975: 64–74).

Murray drew up this list of functions with imperialist states in mind. We shall
see that dependent Third World states also perform these functions in greater
or lesser measure. Nonetheless, this structural/instrumental approach to the
study of the state does not tell us when the state changes to perform some of
these functions differently, and why it undertakes such changes at particular
times and places.

These limitations in the political-economic study of the state in capitalist
society are even more evident when it comes to the study of states in the
Third World, with their different historical, technological, economic, social,
cultural, and therefore political development. The common dependence of
the Third World countries (in various forms) has also hindered the analysis
of the state in the Third World. In his critique of some of the analyses cited
below Colin Leys (1976: 43) admonished that "in order to understand the
significance of any state for the class struggle we must start out from the class
struggle, not the state." His point is well taken, but it offers no ready means of
analysis as long as the classes and their sectors are not readily identifiable,
and as long as their struggle takes place within the broadened context of a
dependent economy, society, and state. The composition and the behavior of
the classes and their struggle to control and transform the state are influenced
by their dependent participation in the process of capital accumulation and
their role in the international division of labor. Thus the limitations of
received theory and the constraints of changing reality necessarily affect any
examination of the position and function of the state in the Third World
during the contemporary crisis of capital accumulation.

Ruy Mauro Marini (1977b: 76) suggests that, "due to a general law of
capitalist society, according to which the relative autonomy of the state is in
inverse relation to the capacity of the bourgeoisie to exercise its class
domination... a strong capitalist state is always the counterpart of a weak
bourgeoisie." Accordingly, Marini argues that one of the characteristics of

dependent societies is the considerable degree of autonomy of their states. But autonomy from whom? From the nonruling classes, since the weaker the ruling classes, the more they need a "strong" state to rule over the nonruling classes. Or perhaps autonomy from particular ruling classes, if there are more than one, or from particular sectors or members of the ruling class; since if their weakness is a result of disunity in their class struggle against the nonruling classes, a temporarily autonomous "Bonapartist" state can manage the affairs of the bourgeoisie during a transitional emergency period. Autonomy from the bourgeoisie itself? That is more questionable, since the bourgeois state and the state bourgeoisie, and indeed the bourgeoisie as a whole, tend to become intertwined. This is particularly true if there is no nonstate bourgeoisie, or if what there is of it has little more than the state at its disposal in order to rule and to extract surplus value from those ruled.

But insofar as Marini's dictum does stand up, it is applicable in the dependent societies to the inverse relation between the strength of the metropolitan or imperialist bourgeoisie and the weakness and consequent lack of autonomy of the dependent state in the Third World. The Third World state may be strong and autonomous vis-à-vis its local bourgeoisie, but it is largely an instrument (and, as we will observe, often the creation) of the imperialist bourgeoisie of the metropolis. Indeed this dependent, and in this sense *weak*, character of the Third World state—dependent financially, technologically, institutionally, ideologically, militarily, in a word politically, on the international bourgeoisie(s) its metropolitan states—may be regarded as its fundamental characteristic. In her analysis of Nigeria Terisa Turner (1976: 64) suggests that "foreign and local businessmen and state officials form a triangle." The imperialist bourgeoisie(s) and its members and states bargain with the local bourgeoisie and its members or sectors through (literally) the good offices and mediation of the Third World state and its officials (who generally receive a private fee, as the Lockhead "scandals" have publicized worldwide). It may be the case, as Marini (1977b: 77) argues with respect to Brazil, that the very weakness of the local bourgeoisie relative to the imperialist one leads it to try to strengthen its bargaining hand by strengthening its "own" national state, in the process making the state more "autonomous" from the bourgeoisie. But experience has shown, as Marini's own analysis should suggest, that the power of the two bourgeois corners of the triangle are very unequal, and that in this economic, political, and military poker game the imperialist forces always have a much stronger and longer suit than the local bourgeoisie. Moreover, imperialism always has some immediate and/or potential aces in the hole in the form of a bourgeois "fifth column" within the local bourgeoisie, and more often than not a military column within the Third World state itself. The economic interests and political actions of these imperialist fifth columns within the Third World bourgeoisie and state are tied to the long-run strategic designs and often to the immediate tactical ends of the imperialist bourgeoisie.

Therefore, in this intraclass conflict between the foreign and the local bourgeoisie or its sectors and members, the state in the Third World is far more an instrument of foreign than of local capital. Someone who was in a position to know, the first Prime Minister of India, Jawaharlal Nehru (1960:221 ff.), referred to the "quisling classes" with vested interests in foreign rule that Britain had organized to divide and rule India. And he observed that "imperialism must function in this way or else it ceases to be imperialism." Nehru (1960: 243) regarded this policy as "natural and understandable . . . and it is a little naive to be surprised at this, harmful from the Indian nationalist point of view though it was." But if Nehru was right about the past, his nationalist point of view is now also a little naive. The development of the post-colonial state in India under Nehru's own administration demonstrated how naive it is to suppose that the state could serve the interests of a local, but hardly nationalist, bourgeoisie more than the interests of imperialism. And if this reality was so oppressive in Nehru's India, it is all the more so today when much smaller and weaker Third World bourgeoisies are much more integrated into and dependent on the imperialist system, not least through the neo-colonial state itself. In this connection, the recent development of the state in the Third World has been analyzed as follows:

> The state in the periphery has the function again to remove economically as far as possible the political border between the world market and the national economic area that this same state brings into existence. . . . The external economic relations are a part of the basic function of the peripheral capitalist state . . . assuring the existence and expansion of the world market in the area of the peripheral capitalist economy (Evers 1975: 84).

The State in Asia, Africa, and Latin America

In an influential essay on "The State in Postcolonial Societies: Pakistan and Bangladesh," in which he also refers to India, Indonesia, and some other countries in Asia, Hamza Alavi (1972, 1973) argues:

> The essential problem of the state in postcolonial societies stems from the fact that it is not established by an ascendant native bourgeoisie but, rather, by a foreign imperialist bourgeoisie. At independence, however, direct command of the latter over the colonial state is ended; yet, by the same token, its influence over the state is by no means brought to an end. The metropolitan bourgeoisie, now joined by other neocolonial bourgeoisies, is present in the postcolonial society. . . . The central proposition I wish to emphasize is that the state in the postcolonial society is not the instrument of a single class. It is relatively autonomous and it mediates the competing interests of the three propertied classes— the metropolitan bourgeoisie, the indigenous bourgeoisie, and the landed classes—while at the same time acting on behalf of all of them in order to preserve the social order in which their interests are embedded,

namely, the institution of private property and the capitalist mode as the dominant mode of production (Alavi 1973: 148).

Looking primarily at some of these Asian states, Alavi (1973: 147) suggests that the ruling classes inherit an "overdeveloped state apparatus and its institutional practices" through which the colonial power had ruled over them and other populations. After independence, the overdeveloped state super-structure is at the disposal of the relatively underdeveloped ruling classes, with regard to whom the state apparatus assumes a certain degree of autonomy—while maintaining a large degree of dependence on the im-perialist powers. However accurately this analysis may fit the major post-colonial states of Asia, it must be amended for the neocolonial states in some parts of East Asia, like South Korea, Taiwan, Thailand, and perhaps the Philippines and Singapore. These neocolonial states were constructed or reconstructed under post–World War II American suzerainty. They are perhaps not overdeveloped in Alavi's sense; and their relative autonomy, where it exists, may be rather more due to the initial strength of the indigenous bourgeoisie, and to the simultaneous nurture of a neocolonial bourgeoisie and the construction of a neocolonial state under American economic, political, and military tutelage (a policy in which Japan sub-sequently played an associated role, particularly in South Korea).

The state in Africa has recently been the subject of attention and analysis in several issues of the *Review of African Political Economy* (RAPE No. 5, 1976, and No. 8, 1977) and elsewhere. Colin Leys (1976), John Saul 1976), Steven Langdon (1977) and others argue that Alavi's thesis of the over-developed postcolonial state does not apply in much of Africa, where in many places the colonial power did not leave behind much of a state apparatus and even less of an indigenous bourgeoisie to take it over. These writers and others (Shivji 1976) disagree among themselves about the relation of the state, or particular states, in Africa to the indigenous classes and their composition. But all of them (except Nicola Swainson, 1977, writing about Kenya, and Paul Kennedy, 1977, on Ghana) agree that the states in just about all the newly independent countries of sub-Saharan Africa (but not considering those that were Portuguese colonies) are first and foremost the instruments of imperialism or neocolonialism and that "there can be little doubt that the *dominant* class is still the foreign bourgeoisie" (Langdon 1977: 91, who gives his own emphasis to a quote from Leys 1976). "It is not an *independent* bourgeoisie emerging in Kenya and itself managing the state apparatus; . . . rather . . . the Kenyan state has a rather subtle and sophisticated role which it is playing rather well; that role is to regulate, extend and defend a growing MNC-state-domestic bourgeois symbiosis in the country" (Langdon 1977: 96; MNC refers to multinational corporation; emphasis in the original). An additional role of the state in Africa is "that of managing the meshing of capitalist and pre-capitalist modes of production" (Langdon 1977: 92) in such a way—or more accurately, manifold ways—as to increasingly couple village society and the production and extraction of economic surplus through "so-called primitive" or "permanent primitive" (Bartra 1974) or "primary" accumulation (Frank 1977a, 1978a) through

"noncapitalist" relations of production to the national and international process of capital accumulation (as analyzed by Rey 1971; by Meillassoux 1975, particularly on the basis of francophone countries; by Mamdani 1976 for Uganda; and by Campbell 1977 for the "commandist" state in Uganda). Thus, "the institutional apparatus of the state has a significant impact on class relations between domestic and foreign bourgeoisie, meshing together domestic and international capital as it meshes together capitalist and noncapitalist modes of production. . . . The state is successfully shuffling prominent Africans into the dominant regulated economy as MNC partners, executives, and even competitors" (Langdon 1977: 97, 96). But foreign capital always holds the long suit and all the aces.

Of course, there are also important differences in class structures and state formations among African countries, which range from outright neocolonial states with *comprador* and productive bourgeoisie like Nigeria, Kenya, and Ivory Coast; bureaucratic bourgeois states staffed by people of petit bourgeois extraction and personified by Emperor Bokassa in the Central African Empire or Idi Amin in Uganda; to "progressive" states like Tanzania in which socialist-minded intellectuals have some influence, but where, according to President Julius Nyerere (IHT 21 April 1977), the goal of socialism is not even in sight. Indeed, according to Shivji (1976), von Freyhold (1977), and others, the supposed goal of socialism is continually receding out of sight of the class forces that manage a weak state, whose weakness consists precisely in its inability to counteract the dependence on imperialism. Even in Nigeria, which is by far the largest country in Africa with the biggest economy and now the highest state revenues and private incomes derived from oil exports at OPEC prices, the state is essentially an instrument of foreign capital interested in maintaining a politically stable outflow of oil and inflow of imports (turmer 1976).

But since many of the states and the local bourgeoisies in Africa are more postcolonial than ex-colonial, the equilibrium between the imperialist forces and the local pretenders for associate status or junior partnership has not yet been stabilized. And inasmuch as state power is *the* source of collective and personal enrichment in Africa, precisely because of the state's crucial triangulation or mediation with imperialist capital, competition for state power in the local corner of the triangle is fierce and violent. More often than not this competition relies on military power as the decisive factor in determining who will use the armed forces and the state to oppress and exploit the masses of the African working population in association with imperialism.

In most of Latin America the formation of postcolonial states began a century and a half ago (Kaplan 1969; Halperin Donghi 1969, 1972; Frank

1972a: Chapter 4; Córdova 1977). This conflictive history and the resulting unstable states in Latin America have sometimes been considered a possible or even inevitable model for Africa today. In a previous book (Frank 1978b) I suggested that the one-to-two-generation-long conflicts over who would form and control the state in Latin America was a sort of luxury Latin Americans could afford so long as their economies were relatively unintegrated into the world economy. This was the case beginning with the economic "Kondratieff" downswing of 1816–1849 when British metropolitan power concentrated its economic and political attention on its Indian colony and on the provision of cotton for its new industries by Egypt and the U.S. South. But perhaps the causation was also the other way around: perhaps Britain and Europe showed relatively little economic and political interest in Latin America (except in Brazil, which inherited an undamaged colonial state) precisely because Latin America lacked states that were strong and stable enough to organize economic activity and to serve as efficient intermediaries in the metropolis-local interest-neocolonial state triangle. In India Britain used direct colonial power to organize a state to serve its interests. In Latin America it lacked the power to do this. It can be argued that the metropolitan economies delayed the incorporation of some regions and peoples in Africa into the world capitalist economy in the nineteenth century, and still do today, precisely for want of local state institutions strong and stable enough to play this intermediary organizing role. Such local state institutions are necessary to mediate between the international or metropolitan economy and the local social formations, some of which are still regarded as precapitalist.

The richer the reserves of raw materials, such as copper and particularly petroleum, and the more attractive the potential market, the greater the effort and the sooner the success in forming and stabilizing a dependent neocolonial state that economically organizes and politically guarantees metropolitan access to these resources and markets. In Latin America these states were finally formed under local "liberal reform" auspices where and when in the classical imperialist period particular raw materials—or in the case of Panama and Nicaragua potential interoceanic canal routes—became economically important (Frank 1972a: Chapter 5). The state still fulfills this role throughout Latin America, almost exclusively so in some "banana republics" (although this denomination has become outmoded). In some countries, including Chile, Peru, Argentina, and Uruguay, the state is again being called upon to intervene to promote the export of raw materials. In the middle third of the twentieth century the state was equally implicated in stimulating and supervising the process of import substitution of industrial products and in organizing regional economic integration. Organizations founded for purposes of economic integration include the Andean Pact and the Central American Common Market, both of which serve less to protect the regional market than to expand and integrate it more effectively into the world market. So the state in Latin America has always responded to—or more accurately resulted from—the exigencies of the uneven and unequal process of world capitalist accumulation of capital and the struggle between and within classes in Latin America to participate in one way or another in this process of accumulation through the international division of labor. The exigencies of world capital accumulation during the contemporary crisis (which vigorously promote export substitution and export promotion) and the class struggle in Latin America about how to participate in this process determine the role and define the character of the state in Latin America today.

The contemporary restructuring of the state in Latin America, and particularly the cruel manifestations of the many new military state regimes, have generated widespread public, intense political, and a new serious scientific interest in the present role and character of the state in Latin America. Few still confuse the new institutional and perhaps corporativist military regimes with the individual *caudillo* military dictators of sorry banana republic fame, of whom hardly any survive. The authoritarian character of the new military regimes is universally recognized, even by their spokesmen and leaders. General Pinochet in Chile likes to call his regime an "authoritarian democracy," which is a rather ludicrous contradiction in terms. Opponents, of course, refer simply to dictatorships or military dictatorships. Others speak of military states, where the armed forces are most visibly in control; of technocratic states, where supposedly "unpolitical" technical cadres occupy most important cabinet and executive positions; or of military-technocratic states, where these features are fused through the technical training of military officers as in Peru and/or through the appointment of "technocrats," such as the team of "Chicago boys" in Chile, to executive positions by the military regime. Political-economic analysis of the economic role and the class character (that is, the class interests that these states and regimes serve rather than the much less important social extraction of their leading personnel) of the regimes in Brazil and the southern cone of South America has led to their denomination as financial-monopoly bourgeois and/or military dictatorships. Such regimes represent and execute the interests of the financial and monopoly bourgeoisie and its association with foreign capital and the world market over, and even against, the interests of local capital tied to the national market.

These state forms have also increasingly been called "fascist," "neo-fascist," or "dependent fascist" (Briones 1975a,b, 1976, 1977; Vuscovic 1978a, b; dos Santos 1977a; Guevara 1977a, b). This terminology may have some justification for the legitimate propagandistic denunciation of authoritarian regimes. But its use is often tied to a political policy of questionable promise, associated primarily with the Communist parties and their immediate allies, which seek to overthrow these regimes through a "democratic," "anti-fascist," pluri-class alliance and to restore "democratic" regimes that would pursue popular national economic policies. Such popular policies—as our analysis elsewhere suggests—are not compatible with the exigencies of world capitalist accumulation at this time. (Among significant

Latin American political personalities and groups, Pedro Vuscovic of the Coordinadora wing of the Chilean Socialist Party and to a lesser extent Roberto Guevara of the Argentina Revolutionary Workers Party [PRT/ERP] are exceptions in that they do explicitly recognize the differences between classical fascist regimes and contemporary Latin American ones and they do reject the political policy of restoring the previous "bourgeois democratic" or even less democratic regimes. Nonetheless they use and defend the terminology derived from "fascism" to refer to present-day regimes and states in Latin America.) Recourse to the term *fascist* for these state forms must be subject to serious reservations after comparison with the major classical examples of fascism in Germany and Italy. These new regimes, far from being nationalist-expansive and mass mobilizing with petit bourgeois support, are internationalist-dependent and necessarily mass suppressive. These dependent and suppressive regimes are outgrowths of the alliance between international capital with limited sectors of the local (antinational) monopoly bourgeoisie (where it exists) or with the bureaucratic and military (petite) bourgeoisie, or a combination of both.

> Contrary to fascism, military dictatorship will not have any margin of flexibility in regard to mass mobilization. Fascism came to power in Germany and Italy when the working class had already been defeated. In Chile, Brazil, Uruguay, Bolivia or Argentina, the task of defeating the labor movement and the workers as a whole is left to the military dictatorship at the cost of foreclosing for it all possibility to maintain the pre-coup mobilization of the petit bourgeoisie and to win over all the proletarians. . . . The Latin American military dictatorships find all solutions of a fascist type foreclosed to them because they essentially have to confront an organized labor movement, decapitate it and its mass organizations and impose the domination of the military state on the whole of society without any counterweight. . . . In Chile this did not permit [them], even in their ideological propaganda, to try to pass as a regime that is equidistant between the classes, which was inherent to the fascist claims about "anti-capitalism," "nationalism," "socialism" and the fight to the death against the bourgeoisie, etc. . . . The armed forces represent the hegemony of the large international financial capital which is socially only very little represented even in the native dominant classes. Therefore its relations with them will often be marked by frictions, due to the discontinuity between the relative social weakness of big capital and its economic power, as politically expressed through the military regime. The gorilla military dictatorship becomes the instrument of big international monopoly capital's attempt to impose its political hegemony on Latin American social formations after having already succeeded in making itself into the axis of their process of capital accumulation. . . . These two features—having the monopoly of violence in the society and being the part of society that is

the least affected by the institutional crisis generated by the greatest sharpening of the class struggle—permit the armed forces to play the role of the political party of big capital and to hegemonize the whole of the ruling classes (Sader 1977: 115–18).

That is why the armed forces in Argentina and elsewhere in Latin America have been called the "military party" (Guevara 1977a, b) or the "foreign political party" and are sometimes accused of being a foreign military occupying force made up of mercenaries who are recruited inside the occupied country and then camouflaged by national uniforms (Echeverria 1977).

The Emergence of the Authoritarian State

The recent development of these state forms in Latin America and many other parts of the Third World was foreshadowed and supported by a "fact-finding" mission that President Richard Nixon sent through Latin America in 1969, which was headed by Nelson A. Rockefeller, then governor of the state of New York and later Vice President of the United States. The resulting report was, of course, confidential, but some of it was subsequently published by the *New York Times* under the title "The Rockefeller Report on the Americas: The Official Report of a United States Presidential Mission for the Western Hemisphere, by Nelson A. Rockefeller." This report reads in part:

Changes in the Decade Ahead

The hemisphere is likely to exhibit the following characteristics in the next few years:—

Rising frustration with the pace of development, intensified by industrialization, urbanization, and population growth;

—Political and social instability;

—An increased tendency to turn to authoritarian or radical solutions;

—Continuation of the trend of the military to take power . . .

—Growing nationalism. . . .

The Challenge to Political and Economic Freedom . . . Our National Objective

The United States must face several important practical issues in trying to shape this new relationship:

1. The United States should determine its attitude toward internal political developments in a more pragmatic way;

2. The United States should decide how it can shift increasing responsibility to the other American nations. . . .

3. The United States should decide how its interests are affected by

insurgency and subversion elsewhere in the hemisphere and the extent to which its programs can and should assist in meeting the security requirements of its neighbors.

The task is difficult but by no means impossible.

Recommendations for Action

1. A Western Hemisphere Security Council.

2. A Western Hemisphere Security Assistance Program. The United States should reverse the recent downward trend in grants for assisting the training of security forces for the other hemisphere countries . . . it is essential that the training program . . . be strengthened.

3. Internal Security Support. The United States should respond to requests for assistance of the police and security forces of the hemisphere nations by providing them with the essential tools to do their job.

4. Military Sales for Defense . . . to permit the United States to sell aircraft, ships, and other major military equipment . . . (Rockefeller 1969: 35–36, 37–41, 63–67).

The U.S. Senate Foreign Relations Committee invited Governor Rockefeller to testify on his report, and the following discussion took place at a meeting of its Subcommittee on Western Hemisphere Affairs:

SENATOR CHURCH: You would acknowledge, would you not, that the military governments that now control Argentina, Peru, Bolivia, Brazil, Panama, and other countries in the hemisphere were not placed in power by the vote of the people?

GOVERNOR ROCKEFELLER: That is correct.

SENATOR CHURCH: They took power by force of arms. Isn't that correct?

GOVERNOR ROCKEFELLER: Yes, in varying degrees.

SENATOR CHURCH: Yes. This strikes me as ironical, because for the past 2 days we have been sitting in executive session with Secretary Rogers and Secretary Laird, reviewing American policy in Vietnam. We have been told that the whole objective of this tremendous effort in Vietnam is to secure self-determination for the people of South Vietnam. When we press for a definition of self-determination, we are told that the purpose of the war is to obtain free election so that the people of South Vietnam can choose their government. This is so important a principle, we are told, that it has warranted the loss of 45,000 Americans and over $100 billion in expenditures in 5 years of what has become the longest foreign war in our history. Well, I find it hard to understand why it is so important for us to secure free elections in South Vietnam, but so unimportant that there be free elections in South America. . . .

But in reading your report, I was disturbed to find language which all but approves the military juntas that have come to power. For example, I read, "In short, a new type of military man is coming to the fore and often becoming a major force for constructive social change in the American Republics. Motivated by increasing impatience with corruption, inefficiency, and a stagnant political order, the new military man is prepared to adapt his authoritarian tradition to the goals of social and economic progress." Well, language of that kind is reminiscent of the time when I was beginning to take my first interest in politics, when similar arguments were put forward in justification of the Fascist military dictatorships in Europe. . . .

GOVERNOR ROCKEFELLER: Well, Mr. Chairman, I appreciate your going to the heart of this question because I think this is probably the most important first step we have to face and understand in facing up to the broader problems of our relations (U.S. Senate 1969: 10–12).

The business perspective on recent and foreseeable developments of state forms and institutions in Latin America was similar. Business International looked ahead in its *Business Latin America* newsletter:

Latin American Issues: How They Stack Up in a 10-year Perspective

Every year at this time, *Business Latin America* attempts to look ahead at the forces at work in the region that will affect the operations of international companies. This year, the tenth anniversary of the publication, BL will peer 10 years ahead.

Political stability. This is an extremely difficult element to predict, but some trends are discernible and should follow through. . . . One generalization of the political situations in Latin America through 1986 forsees five to six years of military and monolithic political systems followed by a change towards more representative government, though not free-for-all politicking.

Policy toward foreign investment: A great wave of positive change is obviously in the making . . . remittance ceilings, rigidly specified equity splits and the like will become less strict. . . . There may even be some efforts to take advantage of what is "international" about international companies, namely their access to steady flows of technology and their ready-made markets within the global marketing network. The idea would be not to force local ownership on firms that were willing to truly and fully plug in the subsidiary to all such advantages.

State role in economy and industry: . . . On the one hand, most governments want to provide services, infrastructure and basic products. On the other hand, they have gotten in a financial bind in doing so. . . . Statism will likely continue but with reassessment of the types of projects the state will embark on. There will be greater effort to promote efficiency including more tie-ins with foreign investment. When foreign debt picks up again after 1980, the statism thrust could intensify. . . .

Labor demands: . . . Governments will try to curtail unions by dictating the level of wage increases. . . . One upbeat note: employers can cease worrying about major worker involvement in management or equity. Social dynamics. Social pressures will probably be contained temporarily between now and 1980.

Special development sectors: Two areas are expected to be the scene for a number of opportunities. One is *agriculture,* which will experience a major reawakening. . . . Another area . . . will be the expected all-out campaign to develop a capital goods industry (BLA 12 January 1977; 9–11).

This same development of authoritarian states in Latin America was observed at high technical levels of the Western strategic and security establishment. Gregory F. Treverton, a staff member of the U.S. National Security Council, writes under the auspices of the (private) International Institute for Strategic Studies in London:

Among the changed circumstances affecting the roles of Latin American states in global politics during the next decade, two are particularly significant: the rise of military-dominated authoritarian governments in Latin America, and the change in the United States role.

The Rise of a New Authoritarianism

The military-dominated authoritarian governments that now rule in Latin America, while of varying ideological colour, are coherent, assertive, and committed to maintaining internal order and to promoting some form of economic development. . . . It now seems painfully obvious that the tensions and frustrations of the process labelled (all too blithely) "modernization" were more likely to strain political democracy than to foster it. In country after country civilian, democratic governments have appeared unable or unwilling to preserve internal order at the same time as promoting a modicum of socioeconomic development in the face of competing internal (and external) demands and entrenched pressures. Those governments have given way to military-dominated authoritarian governments. The governments of the new authoritarian regimes have been given a variety of labels: "bureaucratic authoritarianism," "patrimonial order" or a new form of "corporatism." All these labels suggest the difference between these governments and the old-style dictatorships of Latin America. The new authoritarian regimes are institutional and not personal. All have a commitment to some form of social and economic change; most of them, in fact, derive their internal legitimacy from that commitment and from their ability to turn the power of a centralized state to that end.

Not all the regimes are static. All restrict effective political participation, but several have permitted limited expression of popular will through elections. While none of the regimes is a stranger to repression, even harsh, most have not been purely repressive. Instead, they have sustained themselves in power by repressing some demands yet responding to a range of other demands, thereby preventing the formation of an opposing coalition which might threaten the government's survival. ... The governing coalition is similar in each case: military officers, plus civilian planners—often sophisticated, the "technocrats" by popular label—with the support of domestic industrial and export sectors and with a string following among the urban middle classes. The regimes rely, in some measure, on corporate means of controlling the demands of interest-groups and they attempt to *structure* the process of articulating demands. The governments of Argentina (after April 1976), Brazil, Peru and Mexico all fit within the category of "new authoritarianism." ...

Military-dominated authoritarian governments will be especially attentive to the traditional concerns of the armed forces. The historic concern, of course, is external security; the new concern, by now traditional, is internal security. The latter concern has not been narrow. ... The authoritarian regimes are likely to be sensitive to, and perhaps over-estimate, potential threats to "national security" (Treverton 1977: 3–5).

We may also invoke the unimpeachable authority of the United States Senate to clarify some of the economic reasons for this kind of political regime and repression. The following document, prepared by the staff of the Senate Foreign Relations Committee, is cited more extensively in another context in Chapter 4, but it may be well to examine a part of it here:

Through close cooperation between the private banks and the IMF, pressure is exerted on countries who have debts because of deficits to balance their external accounts through internal austerity measures. ... Countries may also be stimulated to create a favorable climate for foreign investment and for the private sector in general. The problem with these measures is that ... they can also lead to greater unemployment, to the reduction of social welfare, and to a lower standard of living for the people. ... The government decision to impose a program of strict economic austerity can create social and political disturbances. ... Finally, as we have shown, in many countries there seems to be a direct correlation between economic difficulties and political repression. ... Creditor demands to implant drastic economic austerity programs ... could only be imposed at the expense of civil liberties in the countries that adopt them (U.S. Senate 1977: 1379–80).

The recent extension of exploitation and intensification of superexploitation through recourse to political police, and military repression by military and military-backed authoritarian civilian regimes and/or the imposition of emergency rule or martial law, have, of course, not been limited to Latin America. We have already discussed such exploitation and repression elsewhere in the Third World in our analysis of foreign debt bondage (in Chapter 4), of unequal development, particularly in "intermediate," "sub-imperialist" countries (in Chapter 1), and of export promotion of raw materials and industrial commodities (Chapter 3) through superexploitation (Chapter 5). And Chapter 6 extensively documents, country by country, how and why this economic exploitation and political repression have in recent years been extended and intensified in each of several dozen Third World countries in East, Southeast, and South Asia; the Middle East and North Africa; west, east, and southern Africa; the Caribbean, Middle America, and Mexico; and in each of numerous countries of South America. The documentation cites the most authoritative business, financial, official, political, independent, and local and international press sources. It shows unambiguously that more and more political repression has been necessary in nearly every part of the Third World to impose and enforce increased economic exploitation. This political-economic exploitation and repression have been promoted, if not required, by these countries' incorporation into the changing international division of labor during the present world capitalist crisis of capital accumulation. Moreover, this documentation showed that despite President Carter's worldwide campaign for human rights, the United States and other metropolitan powers have effectively, and sometimes expressly, supported and defended this political and economic repression in the Third World.

Some further documentation and analysis are in order here concerning the economic, political, military, and ideological instrumentality of the state at this juncture of the class struggle, the division of labor, and the process of capital accumulation. We need to see just why the functions and the character of the state are being transformed and reinstitutionalized now. That is, we must examine the Third World state as an instrumental relation that is undergoing transformation as part of the historical process itself.

Economic Crisis and State Intervention

The analysis of the role and transformation of the Third World state and its participation in this historical process is complicated by the complex of important commonalities and growing differences that characterize Third World societies (see, for instance, Chapter 1 on unequal accumulation and development). One important commonality is the part Third World states are being called upon to play in organizing national and international economic activity within the international division of labor at a time of world economic crisis. Another, related commonality is the Third World state's function in the struggle between and within classes with regard to their participation in the benefits from this division of labor. A significant difference between states in the Third World derives from their differential insertion and participation in this common international division of labor. Some differences in the type and development of the forces and relations of production are examined in Chapter 1 on unequal accumulation and Chapters 2 and 3 on agricultural, mineral, and manufacturing export. These differences determine that the most important, and in some cases almost the entire, economic process in some Third World countries depends on the process of the accumulation and its cyclical swings in the world economy; while in other countries, such as Brazil and India, the process of accumulation follows a partially autonomous, though not independent, cyclical course. Accordingly, the class structure and the class struggle through the state also differ among these countries. The emphasis here will be on the commonalities, though some account is taken of differences in particular instances.

The most important commonality remains the use, role, and place of the power and functions of the state in the class struggle. The kind and form of state and its intervention, of course, depend on the relations between the local class structures and the international division of labor: how the local class struggle determines and is determined by the local contribution to the process of capital accumulation on the local and world scale at each particular time. Whenever there is a determined effort to incorporate new sources of raw materials and/or labor and markets into the national and international process of accumulation, the social institutions, economic functions, and political power of the state are engaged to integrate resources and people into this process in new and more effective ways, including "primitive" or "primary" accumulation. Thus in many countries of Africa, and in some of Asia and Latin America, the state "mediates" between the national and international capitalist economy and "precapitalist" sectors that are increasingly integrated into agricultural, mining, and manufacturing production and into services for, as well as purchases from, this capitalist market (as examined in Chapters 2, 3, and 5.) In East and Southeast Asia, the Caribbean, and elsewhere state economic functions, and particularly political power and repression, are used to incorporate new sources of labor supply into export manufacturing (Chapter 3). Where the entire population was already fully participating in the international division of labor and the process of capital accumulation, as in the southern cone of South America, repressive state power is the principal instrument used to enforce a substantial cut in the wage rate and a reorientation or production and employment toward the world market.

The principal contradiction or conflict in this entire process remains that between capital (both international and national), the state, and their various easy or uneasy combinations on the one hand, and labor in its various forms and groups on the other. We have observed how the exigencies of the contemporary crisis of capital accumulation require the extended exploitation and increased superexploitation of labor in the Third World (as well as increased exploitation and austerity in the industrialized and socialist countries). It is in the management of this principal conflict and its resolution in favor of capital that the bourgeois and bureaucratic state in almost all Third World countries is called upon to intervene most actively. The state intervenes through the economic, political, forceful, and ideological discipline and repression of labor and the poor in general. It uses its power to cut wages, reduce employment, eliminate social services, crush unions, disorganize and silence political opposition and public opinion, and to repress countless individuals through death, imprisonment, torture, terror, unemployment, and many other measures. These measures are often enforced under emergency rule, martial law, military government, and other emerging institutional forms (documented in Chapter 6).

The widespread recent recourse to military regimes to enforce this repression merits special attention and analysis. For Latin America, at least, military regimes have assumed the double role of repressing workers, peasants, and part of the petit bourgeoisie when the democratic bourgeois state was no longer able to do so effectively, *and* of repressing or at least neutralizing certain sectors of the local bourgeoisie as well. These sectors are principally those that produced for the low-income wage-goods consuming and domestic middle-income market, whose economic base is being sacrificed to national financial and monopoly (and in some cases large agrarian) capital's alliance with international capital in the production for export to the world market. This recent tendency and pattern in Latin America has been the subject of substantial analysis (Vuscovic 1975, 1978a, b; Vuscovic and Martinez 1977; Briones 1975, 1976; dos Santos 1977, 1978; Valenzuela 1976; Marini 1977a, b; Sader 1977; Lowy and Sader 1977; Frank 1976a, b, 1977c, d; and many others).

The succinct analysis of Thomas Vasconi may be cited here:

> It is not only and simply a matter of saving capitalism "in general" from its present crisis. In the period through which Latin America is now passing, it is a matter of assuring the hegemony of the financial oligarchy, which is associated with imperialism, over the other bourgeois fractions and sectors inside the power bloc; and the military dictatorships (Brazil 1964, Argentina 1966, Bolivia 1972, Chile 1973) appear more and more as the privileged instrument to do so. The suppression of *all* political interplay thus has the double objective of resolving the principal contradiction [between capital and labor] in favor of the bourgeoisie and to resolve the secondary (intrabourgeoisie) contradictions in favor of the monopoly bourgeoisie associated with imperialism. . . . The problem of hegemony that the political interplay was unable to solve is now solved through the recourse to authority. That is why it is imperative to "depoliticize" the country . . . (Vasconi 1976: 44–45, emphasis in original).

The course of the class struggle in the Third World today is thus importantly influenced, if not determined, by the actions of Third World states to increase their contribution to the process of world capitalist accumulation in its present crisis. A common symptom of the world capitalist economic participation in the international division of labor of most Third World countries today is these nations' rapidly and greatly increasing balance-of-payments problems and deficits (see Chapter 4). These deficits, in turn, exert increased pressure for export promotion (Chapters 2 and 3), for domestic austerity measures, and for superexploitation through the reduction of the wage rate and other measures. The balance-of-payments deficits also stimulate reliance on various methods of primitive or primary accumulation (Chapter 5). It has already been emphasized (Chapters 1 and 3) that the shift in emphasis or in "growth model" from "import substitution" to "export substitution"—and more capital-intensive production for the domestic market and particularly for public demand—involves significant shifts in the allocation of economic resources. These shifts have widespread social consequences and therefore are only possible with severe political conflict and its temporary resolution. Inefficient small capital enterprises, and medium and even big national capital tied to the production of industrial and primary commodities for the domestic market, are sacrificed in favor of the expansion of export and capital-intensive production by bigger and often financial or monopoly and state capital associated with foreign capital. The wages and income of workers in manufacturing, mining, agriculture, and public and private service are seen solely as costs that must be reduced through real wage cuts and unemployment. Worker income is no longer an important source of effective demand to be maintained on the domestic market; hence the capitalists and workers who produce wage goods for domestic consumers, and of course the consumers themselves, are damaged through export promotion. Even in economies like that of Brazil, where export promotion is important but not dominant, the process of capital accumulation today depends on and is perhaps led by capital-intensive production. And the state is becoming not only the principal source of investment capital but also of effective military and civilian or combined demand, as Marini (1977b) argues. The acquisition of nuclear reactors (and bombs) by Brazil—with 70 percent of the components to be supplied by national industry (Marini 1977b: 82)—and by Iran (not incidentally with Brazilian and South African collaboration) are significant instances of this trend, which has been well publicized because of U.S. opposition to European participation in this business and in the profits to be derived therefrom. Related capital-intensive weapons projects in these and other countries are examined in Chapter 8. All these projects require a reduction in the production of (and market for) wage goods for mass consumption, and even for some durable consumer goods for the relatively high-income market. In the majority of Third World countries the trend to export promotion is more dominant and exclusive than it is in Brazil.

The state is an essential instrument in the promotion, organization, and enforcement of this economic transformation. The state also uses its powers of regulation and licensing, import tariffs and controls, export subsidies, foreign exchange control, monetary, fiscal, and price measures, tax penalties and incentives, credit facilities, financial subsidies—and, of course, its own investment resources and market purchases—to promote and enforce the changing selection and conditions of production, sale, and purchase of commodities. The more drastic or rapid the economic change, the stronger the state intervention and the more severe its enforcement of this change.

The present economic crisis has generated a modification of the international division of labor and the need or desire of some local capital, as well as the obligation of local labor, to participate in it. Such participation is furthered by the state. The state in many Third World countries is called upon to promote and enforce a shift in resources, production, and profits from national capital supplying the domestic market to national and international capital supplying the world market. To do this, the state must promote the association between national and multinational capital, and often participate itself in joint and mixed enterprises. Hence the state must also encourage or enforce the "denationalization" or "foreignization" of private and public national capital. Where state capital is substantial thanks to previous "nationalization" (or more properly "statization") and/or to earlier state investment of public funds, the state is divesting itself of some of its enterprises, which are bought at bargain prices by private, usually foreign, capital. These changes in ownership are in evidence today in Chile, Argentina, Peru, Nigeria, Egypt, Bangladesh, and other Third World countries (documented in part in Chapter 6). Where state ownership and investment are smaller (and sometimes even where it is substantial), the state is increasing its investment in public, mixed (state capital-private capital), and joint (state capital-foreign capital) enterprises. Such investment encourages the state to subsidize private capital with subsequent state-subsidized production and sale of cheap inputs of electricity, steel, equipment, transportation, improved land and/or water resources, technological research, and other facilities to national and foreign private enterprise. There is hardly a Third World (or other capitalist) country in which this process is not visible.

Almost all Third World states have promoted or enforced measures to centralize and concentrate the structure and ownership of production. These measures favor sectors of large national capital that are associated with foreign capital and/or the state, and they promote the export market and the kind of public and/or private demand that is stimulated or financed by the state. Whole sectors of national capital often suffer partial or total exclusion from state favors and from the market. Various instruments of state policy are available to promote these transformations in the allocation of investment, the structure of production, and the changes in ownership and control of capital. The most important are the state's influence over the distribution of income through its control of monetary and fiscal policy, state employment and expenditures, and the state's substantial economic and political control over prices and particularly wages. Income is being shifted from the poor to the rich, from labor to capital, and from the national economy to the imperialist capital (Chapter 5; WE: Chapter 1). These shifts in distribution of income are both a requisite and an effect of the Third World's present participation in the international division of labor. In addition to changing the *distribution* of income, in many cases the state has intervened to reduce the *level* of income by aggravating or even inducing a severe recession in industrial production, viz. Chile and Argentina. The result is that denationalization, monopolization, and inequality in the economy are aggravated still further. Of course, international and national capital do not enforce their economic and political programs only through the domestic political policy of Third World states. Rather they also seek to promote their interests through state foreign and military policy, including war (see Chapter 8); for a discussion of "subimperialism" see Chapter 1 and Marini 1974, 1977a).

Through this entire process the Third World countries are increasing their contribution to world capitalist accumulation and are helping the capitalist system overcome its crisis through the modification of the international division of labor by state intervention. The resulting conflicts between international capital (and its sectors) and national capital, and between the various sectors and different interests of national capital in the Third World countries, are important, but nonetheless secondary. The primary contradiction remains that between all these sectors of international and national capital on the one hand, and labor on the other.

State Expenditure Patterns

The state not only intervenes in the class struggle around the (re)organization of the "private" sector; it also modifies its own investment, production, expenditure, and consumption activities in the "public" or "state" sector. The class struggle between capital and labor and among various sectors of the international and local bourgeoisies also involves the attempt by each class, sector, interest group, and often particular firms and individuals to serve their particular economic and political interests through the redirection of public revenues and expenditures. Control of these revenues and expenditures for their own benefit is certainly one of the important reasons for the competition for public employment by individuals, for government contracts by individuals and firms, and for state power by social classes, economic sectors, political parties, and other groups.

The struggle between and within classes in the recent years of world economic crisis has therefore also affected the amount, pattern, and direction of public revenues and expenditures in the Third World (and, of course, elsewhere as well). Despite the differences from one country to another, the dominant trend is less taxation of and greater public expenditure in favor of major international capital and associated local capital that supplies the world and high-income and/or public national demand. This dominant trend signifies the relative neglect of domestically and particularly mass consumer–oriented capital, and the absolute neglect and reduction of public expenditures favorable to the working classes and the poorest populations (in the industrial countries as well as in the Third World). This neglect is often coupled with increased indirect taxation of the least favored classes. The pattern is increased absolute or relative state infrastructural and capital investments and government purchases of commodities and particularly armaments, which favors foreign and local monopoly capital. Thereby the state promotes the economic fortunes or monopoly position of these sectors of capital. The same dominant trend is reflected in the nearly universal decline in "unproductive" expenditures on social and welfare services. The widespread attack on and dismantling of the few existing welfare states in the Third World and in the industrial capitalist countries is symptomatic. The current policy might well be expressed by the motto "Welfare: farewell." We will now examine this dominant trend in greater detail.

Let us first consider a United Nations Economic and Social Council document on "The Role of the Public Sector in Promoting the Economic Development of Developing Countries":

The Public Sector

Total government consumption plus general government and public enterprise investment [means] concentrating on public expenditures on goods and services, not including transfer payments. . . . In recent years the public sector, as measured in the above sense, has ranged from about one tenth to one third of the gross domestic product in developing countries. For an overwhelming majority of these countries the share of the public sector has been less than one fifth of the total. This is generally lower than in developed countries. . . . The typical share of public consumption in the total public sector is around two thirds, although the range extends from less than one half to almost nine tenths. . . . The share of general public services for many countries appears to have decreased from a range of 20 to 44 per cent to about 15 to 29 per cent. The share of defense on the other hand increased for most countries. . . .

Public Investment

Although the public sector is generally smaller in developing countries than in developed countries, the reverse is generally true for public investment. In relation to gross domestic product, public investment in developing countries has frequently been more than 6 or 7 per cent of gross domestic product. . . . The relatively high share of public investment . . . is even more strikingly reflected in the share of public investment in gross fixed capital formation. In many developing countries . . . the share has been more than one half; this is in sharp contrast with that in developed market economies of generally under one quarter. . . . Among developing countries, the least developed tend to have the highest share of public investment in gross capital formation and vice versa. . . . Over the last 10 years, there has been a trend towards public ownership of existing public utilities and direct government

financing of new ones. . . . Transport and communication absorb a
significant part of total investment. . . . Highway development has been
accorded priority by Governments. . . . Railways are almost invariably
dominated by public enterprise. . . . There is a marked importance of
state-owned shipping lines. . . . The public sector controls air transport. . . . Public irrigation projects have received high priority in many
development plans. . . . In some countries government participation in
trade in agricultural commodities has been undertaken. . . . State trading
is carried out through . . . marketing boards, purchasing agencies, food
agencies and import or export offices. . . . In many instances, countries
have resorted to nationalization of natural resource production facilities. . . . The assumption of ownership by the public sector [in the mining
and petroleum sectors] is frequently accompanied by efforts to gain
greater participation in almost all aspects of downstream facilities,
especially regarding processing, but also including transportation,
fabrication and marketing. . . .

Manufacturing Industry

Although many development plans do not reveal the precise role of the
public sector in industrial development, an analysis of 11 countries, for
which data on planned investment in manufacturing by public and
private components are available, indicates that the public component is
envisaged as being more than 30 per cent of the planned investment in
manufacturing in five of them; in the remaining countries, it is in the range
of 10 to 29 per cent. . . . Often the role of the public sector has been
indirect rather than direct. Attention has been focused particularly on
institutional, financial and promotional frameworks within which the
private enterprise is to act and on the establishment of industrial
infrastructure. Apart from the development of transport, communications and power facilities required for industry, industrial zones or
estates have been created for private enterprise. . . . With respect to
more direct public participation in manufacturing enterprises, measures
range from the establishment of wholly owned corporations, to joint
enterprises with national or foreign investors in which the Government
holds a majority or minority interest. . . . The role of the public sector is
especially large in "key," "priority" or "strategic" industries, although
the degree of necessary ownership or control varies. . . . In many Latin
American countries, the largest steel enterprises are owned by Governments. . . . Attempts to organize public enterprise on an autonomous
basis . . . poses problems of accountability . . . especially . . . where the
public enterprises enjoy explicit or implicit subsidies from the Government (UNECOSOC 1975: passim).

This review of "the role of the public sector" testifies to the predominant
and increasing role of the state in promoting, organizing, financing, and
subsidizing capitalist capital accumulation in general and fixed investment in

particular at the service of private enterprise—national, foreign, and "joint"—throughout most of the Third World. Supplementary information in the statistical annex of the same report and elsewhere sheds further light on this trend toward "state capitalism." For instance, in Chile (which unfortunately is not included in the above-quoted review of ninety-one countries) direct public investment accounted for 50 percent (the order of magnitude indicated for other countries in the quote) or gross capital formation in 1970—that is, before the nationalizations of the Allende government. But since the state also financed 50 percent of the private sector's half share of total investment, the state actually accounted for 75 percent of gross fixed capital formation (Frank 1972b, 1974, from official Chilean documents). It is not clear how much the investment shares for other countries cited in the above quote would have to be similarly adjusted to reflect the true participation of the state. In Chile and elsewhere the state uses the general budget to subsidize state enterprises; and the state enterprises, in turn, subsidize the private enterprise sector by supplying it with subsidized and therefore cheap electricity, steel, and other inputs, not to mention infrastructure. Throughout the Third World, mixed or joint enterprises between the state and national and/or foreign capital are the order of the day. Under these arrangements the state supplies the capital and foreign enterprise supplies the "advanced technology," "efficient management," and "marketing channels." Since their respective 1976 military coups, Argentina and Thailand, for instance, have changed their foreign investment laws and regulations to permit local and state supply not only of long-term capital credits for investment but also of short-term credit for working capital to joint and foreign enterprise.

Besides state expenditures on investment and production, it is important to examine the much greater two-thirds of state expenditures on "public consumption." Among the ninety-one Third World countries examined in the report cited above, those with less than 10 percent of gross domestic production devoted to public consumption declined from 31 percent to 18 percent of the sample, and those with between 10 and 15 percent of gross domestic product declined from 41 percent to 37 percent of the sample; while the number of countries spending 15–25 percent increased from 26 percent to 38 percent of the total, and those spending over 25 percent of their gross domestic product on public consumption increased from 2 percent to 7 percent of the sample between 1961 and 1971 (UNECOSOC: E/5690/add.1 Table 4). These figures show a clear increase in the importance of public consumption during the 1960s. The study distinguishes three major categories of public consumption: economic services to industry and infrastructure or public utilities; community services, including general government administration, police, and defense; and social services for the welfare, health, and education of the population. Data on the changes in the composition of public consumption are spotty. Nonetheless, from the evidence of the same U.N. report (UNECOSOC 1975: 6, Tables 16 and 17), we may make some observations. The share of expenditures on economic services was roughly stable during the 1960s (p. 6) but tended to increase in the 1970s, which also saw an upward trend in absolute expenditures: "community services" have certainly increased and continue to do so. A large share of these "community services" are for "defense"—against both external and internal threats to the rulers—and for police and other forces of repression. In India, for instance, identifiable defense expenditures have risen from 30 percent to 42 percent of the general budget since 1961 (VP Gandhi 1974: 1491), and police expenditures doubled in six years. In the Third World as a whole military expenditures have increased from 3.4–3.7 percent of gross national product in 1960–1962 to 4.3–4.6 percent in 1970–1974 and 5 percent in 1977 (computed from Sivard 1976: 20 and 1979: 25). Other expenditures for state administration have also been rising, though probably not as fast as those directly devoted to repression, defense, and support of foreign and domestic arms producers. Of the public expenditures for social services, only those for education showed a marked increase during the 1960s. Other social service and welfare expenditures probably declined as a share of the budget and total public consumption.

A study on *World Military and Social Expenditures 1976* finds that

> In a world of enormous economic potential, the number of people unable to attend school, to read or write, to see a doctor, to have a minimum diet for health, is continually growing larger. . . . The governments of developing countries, where needs are most acute, were spending less than one-fourth as much on health as on their military programme. Their expenditures for education and health care combined were less than military expenditures (Sivard 1976: 19,12).

Moreover, the evidence is accumulating that as a result of the capitalist crisis of capital accumulation, the underdeveloped capitalist countries no less than the developed ones are reducing their expenditures on welfare services relative to gross national product and/or state budgets, and even absolutely.

The case of India is illustrative:

> As part of the effort to deal with "the worst manifestations of poverty" the draft Fifth Plan contained a "national programme of minimum needs." The programme, designed to provide a "minimum level of social consumption for different areas and sections of the community," covered elementary education, rural health, nutrition, water supply, rural roads, house-sites for the landless, slum improvement and rural electrification. . . . Among the more conspicuous changes now effected in the final version of the Fifth Plan is the omission of the national programme of minimum needs as well as the chapter on objectives and policy-frame. The significant implications of these omissions are confirmed by the changes made in the sectoral distribution of the Plan outlay. The size of the Fifth Plan has shrunk in real terms because of the rise in prices. . . . However, the allocation under a number of heads has been reduced

even in financial terms in the final Plan as compared with the draft. What is significant is that most of the programmes which have met with this fate are precisely the ones which had constituted the draft Plan's programme of minimum needs . . . enumerated by the Prime Minister in her 1972 address . . . as necessary to "eliminate the worst manifestations of poverty."

The outlay on education has been reduced . . . by over one fourth. . . . The outlay on elementary education has been slashed . . . by nearly 45 percent. . . . The same treatment has been meted out to health programmes, the outlay on which has been reduced . . . by 14 percent. The emasculation of the nutrition programme is much more complete. The draft Plan had provided for an outlay of Rs 400 crores . . . which has now been slashed to a mere Rs 116 crores. . . . In the same vein the allocation for social welfare, which covers programmes of family and child welfare, women's welfare and welfare of the handicapped, has been reduced from Rs 229 crores to Rs 86 crores. And to complete the story, the cuts made in the outlays on urban development, from Rs 543 crores to Rs 362 crores, and on water supply schemes, from Rs 1,022 crores to Rs 927 crores, may just be enumerated.

In the aggregate the outlays on education, health, nutrition, social welfare, urban development and water supply taken together have been reduced from Rs 4,716 crores to Rs 3,458 crores or by well over one-fourth. In the Draft Plan these programmes accounted for 12.6 per cent of the total Plan outlay. This proportion has now been brought down to 8.8 per cent. Surely there is a story hidden in this jumble of figures? (EPW 16 October 1976: 1641–2).

The hidden story is emerging throughout the world; in order to deal with the accumulation crisis, capital and the state have cut expenditures on "unproductive" social welfare and put these monies at the disposal of capitalists who are supposed to use it for "productive" investment. In Brazil the relative percentage shares of welfare (Ministry of Social Assistance and Social Insurance, Ministry of Health, and Ministry of Labor) and defense (air force, army, navy, and justice—including police—ministries) in the federal budget have changed as follows under the military government, which was installed in 1964:

	1961–1963	*1964–1966*	*1967–1969*	*1970–1973*	*1974–1977*
Welfare	6.5	4.8	4.0	2.0	2.7
Defense	14.7	17.9	24.1	22.8	13.4

SOURCE: IBGE Anuarios Estadisticos.

Thus while the percentage share of welfare expenditures fell by nearly two-thirds, the share of defense expenditures rose more than one-half. (The registered drastic decline of defense expenditures between 1970–1973 and 1974–1975 looks suspicious, particularly when we observe that "government and administration" expenditures, under which defense expenditures can be camouflaged, increased from 42 percent to 58 percent those same years.) Over the same period, expenditures on "human capital" (that is, mostly education) first rose from 7 to 8 percent and then fell back to 5 percent of the federal budget. Provincial expenditure patterns do not show any clear trend during the same period, though they do register a relative increase of welfare expenditures according to the same source.

In Chile public expenditures on health, housing, social security, education, and regional development were as follows (in millions of 1976 U.S. dollars):

1970	1971	1972	1973	1974	1975	1976
875	1332	1404	1078	1002	724	727

SOURCE: Mensaje March 1977: 114, cited in *Chile-America* No. 31–32, May–June 1977, p. 150.

Thus these social expenditures nearly doubled between 1970 and 1972 during the Popular Unity government of President Allende, and were then cut in half after 1973 by the military junta to below their 1970 level. A comparison of state expenditures for social services and welfare in 1970 and 1976 (which disregards their sharp rise under Allende in 1971–1973 and their sharp decline in 1973–1975) shows that per capita expenditures for health declined 22 percent, for housing 40 percent, for social security 18 percent, and for education 22 percent. For the four sectors combined, they declined from $91 in 1970 to $70 in 1976 (Pinera and Meller 1977: 568). If we consider as public social expenditures not only those by the state but also those by public corporations in social service sectors such as housing, health, and social security, it has been estimated that relative to the pre-Allende year 1970, these expenditures were 10 percent lower in 1974 (including 16 percent less for health and 26 percent less for social security), 30 percent lower in 1975, and 19 percent lower in 1976. Per capita expenditures (which also had risen between 1970 and 1973) declined (in pesos of 1976 value) from 5600 pesos in 1970 to 4700 pesos in 1974, 3500 pesos in 1975, and about 4000 pesos in 1976 (Foxley and Arrellano 1977b: 417). Included in the above-cited budget figures, whose level they helped to maintain, were increases in expenditures on "welfare and work": from $10 million in 1970–1972 to $52 million in 1975 and $130 million in 1976. These expenditures reflect the "minimum employment program" of the junta, through which it pays literally starvation wages (below the legal minimum and without any social security rights) in municipal "employment" to segments of the unemployed (unemployment rose from 3 to 20 percent of the labor force over the same period) (Frank 1976a).

To bolster its rule, the military junta has imposed a virtual cultural blackout on Chile. This is expressed in significant declines in attendance at schools and universities (not to mention changes in curriculum and educational philosophy) and in continually falling average scores on reading tests and university entrance examinations. The number of books published in Chile has declined by half; and newspaper circulation, as well as expenditure on books and magazines, has fallen by three-quarters (that is, to one-quarter of earlier levels). Academic, professional, and technical personnel have migrated abroad—sometimes in groups or research teams—in numbers that far exceed the usual "brain drain" from Third World countries. These emigrants are not just from the social sciences and the humanities, where political repression has been particularly severe, but from such fields as medicine (500 doctors), the physical and biological sciences (30 percent exodus), mathematics (50 percent exodus), and engineering (30 percent exodus). This is an exodus primarily of the best-trained professionals who were engaged in research. It has literally emptied some university faculties and technical departments in private enterprises and public services (MEN 264, November 1977; CHA 35–36, September–October 1977, and Nos. 39–40, January–March 1978). Similar (though perhaps less massive) brain drains have occurred from other Third World countries with military regimes, e.g. Argentina, Uruguay (even more than from Chile), and from some countries of Asia and Africa.

In summary, the "Brazilian model" for intermediate economies and the University of Chicago–inspired "Chilean model" for other underdeveloped economies have produced a drastic reduction in social and welfare expenditures as part of a calculated "reallocation of resources" from "unproductive" uses to "productive" investment (Frank 1976; Chossudowsky 1976). In fact, the imposition of crisis "austerity" plans throughout the Third World has meant first and foremost the sacrifice of state expenditures for social welfare and consumption subsidies that had to a small extent been ameliorating superexploitation. Since this reduction of public welfare expenditures has come at the same time as the crisis-generated cut in direct real wage payments, the effects on labor and the poor have been aggravated. The result is increasing direct and indirect superexploitation and pauperization of larger numbers of people (examined in Chapter 5).

Economic Crisis and State Power

The contemporary world capitalist crisis of capital accumulation, and the state's economic and political intervention in the course of the class struggle and redirection of the international division of labor, has involved—indeed, required—frequent and brutal recourse to states of "exception," "emergency" rule, martial "law," and military "government" (see Chapter 6). The time and way to establish—and then often to institutionalize—these state forms are determined by the course of the class struggle. When democratic and other forms of the bourgeois state are no longer adequate to meet capital's need to contain local class struggles and/or to redirect the ownership and use of local resources, a coalition of foreign and national capital act through their political police and military representatives to take control of the existing state form and/or impose a new one that offers them more power. In selected strategically important areas (e.g. Korea, Taiwan, and Vietnam) authoritarian state forms were imposed in the interest of international capital in the region as a whole. Usually, the repressive measures and authoritarian state forms were imposed after peasants, proletarians, and some members of the petite bourgeoisie had or were mobilized in alliance with one sector of national capital against another and international capital. This mass movement was crushed and its alliance with a sector of national capital in a reformist government was broken through state—and usually military—action with or without foreign intervention. Such popular mobilization and populist reformist alliances against the dominant and internationally allied sector of capital, and the latter's violent reaction, have frequently occurred in connection with economic and political problems during or in the aftermath of cyclical recessions in the national economy. These recessions, in turn, have usually been part of the world capitalist cycle of capital accumulation.

In the past two decades civil or military bourgeois reform governments everywhere in the Third World (with the exception of Cuba "that proves the rule" and so far of the newly established regimes in Southern and East Africa) either degenerated or were overthrown by the right. Domestic right-wing military coups with imperialist intervention, or at least support, have toppled most of the reform governments after a few months or years, and replaced them with domestically repressive ones that made important concessions to local and international capital. The other "national," "democratic," "popular," or "socialist" reform governments all degenerated after a few years or a decade through "palace revolts" (sometimes even while maintaining the same personalist leader or head of government) into more repressive regimes that turned on the original "ideals." The new regimes have then made increasing concessions to private and bureaucratic capital at home and Western imperialist capital abroad. Not a single one of these bourgeois reformist regimes in the Third World has made the "transition to socialism." In the sole exception, Cuba, the orginal reformist government of 1959–1960 was set up and supported by the armed power of irregular popular "rebel" armed forces.

Particularly important authoritarian state forms were imposed in Iran in 1953, Lebanon in 1958, Congo (now Zaire) in 1961, Brazil in 1964, Indonesia in 1965, and Ghana and Argentina in 1966 (Argentina enjoyed a brief "democratic" interval in the early seventies). In the 1970s important reactionary movements occurred in Bolivia and Ceylon (now Sri Lanka) in 1971, the Philippines in 1972, Uruguay and Chile in 1973, Egypt in 1973 and 1977, India in 1975, Thailand, Peru, and Argentina (again) in 1976, Lebanon (again), Palestine (still), Pakistan, and Tunisia in 1977–1978. During that same decade important victories of liberation and popular movements occurred in Indochina, in the ex-Portuguese colonies in Africa, and with more questionable results in Somalia, Ethiopia, and some other African countries such as Congo (Brazzaville) and Equatorial Guinea. Apart from these exceptions, "emergency" or military rule has not (yet?) been imposed in the Third World only where it has been possible to buy off popular and petit bourgeois protest, e.g. with oil money, as in Venezuela; when it was possible in critical times to persuade the masses to accept lower incomes through co-optation of their leadership, as in Mexico; or where there are few economic political or strategic interests at stake, as (so far) in Tanzania; or where the masses have been unable to organize sufficiently even to serve as the pawn of one sector of capital against another (much less to pose a challenge of their own), as is still the case in several countries in Asia, Africa, and Latin America. The international and domestic economic and political pressures and emergencies generated by the contemporary world economic and political crisis, however, promise to continue to lead to further recourse to emergency rule, martial law, and military regimes.

States of "exception," "emergency," or "martial law" (often including nightly curfews, sometimes for extended periods, as in Chile where the curfew lasted uninterruptedly for several years) were in force for all or some of 1976 in the following countries by my (certainly incomplete) recollection:

Indonesia	South Africa	Brazil
South Korea	Zambia	Argentina
Philippines	Uganda	Uruguay
Singapore	Benin	Paraguay
Malaysia	Morocco	Chile
Thailand	Algeria	Bolivia
Bangladesh	Egypt	Peru
Sri Lanka	Ethiopia	Ecuador
India	Sudan	Colombia
Pakistan	Rhodesia	Nicaragua
Iran	Zaire	Honduras
Lebanon		El Salvador
Iraq		Jamaica
		Guatemala

To judge by the frequency and length of "emergency" rule and the number of countries with states of "exception" they have become normal rather than an "exceptional" emergency. Amnesty International observes:

> Emergency laws have been misused to legalize repression—even when by objective standards there are no emergencies. . . . An estimated 80% of the population of Latin America lives under military rule. A common feature of such regimes pointed out by the International Commission of Jurists (ICJ), in a commentary entitled "Military Regimes in Latin America" (ICJ Review No. 17, December 1976), has been the declaration and implementation of a "permanent state of

emergency." Such governments regularly invoke special powers which, over a period of time, inevitably lead to the erosion of civil liberties, to the institutionalization of practices such as arbitrary arrest and torture of suspected dissidents, and to a "repression which oversteps all constitutional and legal bounds, violating the most elementary standards of humanity" (ICJ *Review*, idem.) (Amnesty International 1977: 9, 116).

Further evidence of the extent and kind of political repression in the Third World today is documented in reports by Amnesty International, the U.S. Department of State, the press, and other sources cited in Chapter 6.

The Militarization of the State, Society, and Economy

Emergency rule and martial law have been so frequently imposed by military regimes in Latin America and Africa that on those two continents they have become "traditional." This is less true in Asia, where military-backed or militarized civilian governments are more common. It is public knowledge that in recent years military takeovers and the extended exercise of executive power through force, legislative rule by decree, and judicial decision through martial law, have spread like wildfire through the Third World. But the militarization of the state—and, indeed, of the economy, society, culture, and ideology—is also spreading beneath the immediately visible surface in one Third World country after another. This phenomenon raises the question of how widely and deeply militarism is being institutionalized throughout the Third World. The "militarization of the world economy" (Sivard 1976: 5) and the "new international military order" (Oberg 1976), which encompass the Third World through the "arms economy," are examined in Chapter 8. Here we will look at some particular aspects of the apparent trend toward military penetration, organization, and management of the state, economy, society, and ideology in many Third World countries.

Thomas Vasconi asks:

> What do we understand by the global "militarization" of society? ... The projections over the whole society of the organizational as well as ideological characteristics that are typical of the armed forces in the bourgeois state. We may here note some of the more general ones: subordination, discipline, efficiency, service, nationalism in its military version, that is "patriotism," etc. etc. Vasconi 1976: 445).

In his review of the "doctrine of national security" Mauricio Ruz observes that:

> the official ideology of the political [military] regimes in question is based on certain conceptions that we can call "technocratic." ... According to the technocratic ideology all the problems of the society can be resolved through the *desideratum* of science and technology.

There is "the" answer for every problem, and contrary conceptions only obscure "the" solution and have to be eliminated. . . . It is obvious that a profoundly elitist conception like this one leads to an authoritarian trend in which "scientific" truth cannot be submitted to the democratic give and take of majorities and minorities; and it is [profoundly] conservative in that it does not admit alternative conceptions of society or structural problems that could be resolved through a different social order (Ruz 1977: 423).

The "doctrine of national security" and the necessity for military rule were defended in strong terms by the elected civilian President Juan Boardaberry, of Uruguay, in his secret "Memorandum Addressed by the President of the Oriental Republic of Uruguay to the Junta of General Officers on 9 December 1975":

It is becoming indispensable to change the Constitution. Power should be definitively vested in the hands of the Armed Forces, and their functions should be clearly defined. . . . The actions of the Armed Forces cannot be judged, since they act on the basis of norms that cannot be called into question. . . . Power has to be strong and national, that is, it must be power and public, which is why the Armed Forces should be its guardians. . . . On this basis, the Government will have the authority and the consensus that are the fruits of the absence of sectoral labor union and economic interests within the government. Political parties will be allowed as currents of opinion, but they will not be able to attain power through their classical methods, meetings, the press, etc. That is, what these currents of opinion will not be able to do is to group themselves to achieve power. . . . The power of the political parties and the power of the Armed Forces are therefore mutually exclusive. . . .

But this necessity entails two unfortunate consequences, according to President Boardaberry:

It is easy to understand that, being the basis of governmental power, the Armed Forces have the natural reflex to mix themselves in all the domains of public affairs, even in the least important ones, since it is they who put their corporative prestige on the line. . . . The first consequence is that the behavior of the Armed Forces in the administration of public affairs is analyzed as though they were a political party. . . . The second consequence is the constant reduction in the number of civilians that are willing to serve in public office under such difficult conditions (published in *extenso* in *Excelsior,* Mexico, 12 April 1976, and extracted in *America Presse,* Paris, No. 24, June 1976).

The doctrine of national security is also embraced by many civilian technocrats, government bureaucrats, businessmen, and some academics.

But, as Ruz points out, it is the military establishment that is capable of imposing it on the remainder of society. Moreover, Vuscovic and Martinez (1977) observe that the officer corps in Latin America and elsewhere is not only marked by traditional military authoritarianism, bureaucratism, and discipline, but also by the technocracy that comes with modern weapons technology. (They also point out that the more technologically and technocratically professional a Third World army and its officers, generally the more dependent they are on the international suppliers of weapons technology.) Today, the ruling military establishment actively propagates authoritarian and technocratic organizational forms and values throughout Third World societies—before, during, and after the exercise of military rule per se.

Even where the military has not assumed full executive authority in the states of the Third World, officers under military discipline are entering positions of high responsibility in the state administration of civil affairs. Meanwhile, the armed forces remain backstage to oversee the play of political forces with a vigilant eye. Even President Allende in Chile filled numerous executive positions in his administration with high-ranking officers and introduced them into his ministry. After gaining administrative and political experience in his government, these officers (with few exceptions) turned against him through a military coup to take power directly. In Venezuela

> there are now various dozens of high ranking military officers of the Venezuelan Armed Forces occupying key posts in the administrative, economic and political life of the country. The presence of officers (mostly in active service) is notable in the directive posts of the "strategic industry." . . . The leading cadres of the Armed Forces today are professional soldiers who at the same time are in the great majority economists, lawyers, engineers of many kinds, geographers, educators, etc. (de Monte 1977: 1–2).

In Argentina and Brazil the armed forces as an institution, as well as individual officers, have long had far-reaching ownership and management participation in the most diverse industries. The same process has also been going on undercover in many Third World countries in Africa, the Middle East, and South and Southeast Asia.

Military regimes accelerate the formation and growth of the "military-industrial complex" (as General Dwight D. Eisenhower baptized it in his Farewell Speech from the U.S. presidency). The role of the military-industrial complex in the arms economy (which President Eisenhower denounced) and the development of weapons and other military-related production and export in Third World countries are discussed in Chapter 8. But the participation of military regimes and their officers in the arms economy is only one noteworthy aspect of the developing military-industrial complex in the Third World.

Military regimes advance and accelerate the development of a military-industrial-state complex that extends into the whole national economy. Through state and military participation in mixed enterprises and joint ventures, the military-industrial-state complex also increasingly extends into the international capitalist economy. Indonesia is a prime example:

> In short, military men have not only landed many of the choicest jobs in Indonesia's non-military sector; they have in some cases used their position to accumulate vast personal fortunes.
>
> Consequently, many people in the outside world now have a stereotype picture of the modern Indonesian army officer. He is fat and wears sunglasses; lives in a lavish house, filled with chandeliers, fish-tanks and sunken sitting rooms; drives a Mercedes.
>
> There is a good deal that is recognisable in that stereotype of course. . . . "The conventional wisdom is that you have to have a general on your board if you are doing business in Indonesia" (FER 13 January 1978).

Militarization of the economy is hardly limited to Indonesia. This process accompanies military rule in all its forms throughout the Third World. Military officers, active and retired, are appointed not only to cabinet ministries but also to top executive positions in state enterprises and other economically important state institutions such as the national bank and the customs service. These officers use their executive authority and political influence to make "corrupt" deals with national and foreign private business. They thereby amass personal fortunes directly and/or obtain board membership and stock ownership for themselves, their family members, and their associates in these same and other firms. These privileges and financial resources are then parlayed into accession to capital ownership and management—in a word, bourgeois status. Officers achieve bourgeois status either licitly or illicitly while still on active service or after early retirement to "private" life in the national and international capitalist economy. Thus on the individual level participation in the military-industrial complex does not end, and sometimes only really begins, with retirement from military service.

The military-industrial complex always survives the transition from military to civilian rule; it may be suggested that this certainty weighs in the decision by some military officers "to return to their barracks." Civilians—now including some ex-military—are allowed to run the ship of state and the economy, in which these military men now wish to pursue their private fortunes unhindered by official responsibilities and professional limitations. This tendency exists in countries where military governments propose to give way to civilian or military-civilian ones in the coming years. Thus the development of the military-industrial complex and the militarization of the economy and society proceed apace before, during, and after the direct administration of Third World countries by military regimes.

Lock and Wulf summarize:

The social and political conditions within most developing countries are marked by two diverging, though complementary trends, namely overproportionate growth of a few restricted, generally export-oriented industrial poles versus absolute and relative impoverishment of a majority of people. The institution of economic apartheid calls for a general militarization on the basis of modern military technology to maintain the economic regime and the class structures which have produced the situation of extreme social cleavage in most developing societies. Thus, perceived threats from outside and general militarization as a means of extreme social control combine for a strong stimulus to introduce advanced military technology into the framework of the nation in the Third World. . . . Arms, their application or threat to apply them, may be indispensable for a continued functioning of the production and the accumulation process as well, but just the same arms expenditures constitute a reduction of the available social surplus. The cost to maintain a certain mode of production and to control social functions by force might rise to a level higher than the total amount of available surplus, a situation some Third World countries are already approaching (Loek and Wulf 1977: viii).

The Ideology of National Security in the Third World

As we have seen, liberal, democratic, and parliamentary institutions are less and less compatible with Third World participation in the international division of labor and the contemporary process of capital accumulation, so they are being replaced by the military corporativist state with its policy of intensive repression. This means that democratic and populist ideology must also be replaced, by an ideology than can more nearly mask and justify this repression both to those who suffer it and those who exercise it. The new ideology being espoused to this effect, particularly in Latin America but also in Asia and Africa, is the "doctrine of national security."

A new ideology is being ever more projected on the American continent. Its name is progressively recognized and accepted: it is the doctrine of National Security. A Brazilian author, professor in the Universities of Campinas and Mackenzie of São Paulo, prepared in the Escuela Superior de Guerra (War College) of Brazil, José Alfredo Amaral Gurgel, recently published in June 1975 a book that is the first synthetic exposition of the doctrine of national security written in Latin America: *Seguranca e Democracia* (Security and Democracy). . . . The doctrine of national security [has been] the official ideology of Brazil since 1964. . . . The Brazilian generals found the major themes of their national security doctrine in the United States. . . . The doctrine of national security presents itself as a synthesis of all the human sciences . . . a synthesis of politics, economics, social psychological sciences, military strategy . . . geopolitics . . . and geostrategy (Comblin 1976).

The Brazilian military regime has served as a model for the new geopolitical concept of the state—a model which has already been adopted in several Latin American countries and which is based primarily on the theses of Gernal Golbery Couta e Silva (head of the civil cabinet of President Ernesto Geisel). . . . The new model begins with the absence of those neutralizing powers which characterize the traditional Western state: those decorative legislatures and insignificant judiciaries. The people are a myth. Only nations exist, and the nation is the state. War belongs to the human condition and all nations live in the state of war. All economic, cultural, and other activities are acts of war either in favor of or against the nation. Consequently it is necessary to strengthen the power of the military as a guarantee for national security. The citizenry must understand that security is more important than welfare and that the sacrifice of individual liberty is also necessary. The armed forces are the national elite responsible for leading the state. This is justifiable in Latin America due to the inconstancy of civilians, who are demagogical and corrupt, and by the exigencies of war (Agencia Boliviana de Noticias in ESP 6 August 1976).

War is the condition of man, today more than ever before. Every man is a threat and a competitor. Every nation lives in a state of war. . . . War is total because it mobilizes the whole citizenry with all its resources. . . . War is total because all peoples and all countries are involved in it. Like it or not . . . war is total because all human activities are acts of war, all acts are acts of war and all tools are arms; the enemy is not on the frontiers, he is infiltrated everywhere. . . . War is total because there is no longer any difference between peace and war. War is permanent. . . . National security is the absolute and unconditional value without restriction or limitation. . . . The total strategy has four parts; a. the economic strategy . . . for the development of national power . . . b. the psychosocial strategy whose purpose is to use ideas and other cultural objects to increase national power . . . c. the political strategy, which consists of orienting and using all the state organs . . . d. military strategy. . . . Who can take on the responsibility of total strategy? . . . Only the Armed Forces can take on this role of strategic elites . . . (Comblin 1976:96–103).

This ideology and strategy have been consecrated by "law" in Brazil, Paraguay, Uruguay, Bolivia, Peru, Ecuador, Argentina, and Chile. In Brazil the law of "national security" makes it a legal offense "to give moral offense to a person clothed with authority for reasons of political inconformity." The Argentinian law of "national security" (No. 20.540) is directed against what it terms the "interior enemy," that is, "those who, in order to achieve their ideological postulates, use or promote means that are contrary to the constitutional order and social peace." Chilean law defines "national security" as "the whole of the means that are useful to conserve the national economic patrimony" and forbids the spreading of "tendentious information" as well as "calumny, insult and defamation" of any civil or military authority whatsoever. The Bolivian law of "national security," "considering that the nation needs a climate of permanent order and tranquility to achieve its goals of development," bans all acts that impede the "achievement of national development" (CIAL 2 June 1976: 30–46).

In Venezuela the recently passed "law of security and defense" permits the executive to declare under military jurisdiction any matter that "threatens the security of the nation" (del Monte 1977: 4).

On the third anniversary of his military coup in Chile (September 11, 1976) President General Augusto Pinochet introduced four new "Constitutional Acts" and declared:

> National security thus understood emerges as a concept destined not only to protect the national integrity of the state, but very specially to defend the essential values that make up the national soul or tradition, since without them national identity itself would destroy itself. And from this firm pedestal, national security projects itself dynamically to the field of development, thus focussing not only on the material plane, but on harmony and at the service of the spiritual progress of man. National security, including the authentic tradition and national development, spiritual as well as material, thus appear as the integral elements of the common good of a particular community. . . .
>
> What, exactly, does this enemy consist of in the world of today? Marxism is not a doctrine that is simply wrong, like so many others in history. Marxism is an intrinsically perverse doctrine, which means that everything that emerges from it, no matter how sane it may appear on the surface, is impregnated with the poison that corrodes its root. That is what it means to say that its error is intrinsic and therefore global, in terms in which no dialogue or transaction is possible with it. Nonetheless, contemporary reality indicates that Marxism is not only an intrinsically perverse doctrine. It is also a permanent aggression, that today is at the service of Soviet imperialism. . . . This modern form of permanent aggression produces a nonconventional war in which territorial invasion is replaced by the attempt to control the state from within. To that end, communism uses two tactics simultaneously. On the one hand it infiltrates the vital nuclei of the free societies, like the university and intellectual centers, the media, the labor unions, the international organizations and, as we have seen, even the church sectors. On the other hand, it promotes disorder in all its forms. . . .
>
> Therefore, the new institutionality is conceived on the basis of a new democracy that is capable of defending itself actively and vigilantly

from those that try to destroy it.... The Constitutional Acts that we promulgate today make all acts of a person or a group that challenges these values illegal and to be punished judicially.... Property rights are also re-enforced.... Freedom of expression and the press, yes; licentiousness, no.... In the labor field, we emphasize as a historic progress that our new constitutional order consecrates formulas of obligatory conciliation and arbitration.... Certainly, excluded are strikes in any enterprise or service whose function is vital for the nation....

The fact that our peoples are victims of a permanent aggression imposes the duty on us to have vigorous and efficient emergency regimes to defeat communist subversion and to neutralize those who ease the way for it.... It is the fruit of the preceding analysis that it is also understood that in the face of a Marxism that is converted into permanent aggression, it is absolutely necessary to root power in the Armed Forces and the Police, since only they have the organization and the means to confront it. That is the deep truth of what is happening in a large part of our continent, although some refuse to recognize it publicly.... The progress in the creation of a new institutionality so far ... should make it very clear that the traditional political parties that are in recess today will not and could not have any place in it; because their structures, leadership, habits and mentality were formed under the inspiration of an institutional regime that has already died for ever (General Augusto Pinochet Ugarte, Presidential Message, 11 September 1976).

To protect the fundamental values on which Chilean society is based, any action of persons or groups intended to spread doctrines that attack the family, promote violence or a conception of a society founded on the class struggle or that are against the constituted regime should be declared illegal and against the institutional order of the Republic. ... The constitutional duties, of every citizen, are ... to contribute to the preservation of national security (Constitutional Act No. 3 Santiago, Chile, 11 September 1976).

In commenting on the September 11, 1976, decrees and Pinochet's speech, the Chilean Jesuit magazine *Mensaje* (No. 253, October 1976) suggests that perhaps there has not been another set of documents "which introduce such substantial changes in our political regime and in the conception of the constitution and the characteristics of the state, sovereignty, human rights, etc." in the 160 years of the Chilean republic. (It should be noted here that in his September 11, 1977, Presidential Message, Pinochet hardly mentioned "national security" and emphasized instead "authoritarian democracy" and its institutionalization.)

The "doctrine of national security" as official ideology is perhaps less advanced in the rest of the Third World (though in states like Israel and South Korea it is even more advanced), but it is beginning to spread in Asia and Africa. Thus the director of the Indian Institute of Defense Studies and Analysis, K. Subrahmanyam, writes in a book appropriately entitled *Our National Security* that security "does not mean merely safeguarding of territorial boundaries; it means, also, ensuring that the country is industrialized rapidly and develops into a cohesive, egalitarian, technological society" (quotation taken from a review of the book, EPW 10 March 1973: 513). Prime Minister Indira Gandhi justified many of the repressive economic and political measures of her Emergency Rule in similar terms and sought to institutionalize them through the Forty-fourth Amendment to the Constitution, which curbed the power of the judiciary to review executive action (Frank 1977b). Political and economic repression and their institutionalization in neighboring Pakistan, Bangladesh, and Sri Lanka are "justified" in similar terms. In Thailand the director of maintenance of internal peace and order announced that industrial strike action is "detrimental to national security" (FER 4 February 1977; quoted more extensively in Chapter 6). President Marcos' martial law and his prohibition of strikes in the Philippines rests on the same "justification."

The political, economic, and ideological tendencies in Africa are similar, despite the differences in historical experience, colonial heritage, and culture. Thus Claude Ake observes in his "The Congruence of Political Economies and Ideologies in Africa":

> All African countries, even the most obviously capitalist, such as Nigeria, Zaire, Ivory Coast and Senegal, have very large public sectors which are getting larger in every case. This type of economy was a legacy of colonialism which could not be maintained without statism. It is precisely such statism and its associated dominance of the public sector that makes the struggle to power in Africa so bitter. It means that, all over Africa, the state has become the major and sometimes the only owner of industry; the control of the machinery of the state is the key to wealth. In such circumstances the premium of political power becomes very high. The trend all over Africa has been an ever greater increase in the role of the state in the economy. The pressures for this development are the same all over Africa . . . (Ake 1976: 208).

> In all African countries, the leaders have held tenaciously to power. Change of government is brought about only by force. The second development is that political systems of Africa have become uniformly monolithic. Power has become centralized, and opposition to those in power is illegitimate. Third, all African countries are now de facto one-party systems in which the masses have been effectively depoliticized, in the sense that their political participation has been reduced to choices that are totally inconsequential. . . . Elections have become a redundant formality all over Africa. Dissident groups, counter-elites

and progressives are intimidated, incarcerated, or murdered. Workers' movements are deprived of all autonomy and effectiveness (Ake 1976: 207, 205).

They do this by punishing with the utmost ruthlessness all nonconformist behaviour, particularly that [which] challenges property rights and behaviour that allegedly undermines the legitimacy of the rulers. The evidence is overwhelming. There is no country in Africa that does not impose unspeakably harsh punishment—sometimes up to a decade in prison—for petty theft. There is no African country which is not freely using state power to imprison, banish, or murder political dissenters. What is happening in Africa is a reflection not of the uniqueness of the character of Africans, but rather of social forces which have the same effect wherever they occur. In all very poor countries where the rulers maintain exploitative relations and where the struggle for the surplus is very grim, the established order can be maintained only by ruthless coercion verging on fascism (Ake 1976: 210).

But the survival of a regime in conditions of intense competition for a meagre surplus demands not only force, but also—perhaps most importantly—the rendering of privilege and exploitation by the rulers invisible. The present rulers of Africa are becoming increasingly aware of this point, and they are taking steps to conceal their privileges and their exploitation (Ake 1976: 210).

These are the realities that have now led to a hasty revision of the ideology of the nationalist leaders presently in power. If we compare the speeches and writings of the nationalist leaders before independence and after, we find that they all revised their ideologies along the following lines: First, their ideology now proclaims the end of internal ideological conflict. . . . Second, emphasis has shifted from liberty to order. They argue that order (in effect, conformism) is necessary for maximum effectiveness in dealing with problems of development. Order has to be maintained to discourage the numerous enemies. . . . Third, the significance of independence is redefined . . . to hard work, not self-indulgence. Legitimate expectations of the material betterment of the masses are now represented as naive or subversive or as reprehensible hedonism. The fourth characteristic of the postindependence ideologies is the emphasis on unity . . . (Ake 1976: 205–6).

The differences between the African countries that are usually classified as progressive and those that are classified as reactionary are more apparent than real. That is not to say that there are no differences. The conspicuous difference is that the progressive countries prefer to take a socialist stance. . . . [In] the economic exploitation of the masses . . . the differences are marginal . . . (Ake 1976: 208).

Though the term *national security* does not appear in this summary of ideology in Africa, many of its components—common sacrifice for the common good, discipline and order, national unity, and, of course, "the end of ideology" or at least of political and ideological conflict—are emphasized.

In the state that was long regarded internationally as the most radical "socialist" state of Africa, Tanzania, its undisputed leader and president, Julius Nyerere, commemorated the tenth anniversary of the Arusha Declaration of 1967 in which he had proclaimed the goal of *Ujamaa* or self-reliant socialism with this observation:

> Tanzania is certainly neither socialist nor self-reliant. The nature of exploitation has changed but it has not been altogether eliminated. There are still great inequalities between citizens. Our democracy is imperfect. A life of poverty is still the experience of the majority of our citizens. . . . Our nation is still economically dependent upon the vagaries of the weather and upon economic and political decisions taken by other peoples without our participation and consent . . . [the goal of socialism] is not even in sight (IHT 21 April 1977).

While President Nyerere claims that "we in Tanzania have stopped and reversed a national drift towards the growth of a class society," other Tanzanians who are a bit more critical than the President, like Issa Shivji, argue that "the silent class struggle" has grown and that the bureaucratic capitalist class is so far winning it, and in the process making more and more concessions to international capital.

The Institutionalization of Authoritarianism and Political Economic Prospects*

Finally, we must ask ourselves if these authoritarian and military states, with all their economic and political repression, are only a passing phenomenon, a nightmare soon to be forgotten. Or are the oppressive organization and the militarization of society in the Third World being institutionalized so that they will likely endure for the foreseeable future? Several considerations oblige us to pose and try to answer this question. On the one hand, President Carter launched a "human rights" campaign, and since 1977 elections have been held or announced in several countries of the Third World. Both of these circumstances have led—and perhaps were meant to lead—many people to believe that political change can be brought about by appeals to goodwill and that there is a renewed trend toward democratization and liberalization of the state and society in many parts of the Third World. On the other hand, the most authoritative spokesmen of almost all shades of the socialist left in the world have been making official declarations to the effect

*This section remains largely as written in April 1978. More recent events are examined in Chapter 9.

that liberation, revolution, and socialism are on the irresistible offensive all around the Third World (and elsewhere). At every official reception in Peking and in major declarations at the United Nations, the Chinese leadership (irrespective of who it has been each time) has solemnly declared that "the situation in the world is excellent . . . and in China too." The Soviet Union and other East European socialist countries say that imperialism and reaction are on the defensive and losing ground. The Communist parties of Europe at their meeting in Berlin, and those of Latin America at the meeting in Havana, declared that popular democracy, national liberation, and socialist revolution are on the advance in most developed and underdeveloped countries, despite temporary setbacks in Latin America. Trotskyists declare that prerevolutionary situations are in the making in several parts of the world. The same optimism is shared by various shades of socialists and revolutionaries in Latin America, Africa, and South and Southeast Asia. These people have been encouraged by popular mobilization, liberalization, and other events in their respective countries and regions, and consider the time for new political activity to be ripe or ripening. And in fact, since the mid 1970s we have witnessed popular victories in Vietnam, Laos, and Cambodia (some of whose less salutary results are examined in Chapter 9 and WE: Chapter 4); the defeat of Portuguese colonialism and then of Western attempts to subvert the victory of MPLA, which now governs Angola; the groundswell throughout southern Africa in Zimbabwe, Namibia, and in Soweto, Port Elizabeth, and other cities inside South Africa itself; and progressive advances in Somalia, Ethiopia, and Eritrea in the Horn of Africa (though developments here have also been the subject of concern and doubt) and some revolutionary advances in Central America and the Caribbean. There also appears to be greater room for progressive political mobilization and maneuver in some other regions or countries of South Asia, Africa, and Latin America. Civil and international war, particularly with foreign participation or intervention, is unsettling some political regimes, or at least governments, in Africa and the Middle East, and it is threatening to do so in Latin America and parts of Asia (see Chapter 8). The loss of a war makes it difficult for a government to remain in power, but this is not necessarily so for a regime. It is of vital importance, therefore, to know the realistic prospects for the foreseeable future, so that those who are wont to act may know how to do so. The answers, of course, must be sought in the concrete analysis of the concrete situation at each place and time.

We have argued that the imposition of authoritarian and military regimes and their militarization of society have been both the prerequisite and the accompaniment of the restructuring of the economy for its participation in the international division of labor during the present capitalist crisis of capital accumulation. We will now examine the extent to which this authoritarian political organization is likely to be required and/or maintainable during the continued promotion of this new international division of labor and/or new international economic order. We will also try to determine whether these recent economic trends are likely to continue or be replaced by others that would require, be compatible with, or permit different states forms and political regimes. We may pose the following questions:

1. If the recent economic trends are to continue, must they continue to be enforced by the same political forms?
2. If the political forms can be changed in a more democratic or even socialist direction, will the recent economic trends be reversed and the present economic model be replaced by another?
3. In what alternative direction, through what action, and with what likelihood could the Third World countries' participation in the international division of labor be changed; and with what possible consequences for their political regimes and state forms?

The answers to these questions are indispensable in determining whether the recent development of a superexploitative economic order and superrepressive political regime is likely to continue or be reversed in particular countries and regions of the Third World. Let us review some of the evidence.

During 1977 and early 1978 some states of emergency were lifted and elections were held (India, Sri Lanka); more often emergency measures were maintained and elections announced or promised for the near or distant future (in various countries of Latin America and the Philippines); or hard-line military dictatorships were replaced by "soft-line" ones through coups (Thailand); or palace-coup attempts to impose even harder-line regimes were repulsed by existing coalitions (Brazil, Argentina, Tunisia until the end of 1977). Various observers have hailed President Carter's "human rights" campaign as the cause of these developments. More realistically, it was mass mobilization and/or pressure and growing conflicts among economic interest groups and military or other political representatives that promoted political changes in some of these countries.

Optimists regard these liberalizing swallows as signs that the winter of repression is being replaced by a democratic spring. Unfortunately, most of these changes are more apparent than real. In all four major countries of South Asia the 1977–78 political-economic coalitions and their civilian representatives (through elections in India and Sri Lanka) or military executors (in Pakistan and Bangladesh) represented a big step to the *right* in terms of the domestic political forces they represent and interpret (though some of these could for a time afford to reduce the degree of political repression).

In Latin America the authoritarian status quo has been maintained despite some "democratic" stirrings. Hard-line right-wing challenges mounted by General Frota in Brazil and General Viola in Argentina were repulsed by Presidents Geisel and Videla; but these victories were hardly definitive and certainly did not signify much liberalization. In Brazil President Geisel's hand-picked successor, General Figueiredo, has permitted an "opening," including the return of political exiles, but continues to threaten a renewed military clampdown. In Peru and Ecuador elections were announced after a sharp shift to the right by the military regimes. These elections and their results were a negotiated or engineered civilian institutionalization of the underlying political-economic interests. Civilian governments in these countries can still move to the *right* of their military predecessors. In Bolivia, Chile, and Uruguay the military is likely to maintain its control irrespective of any and all plebiscites, the incorporation of "civilians" into the cabinet, and electoral or negotiated *salidas* or exits. In the Philippines President Marcos himself stated that his "elections" would not eliminate martial law, and certainly would not change the locus of power. The elections were held and were universally denounced as a farce; those who charged that they were fraudulent were imprisoned, and martial law remained in force (IHT 17 April 1978).

More significant than these immediate political developments is the institutionalization of the more authoritarian state forms. Nearly everywhere the executive has encroached increasingly on the legislative domain. The relative independence of the judiciary has been challenged and often circumvented, or simply repressed, particularly by military governments. In Pakistan the courts were deprived of judicial jurisdiction over civil rights cases and were denied judicial review of the state of emergency declared by the executive (EPW 4 June 1977). In Chile and several other Latin American countries the courts have lost effective jurisdiction over most "political" cases, which are tried by courts-martial, if at all (often victims simply "disappear"). In Argentina the judges who maintained a modicum of independence from the military authorities were simply replaced wholesale. Executive control increased over the press, the universities, and other institutions. Perhaps most significant, constitutions have been fundamentally amended (India, Pakistan), or otherwise extended through "Constitutional Acts" (Chile) or "Institutional Acts" (Brazil). Constitutions have also been or are in the process of being replaced by wholly new ones (Chile, Ecuador) in order to consecrate and legitimize the measures that were taken under "emergency" rule or martial "law."

> The changes that the state apparatus suffers in the Military state are too radical to be interpreted simply as transitory forms aimed at restoring the former civil state with its bourgeois-democratic liberties after a reasonable delay. These radical changes include the occupation of the state by a military-technocratic elite; the inexistence or absolute subordination of the legislative and of the judiciary under the executive branch, which is in the hands of the military; control of the apparatus of repression by the Armed Forces; militarization of the whole society— universities, education, ideology, etc.—these changes are *structural changes*, which permit big monopoly national and international capital the development of a new superstructure that can bring life to its model

of accumulation, integrate the dependent economy into the new forms of the international division of labor, and—possibly—permit the political and/or economic domination of more backward countries of the regions (Brazilian sub-imperialism) (Petzoldt 1976: 17).

Does this mean that the same kind and degree of political repression will (have to) be maintained into the foreseeable future? On the contrary; insofar as the present holders of power are able to consolidate their rule and to institutionalize their political measures, they will no longer require so much brute force to maintain themselves in power and to pursue their economic model. The deeper the economic crisis and the more radical the economic change, the more violent the political midwife force necessary to impose an alternative economic model to "solve" the economic crisis. But once the new course of economic development or underdevelopment has been well launched, less political force is necessary to keep it on course. Thus the answer to the first question posed above would seem to be that the most violent political forms may not be so necessary in the future. It will depend on the "prosperity" of the new economic course, a prosperity gained at great cost to the people ("the economy is doing fine, the people are not," as President Geisel of Brazil accurately summarized). Violent political forms will also diminish when the functions of the most aberrant political forms have been otherwise institutionalized. This stage seems to have arrived, at least temporarily, in India and Sri Lanka, and in the Latin American countries that announced or began some democratization or liberalization. Such "democratization" includes forms of elections, as well as the possible partial return of the military to their barracks. In none of these countries, however, does this change signify the departure from economic and political power of those who only recently assumed or consolidated their hold on it. The displacement of Somoza by the Sandinistas in Nicaragua and the challenge to entrenched rule in El Salvador and perhaps Guatemala in opposition to regimes of long standing, are facilitated by these regimes' loss of some of their bourgeois support, perhaps because they have been unable to adapt to changing economic and political requirements.

Do political changes in these new regimes signify the abandonment or even the modification of the economic model of capital accumulation and participation in the international division of labor to which these political regimes gave birth or nurturance? Many people entertain hopes of political democratization. Some even have hopes (or illusions) that a new era of economic democratization is in the offing. It is said that the wage rate has been reduced so much that the time must be arriving to raise it again, both for the sake of the wage earners and in the interest of producers of agricultural and industrial commodities for the internal market. These people therefore expect political democratization to be accompanied by economic democratization through the abandonment or radical modification of the economic model of recent years.

In India Prime Minister Desai and his socialist Minister of Industries,

George Fernandes (who had been imprisoned by the previous government for his labor union and strike leadership), certainly did not deliver anything of the kind during the Janata government. The 1977 budget, announced soon after the election, "broke no new ground" and was "in the same mould" as that of the previous government (EPW 18 June and 9 July 1977). The budget and the "new" industrial policy announced in early 1978 presented only "confused goals, ineffective tools, to little purpose," and there was little to distinguish them from their predecessors (EPW 28 January, 4 March, and 11 March 1978). In agriculture, where the Janata party had particular strength, peasants were even more exploited and politically repressed by local landlords with police support than they had been before. The return of Indira Gandhi as Prime Minister is hardly more promising (see Chapter 1). The elected Communist Party of India (Marxist 6) of CPI (M) government of Jyoti Basu in West Bengal (55 million population) became engaged in "putting up a moderate front" (FER 18 November 1977) and "tight-rope walking" (EPW 7 August 1977). And "the business community [was] assured that the government would not allow a rash of labour troubles to break out" (EPW 27 August 1977: 1530). National and foreign industry found it easy to work with the state Chief Minister Basu and his renowned Communist Finance Minister, Ashok Mitra (as they did with the socialist union leader Fernandez). As Ashok Rudra (1977: 1565) pointed out, the government had "two courses of action open to it. It [could] choose the course of encouraging class struggle . . . [with the] clear understanding that such course of action cannot possibly be pursued for any length of time, however." Or it could have chosen to follow the second course, which was "to stick on to the state government power for as long as possible *just for the sake of it. . . .* That means using the administrative services for the purposes for which they are meant—namely protecting and promoting capitalist and landlord class interest." The CPI(M) government in West Bengal has certainly followed the second course of action, and the bourgeois press there and elsewhere has been "full of praise for the newly discovered virtues of Leftist ministers" and "an enthusiastic defender and supporter of the Left Front government." Meanwhile, in Sri Lanka conservative Prime Minister Jairus Jayawardene had only just begun to implement his new economic model, complete with his long-announced free production zone.

The most radical new economic departures with the most brutal political repression have been in Latin America. It is there that the domestic market, worker income, consumer purchasing power, and local manufacturing sales have been most violently sacrificed to the new model of export promotion. Is a degree of political liberalization or even democratization in Latin America likely to effect the abandonment of this model? Or is the *same* economic model likely to be extended and refined through greater foreign investment attracted by the new political "stability"? And would greater domestic political support for this economic model be won by permitting wider bourgeois participation in its benefits—that is, profits—once the model has been made to operate more steadily? Our analysis of the political economy of export promotion today, and at least circumstantial evidence of who is promoting what changes in some of the countries of Latin America, suggest an answer to the second question: Forseeable political changes are not likely to replace, but to consolidate the present economic model. In Argentina, for instance, a spokesman for "democracy" has been Admiral Massera, whose navy has been the most hard-line representative of the interests of the landed oligarchy. A fundamental change of policy by Massera and those he represents would really be a case of the leopard changing his spots. President Videla may be able to keep the army hard liners at bay (though it is still quite possible that the hard line Viola faction will topple him). And he may, like President Llanusse before him, be able to arrange some sort of military-civilian coalition government. But the essential economic policy of the Argentine state is not like to change. We may agree with *Latin American Political Report* (LAPR 24 March 1978: 90) when it suggests that "the return to democracy will involve a civilian-military political structure in which ultimate control will rest with the military. The process will require a long period of transition. . . . The army is also seeking as a prior condition to implementation of its plan that there should be no major modification of the economic strategy of José Martinez de Hoz until 1980 at the earliest. This does not, however, mean that the minister himself must remain at his post."

In Chile Air Force General Leigh became a military spokesman for "democracy" after having been the most outspoken member of the junta for fascist policies and groups. The Christian Democrats, led by ex-President Frei, also rediscovered the virtues of "democracy" after having plotted for and welcomed General Pinochet's military coup and regime. In a book of political reflections Eduardo Frei (1976) made it clear, however, that a return to the sort of democracy that existed before the coup—even during his own presidency—is out of the question and that much more authoritarianism is the order of the day. The Chilean economic program of Frei and his political and economic allies (which include U.S capital and the U.S. government) proposed that the recently neglected industrial bourgeoisie should be given more participation and a greater share of the profits—as part of essentially the same export-oriented economic model that the junta has imposed. Even the economic program of the Popular Unity parties, which had formed the Allende government that Pinochet so brutally overthrew, reserves a most important place for new exports and foreign investment in the Chilean economy. The Popular Unity and Christian Democratic economic programs for a future Chile under their hoped-for rule (jointly or separately) are remarkably similar in most respects; although the Christian Democratic program appears *more* restrictive with regard to foreign investment than the Communist-Socialist Popular Unity program! (Guerrero y Varela 1977). The Popular Unity parties, of course, do not have much hope for significant participation in any foreseeable future government in Chile. What can be expected from a military-civilian coalition government with Christian Democratic or even some Popular Unity participation? Only maintenance of the same export-promoting economic model with some cosmetic improvements and/or modifications to widen its foreign and domestic economic and political support. And although the population would suffer less political repression, its economic fortunes would not improve much.

Economically, the most important country in Latin America today is Brazil. The "economic miracle" there faded in 1974 (see Chapter 1). Since then, there has been continual talk about changing the economic model to one that would give renewed emphasis to the expansion of the internal market. But the feasibility of such a change is doubtful for both national and international economic and political reasons. Marini (1977b) observes that Brazil's present model of capital accumulation and participation in the international division of labor is based on luxury consumption, exports, and state purchases. Only the second and third categories offer any significant or substantial escape from the renewed crisis of Brazilian capital accumulation; and part of the first may have to be sacrificed to the other two. But ultimately, the extent to which exports remain an important motor force of accumulation and economic activity in the Third World depends not only on how much anyone in the Third World wants to export, but also on how much the rest of the world wants to import.

In Africa military regimes are the rule and in 1978 only three countries (Gambia, Botswana, and Mauritius) out of the fifty members of the Organization of African Unity were said to have had functioning multiparty governments (IHT 31 January 1978). Military coups have been commonplace since independence. But recently there have been some moves in the direction of "democratization" or institutionalization of state rule in Africa, especially in western Africa. Senegal is "edging toward a multiparty state." Referendums and other moves toward elections and civilian (or civilian-military or military-backed "civilian") governments took place in 1979 in Upper Volta, Ghana, and Nigeria. But all these states have imposed severe limitations on their "democracy." In Upper Volta the number of political parties is limited by the constitution. Before the coup by Lieutenant Rawlins in Ghana the military government presented voters with a Hobson's choice between a civil-military "union government" without political parties and an alternative that left its own perpetuation or parliamentary choices undefined. After fraudulent balloting in which the military government supposedly received a 54 percent majority, opposition leaders were rounded up and put in jail (IHT 26 January 1978; ICP 1 May 1978). The progressive Rawlins coup altered the pre-electoral power alignment in Ghana, and yet the government that emerged from the elections continues the same export promotion policy as its predecessors. In Nigeria electoral plans were designed to exclude regional or tribal parties, and other restrictions and prospects made some labor union leaders fearful that they and their worker constituents would fare even worse after elections (IPC 30 January 1978). The elected civilian government has pursued essentially the same economic policies as its military predecessors, except of course that economic circumstances no longer permit the previous spending spree. Thus, despite deceiving appearances, there "is no sudden blossoming of democracy in Africa" after all (IHT 31 January 1978).

The third question posed above was what alternative international division of labor may be in the offing and what prospects it may offer for the modification of political regimes and state forms in Third World countries. One of these alternatives is a renewed turn to protectionism by the industrial nations (examined in WE: Chapter 5).

The sharpening of the economic and political conflicts generated in the world economic crisis may lead to substantially increased metropolitan protectionism and to a breakdown of the international financial and economic system, and therefore also to a reduction of western imports from Third World countries. In that case, the Third World countries will not be able to carry out the role now assigned to them in the "new international division of labor" or to pursue their present policies of "export promotion." This international economic breakdown, of course, would severely undermine the economic basis of the new authoritarian regimes. A weakened economic basis could perhaps alter the political coalitions and alliances in some Third World countries in the direction of the nationalist-populist alliances and internal market policies of the "import substitution" era of the 1930s–1950s. Some important pressures and tendencies in this direction are already visible in both the metropolis and parts of the periphery. Some American business and labor interests are already calling for the "human rights" enforcement of minimum wage and labor standards in Third World countries whose exports compete with domestic production and jobs.

At least two other intermediary alternatives are visible on the horizon: limited export promotion in very specialized product lines in particular Third World countries, which may or may not permit regeneration of production for an internal market and its expansion; and the formation of economic and political blocs—e.g. United States—Latin America, Europe—Africa, Japan—Southeast Asia—in which more limited or specialized export promotion and some expansion of the internal market might be reserved for Third World countries in the respective imperial area. The second alternative would make it likely that the metropolitan political regimes in each bloc would experience marked shifts to the right, with concomitant political repercussions in the neocolonies. The productive apparatuses of the Third World countries would then be even more dominated by the metropolitan capital of their respective bloc than they are now.

In short, the immediate prospects for a democratic summer since the 1977–1978 liberalizing spring are not very bright. Mr. Carter's "human rights" campaign never held much promise for the Third World, and it is now being abandoned for domestic economic and foreign policy reasons anyway in concert with renewed recession (see WE: Chapters 3 and 6). Prospects for a democratic summer will remain dim unless and until popular revolutionary movements are organized, as in Nicaragua and Iran, on a new basis in the Third World countries themselves, in the imperialist ones, and perhaps in the socialist ones as well.

Chapter 8
The Arms Economy and
Warfare in the Third World

A new world military order is being forged much more successfully and rapidly than a new international economic order. Third World arms imports have skyrocketed in response to pressures to export ever more sophisticated and expensive military equipment from the North and sometimes competitive pressures by military or militarily threatened governments in the South to import these weapons. Additionally, more and more Third World countries are increasing their own production of arms, including sophisticated weapons systems, both for their own use and for export. From an economic point of view, armaments are just another major world industry that is adapting to the changing international division of labor. Military conflicts in the Third World, including international wars, civil wars, and military coups, are increasing. This is not necessarily because of the growing stocks of armaments in Third World states. Military conflicts are also provoked by pressures and incentives produced by the world economic crisis. Third World governments are affected both directly and indirectly by the growing international geopolitical tensions and the competition between the great powers. These conflicts are likely to provide the setting and opportunity for further political change in many parts of the Third World, but they are not likely to further the cause of socialism.

The Arms Trade

The progressive militarization of society and the growing arms economy in the Third World are part of the "militarization of the world economy" (Sivard 1976: 5) and of the "New International Military Order" (Oberg 1976 and n.d.; Lock and Wulf 1977: vi). The trend to an arms economy is among the most significant *real* characteristics of the *real* emerging "New International Economic Order" lately heralded at international meetings and in the press (see WE: Chapter 5). We argued in Chapter 7 that the militarization of the state and society in the Third World is the logical derivative of the economic exigencies of capital accumulation in the Third World, which in turn is essentially determined by the process of world capital accumulation, especially during its present period of crisis. Of course, this militarization has consequences in policy and action, including war, that are also directly derived from or related to international political, strategic, and military concerns in a world of bi- and multinational alliances and their shifts. Clearly, the superpowers seek political and military alliances with the states and military establishments of the Third World, particularly in politically sensitive or strategically important areas. The fragile nature of most of these alliances and the frequent changes, often for economic or economically determined political reasons, from one side to another are illustrated by Sadat's shift of Egypt from the Soviet camp to the American, by Quadaffi's constant shifting of Libya from one ally and enemy to another, and by the "exchange" of Ethiopia and Somalia in the system of international alliances. Some military alliances are more long-standing and have more far-reaching consequences, however.

The military alliance between the United States and certain Third World countries, for example, has a relatively stable tradition. Since World War II a few Western countries have trained well over half a million military personnel from the Third World. The United States alone has trained almost four hundred thousand, of whom two-thirds were officers; 80 percent of these were trained within the United States itself or in its Canal Zone possession (Wolpin n.d.: 7). In addition, the United States has given advanced training to ten thousand foreign policemen at its International Police Academy in Washington and has provided training to over one million policemen in the Third World through its "public safety advisers" in forty countries. Because of repeated scandal, the police training programs were canceled by Congress in 1973 and 1974. Yet many of these same activities and related supply programs (of military and police equipment) continue under the overseas operation of the "Drug Enforcement Administration," whose expenditures now match those of the discontinued training programs (NACLA July–August 1976: 31). The military and police programs of the United States have political and ideological objectives. In countless testimonials it is declared that they are designed to "win friends and influence people" destined one day to be in positions of power or poised to take power in their respective countries. The ideological direction of these programs has been to inculcate participants with negative images of "communism, neutralism, leftist revolution, forces of disruption, revolutionary ideas, political dissidents, insurgents, extremists, radicals, ultranationalists, and political instability in general" (Wolpin n.d.: 8). Third World military personnel have also been trained and supplied in or by the socialist countries, with a different ideological direction, of course. But this has not prevented many of them—for example, in Egypt and Syria—from putting their expertise at the service of local and international reaction. In some cases the socialist countries have sent military missions to support outright reactionary regimes that openly collaborate with the West and international capital, such as those in Pakistan and India. The socialist countries have even supported rulers who were placed in power by and remain subservient to the U.S. CIA, like Mobutu in Zaire. In exceptional circumstances, U.S. and other Western military training programs have also backfired in that a dominant sector of the armed forces, as in Peru, has turned moderately "nationalist" against the imperial power and individual trainees have become nationalists or even revolutionaries. By and large, though, Western and particularly U.S. military training and "assistance" programs have been eminently successful in introducing an armed fifth column to defend "Western values" into the societies of the Third World.

Military and economic "aid" have gone hand in hand, with much of the former disguised as the latter. The vast bulk of American "economic" aid to the Third World has gone to a few countries of special strategic political and military importance: South Korea, Taiwan, Indochina, and Israel. Outright U.S. military aid exceeded economic aid by five to four in fiscal year 1974 and, according to Western estimates, Soviet military aid was double its economic aid in the same year (Sivard 1976: 8). Furthermore, military aid has progressively given way to military sales on a simple commercial basis. In the United States military grants predominated in the 1950s; grants and sales were roughly equal in the 1960s; and in the 1970s grants have been increasingly replaced by commercial arms sales. In response to the cut in the space program, the end of the Vietnam War, the 1973–1975 recession, and the American balance-of-payments crisis, U.S. sales of armaments abroad increased from about $1 billion in 1970 to $10 billion in 1975. Other Western manufacturers also launched arms sales drives, if only to extend their production series and pay for the enormous fixed overhead costs of increasingly expensive weapons that their own armed forces cannot use in sufficient quantities to lower unit costs. Armaments have become the number-one export industry of France. Without it, the already weak French economy would suffer a grave crisis. "The equilibrium of our foreign trade is, it is true, a function of our arms sales," French Socialist Party leader François Mitterand, has admitted (LM 12 November 1976). Lock (1979:33–38) estimates that military exports as a proportion of all machinery and transport equipment exports (Standard International Trade Classification—SITC 7) are about 19 percent for the United States and Italy, 12 percent for France and 7 percent for Britain—and 60 percent for the Soviet Union. Lock identifies arms imports as 12 percent of Third World imports of SITC 7 imports of equipment and technology but thinks that including the arms imported as "transport equipment" etc. it is safe to assume that arms transfers to the Third World countries exceed 20 percent of their imports of production technology.

TABLE 8.1

Total Arms Transfers, by Suppliers and Recipient Regions 1965–1974 ($ million)

Recipient Regions	Major Capitalist Suppliers					Major Socialist Suppliers			Other Suppliers	Total
	U.S.A.	France	U.K.	West Germany	Canada	U.S.S.R.	Czechoslovakia and Poland	China		
World Total	31,563	2,826	2,089	1,221	1,187	18,793	2,481	2,119	2,125	64,404
NATO	8,447	770	505	724	893	—	—	—	515	11,854
Warsaw Pact	—	—	—	—	—	5,674	1,888	5	35	7,602
OPEC	2,374	668	662	154	89	2,152	136	—	570	6,825
East Asia	14,640	40	145	23	32	4,049	15	1,616	321	20,881
South Asia		271	98	36	10	1,706	159	335	36	2,922
Middle East	5,628	461	603	181	45	5,733	337	1	2	465	13,455
Africa	341	669	258	73	17	711	68	81	263	2,481
Latin America	811	463	269	137	172	323	2	—	229	2,406

Source: Robin Luckham, *Militarism: Arms and the Internationalization of Capital* IDS Bulletin Vol. 8, No. 2, March 1977, p. 47.

The purchasers of these economically generated metropolitan arms manufactures are largely in the Third World. Third World countries imported 66 percent of these arms in 1970 and 85 percent or $7.4 billion worth in 1973 (Albrecht et al. 1976: 13). A summary of suppliers and recipients of arms transfers until 1974 appears in Table 8.1. Since then, encouraged by the war and the petroleum price increase in the Middle East in 1973, Third World countries have increased their arms purchases enormously, by 40 percent in 1974 and by another 40 percent in 1975 (Kaldor 1976: 293). Between 1960 and 1977–1978 (when they levelled off, but perhaps only temporarily) Third World military expenditures increased four fold in constant prices and reached approximately US 86 billion in 1978. By comparison, total world military expenditures increased by about 70 percent and reached $425 billion (Sivard 1979: 5–7). Previously these countries had usually bought obsolescent or second-hand arms, though with a component of modern arms. Today they are increasingly purchasing the most modern, technologically sophisticated, and incredibly expensive military equipment from the metropolitan powers. Iran took the lead by purchasing the American F-14 Tomcat fighter plane weapons system, which "is so complicated that even the U.S Navy is having trouble keeping it operational; Iran's Spruance class destroyer will be even more sophisticated than those being procured by the U.S. Navy" (IHT 6 August 1976). Under the Shah's policy of buying "tomorrow's weapons, not today's," Iran ordered $9 billion worth of arms from the United States alone, most of them following the 1973 increase in oil prices, including $3.9 billion in 1974 and $2.6 billion in 1975, after oil revenues began to decline again (Chubin 1976: 8).

It is practically impossible to give an accurate accounting of Third World arms purchases, since in official trade statistics arms are frequently camouflaged as "transportation" and other equipment. In some cases, however, armaments reach one-fourth to one-third of total expenditures on imports (as in South Korea in 1965 and Egypt in 1969) and one-third to one-half of foreign technology imports during particular years. As many Third World countries have learned, the initial purchase price of military equipment often represents only half the total expenditure necessary to keep it operational—spare parts and supporting equipment account for the rest. Then when the arms race makes the equipment obsolete, it must be replaced by much more expensive equipment. To these costs must be added the interest payments on the debt incurred to purchase the equipment (Lock and Wulf 1977: xxiii–xxvii).

> It is in the nations of the developing world—in Asia, Africa, and Latin America—that the most pronounced relative increase in military expenditures has occurred. In fifteen years, military spending in developing countries has more than doubled, from $15 billion in 1960 to $39 billion in 1974 (in constant 1973 dollars). The mildest increase was in Latin America [which already spent most], where expenditures were up two-fold, the sharpest in the Middle East, where they were up

eight-fold. In the developing world as a whole, military expenditures increased twice as fast as the economic base to support them. . . . The growth of [armed] forces has exceeded both the rapid growth of population and the development of an industrial base. In the developing countries, on average, there are now four soldiers in the regular forces to ten workers in manufacturing industry. In developed countries, the ratio is about one to ten. . . . For at least some fragile industrial economies, the military is the fastest growing sector of the economy (Sivard 1976: 6–7).

Between 1960 and 1973 military expenditures—conservatively estimated, since military imports are difficult to identify—rose from 3.4 percent to 4.4 percent of Third World gross national product (calculated from Sivard 1976: 20). Since then, of course, the absolute and relative growth of military expenditures in the Third World has shot up (it was 5 percent of Third World GNP in 1977, calculated from Sivard 1979: 25). An important contributing factor has been the crisis-generated accession of military governments, which are particularly prone to expanding the size of the armed forces—they have doubled in size in Chile since the military coup, for example—and to supplying themselves with military hardware. Another contributing factor has been the (usually unsuccessful) attempt by civilian governments to buy off their coup-prone and trigger-happy military brass. A third factor in the increase has been the worldwide arms race fired by international tensions and national political ambitions.

Ninety-three countries in the Third World are receiving arms from abroad (Leitenberg 1979: 15). In 1974, 57 percent of these nations devoted over 10 percent of their government budgets to military expenditures, 30 percent spent over 20 percent, and 25 percent spent over 25 percent of their budgets on the military (Leitenberg and Ball 1977: 311). Since then, not only the amounts of military expenditures but also their shares of national income and government budgets have increased greatly. In Africa the annual growth of military expenditures increased from 8 percent in the five-year period before 1973 to 15 percent in the five-year period following that year. The biggest increases and the largest amounts spent on the military have been in the Middle East. There total arms expenditures approximately equal those of the rest of the Third World put together. Middle Eastern military expenditures were about 11 percent of regional GNP in 1973 and 17 percent in 1975. In 1974 military expenditures as a percentage of GNP were 32 percent in Israel, 23 percent in Egypt, 14 to 15 percent in Saudi Arabia, Syria, Iraq, and Jordan, and 9 percent in Iran. In 1977 military expenditures were $7.9 billion (or 24 percent of the government budget) in Iran, $7.5 billion in Saudi Arabia, $4.4 billion (or 37 percent of the budget) in Egypt, and $4.3 billion (or 35 percent of the budget) in Israel (data from SIPRI 1979; Metra 1978; and Chubin 1976, citing the International Institute of Strategic Studies).

The same pattern of military expenditures, albeit on a lesser scale, is apparent elsewhere:

Since South Vietnam's Fall World's Arms
Salesmen Find Southeast Asia a Big Market

The non-Communist nations of Southeast Asia, all strengthening their military forces in the wake of South Vietnam's defeat, have become a big market for international arms salesmen ... [with] concluded or pending deals that total about $1.1 billion. . . . The forces are being strengthened far less for any external threat than to counter local insurgencies. . . . Cash deals exceed military aid to the area for the first time. The biggest arms purchaser may be Thailand. . . . (IHT 18 January 1977).

Mary Kaldor argues that

high levels of military spending ... can be partly explained by the direct role of the armed forces in the allocation of resources, absorbing surplus product created in the countryside and mobilizing its expenditure in towns. . . . The benefits accrue to small groups in towns and the metropolis. . . . Whereas military expenditure previously consisted largely of expenditure of foreign exchange and could be seen as a method of channelling resources from the periphery to the metropolis, now the bourgeoisie can claim a larger share of the surplus product and military expenditure can also be seen as a method of channelling resources from countryside to town. Military expenditure is paid largely out of surplus generated in the countryside but it is spent in the metropolis and the towns. . . . This is the role that the industrial army plays in the allocation of resources. It is a role that is not peculiar to arms expenditure (Kaldor 1976: 297).

Third World Arms Manufacture

Arms manufacture is one of the fastest-expanding, most important—and most profitable—industries in many countries of the Third World. Lock and Wulf (1977) found that forty-one Third World countries—eight in Latin America, twelve in Africa, five in the Near East/West Asia, and sixteen elsewhere in Asia—plus five in the southern periphery of Europe were engaged in or preparing for the domestic manufacture of arms in the late 1970s:

The level of domestic arms production attained so far in the respective countries differs by a wide margin. Most industries are restricted to the manufacture of small arms or ammunition in relatively small quantities, others are specialized in the construction of small naval craft only. In some countries, however, domestic arms production has attained a considerable level and a relatively high degree of diversification including even production for export. Argentina, Brazil, India, Israel, South Africa, Spain, possibly Taiwan and Yugoslavia are to be mentioned while other nations like Egypt, Iran, Pakistan and Turkey are pursuing an expansion of their domestic arms industry. . . .

Modern fighter aircraft, jet trainer or aeroengines are built in 12 developing countries, generally under license, while light aircraft are manufactured in 14 nations of the Third World. Eight aircraft manufacturers in 14 nations of the Third World produce or assemble helicopters, for missiles and rockets the corresponding figure is 11, for military electronics and avionics nine. The construction of hulls for small naval craft and fighting ships takes place in more than 30 developing countries, while engines, armament and electronic equipment are normally imported. About ten developing nations have constructed warships for their navies above 500 ts or plan to do so, while eight countries produced armoured personnel carriers or even tanks. At present more new projects than ever are still in the pipeline, some of them quite demanding. Eight more countries, alone, pursue plans to take up the production of modern fighter aircraft or jet trainers. Additional countries are certain to enter the register of domestic arms production soon. Other countries will expand and diversify their present productive capacity. . . . Quite often the share of locally added value in the production of weapon systems is minimal.

The production of modern weapon systems imposes itself by backward and forward linkages on previous and subsequent production stages. The choices of techniques in large sectors of industry are predetermined by the technological imperatives of arms production. Capital-intensive, minimum scales of production, quality otherwise not warranted and too expensive for civilian production [such as quality steels and other metal alloys] are determining industrial standards of incipient industries in these developing countries (Lock and Wulf, 1977: x–xi, xxii).

Especially remarkable in this regard is the country with by far the largest number of the poorest people in the world—India. With its one-million-man armed forces complemented by another 800,000 police and para-military forces, India occupies a proud fourth place in military manpower behind the United States, the Soviet Union, and China. In terms of military expenditures, India occupied fourteenth place in the world in 1973, second after Israel in the Third World (this was before Iran and Saudi Arabia vastly increased military expenditures following the oil price increases). If some 240,000 civilians employed by the armed forces and 200,000 workers employed in the Indian armaments industry and ordnance are added in, the number of Indian workers directly dependent on the military apparatus is of the order of 2,240,000—nearly half the 5,100,000 workers engaged in manufacturing, excluding mining and energy. India's direct military defense expenditures, excluding nuclear, missile, and some other development expenditures, consumes about 3.7 percent of GNP, compared with an average of 2.1 percent for Latin America and 2.2 percent for Africa, regions that are known for their military establishments. The 16.5 percent annual growth rate of Indian military spending between 1961 and 1971 exceeded the average growth rate of 12 percent in the Third World and was higher than that of nearly all North and Latin American and European countries and China. Thus after increasing by about 65 percent during the 1950s, Indian military expenditures multiplied about five times during the decade of the 1960s and nearly doubled again in the first half of the 1970s. Not surprisingly, military expenditures shot up during the Sino-Indian border conflict of 1961–1962, and again during the Indo-Pakistani War of 1971–1972, but declined during the first Indo-Pakistani conflict of 1965, which was quickly settled. Significantly, these expenditures show a striking and consistent correlation with periods of economic crisis—in 1961–1962, and again for the whole period since 1967! (All data in this paragraph are from V. P. Gandhi 1974 and Albrecht et al. 1976: 105–31.) It is reasonable to suspect that the Sino-Indian War—whose initiation by India has been proved beyond any legitimate doubt—and the second Indo-Pakistani War, as well as related military expenditures, were provoked by and for economic-political reasons. However that may be,

> when "development" was the aim of the nation, the Central government was able to raise the revenue ratio [of taxes to GNP] by 1.5 per cent in a whole decade. But then, when "defence" was called for, the government was able to achieve a similar percentage in a matter of two years—from 6.4 percent in 1961–62 to 7.9 per cent in 1963–64. ... [The ratio declined again] and then there was a war and we raised our revenue ratio again to 7.7 percent. What this suggests is that in the sixties we have needed wars to motivate us to undertake substantial revenue efforts—as if development was not a serious aim to make tax efforts for! (V. P. Gandhi 1974: 1491).

In fact, it *is not!* On the other hand, taxation to finance military ventures that are profitable to capital *is* a serious aim; serious enough to absorb 30 percent of the Indian central government's allocable expenditures in 1961–62 and 42 percent in the early 1970s. Some estimates of hidden military expenditures in the Indian budget indicate that the total is three times greater than the officially admitted figure—or over 80 percent of the budget, which seems exaggerated (FER 7 May 1975).

What perhaps most distinguishes the military establishment in India from that in other Third World countries is the scope and development of military production within the country itself. This phenomenon argues for the economic importance or rationale of military expenditures for Indian capital:

> The far-reaching and broad scoped production program of the Indian ordnance factories and armaments enterprises includes not only small arms, munitions and uniforms, but also complex weapons systems like

supersonic fighters, jet trainers, fighter bombers, helicopters, medium and light tanks, antitank and ground-to-air missiles, destroyers and patrol boats. Additionally, electronic equipment and precision machine tools are produced. The newest production line of state armaments enterprise is the fabrication of special metals and high quality materials for the construction of airplanes, missiles and electronic equipment and instruments (Albrecht et al. 1976: 120).

Most famous, perhaps, is the Indian production of Soviet-designed Mig-21 fighters, the spare parts for which India sought to sell to Egypt after its break with the Soviet Union. When the Soviets refused to allow India to proceed with this sale, the Chinese offered to replace the parts for free! India has been more successful in the export of other heavy weaponry to other Middle Eastern countries.

Lock and Wulf distinguish two development models of arms production. One attempts, but largely fails, to achieve self-sufficiency in a vertically integrated arms industry. With the much more common model—which is part of the general "industrialization" model—arms are manufactured through licensing and/or subcontracting by Western and Eastern producers. This results in a high dependence on imported components, the costs of which absorb all the potential foreign exchange savings of local production, and also in direct and indirect production costs that make domestic production even more expensive for the national economy than importing the same equipment outright (Lock and Wulf 1977: xv–xxii; see also their contributions to Albrecht et al. 1976). The second model of arms production—which, like other industrial production, results in a great dependency on imports— satisfies the desire of metropolitan manufacturers to transfer part of their productive operations to cheap-labor economies that do not impose political restrictions and may even offer political advantages for export to Third World countries. An example is West German arms manufacture in Thailand, through which the German firm circumvents West Germany's legal restrictions of arms exports to countries with certain political tensions. This model, of course, generates incentives in the Third World countries to emulate the metropolitan countries in reducing unit production costs by producing more than local demand can absorb and then exporting the excess. This export of arms also seeks to ally balance-of-payments problems, including those that arms production itself generates. Arguments justifying such arms production in terms of "national security" abound, of course, but they are frequently be-lied by the resulting dependence on the metropolitan producers and their governments, which reserve the right to veto the use and sale of these arms and can enforce this veto by suddenly cutting off the vital flow of supplies, com-ponents, spare parts, and so on. Pakistan, India, and Israel, for example, have in recent years found their ability to use or dispose of arms built with foreign licenses or components compromised by such vetoes. This dependence, then, affects not only the use of the specific armaments concerned, but extends to other aspects of foreign and domestic policy. In a sense, these armaments industries are hostages that make their manufacturers most vulnerable to blackmail precisely when these arms are most needed for "national security."

The ideological defense of military expenditures—as well as a host of other measures (discussed in Chapter 7)—through the appeal to "national security" obscures much more concrete and immediate economic and political interests.

It is persuasively arguable—and in some cases, e.g. India and Israel, demonstrable—that arms production is demanded by the vested economic and political interests of capital accumulation through the capital goods and exports sectors. This is, of course, especially the case when domestic civilian demand is—as both an instrument and a consequence of this same accumulation model—insufficient to permit the full or even adequate utilization of installed capacity in steel and other industries or to permit sufficient profits in some manufacturing sectors. As a result of this kind of accumulation crisis, public expenditures on domestic arms production, whether directly by private enterprise or by state-owned enterprises that purchase inputs from the private sector, are a welcome source of demand, insistently promoted by precisely those industrial interests with economic and political influence in the state. They, and their spokesmen in the press and elsewhere, become the loudest defenders of "national security." This political-economic demand extends, where possible, to nuclear power and the atomic bomb, the most capital-intensive industry and armament of all. Here—and not in threats from Pakistan or even China, from Argentina, or from the African front states— lies the explanation for the Indian atomic bomb and the Brazilian and South African plans to build one, and the Pakistani and Argentine plans to follow suit. (For India, see Frank 1973, 1977b; for Brazil, see Marini and Pellicer 1967–1968.)

This economic reason, derived from the profit conditions of capital accumulation on the national and international level, also explains away the paradox—remarked upon by Albrecht, Lock, and Wulf (1976)—of "irrationally" producing armaments that cost more in total expenditures and/or foreign exchange than they would if imported outright. The overriding objective of such arms production is not to save or minimize production costs through domestic manufacture, but rather to *maximize public expenditures* on, and hence profits in, domestic capital goods and machine-building industry—even at the cost of high expenditures of foreign exchange. These high expenditures (not coincidentally) benefit the foreign producers who are engaged in joint ventures with local producers.

Thus the production—not to mention the subsequent use and replacement—of armaments, especially those with the most capital-intensive advanced technology, becomes a "growth industry" with "public sector" demand par excellence. What better ideological justification is there for this "growth industry" than "national security," and what better arguments are there for blue-collar workers than "jobs" and for white-collar employees than R & D and engineering positions? According to the Shah of Iran, huge military expenditures constitute the shortest and quickest route to increased productivity and a highly trained work force (Chubin 1976: 38–39). Others have developed ideological arguments supporting military expenditures and production as the "growth industry" best suited to "generate growth." Thus, a peace-loving Quaker under contract to the Pentagon, Emile Benoit, has even claimed to demonstrate in his *Defense and Economic Growth in Developing Countries* that a "strong positive correlation between high defense burdens and rapid growth rates" shows that "it seems clear that in sample countries higher defense burdens stimulate growth" (Benoit n.d.: 2,8), and not vice versa. Such growth comes especially through military training but also through military equipment and production. When Benoit discussed his thesis at a symposium

> a large number of concerns were expressed regarding the methodology and the conclusions of the paper. . . . Serious questions were raised, particularly with respect to the statistical treatment of the available data on military expenditures and GDP as a measure for development [which] most participants felt . . . is not a satisfactory measure since the effect on welfare of people may be negligible or even be negative for a large part of the population. . . . [The inference from the correlation] could be challenged by pointing out that other causal relationships could be presented to explain this phenomenon. For instance, high economic growth rates achieved in a developing country, especially exported growth under world market conditions, might antagonize large sectors of the population. Since inequalities are increased in such a situation, social frictions could lead to an expansion of military expenditures to ensure, by means of repression, sustained industrial growth. Furthermore, it was pointed out that militarization in the Third World often correlates with crisis situations in the capitalist system. . . . Nonetheless some participants expressed their interest in [Benoit's] approach and recommended that it [be] given further study (*Pugwash Newsletter*, January 1977: 90–91).

This is how the necessity of "national security" yields the virtue of "development." According to the Shah of Iran, there is no dichotomy between guns and butter. On the contrary, for economic development, defense expenditure "is not only compatible but essential. The one is worthless without the other. There is no economic power without military power" (from an interview quoted in Chubin 1976: 23). Of course, the Shah was right, if he meant the development of the profit and power of the powerful over the powerless.

War and Other Military Conflicts in the Third World

It is almost impossible to define and measure the use of military organization, equipment, and manpower in military conflict. Their very existence is a threat, and the threat itself constitutes a use. Indeed, most of the time the mere possession of weapons and the threat to use them—nuclear bombs, an action-ready army or police force, or a simple gun in the hands of a bank robber—produce the effect for which the weapons and the armed organization behind them were designed. The perpetual threat of military "intervention" in the political process in Third World countries, no matter how apparently "free" and "democratic" their elections may seem, constitutes military-political intervention. The difficulty of defining military action and conflict applies equally to "international" conflicts across the borders of two or more states. But in this case the difficulty is augmented by that of defining and identifying "international," since the participation or intervention of a second or third state in any particular conflict is often deliberately vague.

Therefore the many attempts to define, identify, count, and analyze military conflicts in the Third World since 1945 are more confusing than clarifying. Depending on the criteria used by the analyst, the number of such conflicts counted has ranged from 30 to 350 (Leitenberg 1979). The often cited responsible studies by Istvan Kende and by the Stockholm International Peace Research Institute (SIPRI) count 119 military conflicts in the Third World between 1945 and 1975, and the latter adds a further 14 conflicts for 1976. According to these studies, then, on the average twelve military conflicts were going on in the Third World on any given day since the Second World War (Leitenberg 1977: 8).

While he was still U.S. Secretary of Defense, Robert McNamara claimed in 1966 that

> In the last 8 years alone, there have been no less than 164 internationally significant outbreaks of violence. . . . What is striking is that only 15 of these 165 significant resorts to violence have been military conflicts between two states. And not a single one of the 164 conflicts has been a formally declared war. Indeed, there has not been a formal declaration of war—anywhere in the world—since World War II (US DSB 6 June 1966, cited in Leitenberg 1977: 8).

Of course, the war Mr. McNamara waged against Vietnam was not declared either. And many of the other "internationally significant outbreaks of violence" were so significant for the United States that it felt impelled to intervene in them in one way or another, usually without declaring it was doing so.

In his study of *Local Wars in Asia, in Africa and in Latin America (1945–1969)* the Hungarian Istvan Kende (1973) summarizes:

> The principal type of contemporary war is one that has the territory of one single country as its place of operation and in which the objective is to change the regime and the government and to overthrow the existing power. In this kind of war, the principal type is . . . war with foreign participation. . . . The participation of foreign powers in the wars is becoming a more and more general trait. . . . Foreign participation is

more frequent in the wars of longer duration. Therefore, one may suppose that foreign intervention probably contributes to their prolongation. . . . Foreign powers are more interested in the overthrow or the maintenance of a regime in power than in border conflicts (Kende 1973: 83–85).

Kende finds the United States most active in this kind of foreign intervention, which is not surprising since it replaced Britain and France in their interventionist roles after 1960. Leitenberg (1977: 3) also emphasizes foreign "military interventions, in relation to wars and conflicts; this is probably the least systematically studied area relating to war and conflict. In fact, it is barely studied at all, systematically or otherwise." The recent revelations of interventions by the CIA may provide the basis for such studies that go beyond the notorious American interventions in Iran in 1953, Guatemala in 1954, Lebanon in 1958, the Congo and Cuba in 1961, Panama (and Brazil?) in 1964, and the Dominican Republic in 1965.

Leitenberg (1979) also reviewed twenty other studies of military coups d'état and used them to compile a list of both successful coups and unsuccessful attempts. Between 1945 and 1975 Leitenberg counts 276 successful coups (and 269 unsuccessful attempts), of which 100 (and 103) took place between 1945 and 1960 and 176 (and 166) took place between 1961 and 1975. (Leitenberg says his figures of 18 successful coups and 18 unsuccessful attempts for 1976 to 1978 are very incomplete, so they are not used here.) Until 1960 most of these coups and attempts were in Latin America. But with the creation of many independent states in Africa after 1961, this continent experienced 71 successful coups and 83 unsuccessful attempts, while Latin America had 44 successes and 36 failures. (These figures suggest, incidentally, that on balance there is a nearly even chance of succeeding in a coup attempt; but in Latin America the chances of winning are better and in Africa less than fifty-fifty.) In the decade after 1966, of the 105 successful coups and 96 unsuccessful attempts, 51 and 58, respectively, were in Africa and 23 and 16, respectively, took place in Latin America. According to David Lamb, writing in the *Los Angeles Times*,

> No military government in Africa has ever surrendered power voluntarily. In fact, no government has ever changed hands peacefully through the electoral process in the 20 years since colonial Africa started breaking up into independent nations (IHT 12 June 1978).

These data suggest that the frequency of military coups increased throughout the 1960s, and then diminished somewhat during the 1970s. The calculations of Kende show that the number of wars and the length of these wars in the Third World have been increasing: from twenty-five years' duration of all wars put together in the period 1945–1949, to thirty-three years' duration in 1950–1954, forty-eight years in 1955–1959, fifty-seven years in 1960–1964, and eighty-nine years in 1965–1969. Kende's graph

(1973: 21) shows a tendency to longer durations since 1964. The number of wars in any given year was, on the average, six in 1945–1954, ten in 1955–1964, and eighteen in 1965–1969 (Kende 1973: 20). The number and length of military conflicts in the Third World therefore seems to have been increasing, particularly since the mid-1960s. This tendency toward more military conflict in the Third World seems to be, at least in part, generated by the world economic and political crisis. The persistence—and probable aggravation—of this crisis is likely to generate still more military conflict in the foreseeable future.

According to popular conceptions, the wider distribution of armaments causes wars and other military conflicts. Indeed, Kende (1973: 73–82) does find positive correlations between military expenditures and arms imports on the one hand, and war on the other. But this correlation does not mean that armaments *cause* war or conflict—though, of course, the prossession of arms constitutes a credible threat. In his discussion of the "causes of the increasing tendency" of war and other military conflicts in the Third World, Kende (1973: 68–72) notes the shift by the United States from a strategy of "massive retaliation" during the cold war era to one of "flexible response" through "limited war" after the Soviet Union achieved nuclear parity; the development of national liberation movements and their repression; the simple statistical increase in the number of states in or among which military conflicts could take place; and the increase of tension within many of these states. We will examine these and related causes of increased military conflict in greater detail.

The American strategic posture since it was set in the postwar period by Secretaries of State Dean Acheson and John Foster Dulles has been dominated by the idea of "containment." It is hardly necessary here to document its application through overt military and covert CIA actions in the substantially successful repression of national liberation movements, and indeed of the most elemental progressive political developments all around the Third World. Dulles used to say that there are "no neutrals" and "those that are not with us are against us" and have to be combated tooth and nail. After the Soviet Union achieved nuclear parity with the United States and thereby produced a nuclear "stalemate," the United States found it expedient to "widen its options" through "flexible response" in "limited local wars." According to the American political strategist Eugene Rostow (1972: 242), Khrushchev confirmed in an interview with James Reston that the Soviet Union had undergone a similar policy shift (NYT 10 October 1957). Khrushchev declared that after Korea, conventional war was too dangerous, because "nuclear weapons don't respect class differences." Therefore, he said, it was necessary to rely on wars of liberation, especially in the Third World. The first major such war was fought in Korea in 1950–1952 with large "conventional" troop formations on both sides. It resulted in a standoff, which is still maintained across the 38th parallel. The Korean experience discouraged subsequent similar troop commitments, particularly because of the increasing threat of escalation into nuclear warfare. The next major such war was waged in Vietnam for two decades and spilled over into neighboring countries in Indochina. The increasing American troop commitment (up to 800,000, of which 500,000 were in the field) in a "nonconventional guerilla war," and particularly the subsequent liberation of Indochina from imperialist occupation, forced the United States into an "agonizing reappraisal" of its military posture. One result was the Nixon Doctrine of disengaging American troops from direct participation as much as possible and maintaining a military presence through arms supplies and other means of using "Asians to fight Asians." A major manifestation of this military posture has been the development of a rapid and flexible U.S. Navy that has modernized "showing the flag" and "gunboat diplomacy," which once seemed to have gone out of fashion, and the design and construction of naval and air forces that permit rapid "deployment" of troops and supporting weapons to "trouble spots" anywhere in the world at a moment's notice. The development and deployment of similar Soviet naval and air capacities and the war between Vietnam and Kampuchea, as well as the presence of Cuban troops in Africa, indicate that the Soviet Union and China may have developed their own versions of the Nixon Doctrine. (Moreover, it is clear that the Chinese welcome, if not demand, an American military presence in Asia.) The other major result of the American reappraisal has been the United States' temporary reluctance to intervene too directly in the Third World, particularly in Africa, where France and Britain seem to be in a better position to do so.

In 1978 "Foreign Aid Is Proposition 1," according to the prestigious *New York Times* columnist James Reston:

> Foreign aid is not a charitable exercise. . . . The major confrontations between Washington and Moscow are no longer taking place over the great industrial complexes of the Ruhr, the Rhineland, and Japan, but in the Middle East, where weapons are clearly important, and in black Africa, Southeast Asia and Latin America, where money, trade, economic assistance, health, education, and population control are likely to be more important than cruise missiles or neutron warheads (IHT 19 June 1978).

But, though foreign economic aid is no doubt important for this major confrontation, other weapons may be still more important:

Gen. Haig Urges NATO to Adjust Strategy for Third World Threats

> Myopic concentration on the Central European front at the expense of equal concern about what happens on our flanks could be self-deluding. As long as we maintain a viable deterrent, the likelihood of conflict in the short-term will be the outgrowth of situations on our

flanks or on the periphery as the Soviet Union exploits targets of opportunity. And these situations will carry the implications of major confrontations. I believe that we must be armed with regional military capabilities which could be employed as deterrent forces to prevent the escalation of Third World dynamics into major conflict. . . .

There is no substitute for in-place ready forces. An allied military presence must be viewed in a global context. . . . It's now a question of the Western nations dealing with the changing nature of the threat—from Eurasian in character to global, which engages the whole nexus of Western vitality, political, economic, and military. . . . The West has to take a collective political decision. . . .

[Question]: You said recently that in 1974 the Soviet Union shipped 50 per cent more than the United States in arms to the Third World and that it is now supplying 20 African states out of 49.

[Answer]: I believe that uninhibited provision of arms by the Soviet Union throughout Africa today is not consistent with the objectives that serve Western interests. . . . I am not espousing an interventionist doctrine but rather a policy that seeks concerted Western assessment (IHT 3 January 1978).

Events in Iran and Afghanistan helped the United States overcome its "Vietnam syndrome." An acute observer had written, before the American reaction to Soviet troops in Afghanistan made the change in American mood and policy painfully obvious:

We begin to gain insight into the wider stakes by reflecting on the comment of a prominent American conservative journalist, William Safire: "The Ayatollah's provocation is heaven-sent." Why? Because it creates a moral and political climate that makes it practical for the United States to take some steps that had been previously favored, but were not taken because of some lingering inhibitions arising out of the Vietnam experience. The Ayatollah's provocation has evidently wiped the Vietnam slate clean in the American public mind, opening the way to a new round of defense budget increases, forward air and naval deployments in the Middle East, the formation of quick-reaction military forces, and rehabilitation of the covert operations capability and mission of the CIA. The net effect of these developments is a new willingness by Washington to set the stage for military intervention in the Third World. As such, it shifts the American governing process in a more rightist direction, especially with respect to Third World revolutionary nationalism.

More specifically, in relation to Iran and the Persian Gulf the United States Government now enjoys a popular mandate to do whatever it wishes, even if it means war, to crush anti-Western political movements and leaders in the region. Such a mandate reinforces the earlier Kissinger-Rockefeller unwillingness to accept the outcome of the

Iranian Revolution as final or irreversible. This unwillingness relates back to the Atlantic Council view that hostile or potentially hostile political forces cannot be allowed to gain control over Middle East oil.

What the Ayatollah's provocation also did for American foreign policymakers was to create a moral foundation for an American crusade against revolutionary nationalism that was neither Marxist-Leninist, nor pro-Soviet. In that sense, it supersedes the Cold War rationale for intervention by one that is openly racist and imperial in its character. By this reasoning, the United States is opposing Islamic fanatics on behalf of "civilized values" and, besides, it must for practical reasons remove the growing threats from nationalism in the region to the oil lifeline of the West.

A principal irony, then, of the Embassy seizure, is that it lends legitimacy to a new type of counter-revolutionary foreign policy for the United States. In an important sense, this mandate is more dangerous than the earlier crusade against Third World Marxism, rationalized by reference to "the containment" of Soviet, or Sino-Soviet, power. Here, the new doctrine is connected with the struggle for control over Persian Gulf oil reserves, the most vital of all geopolitical stakes. It occurs in a highly militarized region, is linked to the explosive Arab-Israeli conflict, and in a general setting wherein it must tempt Soviet leaders to interject their military power at least to the extent of letting the flames of nationalism ravage the pro-Western political orders of the area. For these various reasons, it is not alarmist to regard the struggle for oil as likely to generate important dangers of world war in the early 1980s (Falk 1980: 4-5).

The result was the Carter Doctrine of protecting the West's oil arteries, if necessary by unilateral military action, which the President announced in his State of the Union message in January 1980.

Expressing a rather different point of view, the *Economic and Political Weekly* in Bombay commented on the "Congress of Helsinki":

> For the first time in more than 50 years, the ideological divide was obliterated; the pigmentation of the skin was the governing criterion for certain governments to meet (EPW 2 August 1975: 1139).

A commentator for the same journal wrote under the title "White Man's Burden":

> The Helsinki summit has, in other words, reinforced an international system dominated by the United States of America and the Soviet Unon. . . . The Europeans agreed that the lines drawn in Europe would stay. The zones of influence would survive. Helsinki has evolved a charter of peaceful co-existence between different zones of influence. . . .
>
> The Helsinki summit has been likened by many to the Congress of Vienna. The analogy seems to be rather fateful. After 1815 Europe did

enjoy peace and security for a whole century till war broke out in 1914. But this so-called peaceful century was also the century of imperialism. In other words, there was peace in Europe, but war, aggression and imperialism in the not-so-fortunate rest of the world.

The Congress of Vienna gave Europe an era of peace with imperialism elsewhere. One hopes the Helsinki summit does not likewise give Europe an era of peace with dominance elsewhere (EPW 9 August 1975: 1192).

A major area of confrontation is in the Indian Ocean and the South Asian and other countries near it. These include Bangladesh, Sri Lanka, Pakistan, Afghanistan, Iran, Saudi Arabia, and the "Horn of Africa." The United States, the Soviet Union, and China seem to have established a modus vivendi with regard to India, under whose terms this country has been able to maintain substantial economic ties to the Soviet Union without accepting the latter's proposed "Asian security" plans directed against China. At the same time, the Soviet-supported Indian public sector of the economy does not impede, and in many respects subsidizes, India's increasing participation in the capitalist international division of labor under American sponsorship; and Sino-Indian relations improved in the face of apparent increases in common interests since the Sino-Indian-Pakistani wars. On the other hand, Indian subimperialist pretensions in the area have been limited by the complicated cross-cutting of her and her neighbors' alliances with the major powers. The April 1978 Soviet-backed coup in Afghanistan, and the September and December 1979 semicoups, followed by the massive introduction of Soviet troops into that country in December 1979 and the strong reaction by the United States, have converted the region into a flashpoint of international crisis and have significantly enhanced political-tribal threats to the stability of Pakistan and therefore India, as well as Iran and Iraq. Countermeasures—which would have Chinese support—cannot be excluded, both for domestic political reasons in these countries and because of the competition between the U.S. and Soviet navies for island (Diego Garcia) and coastal bases, as well as for influence in governments farther inland. Moreover, the Indian Ocean washes the coasts of part of the Middle East and includes the Arabian Sea and the Persian Gulf through which passes the West's petroleum "lifeline."

During the war in Vietnam the influential American economic and political strategist and sometime Under Secretary of State George Ball suggested that "South Vietnam has little significance for either economic or geographic reasons" and that "proponents of the war have had to devise the dubious argument of the 'domino theory' to establish any serious importance at all." On the other hand, Ball argued and predicted (*New York Times Magazine,* July 28, 1970), "Suez is the front to watch":

NATO military officials increasingly believe that recent Soviet activities in Egypt have so altered the miltary situation that Israel may not much longer be sure of defending all of her frontiers, while certain American military experts see a serious possibility that the Soviet Union may seek to—and indeed be able to—neutralize the Israeli Air Force. . . .

For the Russians to gain dominion over the Middle East would clearly mean a breach of a vital line at a vital point. Why should the Soviet domination of the Middle East affect the power balance more decisively than a North Vietnamese victory over Saigon? The answer is twofold: because the nature of the antagonists is widely different and because there is a disparity in the significance of the two areas. . . .

The Middle East . . . is an economic prize of extraordinary value. Supplying a substantial part of the energy requirements of Western Europe and even Japan, it is an area of concentrated American investment providing a major source of our foreign-exchange earnings. . . . In marked contrast to Vietnam, the Middle East *does* lie near the center of world power—just below Central and Western Europe— and what happens in the U.A.R. and Israel would have a profound effect on millions of people in the industrially advanced countries . . . [which] vitally relates to the power balance and thus to the maintenance of world peace. . . . The south and east coasts of the Mediterranean remain critical to Western survival, and a dominant Soviet position throughout the Arab world would threaten our most vital interests. . . .

Russia has, after centuries of yearning, become a Mediterranean power, and—short of nuclear war—we cannot dislodge her. What we can do is require strict limits and ground rules for her military personnel and insist that together we find the key to peace in the Middle East. . . . To transform the public mood, equipping America to face up to the Middle East crisis, will require a great deal of clear thinking and straight talking (Ball 1971: 222–35).

It is hardly necessary to record how clairvoyant Mr. Ball was. Similarly, Eugene Rostow wrote under the title "Does the Third World Matter? The Middle East" that "the protracted conflict between Israel and some of her Arab neighbors is not the cause of the Middle Eastern crisis but its symptom and consequence. . . . The Middle Eastern crisis is a NATO crisis, not an Arab-Israeli quarrel. It is a fissure in the foundation of world politics—a Soviet challenge to the relationship of Western Europe and the United States, and therefore to the balance of power" (Rostow 1972: 250). Of course, these American strategists consider Israel a Western pawn—albeit a rebellious one at times. (Israel's role as a "subimperialist" power is discussed in Chapter 1.)

Decolonization in Africa since 1960 has resulted in the creation of many new states that have inherited the boundaries, internal social and tribal composition, and bureaucratic machineries established under colonialism. Many of these states—most notably the Ivory Coast, Senegal, Kenya, and

Malawi—became outright neocolonial dependencies of the Western capitalist powers. Some countries in West Africa initially joined the so-called Monrovia group of nations, named after the capital of Liberia, where the group's first meeting took place. Others—including Ghana, Guinea, and Mali in particular—formed the Casablanca group, which aspired to more progressive internal and more independent foreign policies, with some support from the Soviet Union. Progressive policies did not prosper, however, and all of these regimes were eventually replaced by reactionary ones through military coups (Nkrumah in Ghana, Modibo Keita in Mali) or else succumbed to the force of circumstances (Sekou Touré in Guinea, who in 1978 smoked the peace pipe with his erstwhile archenemies in the Ivory Coast, Senegal, and Liberia). Thus only modest intervention supplemented by considerable pressure by the West was necessary to (literally) right things in this region. In the Congo, on the other hand, it was necessary to send in United Nations troops and to take various other direct actions to eliminate Patrice Lumumba and eventually to replace him and the Belgian puppet Moise Tshombe by the CIA-appointed Mobutu, who still reigns today, albeit barely and very unsatisfactorily from the Western point of view.

Otherwise, the situation in Southern Africa appeared to be as Henry Kissinger described it in his notorious secret U.S. National Security Council Memorandum 39 in 1969:

A. The Area. The black states of Zambia, Malawi, Swaziland, Lesotho and Botswana. The white minority area of South Africa, South West Africa, Southern Rhodesia, Mozambique and Angola. Tanzania, while not in the area designated, is closely linked to the problem.

B. The Problem. Racial repression by white minority regimes and the black African opposition to it pose two problems for U.S. interests in the area: 1. Our interests in the white states to the degree that they are seen as at least tacit acceptance of racism affect our standing with African and other states. 2. The prospects of increasing violence in the area growing out of black insurgency and white reprisal could jeopardize our interests in the future. Our interests in the region are important but not vital. Our investments, primarily in South Africa, total about $1 billion and our trade yields a highly favorable balance of payments. This geographically important area . . . can be useful to our defense forces. . . . Outside of the region our investments in Africa total about $1.5 billion and profitable trade relations are expanding. . . .

C. U.S. Objectives. . . . Arranged without intent to imply priority, they are: to improve the U.S. standing . . . to minimize the likelihood of escalation of violence in the area and the risk of U.S. involvement. To minimize the opportunities for the USSR and Communist China . . . to encourage moderation . . . to protect economic, scientific and strategic interests and opportunities in the region, including the orderly marketing of South Africa's gold production. . . .

D. The Policy Dilemma within the U.S. Government. There is agreement that: 1. the U.S. does not have vital security interests in the region. . . . There is disagreement over: 1. Whether there is any prospect for non-violent change. . . . 3. The extent to which pursuit of our tangible interests in the white states is likely to do appreciable damage to our present or long term political interests in the black states of the region, in the rest of Africa, or elsewhere, including in the UN. . . .

F. The Options. Option One: Closer association with the white regimes to protect and enhance our economic, strategic and scientific interests. Premise: Our disagreement with the domestic policies of either side should not inhibit our relations with them. . . . Option Two: Broader association with both black and white states in an effort to encourage moderation. . . . Premise: The blacks cannot gain political rights through violence. Constructive change can come only by acquiescence of the whites.

Situation, Prospects and U.S. Interest

Over the past 20 years, South Africa's racial policies have steadily hardened . . . expenditures for defense have increased seven hundred per cent. . . . For the foreseeable future South Africa will be able to maintain internal stability and effectively counter insurgent activity. . . . South West Africa. No solution in sight. . . . Southern Rhodesia. . . . Despite the effects of sanctions, the white regime can hold out indefinitely with South African help. . . . Portuguese territories. . . . The outlook for the rebellions is one of continued stalemate. . . . There is no likelihood in the foreseeable future that liberation movements could overthrow or seriously threaten the existing white government. . . . Both the USSR and Communist China can be expected to exploit targets of opportunity so long as they are available (Kissinger 1975: 43–47, 77–98).

On the basis of these premises, Kissinger recommended hard-line policies of support for the white and colonial regimes in Africa, but without much concern or involvement.

Unfortunately for Kissinger and those he represents, he miscalculated very badly. The liberation movements in the "Portuguese territories" won and completely changed the balance of power in the entire region. This made the other premises about Namibia (South West Africa) and Zimbabwe (Rhodesia) and even South Africa itself obsolete at the very time that the United States was forced out of Indochina. This change obliged the United States and its Western (as well as African) allies to submit their African policy to an "agonizing reappraisal." For a while, the "Vietnam trauma" partially immobilized the United States, particularly while the MPLA (Movimento Popular de Liberacão de Angola) was fighting for power in Angola (though this paralysis was not complete enough to prevent the CIA from secretly helping the MPLA's enemies, as was subsequently revealed). Then Jimmy Carter took over the White House and appointed his friend Andrew Young as a roving black-dove Ambassador to the United Nations and particularly to Africans—and to balance him, he appointed the hawk Zbigniew Brzezinski to oversee U.S. global interests from the National Security Council. For a while, there was another "policy dilemma within the U.S. government" in which these two personages represented, respectively, the soft or "cool" and hard lines toward Africa. But after November 1977 the hard line advocated by Brzezinski won out "and the 'cool' approach advocated by Mr. Young went by the board" (IHT 14 February 1978). By May 1978, according to the *Washington Post*, "an ever-larger segment of the political community, we note, seems to think that . . . the United States [has] overreacted to the Vietnam trauma" and that the time had come of "taking the African problem seriously. . . . [However] its leadership responsibilities do not require the United States to do everything itself" (IHT 20–21 and 22 May 1978). By June 1978, the *New York Times* could observe that

> the fact is that President Carter and Mr. Brzezinski have now settled comfortably into the chairs of their predecessors and are globally advocating something very close to what Presidents Nixon and Ford and Mr. Kissinger sought: a hard-headed deal with Moscow . . . a cozying up to China . . . a determination to resist Soviet penetration elsewhere, notably in the Middle East and Africa, provided Congress can be persuaded. . . . (IHT 1 June 1978).

> The techniques of crisis management were being born again in Washington, plainly to test the nation's tolerance for involvements that it has bitterly opposed since the final escape from Southeast Asia. . . . American involvement accomplished three things: it signalled U.S. support for Mobutu, it showed a willingness to back up West European intervention more quickly than last year, and it demonstrated willingness to commit forces overseas. . . . We confess to a certain sympathy for this desire over the weekend to demonstrate something more than rhetoric that American restraint in Africa these days is a matter of choice and not of political paralysis (NYT 22 and 23 May 1978, cited in ICP 5 June 1978).

The *Washington Post* chimed in:

> Just as the Administration seems more primed to counter another communist-backed advance in Africa, however, so the public would also probably be readier to go along (WP 16 May 1978, cited in ICP 5 June 1978).

Thus "Carter, Giscard [are] reported agreed on Africa defense . . . against 'destabilizing external forces' " (IHT 31 May 1978), and:

Things can't go on this way. Thus the French effort to spread the burden among moderate Africans, and the growing U.S. awareness that it's time to shake off the Vietnam trauma as far as Africa is concerned; witness President Carter's impatience with congressional restrictions on his freedom to deploy at least covert resources and aid in Zaire and Angola (IHT 7 June 1978).

According to a headline in the spring of 1978, "Carter Said to Seek End to Angola Curbs. Reportedly Wants to Aid UNITA Rebels" (IHT 25 May 1978). At the same time, "France is being called the 'gendarme of Africa'; reference is made to a nostalgia for colonial status and to a brazen attempt to 'grab' Belgian economic assets in Zaire" (IHT 7 June 1978). There was indeed a sharp conflict between France and Belgium with regard to their respective "aggressive" and "humanitarian" intervention in the second Shaba crisis in May 1978 (IHT 23 May 1978). The Foreign Minister of Belgium declared that "France is particularly interested in the wealth of Zaire, and Belgium perceives this as an international rivalry" (LM 21 May 1978). No wonder, considering that Belgium owns 80 percent of the foreign investments in its ex-colony. The Belgians once tried to separate the mineral-rich Katanga region from the Congo and to convert it into a client state under Tshombe. Now, however, they and the French, indeed the entire West, are in agreement that any attempt to destabilize Mobutu in Zaire by paralyzing the copper and diamond mines of Shaba (Katanga) that support (however badly) the economy of Zaire must be resisted. It is vital for all the Western capitals, however strong the rivalry among them, to prevent the secession of Shaba and its diplomatic recognition as an independent state by the Soviet Union in exchange for delivery of its riches to the latter. Finally, as the attempt to separate oil-rich Biafra from Nigeria showed, all other African states, no matter what their political line, regard any attempt to alter state boundaries as anathema because it would provide a precedent for their own dismemberment. Hence the African opposition to aspirations to form a "Greater Somalia" that would bring under its flag all the Somalian peoples.

The French plan "to spread the burden among moderate Africans" by creating a "pan-African security force" to intervene around the continent with the support of Gabon, Senegal, the Ivory Coast, Zaire, and Uganda has faltered so far over the natural opposition of Libya, Tanzania, Liberia (surprisingly), and even some French-speaking countries, as well as Angola and Mozambique (IHT 9 June 1978). Tanzania's President Julius Nyerere declared that the meeting of the presidents of French-speaking African countries with French President Giscard in Paris to explore this proposal and the discussions at Western meetings about Shaba, Zaire, and Africa in Paris and Brussels

> are by no means about the liberty of Africa. They are discussing continued domination, continued use of Africa by the Western powers. These meetings, if taken together, are put on to become a second

Conference of Berlin [at which the colonial powers carved Africa up among themselves in 1884]. . . . The question is one of neocolonialism in Africa, and that for economic interests . . . this [neocolonial attempt] is being led by France. The second point on the agenda is about the use of Africa in the East-West conflict. Here the USA is the leader. These two intentions are being coordinated so that they will complement each other; and the distribution of the expected profits—as well as of the related costs—are being arranged at these meetings (FR 26 June 1978).

The real problems in satisfactorily concluding this interventionist enterprise were pointed out, surprisingly, by King Hassan of Morocco, who had sent his troops to Shaba during the first crisis in 1977:

"Moderate" African countries could form such a force, he said, but it would trigger a move by more radical states, with larger armies, "to form another inter-African force . . . much more powerful than the moderates" and able to count on the Soviet bloc for more support than the West could give its allies (IHT 31 May 1978).

This would revive the "Monrovia" vs. "Casablanca" kind of division of the 1960s, but at a much more explosive level. But why should the West be able to give less support than the Soviet Union? George Ball provides a clue to this problem, the political parameters of which have changed since Mr. Kissinger thought everything in Africa was under control.

Rethinking U.S African Policy

If we are prepared to recognize the primacy of European interests in areas where they can effectively employ their limited power and resources, may we not expect some key European countries to extend political and military as well as economic assistance? Africa is the logical place to test that hypothesis. It lies in the same geographical relation to Europe as does Latin America to the United States, while solid European relationships already exist with certain African states. France has long furnished substantial economic aid. . . .

Although our bureaucrats cherish their freedom of maneuver and our specialists in African affairs decry any European involvement in Africa as neocolonialism, such preferences or prejudices should not deter us from recognizing the primacy of European responsibility for such areas as Zaire and the French-speaking states. . . .

The nightmare haunting the State Department is that, unless a general settlement is reached in Rhodesia, Cuba may not only provide training but deploy substantial forces to assist the Patriotic Front against the fragile government in Salisbury. In that event, Western resistance would be paralyzed since we could not afford the appearance of siding with the whites against the blacks (IHT 20 June 1978).

Or as President Kenneth Kaunda of Zambia put it, "At that point the American people might find themselves fighting on the wrong side. America might well find herself fighting Africa. The United States cannot pursue a policy of liberation at home and reaction in Southern Africa" (IHT 20–21 May 1978). With twenty million Afro-Americans (over a million of them unemployed), "fighting on the wrong side" of the color bar would create immense problems at home for the United States. The election of Robert Mugabe appears to have defused the situation in Zimbabwe—or made the fuse longer—but the dilemma persists in Namibia and South Africa, where, paradoxically, the Zimbabwian "solution" may have exacerbated the situation.

Finding oneself on the wrong side is not a monopoly of the United States or the West. China has come down on the wrong side in one conflict after another in recent years and continues to do so in Shaba, Zaire, and Africa, where it supports Mobutu and Company, whom the Chinese Foreign Minister visited for four days right after the second Shaba invasion. And Cuba has made an effort not to find herself on the wrong side of the national liberation struggle in Eritrea—and perhaps also in the conflict between rival progressive revolutionary forces in Angola, where American journalist Harrison Salisbury claimed that the Cubans, with Soviet instigation, supported Agostinho Neto against the pretensions of Nino Alves (IHT 16 November 1977), or in South Yemen, or even in Ethiopia itself.

With the single exception of Tanzania—where, however, President Nyerere has admitted that socialism is not yet feasible—no state in Africa has maintained its originally revolutionary or even progressive regime for very long. Perhaps Angola and Mozambique, where MPLA, Frelimo, and their peoples were schooled through long years of fighting, will transform this sad record. But the Chinese were even better schooled in political and military battle, and this has not prevented them from supporting one reactionary cause after another. And Somalia, whose significant progressive social transformations were greeted and supported as "socialist" in Africa until very recently, found no visible difficulty in switching alliances and becoming an instrument of Western and reactionary Arab pressure against its neighbor Ethiopia. In that country an initially progressive regime began profound social transformations but then put a brake on them and organized a nationwide manhunt against the most revolutionary cadres while simultaneously embarking on a war of annihilation against the Eritreans, who were forcefully incorporated into Haile Selassie's empire two decades ago. This situation has led to the saying that "you cannot buy an African government, you can only rent it for a day. Allegiances change fast, and ideologies, like friendships, often are available to the highest bidder" (IHT 6 February 1978). For the time being, the highest economic and political bidder is capitalism and its powers, even if they are subject to some circumstantial military constraints. And if recent experience is any guide, a particular government may resist being bought, but it may not be able to resist a military coup by those who are bought and know which side their bread is buttered on—the right side.

Claude Gabriel, writing in the Trotskyist *Intercontinental Press*, has realistically suggested that

> In the last analysis, however, such [Soviet] intervention is in no way aimed at aiding the rise of socialist revolution, but to the contrary at stabilizing the situation and blocking the unfolding anticapitalist developments. The payoff for this policy is the utilization by the Soviets, for a certain length of time, of economic and diplomatic advantages gained in this way in one country or another.
>
> But overall the Soviets are not the masters of the game. To conduct such a policy, they must tail behind the bourgeois or petty-bourgeois leaderships to whom Soviet aid is temporarily necessary. Once the indigenous leaderships have passed through their rough times, an alliance with imperialism will appear to them as a better guarantee against mass movement. The Soviets are thus forced to continually reexamine their whole system of alliances in a continent like Africa.
>
> Such continual shifts are not, as the Western press pretends to think, the result of calculated cynicism and crafty maneuvers on the part of the Soviets. In fact, it follows from their attachment to "peaceful coexistence."
>
> In this sordid game, the Chinese have demonstrated their ability to compete with the Soviets in the field of opportunism. Over the past few years the Soviets have skilfully managed to milk the advantage of happening to be on the progressive side [except in Cambodia, Uganda, Argentina], while the Chinese, as in Angola, ended up in the camp with the CIA and South African advisers. This does not, however, alter the identical character of their policies (ICP 29 May 1978:641).

The situation in Latin America is related but different. It is related through Latin America's participation in common with other areas of the world in the system of international economic relations and political tensions, as well as through Latin America's close relations to the United States. One manifestation of these relations is the proposal, especially since the liberation of the Portuguese colonies in Africa, for a South Atlantic Treaty Organization (SATO) to bolster the "security" of this area and its Middle Eastern oil route to Europe and America against Soviet incursions and excessively progressive domestic policies in some African countries. Besides the United States as patron and South Africa as senior partner on the eastern side of the South Atlantic, the proposed members would be Brazil, Argentina, Uruguay, Chile, and (pro forma) Paraguay and Bolivia. Indeed, it is these latter countries' military governments, which have little business in Africa, that have shown the greatest enthusiasm for this unholy alliance against "international communism." Argentina and, especially, Brazil display considerable official reluctance to be branded by a formal alliance with the South African pariah, since this mark might burn the commercial bridges they are carefully constructing to the remainder of Africa, including Angola. The formal establishment of SATO, therefore, depends on a satisfactory "settlement" in Rhodesia and South Africa. One analyst suggests that it is probable that SATO will never be a formal alliance, but this does not matter much since it can certainly function informally, and to a certain extent it already does. The Falkland Islands/Malvinas, whose ownership has been disputed by Britain and Argentina for over a century, have been proposed as a major naval base for SATO (Waksman 1977).

A major difference between other parts of the Third World and Latin America is that, with the exception of Cuba, the whole continent is regarded as the "backyard" of the United States, its private political hunting ground. A historical "accident" permitted the Cuban Revolution, and the Soviet alliance has guaranteed its survival. Otherwise, the Soviet Union respects Latin America as a U.S. "zone of influence," a respect confirmed in the Nixon-Brezhnev agreements, pursuant to which the Soviet Union declined to give any but the most insubstantial aid to the beleaguered Allende government in Chile. The recognition of U.S. preeminence in Latin America has not impeded West European investments and trade, including armaments and nuclear sales, with Latin America, nor, to a lesser extent, Soviet and Chinese investment and trade. The Soviet Union has become the largest importer of Argentine products under the Argentine military junta, and Peru has bought Soviet fighter-planes. China has offered economic and political support to Pinochet in Chile and other military dictatorships in Latin America and is trying to compete with the Soviet Union in Argentina and Brazil. Nonetheless, so far and for the foreseeable future, Latin America is by mutual agreement excluded from Soviet-American contention.

Another major difference between Latin America and the rest of the Third World, especially Africa, is that most Latin American countries have been formally independent for over a century and a half. During that time almost every one of these states acquired a military organization and tradition of long standing. Certainly all the major Latin American states and most of the minor ones have an economic, technological, political, and military base far stronger and relatively more independent than that possessed by any of the new African states. This difference is seen in the much better military equipment, organization, training, and internal/external fighting capabilities of the armed forces in Latin America, which are comparable to the "best" in the Middle East and capitalist Asia, perhaps excepting only Israel (and to some extent Iran in equipment and India in manpower). For this reason it is more difficult to attempt a military coup in Latin America without substantial agreement from the upper command of the armed forces, but once this is reached, the attempted coup is more likely to be successful than in Africa.

Under these circumstances, the outbreak of international warfare in Latin America is much more determined by the respective countries' relations to the United States, to one another, and to internal economic and political tensions. The major international conflict within Latin America, of course, is that between its two major powers, Brazil and Argentina, whose rivalry goes back well into the nineteenth century. Recently, the terms of this rivalry have been altered by the successful establishment of Brazil as the dominant economic and subimperialist power on the continent, with privileged American support. The Carter administration, however, has reduced U.S. support for Brazil; and Paraguay and Bolivia, which seemed to have thrown in their lot with their larger neighbor to the northeast, are trying once again to walk a tightrope between Brazil and Argentina. This fragile equilibrium is particularly evident in negotiations about the use by Brazil and Argentina of hydroelectric power from dams on Paraguay's borders and the connecting grids to supply electric power to the industries of São Paulo and Buenos Aires. (Argentina and Brazil also have a cycle difference in their electric systems, and Paraguay has been under pressure to change its own to that of Brazil.) The iron ore deposits in the Mutua region of Bolivia and the electric power necessary to smelt them are additional points of contention. The Foreign Minister of Argentina felt it necessary to declare (to the newspaper *Clarin*, Buenos Aires, 5 August 1977) that he did not share "the evaluations of some circles who mention the possibility of a possible armed conflict with Brazil if the Itaipú dam begins to operate without being aligned with that of Corpus" (cited in Ampuero 1977:270). But with so much smoke, there may be an outburst of fire. Whether or not the spark is found to light this fire perhaps depends on American policy; the political-economic situation in these countries, the region, and the world; and, of course, the political-military situation in the region as a whole.

For Argentina is also involved in a long-standing dispute with neighboring Chile, ostensibly about sovereignty over the Beagle Canal and adjoining islands at the southern tip of the continent. The real issue is sovereignty over probable offshore petroleum resources and conflicting claims in mineral-rich Antarctica, whose new economic importance is reawakening old territorial disputes. Chile, in turn, has border disputes with Bolivia, which continues to press its demand for an outlet to the sea, and with Peru, whose territory Chile conquered in the Pacific War of 1879, thereby denying Bolivia access to the sea. These disputes make Chile the natural ally of Brazil, and Bolivia and Peru the natural allies of Argentina. However, Chile is also a natural ally of Ecuador, since this country has not renounced its claims to a large territory that Peru obtained in the unequal treaty of 1942. By this treaty, Ecuador lost access to the Amazon region, which is acquiring new economic importance. Brazil has been trying to "coordinate" the future exploitation of the Amazon region through consultations under its initiative and "leadership" with bordering Peru, Colombia, and Venezuela. The latter two countries, in turn, have engaged in long-standing border conflicts near Venezuela's oil-rich Maracaibo region and probable offshore oil reserves. And coming full circle in South America, Guayana seeks the support of Brazil against Venezuela, which is laying claim to parts of Guayana that are rich in iron ores, bauxite, and timber.

When Chile and Peru had relatively progressive governments, these economic rivalries were supplemented by political ones that combined in attempts to isolate one or both of these countries. After the progressive governments were replaced by right-wing regimes, the economic rivalries advanced to the foreground—as they did in the "football" war between El Salvador and Honduras elsewhere within the faltering Central American Common Market. In South America each of these border conflicts is related to the next one, not only through the "enemy of my enemy is my friend" line of thinking that results in a chain of alliances, but also through the natural inclination of each state to exploit the weaknesses of its neighbor by, say, obliging Chile and Peru to fight on their respective southern and northern fronts simultaneously. Moreover, these international rivalries are managed if not fueled through internal political tensions.

Internal political tensions, in turn, are fueled in Latin America and elsewhere by the worsening world economic crisis. We have already re-marked (in Chapters 1, 3, and 5) that the economic crisis is accelerating the modification of the international division of labor and the mechanisms of exploitation and superexploitation of the masses in the Third World, thereby generating more authoritarian state institutions and repressive governments. But these economic, social, and political transformations are not automatic. On the contrary, they are imposed by force—often of arms—through the intensification of the class struggle between capital and labor and also among the different sectors of capital, the bureaucracy, and the armed forces. As we have seen, the internal political process in many Third World countries is intimately connected to often complicated and shifting international alliances and interventions between the contenders on the national scene and major political powers and potential emerging economic blocs in the world political arena. It is not surprising, then, that there are frequent attempts—which will most likely increase as the economic and political crisis worsens—to eliminate or at least neutralize internal political opponents *and* allies through appeals to "national unity" in the face of real, perceived, or conjured external threats, attacks, or adventures. Thus in times of economic and political crisis, internal "tension management" can inflame external political tensions that may well lead to international war between neighboring Third World countries. And in times of crisis, political-military tensions between states are aggravated by economic rivalry for raw materials or—as between Brazil and Argentina or India and Pakistan—for external markets.

It would be hazardous to predict the political consequences of all these internal and external conflicts in the short and medium terms. But we may note some implications. Unless such conflicts—as well as international economic and political developments—alter the regional and national polit-ical dimensions immensely, the prospects for substantial progressive, let alone revolutionary socialist, political modifications in South America appear to be very dim. Elsewhere in the Third World, progressive movements have certainly scored some important victories in recent years with prior or subsequent support from the Soviet Union and/or China. But as the daily press records (see WE: Chapter 4), other progressive movements have been denied such material support, or it has been suddenly withdrawn. The Soviet Union and China and other socialist powers have not hesitated to support reactionary movements, causes, and states when it suits their interests. So the prospects for socialism in the Third World in the immediate future are uncertain at best. The political insurgent movements in Southeast Asia (Thailand, Malaysia, and to some extent the Philippines and Burma) have received scant material support from Vietnam and China, whose political rivalry precludes unified revolutionary action in this area in the near future. Revolutionary movements in South Asia have been disorganized or decimated, and political tensions seem to be taking on a nationalist or regionalist character. In the Middle East the Arab-Israeli stalemate appears to have had a debilitating effect on the Palestinians and the few remaining progressive forces among both the Arabs and the Israelis. The increasingly militant nationalist movements and the great power rivalry in the region of Afghanistan, Iran, Iraq and Turkey create a very explosive combination; but they hardly promote socialism. In North Africa it is difficult to discern any far-reaching socialist mass movements, though the aggravation of tensions between Libya and her neighbors or among the three Maghreb countries that are contending for the phosphate-rich ex-Spanish Sahara might suddenly radicalize the region—but more likely to the right than to the left. This leaves sub-Saharan Africa, particularly southern Africa, and the Central American-Caribbean regions that today inspire the greatest hopes or fears (depending on which side one is on) of radical-progressive social and political transformation in the near future. But even there it would be prudent to maintain a realistic historical perspective that takes due account of past experience and the economic, social, political, and military limitations circumstances impose on the prospects for development.

Chapter 9
Development of Crisis and Crisis of Development: A Summary Conclusion About Living in the Real World

> This conclusion, which is similar to that in *Crisis: In the World Economy,* is deliberately not footnoted, since it represents a summary of the argument set out and documented in the preceding chapters and in WE on the development of the present crisis in the industrial capitalist West, the socialist East, and the underdeveloped South. Further questions are also raised about the recent and foreseeable development of nationalism and its implications for socialism.

Many people throughout the world believe that we are living in a prerevolutionary era analogous to the one at the end of World War I during which the world's first socialist revolution occurred in what is now the Soviet Union. This belief in the present progress of revolution and socialism has been promoted and sustained especially by the developments of the past decade and a half in Cuba and Vietnam, Angola and Mozambique, Ethiopia and Iran, and even Afghanistan, and by current or prospective developments in Zimbabwe and Namibia, Nicaragua and other parts of the Caribbean area, and other places in the Third World. The belief in prerevolutionary progress is also based on the widespread mass movements in Europe and North America during the late 1960s and early 1970s; the subsequent fall of the dictatorships in Greece, Portugal, and Spain; and the recent worker, women's, and populist mobilizations, especially against economic and social policies, that seem to be sweeping through many industrial capitalist, underdeveloped and socialist countries (the last of which seems particularly significant to some observers) since 1976–1977. On the other hand, the industrial capitalist West, the socialist East, and the underdeveloped Third World South are also being swept by very strong conservative or reactionary, counterreformist or counterrevolutionary, and militantly nationalist winds.

To what extent is revolution or counterrevolution likely in the foreseeable future? As in any prerevolutionary or supposedly prerevolutionary situation, the answer depends on which way the class struggle and the imperialist struggle will go. The subjective political element or forces in this class struggle are in part limited and shaped by the objective economic factors. The subjective and ideological factors were elevated to particular prominence in Cuba, China, and Vietnam in the recent past, and there has been some considerable disappointment in the efficacy of these subjective factors in or starting from the countries named. This disappointment has marked their own leadership—suffice it to mention Mao Zedong, whose Cultural Revolution was obviously defeated—and many others both in these countries and in the world as a whole. Therefore, it may not be amiss to devote greater care to the objective economic factors in the fight for liberation and socialism. Recent events may raise some doubts about whether the objective truth is always revolutionary, as the old adage says, but surely it is still true that subjective illusion or falsehood can never be revolutionary.

According to the official pronouncements about the world and the above-mentioned apparent revolutionary advances, the Chinese say at every opportunity that the present situation is excellent. The Soviet Union says that socialism is advancing on the world at a giant's pace. The Eurocommunist and other Communist parties say that social mobilization and popular advances are accelerating and virtually carrying the world before them, although there have been temporary localized reverses in Latin America until recently. At the Conference of the Nonaligned in Havana and particularly since the events in Nicaragua and elsewhere, popular mobilization is said to be advancing by leaps and bounds around the Third World. Trotskyists say that at least in several countries of Southern Europe— in Portugal, Spain, France, Italy, and maybe Belgium—the revolution is practically around the corner or at least that the revolution could be around the corner if revolutionaries play their cards correctly. Even the United States is said to be marked by new large-scale popular movements. To what extent are these pronouncements objectively correct? To what extent is this optimism, which we should all support subjectively, really merited by objective political economic considerations? Indeed, calling them objective or subjective considerations, do existing revolutionary theory, organization, and leadership, which certainly all socialists and revolutionaries regard as essential to convert a prerevolutionary situation into a revolution, justify this revolutionary optimism? There are objective reasons to doubt it.

In fact, a good part of this contemporary revolutionary and national liberation mobilization is a defensive outgrowth of a growing world economic and political crisis and is so far objectively severely limited. The crisis is perhaps not entirely unlike previous crises, particularly the one that began in 1913 and lasted through World War II. This crisis included the two wars, the depression of the 1930s, the October Revolution, and the Chinese Revolution. The same crisis included the rise of facism as a counterrevolutionary movement, with some considerable success at least in certain times and places. An earlier analogous major crisis of capitalist development occurred between 1873 and 1895 and was associated with the rise of monopoly capitalism in the central economies and the rise of classical imperialism and colonialism from the central economies to the periphery—or more accurately within the world economy and political system that includes them both. My suggestion is that since the 1960s the world, or at least the capitalist world, has entered another analogous long crisis period of overaccumulation of capital and overproduction. The companion volume, WE, has examined the development and manifestations of this crisis in the West, East, and South combined. This book has examined in detail the manifestations of this world crisis in the underdeveloped countries.

The postwar industrial expansion, like previous major expansions, produced more capital relative to the labor used (in Marxist terminology, an increase in the organic composition of capital), particularly in industry. Associated with relative overinvestment in capital equipment in industry there was relative underinvestment in productive capacity in the mining and agricultural sectors in most of the capitalist world. Not incidentally, this primary sector underinvestment is substantially responsible for the oil and agricultural crises of the 1970s and perhaps the 1980s. The increase in the organic composition of capital (an increase in the capital/labor ratio) and productivity, and the partly associated increase in worker bargaining power and militancy, have since the mid-sixties led to a decline in the industrial economies in the rate of profit and a reduction in the rate of growth, in some instances to an absolute reduction in the demand for industrial commodities and most particularly of capital or investment goods. The previous imbalance may now perhaps lead to a relative increase in the provision of raw materials from mineral (including seabed and perhaps Antarctic) and agricultural (especially agribusiness) sources. Additionally, productivity and production have grown at different rates in the major industrial capitalist economies. Productivity in Western Europe has grown at twice the American rate, and Japan's productivity, until recently, grew at twice the European and four times the American rate.

These developments have led to the following major consequences and manifestations. One has been the attempt to postpone or restrain, or indeed in some monopolized sectors to prevent, the decline in the rate of profit and restriction in the market through mass programs of printing money and credit creation. This effort took its most spectacular form in the United States through the deficit financing of the war against Vietnam, which flooded the world with dollars. Secondly, competition increased, particularly among national sectors of capital from one country to another, for the remaining market. This competition manifested itself most particularly in the repeated devaluations of the dollar, which were an attempt to maintain or increase the overseas market for American exports and to protect it and the American home market against the incursions particularly of Germany and Japan. Their currencies have been revalued and have risen very markedly against the dollar, without so far turning the balance in favor of the United States on the world market. The decline of the dollar has, however, cheapened American wage and property costs relative to those in Europe and Japan and has therefore reversed the flow of foreign investment, which is now going from these areas into the United States. Slack demand and increased competition have also accelerated bankruptcies and monopolization nationally and aggressive export drives and renewed protectionism internationally.

Another major manifestation of overproduction and inadequate demand has been an increase in unutilized excess productive capacity in industry. This industry-wide problem is particularly visible in the steel industry, which has been in a worldwide slump for some years and, after shutting down a number of steel mills, is still working at only 60 or 70 percent capacity in various parts of the industrialized world. In consequence there has also been of marked slump in investments. With excess but unused capacity and low profits, business sees no good reason to engage in mammoth new investment. The 1973 level of investment in the industrialized economies was not reattained until 1978, and in Britain has still not been reached. Thus, there is a gaping investment hole from 1973 to 1978. Now investment is threatening to decline again, because of a new recession. Moreover, the nature of investment has changed. Expansive investment to provide new productive capacity for more and new goods has increasingly been replaced by rationalizing investment designed to produce at lower costs and most particularly with lower labor costs.

There has been much talk about new technology in the energy supply and in a number of other fields. Despite the fact that the price of energy has shot up rapidly since 1973 and did so again in recent months, there have not been any major new investments in the energy field except for prospecting and drilling for petroleum, which has increased markedly since 1973. There has been no major new investment in petroleum refining, which is one reason for the recent bottlenecks. There also has been no major new investment in alternative sources of energy from shale oil, coal, or nuclear fuel. The nuclear industry is economically in a virtual shambles, which explains much of the adamant drive to sell nuclear reactors at home and abroad and has led to the strong competitive reactions and squabbles internationally (e.g., between the United States and West Germany over Brazil and between the United States and France over Pakistan) and the strong "no nukes" reaction in many parts of the world. Alternative sources of energy, including solar energy and synthetic fuels, have been the subject of much talk, but so far it is all talk and no action. The main reason is that the general rate of profit and prospective markets do not yet justify major investment either in the energy field or in any other. The apparent exception of the computer industry and particularly the use of microchips is so far primarily a rationalizing investment designed to reduce labor costs of production and is not yet a major innovation that puts production on new footing. Before a major new investment program can be undertaken and such major new technology put into place, the profit rate has to be elevated again. In order to do that, vast economic, social, and political transformations on a world scale will be necessary. (The beginnings of some of these transformations are reviewed in the preceding chapters and in the companion volume on the world economy and they are summaried below.)

Instrumental in both the decline in profits and their possible future recovery are another set of consequences and manifestations of the development of this crisis through recurrent and deepening recessions. Since the mid-1960s, recessions have become increasingly frequent, increasingly long, increasingly deep, and increasingly coordinated from one major industrial country to another. An index of the growth of these recessions is their impact on unemployment in the industrial countries of the OECD. In North America, Europe, Japan, Australia, and New Zealand, registered unemployment rose to 5 million during the recession of 1967, in which the United States barely participated because, so to say, it kept the recession wolf from the door with the war against Vietnam. By the recession of 1969–1971, which did hit the United States, registered unemployment rose to 10 million in the industrialized countries. Unemployment then fell back to 8 million in the subsequent recovery from 1972 to 1973. In the next recession, which hit almost the whole capitalist world simultaneously from 1973 to 1975, and which was the deepest one so far since 1930s, registered unemployment rose to 15 million in the industrialized countries, of which roughly 9 million or 9 percent were in the United States. Since then, unemployment again declined to less than 6 million in the United States but continued to rise in the industrial capitalist countries of Europe and Japan, as well as Canada and Australia. Indeed, the number of unemployed in these countries rose so much during the so-called recovery after 1975 that total OECD registered unemployment increased from 15 million at the bottom of the last recession to 17 or 18 million in late 1979.

A new recession began in 1979–1980 in the United States and Britain and is visibly threatening elsewhere. No one knows for sure how long the recession will last. The Carter administration was talking about a so-called soft landing and hoped that the recession would be relatively mild and not very long, if only because of the 1980 presidential election. To the express dismay of President Carter, a confidential document leaked out of his administration, which objectively projected a much deeper recession, lasting into 1981, with unemployment rising again to at least 8 percent. Furthermore, there are very substantial reasons to anticipate the 1979–1980 (81?) recession may turn out to be even more severe than the one of 1973–1975. One reason is that this recession is more welcome and "needed" than the previous one, which did not drive enough capital into bankruptcy to clean up the capitalist house sufficiently and did not successfully break the back of labor organization and militancy. Therefore, the capitalist states will do even less to combat this recession domestically than they did the last one. The Debt Economy, as *Business Week* aptly calls it, has grown so spectacularly in the attempt to keep the wolf from the door, that further acceleration in the growth of debt threatens to aggravate a possibly impending crash of the already excessively unstable financial house of cards; this has made worried bankers even more prudent and has reinforced economic conservatism.

At the same time, the previously available financial and institutional resources against the spread of recession, such as the development of speculative Euro- and Asian-currency markets, and, to counteract them, the introduction of flexible exchange rates and international economic coordination through economic summit conferences and the like, have already been substantially exhausted or have failed outright. Internationally, moreover, the safety valve or net that the socialist and OPEC countries offered to capital through increased demand for Western exports is already significantly diminished and likely to be far less available during this new recession. After their last expansion, these economies have a limited capacity to pay or to absorb imports, and are not likely to come to the rescue of Western capital again as they did after 1973. Thus, there would seem to be significant limits to consumer, investment, and export demand during this new recession. The only obvious alternative and additional source of demand is increased military spending.

The new recession is beginning at a level of unemployment, particularly in Europe and Japan, that is vastly higher than the level prior to the 1973–1975 recession, and a level of investment that has only just reattained the 1973 level. Most serious "scientific" projections from official and institutional forecasters seem to be unable or unwilling to take due account of these factors in the preparation of their generally overoptimistic forecasts. The September 1979 Annual Report of the International Monetary Fund predicted a long and hard worldwide recession starting in 1980 as a consequence of the weakness of the American economy. At its annual meeting in Belgrade in September 1979, the IMF amended its forecast further downward for 1980 and said "world economic growth will be lower than the percentage shown in the annual report." We are facing the prospect of a recession that may be even more severe than the one of 1973–1975, at a time when the economic, social, and political manifestations and consequences of the last recession—including 17 million unemployed in the OECD countries—have not by any means been overcome. This sobering circumstance is itself a mark of the deepening crisis.

Another consequence—indeed an essential part—of this process of deepening crisis through successive recessions has been the attempt to reduce costs of production through austerity policies and cuts in welfare, which has resulted in increased unemployment. It was demonstrated in WE that in most industrial capitalist countries there has been a deliberate policy of unemployment.

The same argument is advanced everywhere in the West and in the Third World: We need to combat and hold down inflation because it hurts all of us equally at home (although inflation characteristically reduces real income from work and raises the real values of property) and particularly because inflation at home would price us out of the world market, cut out export capacity, and therefore create unemployment. The principal cause of inflation supposedly is high public spending and high wage demands (although wage costs are a small and declining component of selling prices, and the evidence shows that prices are pushed up by the attempt to protect profits in monopolized industry). These same arguments are used everywhere to defend the imposition of austerity policies and to demand political restraint in public spending (except for defense and other business expenditures) and in "responsible" union wage demands, which are to be kept below the rate of inflation (both of which result in a decline of real wages and income, especially at the lowest end of the income scale).

Austerity policies have been imposed in every one of the major and minor capitalist economies in an attempt to get workers to tighten their belts. This attempt has been more successful in some places, less successful in other countries of the West, but it has been successfully imposed—often by force—throughout the Third World. Indeed before—and if—capital is to recover "adequate" levels of profit and to launch a renewed investment drive that could bring capitalism out of its present crisis of accumulation and into a new period of expansion, not only will capitalism have to have a new technological base, but both the profitable introduction of new technology and such investment will have to be based on another major political defeat of labor in the West, as happened between the 1920s and 1940s, and a major contribution from the South and perhaps from the East.

These circumstances have led to very marked shifts to the right of political center in many countries. Britain and West Germany are obvious cases in point and so is the United States. As I write this, the extremely right wing Franz Josef Strauss as the next Prime Minister of Germany is a real prospect. Marked shifts to the right are not only manifest on these domestic political levels, but in more aggressive if not bellicose international policies, as manifested by the installation of mobile intercontinental MX missiles in the western United States, the NATO decision to station a new generation of American nuclear missiles in Western Europe, the U.S. Senate's apparent refusal to accept SALT II, and the Pentagon's plans for a new mobile intervention force, all of which were decided *before* the new Soviet push into Afghanistan (and which certainly entered into Soviet calculations of whether an invasion would lead the West to pose any *additional* threats and costs to the Soviet Union beyond aforementioned and the Sino-American alliance). The Western shifts to the right also manifest themselves in a whole variety of other fields, such as in education (as a counteroffensive against the progressive measures of the 1960s), health, immigration, and race and sex relations (against the women's movement), and on the ideological level in general, where the "new right" is advancing by leaps and bounds in most industrial capitalist countries. In many Third World countries the real advance of the right has been even greater, as was documented above. The social democrats and liberals find themselves relatively unarmed against these shifts to the right and suffer from a severe crisis of confidence.

It is open to question whether the left has escaped this crisis of confidence and of ideology. The previously quoted official and officious statements to the effect that everything is going fine may be no more than not very substantial fig leaves covering a serious ideological crisis on the left as well. This ideological crisis of the socialist left and Marxism is a reflection or counterpart of a real economic and political crisis and also manifests itself importantly in the so-called socialist countries from the Soviet Union to China and the smaller socialist countries of Eastern Europe and Southeast Asia and perhaps also Cuba. These countries are caught up in the political economic crisis of the West as well as in one of their own, which may both be part of a single crisis in a single world system. Although it is not good to appeal to authority, it is perhaps convenient to cite Comrade Brezhnev from the Soviet Union, who says, "Because of the broad economic links between capitalist and socialist countries the ill effects of the current crisis in the West have also had an impact on the socialist world." The Prime Minister of Bulgaria, Comrade Zhikov, goes one step further and says: "It may be hoped that the crisis which is raging in the West may come to a rapid end; since it affects and creates uncertainties for the Bulgarian economy, which to a certain extent is dependent on trade with the countries of the West." Not only do these leaders of "socialist" countries recognize that the world capitalist crisis affects them, and does so negatively in their estimation, they also hope and ask that this crisis go away so that they can continue with business as usual. That in itself is both an element of and a manifestation of very serious crisis in socialism and Marxism, because in the past and even during the last serious crisis of capitalism between the two world wars, Marxist socialists welcomed such a crisis on the theory that it would lay the basis for the possible revolutionary destruction of captialism and its replace- ment with socialism. The fact that the "socialist" Soviet Union, Bulgaria, and other countries in Eastern Europe, not to mention China, which has entered into a political and economic alliance with the United States and Japan against the Soviet Union, now all hope that the crisis will go away and that they are actively collaborating with the capitalists to overcome the crisis (and even compete with each other in helping capitalism to do so) means that socialism and Marxism itself are in very serious ideological trouble. The "socialist" countries are very clearly committed in words, and even more so through their actions, to the maintenance—and even prosperity—of capi- talism in the West, and these "Marxist socialists" seem to all intents and purposes literally to have abandoned any hopes and any policies to con- tribute in one way or another to the demise of capitalism in the West. This socialist integration in and apparent commitment to the world capitalist system is documented in WE: Chapter 4 and summarized below.

That "socialism" is banking on the capitalist West is visible in the economic arena through the accelerated integration or reintegration of the socialist economies in the capitalist international division of labor through trade and production. During the last decade the "socialist" countries have vastly increased their trade with the West in order to import Western technology. As a result they have run a balance of payments deficit with the West, which they have covered in part by running up vast debts that have risen from about $7 billion in 1971 to approximately $60 billion today. In part—and this is particularly significant politically—the socialist countries cover their deficit with the West through their balance of payments surplus with the underdeveloped countries of the Third World with which they are also increasing trade ties. Thus, the socialist countries import technology from the West and to pay for it export two thirds fuels and raw materials and one third manufactures. But in turn their exports to the Third World consist of two thirds manufactured commodities of a lower order of technological development, and their imports from the Third World consist of two thirds raw materials. The socialist economies occupy an intermediate place in the international division of labor in which the pattern of the Socialist East-Third World South relations are similar to the Capitalist West-Socialist East relations.

This policy of economic integration and cooperation between the socialist countries and the capitalist ones in the West and South goes beyond simple trade and increasingly includes the most complex network of productive arrangements. Western firms increasingly produce in the socialist countries through complex arrangements ranging from licensing to foreign investment, in which the Western firms provide the technology, know-how, and often the management and marketing, and the socialist economies provide cheap skilled labor and labor discipline, that is, no strikes. Even China, which was famous for its policy of self-reliance, and Vietnam, which won the war against American imperialism in large part because of its policy of political and military self-reliance (despite military aid from the Soviet Union and China), have now permitted and indeed encouraged foreign investment in their countries—in Vietnam's case with 100 percent foreign ownership to produce manufactured commodities for the world market. Thus, the capitalist West increasingly produces in the socialist countries at low cost through a variety of complex production agreements for export to the West and to the Third World.

From the point of view of capital in the West, this increasing production and trade with the socialist economies represents one of the important means of trying to stem and reverse the tide of the growing economic crisis. This "socialist" safety valve for capitalist crisis manifested itself in particular ways in the 1973 to 1975 recession, when the capital equipment which then found no market in the West was bought by the East and OPEC countries, and thus helped to keep Western business afloat during that recession. The same socialist helping hand to capitalism manifests itself economically through the reduction in production costs which are lower in the East, and subsidized by "socialist" society, and politically through the already several times exercised capitalist threat to move production facilities to a socialist country if union militancy does not exercise "self-discipline" at home.

In WE we questioned whether the "socialist" countries form a "socialist world" outside and apart from the world capitalist system and argued that these countries are increasingly an integral part of the world capitalist division of labor, production, and trade—and concomitantly of the world capitalist social and political system. Stalin claimed a year before he died that there were two world markets, and though history has shown him to have been wrong, many people still claim that there are two social systems (though hardly anyone would claim only two political systems). Indeed, many Marxists and others argue that, though there may be only one (capitalist) world market, the capitalist law of value, and that market forces do not operate within the socialist economies. These capitalist forces clearly do operate, however, in Yugoslavia, complete with competition, monopoly, and unemployment; and the evidence is increasisng that they also operate in "socialist" Eastern Europe. Rumania's violation of Comecon agreements by suddenly charging East European tourists high prices in hard (capitalist) currencies for gasoline at the roadside pump is only a spectacular manifestation of the eastward spread of the capitalist world inflation and the economic reorganization. This economic "reform" has been most deliberate in Hungary to adapt the organization, financing, prices, varieties, quality, work processes, and marketing of domestic production to the exigencies of competition on the capitalist world market. Moreover, although the socialist countries can plan their economies, the underfulfillment by nearly half of the growth targets in the current five-year plans in the Soviet Union and similarly in most of Eastern Europe suggests that whatever their considerable domestic difficulties are, they are not unrelated to the development of the crisis in the West, which particularly in Eastern Europe has increased import costs while restricting export possibilities to pay for them. Therefore, the capitalist law of value (and not just a separate socialist one as Stalin argued) does seem to operate within the socialist economies, although perhaps less so in the relatively more autonomous Soviet and Chinese economies (though they also have followed the OPEC oil price upward in their external sales including those to other socialist countries). If some òf these socialist economies are successful in solving these problems during the current crisis (as Deng Xiaoping promises for China by the year 2000 through the four modernizations), the further question arises whether ironically only some countries that have passed through a socialist revolution will therefore be able to join the inner circle of metropolitan economies in the world capitalist system—while intermediate capitalist economies, like Brazil or Iran when ruled by the Shah, fail to do so. However, the intensive rivalry to the point of war between "socialist" states poses a serious obstacle to their success, as each—so far the Soviet Union, China, and Vietnam—is intent on preventing the success of another rival. (This most intense rivalry among socialist states contending for world and regional leadership positions and the resulting otherwise surprising alliances with capitalist nations are reminiscent of the similarly intense competition and alliances for the mantle of declining British world and regional leadership positions among the United States, Germany, France, Russia, and Japan during the periods of world crisis and wars over the past century.)

The socialist integration in the capitalist world has been all the more visible in the détente between the Soviet Union and the United States, which has been due not simply and perhaps not even primarily to peaceful co-existence under the nuclear sword of Damocles, but also to the political counterpart of growing economic integration. Perhaps it is appropriate to quote Mr. Kissinger in this regard: "The key to U.S. strategy towards the U.S.S.R. has been to create mutual vested interests in the preservation of the international order. Relations between the U.S. and the U.S.S.R. have become so stable that dramatic new departures could no longer be expected." For his part Mr. Brezhnev added, "We will be happy if our efforts to better Soviet American relations help draw more and more nations into the process of détente, be it in Europe or Asia and Africa or Latin America, in the Middle East or in the Far East." On the other hand, the emerging Washington-Peking-Tokyo axis requires little comment, and the Chinese foreign policy of visible and invisible alliance with anyone they hope will aid and abet their anti-Soviet policy speaks for itself. The Chinese policy seems to be simply that "the enemy of my enemy is my friend," no matter whether that be the Shah of Iran, the CIA puppets in Africa, Senator Henry Jackson in the United States or Franz Josef Strauss in West Germany, all of whom have been Chinese favorites because they represent the most avid anti-Soviet forces in the West. This is not to suggest that the Soviet policy is vastly better in that respect, because the record of recent years shows that although the Soviet Union has supported some progressive causes, it has also supported some very reactionary ones—Lon Nol in Cambodia, the Videla regime in Argentina, and Morocco, with which the Soviet Union has vastly increased trade ties. Despite certain support for national liberation movements here and there, and notwithstanding some claims among the Nonaligned, it seems objectively less than realistic, indeed unjustifiably optimistic, to hope that Soviet, let alone Chinese or Vietnamese foreign economic, political, or military policy will in the foreseeable future support the transformation of any movement of national liberation into a socialist revolution in Africa or elsewhere, especially if their own interests counsel that others' national or socialist interests be abandoned to their fate or even opposed, as in Somalia, Eritrea, and Southeast Asia. The motto of "proletarian internationalism" rings increasingly hollow.

The Third World was and is an integral and important part of the world capitalist economy. (This integration is documented above and in WE: Chapters 1 and 5.) Unless the working class in the West and the working class in the South can prevent it, the Third World is destined to play a major role in the attempt of capital in the world capitalist economy to stem and reverse the tide of the growing economic crisis. In the first place, since the Third World is an integral part of the capitalist world, the crisis is immediately transmitted from the center to the Third World through growing balance of payment deficits. As demand in the industrialized countries declines or grows more slowly, prices for exported raw materials other than petroleum decline or grow more slowly. At the same time, the vast world inflation in the industrialized economies increses prices of manufactured commodities imported by the Third World. Therefore, the terms of trade have been shifting again against the underdeveloped countries during this crisis (despite a temporary raw materials price boom in 1973–1974 which was completely reversed again after 1974), and the nonpetroleum-exporting underdeveloped Third World countries have faced increasingly serious balance of payments problems and a mushrooming foreign debt. Moreover, it is not accidental or incidental that the OPEC surplus is more or less equivalent to the increase in the balance of payments deficit of the Third World, suggesting that most of the increases in the prices of petroleum since 1973 have ultimately been borne by the Third World.

A significant portion of the OPEC surplus has been recycled through the banks in the imperialist countries to the Third World to cover their balance of payments deficits through private loans at increasingly onerous conditions and costs. Their growing debt, in turn, is then used increasingly as a political instrument to impose austerity and superausterity policies in the Third World. This blackmail through the renegotiation and extension of debts has received many newspaper headlines in the cases of Peru and Zaire, but it has also become standard International Monetary Fund (IMF) and private banking operating procedure elsewhere throughout the Third World. As these countries' foreign debt increases, they have to get the debt refinanced both through private banks and through official loans. The IMF then declares that if the government does not devalue the currency to make exports and foreign investment cheaper, lower wages, cut the government budget especially for welfare expenditures and take other antipopular measures, and if it does not throw out Minister A and replace him with Minister B who is more likely to institute the IMF-supported policies, then the country will not get the IMF certificate of good behavior and without it neither official loans nor loans from private banks will be forthcoming. This political-economic club has been used to beat governments into shape to adopt policies of superausterity throughout the Third World. Moreover, the same thing has also happened to Portugal and it has happened to Great Britain. However, just as unemployment and recession are not simply or even primarily due to government policy decisions, so are superausterity measures in the Third World not simply the result of pressure from the industrialized capitalist countries through the IMF. These external political pressures are simply reinforcing tendencies that have another much broader economic base in the capitalist attempt to maintain or revive the rate of profit by producing at lower costs in the Third World (and also in the socialist countries) with national political support for these repressive measures.

Costs of production are reduced by moving industry to the Third World, particularly labor-intensive industries, such as textiles and certain kinds of electronic equipment, but also some very capital-intensive industries, such as steel and automobiles. It is perhaps symbolic that the Volkswagon beetle is no longer produced in Germany but is now made in Mexico for export to the other parts of the world. From the point of view of the world capitalist economy this is a transfer of part of industrial production from high- to low-cost areas. From the point of view of the Third World, this move represents a policy of export promotion, particularly of so-called nontraditional industrial exports. Third World manufacturing export promotion has two seemingly different origins. In the first case, the economies that had advanced most in the process of import substitution, like India, Brazil, and Mexico, have turned to export some of their manufactures that began as import substitutes, from textiles to automobiles, some produced by multinational firms. In the second case, from the very beginning foreign capital went to other Third World countries to set up manufacturing facilities to produce for the export rather than for the domestic market. This movement started in the 1960s with Mexico (which combined both kinds of industry but in different regions) on the border with the United States and in South Korea, Taiwan, Hong Kong, and Singapore. In the 1970s it spread to Malaysia, the Philippines, and increasingly through India, Pakistan, Sri Lanka, Egypt, Tunisia, Morocco, the Ivory Coast, and to virtually every country on the Caribbean. These economies offer cheap labor, and they compete among each other with state subsidies to provide plant facilities, electricity, transportation, tax relief, and every kind of incentive for foreign capital to come to their countries to produce for the world market. In the case of Chile the military junta went so far as to offer to pay part of the otherwise starvation wages so that foreign capital could keep its costs down.

To provide these low wages and indeed to reduce wages from one country to another competitively, as each tries to offer more favorable conditions to international capital, requires political repression, the destruction of labor unions and/or the prohibition of strikes and other union activity, the systematic imprisonment, torture, or assassination of labor and other political leaders and in general the imposition of emergency rule, martial law, and of military government. In fact, the whole state apparatus has to be adapted to the Third World role in the new international division of labor.

This repressive movement has swept systematically through Asia, Africa, and Latin America in the course of the 1970s and is demonstrably not simply due to some kind of autonomous political force to combat communism (which has become a rather doubtful policy at a time when even the United States has socialist allies and some socialist countries collaborate with the repressive regimes). Demonstrably, this repressive political policy has the very clear economic purposes and functions of making these economies more competitive on the world market by lowering wages and by suppressing those elements of the local bourgeoisie who are tied to the internal market. This sector of the bourgeoisie pressured for certain kinds of mild restrictions on the operations of multinational corporations in a number of Third World countries during the late 1960s and early 1970s. Since then, these restrictions have increasingly been removed, and one government after another is falling over itself to offer favorable conditions to international capital.

The motto now is to work for the world market rather than for the internal market. Effective demand on the national market is not and is not intended to be the source of demand for national production—demand on the world market is. There is no reason to raise the wages of the direct producers, because they are not destined to purchase the goods that they produce. Instead, the goods are meant to be purchased far away on the world market. An important exception is the small local market of high income receivers, which is supposed to expand. Thus, there is a polarization of income not only between developed and underdeveloped countries on the global level, but also on the national level. Within the underdeveloped countries the poor are getting poorer, both relatively and often absolutely, and the rich are getting richer. In some cases, such as in Brazil until 1974 but less so since then, the attempt to develop a high income market for part of local industry has been very successful. However, in Brazil as elsewhere in the Third World, this "development model" is based on the depression of the wage rate (which as a consequence has been cut by about half in Brazil, Uruguay, Argentina, and Chile and is increasingly being forced down in Peru and elsewhere) and the forced marginalization and unemployment of labor (which has already increased vastly in the Third World and continues to do so.) Both of these processes are rapidly increasing the misery of the masses and the polarization of society in the Third World. Moreover, since in general the internal market is being restrained and restricted, the sector of the bourgeoisie that depends on the internal market, as in Chile and Argentina, also has to be repressed. Therefore, big capital must institute a military government that will repress not only labor but even a sector of the bourgeoisie and the petit bourgeoisie. The governing alliance is between the sector of local capital allied with international capital and their military and other political executors. This arrangement involves a very substantial reorganization of the state or even militarization, so that the Third World can more effectively participate in the international division of labor in the interests of facing an economic crisis in the imperialist countries and its state monopoly capital allies in the Third World itself.

In some places since late 1976, in others since 1977 and 1978, there appears to have been a reversal of this tendency toward military coups, emergency rule, and martial law. There have been elections in India and Sri Lanka, pseudo elections in Bangladesh and the Philippines, elections in Ghana and Nigeria with promise that their military regimes will step down and hand over power to civilian rule, announced elections in various parts of Latin America, and some perhaps significant liberalization in the military regime in Brazil. Some people attribute these developments to President Carter's human rights policy, though it is a bit difficult to sustain the efficacy of this policy when in quite a few crucial cases it either was absent or was restrained in the higher "national interest" of the United States. Other people attribute the liberalization to increasing mass mobilization in many parts of the Third World, or to a supposed failure of the new policy of export promotion and—certainly according to many Brazilians—to the renewed and prospective importance of a policy of import substitution and the widening of the internal market. However, at this time any such redirection of the Third World economies generally is hardly observable. Such a renewed import substitution in the Third World would be objectively aided and abetted by a far-reaching protectionist drive or the substantial breakdown of the system of international trade and finance elsewhere in the world. As the world economic crisis deepens, this eventually is admittedly a distinct possibility; but so far it has not come to pass. In the Third World progressive import substitution of consumer goods—though less so of capital goods producing for the export market—would require a relatively more equal distribution of income and a politically more benign regime to permit or reflect a broader coalition or alliance of classes and sectors. In other words, these people argue that the dark days of the mid-seventies are over and that we are again facing the prospect of a redemocratization or at least of limited democracy in many parts of the Third World. Even a measure of democracy would offer better conditions for popular mobilization and for the continuation or acceleration of national liberation movements and of socialist revolutions in the Third World.

On the other hand, it may also be argued with considerable evidence that these recent developments do not represent the reversal of the emerging new model of economic integration of the Third World in the international division of labor in response to the development of the world crisis, but rather that this apparent democratization is simply the institutionalization of the new model of economic growth based on export promotion. It was necessary to have very severe political repression as a midwife to institute this new model; but once the model is in place and more or less working, it is possible to ease off a bit on the political repression. Then, indeed, it is not only possible, but it becomes politically necessary and desirable to get a wider social base for the political regime and to institute a kind of limited political democracy by handing over the government from military to civilian rule. But these political modifications would not be made in order to overturn the present economic order and again to promote import substitution, let alone so-called noncapitalist growth or some variety of "socialism." Instead, this supposed redemocratization would be to maintain and to institutionalize the new insertion of the Third World in the international division of labor as low-wage producers during the present world economic crisis. If we look realistically at what is happening in Asia, Africa, and Latin America, there is very considerable economic and political evidence for this latter explanation of what is politically going on today in the Third World.

A political counterpart of this economic alternative is a renewed populist alliance of labor and other popular forces and parties with some bourgeois ones. This alliance would press for the amelioration of politically repressive regimes and their gradual replacement by formally or superficially more democratic but essentially technocratic ones to implement the same fundamentally exclusivist and antipopular economic policy. In the pursuit of such unholy alliances around the Third World, it has become opportune(ist) to resurrect all kinds of bygone politicians or even their ghosts. These politicians did not have left wing support in their heyday when they did not pursue very progressive policies, but they now receive support from the left to implement policies that are far more rightist than their previous ones. However, these rightist policies now appear as the lesser evil compared to more recent, often military, governments and policies. For lack of better alternatives the opposition, including the left, is now rallying behind bygone civilian political figures like Frei in Chile, Siles Suarez in Bolivia, Magalhaes Pinto in Brazil, Awolowo and Azikwe in Nigeria, Aquino in the Philippines, Pramaj in Thailand, Indira Gandhi in India, and even the ghost of Bhutto in Pakistan, as well as accepting new old men like the Ayatollah Khomeini in Iran to lead "progressive" movements, which are likely to maintain the essentials of the status quo and certainly will not offer any real development alternatives.

To the extent that these policies and politicians are a realistic political alternative in the Third World, orthodox development theory and ideology, as well as progressive dependence or even (not as revolutionary as hoped) new dependence theory—not to mention the Chinese "three worlds" theory and the Soviet supposedly "noncapitalist" third way to national liberation, democracy, and varieties of socialism—are all completely bankrupt. Today none of these theories and ideologies can offer any realistic policy alternatives and practical political economic guidelines for the pursuit of economic development or national liberation, let alone of socialist construction. Independent national development in the Third World has proved to be a snare and a delusion; and self-reliance, collective or otherwise, is a myth that is supposed to hide this sad fact of life in the world capitalist system. Political compromises with the capitalist status quo by the avowedly revolutionary socialist parties and particularly the Communist parties around the Third World are another part of the ideological crisis of the left in the face of the present world crisis.

In addition to the recent invasions of Kampuchea by Vietnam and of

Vietnam by China, current developments in Africa and Latin America also illustrate—indeed manifest—these dilemmas. Despite (some now even contend because of) Cuban aid and Soviet backing, Angola gives little evidence of moving toward self-reliance, let alone socialism, and has repressed some internal political forces that wanted to move faster or farther in that direction. Instead, after the express Soviet demonstration that the Soviet Union does not want an Angolan-sized Cuba on its hands, the MPLA government in Angola is turning its best efforts to maintaining and increasing its economic ties with the West and is encouraging capitalist foreign investment. Angola is also cultivating the friendliest possible relations with Mobutu to the north and with those who want a settlement in Namibia to the south. Freilimo is making greater efforts to promote national development through self-reliance, but so far without being able to extricate Mozambique from heavy dependence on South Africa and cautious involvement with Zimbabwe. Socialist backing of the Mengistu regime in Ethiopia has also acquiesced in widespread repression not only of reactionaries but also of revolutionaries inside Ethiopia, not to mention the sacrifice of progressive forces in Somalia and the fierce combat against national liberation and socialist forces in Eritrea.

On the other hand, while Cuba has made its presence strongly felt in Africa, Cuba's presence and open material support has, no doubt for very good objective reasons, until recently been in conspicuous in Nicaragua and elsewhere in Latin America. Moreover, after the Sandinistas had ousted the Somoza dictatorship, Fidel Castro invited their leadership to his 1979 Twenty-sixth of July celebration and in their presence emphatically said in his speech-as it was interpreted by the *New York Times* and American television commentators—that Nicaragua will not become another Cuba but another Nicaragua. This assurance probably reflects Fidel's realistic assessment of or legitimate doubts about the objective and subjective prospects arising out of the composition of the junta and of the Sandinista movement itself (which was, after all, backed by the anti-Somoza bourgeois forces within Nicaragua and the hardly revolutionary governments of Costa Rica, Panama, and Venezuela on the outside, although the Sandinistas have shown surprising independence since then). Fidel's statement perhaps also reflects the politico-economic limitations set by the ravage of the economy and the consequent need for outside aid in Nicaragua as well as other objective limitations elsewhere in Central America, Latin America, and the world as a whole, as well as most particularly the limitations which Cuba and the Soviet Union themselves experience and transmit. These objective limitations should make us consider again whether the situation is really excellent, as the Chinese say, and whether socialism is really making great strides. We would do well to remember that, as Marx said, man (he wrote before the feminist movement) or people make their own history, but they do not make it entirely as they wish but subject to certain objective limitations.

These reflections on living in the real world raise three further considerations that partly extend beyond the confines of this book. These considerations are war, nationalism, and—particularly in view of both—whether the
real world we are living in consists of two or more subjectively perceived
economic, social, and political systems and countless national ones, or
whether the real world in crisis we are living in is objectively only *one.*

The development of crisis or the crisis of development generates growing
nationalist attempts to manipulate or even escape from reality and increasingly belligerent attempts to resolve the crisis. Heightened economic competition and political rivalry increasingly take the form of threatened or actual
warfare around the Third World and now among socialist states. Armed
conflict occurs over border problems posed by adjacent or off-shore resources, national and religious allegiances, and most particularly the political
position and composition of the neighboring governments (as in Kampuchea,
Uganda, Nicaragua), which are defended and challenged if not overthrown
through a coalition of domestic, neighboring, faraway, and superpower
political and military forces. The pretended ideological justifications for
these policies frequently appear as pretexts to cover other publicly less
defensible interests, and the ideological lines and alliances are rapidly
adapted to changing circumstances, as in or over Kampuchea in Southeast
Asia and Ethiopia and its neighbors in the Horn of Africa.

The apparently most widespread and powerful moving force in this crisis
development is nationalism, sometimes combined with religion. Varieties of
nationalist, ethnic, and religious interests and allegiance seem to move the
superpowers, their challengers, and the other states in their mutual rivalries
to participate in world development. Tensions and conflicts that often have
their sources in the constraints and readjustments imposed by the world
economic crisis find their politically most viable expression through combinations or coalitions of national, regional, ethnic, and religious movements
within "nation" -states and their zones of influence. In Eastern Europe anti-
Soviet, anti-Communist, and religious sentiments (probably in that order of
importance) have expressed themselves through Polish Catholic (probably
far more nationalist than religious) sentiment, which brought five million
people out to see the Pope when he visited his native land in 1979.
Nationalist, regionalist, and religious sentiment, however, is also becoming
the most popular vehicle of opposition elsewhere in Eastern Europe and
particularly in the Central Asian and other non-Russian regions of the Soviet
Union. In China, also, the recent struggles over ideological lines and political
power have been combined with nationalist/regionalist non-Han rumblings.
The exodus from Vietnam of the largely ethnic Chinese "boat people" and of
others overland into China, as well as the politically significant expulsion of
ethnic Chinese and other minority functionaries from their positions of
leadership in the Liberation Army and the Communist Party of Vietnam,
bode for alarming if not terrifying possibilities for the near future: What if,

with the deepening crisis through another recession, Malays, Japanese, and others in Southeast Asia take a cue from Vietnam and launch anti-Chinese programs in their multiethnic societies?

Nationalist, regional, ethnic, and religious movements are also defining factors in Philippine Mindanao, Tamil Sri Lanka, in all three corners of India, through Pakistan and Afghanistan, in Iran thanks to the Baluchis and others, among Kurds and other minorities in Iran, Iraq, and Turkey (as well as the Soviet Union), and of course throughout the Israeli-Palestinian-Arab conflict. In Africa, existing ethnic allegiances condition the attempts to build national states without nations. In Europe, the authority of existing national states is challenged by regional ethnic movements (from Scotland to Euzkadi and Sardinia, and throughout Yugoslavia), which offer possibly false promises of salvation in a time of national and international economic and political crisis. In Mexico, where the Catholic Church has played a minor role for a long time, the Pope's visit still attracted three million people to the streets. In the United States, Spanish-speaking people of Mexican, Puerto Rican, and other Latin American origin are fast becoming not only the largest but also the most self-consciously militant minority. They have also contributed to the resurgence, particularly in the West and Southwest, of strong regional consciousness. Quebec nationalism now poses a supposed threat to the survival of the Canadian state and has encouraged regionalism in other provinces as well, including petroleum-rich Alberta.

Most of this contemporary nationalist resurgence is no longer a component of a drive for national liberation, let alone to socialism, as nationalism was during much of this century. On the contrary, not unlike a century ago, the question arises whether these nationalist movements merit support by virtue of their possible contributions to progressive and socialist causes or whether much of this new nationalism deserves condemnation and opposition for its probable reactionary and even counterrevolutionary consequences. Certainly, the nationalism that contributes to war between socialist states or even to the abandonment of socially progressive movements, policies, or governments can only be the largest stretch of the ideological imagination be supported as conducive to liberation and socialism—except on purely nationalist grounds. Many other nationalist, regional, ethnic, and religious movements in the East, South, and West are also exposed to manipulation and use by conservative and reactionary class forces far more easily than they are of use to progressive, let alone socialist, forces. At best, nationalism now increasingly threatens to confuse and divide popular and proletarian forces; at worst, nationalist and religious sentiments threaten to be increasingly manipulated outright by reaction. The threat is very real that socialism will be sacrificed on the alter of nationalism.

Finally, we may pose the question: Are we living in many different societies that are going through various crises simultaneously, or are we really living in a single world that is going through one crisis, albeit with different manifestations? The resurgence of so many different separate and separatist political, nationalist, ethnic, traditionalist, and religious movements, many in response to varied perceptions of social and personal crisis, might suggest that the world consists of or is breaking up into little pieces, each of which is reaffirming its traditional culture and life. An alternative suggestion is that most of these movements are little more than desperate reactions—and often with reactionary consequences—to the varied sensations of crisis generated by the development of a single world system, which is itself in a crisis of development as it rapidly engulfs all the inhabitants of the entire globe. This alternative suggestion rises out of the study of the historical development of the capitalist world system and its spread to incorporate all parts of the globe.

Moreover, the one-world view seems to be supported by evidence from the social movements that in recent times have posed the strongest and most successful challenges to the reality and the received theories of our world, and have caused the most widespread surprise and alarm: the revolutions led by Khomeini in Iran and by Pol Pot in Kampuchea. The apparent extremism of both revolutions—symbolized by the return to the Koran in Iran and the abolishment of money in Kampuchea—and their leaders' ability to elicit the acdeptance, sometimes grudging or enforced, of these and other measures by their mass bases is in reality an expression of how widely and deeply these peoples have been literally impressed by their accelerated incorporation into the operation of the single world system during the past decade. The popular reaction against the system and the rejection of the costs their incorporation had imposed on them only shows how much they are a part of the system and does not mean that they have escaped it. Pol Pot's revolution in Kampuchea has already come to a sad end (and his deputy, Ieng Sary, made a public declaration in Colombo that an alliance with any and all class and international forces is acceptable so long as it is anti-Vietnamese). There has been a resurgence of economic and regional geopolitical realism in Iran—perhaps only temporarily interrupted by the American embassy hostage affair, but again manifested by the new president—which seemed intent on repairing Iran's economic and political ties with the West and reassuming its policeman role in the Gulf region. These Kampuchean and Iranian accommodations to world reality suggest that their leadership itself now acknowledges that although people make their own social and national history, they make it within the objective political economic conditions and limitations of living in one real world system in crisis.

We must also ask ourselves what the implications of events in China and Southeast Asia are for the compatibility or competition between socialism and nationalism. Vietnam fought for its liberation for a generation under the banner of socialism and then treated the collaborators of the previous genocidal regime with kid gloves, sought maximum reintegration into world capitalism and failed to achieve it only because of capitalist recalcitrance (and the opposition of its socialist neighbor to the north), but then invaded socialist Kampuchea and expelled cadres of long standing from its own Communist Party and Liberation Army in the name of nationalism disguised as socialism. The Communist Party of Kampuchea initiated the most far-reaching mass-based social transformation ever attempted in an agrarian society, but then stratified to an extreme degree and reverted to the most brutal repression before being displaced by Vietnamese socialists, after which the Kampucheans offered to make a pact with the devil—any devil—to oppose their invading neighbors. China, the world's most populous country and most self-conscious socialist society, has pursued a steady course of policy zig-zags violating all tenets of its supposed mass line; it has defended the need to sacrifice egalitarianism to modernization at home, self-reliance to foreign technology, and other accommodations to capitalism abroad; it pursues the haughtiest nationalist foreign policy and even military adventures against its socialist neighbor in the supposed defense of socialism.

Should these developments lead us to suspect that the banner of "socialism" is little more than a fig leaf for naked nationalism, perhaps combined with racism? Should we regard this national assertion to be the attempt by a ruling class to promote its own interests where possible and to accommodate them to the limitations of reality in the capitalist world system? It is possible that often the emphasis on and utilization of socialist ideology are really nonideological attempts by pragmatically striped nationalist cats in socialist disguise to gain access to the super-privileged or at least relatively privileged core positions and benefits of the capitalist world system and its continuing development? Are appeals to socialism sometimes more effective to this nonsocialist end in the Third World than appeal to outright reactionary ideology or to a supposedly technocratic end-of-ideology would be? If so, or even if any of the above are partially so, how much rethinking of socialism and nationalism are now necessary by those who profess one or the other or both as a real alternative to the dehumanizing reality of the world capitalist economy?

Abbreviations

Organizations

AEI	American Enterprise Institute, Washington
AI	Amnesty International, London
APHA	American Public Health Association, Washington
BIS	Bank for International Settlements, Basel
CIAL	Centro de Información de America Latina, Paris
CMEA	Council for Mutual Economic Assistance, "Comecon," Moscow
ECE	UN Economic Commission for Europe, Geneva
ECLA	UN Economic Commission for Latin America, Santiago
EEC	European Economic Community (Common Market), Brussels
FAO	UN Food and Agricultural Organization, Rome
GATT	General Agreement on Tariffs and Trade, Geneva
GEREI	Groupe d'Etude des Relations Economiques Internationales, Paris
IBRD	International Bank for Reconstruction and Development (World Bank), Washington
IDEP	UN African Institute for Economic Development Planning, Dakar
ILO	UN International Labor Office, Geneva
IMF	International Monetary Fund, Washington
INRA	Institut de Recherche Agronomique, Paris
NACLA	North American Congress for Latin America, New York
OECD	Organization for Economic Cooperation and Development, Paris
OPEC	Organization of Petroleum Exporting Countries, Vienna
PCI	Partido Communista Italiano, Rome
PRIO	Peace Research Institute, Oslo
RBI	Reserve Bank of India, New Delhi
SIPRI	Stockholm International Peace Research Institute
UNCTAD	United Nations Conference on Trade and Development, Geneva
UNDESA	United Nations Department of Economic and Social Affairs, New York
UNECAP	United Nations Economic Commission for Asia and the Pacific, Bangkok

This listing includes works cited in *Crisis: In the World Economy* and in *Crisis: In the Third World*.

UNECE   United Nations Economic Commission for Europe,
             Geneva
UN ECOSOC   United Nations Economic and Social Council, New York
UNIDO   United Nations Industrial Development Organization,
             Vienna
UNITAR   United Nation Institute for Training and Research, New
             York
URPE   Union for Radical Political Economics, New York
USBLS   U.S. Bureau of Labor Statistics, Washington
USDA   U.S. Department of Agriculture, Washington
WBG   World Bank Group, Washington

Periodical Publications

AEI   *AEI Economist,* Washington
AEP   *Actualidad Económica del Peru,* Lima
AER   *American Economic Review,* Menasha, Wis.
ALT   *Alternativa,* Bogotá
AMPO   *Japan Asia Quarterly,* Tokyo
AP   Associated Press, USA
APR   *America Presse,* Paris
BA   *Business Asia,* Hong Kong
BCS   *Bulletin of Concerned Asian Scholars,* San Francisco
BD   *Brasil Dossiers,* Paris
BDS   *Bulletin of the Department of State,* Washington
BE   *Business Europe,* Geneva
BI   *Business International,* New York
B3W   *Blätter des Informationszentrum Dritte Welt,* Freiburg
BLA   *Business Latin America,* New York
BS   *Business Standard,* India
BSR   *Business and Society Review,* New York
BW   *Business Week,* New York
CA   *Commerce America,* Washington
CC   *Capitalism and Class,* London
CE   *Comercio Exterior,* Mexico
CEE   *Commercio Exterior,* English-language abridged edition, Mexico
CHA   *Chile-America,* Rome
CJB   *Columbia Journal of World Business,* New York
CON   *Contemporary Crises,* Amsterdam
CP   *Cuadernos Politicos,* México
CRI   *Critique,* Glasgow
CS   *Current Scene,* Hong Kong
DA   *Dialectical Anthropology,* Amsterdam
DAS   *Deutsches Allegemeines Sonntagsblatt,* Germany
DB   *Debate Proletario,* México

DC	*Development and Change,* The Hague
EBE	*Economic Bulletin for Europe,* UNECE, Geneva
ECO	*Economist,* London
EDC	*Economic Development and Cultural Change,* Chicago
EE	*Eastern Economist,* India
EIU	*Economist Intelligence Unit, Quarterly Economic Review,* London
EJ	*Economic Journal,* Cambridge, England
ELJ	*El Jarida,* Algiers
EO	*Economic Outlook,* OECD, Paris
EPA	*El Pais,* Madrid
EPW	*Economic and Political Weekly,* Bombay
ES	*Economy and Society,* London
ESE	*Economic Survey of Europe,* UNECE, Geneva
ESP	*O'Estado de São Paulo*
FA	*Foreign Affairs,* Lancaster, Penn.
F & D	*Finance & Development,* IMF and World Bank, Washington
FAZ	*Frankfurter Allgemeine Zeitung*
FER	*Far Eastern Economic Review,* Hong Kong
FEX	*Financial Express,* New Delhi
FMT	*Financial Market Trends,* OECD, Paris
FOR	*Fortune,* New York
FT	*Financial Times,* London
GM	*Gazeta Mercantil,* São Paulo
GUA	*The Guardian,* London
GUW	*The Guardian Weekly,* London
HB	*Handelsblatt,* Hamburg
HBR	*Harvard Business Review,* Cambridge, Mass.
HOL	*Holiday,* Dacca
HS	*Historia y Sociedad,* México
ICP	*Intercontinental Press,* New York (incorporating Inprecor, Brussels)
IDS	*Institute of Development Studies Bulletin,* Sussex
IE	*Indian Express,* India
IHT	*International Herald Tribune,* Paris
INF	*Informativo,* Paris
IPC	*Inprecor,* Brussels, Paris
IPW	*IPW Berichte,* Berlin, DDR
IRP	*Instant Research on Peace and Violence,* Tampere
IT	*India Today,* Delhi
JCA	*Journal of Contemporary Asia,* Stockholm
JEL	*Journal of Economic Literature,* Menasha, Wis.
LAER	*Latin American Economic Report,* London
LAPR	*Latin American Political Report,* London
LEV	*Leviathan,* Frankfurt
LM	*Le Monde,* Paris

LMD	*Le Monde Diplomatique,* Paris
LT	*The Times,* London
LTM	*Les Temps Modernes,* Paris
MAR	*Mining Annual Review,* Mining Journal, London
MBS	*Monthly Bulletin of Statistics,* United Nations, New York
MD	*Marxismus Digest,* Frankfurt
MEI	*Main Economic Indicators,* OECD, Paris
MEN	*Mensaje,* Santiago
MR	*Monthly Review,* New York
MRC	*El Mercurio,* Santiago
MRP	*Report* (Middle East Research and Information Project) *Report,* Washington
NIB	*New India Bulletin,* Montreal
NJ	*National Journal,* AEI, Washington
NLA	*NACLA Latin America and Empire Report,* New York
NLR	*New Left Review,* London
NS	*New Statesman,* London
NT	*New Times,* Moscow
NW	*Newsweek,* New York
NYT	*New York Times*
NYTM	*New York Times Magazine*
NZZ	*Neue Zürcher Zeitung,* Zürich
OBS	*Observer,* London
OO	*OECD Observer,* Paris
PD	*Problemas del Desarrollo,* México
PF	*Punto Final,* Santiago
PN	*Pugwash Newsletter,* London
PR	*Peking Review*
QB	*Quarterly Bulletin* (Bank of England), London
RAPE	*Review of African Political Economy,* London
RBI	Reserve Bank of India, *Reports on Currency and Finance,* New Delhi
SA	*Scientific American,* New York
SAC	*Southeast Asia Chronicle,* Berkeley
SCB	*Survey of Current Business,* Washington
ST	*Sunday Times,* London
SZ	*Süddeutsche Zeitung,* München
TE	*El Trimestre Económico,* México
TI	*Times of India,* New Delhi
TIM	*Time,* New York
TRA	*Transaction,* New York
UBS	*Union de Banques Suisses Report,* Zürich
USN	*U.S. News and World Report,* Washington
WD	*World Development,* Oxford
WDR	*World Development Report,* World Bank, Washington

WER	*World Employment Report*, ILO, Geneva
WDT	*World Debt Tables*, World Bank, Washington
WK	*Wirtschaftskonjuntur*, Berlin
WP	*Washington Post*
WSJ	*Wall Street Journal*, New York
WW	*Wirtschaftswoche*, Frankfurt
WWA	*Weltwirtschaftliches Archiv*, Kiel
YLS	*Yearbook of Labour Statistics*, ILO, Geneva
ZA	*Zona Abierta*, Madrid
ZT	*Die Zeit*, Hamburg
ZW	*Zerowork*, New York

Bibliography

Abercrombie, K. C. (1975) The International Division of Labour and of Benefits in Food and Agriculture. Paper presented at Society for International Development Conference on World Structures and Development-Strategies for Change. Linz, Austria, September 15–17, 1975.

Adler-Karlsson, Gunnar (1971) *Der Fehlschlag. Zwanzig Jahre Wirtschaftskrieg zwieschen Ost und West.* Wien: Europa Verlag.

Ake, Claude (1976) "The Congruence of Political Economies and Ideologies in Africa" *The Political Economy of Contemporary Africa.* Peter C. W. Gutkind and Immanuel Wallerstein, eds. Beverly Hills, London: Sage.

Alavi, Hamza (1972) "The State in Postcolonial Societies: Pakistan and Bangladesh" *New Left Review,* London, No. 74, July–August reprinted in Kathleen Gough and Hari P. Sharma, eds. *Imperialism and Revoluion in South Asia.* New York: Monthly Review Press, 1973.

Albrecht, Ulrich; Ernst, Dieter; Lock, Peter und Wulf, Herbert, (1976) *Rüstung und Unterentwicklung. Iran, Indien, Grichenland, Turkei. Die verschärfte Militarisierung.* Hamburg: Rowohlt.

Altavater, Elmar et al. (1974) "On the Analysis of Imperialism in the Metropolitan Countries. The West German Example" *Bulletin of the Conference of Socialist Economists,* London: Spring.

Amerongen, Otto Wolff von (1977) "Protectionism—a Danger to Our Prosperity" *Intereconomics,* Hamburg, No. 11–12.

Amin, Samir (1970) *L'accumulation à l'échele mondiale. Critique de la théorie du sous-développement.* Paris: Editions Anthropos.

—— (1973) *Le développement inégal. Essai sur les formations sociales du capitalisme périphérique.* Paris: Les Editions de Minuit.

—— (1976) After Nairobi—Preparing the Non-Aligned Summit in Colombo. An Appraisal of UNCTAD IV. Dakar, United Nations African Institute for Economic Development and Planning, DIR/2747, June.

—— (1977) *The Future of Southern Africa.* Introduction. Dakar, IDEP reproduction 402; Dar es Salaam: Tanzanian Publishing House.

——, Frank, Andre Gunder and Jaffe, Hosea (1975) *Quale 1984.* Milano, Jaca Book. Also in Spanish *Como será 1984.* Madrid: Zero, 1976.

—— et al. (1975) *La crise de l'impérialisme.* Paris: Les Editions Minuit.

Amnesty International Report 1976. London: Amnesty International Publications.

Amnesty International Report 1977. London: Amnesty International Publications.

AMPO (1977) "Free Trade Zones and Industrialization of Asia" *AMPO, Japan-Asia Quarterly Review,* Tokyo, Pacific Resources Center, Special Issue.

Ampuero, Raúl (1977) "El nuevo poder militar" *Nueva Politica,* Mexico, v. II, Nos. 5–6, Abril–Septiembre.

Amuzegar, Jahangir (1977) "A Requiem for the North-South Conference" *Foreign Affairs,* Lancaster, Penn., October.

—— and Fekkrat, M. Ali (1971) *Iran: Economic Development under Dualistic Conditions.* Chicago, The University of Chicago Press.

Annual Register of Political Economy (1978) *La Crise Contemporanea.* Milano: Jaca Book.

APHA (1975) *Health and Work in America: A Chart Book.* Washington, American Public Health Association, U.S. Government Printing Office.

Armstrong, P. J., Glyn, A. J., Harrison, J. M. and Sutcliffe, R. B. (1976) Reconstruction: Metropolitan Capitalism from the Second World War to Korea. Oxford, University of Oxford Institute of Economics and Statistics, January Mimeo.

Arrighi, Giovanni and Saul, John (1973) *Essays on the Political Economy of Africa.* New York: Monthly Review Press.

Arroio Junior, Raimundo (1976) "La miseria del milagro brasileño" *Cuadernos Politicos,* México, D. F., No. 9, July–September.

Arroyo, Gonzalo (1976) "Capitalisme transnational et agriculture traditionelle: Formes d'integration" *Political Economy of Food* Proceedings of an International Seminar. Tampere Peace Research Institute. Research Reports No. 12.

Aziz, Sartaj (1977) "The World Food Situation and Collective Self-Reliance. *World Development,* Oxford, v. 5, Nos. 5–7, May–July.

Baade, Fritz (1960) *Der Wettlauf zum Jahre 2000.* Oldenburg.

Bairoch, Paul (1973) *Urban Unemployment in Developing Countries.* Geneva: International Labour Office.

Bajit, Alexander (1971) "Investment Cycles in European Socialist Economies: A Review Article: *Journal of Economic Literature,* Menesha, USA, 9. No. 1.

Balakrishnan, K. (1976) "Indian Joint Ventures Abroad—Geographic and Industry Patterns" *Economic and Political Weekly,* Bombay, May.

Ball, George W. (1971) "Suez Is the Front to Watch" in *After Vietnam. The Future of American Foreign Policy,* Robert W. Gregg and Charles W. Jr. Kegley, eds. Garden City, New York: Anchor Books.

—— (1976) *Diplomacy for a Crowded World. An American Foreign Policy.* Boston: An Atlantic Monthly Press Book.

Bank for International Settlements (1978) Forty-eighth Annual Report, 1 April 1977–31 March 1978. Basel, 12 June.

—— (1979) Forty-ninth Annual Report, 1 April 1978–31 March 1979. Basel, 11 June.

Bartra, Roger, (1974a) *Estructura agraria y clases sociales en México.* México: Ediciones Era.

—— (1974b) "Modos de producción y estructura agraria en México" *Historia y Sociedad,* México, D. F., 2. época, No. 1.

BCC (1975) Can Business Help Solve the World Food Problems. Exploring the Alternatives. Business Communications Co. First Annual Food Conference Held March 19.

Behrman, Jack N. and Wallender, Harvey (1976) *Transfers of Manufacturing Technology within Multinational Enterprises.* Cambridge University.

Bein, David O. (1977) "Rescuing the LDCs." *Foreign Affairs,* Lancaster, Penn., v. 55, No. 4, July.

Belassa, Bela (n.d.) "The Firm in the New Economic Mechanism," *The New Hungarian Quarterly.*

Benaim, Raymond (1976) Une firme multinationale d'elevage au Maroc: Le King Ranch. Paris, Institut National de la Recherche Agronomique. Mimeo.

Benoit, Emile (1973) *Defense and Economic Growth in Developing Countries.* Lexington Mass.: Heath

—— (n.d.) Growth Effects of Defense in Developing Countries. Mimeo.

Bergmann, Denis (1977) "Agricultural Policies in the EEC and their External Implications" *World Development,* Oxford, v. 5, Nos. 5–7, May–July.

Berlinguer, Enrico (1977) *La cuestión comunista.* Barcelona: Editorial Fontanara.

Bhagat, S. (1977) "India: Gandhi Aims at 'Normalisation'" *Inprecor,* Bruxelles, No. 65, January 13.

Bitran, Daniel y König, Wolfgang (1977) "Las empresas transnacionales y las exportaciones de manufacturas de América Latina. Algunas consideraciones." *Comercio Exterior*, México, D. F., v. 27, No. 7, Julio.

Blaikie, Piers, Cameron, John and Seddon, David (1979) The Logic of a Basic Needs Strategy: With or Against the Tide? Norwich: University of East Anglia, School of Development Studies, June (mimeo).

Blair, John M. (1974) "Market Power and Inflation: A Short-Run Target T Return Model" *Journal of Economic Issues,* v. VIII, No. 2, June.

Block, Fred (1975) "Contradictions of Capitalism as a World System" *Insurgent Sociologist*, Eugene, Oregon USA, v. 1, No. 2, winter.

Boddy, Raford and Crotty, James (1976a) "Wages, Prices and the Profit Squeeze" *The Review of Radical Political Economics,* New York, URPE, v. 8, No. 2, Summer.

—— (1976b) "Wage-Push and Working Class Power" *Monthly Review,* New York, v. 27, No. 10, March.

Bondestam, Lars (1976) "The Politics of Food in the Periphery with Special Reference to Africa" *Political Economy of Food.* Proceedings of an

International Seminar. Tampere, Peace Research Institute. Research Reports, No. 12.

Bratenstein, Roger (1974) "First Steps Towards a Cyclical Theory for LDC" *Intereconomics* No. 10, October.

Braun, Oscar (1976) The New International Economic Order from the Point of View of Dependence Theory. Paper presented at First Congress of Third World Economics. Algiers, January.

Braverman, Harry (1974) *Labor and Monopoly Capital. The Degradation of Work in the Twentieth Century.* New York: Monthly Review Press.

Briones, Alvaro (1975a) "El neofascismo en América Latina" *Problemas del Desarrollo,* México, D. F., No. 23.

────── (1975b) "Neofascismo y nacionalismo en América Latina" *Comercio Exterior,* México, D. F., Julio.

────── (1976) "América Latina: crisis enconómica y fascismo dependiente" *Comercio Exterior,* México, D. F., Agosto.

Buira, Ariel (1977) "Diálogo Norte-Sur: final del juego" *Comercio Exterior,* México, D. F. v. 27, No. 9, September.

Buring, P. (1977) "Food Production Potential of the World" *World Development,* Oxford, v. 5, Nos. 5–7, May–July.

Burns, Arthur F. (1977) "The Need for Order in International Finance" *Columbia Journal of World Business,* New York, v. XII, No. 1, Spring.

Busch (Klaus), Schöller und Seelov (1971) *Weltmarkt und Weltwährungskrise.* Bremen: Margret Kuhlman für Gruppe Arbeiterpolitik.

Buxedas, Martin (1977) "El comercio internacional de carne vacuna y las exportaciones de los países atrasados" *Comercio Exterior,* México, D. F., v. 27, No. 12, Diciembre.

Campbell, H. (1977) The Commandist State in Uganda. University of Sussex, England. Political Studies Research in Progress Seminar Paper, April.

Cardoso, Fernando Henrique (n.d.) O"modelo brasileiro" de desenvolvimento: dados e perspectivas. (Uma interpretaçao socioeconómica.) Mimeo.

Carlo, Antonio (1975) "Die strukturellen Ursachen der Sowietischen Koexistenzpolitik" in *Sozioökonomische Bedingungen der Sowietischen Aussenpolitik,* Jahn, Egbert, ed. Frankfurt: Campus Verlag.

Carrillo, Santiago (1977) *"Eurocomunismo" y estado.* Barcelona: Editorial Crítica.

Castells, Manuel (1976) *La crise économique et la société américaine.* Paris: Presses Universitaires de France.

Chenery, Hollis et al. (1974) *Redistribution with Growth.* London.

Chile-America (1977) "Améica Latina bajo la hegemonia militar" Seminario de Bolonia. *Chile-América,* Nos. 33–34, Julio-Agosto.

Chomsky, Noam (1974) *Peace in the Middle East? Reflections on Justice and Nationhood.* New York: Vintage Books.

Chossudowsky, Michael (1975) "The Neo-Liberal Model and the Mechanisms of Economic Repression. The Chilean Case." London: Coexistence.

—— (1976) La recesión económica argentina. Julio. Mimeo.

—— (1977) "Legitimised Violence and Economic Policy in Argentina" *Cahier de Recherche,* Ottawa, Dept. of Economics, University of Otawa, No. 7613. Mimeo. Published in *Economic and Political Weekly,* Bombay, April 16, 1977.

Chubin, Shahram (1976) Implications of the Military Build-Up in Non-Industrial States: The Case of Iran. May. Mimeo.

CIAL (1976) La militarización del estado en América Latina. Paris, Centro de Información América Latina, No. 1. Mimeo.

Clairmont, Edmond de (1975) "Dialogue ou Confrontation Nord-Sud? *Le Monde Diplomatique,* Paris, December.

Clairmonte, Frederick F. (1975) "Dynamics of International Exploitation" *Economic and Political Weekly,* Bombay, August 29.

Claudin, Fernando (1970) *La crisis del movimiento communista. v. 1 De la Komintern al Kominform.* Paris: Ediciones Ruedo Ibérico.

—— (1977) *Eurocomunismo y socialismo.* Madrid: Siglo XXI.

Cleaver, Harry (1976) "The Political Economy of Malaria de-Control" *Economic and Political Weekly,* Bombay, September 4.

—— (1977) "Malaria and the Political Economy of Public Health" *International Journal of Health Services,* Farmingdale, New York, v. 7, No. 4.

Cleveland, Harold van B. and Brittain, W. H. Bruce (1977) "Are the LDCs in over their Heads?" *Foreign Affairs,* Lancaster, Penn., v. 55, No. 4, July.

Collins, Joseph D. (1971) "The World Bank and the 'Small Farmer' in Guatemala" *Notes du G.E.R.E.I.,* Paris, Institut National de Recherches Agronomiques, No. 3.

Comblin, Joseph (1976) "La doctrina de la seguridad nacional" *Informativo,* Paris, Centre Ecumenique de Liasons Internationales, No. 23, Julio.

Comité Brésil pour l'Amnistie (n.d.) Bresil Dossiers, Paris, v. 1.

COMITEXTIL (n.d.) The European Textile and Clothing Industries and the International Division of Labour. Bruxelles, Comité de Coordination des Industries Textiles (1977). Mimeo.

Committee for Freedom in India (n.d.) *Democracy or Dictatorship in India?* A Handbook of Facts Documents Analysis. Chicago.

Córdova, Arnaldo (1977) "Los orígenes del Estado en América Latina" *Cuadernos Políticos,* México, D. F., No. 14, October–December.

CPI-ML (n.d.) Soviet Social Imperialism in India. A CPI-ML Publication. Reproduced by IPANA, Wesmount, Quebec, Indian People's Association in North America (1976).

CSE (1976) The Labour Process and Class Strategies, Pamphlet No. 1. London, Conference of Socialist Economist.

Dandekar, V. M. and Rath, Nilakantha (1971) "Poverty in India" *Economic and Political Weekly,* Bombay, January 2 and 9.

De, Sankar (1975) "Foreign Aid and the Communist Bloc" *Economic and Political Weekly,* Bombay, December 13.

Declaration by the Socialist Countries . . . at the Third Session of the United Nations Conference on Trade and Development (1972) UNCTAD, TD/154, 25 April.

Del Monte, Matías (1977) El caso venezolano: reflexiones sobre una nueva variante de militarización en un país latinoamericano. Mimeo.

Demac, Donna and Mattera, Philp (1977) "Developing and Underdeveloping New York: the 'Fiscal Crisis' and the Imposition of Austerity" *Zerowork,* Political Materials, New York, No. 2.

Denison, Edward F. (1979) "Explanations of Declining Productivity Growth," *Survey of Current Business,* vol. 59, no. 8, part II.

Devron, Jean-Jacques (1976) Dévéloppement rural et technologies alternatives dans la strategie de la Banque Mondiale. Paris, Institut National de la Recherche Agronomique. Mimeo.

Diwan, Romesh (1977) "Projections of World Food Demand for and Supply of Foodgrains: An Attempt at Methodological Evaluation" *World Development,* Oxford, v. 5, Nos. 5–7, May–July.

Domhoff, G. William (1967) *Who Rules America?* Englewood Cliffs, N.J.: Prentice-Hall.

Dos Santos, Theotonio (1975) Imperialismo y dependencia. Ensayos sobre la crisis actual del capitalismo. México, Ms. 3vs. Published as Dos Santos 1978.

—— (1977a) "Socialism and Fascism in Latin America Today" *The Insurgent Sociologist,* Eugene, Ore. USA, v. VII, no. 4, Fall.

—— (1977b) "La crisis del milagro brasileño" *Comercio Exterior,* Mexico, D. F., v. 27, No. 1.

—— (1978) *Imperialismo y dependencia.* México, D. F.,Ediciones Era.

Du Boff, Richard (1977) "Unemployment in the United States" *Monthly Review,* New York, v. 29, No. 6, November.

Echeverría, José (1977) "Fascismo y colonialismo en el caso chileno" *Chile-América,* Roma, Nos. 33–34, Julio–Agosto.

Edwards, Richard C. (1975) "The Impact of Industrial Concentration on Inflation and the Economic Crisis" in *Radical Perspectives on Economic Crisis of Monopoly Capitalism,* by URPE/PEA. New York: Union for Radical Political Economics.

Ehrensaft, Philip (1976) "Polarized Accumulation and the Theory of Economic Dependence: The Implications of South African Semi-Industrial Capitalism" in Peter C. W. Gukind and Immanuel Wallerstein, eds., *The Political Economy of Contemporary Africa,* Beverly Hills, London: Sage Publications.

Ellman, Michael (1975) "Did the Agricultural Surplus Provide the Resources for the Increase in Investment in the USSR during the First Five Year Plan? *The Economic Journal,* Cambridge, Eng., December.

Engellau, Patrik and Nygren, Birgitta (1979) *Lending without Limits—On International Lending and Developing Countries.* Stockholm: Secretariat for Future Studies, Liber Forlag.

Epstein, Edward C. (1975) "Politicization and Income Redistribution in Argentina: The Case of the Peronist Worker" *Economic Development and Cultural Change,* Chicago, v. 23, No. 4, July.

Erb, Guy F. (1975) "The Developing World's 'Challenge' in Perspective" in Guy F. Erb and Valerina Kalbab, eds., *Beyond Dependency. The Developing World Speaks Out.* New York: Overseas Development Council.

Erdman, Paul E. *(1977) The Crash of '79.* New York: Pocket Books.

Evers, Tilman (1975) Subdesarrollo y estado. Elementos de una teoría del estado en el capitalismo periférico. Berlin, Instituto Latinoamericano de la Universidad Libre de Berlin. (Ponencia para el coloquio sobre "Procesos de Urbanización en el capitalismo desarrollado y subdesarrollado" 29 September, 2 October 1975. Giessen, Alemania Federal) Mimeo.

Eyer, Joseph and Sterling, Peter (1977) "Stress-Related Mortality and Social Organization" *The Review of Radical Political Economics,* New York, URPE, v. 9, No. 1, Spring.

Faire, Alexandre et Sebord, Jean-Paul (1973) *Le nouveau déséquilibre mondial. Une prospective des rapports internationaux.* Paris, Bernard Grasset.

Falk, Richard (1980) *The Iran Crisis and International Law.* International Conference on Alternative Development Strategies and the Future of Asia, New Delhi, March 11–17.

FAO (1974) "Population, Food Supply and Agricultural Development" Chapter 3 in *The State of Food and Agriculture 1974.* Rome, Food and Agricultural Organisation, also prepared for and incorporated in United Nations World Food Conference. Assessment of the World Food Situation. Present and Future. E/Conf. 65/3.

Farer, Tom J. (1975) "The United States and the Third World: A Basis for Accommodation" *Foreign Affairs,* Lancaster, Penn., October.

Feder, Ernest (1973–74) "Six Plausible Theses about the Peasants' Perspectives in the Developing World" *Development and Change,* The Hague, v. V, No. 2.

—— (1974) "Notes on the New Penetration of the Agricultures of Developing Countries by Industrial Nations" *Boletin de Estudios Latinoamericanos y del Caribe,* Amsterdam, No. 16.

—— (1976a) "Agribusiness in Underdeveloped Agricultures. Harvard Business School Myths and Reality" *Economic and Political Weekly,* Bombay, July.

——— (1976b) "McNamaras's Little Green Revolution. World Bank Scheme for Self-Liquidation of Third World Peasantry" *Economic and Political Weekly*, Bombay, v. XI, No. 14.

——— (1977a) Capitalism's Last-Ditch Effort to Save Underdeveloped Agricultures: International Agribusiness, The World Bank and the Rural Poor. The Hague, Institute of Social Studies. also published in *Journal of Contemporary Asia*, Stockholm, v. 7, No. 1.

——— (1977b) "Agribusiness and the Elimination of Latin America's Rural Proletariat" *World Development*, Oxford, v. 5, Nos. 5–7, May–July.

——— (1977c) "Regeneration and Degeneration of the Peasants. Three Divergent but not Incompatible Views about the Destruction of the Countryside." Published in Spanish as "Campesinistas y descampesinistas" *Comercio Exterior*, México, Diciembre.

——— (n.d.a) The New Penetration of the Agricultures of the Underdeveloped Countries by the Industrial Nations and their Multinational Concerns. Den Haag, Institute of Social Studies and Institute of Latin Ameican Studies, Glasgow, Occasional Paper No. 19, 1975.

——— (n.d.b) Strawberry Imperialism. An Enquiry into the Mechanisms of Dependency in Mexican Agriculture. Den Haag, Institute of Social Studies also published in México, Editorial Campesina, 1977 (distributed in England by America Latina) in Spanish: *El imperialismo fresa. Una investigacion sobre los mecanismos de dependencia de la agricultura mexicana*. México, Editorial Campesina, 1977.

Fellner, William ed. (1979) with contributions by Denison, Kendrick, Perlaman, and others on productivity. *Contemporary Economic Problems 1979*. Washington: American Enterprise Institute for Policy Research.

Foxley, Alejandro y Arrellano, José Pablo (1977a) "El Estado y las desigualdades sociales" *Mensaje*, Santiago, Chile, No. 261, agosto.

——— (1977b) "El tamaño y el papel del Estado" *Mensaje*, Santiago, Chile, No. 262, Septiembre.

Frank, Andre Gunder (1966) "The Development of Underdevelopment" *Monthly Review*, New York, September (reprinted in Frank 1969, chapter 1 and elsewhere).

——— (1967) *Capitalism and Underdevelopment in Latin America*. New York: Monthly Review Press, 1967, 1969. London: Penguin, 1971.

——— (1969) *Latin America: Underdevelopment or Revolution*. New York: Monthly Review Press.

——— (1972a) *Lumpenbourgeoisie and Lumpendevelopment. Dependency, Class and Politics in Latin America*. New York: Monthly Review Press.

——— (1972b) "La política ecónomica en Chile: del Frente Popular a la Unidad Popular. *Punto Final*, Santiago, sup. del No. 153, 14 Marzo.

——— (1973) "Reflections on Green, Red and White Revolution in India" *Economic and Political Weekly*, Bombay, January 20.

—— (1974) *Carta abierta en el aniversario del Golpe Chileno.* Madrid, Alberto Corazon Editor, Serie Communicación B No. 40 (incorporating Frank 1972b).

—— (1976a) *Economic Genocide in Chile. Monetarist Theory versus Humanity.* Nottingham, Spokesman Books, Spanish edition, Madrid: Ediciones Zero, 1976.

—— (1976b) "Economic Crisis, Third World and 1984" *World Development,* Oxford, v. 4, Nos. 10–11.

—— (1977a) "On So-called Primitive Accumulation" *Dialectical Anthropology,* Amsterdam, No. 2.

—— (1977b) "Emergence of Permanent Emergency in India" *Economic and Political Weekly,* Bombay, v. XII, No. 11, March 12.

—— (1977c) *Reflexiones sobre la crisis económica.* Barcelona, Anagrama, also published as *Reflexions sur la nouvelle crise economique mondiale.* Paris: Maspero, 1978 (incorporating Frank 1976b and 1977d). English ed.: *Reflections on the New World Economic Crisis.* New York: Monthly Review Press, 1981.

—— (1977d) "World Crisis and Underdevelopment" *Contemporary Crisis,* Amsterdam, No. 1.

——(1978a) *World Accumulation 1492–1789.* London: Macmillan and New York: Monthly Review Press.

—— (1978b) *Dependent Accumulation and Underdevelopment.* New York: Monthly Review Press and London: Macmillan.

—— (1978c) "Mainstream Economists as Astrologers: Gazing through the Clouded Crystal Ball" *U.S. Capitalism in Crisis,* New York: Union for Radical Political Economics.

—— (1978d) "The Economics of Crisis and the Crisis of Economics." *Critique,* Glasgow, No. 9 (incorporating Frank 1978c) in Spanish *Cuadernos Políticos,* México, No. 12, April–June 1977, and *Zona Abierta,* Madrid, No. 13, 1977.

—— (1978e) "Equating Economic Forecasting with Astrology is an Insult to Astrologers." *Der Gewerkschafter,* Frankfurt, v. 26, No. 1976, *Transicion,* Barcelona, vol. 1, no. 1, October. University of East Anglia School of Development Studies, Discussion Paper no. 52, mimeo. *Contemporary Crises,* vol. 4, no. 1, Jan. 1980.

—— (1978f) "Is a Left Eurocommuism Possible?—A Review of Claudin" *New Left Review,* London (original published as "Es posible un Euro-comunismo de izquierdas?" *Cuadernos para el Diálogo,* Madrid, 21 Enero 1978). Also in *Kritik,* Berlin, v. 6, no. 17.

Frei Montalva, Eduardo (1976) "El mandato de la historia y las exigencias del porvenir" *Chile-America,* Roma, Nos. 14–15, Enero–Febrero.

Freyhold, Michaela von (1977) "The Post-Colonial State and its Tanzanian Version" *Review of African Political Economy,* London, No. 8, January–April.

Fröbel, Folker; Heinrichs, Jurgen and Kreye, Otto (1976) "Tendency towards a New International Division of Labour. Worldwide Utilisation of Labour Force for World Market Oriented Manufacturing" *Economic and Political Weekly,* Bombay, Annual Number, February.

———— (1977) *Die neue internationale Arbeitsteilung. Strukturelle Arbeitslosigkeit in den Industrieländern und die Industriealisierung der Entwicklungsländer.* Hamburg, Rowohlt. A few citations of quotations, whose pagination here is preceded by roman numerals, were taken over from these authors' original manuscript and were not included by them in the final published book. Wherever possible, their quotations from English language sources were used in the English original generously supplied by the authors. English ed.: *The New International Division of Labour,* Cambridge University Press, 1980

Galtung, Johan (1975) Self-Reliance and Global Interdependence. Some Reflections on the 'New International Economic Order.' Society for International Development, European Regional Conference, Linz, Austria, Conf. Doc. No. 12-e.

Gandhi, Ved P. (1974) "India's Self-inflicted Defence Burden" *Economic and Political Weekly.* Bombay, August 31.

GATT (1972) *El comercio internacional en 1971.* Geneva, General Agreement on Tariffs and Trade.

———— (1976) *International Trade 1975/76.* Geneva, General Agreement on Tariffs and Trade.

———— (1977) Prospects for International Trade. Main Conclusions of GATT Study for 1976–77 Published. Geneva, General Agreement on Tariffs and Trade. Press Release GATT 1196, 7 September.

———— (1979a) "The Outlook for International Trade and the Management of Interdependence." Speech by Olivier Long, GATT director general. GATT Press release 21 June.

———— (1979b) Prospects for International Trade. Main Conclusions of GATT Study for 1978–79 Published. Geneva, General Agreement on Tariffs and Trade. GATT Press Release 4 September.

George, Susan (1976) *How the Other Half Dies. The Real Reasons for World Hunger.* Harmondsworth, England: Penguin Books.

Ghai, Dharam (1975) The Unemployment Crisis in the Third World. Society for International Development European Regional Conference, Linz, Austria, Conference Doc. 14-e.

Glyn, Andrew (n.d) "Capitalist Crisis: Alternative Strategy: Socialist Plan," Oxford, mimeo (1977), published in revised form as *Capitalist Crisis: Tribune's "Alternative Strategy" or Socialist Plan,* London: Militant, 1979.

———— and Sutcliffe, Bob (1972) *British Capitalism, Workers and the Profits Squeeze.* Harmondsworth, England: Penguin Books.

Gordon, David M. (1975) "Capital v. Labor: The Current Crisis in the Sphere of Production" in *Radical Perspectives on the Economic Crisis of Monopoly Capitalism,* by URPE/PEA. New York: The Union for Radical Political Economics.

—— (1978) "Up and Down the Long Roller Coaster" in *U.S. Capitalism in Crisis,* by URPE. New York: The Union for Radical Political Economics.

—— (1980) "Stages of Accumulation and Long Economic Cycles" in T. K. Hopkins and I. Wallerstein, eds., *Processes in the World-System,* Beverly Hills, Calif.: Sage Publications.

Griffin, Keith (1972) The Green Revolution: An Economic Analysis. Geneva, United Nations Research Institute for Social Development.

—— and Azizur Rahman Khan, eds. (1976) Poverty in Asia. Geneva, ILO, Mimeo.

Guerrero, Hernán y Varela, Andrés (1977) "Y después de Pinochet, que?" *Comercio Exterior,* México, D. F., v. 27, No. 10, October.

Guevara, Roberto (1977a) Nuevas formas de militarismo en América Latina. Belgrado, Semana Latinoamericana, 7–14 de Noviembre. Mimeo.

—— (1977b) "El partido militar en América Latina" *Chile-América,* Roma, Nos. 33–34, Julio–Agosto.

Gustafsson, Mervi (1977) Food Aid in International Relations: The Case of the United States. Tampere, Finland, Peace Research Institute, Research Report No. 14.

Halperin Donghi, Tulio (1969) *Historia Contemporánea de América Latina.* Madrid: Alianza Editorial.

—— (1972) *Hispanoamérica después de la Independencia. Consecuencias sociales y económicas de la emancipación.* Buenos Aires: Ed. Paidós.

Haq, Mahbub ul (1976) *The Poverty Curtain: Choices for the Third World.* New York: Columbia University Press.

Harrington, Michael (1977) *The Vast Majority: A Journey to the World's Poor.* New York: Simon and Schuster.

Harrison, John (1974) "British Capitalism in 1973 and 1974: The Deepening Crisis," *CSE Bulletin,* Spring.

Hayes, Carlton J. H. (1941) *A Generation of Materialism 1871–1900.* New York: Harper & Brothers.

Helleiner, G. K. (1976) "Transnational Enterprises, Manufactured Exports and Employment in Less Developed Countries" *Economic and Political Weekly,* Bombay, Annual Number, February.

Heller, Walter W. (1975) "What's Right with Economics?" Presidential Address delivered to the American Economic Association, December 29, 1974. *American Economic Review,* Menasha, Wis., March.

Hewett, Edward A. (1975) "The Economics of East European Technology Imports from the West" *American Economic Review,* Menasha, Wis., May.

Hewitt de Alcatara, Cynthia (1976) Modernizing Mexican Agriculture:

Socioeconomic Implications of Technological Change 1940–1970. Geneva, United Nations Research Institute for Social Development.

Heyman, Hans (1973) "La economía soviética. Problemas de la productividad de la economía soviética" (Translation from the English original in) *El Mercurio,* Santiago, 24 Abril.

Heyne, H. (1976) "Neue Weltwirtschaftordunung—Veränderung für die Dritte Welt?" *Blätter des Iz3w,* Freiburg, Germany, No. 54, June.

Hinkelammert, Franz (1970) "Teoría de la dialéctica del dearrollo desigual" *Cuadernos de la Realidad Nacional,* Santiago, CEREN, No. 6 especial, Diciembre.

Holloway, John and Picciotto, Sol (1977) "Capital, Crisis and the State" *Capital and Class,* London, No. 2, Summer.

Hong Kong Research Project (1974) *Hong Kong: A Case to Answer.* Nottingham: Spokesman Books.

Hopper, David (1976) "The Development of Agriculture in Developing Countries. It Needs Additional Technology and Capital from the Development Countries" *Scientific American,* New York, v. 235, No. 3, September.

Hudson, Michael (1972) *Super Imperialism. The Economic Strategy of American Empire.* New York: Holt, Reinhart and Winston.

―――― (1977) *Global Fracture. The New International Economic Order.* New York: Harper and Row.

Hveem, Helge (1975) "The Political Economy of Raw Materials and the Conditions for their OPECization." Oslo, International Peace Research Institute, March. Mimeo.

――――(1976) "The Political Economy of Producer Associations." Oslo:, International Peace Research Institute, mimeo. Published as *The Political Economy of Third World Producer Associations.* Oslo: Norwegian Universities Press, 1977. Available from Global Book Resources Ltd., London, and Columbia University Press, New York.

IBGE *Annuario Estadistico.* Rio de Janeiro, Instituto de Geografia e Estadistica.

IHT (1977) "The Euromarket" *International Herald Tribune,* Zurich, December Part I.

ILO (1975) *1975 Year Book of Labour Statistics.* Geneva: International Labour Office.

―――― (1976) *Employment, Growth and Basic Needs: A One World Problem.* Report of the Director General of the International Labour Office to the Tripartite World Conference on Employment, Income Distribution and Social Progress and the International Division of Labour. Geneva: International Labour Office.

IMF (1977) "La deuda externa de 75 países en desarrollo no petroleros aumentó notablemente en 1976" *Boletin del FMI—Bulletin IMF,* v. 6, No. 17, Washington, September in *Comercio Exterior,* México, D. F. December.

Ivanov, Ivan (1975) Tripartite Industrial Co-operation: Recent Situation, Problems and Prospects. Discussion Paper. Geneva, UNCTAD, TAD/SEM.1/7, 12 November.

Jacoby, Erich H. (1975) "Transnational Corporations and Third World Agriculture" *Development and Change,* The Hague, v. 6, No. 3, July.

—— (n.d.) Agri-Business and the United Nations System. Stockholm: University of Stockholm.

Jahn, Egbert (1975) *Sozioökonomische Bedingungen der sowjetischen Aussenpolitik.* Frankfurt: Campus Verlag.

Jolly, Richard; Kadt, Emmanuel de; Singer, Hans and Wilson, Fiona, eds. (1973) *Third World Employment. Problems and Strategy.* Harmondsworth: Penguin Books.

Kaiserlich Iranischer Botschafter (1976) *Iran Wirtschaftsdaten und Investitionsmöglichkeiten.* Bonn.

Kaldor, Mary (1976) "The Arms Trade and Society" *Economic and Political Weekly,* Bombay, Annual Number, February.

Kaplan, Marcos (1969) *Formación del estado nacional en América Latina.* Santiago: Editorial Universitaria.

Kende, István (1973) *Guerres Locales en Asie, en Afrique et en Amerique Latine (1945–1969).* Budapest, Centre pour la Recherche de l'Afro-Asie de l'Academie des Sciences de Hongrie.

Kennedy, Paul (1977) "Indigenous Capitalism in Ghana" *Review of African Political Economy,* London, No. 8, January–April.

Khanna, Sushil (n.d.) "Petrochemical Industry and Industrial Stagnation in India." Calcutta: Indian Institute of Management, mimeo.

Kim, Chang Soo (1977) "Marginalization, Development and the Korean Workers' Movement", *AMPO,* Tokyo, vol. 9, no. 3.

Kindleberger, Charles P. (n.d.) *Manias, Bubbles, Panics and Crashes and the Lenders of Last Resort.* Cambridge, Mass.: M.I.T. Mimeo.

Kissinger, Henry A. (1975) *The Kissinger Study of Southern Africa.* Nottingham, U.K.: Spokesman Books.

—— (1976) "UNCTAD IV: Expanding Cooperation for Global Economic Development" Address by Secretary Kissinger. *Department of State Bulletin,* Washington, No. 1927, May 31.

Klein, Dieter (1976) "Politökonomische Aspekte des Kampfes zwischen Sozialismus und Kapitalismus" *IPW Berichte,* Berlin, DDR, No. 3.

Kolko, Gabriel (1968) *The Politics of War. The World and United States Foreign Policy, 1943–1945.* New York: Random House Vintage Books.

Kolko, Joyce (1974) *America and the Crisis of World Capitalism.* Boston: Beacon Press.

Kondratieff, Nikolai D. (1935) "The Long Waves in Economic Life" *The Review of Economic Statistics,* Cambridge, USA. Reprinted in The American Economic Association, *Readings in Business Cycle Theory.* Philadelphia, 1944.

Kowarick, Lucio (n.d.) The Logic of Disorder in Capitalist Expansion in the Metropolitan Area of Greater São Paulo: São Paulo, CEBRAP, University of São Paulo. Mimeo.

Krishnappa, S. (1973) "Politics of Defence" *Economic and Political Weekly,* Bombay, March 10.

Labrousse, C. E. (1932) *Esquisse du mouvement des prix et des revenues en France au XVIIIe siècle,* Paris Lib. Dalloz, 2 vols.

Lacharriere, Guy de (1975) The Role of East-West Co-operation in the Development of Tripartite Co-operation. Paper prepared by Mr. Guy de Lacharriere, Consultant. Geneva, UNCTAD TAD/SEM.1/16, 18 November.

Laclau, Ernesto (1977) *Politics and Ideology in Marxist Theory. Capitalism, Fascism, Populism.* London: New Left Books.

Ladejinsky, Wolf (1973) "How Green Is the Indian Green Revolution?" *Economic and Political Weekly,* Bombay, December.

Langdon, Steve (1977) "Debate: The State and Capitalism in Kenya" *Review of African Political Economy,* London, No. 8, January–April.

Lavigne, Marie (1973) *Le programme du Comecon et l'intégration socialiste.* Paris: Editions Cujas.

Legassick, M. (1974) "South Africa: Capital Accumulation and Violence" *Economy and Society,* London, v. 3, No. 3.

Leitenberg, Milton (1977) A Survey of Studies of Post W.W. II Wars, Conflicts and Military Coups. Ithaca, Cornell University Center for International Studies. Peace Studies Program. Mimeo.

—— (1979) "The Military Implications of Arms Sales to the Third World: What Do We Know, and What Don't We Know." Cornell University, Center of International Studies.

Leitenberg, Milton and Ball, Nicole (1977) "The Military Expenditures of Less Developed Nations as a Proportion of their State Budgets/A Research Note." *Bulletin of Peace Proposals* v. 8, No. 4.

Leontief, Wassily et al. (1977) *The Future of the World Economy. A United Nations Study.* New York: Oxford University Press.

"Les intellectuels communistes dans la tormente" (1978) *Les Nouvelles Littéraires,* Paris, No. 2639, 15 Juin.

Leys, Colin (1976) "The 'Overdeveloped' Post Colonial State: A Re-evaluation" *Review of African Political Economy,* London, No. 5, January–April.

Lietaer, Bernard A. (1978) "El próximo conflicto Norte-Sur" *Comercio Exterior,* México, D. F., v. 28, No. 3, Marzo.

Lock, Peter (1979) "Obstacles to Disarmament Relating to the World Economic and Political Order: International Economic Structures." Hamburg: Study Group on Armaments and Underdevelopment, Revised Version, April (mimeo).

Lock, Peter and Wulf, Herbert (1977) Register of Arms Production in

Developing Countries. Hamburg, Arbeitsgruppe Rüstung und Unterentwicklung. Mimeo.

Lockwood, Lawrence (1973) "Israeli Subimperialism?" *Monthly Review,* New York, v. 24, No. 8, January.

Long, Olivier (1977) "The Protectionist Threat to World Trade Relations" *Intereconomics,* Hamburg, No. 11–12.

Lowy, Michael and Sader, Eder (1977) "La militarización del Estado en América Latina" *Cuadernos Políticos,* México, No. 13, Julio–Septiembre.

Luckham, Robin (1977) "Militarism: Arms and the Internationalisation of Capital" *IDS Bulletin,* Sussex, England, v. 8, No. 2, March.

Lund (1978) Letter on Science, Technology and Basic Human Needs, December.

—— (1979) Letter on Science, Technology and Basic Human Needs, March.

McCracken, Paul (1977) *Towards Full Employment and Price Stability.* Summary of a report to the OECD by a group of independent experts. Paris: OECD.

—— et al. (1977) *Towards Full Employment and Price Stability.* Summary to the OECD by a group of independent experts. Paris: OECD.

MacEwan, Arthur (1975) "Changes in World Capitalism and the Current Crisis of the U.S. Economy" in *Radical Perspectives on the Economic Crisis of Monopoly Capitalism.* New York: Union of Radical Political Economics.

MacKay, Donald, ed. (1977) *Scotland 1980 the Economics of Self-Government.* Edinburgh: Q Press.

McNamara, Robert S. (1973) Address to the Board of Governors World Bank Group. Nairobi, September.

—— (1974) Address to the Board of Governors World Bank Group. Washington, D.C., September 30.

—— (1977) Address to the Board of Governors, World Bank Group. Washington, D.C., September 28.

Magdoff, Harry (1969) *The Age of Imperialism. The Economics of U.S. Foreign Policy.* New York: Monthly Review Press.

Mamdani, Mahmood (1976) *Politics and Class Formation in Uganda.* New York: Monthly Review Press.

Mandel, Ernest (1975a) *Late Capitalism.* London: New Left Books.

—— (1975b) "Prospects for the International Capitalist Economy" *Intercontinental Press,* New York, July 7.

—— (1975c) "Folgen der Weltwirtschaftkrise auf die Entwicklung der Arbeiterkämpfe im EG-Bereich" Ein Interview mit Ernst Mandel von Adelbert Reif. *Monthly Review,* Deutsche Ausgabe, Frankfurt, v. 1, No. 5, Oktober.

—— (1978) *Crítica del eurocomunismo.* Barcelona, Editorial Fontanara. *Critique of Eurocommunism.* London: New Left Books.

Mansour, Fawzy (1977) Third World Revolt and Self-Reliant Auto-Centered Strategy of Development (A Draft). Dakar, United Nations African Institute for Economic Development and Planning, Reproduction 406.

Marchais, Georges (1973) *Le défi démocratique.* Paris: Bernard Grasset.

Marini, Ruy Mauro (1973) *Dialéctica de la dependencia.* México: Ediciones Era.

—— (1974) *Subdesarrollo y revolución.* Ed. Rev. México: D. F. Siglo XXI.

—— (1977a) "La acumulación capitalista mundial y el subimperialismo" *Cuadernos Políticos,* México, D. F., No. 12, Abril–Junio.

—— (1977b) "Estado y crisis en Brasil" *Cuadernos Políticos,* México, No. 13, Julio–Septiembre.

—— y Pellicer de Brody, Olga (1967–1968) "Militarismo y desnuclearización en América Latina" *Foro Internacional,* México, El Colegio de México, v. VIII, No. 1.

Marx, Karl (n.d.) *Capital.* Moscow: Foreign Languages Publishing House. 3 v.

Mato, Daniel (1977) "La deuda externa de América Latina" *Comercio Exterior,* México, v. 27, No. 11, November.

Meadows, Donelle and Dennis (1972) *The Limits to Growth.* New York: Universe Books

Meillassoux, Claude (1975) *Femmes, greniers et capitaux.* Paris: François Maspero.

Melman, Seymour (1974) *The Permanent War Economy: American Capitalism in Decline.* New York: Simon and Schuster.

Menob, Kitty (1979) "India's Economic Crisis: A Comment," *Economic and Political Weekly,* Bombay, September 15.

MERIP (1977) "Labor Migration in the Middle East" *MERIP Reports,* Washington, No. 59, August.

Mesarovic, M. and Pestel, E. (1974) *Mankind at the Turning Point.* New York: Dutton.

Metra Consulting Group (n.d.) *Iran: A Business Opportunity.* London: Financial Times Limited.

—— (1977b) "La Conferencia de Paris: un final esperado" *Comercio Exterior,* México, Septiembre.

Meyer, Herbert E. (1974) "A Plant that Could Change the Shape of Soviet Industry" *Fortune,* Chicago, November.

Michalet, Charles-Albert (1976) The Multinational Companies and the New International Division of Labour. Geneva, ILO World Employment Programme Research Working Papers, WEP 2–28, WP 5, November.

Miliband, Ralph (1969, 1973) *The State in Capitalist Society. The Analysis of the Western System of Power.* London: Quarter Books.

Mills, C. Wright (1956) *The Power Elite.* New York: Oxford University Press.

Mishra, H. K. N. (1974) "Progress of Industrial Sector in the Fourth Plan 1969–74" *Economic and Political Weekly,* Bombay, June 8.

Moran, Theodore H. (1971–72) "New Deal or Raw Deal in Raw Materials" *Foreign Policy,* Winter.

—— (1973) Transnational Strategies of Protection and Defense by Multinational Corporations: Spreading the Risk and Raising the Cost for Nationalization in Natural Resources. *International Organization,* Madison. v. 27, no. 2, Spring.

Morris, Jacob (1975) "The Weird World of International Money" *Monthly Review,* New York, v. 27, No. 6, November.

Münster, Anne Marie (1977) Der Ubergang von der Elektromechanik zur Elektronik und die damit verbundenen Verwertungsmöglichkeiten im Rahmen transnationaler Produktion. Starnberg. Mimeo.

Murray, Robin (1975) *Multinational Companies and Nation States. Two Essays.* Nottingham: Spokesman Books.

NACLA (1975a) "The Food Weapon-Mightier than Missiles" *Latin America and Empire Report,* New York, v. IX, No. 7, October.

—— (1975b) "US Grain Arsenal" *Latin American and Empire Report,* New York, v. IX, No. 7, October.

—— (1976) "Merchants of Repression: U.S. Police Exports to the Third World," *NACLA Latin America and Empire Report,* vol. X, no. 6, July–August.

—— (1977) "Electronics: The Global Industry" *Latin America and Empire Report,* v. XI, No. 4, April.

—— (1978a) "Agribusiness Targets in Latin America" *NACLA Report on the Americas,* New York, v. XII, No. 1, January–February.

—— (1978b) *Report on the Americas* (1978b) v. XII, No. 2, March–April.

Nairn, Tom (1977) *The Break-Up of Britain. Crisis and Neo-Nationalism.* London: New Left Books.

Navarrete, Jorge Eduardo (1977a) El diálogo Norte-Sur. Una búsqueda negociada del nuevo orden económico internacional" *Nueva Política,* México, v. 1, No. 4, Octubre–Marzo.

—— (1978) *Iran: A Business Opportunity for the 1980s.* London: Metra Consulting Group Limited.

Nayyar, Deepak (1975a) The Impact of Transnatinal Operations on Exports of Manufactures from Developing Countries. A study prepared for the UNCTAD Secretariat, August.

—— (1975b) Socialist Countries and the Third World. Towards a Political Economy of the Relationship. Paper presented at a conference on New Approaches to Trade. Sussex, England, Institute of Development Studies, September. Mimeo.

—— Ed. (1975c) "Special Issue on Economic Relations between the

Socialist Countries and the Third World" *World Development,* Oxford, v. 3, No. 5, May.

—— (1976a) Transnational Corporations and Manufactured Exports from Poor Countries. Sussex, England, University of Sussex, Economics Seminar, Paper Series 76/17.

—— (1976b) "India's Export Performance in the 1970s" *Economic and Political Weekly,* Bombay, May 15.

Nehru, Jawaharlal (1960) *The Discovery of India.* New York: Doubleday Anchor.

Nordhaus, William (1974) "The Falling Share of Profits" in A. Okun and L. Perry, eds., *Brookings Papers on Economic Activity* no.1.

Oberg, Jan (1976) "Towards a New Military World Order. A Sceptic Contribution to the Discussion of a New Economic World Order." Lund, Department of Peace and Conflict.

—— (1977) "The New International Economic and Military Orders as Problems of Peace Research", *Bulletin of Peace Research Proposals,* vol. 8, no. 2.

——(n.d.) "The New International Military Order—The Real Threat to Human Security/An Essay on Global Armament, Structural Militarism, and Alternative Strategy." Lund: University of Lund, Department of Peace and Conflict Resolution.

O'Connor, James (1972a) *The Fiscal Crisis of the State.* New York: St. Martin's Press.

—— (1972b) "Inflation, Fiscal Crisis, and the American Working Class" *Socialist Revolution,* San Francisco, No. 8, March–April.

OECD (1976a) *Collective Bargaining and Inflation: New Relations Between Government, Labour and Management.* Final Report on an Internatinal Management Seminar Convened by the OECD. Paris: Organisation for Economic Co-Operation and Development.

—— (1976b) *Study of Trends in World Supply and Demand in Major Agricultural Commodities.* Paris: Organisation of Economic Co-Operation and Development.

—— (1979) *Economic Surveys, United States.* Paris: Organisation of Economic Co-operation and Development, November.

Oliveira, Francisco (1973) "La economía brasileña: crítica a la razón dualista" *El Trimestre Económico,* México, D. F., v. XL (2), No. 158.

Osorio Urbina, Jaime (1975) "Superexplotación y clase obrera: el caso mexicano" *Cuadernos Políticos,* México, D. F. No. 6, Octubre.

Owen, Henry and Schultze, Charles L. eds. (1976) *Setting National Priorities: The Next Ten Years.* Washington: The Brookings Institution.

Pajestka, Josef and Kulig, Jan (1979) The socialist countries of Eastern Europe and the New International Economic Order. Trade and Development, An UNCTAD Review. Geneva, no. 1, Spring.

Parvus et al. (1972) *Die langen Wellen der Konjunktur Beitrage zur*

Marxistischen Konjunktur- und Krisentheorie, von Parvus, Karl Kautsky, Leo Trotzki, N. D. Kondratieff und Ernst Mandel. Berlin: Prinkipo.

Paul, Samuel (1974) "Growth and Utilisation of Industrial Capacity" *Economic and Political Weekly,* Bombay, December 7.

Payer, Cheryl (1976a) "Third World Debt Problems: The New Wave of Defaults" *Monthly Review,* New York, v. 28, No. 4, September.

——— (1976b) "Third World Loans Might Make our Banks Beggars" *Business and Society Review,* New York, No. 20, Winter.

Pérez Guerrero, Manuel (1977) "Un nuevo orden económico internacional" *Nueva Política,* México, v. 1, No. 4, Octubre–Marzo.

Petzoldt, Volker, (1976) "Consideraciones sobre el estado militar en América Latina" *Actualidades,* Caracas, v. 1, No. 1.

Piñera, Sebastian y Meller, Patricio (1977) "Pobreza, distribución del ingreso y rol del estado" *Mensaje,* Santiago, No. 263, October.

Pinochet Ugarte, Augusto (1975) Objetivo Nacional del Gobierno de Chile. Santiago, 23 de diciembre.

Pinto, Aníbal y Knakal, Jan (1973) El sistema centro-peripheria 20 años después. Santiago, Instituto Latinoamericano de Planificación Económica y Social. Mimeo.

Plaschke, Henrik (1975) "International Subcontracting: on the Migration of Labour-Intensive Processing from the Center to the Periphery of Capitalism" in *Instant Research on Peace and Violence,* v. V.

Poulantzas, Nicos (1968) *Pouvoir politique et classes sociales.* Paris, Maspero. 2 vs., in English *Political Power and Social Classes.* London, New Left Books, 1973.

PREALC (1976) (Regional Employment Program for Latin America and the Caribbean) The Employment Problem in Latin America: Facts, Outlooks and Policies. Santiago, ILO, April.

Prebisch, Raúl (1979) "Aspects of international economic co-operation: Some reflections on the vicissitudes of development." *Trade and Development, An UNCTAD Review.* Geneva, no. 1, Spring.

Radice, Hugo (1975) East West Industrial Cooperation and the Transition to Socialism. Paper prepared for a conference on New Approaches to Trade. Sussex, England, Institute of Development Studies, September. Mimeo.

Raj, K. N. (1976) "The Economic Situation" *Economic and Political Weekly,* Bombay, July 3.

Resnick, Idrian (1975) "L'état dans l'Afrique Contemporaine" in *Les inégalités entre états dans le système international: origines et perspectives,* Ed., par Immanuel Wallerstein. Quebec: Choix.

Revelle, Roger (1976) "The Resources Available for Agriculture" *Scientific American,* New York, v. 235, No. 3, September.

Review (1979) Special Issue on Cycles and Trends. *Review* vol. II, no. 4, Spring.

Rey, Pierre-Philippe (1971) *Colonialisme, néo-colonialisme et transition au capitalisme. Exemple de la "Comilog" au Congo-Brazzaville.* Paris: Francois Maspero.

Roberts, Dick (1977) "Imperialism and Raw Materials," *International,* London, vol. 4, no. 1, Autumn.

Rockefeller, Nelson A. (1969) *The Rockefeller Report on the Americas. The Official Report of a United States Presidential Mission for the Western Hemisphere.* Chicago: Quadrangle Books.

Rodríguez, Mario V., (1976) "Fundamento de la nueva institucionalidad (El concepto de Seguridad Nacional)" *Mensaje,* Santiago, No. 253, October.

Rosefielde, Steven (1974) "Factor Proportions and Economic Rationality in Soviet International Trade 1955–1968" *American Economic Review,* Menasha, Wis., v. LXIV, No. 4, September.

Rostow, Eugene V. (1972) *Peace in the Balance. The Future of American Foreign Policy.* New York: Simon and Schuster.

Rostow, W. W. (1978) *The World Economy: History and Prospect.* Austin, University of Texas Press.

Roy, Ajit (1980) "Monopoly Capital in India and Prospects of Social and Political Changes." International Conference on Alternative Development Strategies and the Future of Asia, New Delhi, March 11–17.

Rudra, Ashok (1977) "The Left Front Government" *Economic and Political Weekly,* Bombay, September 3.

Ruz, Mauricio F. (1977) "Doctrina de seguridad nacional en América Latina. Contribución a un debate" *Mensaje,* Santiago, No. 261, Agosto.

Sabolo, Yves and Trajtenberg, Raúl (1976) The Impact of Transnational Enterprises on Employment in the Developing Countries. Preliminary Results. Geneva, ILO, WEP 2-28/WP 6.

Sachverständigenrat (1974) Jahresguatchten 1974, Bonn.

Sader, Emir (1977) "Fascismo y dictadura militar" *Chile-América,* Roma, No. 33–34, Julio–Agosto.

Salvi, P. G. (1971) *Comecon and the Emerging Nations.* New Delhi: Writers and Publishers Corporation.

Sarkar, N. K. (1974) Industrial Structure of Greater Bangkok. Bangkok, United Nations Asian Institute for Economic Development and Planning.

Sau, Ranjit (1973) "Growth and Fluctuation in Indian Economy" *Economic and Political Weekly,* Bombay, Special Number August.

—— (1977) "Indian Political Economy, 1967–77. Marriage of Wheat and Whisky" *Economic and Political Weekly,* Bombay, April 9.

—— (1979) "India's Economic Crisis: Dialectics of Sub-Imperialism," *Economic and Political Weekly,* Bombay, March 3.

Saul, John S. (1976) "The Unsteady State: Uganda, Obote and General

Amin" *Review of African Political Economy,* London, No. 5 January–April.

Saul, S. B. (1969) *The Myth of the Great Depression, 1873–1896.* London: Macmillan.

Schertz, Lyle P. (1974) "World Food: Prices and the Poor" *Foreign Affairs,* Lancaster, Penn., April.

Schui, Herbert (1976) "Die Unternehmer haben die Krise selbst verschuldet" *Frankfurter Rundschau,* March 6.

Schumpeter, Joseph A. (1939) *Business Cycles.* New York: McGraw Hill.

Sebastian, M. (1973) "Does India Buy Dear from and Sell Cheap to the Soviet Union?" *Economic and Political Weekly,* Bombay, December 1.

Sebord, Jean-Paul (1977) *D'un deuxième monde à l'autre. Essai prospectif sur l'Europa du sud et le Monde Arabe.* Paris: Editions Anthropos.

Sen, Ranjan (1980) "The Steep Descent," *Frontier,* Calcutta, v. 12, No. 28, March 9.

Senghaas, Dieter (1977) *Weltwirtschaftsordunung und Entwicklungspolitik. Plädoyer für Dissoziation.* Frankfurt: Edition Suhrkamp.

Senghaas-Knobloch, Eva (1976a) "The Impact of Periphery Capitalism on Constitution and Composition of the Labour Force. Some Reflections on the New ILO Strategy for Employment and Development." Västerhaninge, Summer. Mimeo.

—— (1976b) "Weibliche Arbeitskraft und Gesellschaftliche Reproduktion" *Leviathan,* No. 4.

Sherman, Howard (1976a) "Class Conflict and Macro-Policy" *The Review of Radical Political Economics,* New York, URPE, v. 8, No. 2.

—— (1976b) "Inflation, Unemployment and Monopoly Capital" *Monthly Review,* New York, v. 27, No. 10, March.

—— (1979) "A Marxist Theory of the Business Cycle." *Review of Radical Political Economics,* vol. 11, no. 1, Spring.

Shetty, S. L. (1973) "Trends in Wages and Salaries and Profits of the Private Corporate Sector" *Economic and Political Weekly,* Bombay, October.

Shivji, Issa G. (1970) *Tanzania: The Silent Class Struggle.* Lund, Zenit Reprint.

—— (1976) *Class Struggles in Tanzania.* New York, Monthly Review Press (incorporating Shivji 1970).

Shourie, Arun (1974) "India—An Arrangement at Stake" *Economic and Political Weekly,* Bombay, June 22.

Shuman, James B. and Rosenau, David (1972) *The Kondratieff Wave.* New York: World Publishing.

Sideri, Sandro (1972) "International Trade and Economic Power" in *Toward a New World Economy.* Rotterdam: Rotterdam University Press.

——— (1973) Manuscript prepared at UN ECLA in Santiago, and no longer available for complete citation.

Siegel, Lenny (1980) "Export-oriented Semiconductor Production in Asia." International Conference on Alternative Development Strategies and the Future of Asia, New Delhi, March 11–17, mimeo.

Simiand, F. (1932) *Les fluctuations économiques à longue période et la crise mondiale,* Paris: Alcan.

Sinha, N. P. (1976) "Malaria Eradication: What went Wrong?" *Economic and Political Weekly,* Bombay, June 26.

SIPRI (1979) *Armaments or Disarmament? The Crucial Choice.* Stockholm, SIPRI.

Sivard, Ruth Leger (1976) *World Military and Social Expenditures.* Leesburg, Virginia USA, WMSE Publications.

——— (1979) *World Military and Social Expenditures 1979.* Leesburg, Virginia, World Priorities.

Smith, Adam (1973) *An Inquiry into the Nature and Causes of the Wealth of Nations,* New York: Random House (original ed., 1776).

Southeast Asia Chronicle (1979) "Changing Role of S. E. Asian Women. The Global Assembly Line and the Social Manipulation of Women on the Job," Berkeley, No. 66, January–February 1979.

Souza, Herbert (1975) "Las multinacionales y la superexplotación de la clase obrera en Brasil" *Problemas del Desarrollo,* México, D. F., Año IV, No. 23, Agosto–Octubre.

Stalin, Joseph (1953) *Economic Problems of Socialism in the U.S.S.R.* Moscow: Foreign Languages Publishing House.

Stewart, Frances (1979) The New International Economic Order and Basic Needs: Conflicts and Complementarities. Unpublished paper presented at the Nordic Symposium on Development Strategies in Latin America and the New International Economic Order, University of Lund Research Policy Institute, September.

Streeten, Paul P. (1979) "Basic Needs: Premises and Promises." Washington: World Bank Reprint Series Number 62. Reprinted from *Journal of Policy Modeling* 1 (1979).

Subrahamanyan, K. (1973) "Indian Defence Expenditure in Global Perspective" *Economic and Political Weekly,* Bombay, June 30.

Swainson, Nicola (1977) "The Rise of a National Bourgeoisie in Kenya" *Review of African Political Economy,* London, No. 8, January–April.

Swamy, Subramanian (n.d.) "What Is Happening in India? Democracy or Dictatorship in India" *Committee for Freedom in India* Chicago.

Sweezy, Paul M. (1953) *The Present as History.* New York: Monthly Review Press.

Terzian, Pierre (1977) "OPEC Surpluses: Myth and Reality" MERIP *Reports,* Washington, No. 57, reprinted from *Arab Oil and Gas,* Paris, March 16.

Testa, Victor (n.d.) "Aspectos Economicos de la Coyuntura Actual 1973–1975." Mimeo.

Tharakan, P. K. M. (n.d.) Multinatinal Companies and a New International Division of Labor. Brussels, European Centre for Study and Information on Multinational Corporations. Mimeo.

Ticktin, H. H. (1973) "Towards a Political Economy of the USSR" *Critique*, Glasgow, No. 1, Spring.

—— (1975) "Das Verhältnis zwischen Wirtschaftreformen und Entspannungspolitik der Sowietunion" in *Sozioökonomische Bedingungen der sowietischen Aussenpolitik*, Egbert Jahn ed. Frankfurt: Campus Verlag.

Tinbergen, Jan (1976–1977) *Reshaping the International Order* (RIO). Amsterdam: Elsevier. Citations here from the German translation: *Wir haben nur eine Zukunft. Reform der Internationalen Ordnung.* Opladen: Westdeutscher Verlag, 1977.

TNI (1974–1975) World Hunger: Causes and Remedies. Report presented to the World Food Conference, Rome. Amsterdam. Mimeo. Published in revised form in *International Journal of Health Services*, Farmingdale, New York, v. 5, No. 1, 1975.

Trajtenberg, Raúl with Jean-Paul Sajhau (1976) Transnational Enterprises and the Cheap Labour Force in Less Developed Countries. Geneva, ILO. World Employment Programme Research, Working Paper WEP 2-28/WP 15, December.

Treverton, Gregory F. (1977) "Latin America in World Politics: The Next Decade" *Adelphi Papers*, London, International Institute for Strategic Studies, No. 137.

Trilateral Commission (1975) *The Crisis of Democracy*, by Michael Crozier, Samuel P. Huntington and Joji Watanuki. Report on the Governability of Democracies to the Trilateral Commission. New York: New York University Press. Copyright © 1975 by the Trilateral Commission.

Triplett, Jr., Glover, B. and Van Doren, David M. Jr. (1977) "Agriculture without Tillage" *Scientific American*, New York, v. 236, No. 1, January.

Turnham, David (1971) *The Employment Problem in Less Developed Countries. A Review of Evidence.* Paris, Development Centre of the Organisation for Ecnomic Co-Operation and Development.

Turok, Ben and Maxey, Kees (1976) "Southern Africa: White Power in Crisis" in *The Political Economy of Contemporary Africa*, Peter C. W. Gutkind and Immanuel Wallerstein, eds. Beverly Hills, London: Sage Publications.

Udry, C. A. (1976) "A New World Order?" *Inprecor*, Bruxelles, No. 61–62, 11 November.

UNCTAD (1972a) Handbook of International Trade and Development Statistics. New York, UNCTAD TD/STAT.4. UN Sales Number E/F.72.II.D.3.

—— (1972b) Trade Relations among Countries Having Different Economic and Social Systems. Review and Analysis of Trends and Policies in Trade Between Countries having Different Economic and Social Systems. Geneva, UNCTAD TD/112, 20 January.

—— (1972c) Declaration by the socialist countries at the third session of the United Nations Conference on Trade and Development, Santiago, UNCTAD TD/154, 25 April.

—— (1974) Problems of Raw Materials and Development. Note by the Secretary-General of UNCTAD. Geneva, UNCTAD/OSG/52, 4 April.

—— (1975a) Tripartite Industrial Co-Operation. Geneva, UNCTAD TAD/SEM.1/2, 25 November.

—— (1975b) Tripartite Co-Operation Arrangements for the Transfer of Technology to Developing Countries. Geneva, UNCTAD TAD/SEM. 1/13, 12 November.

—— (1975c) Financial Flows to and from Developing Countries. Geneva, UNCTAD TD/B/XV/Misc. 3, 3 June.

—— (1975d) The Scope of Trade-Creating Industrial Co-Operation at Enterprise Level between Countries having Different Economic and Social System. New York, UNCTAD TD/B/490/Rev. 1.

—— (1975e) Trade Relations among Countries having Different Economic and Social Systems. Review of Trends and Policies in Trade between Countries having Different Economic and Social Systems. Geneva, UNCTAD TD/B/560. 30 June.

—— (1975f) Review of the World Commodity Situation and Report of International Action on Individual Commodities. Commodity Trade: Review and Outlook. Report by the UNCTAD Secretariat. Geneva, UNCTAD TD/B/C.1/174. January.

—— (1975g) An Integrated Programme for Commodities. A Common Fund for the Financing of Commodity Stocks: Amounts, Terms and Prospective Sources of Finance. Report by the Secretary-General of UNCTAD. Geneva, UNCTAD TD/B/C.1/184. 24 June.

—— (1975h) An Integrated Programme for Commodities: The Impact on Imports, Particularly of Developing Countries. Report by the UNCTAD Secretariat. Geneva, UNCTAD TC/B/C.1/189. 13 June.

—— (1975i) Report of the Committee on Manufactures on Its Seventh Session. Geneva, UNCTAD TD/B/C.2(VII)/Misc. 3.

—— (1976a) New Directions and New Structures for Trade and Development. Report by the Secretary-General of UNCTAD to the Conference, Nairobi, TD/183.

—— (1976b) Preservation of the Purchasing Power of Developing Countries' Exports (Item 8-Supporting Paper) Geneva and Nairobi, UNCTAD TD/184/Supp. 2, May.

—— (1976c) Trade Relations among Countries having Different Economic and Social Systems. Nairobi, UNCTAD TD/193 May.

—— (1976d) International Specialization in Industrial Production and its Impact on the Expansion of Trade and Economic Relations between the Socialist Countries of Eastern Europe and the Developing Countries. Geneva, UNCTAD/TSC/24. 21 January.

—— (1977a) The Evolution of a Viable International Development Strategy. Report by the Secretary-General of UNCTAD. Geneva, TD/B/642, 30 March.

—— (1977b) Implementation of International Development Policies in the Various Areas of Competence of UNCTAD. Report by the Secretary-General of UNCTAD. Geneva, TD/B/642/Add.1. 31 March.

—— (1977c) The Recent Economic Experience of Developing Countries in Relation to United Nations Development Objectives. Report by the UNCTAD Secretariat. Geneva, TD/B/642/Add.2. 13 April.

—— (1979a) Trade relations among countries having different economic and social systems. Geneva, UNCTAD TD/243.

—— (1979b) Statistical review of trade among countries having different economic and social systems. Geneva, UNCTAD TD/243/Suppl. 1.

—— (1979c) Tripartite industrial co-operation in third countries. Geneva, UNCTAD TD/243/Suppl. 5.

—— (1979d) Restructuring the international economic framework. Report by the Secretary-General of UNCTAD to the fifth session of the Conference. Geneva, UNCTAD TD/221.

—— (1979e) Evaluation of the world trade and economic situation and consideration of issues, policies and appropriate measures to facilitate structural changes in the international economy. Geneva, UNCTAD TD/224.

—— (1979f) Evaluation of the world trade and economic situation and consideration of issues, policies and appropriate measures to facilitate structural changes in the international economy. Geneva, UNCTAD TD/224/ADD. 1.

UNDESA (1974) *1974 Report on the World Social Situation.* New York, United Nations, Department of Economic and Social Affairs. E/CN.5/521/Rev.1.ST/ESA/24.

UNECE (1974a) A Review of Commercial Policy Developments Affecting East-West Trade, 1968 to 1973. Part B of pre-publication text of the *Economic Bulletin for Europe,* Geneva, v. 25, UNECE, TRADE (XXII)/1 Add.1, n.d.

—— (1974b) *Bulletin Economique pour l'Europe,* Geneva, UNECE, v. 25.

—— (1974c) "Recent Economic Developments in Eastern Europe and the Soviet Union" Chapter 2 in *The European Economy in 1974.* Pre-publication text of the *Economic Survey of Europe 1974.* Geneva, UNECE (XXX)/1 Add.1.

——(1975a) Recent Changes in Europe's Trade. Pre-publication text of the *Economic Bulletin for Europe*, v. 27. Geneva, UNECE (XXIV)/1, 17 November.

—— (1975b) "Recent Economic Development in Eastern Europe and the Soviet Union" Chapter 2 in *The European Economy in 1975.* (Prepublication text of the *Economic Survey of Europe 1975*) Geneva, UNECE (XXXI)/1 Add.1.

—— (1975c) Long-Term Economic Growth of East European Countries: Objectives, Major Factors and Patterns between 1960 and 1990. Geneva, UNECE, EC.AD. (II)/AC.1/R.1/Add.3, 14 July.

—— (1976) "Recent Economic Development in Eastern Europe and the Soviet Union" Chapter 2 in *The European Economy in 1975.* Geneva, UNECE (XXXI)/1 Add.1.

UNECOSOC (1975) The Role of the Public Sector in Promoting the Economic Development of Developing Countries. Report of the Secretary-General. New York, E/5690 and E/4690/Add.1. Mimeo.

UNIDO (1974) Industrial Development Survey. Special Issue for the Second General Conference of UNIDO. New York, ID/CONF. 3/2 (ID/134).

——(n.d.) "Industrial Free Zones as Incentives to Promote Export Oriented Industries," mimeo.

——(1979) "World Industry since 1960: Progress and Prospects." Special issue of the Industrial Development Survey for the Third General Conference of UNIDO. New York: United Nations ID/CONF. 4/1 (ID/229).

Union Bank of Switzerland (1976) Prices and Earnings around the Globe. A Comparison of Purchasing Power in 41 Cities. Zurich.

—— (1978a) Prices and Earnings around the Globe. A comparison of Purchasing Power in 41 Cities. Zurich.

—— (1978b) Business and Technology Today and Tomorrow. Zurich: UBS Publications in Business, Banking and Monetary Problems, No. 52.

UNITAR (n.d.) Progress in the Establishment of a New International Economic Order: Obstacles and Strategies. New York: United Nations Institute for Training and Research.

URPE (1975) *Radical Perspectives on the Economic Crisis of Monopoly Capitalism* with Suggestions for Organizing Teach-Ins and Teach-Outs. New York. URPE/PEA.

—— (1977) Special Issue on the Political Economy of Health, *Review of Radical Political Economics*, v. 9, No. 1, Spring.

—— (1978) *U.S. Capitalism in Crisis.* New York: Union for Radical Political Economics.

U.S. Senate (1969) Hearing before the Subcommittee on Western Hemisphere Affairs on the Committee on Foreign Relations. United States Senate, Ninety-first Congress, First Session, November 20.

—— Foreign Relations Committee (1977) Foreign Debts, the Banks and

U.S. Foreign Policy. Washington, Aug. from spanish translation *Comercio Exterior*, México, November 1977.

U.S. Tariff Commission (1970) Economic Factors Affecting the Use of Items 807.00 and 806.30 of the Tariff Schedules of the United States, Report to the President. Washington, TC publications 339.

Utrecht, Ernst (1976a) Industrial Estates and Australian Companies in Singapore. Sydney, Transnational Corporations Research Project. Research Monograph No. 2.

—— (1976b) Transnational Corporations in the Developing World. Transnational Corporations Research Project, University of Sydney. Research Monograph. No. 1.

Vaitsos, Constantino V. (1976) Employment Problems and Transnational Enterprises in Developing Countries: Distortions and Inequality. Geneva, ILO. WEP 2-28/WP 11. October.

Vajda, Imre and Simai, Mihály eds. (1971) *Foreign Trade in a Planned Economy*. Cambridge: At the University Press.

Valenzuela, Carlo J. (1976) "El nuevo patrón de acumulación y sus precondiciones. El caso chileno: 1973–1976" *Comercio Exterior*, México, Septiembre.

Vasconi, Tomás Amadeo (1976) El estado militar en América Latina. El caso chileno. Enero. Mimeo.

Vernon, Raymond (1971) *Sovereignty at Bay. The Multinational Spread of U.S. Enterprises*. New York: Basic Books.

Vuscovic, Pedro (1975) "América Latina: la crisis de un patrón de desarrollo y sus consecuencias políticas" *Comercio Exterior* México, v. 25, No. 12, Número aniversario 25 años.

—— (1978a) "La restructuración del capitalismo mundial y el nuevo orden económico internacional" *Comercio Exterior*, México, v. 28, No. 3, Marzo.

—— (1978b) "El neofascismo en América Latina" *Zona Abierta*, Madrid, No. 14/15.

—— y Martínez, Javier (1977) Once proposiciones sobre la situación actual de América Latina. Mimeo.

Waksman Schinca, Daniel (1977) "El proyecto de la OTAS" *Nueva Política*, México, v. II, Nos. 5–6, Abril–Septiembre.

Wallenstein, Peter (1976) "Scarce Goods as Political Weapons: the Case of Food" *Journal of Peace Research*, Tampere, XIII, No. 4.

Wallerstein, Imanuel (1974) *The Modern World. Capitalist Agriculture and the Origins of the European World-Economy in the Sixteenth Century*. New York: Academic Press.

—— (n.d.) Semi-peripheral Countries and the Contemporary World Crisis. Mimeo. Published in *The World Capitalist System*. Cambridge University Press, 1980.

Watanabe, Susumu (1976) "Minimum Wages in Developing Countries:

Myth and Reality" in *International Labour Review,* Geneva, V. 113, No. 3, May–June.

Weisskoff, Richard y Figueroa, Adolfo (1977) "Examen de las pirámides sociales: Un estudio comparativo de la distribución del ingreso en América Latina" *El Trimestre Económico,* México, v. XLIV(4), No. 176, Octubre–Diciembre.

Weisskopf, Thomas E. (1978) "Marxist Perspectives on Cyclical Crisis" in *U.S. Capitalism in Crisis,* by URPE. New York: Union for Radical Political Economics.

—— (1979) "Marxian Crisis Theory and the Rate of Profit in the Postwar U.S. Economy." *Cambridge Journal of Economics,* vol. 3, no. 4, December.

Wilczynski, J. (1969) *The Economics and Politics of East-West Trade. A Study of Trade between Developed Market Economies and Centrally Planned Economies in a Changing World.* London: Macmillan.

Wionczek, Miguel S. (1976) "La IV UNCTAD: exámen de problemas reales" *Comercio Exterior,* México, Mayo.

—— (1977) "La deuda externa de los países de menor desarrollo y los euromercados: un pasado impresionante y un futuro incierto" *Comercio Exterior,* México, v. 27, No. 11, Noviembre.

Woddis, Jack (1960) Africa. *The Roots of Revolt.* New York: The Citadel Press.

Wolpe, Harold (1972) "Capitalism and Cheap Labour-Power in South Africa: from Segregation to Apartheid" *Economy and Society,* London, November.

Wolpin, Miles D. (n.d.) Military Dependency vs Development in the Third World. New York, Department of Political Science, State University of New York. Mimeo.

World Bank (1975) *Undernutrition and Poverty.* Washington, International Bank for Reconstruction and Development. Bank Staff Working Paper, No. 202, April.

Yago, Glenn (1976–1977) "Whatever Happened to the Promised Land? Capital Flows and the Israeli State" *Berkeley Journal of Sociology,* Berkeley, California, XXI.

Zarnowitz, Victor ed. (1972) *The Business Cycle Today.* New York, National Bureau of Economic Research, Distributed by Columbia University Press.

Index

made, have good balance and fruit, and are in a forward, drinkable style. The Merlot, especially, has been a big prizewinner—it shows tart, cherrylike fruit and is considerably lighter than many Merlots, a good style for this sometimes difficult grape.

The unusual wine is the moderately sweet Sauvignon Blanc, which Gordon says people like because it has more flavor than Riesling. He's the only one making wine like this, but sometimes it doesn't hurt to be different. Those who like their Sauvignon Blanc light and crisp should look elsewhere.

CHARDONNAY ($$) ★★★ A very forward, appealing wine, with an oaky-buttery nose, and rich, soft, apple fruit. Well rounded.

CHENIN BLANC ($) ★★½ Pungent apple nose, good fruit, nice bite.

MERLOT ($$) ★★★½ Fresh, tart, bright cherry fruit, with nice oak flavors—a good example of the forward style.

RIESLING ($) ★★½ Rich, spiced apple fruit—some tendency toward overripeness.

SAUVIGNON BLANC ($$) ★★ There's lots of herbaceous Sauvignon flavor, but the moderate sweetness is disconcerting. Good acid, but not really a dinner wine style.

HAVILAND VINTNERS
Woodinville (1981)

The ambitions of founder George de Jarnatt were not small: This young winery described itself as "Washington's premier limited production, world-class winery." But de Jarnatt's expertise ran more to promotion than winemaking, and the wines never matched the claims. Rapid expansion, including an elaborate new production facility, led to the winery's financial collapse in late 1987. Remaining wines and the winery's equipment were sold off in 1988, and Columbia Winery purchased the facility.

HINZERLING VINEYARDS
Prosser   (1976)
3,000 cases

Hinzerling was the first small winery established in the Yakima Valley (earlier wineries trucked their grapes across the mountains to Seattle area facilities). The Wallace family moved across the mountains to settle in Prosser and realize winemaker Mike Wallace's dream. Wallace was one of the first winemakers native to the state to have been thoroughly trained as an enologist, at the University of California at Davis, and he was instrumental in getting the young wine industry off the ground. Ironically, Hinzerling's production, never large, has fallen in the past several years, as the wines have faced greatly increased competition in the marketplace. In 1988 the Wallaces sold the winery to Californian Don Allen, but the leading influence at the winery will probably be Allen's brother-in-law, Bill Broich. Broich, the original winemaker at Idaho's Ste. Chapelle, has established a reputation especially for Chardonnay, and the new emphasis will be on whites.

Wallace's wines were shaped not by the market but by his own uncompromising standards. The largest portion of the twenty-three acres of vineyards is committed to the classic grapes of Bordeaux—Cabernet Sauvignon, Merlot, Cabernet Franc, and Malbec. The Cabernet Sauvignon (which in some vintages has some Merlot in it) is a great wine for the patient—tough and unyielding in youth, it develops fine complexity with age. (The '77 is still going very strong.) This wine is underpriced and overlooked. In addition to the regular Cab, there's a Cabernet-Merlot-Malbec blend that is more forward, with lots of fruit and a softer touch.

Of the whites, the Gewürztraminer is a fine, ripe example, and there are some excellent Late Harvest wines. Wallace was one of the first in the valley to make sweet dessert wines from botrytised grapes and has some memorable wines to his credit, including one fabulous wine called Die Sonne from Gewürztraminer grapes allowed to dry out in the sun. Pungent and aggressive young, this wine has aged very graciously.

A second label, Prosser Falls, is in use for some white wines.

ASHFALL WHITE ($) ★★ Lively, lots of flavor, slightly sweet.

CABERNET-MERLOT-MALBEC ($$) ★★★½ The nose is slightly weedy at first, but opens into rich, spicy, oaky flavors with more pronounced fruitiness and less tannin than the regular Cab.

CABERNET SAUVIGNON ($$) ★★★★ In youth, dark, tough, lean, tannic. But with age the wine develops complex spice while retaining powerful fruit. Always long-lived.

CHARDONNAY ($) ★½ Pungent, woody, and slightly weedy—it doesn't have the fresh fruit of most others.

GEWÜRZTRAMINER ($) ★★★ Varies from slightly sweet to totally dry, but always spicy, tart, full-flavored.

RIESLING, LATE HARVEST ($$) ★★★½ Older vintages are lovely, with an old Riesling nose and lots of rich, honeylike flavors—not too heavy.

SONNE, DIE (GEWÜRZTRAMINER) ($$$) ★★★★½ The '77 is an amazing old sweet Gewürztraminer with huge flavor, excellent spice, and great weight. The '85 is dense, nutty, viscous, and spicy.

1976 Hinzerling Vineyard
Yakima Valley
CABERNET SAUVIGNON

Produced and Bottled by Hinzerling Vineyards, Prosser, Wa.
Alcohol 12.2% by volume

HOGUE CELLARS
Prosser (1982)
60,000 cases

In five years Hogue has become one of the best-selling and highest-quality producers in the state—an extraordinary success story. The members of the Hogue family are no strangers to success, having built up a prosperous and diversified farming business on their 1,200 acres of land in the Yakima Valley (200 of which are now planted with grapes). They jumped into the wine business with a stylish Chenin Blanc and Riesling (made by Mike Conway of Latah Creek), which proved immediately popular and which have been models for other developing wineries. But increasingly, the winery is emphasizing more prestigious varietals, like Chardonnay, Fumé Blanc, and Cabernet Sauvignon, as well as a Champagne-method sparkling wine.

Hogue winemaker Rob Griffin (who also has his own small winery—see Barnard Griffin) has been making wine in Washington longer than most, having started with Preston Cellars in 1976. Griffin has a solid background from training at UC Davis and while at Preston established a reputation especially for fine Chardonnay and Fumé Blanc. His trademark has always been very fresh fruit and clean, technically excellent winemaking, and the Hogue commitment to a first-class product supports this approach. And Griffin has demonstrated the ability to handle a large number of varietals and maintain quality in a large facility.

The Chenin Blanc and Riesling continue to be fine examples of these varietals in the state, though increased production seems to have taken a little varietal intensity out of the wines. The Fumé Blanc shows a character rather similar to the trend-setting Sauvignon Blanc at Arbor Crest—with the herbaceous quality of the grape toned down by judicious use of American oak, which plumps the wine up a bit, too (the Hogue wine has a bit more backbone than most). There's a real contrast between the regular and Reserve Chardonnays—the former (a great bargain) should appeal to those who like ripe Chardonnay fruit while the latter, completely barrel-fermented in French oak, is great for those in love with a big, buttery oak style.

Hogue's very first Cabernet Sauvignon, a 1983 Reserve, took Best of Show at the large Atlanta Wine Festival. It is a monster wine with loads of fruit and lots of spicy oak (Griffin prefers American oak for the reds because of the more intense, "showier" oak character it imparts to the wine). Red wines have been in limited production here, but that is changing, and there are now regular as well as Reserve bottlings of both Merlot and Cabernet Sauvignon.

Hogue was also one of the first in the state to produce a Champagne-method sparkling wine made primarily from Riesling grapes. With the '86 vintage Griffin had developed a very attractive style for this wine, toning down the fruitiness of the Riesling with the addition of a little Chardonnay. It's hardly French Champagne but has a very appealing character of its own.

All the wines are reasonably priced.

BRUT ($$$) ★★★★ Most recent style shows a lovely, subdued nose of apples and melon, with lots of bubbles and good body.

CABERNET SAUVIGNON ($$$) ★★★ Fairly light color with forward berry-oaky nose. Fruity, tart, light tannins, straightforward.

CABERNET SAUVIGNON, RESERVE ($$$$) ★★★★½ Intense blackberry-vanilla nose, very full body—but surprising softness. Solid tannin and acid without harshness. Lovely.

CHARDONNAY ($$) ★★★½ A hefty wine with lots of rich, appley fruit and a bit of oak. More emphasis on fruit than in the Reserve.

CHARDONNAY, RESERVE ($$) ★★★★ An intensely buttery nose, with a soft feel to it—the fruit really gives way to oak. Lovely texture, though perhaps not as complex as one might like.

CHENIN BLANC ($) ★★★½ One of the best examples of this grape. Light, balanced, with wildflower aromas and fine crispness. Just a bit of prickle on the tongue.

FUMÉ BLANC ($$) ★★★★ A rather fat Fumé, with a subdued, grassy nose, forward fruit, good tartness, and a rounded feel from light oak aging.

MERLOT ($$$) ★★★½ Intense nose with good fruit, some spice, and fine balance. Softer than the Cabernet.

RIESLING ($) ★★★ Pears and wildflowers in the nose, lively, fresh flavors—fairly lean.

RIESLING, LATE HARVEST (MARKIN) ($$) ★★★★ Forceful, rich, sweet wine—tons of fruit and spice. Not really delicate or complex, but very tasty.

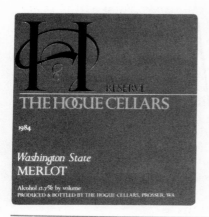

HOODSPORT WINERY
Hoodsport   (1980)
12,000 cases

Sixty percent of production at this little winery, well off the beaten track on the Olympic Peninsula, is fruit and berry wines, with the remaining 40 percent grape wines (most of the grapes come from eastern Washington, including the excellent Kiona Vineyard). Dick Patterson, who owns the winery and makes the wine, began as a hobbyist (he still teaches part-time at a nearby community college). The wines are sound in quality, if not exciting, with the style of the grape wines emphasizing straightforward fruit flavors. The one stand-out wine is the raspberry—fresh and luscious without being heavy. It's hard to fault the gooseberry wine—it tastes like gooseberries, nice if you like that fruit. The winery recommends it with spicy Asian cuisine.

The most unique Hoodsport wine is the Island Belle, a red wine from a native American grape. Some identify

Island Belle with the Campbell Early grape, while others contend it is a cross. In any case, the grapes come from some of the oldest vineyards in the Northwest, on Stretch Island in South Puget Sound. First planted in the late nineteenth century, the vineyards survived Prohibition and prospered until rising land values and competition from eastern Washington and California ruined the market for the grape. But the Pattersons began purchasing it for their winery in 1981 and have made a small amount every year since. Island Belle has the "foxy," grapy character of labrusca grapes, though considerably toned down.

Rapid increases in production and sales have led to ambitious plans for expansion, including two possible new facilities in the South Sound area.

CHARDONNAY ($$) ★★★ The emphasis is on fresh apple-melon fruit, with quite viscous body and a good oakiness.

GEWÜRZTRAMINER ($$) ★★ Floral, sweetish, soft, fruity.

ISLAND BELLE ($$) ★★½ A bright red wine with a "foxy," grapy nose and lots of tart flavor. Fairly dry—interesting if not elegant.

MERLOT ($$) ★★★ Good berry nose with considerable fruit and body—without oak flavor.

RIESLING ($) ★★ Light wildflower nose, just off-dry. Clean flavors.

GOOSEBERRY ($) ★★ Wild forest aroma of gooseberry, with a balance of tart and slightly sweet. Distinctive.

LOGANBERRY ($) ★★★ Bright red, with a very fresh nose—fairly sweet but not heavy.

RASPBERRY ($) ★★★★ Lovely, fresh, crisp flavors—slightly sweet. A truly delicious example.

CHARLES HOOPER FAMILY WINERY
Husum   (1985)
1,000 cases

After more than twenty years in Europe, having discovered the pleasures of German wine, the Hooper family returned to the United States to settle in the Columbia Gorge and make wine. Their six-acre vineyard, planted largely to Riesling, is on a very steep slope high in the hills, looking south across spectacular scenery toward Oregon's Mount Hood. Charles and son Chris are basically amateur winemakers, without formal training, though they did gain some experience in German vineyards. Production is tiny, and the winery is very much a family enterprise.

The wines are fruity, if not as fresh as those made in larger commercial wineries. (A new facility is in the works.) Most interesting are the Chardonnay, from a mixture of Oregon and Washington fruit, and the Riesling, which shows more of a piney than applelike character.

CHARDONNAY ($$) ★★   Interesting herbal nose, some nice viscous fruit, slight oak character—not really classic flavors, but decent.

GEWÜRZTRAMINER ($) ★   Dry, fairly biting, a bit tired out—good body.

RIESLING ($) ★½   A somewhat piney nose and fairly full body—dry and tart, slightly harsh, not that fresh.

HORIZON'S EDGE WINERY
Zillah   (1983)
3,000 cases

This small winery has attracted little attention so far, but its first releases of Chardonnay (the wine it plans to specialize in) showed great promise. Owner-winemaker Tom Campbell has worked at a number of other Yakima Valley wineries, including Ste. Michelle and Stewart, and helped start Montana's first winery (Mission Mountain). He is a devotee of barrel fermentation, aiming more for richness and complex flavors than fresh fruit in his wines.

Despite its small size, the winery has several different bottlings of Chardonnay (you have to check the fine print on the label to know which is which). Chardonnay from the Celilo Vineyard in the Columbia Gorge is quite different from the others—not only is it a different clone, but the climate is cooler. Most Chardonnay lovers will probably favor the wines from Yakima Valley or Columbia Valley grapes. Chardonnay also provides the base for a Champagne-method sparkling wine, which has the toasty richness of the other Chardonnays.

The initial release of Cabernet Sauvignon showed some promise, though the remaining wines are unremarkable. Still to come is Pinot Noir. Campbell is convinced Pinot grown in cooler sections of the Yakima Valley (his own twenty-acre vineyard is north-facing) can have the elegance of Oregon Pinot Noir.

CABERNET SAUVIGNON ($$$) ★★½ Deep purple-red, ripe, oaky nose, lots of flavor. It has the strong, spicy quality of American oak, with lean, rather herbal fruit. Still tart, it needs some age.

CHAMPAGNE ($$$) ★★★ One hundred percent Chardonnay, this wine has the toasty nose of the other Chardonnays, is quite tart, and has lots of fine bubbles. A good sparkler.

CHARDONNAY (CELILO) ($$) ★★½ An interesting, slightly stewed nose, fruity and tart. There's not much oak showing and the wine seems fairly simple.

CHARDONNAY (FAIR ACRE) ($$$) ★★★½ A very appealing wine in a soft, ripe, toasty oak style, made from

Yakima Valley grapes. Flavors are assertive but not harsh. Needs some time to smooth out. The best of these bottlings.

CHARDONNAY (GREEN LABEL) ($$) ★★½ The entry-level Chard here, with pleasant, crisp varietal fruit and fresh flavors. Well made.

CHARDONNAY (MCKINNON) ($$$) ★★★ Lighter, oakier, softer, more open than the Fair Acre, with appley fruit and nice balance.

GRENACHE ($) ½ Made in a light blush style, it tends toward vegetal, bell pepper flavors, with slight sweetness. It will probably seem very odd to most blush lovers.

RIESLING ($) ★★ Light, fruity, crisp, not notable.

HUNTER HILL VINEYARDS
Othello   (1984)
4,000 cases

The location is somewhat isolated from the rest of the Columbia Valley wineries, northeast of the Wahluke Slope, a good twenty miles from the river. Twenty-eight acres of vineyard were planted in the early eighties by commercial pilot Art Byron, and a new winery was completed in time for the 1987 crush (previous vintages were made at another local winery). It's too early yet to know whether this subregion will be favorable for wine grapes—based on limited samples, the wines have seemed ordinary. (Gary Graves of Pacific Crest recently became consulting winemaker.)

CHENIN BLANC ($) ★ Light color and nose, slightly sweet, not much character.

RIESLING ($) ★★ Scents of wildflowers and clover, with fairly full body and sweetness.

HYATT VINEYARDS WINERY
Zillah   (1987)
8,500 cases

The newest winery in Zillah (fast becoming the center of mid–Yakima Valley winemaking), Hyatt is frankly an effort by owner Leland Hyatt to deal with an oversupply of grapes from his seventy-three-acre vineyard. Hyatt shakes his head over the recent prices for wine grapes (he gets more for his Concords than for some varieties of wine grapes). The plan is to process some bulk wine to sell to other wineries while keeping the best to bottle under his own label, as well as the label of his winemaker, Wade Wolfe, a noted viticulturist.

Wolfe, who used to work for Ste. Michelle and now acts as vineyard consultant for a number of properties, is most interested in dessert wines and will release these under a separate label. His most unusual project is Black Muscat, a little-planted red Muscat grape grown only in one nearby vineyard, which he has made into a fortified, heady sweet wine.

Hyatt will concentrate on higher-end wines, including Chardonnay, Sauvignon Blanc, and Merlot (Wolfe feels the earlier-ripening Merlot does better in the cooler sections of the Yakima Valley). Barrel samples of the wines showed considerable promise; first releases were in the fall of 1988.

JOHNSON CREEK WINERY
Tenino   (1984)
2,000 cases

One of a very small number of intrepid vineyardists in western Washington, Vince De Bellis has planted mostly

Müller-Thurgau, a cool-climate grape, in his three-acre vineyard southeast of Puget Sound. While the vines mature he is buying grapes from the good-sized Brookside Vineyard in southwest Washington, as well as warmer-climate grapes from small growers in the Yakima Valley. Although he hopes to specialize in Müller-Thurgau, a wine that has proved surprisingly popular, the winery makes a fairly full line of white and red varietals.

The winery, in the European tradition, is alongside the popular restaurant that wife Ann runs, and much of the wine is sold through the restaurant. The De Bellises, long-time home winemakers, got the itch for a commercial winery when they entered a national amateur wine competition as a lark and won three first prizes. The wines are all decently made and fairly priced, without being fancy. The Müller-Thurgau, full-flavored and earthy, is a very nice example of this little-known wine, while the new Cabernet Sauvignon has lots of straightforward flavor.

CABERNET SAUVIGNON ($$) ★★★ Lots of lively oak-berry flavors, fresh and straightforward. Good drinking.

CHENIN BLANC ($) ★★ Pungent nose of tropical fruit, with fresh fruit and some liveliness.

MERLOT ($$) ★★ Ripe, oaky blackberry nose, spicy, tannic, rough and ready.

MÜLLER-THURGAU ($) ★★★½ Earthy-flowery nose—almost Muscaty; off-dry, strong-flavored, with more body than is typical.

PINOT NOIR ($) ★★ A very light-styled Pinot, with a ripe cherry nose, good acid, and a slight harshness. Not for aging.

RIESLING ($) ★½ Apple nose, slightly overripe flavors, decent acid.

RIESLING, PINK ($) ★½ Salmon color, quite sweet, decent fruit.

KIONA VINEYARDS
Richland   (1980)
8,500 cases

Kiona has been a consistent award winner in national competitions, attracting attention as one of the consistently best small producers in the state. A thirty-acre vineyard was planted in 1975 in a previously wild section of hills (known locally as Red Mountain) at the warm eastern end of the Yakima Valley, and it has proved a fine site for grapes: Kiona grapes, particularly Cabernet Sauvignon, have made impressive wines under labels like Woodward Canyon and Quilceda Creek. More recently a number of other new vineyards, like Blackwood Canyon, have been established in the area.

Kiona is the product of a partnership between Jim Holmes, a longtime home winemaker who describes winemaking as a "compelling hobby," and John Williams, an experienced farmer. Clearly the fruit is excellent, and the wines have all been well made. Riesling and Chenin Blanc are made in a light, soft style, but the barrel-fermented Chardonnay is very serious wine, not heavy, but with lots of well-rounded flavors.

Lemberger is Kiona's most interesting contribution to the state's wine lineup. A German variety, this red grape makes light, unremarkable wine in its native land. But in the Yakima Valley it has the character of a big red wine without the harshness of Cabernet. "It's ideal for those who would like to have a red but might be put off by it," says Holmes. Kiona's version is very pleasing, with dark colors, a rich raspberry nose, and soft smooth flavors. Production is small, but other area vineyards are beginning to plant the grape.

Holmes is also enthusiastic about Cabernet, believing

(with others) that the region will become a premier area for this varietal. His Cabernet, aged in French and old American oak, is dark, rich, and spicy—appealing when young but very ageable. It's one of the better ones in the state and, like all the wines, reasonably priced.

Rosé lovers will appreciate the very tasty Merlot Rosé.

CABERNET SAUVIGNON ($$$) ★★★★ Very rich, deep, chocolaty nose, thick and full of fruit, with delightful spice. Tart and strong. The aggressive flavors are not to everyone's taste.

CHARDONNAY ($$) ★★★★ Lovely, rich aromas of melon and toasty oak. Good weight but rounded flavors and nice spice. Barrel-fermented. Excellent value.

CHENIN BLANC ($) ★★ Light nose, tart, grapefruity flavors.

LEMBERGER ($$) ★★★★ Fresh and full of raspberry fruit, with a good hint of oak. The wine is deceptive—the tannins are soft, but there is surprising weight here, and it ages quite well.

MERLOT ROSÉ ($) ★★★ Fresh, fruity, but with considerable backbone.

RIESLING ($) ★★★ This has a light, pleasing spritz on the tongue, with baked-bread aromas. Moderate sweetness and full body.

RIESLING, LATE HARVEST ($$) ★★★ Straightforward apple-pie or grapefruity flavors, slightly harsh feel. Smooths out with age.

F. W. LANGGUTH WINERY   *See* SNOQUALMIE WINERY

LATAH CREEK WINE CELLARS
Spokane   (1982)
15,000 cases

In 1982 Mike Conway, a winemaker who had apprenticed at Parducci in California, struck a deal with Mike
Hogue, a Yakima Valley farmer who wanted to diversify
into the wine business. Conway would make wines for
Hogue and in turn Hogue would help finance Conway's
own winery. The plan turned out well for both—Conway's
touch, especially with Chenin Blanc, helped Hogue establish a quality reputation early, and Conway now is running his own show at Latah Creek. Latah is a small winery
by California standards, but Conway doesn't classify himself as a "boutique" winemaker, aiming for a specialized
market. Instead, he takes Parducci (of which he is a frank
admirer) as a model: to make consistent, drinkable wines
in a popular style and at a fair price. He may get written

off by the snobs, but the fact is the wines, if not really distinctive, are fresh, fruity, and very well made.

The winery is outside Spokane—not a grape-growing area—so grapes are purchased from vineyards in the Yakima Valley and the Wahluke Slope. All the wines have an attractive fruit quality, and almost all are finished with just a bit of sweetness to make them more appealing. Chenin Blanc is the grape that Conway has really made his mark with, both at Hogue and at Latah Creek—it is livelier and more delicately fruity than most Chenins, with a faint spritz on the tongue from trapped carbon dioxide. A recent release was a Reserve Chenin Blanc, surely the first in this country (Chenin Blanc is not a big seller). Conway made some very attractive Fumé Blanc originally, but has switched to Semillon, which he feels is even better. Like many successful Sauvignons, it is finished with a tad of sweetness and a hint of oak.

Conway made some excellent Merlot early on and then dropped it from his repertoire for several vintages. Now both Merlot and Cabernet are in production, with Merlot the more successful. Also of interest here is the Maywine, a traditional German wine of Riesling flavored with the herb woodruff, which imparts a tangy, woody flavor. It's something of a curiosity but can be a refreshing change of pace.

CABERNET SAUVIGNON ($$$) ★★½ A decidedly oaky and closed-in wine, dark-colored—it needs some time.
CHARDONNAY, FEATHER ($) ★★ Light, fruity, appley, pleasant.
CHENIN BLANC ($) ★★★½ Lively, grapefruity flavors, with some prickle on the tongue and excellent crispness. A model Chenin Blanc.
CHENIN BLANC, RESERVE ($) ★★★½ Richer and sweeter than the regular bottling, with less assertive fruit and good balance.

MAYWINE ($) ★★½ Riesling flavored with woodruff. Dusky color, with definite herbal spiciness. Interesting and good.

MERLOT ($$) ★★★★ A full-bodied wine showing excellent berry fruit and good tartness—ages nicely. One of the best examples in the state.

MUSCAT CANELLI ($) ★★★½ This is not a terribly sweet or full-flavored Muscat, but it has lots of floral character, light body, and nice acid.

RIESLING ($) ★★ Fairly simple applelike flavors, with good bite.

RIESLING, LATE HARVEST ($$) ★★½ Flowery nose, with fresh crisp flavors, moderately sweet.

SEMILLON ($) ★★★ Soft, lively, with fruity-grassy nose. Rounded, subtle flavors.

L'ÉCOLE NO. 41
Lowden   (1983)
2,000 cases

The Fergusons, Jean and Baker, make no bones about the style of their two principal wines, calling them "big, gutsy wines . . . not for everyone." The winery, one of several in the Walla Walla area, is a retirement project for the couple; Jean is the winemaker, with skills mostly picked up from summer enology courses at UC Davis. Production in the old schoolhouse that is home to the winery is small, and L'École has no vineyards, buying grapes mostly from Gordon Brothers and Balcom and Moe. The Fergusons look for grapes with a high degree of ripeness and sugar (picking after almost everyone else), to give the wines richness and power—and usually high alcohol.

This winery has eschewed the better-known Riesling, Chardonnay, and Cabernet in favor of Semillon and Merlot, two grapes that the Fergusons feel do particularly well in the area (Baker is still convinced that Semillon has probably the most promise of any white grape in eastern Washington). The Semillon has almost a yellow color from long skin contact and is aggressively varietal and heavy; the Fergusons call it a "red wine drinker's white wine." The Merlot is quite incredible: a purple monster of high alcohol and biting tannin. The question is whether time will tame and smooth it out before the fruit fades away. Don't look for elegance or finesse here, but if you're tired of taste-alike commercial wines and have a palate that can absorb powerful flavors, these wines may be appealing.

There's also quite a pleasant Chenin Blanc for the tourists.

MERLOT ($$$) ★★★½ A controversial wine: dark, cloudy, with heaps of fruit and very hot, alcoholic flavors—will age tone it down? Some love it and some don't. It may be better from lighter vintages.

SEMILLON ($) ★★ A very full, heavy, sharp-flavored style—but it comes off rather flat and charmless, for all its flavor.

WALLA VOILÀ (CHENIN BLANC) ($) ★★½ Fresh, appley, medium sweet, a bit of spritz.

LEONETTI CELLAR
Walla Walla (1978)
1,700 cases

Gary Figgins figures he has devoted twenty years to making the quintessential red wine, and he has come remarkably close. A Walla Walla native, he was strongly influenced by his Italian grandfather, a home winemaker. Figgins began making wine at home, shared his dreams with friend and fellow drill sergeant Rick Small (now of

Woodward Canyon), and finally made his first commercial vintage of Cabernet Sauvignon in 1978.

Cabernet Sauvignon and Merlot are the whole story at this tiny winery, but they are a big story. That first Cabernet, which is aging beautifully, was named Best in the Country by a national wine consumers' magazine, and the wines have become expensive and very much sought after. Figgins has kept his enterprise on a small scale, maintaining a regular full-time job until 1988, and making wines literally in his cellar. (He is slowly building himself a little winery out in back.)

Figgins and Small share much the same approach to their red wines. Both must purchase essentially all their red grapes (Figgins has just one acre of very vigorous Merlot) from growers in the Walla Walla, Columbia, and Yakima valleys. Both use all new French cooperage for aging their wines, and both are looking for a big, deep wine with long aging potential. One significant difference: Figgins likes to blend Merlot into his Cabernet, and vice versa, while Small's Cabernet is nearly 100 percent. Blending seems really at the heart of Figgins's work ("building complexity," he calls it), the different lots of Cabernet and Merlot from different vineyards complementing each other, filling in gaps and smoothing out rough edges. While the wines are massive, they don't seem angular or harsh but have a rounded, complete feel.

The Leonetti Merlot is very good, certainly one of the best in the state, with lots of bright berry flavor, though it's occasionally bothered by a herbal tinge. But the Cabernet is extraordinary, one of those wines that improves for several days after the bottle is opened. It may be the most powerful in the state, and should require considerable aging. Although a believer in blends, Figgins has produced a spectacular Cabernet from the Seven Hills Vineyard, just south of Walla Walla, near Milton-Freewater (the vines are actually in Oregon). And soon to be released is his first Reserve Cabernet, from the '83 vintage, an incredibly powerful wine. Very French in style, it may prove to be his best yet and certainly rates high marks.

Though the number of acres remains small, the Walla Walla area has tremendous potential for red grapes (Figgins notes that the Seven Hills Vineyard gets the same number of heat units as St. Helena in the Napa Valley) and he would like to see more planted.

CABERNET SAUVIGNON ($$$$) ★★★★★ A classic Cabernet nose, though closed in. Huge, ripe chocolaty-berry flavors, with lots of tannin and great spice. Yet all is in balance. A premier Washington Cabernet.

CABERNET SAUVIGNON (SEVEN HILLS) ($$$$) ★★★★½ An absolutely classic Cabernet, with cedary, cigar-box scents and huge, mouth-filling body. Should be a blockbuster.

CABERNET SAUVIGNON, RESERVE ($$$$) ★★★★★ A mountainous wine, dense and extraordinarily rich. Cedary, spicy, very oaky. This will stand up to any Cabernet, anywhere.

MERLOT ($$$) ★★★★ Very deep color, with a herbal-berry nose and rich, spicy fruit. Tremendous potential here, as the tannin and vegetal qualities fade.

LOST MOUNTAIN WINERY
Sequim   (1981)
500 cases

Don't look for Lost Mountain in the wine country. It sits in the fir-covered hills of the Olympic Peninsula, where former research chemist Romeo Conca has his retirement home. Conca takes his Italian heritage seriously and has been making full-blown, rather rough-edged red wines— the kind that go so well with hearty Italian *cucina*—for a number of years, first as an amateur and now commercially. Owning no vineyards, Conca will go far afield for the kind of grapes he wants: Cabernet and Merlot from eastern Washington, Pinot Noir from Oregon, and Zinfandel and Petite Syrah from California's Dry Creek Valley in Sonoma.

Lost Mountain's first releases were decidedly rustic— tart, tannic, and oxidized. But newer vintages have shown much more freshness and drinkability, while maintaining a full-bodied style—zesty and alcoholic—for immediate enjoyment. Conca uses only old oak for aging, so the emphasis is on fruit flavors. The Lost Mountain Red (which Conca cheerfully calls "Dago Red") is an interesting blend of red grapes with some Muscat, the pungent aromas of which add to the fruitiness of the wine.

Conca wants as natural a product as possible and uses no sulfites in his wines, so they are best drunk young.

CABERNET SAUVIGNON ($$) ★★½ Plum-cherry nose, fruity, somewhat harsh.
LOST MOUNTAIN RED ($) ★ Very purple, very aromatic, very alcoholic.
MERLOT ($$) ★★★ Lovely, fresh, spicy blackberry flavors. A very forward and fruity wine. Delightful.

PETITE SYRAH–ZINFANDEL (DRY CREEK) ($$) ★★½
Raspberry nose, fresh fruit with nice bite.
PINOT NOIR (WILLAMETTE) ($$) ★★½ Bright color,
spicy cherry nose, full-bodied and slightly sweet. Very
Italian in style.

LOWDEN SCHOOLHOUSE WINERY *See* L'ÉCOLE No. 41

MERCER RANCH VINEYARDS
Alderdale (1984)
1,700 cases

Certainly one of the premier Cabernet vineyards in the
state, Mercer Ranch is now producing small quantities of
estate wines, and they promise to be excellent. The Mercers are an old family (more than 100 years) in these parts,
and the 132-acre vineyard occupies but a small parcel of
the family's 30,000-acre ranch in the Horse Heaven Hills.

This is a spectacular and empty ridge of hills that sits
between the Yakima Valley and the Columbia. Dry-farm
wheat and sheep were all the land would support until
private irrigation arrived twenty years ago; now the deep
soils support a variety of vegetable crops. Don Mercer, an
architect by background, returned from the Puget Sound
area to help with the family's irrigation project, and in
1972 he planted the first vines—mostly Cabernet, since his
own tastes ran to red. Although the mailing address is
Prosser, the vineyard lies just a couple of miles from the
Columbia, not far downriver from the Columbia Crest
vineyards at Paterson.

The Mercers still sell over 90 percent of their grapes, and
Mercer Ranch Cabernet has gone into some of the best-
known wines in the state, including Woodward Canyon

and Quilceda Creek. These wines from the "Old Block" (Block 1) Vineyard share a dense, concentrated, tannic quality with some minty overtones—all destined for long lives. Why this particular block should be so distinct is unclear, but Don Mercer thinks that the deep outcropping of heavier, claylike soil on which the vineyard grows may be the answer. Mercer also has one of the largest blocks of Lemberger (here called Limburger, an alternative spelling) in the state, much of which again is sold to other wineries.

From 1985 to 1987 the Mercer Ranch wines were made by Steven Redford, the talented but mercurial brother of Amity's Myron Redford, who has now left. Redford's first batches of Cabernet for Mercer Ranch turned out extremely well—both the Old Block wine and the more delicate and fruity wine from Sharp Sisters Vineyard. The Limburger, which the Mercers feel is the perfect match for lamb, is in a serious style, though Mercer is contemplating releasing some without oak aging to test the market (the grape makes inherently soft wine). And although reds are the first order of business here, not to be overlooked is an absolutely excellent Muscat Canelli, packed with flavor.

CABERNET SAUVIGNON (MERCER RANCH BLOCK 1) ($$$) ★★★★ A very big, tough, almost minty wine, with lots of tannin—should be great.
CABERNET SAUVIGNON (SHARP SISTERS) ($$$) ★★★½ More forward than the Old Block, softer, but with tight Cabernet character.
LIMBURGER ($$) ★★★★ Lots of fruit, varying from berry to plummy. A big wine, but with a velvety feel. Quite approachable.
MUSCAT CANELLI ($$) ★★★★ Wonderful intense aromas of sweet melon—not too flowery. Sweet, but lots of acid. Very tasty indeed.
SADIE LOUISE (BLUSH) ($) ★ Pungent, light, off-dry.

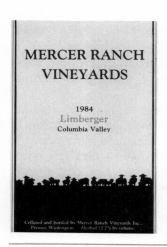

MERCER RANCH
VINEYARDS

1984
Limberger
Columbia Valley

Cellared and bottled by Mercer Ranch Vineyards Inc.,
Prosser, Washington   Alcohol 12.7% by volume.

MONT ELISE VINEYARDS
Bingen   (1975)
7,000 cases

Chuck Henderson established the first winery (originally called Bingen Wine Cellars) in the Columbia Gorge in 1975, planting grapes on fifty-five acres of vineyards high above the Columbia River, and his pioneering efforts have led to more vineyards and several newer wineries. The windswept gorge, spectacularly beautiful, has a climate somewhere between the hot, dry conditions of eastern Washington and the cool, moist weather of the western part. Not surprisingly, Gewürztraminer, which loses some character in heat, does well in the gorge, producing a wine with good spice. The winery could be making more Gewürz than it is; unfortunately, the market for dry Gewürztraminer is slim. Mont Elise has also had good success with Chenin Blanc.

Henderson's emphasis has always been on growing the grapes—his background is in growing fruit. But the winery, housed in an old fruit warehouse, is not one of the more up-to-date facilities in the state. Now, while Chuck senior tends the vineyards, his son Charles junior, trained in enology at California's Davis campus, has taken over the winemaking, and he may bring a more professional approach to wine production.

Although Pinot Noir was one of the original plantings, the wine has never come out very well, so production is now being steered into a sparkling Blanc de Noir, as well as lighter picnic wines. The first vintage of sparkling wine spent more than three years on the lees before release, much longer than most Northwest sparkling wines, but similar to the aging that French Champagne gets. The style is lean and tart, but the wine is very nicely made. There is a successful red wine, Gamay Beaujolais, made in a very light, grapy style that has been consistently popular (the winery has trouble keeping up with demand). All the wines are reasonably priced.

BLANC DE NOIR BRUT ($$$) ★★★ It's Brut, all right. This dry and very tart wine really needs some food to accompany it. But there are fine bubbles, some good Pinot aromas, and decent body.

CHENIN BLANC ($) ★★½ Pungent nose of clover, quite sweet and full-bodied.

GAMAY BEAUJOLAIS ($) ★★½ Pink-red color, very grapy nose with light, tart fruit. Fine wine for a summer picnic.

GEWÜRZTRAMINER (MONT ELISE VINEYARD) ($) ★★★½ Dry, tart, spicy. Good apple fruit without floweriness, some richness. Can be a bit harsh. There is also a bottling from Celilo Vineyard, which is not as good.

PINOT NOIR ROSÉ ($) ★★½ Rather nice, strawberry-rhubarby nose, soft, slightly heavy.

RIESLING ($) ★½ Very pungent, apricoty nose, medium sweet, quite full—occasional nuttiness. Could use some finesse.

MOUNTAIN DOME WINERY
Spokane (1984)
300 cases

Very much a home-style operation, this tiny family winery's goal is to make top-quality vintage Champagne-method wine from two-thirds Pinot Noir and one-third Chardonnay—grapes come from the Moreman Vineyard, near Pasco. The first vintage was crushed in 1984 and is still aging on the lees, with no date set for its bottling and release. The owner and winemaker is Michael Manz. First release is planned for 1992. Wines not tasted.

MOUNT BAKER VINEYARDS
Deming (1982)
9,500 cases

Every western Washington vineyard is an expression of individual determination; Mount Baker's is the product of Al Stratton, a retired physician. Stratton experimented with numerous grape varieties on behalf of the nearby Washington State University Research Station, and the vines in commercial production represent the fruit of that research. Müller-Thurgau, a German cross; Madeleine Angevine, an old French cross; and Okanogan Riesling, a Canadian grape (yes, that's right) are the principal local plantings. The Okanogan Riesling (not a true Riesling) is nothing to get excited about, but the other two are always interesting and flavorful, if not to everyone's taste. The winery's style for whites stresses flowery fruit and fairly full body.

Though the twenty-five-acre vineyard is hardly large, it is the biggest of any Puget Sound winery growing its own grapes. Its northerly location, almost on the Canadian border, looks suspect, but the Nooksack Valley, nestled up against the Cascades, lies in the "rain shadow" of the Olympic Mountains, so it's actually a little drier and gets slightly more sunshine than most of the rest of western Washington.

Mount Baker may be in the "banana belt," but for late-ripening grapes like Cabernet Sauvignon and Riesling it must go to eastern Washington. The Cabernet (temporarily out of production) has proved surprisingly good for a winery that has devoted itself to soft white wines. The Chardonnay has been rather clumsy.

Perhaps most impressive have been the sweeter wines, especially the Select Cluster Riesling, which is very sweet and quite luscious.

Partner and winery manager Jim Hildt has been active in selling wines in Japan—not surprisingly, Mount Baker's plum wine has proved a huge success among Japanese consumers. Another good sign for the winery is recent federal approval of a Nooksack Valley appellation, which may attract some more serious attention to this unique growing area.

As this book went to press, Al Stratton had decided to relinquish his share of the winery, which was looking for additional investors, so its future course is somewhat uncertain.

CABERNET SAUVIGNON ($$) ★★★   Soft, oaky, slightly vegetal, very forward and pleasant.

CHARDONNAY ($$) ★★   Has varied from very oaky to light and somewhat vegetal. Recent vintages show some improvement.

GEWÜRZTRAMINER ($) ★★   Less assertively varietal than most, soft, off-dry.

MADELINE ANGEVINE, RESERVE ($$) ★★★½   A fascinating nose of tropical fruit, sweet, but quite light and crisp.

MÜLLER-THURGAU ($) ★★★   Flowery, nicely balanced
sweetness, bit of spritz—very attractive.

RIESLING, SELECT CLUSTER ($$$) ★★★★   Very sweet,
but there's more than sugar—apple-like fruit with some
nice complexity. Delicious.

NEUHARTH WINERY
Sequim   (1979)
1,500 cases

Sequim, on the rainy Olympic Peninsula in western
Washington, seems an unlikely location for a winery, but
this small place is the pet project of a retired California
grape grower, Gene Neuharth. Neuharth is not trying to do
anything too fancy, just make good, consistent wines that
reflect the fruit of the grape and that will accompany food.
He is careful in his choice of grapes ("I know what good
grapes taste like"), ages all the wines including Riesling in
a combination of French and American oak, and takes
care that each wine is clean. The results have been im-

pressive—Neuharth has been making excellent wine since the first vintage.

Although Sequim is in what is optimistically termed the peninsula's "banana belt," it's too cold to grow grapes (though Neuharth has a number of experimental hybrids planted). Grapes for the wine come from Sagemoor Farms near Pasco in eastern Washington. The Chardonnay and Cabernet Sauvignon are both noteworthy: The Chardonnay is beautifully oaky and balanced, while the Cabernet, though it doesn't have the weight of some others, has a lovely cedary nose and plenty of flavor—balance is its keynote. All the wines here are relatively lean, have sturdy acid backbones (they show best with food), and age well.

CABERNET SAUVIGNON ($$) ★★★★ Lean, balanced, with lots of sweet oak and some slight herbaceous qualities. Not a knockout wine, but excellently made.

CHARDONNAY ($$) ★★★½ Rich oaky-lemony nose; not a big wine, but very good structure.

DUNGENESS RED ($) ★★½ A wonderfully fruity wine with fresh cherry flavors made in Beaujolais style, from Merlot.

DUNGENESS WHITE ($) ★★ Flowery nose, slightly sweet fruit, with some extra body from oak.

MERLOT ($$) ★★★ Light, herbaceous nose with a bit of blackberry, tart and spicy.

RIESLING ($$) ★½ This oak-aged wine has pungent, cooked-apple aromas, lots of flavor, and medium sweetness. Unusual.

NEUHARTH

19 Washington 80
Cabernet Sauvignon
Aged in Oak

PRODUCED AND BOTTLED BY
NEUHARTH WINERY, INC.
SEQUIM, WA BONDED WINERY NO. WA-74
ALCOHOL 12.6% BY VOLUME

NEWTON AND NEWTON VINTNERS *See* WHITTLESEY-MARK

NORTHWEST DAILY
(1986)

These wines, which were made for a local *négociant,* are no longer in production, although they may still be found in the marketplace.

CABERNET SAUVIGNON ($) ★★   A bit of vanilla oak and some Cabernet character, light and soft.

CHARDONNAY ($) ★½   Not much varietal character, though there's some wood.

CHENIN BLANC ($) ★★½   A ripe, floral bouquet with solid fruit—a nice wine.

RIESLING ($) ★   Not nearly the character of the Chenin—candylike in the nose.

WHITE TABLE ($) ★★   A lively blend, with a flowery nose and good, tart fruit.

OAKWOOD CELLARS
Benton City   (1986)
3,000 cases

This small, new winery outside of Richland is another that grew out of the enthusiasm of a home winemaker—in this case Robert Skelton, a chemical engineer. Skelton has a tiny three-acre vineyard of Riesling, but most of the grapes are purchased from various Yakima Valley locations, including reds from vineyards on nearby Red Mountain (already acquiring a reputation for Cabernet). The cramped winery is short on space and equipment, but the confident Skelton has improvised and is aiming for top-quality wines in a traditional big style.

Best bets here are the barrel-fermented Chardonnay (Skelton is experimenting with American oak as well as French), in the ripe, fat style, and the regular Riesling, which has lots of nice, full fruit flavors. The first release of Merlot was boisterously flavorful, but samples of Cabernet and Lemberger to come showed some promise—these wines should be big and oaky. Skelton is also planning a dry-style Riesling.

CHARDONNAY ($$) ★★★½   Some nice, toasty, ripe pineapple flavors—oaky and fairly rich. Quite appealing.

MERLOT ($$) ★★   Cherry and oak flovors, some sharpness. Zesty, not refined.

RIESLING ($) ★★★   Haylike aromas accompany strong, appley fruit. The style is full and fruity, with good acid.

RIESLING, LATE HARVEST ($$) ★   Some piney flavors, could be fresher.

ROSÉ OF CABERNET ($) ★   Rather herbaceous, crisp, fresh—OK.

OREGON CHAMPAGNE CELLARS *See* WHITTLESEY-MARK

PACIFIC CREST WINE CELLARS
Marysville (1985)
500 cases

Despite the small size, this winery has not stinted on first-rate equipment—there's a strong belief here that high tech can make a difference. On the other hand, winemaker and partner Gary Graves, a TV broadcaster turned enologist, also believes in high-quality grapes and is working with the vineyards in the Yakima Valley from which he buys to improve quality by reducing yield. Graves is a self-described "Chardonnay freak" who hopes to make a big, barrel-fermented Chardonnay in the Burgundian style. He is also producing Late Harvest Riesling and Gewürztraminer in a higher-alcohol style than is usual ("I'm notorious for alcoholic wine"), letting them sit in the tank for at least a year to acquire needed age. Initial releases of these sweeter varietals showed a tendency toward very ripe wines, but the winemaking seems competent.

Current capacity is small, about 5,000 gallons, but Graves hopes to move the winery, now in a small town north of Seattle, perhaps to an eastern Washington location and eventually increase capacity to the 30,000-gallon range.

GEWÜRZTRAMINER, LATE HARVEST ($$) ★★★ Although slightly harsh, this wine has lots of ripe lychee flavors with interesting clove accents. Medium sweet.

RIESLING ($) ★★★ Very ripe wine—flowery, full-flavored, with balanced sweetness.

PONTIN DEL ROZA
Prosser   (1984)
4,000 cases

A long-established Yakima Valley farming family has recently turned to winemaking, using grapes from its own small vineyard and from other vineyards on the Roza, a section of south-facing slope in the middle of the valley. The first wines were made at nearby Coventry Vale, but Pontin has its own facility now. Youthful Scott Pontin, trained at UC Davis, is the winemaker, while other members of the family all seem to be involved, in the Italian tradition (Scott's Italian grandfather arrived in the valley in the twenties).

Like many small wineries just getting started, Pontin has had uneven results. The whites tend to the simple and sweet. Some of the Chenins have been very pleasant, in a soft picnic style. But other wines have not fared as happily and have seemed clumsy or overripe. The wines also seem to have the problem of tasting old rather quickly. Nevertheless, if you like sweet whites with lots of fruit, these may fit the bill.

CABERNET SAUVIGNON ($$) ★★ Sweet oaky nose with rather biting, herbaceous flavors. OK for oak lovers.

CHARDONNAY ($$) ★ This wine shows signs of improvement. The fruit is decent though not terribly varietal. Soft.

CHENIN BLANC ($) ★★ Light, apple-flower nose, pleasant flavors, off-dry style.

RIESLING ($) ★ This is not bashful wine. Ripe apricot flavors, quite sweet and rather cloying, as it lacks acid. Not always fresh.

ROZA SUNSET ($) ½   This blush wine based on Chenin and Riesling has a funny, earthy nose—pepper and stewed vegies.

PORTTEUS VINEYARDS
Zillah   (1986)
2,000 cases

The Portteus family (Paul senior and Paul junior are the owners, with Paul junior the winemaker) avoided the problems of the many Yakima Valley growers when it eschewed Riesling and Chenin Blanc in favor of Chardonnay, Cabernet, and Semillon in its vineyard. The 36 acres of vines, planted in 1982, sit on a ridge above the valley floor—at 1,400 feet this is one of the loftier vineyards in the area, which helps it avoid the worst of winter frosts. Paul Portteus, Jr., had actually hoped to find land in California when he conceived the idea of starting a winery ten years ago, but the Seattle native liked the idea of being closer to home.

Portteus, whose knowledge comes largely from hands-on helping at several local wineries, is aiming for the upper end of the market, with a Chardonnay 100 percent fermented in French oak (he's looking for a ripe style) and Cabernet (he prefers the more aggressive American oak for this wine). Of interest, too, is a small patch of Zinfandel that seems to be growing just fine. First vintage was in 1986, with the wines to be released in late 1988 or early 1989. Production will probably grow to something over 10,000 cases. Wines not tasted.

PRESTON WINE CELLARS
Pasco   (1976)
55,000 cases

Bill Preston was a highly successful farm-equipment dealer who enjoyed his trips to the Napa Valley so much he decided to try making his own wine in the desert near Pasco. Preston Cellars, for years the state's second-largest winery after Ste. Michelle, established a solid reputation while Rob Griffin (now at Hogue Cellars) was making the wines. Griffin made some exciting Chardonnays in the early years (including a '77 that won many awards) and also showed a firm command of Fumé Blanc and Riesling. Since Griffin's departure the winery has lived through a succession of winemakers; Wayne Marcil, formerly of Covey Run, was made winemaker in time for the 1988 crush. If Marcil stays, his track record of well-made wines, especially whites, bodes well for the winery.

The 180 acres of vineyard were first planted in 1972. The hot surrounding country has none of the green lushness of the Yakima Valley, but the vines are kept very green, and cool, by overhead sprinklers. (Unfortunately, this kind of watering makes the vines more vulnerable to winter frost.) Preston's initial success was based as much on novelty and its pioneer status as on quality and marketing skill—as competition has gotten stiffer and newer wineries have received the acclaim, sales have suffered.

The list of varietals is long, and the wines have not always been consistent in the last several years, a problem compounded by slow sales, since some of the whites on the market are clearly too old. (One advantage, though: Reds available already have considerable bottle age.) There has also been a proliferation of lower-end proprietary blends with names like Desert Blossom.

If you stick with the basics here, you can do very well. The Fumé Blanc, aged in oak, will appeal to those who like an assertive Sauvignon Blanc—it has always been one of the better ones in the state. The Chardonnay, which used to be light, lemony, oaky, now has riper fruit flavors. There is also a confusing assortment of Late Harvest Rieslings in different bottlings—some of these can be fine in a straightforward, grapefruity way and are worth trying when the price is right.

Second-label Columbia River Cellars wines are inexpensive, and the Merlot, very ripe, has consistently been a good value.

CABERNET SAUVIGNON ($$) ★★   A soft but rather hot wine that tends toward the herbal, with some berry fruit.

CHAMPAGNE ($$$) ★★   Made from Riesling, it is fruity and frothy, but a bit sweetish and lacking acid. Expensive.

CHARDONNAY ($$) ★★★   The latest one ('86) has very ripe apple aromas, a nice hit of oak, and some bite. Straightforward and flavorful.

DESERT BLOSSOM ($) ★   Very exotic fruit, soft, sweet, "hot-tub wine."

FUMÉ BLANC ($$) ★★★½   Ripe, intense, full of herbaceous fruit—it's quite an aggressive style. Partisans of this style will love it. Well made.

RIESLING ($) ★★   Used to be one of the best, characteristically ripe and full-flavored, with lots of appley fruit, but recent vintages have seemed less interesting.

RIESLING, SELECT HARVEST ($$) ★★★   Straightforward grapefruity flavors, medium sweet.

COLUMBIA RIVER CELLARS MERLOT ($) ★★   Pleasant, woody, rounded flavors with lots of body. A fine, simple wine.

PROSSER FALLS   *See* HINZERLING VINEYARDS

QUAIL RUN VINTNERS   *See* COVEY RUN VINTNERS

QUARRY LAKE WINERY
Pasco   (1985)
20,000 cases

Balcom and Moe Vineyard is one the largest and best-established independent vineyards in eastern Washington, with 110 acres of vines just north of Pasco and more being planned. Now, in what was originally a joint venture with the enormous Langguth Winery, it is producing its own wines. Balcom and Moe began in the potato business (it supplies Wendy's, among other large customers, and has extensive apple and cherry orchards as well), but grapes represented a way to diversify, as they did for Hogue Farms, or the Symms Ranch in Idaho.

The vineyard was first planted in 1971, and for years Balcom and Moe supplied grapes to many Washington wineries. Finally, manager Maury Balcom, trained in viticulture and enology in California, decided it was time to make his own wines. Lacking his own winery, he has used the state-of-the-art facility at Langguth to crush, ferment, and bottle the wines, with his own separate location for aging. The initial releases seemed decidedly awkward, but the wines have improved steadily with a little age, and with newer vintages Balcom has demonstrated a surer style. The Chardonnay especially, 30 percent barrel-fermented, has attracted national attention—its fresh, balanced flavors make it a perfect restaurant wine. The first Sauvignon Blancs were pretty unyielding, but the '87 has more fruit and rounder flavors. All the wines are in a lighter, more subtle mold than is standard in eastern Washington.

The initial releases of reds also showed promise—especially a well-structured Cabernet that asks to be aged. Both Cabernet and Merlot avoid the herbal flavors of so many Washington reds: Balcom (who likes to spend lots of time in the vineyard) is convinced that careful management of irrigation and thus foliage canopy is the key to this problem. With reasonable prices and dedication to careful grape growing, Quarry Lake is a winery to watch.

CABERNET SAUVIGNON ($$) ★★★½ Tight, tart, and tannic style in its first offering (1985)—shows good structure and some berry flavors. Age.

CHARDONNAY ($) ★★★ Strong improvement over the last several years: The latest release is light, balanced, with hints of oak and lemon. A fine food wine.

CHENIN BLANC ($) ★★½ Light, off-dry, some pleasant wildflower aromas.

RIESLING ($) ★★½ Light, tart, fresh, appley—quite pleasant.

SAUVIGNON BLANC ($) ★★★   Style still evolving: The most recent release shows more fruit, with slight grassiness and sweetness. Good acid, great with seafood.

QUILCEDA CREEK VINTNERS
Snohomish   (1979)
900 cases

Cabernet Sauvignon is Quilceda Creek's one wine, and what a wine it is. Since the first vintage (1979) won the Grand Prize at the Enological Society of the Pacific Northwest's competition in 1983, this winery has gone from strength to strength. In 1987, in a blind tasting pitting Washington Cabernets against some of Bordeaux's top wines, the '83 Quilceda finished second overall. It's perhaps not surprising to learn that the old pro behind this operation is André Tchelistcheff, who created Beaulieu Vineyard's great Cabernets and got Ste. Michelle started. Tchelistcheff is uncle to Alex Golitzin, a chemical engineer who turned his home winemaking experiments into a commercial winery at Tchelistcheff's urging. The results have been first class and have put Quilceda Creek in an elite group of other small state wineries producing deep-flavored, long-lived Cabernet Sauvignon that can stand with the best in the world.

Quilceda Creek is in Snohomish, just north of Seattle. Currently, the winery is purchasing grapes from both Kiona Vineyards and Mercer Ranch Vineyards, both in the Yakima Valley, both acknowledged as among the best sources of Cabernet Sauvignon in the state. The wine, unfiltered and unfined, is a powerhouse, loaded with deep blackberry fruit. There are no apologies for the tons of tannin or the pronounced oak character, although the wines are held back until four years after the vintage. Even so, they need considerably more time to develop.

CABERNET SAUVIGNON ($$$) ★★★★★ Absolutely black in youth, with a huge, spicy oak nose, deep blackberry fruit, lots of spicy tannin. Very ripe. World class. Will need lots of time to be at its best.

REDFORD CELLARS
(1978)
600 cases

Redford Cellars has gone for ten years without a winery to call its own. Stephen Redford, a true Northwest winemaker, since his interests span the Columbia, started out making a blend of Cabernet Sauvignon and Merlot from Washington and Oregon grapes at his brother Myron's winery, Amity Vineyards, in Oregon. Attracted to eastern Washington by its potential for Cabernet Sauvignon, Redford in 1985 became winemaker for grape grower Don Mercer, when the latter decided to start his own winery. Using the Mercer Ranch facility, Redford continued to make his Cabernet-Merlot blend, plus a varietal Cabernet Sauvignon, from grapes purchased from various vineyards in the Yakima and Columbia valleys (though he uses Oregon fruit when he can find it—the Merlot for the '84 blend, for example, all came from Oregon). In 1988 Redford parted company with Mercer and at press time was still looking for a facility in the Seattle area where he could set up shop. Though a talented winemaker, he has not been able to attract backing for his own winery.

Redford's model is Bordeaux, and the blend of grapes is based on Bordeaux tradition. (The earlier vintages were aged in American oak, but recent ones have been in French.) The wines are not blockbusters but have the virtues of balance and smoothness.

CABERNET-MERLOT ($$) ★★★½ A rich, warm, oaky nose, with considerable body. Lean, tart, balanced.

RUSHCUTTER BAY *See* PAUL THOMAS

SETH RYAN WINERY
West Richland   (1986)
300 cases

A tiny home-based winery run by the Brodzinski and Olsen families, Seth Ryan hopes to focus on specialty Rieslings. The year 1988 should see releases of several experimental lots of wine, including an oak-aged Riesling. There will also be Chardonnay and Gewürztraminer.

RIESLING ($) ★½ Solid body and some flowery qualities, but it doesn't seem entirely fresh.

SADDLE MOUNTAIN WINERY *See* SNOQUALMIE WINERY

SALISHAN VINEYARDS
La Center   (1976)
4,000 cases

Salishan stands practically in the shadow of Mount St. Helens, in a hilly area along the Columbia, north of Portland, that had never been planted to grapes until Joan and Lincoln Wolverton arrived in the early seventies. They were looking for a climate approximating that of the Willamette Valley, forty miles to the south, and while their harvest is usually a week or so behind the Willamette vineyards, the same varieties, especially Pinot Noir, do well here. Though western Washington had been written off for any but hybrid grapes, the Wolvertons planted 12 acres, and there are now 200 or so acres of vines in the hills around Salishan.

Salishan impressed wine lovers early on with delicious Pinot Noirs from the warm vintages of 1978 and '79—they were Burgundian-style wines with delicate texture but big, smoky noses. These early vintages were actually made at several Oregon wineries, in the days when the Wolvertons were still commuting from Seattle to tend the vineyard. Since 1982 Joan Wolverton has been making the wines, and while they have had difficulties with the weather in several vintages, '85, '86, and '87 were all fine years.

The wines here are in a totally dry, fairly austere style. The Pinot Noir tends to be a bit lighter and gentler in texture than Willamette Pinots (some liken it to Volnay). Besides the Pinot, the most interesting wine is the dry

Chenin Blanc; although Chenin is a cool-climate grape in France's Loire, it is little planted in cool areas in the United States. While it doesn't get terribly ripe in the Wolvertons' vineyard, the wine is richly fruity, with tangy flavors that make it great with seafood—a lovely wine. Chardonnay is a bit iffy here—the climate is pretty marginal—but can be very good in the warm years. All the Salishan wines are modestly priced.

CHARDONNAY ($$) ★★★ Quite a lean style with plenty of oak and fruit that varies from lemony to appley. Very much a food wine.

CHENIN BLANC, DRY ($) ★★★★ Rich, grapefruity, bready nose with lots of flavor in a very dry style. Crisp acidity makes it great with seafood, and it actually needs some age to develop.

PINOT NOIR ($$) ★★★½ In the best years, this has light color but a round, smoky, oaky bouquet and silky textures. Always tart, in some years it is a bit green and unyielding. Produced in different lots.

RIESLING, DRY ($) ★★★ Fresh, lemony, grassy nose; light, delicate, quite dry. Not quite the depth of the Chenin.

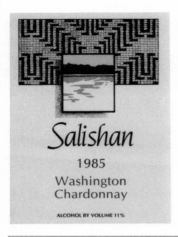

Salishan
1985
Washington
Chardonnay

ALCOHOL BY VOLUME 11%

SALMON BAY WINERY
Woodinville   (1982)
4,500 cases

Salmon Bay, under the name Vernier, got off to a rocky start from which it is gradually recovering. Seattle sommelier Bruce Crabtree, with strong connections to the local restaurant industry, decided with some friends to make wines they could sell to restaurants. But Crabtree didn't prove successful as a part-time winemaker, and he has started over, with a new name and professional help with the wines.

The winery is still in transition. Winemaker Louis Facelli, who made a fine reputation in Idaho, brought out many of the current releases but then moved on to Haviland Vintners. Salmon Bay has just moved to a new location in suburban Woodinville and is currently hunting for a new winemaker—the '86 and '87 vintages were made at eastern Washington wineries. Grapes come from several eastern Washington vineyards.

The current wines, moderately priced, are a slightly mixed bag, with the Chardonnay tasting best. Not a big Chardonnay, and not heavily oaked, it nevertheless has nice melony fruit and medium body. The reds have their origins in less happy times, but they're perfectly decent. Look for newer vintages to be improved.

CABERNET SAUVIGNON ($$) ★★   The flavors are rather tired out and woody, but there's good body.
CHARDONNAY ($$) ★★★   Tart, okay, melony flavors—fresh, straightforward.
MERLOT ($$) ★★   Ripe, soft, but the flavors are a bit weedy.
RIESLING, SELECT ($)   The '85 is foul and should be avoided.
SAUVIGNON BLANC ($$) ★½   There's lots of flavor, but it doesn't quite all hang together. Sharp.

SNOQUALMIE WINERY
Snoqualmie   (1983)
SADDLE MOUNTAIN WINERY
Mattawa
330,000 cases (capacity)

Snoqualmie was the creation of Joel Klein, a strong-willed and enthusiastic bear of a man who helped shape Washington's wines in the seventies as the first winemaker for Chateau Ste. Michelle. He left Ste. Michelle in 1983 to start his own winery in the foothills of the Cascades (not far from Seattle), with ambitious plans for a large winery turning out wines with broad appeal—lighter-bodied, fruity, quite soft. Then in 1986 Snoqualmie bought control of the large (now up to 800,000 gallons), technologically sophisticated F. W. Langguth Winery (now called Saddle Mountain) in Mattawa, near the Columbia River. Built in

1981, Langguth had represented a large commitment by the big German wine company of the same name to produce Riesling from Washington grapes, but the wines ran into stiff competition from the locals and the Germans never quite figured out the marketplace.

The amalgamation of Snoqualmie and Langguth (producing the perhaps unfortunate nickname of Snoguth) makes it the fourth-largest winery facility in the state, after Columbia Crest, Ste. Michelle, and Coventry Vale. (For now, all the wines, including Snoqualmie's, are being made at Mattawa, although ambitious expansion plans call for a new production facility at Snoqualmie's original site outside Seattle.) But much of the winery's capacity has been turned over to custom-crushing grapes for other operations. The F. W. Langguth label, never terribly successful, will be phased out for all except a small selection of Late Harvest Rieslings. Instead, the winery has introduced a list of inexpensive varietals under the Saddle Mountain name, which are intended to be "good-tasting, affordable wines." The Snoqualmie line will remain slightly upscale, without forsaking an approachable style.

Klein is no longer the winemaker, and Mike Januik, a very successful winemaker at Stewart Vineyards (and well known for excellent late-harvest wines), has been hired to run the Mattawa facility. With Langguth came 280 acres of young vines on the Wahluke slope, a relatively warm section of the Columbia Basin, but the winery also has contracts with a number of growers in the Yakima and Columbia valleys.

With all the changes taking place at this winery, it is perhaps misleading to comment on the wines. Certainly one would hope for improvement in the Langguth and Saddle Mountain lines—the Langguth Rieslings have been quite ordinary and the Saddle Mountain varietals inconsistent at best. (Most recent Saddle Mountain releases, under a redesigned label, show marked improvement.) The Snoqualmie wines, though well made, have seemed a shade light and are quite soft; Klein believed in harvesting his fruit later than most, to achieve greater maturity, and bucked the trend to higher-acid wines. This seems to work very nicely for Chenin Blanc, which shows some richness, and Semillon, full of ripe flavors. The reds are quite forward and fruity. A new Fumé Blanc has been very successful.

CABERNET SAUVIGNON ($$) ★★★ Very forward and fruity (berries) with good structure.

CHARDONNAY ($$) ★★½ Light nose (a little oak), soft, not much varietal intensity.

CHENIN BLANC ($) ★★★½ Intriguing nose of clover, slightly sweet, with soft, restrained fruit. More interesting than most.

FUMÉ BLANC ($$) ★★★ A nicely grassy nose with rounded fruit and a hint of sweetness. Well made.

MERLOT, RESERVE ($$) ★★★ Intense, jammy nose with soft, forward fruit and a bit of oak.

MUSCAT CANELLI ($) ★★★ Pungent Muscat nose, with lovely balance of sugar and acid. Very tasty.

RIESLING ($) ★★½ Full, apple-apricot nose, straightforward.

SEMILLON ($) ★★★ Intense nose of honey and hay. Soft, round. Good light-food wine.

LANGGUTH RIESLING, SELECT CLUSTER ($$$) ★★★★ Extremely sweet and nectarlike, with creamy texture. Heavy, but good balance.

LANGGUTH RIESLING, SELECT HARVEST ($$) ★★½ Full, sweet flavors, but without much delicacy or balance.

SADDLE MOUNTAIN CHARDONNAY ($) ★★½ Very warm, appley fruit, light and soft on the palate. A very nice example of fruity Chardonnay.

SADDLE MOUNTAIN GEWÜRZTRAMINER ($) ★★½
Sweet, fruity style, with good body and some underlying spice.

SADDLE MOUNTAIN RIESLING ($) ★★   Big nose, but not that fruity.

STATON HILLS VINEYARD
Wapato and Seattle   (1984)
35,000 cases

One of the fastest-growing wineries in the state, Staton Hills has hit the market with a large number of reasonably priced wines under a variety of labels. The quality, with a couple exceptions, is fairly ordinary, but owner David Staton, a savvy and experienced businessman, has done some innovative things to sell his wine. He introduced the idea of "Pink Riesling"—Riesling with a small amount of red juice added to give it a little extra color and flavor—to compete with California blush wine (and to help deal with the state's Riesling glut). He has been one of the pioneers in selling Washington wine in the Far East (speaking Japanese certainly helps), producing special labels for wines in Japan. And he has decided to challenge New York and California in the inexpensive bulk Champagne business. The state's industry could use a few more leaders with his enthusiasm and sense of vision. In 1988 vineyard holdings had reached 300 acres, and the winery was planning to increase production yet again. The winemaker is Rob Stuart.

The small vineyard lies in a warm south-facing section of the narrow (and generally cooler) western end of the Yakima Valley, and Staton has used several different innovative trellising techniques to encourage better ripening. Given the first-class winemaking facility that Staton has, one would wish that the wines were a little more impressive. The wide range of offerings may dilute the quality of individual wines. Best bet is a fresh and fruity Sauvignon Blanc. The semisweet whites are made in a popular style, while the dry whites are clean but sometimes seem to lack varietal fruit. The red wines so far have been fairly tough and unyielding—surprisingly, Pinot Noir (from Oregon) may be the best of these.

A partnership with wine label artist Sebastian Titus has produced two additional labels: Status and Titon, and the Ridgemont label has also been used for wines from California grapes. A small satellite winery operates in downtown Seattle, mainly to provide a tasting room facility.

CABERNET SAUVIGNON ($$) ★★½ Sweet oak nose, with herbal tones dominating, quite soft.

CHARDONNAY ($$) ★½ Light, woody flavors, without much varietal fruit.

CHENIN BLANC ($) ★★ Very tart, a hint of oak in the finish—thin fruit.

GEWÜRZTRAMINER ($) ★★★ One of the nicer wines here—good varietal fruit, tart, zippy. Slightly sweet.

MUSCAT CANELLI ($) ★½ Thick Muscat flavors, sweet and viscous. A bit heavy-handed.

PINOT NOIR (OREGON) ($$) ★★★ Ripe, oaky flavors with a bit of tannin—quite soft.

RIESLING, JOHANNISBERG ($) ★★ Simple fruit, crisp, light.

RIESLING, PINK ($) ★★ Good fruit, sweet, but there's enough acid here to balance the sugar. Merlot and Baco Noir give the color. All in all, a nicer wine than it sounds.

SAUVIGNON BLANC ($) ★★★ Best of the dry wines—nice, ripe, spicy flavors with lots of fruit.

SEMILLON ($) ★★ Fruity, light, tart, simple—slightly herbaceous.

RIDGEMONT CABERNET SAUVIGNON ($) ★★ Good, oaky nose, lean tannic flavors.

STATUS CHAMPAGNE, PINK ($) ½   The price is right, but there's not much fruit and some chemical flavors. The Brut is about the same.

TITON CHARDONNAY ($) ★   This lean wine has oaky, mushroomy aromas and tart flavors. Cleanly made but not terribly varietal.

STEWART VINEYARDS
Sunnyside   (1983)
8,500 cases

Although the winery has been open only since 1983, Dr. George Stewart planted his first vineyard back in the late sixties, on Harrison Hill near Sunnyside in the Yakima Valley, a historic site that had been home to early grapevines during the thirties and then to Associated Vintners' first vineyard in the early sixties. Stewart was also the first to plant vinifera grapes on the Wahluke Slope near the Columbia River north of the Yakima Valley, an area that has since seen many more acres of vineyard planted. The Wahluke is warmer than the Yakima Valley and a good home to varieties like Muscat that are more susceptible to the cold. Before the winery opened, grapes from the seventy acres of vineyards were used for several fine wines at other wineries.

The original winemaker was Mike Januik, a well-trained professional from the University of California at Davis enology program, who demonstrated a deft touch with Late Harvest Riesling and made some fine fat Chardonnays (which haven't aged very well). The winery now has a deserved reputation for appealing, ripe, fruity wines at good prices. New winemaker Scott Benham apprenticed with Rob Griffin at Hogue Cellars and plans largely to carry on in the same style, looking for perhaps a bit more subtlety and complexity in the Chardonnay through barrel fermentation.

There is little to quarrel with in the wines here. Although the Cabernet Sauvignon, while well made, lacks the depth of some others, the whites are uniformly fresh and fruity. The Chardonnay is a model for this wine made in a plump, popular style (drink it up young). The Late Harvest Rieslings are some of the very finest in the state, with consistent richness of flavor and excellent balance—there is little doubt that they can match flavors with the best dessert Rieslings from anywhere in the world (at much lower prices).

CABERNET SAUVIGNON ($$) ★★½ Bright red, fairly oaky, with a dusty nose. Not a heavyweight—cleaned up a little too much?

CHARDONNAY ($$) ★★★½ Ripe, toasty-oaky nose, with lots of apple. Rich, viscous, tangy, ripe. A very open and appealing wine with a long finish. Excellent value.

GEWÜRZTRAMINER ($) ★★½ Light, varietal fruit, with soft, fresh flavors. Very slight sweetness.

MUSCAT CANELLI ($$) ★★★½ Lovely, deep, rich Muscat nose—tart and fresh on the palate. Full-flavored style.

RIESLING, JOHANNISBERG ($) ★★★★ Rich nose, heavier than most, with peachy flavors and soft acidity. A Riesling lover's Riesling, not shy on flavor.

RIESLING, LATE HARVEST ($$$) ★★★★★ Very sweet and quite delicious, with intensely ripe apricot flavors, some spice, and fine acid balance. Hard to resist. Excellent year in and year out.

RIESLING, WHITE ($) ★★ Medium sweet, with ripe, spiced peach nose. Good acid, but the fruit seems to drop off a bit.

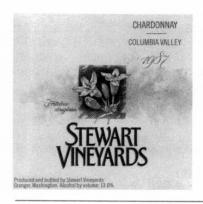

TAGARIS
Othello (1987)
15,000 cases

Michael Taggares's Greek grandfather (who spelled his name Tagaris) planted some of the first grapes in the Columbia Valley in 1911, and the Taggares family today holds the largest Concord grape acreage in the world. Now the grandson has a 120-acre vinifera vineyard, first planted in 1982, on the Wahluke Slope north of the Columbia River—at 1,300 feet one of the higher vineyards in the state. The leading variety initially will be Chardonnay, but the winery also has high hopes for Cabernet Sauvignon as well as for Pinot Noir (planted on a north-facing slope to lengthen the growing season).

Winemaker Peter Bos has a varied background in the wine industry, having served as cellarmaster at Preston under Rob Griffin (now at Hogue Cellars), managed vineyards for Balcom and Moe, sold wine as a supermarket wine specialist, and worked as assistant winemaker for David Lake at Columbia. Although a winery is in the plan, initial vintages are being made at the Coventry Vale custom winery.

The new Chardonnay is quite agreeable, with a good hit of new oak, while the other varietals, fresh and clean in flavor, are fine but unremarkable. Production is planned to increase to around 50,000 cases.

CHARDONNAY ($$) ★★½   Apple and oak flavors, fruity and forward.

FUMÉ BLANC ($) ★★   An aggressive Sauvignon, with slightly harsh, herbal flavors.

RIESLING ($) ★★   Very appley flavors, soft, simple, medium sweet.

PAUL THOMAS
Bellevue   (1979)
17,000 cases

The winery has a well-deserved reputation for producing some of the best fruit wines in the Northwest (and probably the United States). But there is a problem: In more recent years it has also established itself as a fine producer of grape wines. As winemaker Brian Carter says, "How do you convince people you can make great Cabernet and great rhubarb wine at the same time?" But owner Paul Thomas, a former schoolteacher, explains his program as making the best wine possible from *all* the fine fruit in the Northwest.

The original premise here was that fruit wines should be taken seriously as dry table wines, and wines like Crimson Rhubarb and Bartlett Pear (the latter goes well with spicy foods and is popular in New Orleans) have a solid following. The fruit comes mostly from western Washington. These are far from the heavy, sweet berry wines of home winemakers—they are crisp, delicate, and balanced.

The vinifera wines from eastern Washington grapes are even better and show the broad range of Carter's talent. The whites are balanced and show good acid; Riesling and Sauvignon Blanc age very nicely and have elegant flavors. Paul Thomas was one of the first in the state to produce a true dry Riesling, which was excellent. Abandoned in the face of consumer apathy, it has now been revived, though the new version is not totally dry. Carter's first Merlot (made as a sort of afterthought in 1984 when Cabernet grapes were not available) was one of the best ever made in the state, and his first barrel-fermented Chardonnay, an understated wine with excellent balance, has walked off with a basketful of gold medals. In fact, each of the wines here is very near the top of its class in the state, making the winery's products a very reliable choice for consumers.

In 1988, Carter, one of the state's most serious talents, left full-time work at Paul Thomas (though he remains consulting winemaker) to branch out into different projects. Paul Thomas has taken over as winemaker, with Mark Cave, formerly at Yakima River, handling day-to-day winemaking chores.

Second-label Rushcutter Bay wines, intended for the restaurant trade, can be good values.

CABERNET SAUVIGNON ($$$) ★★★★ At five years, still youthful, chocolaty nose, with balanced yet intense flavor, well structured, tart, tannic. Very nicely made. Demands aging.

CHARDONNAY ($$) ★★★½ This regular bottling emphasizes fresh fruit, with a hint of buttery oak and a hint of sweetness. The ultimate restaurant Chardonnay.

CHARDONNAY, PRIVATE RESERVE ($$$) ★★★★ An austere nose opens gradually to a nice toastiness; the fruit is restrained, with a good acid backbone, and all is in balance. Lovely.

CHENIN BLANC ($) ★★★½ Light, apple nose, straightforward flavor, slightly sweet—some fresh clove and bread dough in the nose.

MERLOT ($$) ★★★★½ Big plummy nose, lots of raspberry flavors, a soft feel, and a touch of oak. A nicely balanced, very attractive wine—about all one could ask for in Merlot.

MUSCAT CANELLI ($$) ★★★½ Slight spritz on the tongue, lush floral nose with lots of sweet fruit. A lovely dessert wine.

RIESLING ($) ★★★★ One of the best in the state— very fruity (apples), very fresh, a big nose. Most appealing.

RIESLING, DRY ($) ★★½ Apple and grapefruit, just off-dry, not quite the character of the regular bottling.

SAUVIGNON BLANC ($$) ★★★½ Very nice, subtle, grassy aromas with very crisp acidity. More subdued than most—a very good seafood wine. Ages well.

BARTLETT PEAR, DRY ($) ★★★★ Full, rather spicy aroma (not immediately identifiable as pear) and delicate flavors. A viscous feel to it and bone dry.

RASPBERRY ($$) ★★★★ If you have ever wanted to taste essence of raspberry in a wine, this is it. Fresh, lovely fruit, just slightly sweet and not too heavy.

RHUBARB, CRIMSON ($) ★★½ Definite rhubarb flavors, just slightly sweet, light, fresh, very pleasant. A nice alternative to a blush.

TUCKER CELLARS
Sunnyside (1981)
5,000 cases

The quintessential family fruit operation, the Tucker farm has been producing fruit and vegetables for three generations—the patriarch of the family planted some of the first vinifera grapes (Muscat, Riesling, Semillon) in the Yakima Valley back in 1933. (The grapes were destined for Upland Winery, which went out of business, and the vines were eventually pulled up.) But it wasn't until 1981 that the family added a winery to its burgeoning roadside fresh-produce stand (a valley landmark), using grapes from its sixty-acre vineyard.

Randy Tucker is the winemaker, but lacking technical expertise with wine, he has retained respected consultant Kay Simon for help. All of the wines are made in a straightforward, fruity style, as one might expect, though there's a tendency toward overripeness. Several of the whites lack distinctive varietal characteristics. The tastiest is the Muscat Canelli, with delicate fruit and very fresh flavor—a good value. The wines are all reasonably priced.

CABERNET SAUVIGNON ($$) ★★ Nice berry nose, tart, fruity, with a little tannin.

CHARDONNAY ($$) ★★ Rather light, woody nose. The fruit is like stewed apples and slightly hot.

CHARDONNAY, RESERVE ($$) ★★½ An older wine when released—yellowing, fat and oaky, overripe and rather clumsy. Some varietal character.

CHENIN BLANC ($) ★½ Somewhat weedy nose, light, medium sweet.

MUSCAT CANELLI ($) ★★★ Lovely, fresh, light Muscat nose (not too floral), good fruit. Very pleasant.

PINOT NOIR ($) ★½   Tired and woody, overripe—OK flavors.

RIESLING ($) ★★   Very peachy-apricot nose, heavy, a bit stewed—but just slightly sweet. It doesn't seem to hold up very well.

RIESLING, LATE HARVEST ($$) ★★   Sweet, simple, lacks richness.

VERNIER WINES   *See* SALMON BAY WINERY

MANFRED VIERTHALER WINERY
Sumner   (1976)
16,000 cases (capacity)

Although this winery claims to make white wines in the style of the German Rheingau, most lovers of German Riesling would be disappointed with the results. Owner Manfred Vierthaler does purchase grapes from some local Puget Sound vineyards (he doesn't like grapes from eastern Washington), but most of the wines are made from grape juice obtained from California; these wines are labeled "American." Winemaker Vierthaler has a German background and interest, but the wines, low in both acid and alcohol, lack the fruit and crispness of fine Rieslings. The varietals don't taste much like varietals, and all the wines seem simple, sweet, and often flat and oxidized. The best advice is to avoid the reds and the inexpensive whites—some of the Select Harvest wines are OK.

Most the wines are inexpensive, but hardly worth it; they are available only at the winery.

BARBECUE RED ($) ½   A very light rosé-style wine, innocuous.

BURGUNDY, SELECT HARVEST ($$) ½   Interesting—a
   dark, sweet, smooth wine with decent fruit. Not bad, but
   most drinkers will find it odd.
GEWÜRZTRAMINER, SELECT HARVEST ($$) ★   Slight
   apple character, soft, pleasant, sweet.
RIESLING, SELECT HARVEST ($$) ½   Sweet, low in acid,
   not much character.

WASHINGTON DISCOVERY *See* COVENTRY VALE

WATERBROOK
Lowden   (1984)
6,000 cases

Another of the cluster of wineries near Walla Walla,
Waterbrook too is taking a handcrafted approach to the
making of wine. Like other local winemakers, Eric and
Janet Rindal come from farming backgrounds—Janet's
family grows alfalfa seed nearby. The energetic Rindals,
who pretty much run the winery by themselves, leaped
into winemaking feet first. One summer they helped their
neighbors the Fergusons with the crush at L'École No. 41;
the next year, after a few mini-classes in enology, they
bought a couple of tanks and started in on their own. Janet
remarks cheerfully that she didn't know anything about
wine when they started, but from the beginning the wines
have been carefully made and very appealing, no doubt
thanks in part to consulting enologist Kay Simon.
   They own no vineyards, procuring their fruit from Co-
lumbia Valley vineyards, including the well-regarded
Moreman Vineyard and Balcom and Moe Vineyard, both
near Pasco. Chardonnay will probably end up the spe-
cialty here, and the winery is producing several different
bottlings, including one entirely barrel-fermented ver-

sion. (The secondary wine has been labeled Pinot Chardonnay, which may cause some confusion.) Although pleased with the results of their French oak barrels, they are also experimenting with the use of (much less expensive) American oak. Rindal feels he can control the aggressive flavors of American oak by cutting back the time the wines spend in it. Other successful wines here have been Sauvignon Blanc, which sees a little time in oak and ends up soft and not too herbaceous (although the '86 vintage refused to ferment dry, leaving an awkward slight sweetness in the wine), and Merlot, which has a nice balance of berry and sweet oak flavors.

CABERNET SAUVIGNON ($$$) ★★★ Lovely balance of oak and berry flavors, quite tart and hard on the palate, with good spice.

CHARDONNAY ($$) ★★★½ An assertively toasty, oaky style, with pineapple fruit, good acid, and some buttery qualities. The Reserve has even more buttery oak qualities.

MERLOT ($$) ★★★½ Intense, sweetish nose, fairly soft and forward, with slight herbaceousness.

PINOT CHARDONNAY ($) ★★ A straightforward wine with applelike fruit, a hint of sweetness, and decent acid.

SAUVIGNON BLANC ($$) ★★★ Slight grassiness is toned down with rich oak. Usually tart and round, though '86 has some sweetness.

WENATCHEE VALLEY VINTNERS
East Wenatchee   (1986)
20,000 cases

The Wenatchee Valley lies up against the eastern side of the Cascade Mountains, toward the northern end of the

Columbia Valley appellation. A well-known apple-growing region, it has not been home to any wineries until Wenatchee Valley Vintners began. The elevation is higher, the climate a touch cooler, and the harvest a little later than in the Yakima Valley. The Hansens, Mike and Debbie, planted their 18-acre vineyard in 1982 with several varieties, including Sauvignon Blanc and Pinot Noir, and they are also using grapes from Mike's father's 250 acres of vineyard near Zillah, in the Yakima Valley, also the location of a new fermentation facility. (The winery already has considerable tank capacity, and production could grow quickly given the ready source of grapes.)

Mike Hansen is not a winemaker by background (consultant Kay Simon of Chinook Wines provided winemaking expertise when they began), but his training as a biochemist makes him a great quality-control man. His aim is to produce full-flavored varietals; of the initial releases, the Riesling seemed better than the Chardonnay, which didn't show much varietal character.

CHARDONNAY ($) ★★ Light and leafy, this wine is soft and a bit thin.

RIESLING ($) ★★★ Lovely apple flavors—tart and refreshing.

WHITTLESEY-MARK (OREGON CHAMPAGNE CELLARS)
Seattle   (1983)
1,500 cases

Formerly Newton and Newton (the name change resulted from a dispute with California's Newton), this is the Northwest's first exclusive sparkling-wine producer, and the first releases of small amounts of Champagne-method wines have been most impressive. Mark Newton's wine background is primarily as a serious wine consumer—he decided on a career making sparkling wine after a visit to California's Domaine Chandon. He has spent time learning the business at several successful Champagne houses in California, including the large French Deutz concern, and he has several consulting enologists from California. But the Northwest is the place for sparkling wine, he thinks.

Oregon fruit—Chardonnay, Pinot Noir, and Pinot Meunier, the classic French Champagne grapes—is perfect for the wine, ripening with low sugars and high acids. The grapes, from the well-known Hyland Vineyard in the Willamette, are crushed and pressed in Oregon, but the rest of the production process takes place in Seattle, making the winery a true Northwest concern.

Newton has managed to achieve what few others in the Northwest have: a delicately fruity sparkling wine reminiscent of French Champagne. It doesn't have quite the yeasty weight of great Champagne (like most new producers, Newton can't afford to let the wine rest on the yeast for three or four years), but it makes up for that with considerable elegance. The wine is well priced, and production should increase in coming years.

Still Chardonnay will be released under a separate label, diStefano.

BRUT (OREGON) ($$$) ★★★★   Rich, fresh, tart fruit with some depth and lovely rounded elegance. A lively and distinctive wine.

ROSÉ (OREGON) ($$$) ★★★½   Not quite as nice as the Brut. Fresh flavors, some nice Pinot character, quite soft.

WINDY RIVER CELLARS   *See* BLACKWOOD CANYON

WOODBURNE   *See* COLUMBIA WINERY

WOODWARD CANYON WINERY
Lowden   (1981)
2,400 cases

From its beginning in 1981 this tiny winery near Walla Walla has been one of the state's top producers of both Cabernet Sauvignon and Chardonnay. Owner and winemaker Rick Small comes from a longtime Walla Walla farming family, but even his relatives numbered among the skeptics in this conservative wheat-and-beef town when Small started his winery. After helping Gary Figgins at Leonetti Cellar (a former fellow drill sergeant in the Army Reserve) make his wines, Small set off on his own, with the same commitment to small quantities of powerful, top-notch wines.

Rick Small isn't sure what the best grape varieties for the young Walla Walla appellation are, but clearly Chardonnay and Cabernet are among them. His own ten-acre vineyard, on a steep south-facing slope ten miles west of town, is planted with Chardonnay, and he feels Walla Walla's slightly cooler temperatures are ideal for this variety. What's interesting about the finished product, though, is that Small manages to work his magic not just with his own grapes, but with fruit from other sources, drawing from Seven Hills Vineyard across the Oregon border (still part of the appellation), Mercer Ranch, Gordon Brothers Vineyards, and various others.

Small was one of the first in the state to produce a barrel-fermented Chardonnay well aged on the lees: It is consistently a big, buttery wine with a soft texture that belies its depth and strength. It has also shown good aging ability. The single-vineyard Chardonnay, from the Roza Bergé Vineyard in the Yakima Valley, shows a slightly different style, with the influence of new oak.

Small's Cabernet is one of the best in the state—a consistent award winner. It's a huge wine, with deep fruit—nearly black in color, and like the Chardonnay aged completely in new French oak. The first vintage, the '81, still looks and tastes young and will take years to develop, but for the patient this is extraordinary wine. The latest Small effort is a blend of 70 percent Merlot and 30 percent Cabernet called Charbonneau (after the Snake River vineyard from which the grapes come). Just released in 1987, this may be the best Merlot-based wine yet from Washington; Small attributes the quality to a meager yield. Riesling is produced for the tourist trade—sold only at the winery. The top wines are expensive and sell quickly but are worth looking for.

CABERNET SAUVIGNON ($$$$) ★★★★★ Big, spicy, oaky nose with tart, lean classic Cabernet fruit. Built for the ages. One of the very best.

CHARBONNEAU ($$$$) ★★★★½ Plummy and rich, with a great whack of oak, extremely tannic, powerful. Exceptional Merlot.

CHARDONNAY (COLUMBIA) ($$$) ★★★★★ Very rich butterscotch-pineapple nose, ripe, round fruit—quite luscious. Lots of fruit and lots of oak. A big style for rich foods. California, watch out.

CHARDONNAY (ROZA BERGÉ) ($$$$) ★★★★½ A lighter, more subtle wine than the Columbia Valley, with a toastier nose and more apparent spicy oak.

RIESLING ($) ★★ Light, tart, apricot flavors.

H.P. ISAACS

woodward canyon

1983

Columbia Valley
Cabernet Sauvignon

Produced and bottled by Woodward Canyon Winery BW-WA-81, Lowden WA 99360
Alcohol by Volume 13.3%

WORDEN'S WASHINGTON WINERY
Spokane   (1980)
18,000 cases

Owner Jack Worden, a longtime fruit grower, has gone through a succession of winemakers, including Mike Conway of Latah Creek and Rollin Soles of Oregon's Crochad operation. The turnover has meant a rather inconsistent style for the wines, though overall quality has improved significantly since the early eighties. (Worden is now making the wines himself.) The winery has had some difficulties in establishing a market niche, but increasing emphasis has been put of late on light, fruity wines, including several pleasant blush-style wines, which have proved to be quite popular.

The winery is outside Spokane, not a grape-growing area, and all the grapes are purchased from Columbia and Yakima Valley vineyards—the majority from the excellent Moreman Vineyard near Pasco. Most of the wines are finished with some residual sweetness and even the reds are made in a soft, forward style, emphasizing fruit. Both the regular and Late Harvest Rieslings are very tasty (the Late Harvest is a sleeper, a very enticing wine at a ridiculously low price), and the various Gamay Beaujolais wines are among the best in their category, with bright flavors and crisp acidity. The leading red wine is a blend of Cabernet and Merlot—Worden likes the effects of blending, with the Merlot softening out the Cabernet. The wines are fairly inexpensive.

The newest marketing effort is the Seafare label, for those wines that the winery feels are particularly suitable with seafood. Of these, the Merlot is the most interesting—almost Beaujolais-like, with light raspberry fruit—though it's a little hard to picture as seafood wine.

CABERNET-MERLOT ($$) ★★½ A light style, with an intense strawberry nose, lots of fruit, and a slight pepperiness. Drink young.

CHARDONNAY ($$) ★★½ Fruity, light, tart, slight oak.

CHENIN BLANC ($) ★★★ Strong nose of apples and wildflowers, slightly sweet, quite soft.

FUMÉ BLANC ($$) ★★★ Definite bell pepper aromas, nicely balanced with a soft finish from French oak.

GAMAY BEAUJOLAIS ROSÉ ($) ★★★ Lovely color, strawberry fruit—delightful flavor and good tartness.

NOUVEAU BLUSH ($) ★★½ Strawberry nose with tart, zippy fruit.

RIESLING, JOHANNISBERG ($) ★★★ It has varied from straightforward, citrusy flavors to a full, peachy style—moderately sweet.

RIESLING, LATE HARVEST ($$) ★★★½ Lovely peach nose, very fresh, balanced, with medium sweetness.

SEAFARE CHARDONNAY ($$) ★½ Light, green flavors, not much interest.

SEAFARE MERLOT ($) ★★½   Beaujolais style, raspberry flavors, light, pleasant.

YAKIMA RIVER WINERY
Prosser   (1979)
18,000 cases

John Rauner loves big red wines, particularly those with a strong oak influence, and that personal preference shows in the wines he makes. Rauner, the owner and winemaker, is a transplanted Easterner and pipe fitter by trade, whose interest in Washington wine was first stimulated when he made wines at home in New York from Washington grapes. One of the older wineries in the Yakima Valley, Yakima River owns no vineyards, preferring to buy grapes from area growers with whom it can build long-term relationships.

There is little pretense in these wines; they are "made with the average consumer in mind," notes Rauner. In fact, they have been fairly rough and ready. Older notes indicate a depressing lack of consistent quality, but in the last few vintages the winery has shown signs of cleaning up its act, especially in the reds. A fairly dull Chardonnay has been dropped and more focus given to red wine. Rauner's current pet project is developing good Pinot Noir in the Yakima Valley—he feels problems with Washington Pinot have been due to poor clonal selection. He has settled on two clones he likes (including the Pommard, well established in Oregon), and initial results look pretty good, though as with Cabernet and Merlot, the use of oak is fairly heavy-handed.

Those who like big, oaky, tannic reds may find some of these wines very attractive, though they often lack depth and complexity. While the Cabernets seem just too tough, the more recent Merlots (like '85) have good fruit, though they are still big wines. There are some decent sweet dessert Rieslings, but here again, they seem to miss out on the fruit and balance that one would like to see. (There is also an occasional Ice Wine.) Moreover, the sweetest are quite expensive.

CABERNET SAUVIGNON ($$) ★★½ Oaky nose and flavors dominate, with some berry qualities. Burly, tannic, rough—but fairly simple.

CABERNET SAUVIGNON, RESERVE ($$$) ★★★ This spent thirty-two months in new oak and shows it. Extremely oaky, lots of vanilla in the nose, spicy, tannic—but not much fruit showing. Will age help?

FUMÉ BLANC ($$) ★★ Very herbaceous, bell pepper nose; aggressive, tart flavors—fairly rough. Good if you like this style.

MERLOT ($$) ★★★ This seems to be lightening up a bit in recent vintages and showing more balance. The '85 had lots of berry fruit, along with a good whack of oak.

PINOT NOIR ($$) ★★½ Nice cherry-oaky nose, lean and tart, with subdued fruit.

PINOT NOIR, WHITE ($) ★½ Pleasant, rhubarby flavors—sweet, clean.

RIESLING, DRY BERRY SELECT ($$$$) ★★★½ Quite yellow, with a spicy, honeyed apricot nose. Very sweet but not terribly rich. Expensive.

RIESLING, SELECT CLUSTER ($$$) ★★ Not as sweet as the Dry Berry, but plenty of sugar. A nice grapefruity nose—but it lacks richness.

ZILLAH OAKES WINERY *See* COVEY RUN VINTERS

WINERIES NO LONGER MAKING WINES
Caroway Vineyards
Cascade Cellars
Daquila Wines
Haviland Vintners
Puyallup Valley Winery
Rainier Valley Cellars

American Wines of the Northwest

10

IDAHO WINES AND WINERIES

CAMAS WINERY
Moscow   (1983)
1,500 cases

G rapes for this tiny winery come from Washington's huge Sagemoor Farms, so the wines don't necessarily represent an "Idaho style." Indeed, the winery is near the Washington border and rather closer to eastern Washington growing areas than to Idaho's Sunny Slope near Boise. The goal of owner-winemaker Stuart Scott (the winery is the Scott basement) is to make fairly light-bodied wines to be consumed young—and Scott likes a soft, slightly sweet style, even in Chardonnay. The most unusual bottling is the Hog Heaven Red, a blend of 60 percent cherry wine and 40 percent Merlot.

CABERNET SAUVIGNON ($) ★½   Light, woody, slightly herbal.
CHARDONNAY ($) ★★   Very oaky, hot, buttery—straightforward and simple.

COVEY RISE
Boise
500 cases

The winery's name is about to change (a result of a dispute with Washington's Covey Run), production is tiny, the owner runs a fish market in Boise, the wines are not generally available, and there is no "winery" (wines are made at another facility). But the Chardonnay under this label, from a small vineyard on the Snake River, is good enough to have attracted the attention of English importer Mark Savage, who is shipping it to the tough English market. Wines not tasted.

DESERT SUN WINERY
Nampa   (1987)
1,200 cases

Owner Brad Pintler is a farmer in the Snake Valley south of Nampa who has converted part of his sugar beet fields into vineyards. The first vintage was crushed at the Stowe Winery in Kuna, but Pintler plans to build his own facility. The first wines were clean and showed good varietal character, especially the Semillon in a fairly aggressive style.

RIESLING ($) ★★   Peachy, soft, clean, off-dry. Very pleasant.
SEMILLON ($) ★★½   Definite Semillon character, with a mixture of citrus and herbaceous fruit. Fairly dry, slightly hot.

DESERT SUN

IDAHO
SEMILLON
1987

Pintler Vineyard
Alcohol 12.6% by Volume

LOUIS FACELLI WINERY *See* PETROS WINERY

INDIAN CREEK
Kuna   (1987)
4,000 cases

Indian Creek's twenty-acre vineyard lies south of Boise, about ten miles east of the established Sunny Slope growing area, and was planted in 1982 to Riesling, Chardonnay, and Pinot Noir (a variety little grown in Idaho). Owner-winemaker Bill Stowe says the grapes grow equally well in his area, the only drawback being greater risk of frost damage in the spring and fall.

Stowe, a retired air force officer, developed a taste for wine (especially dry Riesling) while stationed in Germany, where he helped out in vineyard and winery. His brother Mike, co-winemaker, is a schoolteacher in Davis, California, where he has had a chance to attend enology and viticulture classes, and provides Stowe with technical assistance.

The dry Riesling, which Stowe says he makes "out of principle," is the most interesting wine. The other wines seem more problematic, lacking true varietal character, and Stowe admits he is still experimenting with his wine-making (the first Chardonnay was barrel-fermented, but he plans to go to tank fermentation, to emphasize the fruit). A second Pinot Noir, from the Stowe Vineyard, will be released in 1989.

CHARDONNAY (KUNA BUTTE) ($) ★½ Some apple fruit, but woody, leafy flavors—OK.

PINOT NOIR (KUNA BUTTE) ($) ½ This first effort misses the mark, with some off flavors, but the winery gets credit for making the effort with this varietal in Idaho.

RIESLING (STOWE) ($) ★★ Appley, simple, soft—finishes dry.

PETROS WINERY
Boise   (1986)

Petros, after an initial splash, is now out of business, though some wines are still available. The winery began life as the project of talented winemaker Louis Facelli, who made a reputation for fine Riesling and Chardonnay under a label bearing his name. Unfortunately, the winery was sold from underneath him to a group of investors, including former Ste. Chapelle winemaker Bill Broich, and renamed Spring Creek. The partnership fell apart under a storm of accusations and lawsuits, and partner Pete Eliopolous, a Boise investor, took control of the winery, which he renamed Petros, in 1987, only to close it under financial pressures in 1988.

CABERNET SAUVIGNON ($$) ★★★½ Dark, with an oaky-vanilla nose, lots of spicy oak, and decent fruit. Tannic, tart, rather rough, but it opens up. One of the Louis Facelli wines.

CHARDONNAY, EARLY SELECT ($) ★★ Very ripe apple nose, with a bit of mushroom, some viscous flavors—a bit hot.

RIESLING, JOHANNISBERG ($) ★★ Pleasant apple-candy nose, lightly sweet, fairly lively.

RIESLING, WHITE ($) ★½ Grapefruity nose, rather herbal on the palate, fairly sweet—not as interesting as the Johannisberg.

SAUVIGNON BLANC ($$) ★½ Light, steely, austere, tart.

PUCCI WINERY
Sandpoint   (1982)
2,000 cases

Sandpoint is several hundred miles to the north of the main grape-growing areas in Idaho (it's not far from Spokane), and the country is more suited to pine than grapevine. In fact, the grapes for these wines come from eastern Washington and from California. Very much a home winery, Pucci is run by Skip Pucci—who comes from a long line of winemakers—in his spare time, using largely homemade equipment. All the wines are fermented and aged in oak, which sets them apart in style from most others in the Northwest. Results have been variable so far.

CHARDONNAY (WASHINGTON) ($) ★ Flavor tends to be a bit cooked and tart, though there is some decent fruit.

RIESLING (WASHINGTON) ($) ★ Not much varietal character—quite light and dry.

ROSE CREEK VINEYARDS
Hagerman   (1984)
4,000 cases

Hagerman is in a picturesque section of the Snake Valley 100 miles southeast of Boise. The forty acres or so of small vineyards in the area are among the most southerly and warm-sited in the Northwest (the town isn't far from the Nevada border), but their high altitude, around 2,800 feet, keeps the fall temperatures cool and the grapes from getting overripe. The local vineyards (some only a few acres) have been developed by Rose Creek owner and winemaker Jamie Martin, who grew up in the area. Martin, who has a viticultural background, has a landscape business and has encouraged clients to plant small vineyards; he manages them and then uses the grapes at his tiny subterranean winery. Pinot Noir grapes come from Oregon and Cabernet Sauvignon from Washington to make the red wines—Martin is happy to go far afield to find what he feels are the best grapes.

The winemaking shows considerable promise. French oak is jammed into the winery, and the partially barrel-fermented Chardonnay is a forward wine with lots of spicy oak. These are not subtle wines (the unfiltered Cabernet is immense and tough), but they have lots of flavor and good balance, and show attention to quality. Idaho has suffered a bit from a reputation for small mom-and-pop wineries, but Rose Creek should be able to compete with the better Oregon and Washington wines; this is the first "boutique" Idaho winery with boutique quality.

CABERNET SAUVIGNON (WASHINGTON) ($$$) ★★★★
Very dark and thick, with herbal-berry-vanilla scents and great depth. Slightly hot. A most impressive first effort.

CHARDONNAY ($$) ★★★★ Ripe, oaky, pineapple nose, viscous, tart, solid. Lovely wine. Should help Idaho's reputation as Chardonnay country.

PINOT ROSÉ VIN GRIS ($$) ★★★ A temporary wine, preceding a red Pinot Noir, but very good anyway. Earthy Pinot fruit, fine backbone—might be a bit drier.

RIESLING ($) ★★½ Interesting peachy-almond nose, tart, off-dry.

ROSE CREEK MIST ($) ★★ Riesling with Cabernet for color. Slightly herbal, crisp, fruity.

STE. CHAPELLE WINERY
Caldwell (1976)
130,000 cases

For most intents and purposes, Ste. Chapelle *is* Idaho wine. Ste. Chapelle is an offshoot of the Symms family's large fruit business on Idaho's Sunny Slope along the Snake River, which underwrote the fledgling winemaking efforts of Bill Broich in the mid-seventies. The winery has grown quickly, helped along by considerable marketing muscle, and is now not only by far the largest winery in Idaho but one of the largest in the Northwest. Although the winery owns extensive vineyards (about 150 acres), it still buys lots of grapes from other growers, including several in eastern Washington.

The high altitude (around 2,500 feet) of this part of the Snake Valley ensures very cool night temperatures during the critical fall season, which preserves the essential acid content of the grapes even while they ripen. This slow ripening seems ideally suited to Chardonnay, Riesling, and Gewürztraminer. Ste. Chapelle under former winemaker Bill Broich made a reputation for excellent Chardonnay, in a big, oaky, ripe style that was very appealing, though the wines didn't age very gracefully. But as production expanded, quality didn't seem to keep up, and the wines, while clean and well made, haven't stood out in the last several years. The best deal has been a lighter and fruiter Chardonnay than the regular bottling, known variously as Blanc de Chardonnay and Canyon Chardonnay.

Broich has moved on, after problems with mislabeling the wines cost the winery some penalties from the Bureau of Alcohol, Tobacco, and Firearms (the mislabeling was quickly rectified). New winemaker Mimi Mook comes to Ste. Chapelle from J. Lohr Winery in California; her only plans for stylistic changes are with Chardonnay, where she would like to see more fruit and a crisper, less oaky style that will age better. The new Mook-made Reserve Chardonnay, rich and spicy, puts the winery back on the fast track for success with this varietal. She also plans to experiment with a dry but fruity Riesling. Plans call for a red Pinot Noir eventually, as new vineyards come into production—Mook is hopeful that Idaho Pinot can have something of the same success that Oregon Pinot has had, though the climate is hardly the same.

Besides pioneering fine table wine in Idaho, Ste. Chapelle has also made a splash with sparkling wine, produced by the bulk Charmat process (in which the second fermentation, to make the bubbles, takes place in pressurized tanks rather than individual bottles). Ste. Chapelle has the only Charmat line in the Northwest (the equipment is terrifically expensive), and it keeps expanding its production. Both Riesling and Chardonnay "Champagne" have been light and fruity and reasonably priced, and the winery has been hard pressed at times to keep up with demand. (A "Champagne Blush" has been added to the line now.)

Ste. Chapelle has recently introduced a separate label, Chapel Hill, for generic red, white, and blush table wines that the winery promises will be made from a preponderance of top-quality grape varieties (e.g., Chardonnay and Riesling for the white).

CABERNET SAUVIGNON (WASHINGTON) ($$) ★★½
An appealing oaky-vanilla nose, but the flavors are slightly vegetal, and there's no great depth.
CABERNET SAUVIGNON, CANYON ($) ★ Hot flavors, quite vegetal and out of balance.
CHAMPAGNE BLUSH ($$) ★½ Floral-herbal nose, decent fruit.
CHAMPAGNE CHARDONNAY ($$) ★★★ This is the best of these Charmat wines—a pleasant fresh-bread nose, with considerable crisp fruit. Fairly dry. Good value.
CHAMPAGNE RIESLING ($$) ★★ Light bubbles and a light peachy nose; clean, tart flavors. Only slightly sweet.
CHARDONNAY ($$) ★★★ Recent bottlings show a fruity, apple-bready nose, with crisp, understated flavors and a bit of viscosity.
CHARDONNAY, CANYON ($) ★★ Doesn't age long, but it has crisp, applelike fruit.
CHARDONNAY, RESERVE (SYMMS) ($$$) ★★★½ Rich, appley nose, with butterscotch underneath; lots of fruit and some complexity.

RIESLING ($) ★★½ Light, grapefruity nose, good tartness, barely off-dry.

RIESLING, LATE HARVEST ($$) ★★★ Lots of apple and spice flavor in a heavy style. Not as elegant as some.

STOWE WINERY *See* INDIAN CREEK

WESTON WINERY
Caldwell   (1982)
4,000 cases

Cheyne Weston left Ste. Chapelle, where he worked briefly, feeling that he could make just as good wine as the big boys. The small ten-acre vineyard is claimed to be, at 2,800 feet, the highest-altitude vineyard in the Northwest, though most in Idaho are quite high. While the vines are maturing, wines are being made with grapes from various Idaho and Oregon vineyards—as well as Cabernet Sauvignon from California. Weston, a former cinematographer, is an experimenter—one of his projects is an Idaho cooler called Blue Moon, made from Riesling, fresh peaches, and a bit of ginger for flavor. It's lighter and crisper than California coolers, and Weston figures it should appeal to those who enjoy more natural flavors.

The quality of the wines is variable, though both the Riesling and Chardonnay from Idaho grapes are flavorful in a straightforward fashion. The Chardonnay is barrel-fermented and aged in French oak and shows some promise. There is also a small quantity of Champagne-method sparkling wine. Prices are very reasonable.

CABERNET SAUVIGNON (AMERICAN) ($$) ★★   Cherry nose, soft, fruity—pleasant, but not much to it.

CHARDONNAY ($) ★★★   Very ripe apple nose with some toasty oak—balanced, viscous flavors in a forward, fruity style. Not complicated, but quite nice.

GEWÜRZTRAMINER ($) ★½   Slightly sweet, with pleasant spice and soft fruit.

RIESLING ($) ★★★   Pleasant appley, flowery nose with medium-sweet flavors, clean, fresh.

WINERY AT SPRING CREEK   *See* PETROS WINERY

WINERY NO LONGER MAKING WINE
Petros Winery

APPENDIX A:
RECOMMENDED WINES, BY VARIETAL
(WINES WITH RATINGS OF 3.0 OR ABOVE)

$	$7 OR LESS
$$	$7 TO $12
$$$	$12 TO $20
$$$$	MORE THAN $20

3.0	VERY GOOD QUALITY, WITH SOME DISTINCTION
4.0	EXCELLENT, AMONG THE BEST IN ITS CLASS
5.0	OUTSTANDING, WORLD-CLASS, UNIQUE QUALITIES

CABERNET SAUVIGNON

WINERY	STATE	WINE	PRICE	RATING
Columbia	WA	Cabernet Sauvignon (Red Willow)	$$$	5.0
Leonetti	WA	Cabernet Sauvignon	$$$$	5.0
Leonetti	WA	Cabernet Sauvignon, Reserve	$$$$	5.0
Quilceda Creek	WA	Cabernet Sauvignon	$$$	5.0
Woodward Canyon	WA	Cabernet Sauvignon	$$$$	5.0

WINERY	STATE	WINE	PRICE	RATING
Columbia	WA	Cabernet Sauvignon (Sagemoor)	$$$	4.5
Hogue	WA	Cabernet Sauvignon Reserve	$$$$	4.5
Leonetti	WA	Cabernet Sauvignon (Seven Hills)	$$$$	4.5
Alpine	OR	Cabernet Sauvignon, Vintage Select	$$$	4.0
Arbor Crest	WA	Cabernet Sauvignon	$$$	4.0
Barnard Griffin	WA	Cabernet Sauvignon	$$$	4.0
Chateau Ste. Michelle	WA	Cabernet Sauvignon	$$	4.0
Chateau Ste. Michelle	WA	Cabernet Sauvignon, Reserve	$$$	4.0
Columbia	WA	Cabernet Sauvignon (Otis)	$$$	4.0
Hinzerling	WA	Cabernet Sauvignon	$$$	4.0
Kiona	WA	Cabernet Sauvignon	$$$	4.0
Mercer Ranch	WA	Cabernet Sauvignon (Mercer)	$$$	4.0
Neuharth	WA	Cabernet Sauvignon	$$	4.0
Rose Creek	ID	Cabernet Sauvignon	$$$	4.0
Paul Thomas	WA	Cabernet Sauvignon	$$$	4.0
Columbia	WA	Cabernet Sauvignon	$$	3.5
Columbia Crest	WA	Cabernet Sauvignon	$$	3.5
Covey Run	WA	Cabernet Sauvignon	$$$	3.5
French Creek	WA	Cabernet Sauvignon	$$	3.5
Hinzerling	WA	Cabernet-Merlot	$$	3.5
Mercer Ranch	WA	Cabernet Sauvignon (Sharp Sisters)	$$$	3.5
Petros	ID	Cabernet Sauvignon (Facelli)	$$	3.5
Quarry Lake	WA	Cabernet Sauvignon	$$	3.5
Redford	WA	Cabernet-Merlot	$$	3.5
Valley View	OR	Cabernet Sauvignon	$$	3.5
Bookwalter	WA	Cabernet Sauvignon	$$$	3.0
Champs de Brionne	WA	Cabernet-Merlot	$$	3.0
French Creek	WA	Cabernet Sauvignon, Reserve	$$$	3.0
Hogue	WA	Cabernet Sauvignon	$$$	3.0

Appendix A

WINERY	STATE	WINE	PRICE	RATING
Snoqualmie	WA	Cabernet Sauvignon	$$	3.0
Waterbrook	WA	Cabernet Sauvignon	$$$	3.0
Yakima River	WA	Cabernet Sauvignon, Reserve	$$$	3.0

CHARDONNAY

WINERY	STATE	WINE	PRICE	RATING
Eyrie	OR	Chardonnay	$$$	5.0
Woodward Canyon	WA	Chardonnay (Columbia)	$$$	5.0
Cameron	OR	Chardonnay, Reserve	$$$	4.5
Tualatin	OR	Chardonnay, Reserve	$$	4.5
Woodward Canyon	WA	Chardonnay (Roza Bergé)	$$$$	4.5
Adams	OR	Chardonnay, Reserve	$$$	4.0
Adelsheim	OR	Chardonnay (Yamhill)	$$	4.0
Barnard Griffin	WA	Chardonnay	$$$	4.0
Bonair	WA	Chardonnay (Puryear)	$$	4.0
Cameron	OR	Chardonnay	$$	4.0
Chinook	WA	Chardonnay, Reserve	$$$	4.0
Covey Run	WA	Chardonnay (Willard Farms)	$$	4.0
Hogue	WA	Chardonnay, Reserve	$$	4.0
Kiona	WA	Chardonnay	$$	4.0
Ponzi	OR	Chardonnay	$$	4.0
Rose Creek	ID	Chardonnay	$$	4.0
Shafer	OR	Chardonnay	$$	4.0
Sokol Blosser	OR	Chardonnay, Reserve	$$$	4.0
Paul Thomas	WA	Chardonnay, Private Reserve	$$$	4.0
Adams	OR	Chardonnay	$$	3.5
Amity	OR	Chardonnay, Reserve	$$$	3.5
Bethel Heights	OR	Chardonnay	$$	3.5
Blackwood Canyon	WA	Chardonnay	$$	3.5
Chateau Ste. Michelle	WA	Chardonnay (Cold Creek)	$$$	3.5
Columbia	WA	Chardonnay (Wyckoff)	$$$	3.5
Elk Cove	OR	Chardonnay, Reserve	$$$	3.5

WINERY	STATE	WINE	PRICE	RATING
Girardet	OR	Chardonnay	$$	3.5
Hogue	WA	Chardonnay	$$	3.5
Horizon's Edge	WA	Chardonnay (Fair Acre)	$$$	3.5
Knudsen Erath	OR	Chardonnay, Vintage Select	$$	3.5
Neuharth	WA	Chardonnay	$$	3.5
Oakwood	WA	Chardonnay	$$	3.5
Rex Hill	OR	Chardonnay (Willamette)	$$$	3.5
Ste. Chapelle	ID	Chardonnay, Reserve (Symms)	$$$	3.5
Stewart	WA	Chardonnay	$$	3.5
Paul Thomas	WA	Chardonnay	$$	3.5
Valley View	OR	Chardonnay	$$	3.5
Wasson Brothers	OR	Chardonnay	$$$	3.5
Waterbrook	WA	Chardonnay	$$	3.5
Adelsheim	OR	Chardonnay (Oregon)	$$	3.0
Alpine	OR	Chardonnay	$$$	3.0
Amity	OR	Chardonnay	$$	3.0
Arbor Crest	WA	Chardonnay (Sagemoor)	$$	3.0
Autumn Wind	OR	Chardonnay	$$	3.0
Bonair	WA	Chardonnay (Outlook)	$$	3.0
Broadley	OR	Chardonnay	$$	3.0
Chateau Ste. Michelle	WA	Chardonnay, Reserve	$$$	3.0
Chinook	WA	Chardonnay	$$	3.0
Columbia	WA	Chardonnay	$$	3.0
Columbia Crest	WA	Chardonnay	$$	3.0
Cooper Mountain	OR	Chardonnay	$$	3.0
Covey Run	WA	Chardonnay	$$	3.0
Flynn Vineyards	OR	Chardonnay	$$	3.0
Gordon Brothers	WA	Chardonnay	$$	3.0
Henry	OR	Chardonnay	$$	3.0
Hood River	OR	Chardonnay	$$$	3.0
Hoodsport	WA	Chardonnay	$$	3.0
Horizon's Edge	WA	Chardonnay (McKinnon)	$$$	3.0
Knudsen Erath	OR	Chardonnay	$	3.0
Oak Knoll	OR	Chardonnay	$$	3.0
Preston	WA	Chardonnay	$$	3.0

Appendix A

WINERY	STATE	WINE	PRICE	RATING
Ste. Chapelle	ID	Chardonnay	$$	3.0
Salishan	WA	Chardonnay	$$	3.0
Sokol Blosser	OR	Chardonnay (Yamhill)	$$	3.0
Paul Thomas	WA	Chardonnay	$$	3.0
Tualatin	OR	Chardonnay	$$	3.0
Tyee	OR	Chardonnay	$$$	3.0
Veritas	OR	Chardonnay	$$$	3.0
Weston	ID	Chardonnay	$	3.0
Yamhill Valley	OR	Chardonnay	$$$	3.0

CHENIN BLANC

WINERY	STATE	WINE	PRICE	RATING
Salishan	WA	Chenin Blanc, Dry	$	4.0
Hogue	WA	Chenin Blanc	$	3.5
Latah Creek	WA	Chenin Blanc	$	3.5
Latah Creek	WA	Chenin Blanc, Reserve	$	3.5
Snoqualmie	WA	Chenin Blanc	$	3.5
Paul Thomas	WA	Chenin Blanc	$$	3.5
Blackwood Canyon	WA	Chenin Blanc, Dry	$$	3.0
Columbia Crest	WA	Chenin Blanc	$	3.0
Eola Hills	OR	Chenin Blanc	$	3.0
Serendipity	OR	Chenin Blanc	$	3.0
Worden's	WA	Chenin Blanc	$	3.0

GEWÜRZTRAMINER

WINERY	STATE	WINE	PRICE	RATING
Hinzerling	WA	Die Sonne (Gewürz-traminer)	$$$	4.5
Airlie	OR	Gewürztraminer	$	3.5
Alpine	OR	Gewürztraminer	$$	3.5
Amity	OR	Gewürztraminer	$$	3.5
Callahan Ridge	OR	Gewürztraminer (Elkton)	$	3.5
Elk Cove	OR	Gewürztraminer, Late Harvest	$$$	3.5
Henry	OR	Gewürztraminer	$$	3.5
Hinzerling	WA	Gewürztraminer	$	3.5

WINERY	STATE	WINE	PRICE	RATING
Mont Elise	WA	Gewürztraminer (Mont Elise)	$	3.5
Pellier	OR	Gewürztraminer	$	3.5
Shafer	OR	Gewürztraminer	$	3.5
Woodburne	WA	Gewürztraminer	$$	3.5
Airlie	OR	Gewürztraminer, Late Harvest	$$	3.0
Elk Cove	OR	Gewürztraminer	$	3.0
Hinman	OR	Gewürztraminer	$	3.0
Pacific Crest	WA	Gewürztraminer, Late Harvest	$$	3.0
Staton Hills	WA	Gewürztraminer	$	3.0
Tyee	OR	Gewürztraminer, Reserve	$$	3.0
Wasson Brothers	OR	Gewürztraminer	$	3.0

LEMBERGER

WINERY	STATE	WINE	PRICE	RATING
Kiona	WA	Lemberger	$$	4.0
Mercer Ranch	WA	Limburger (Lemberger)	$$	4.0
Covey Run	WA	Lemberger	$	3.5
French Creek	WA	Lemberger, Reserve	$$	3.5

MERLOT

WINERY	STATE	WINE	PRICE	RATING
Paul Thomas	WA	Merlot	$$	4.5
Woodward Canyon	WA	Charbonneau (70 percent Merlot)	$$$$	4.5
Chateau Ste. Michelle	WA	Merlot, Chateau Reserve	$$$	4.0
Latah Creek	WA	Merlot	$$	4.0
Leonetti	WA	Merlot	$$$	4.0
Arbor Crest	WA	Merlot (Bacchus)	$$	3.5
Chateau Ste. Michelle	WA	Merlot	$$	3.5
Chinook	WA	Merlot	$$	3.5

WINERY	STATE	WINE	PRICE	RATING
Gordon Brothers	WA	Merlot	$$	3.5
Hogue	WA	Merlot	$$$	3.5
L'École No. 41	WA	Merlot	$$$	3.5
Valley View	OR	Merlot	$$	3.5
Waterbrook	WA	Merlot	$$	3.5
Columbia	WA	Merlot	$$	3.0
Columbia Crest	WA	Merlot	$$	3.0
Covey Run	WA	Merlot	$$	3.0
Hoodsport	WA	Merlot	$$	3.0
Knudsen Erath	OR	Merlot	$	3.0
Lost Mountain	WA	Merlot	$$	3.0
Neuharth	WA	Merlot	$$	3.0
Quarry Lake	WA	Merlot	$$	3.0
Snoqualmie	WA	Merlot, Reserve	$$	3.0
Yakima River	WA	Merlot	$$	3.0
Yakima River	WA	Merlot (Ciel du Cheval)	$$	3.0

MÜLLER-THURGAU

WINERY	STATE	WINE	PRICE	RATING
Airlie	OR	Müller-Thurgau	$	3.5
Johnson Creek	WA	Müller-Thurgau	$	3.5
Tualatin	OR	Müller-Thurgau	$	3.5
Bainbridge Island	WA	Müller-Thurgau	$	3.0
Mount Baker	WA	Müller-Thurgau	$	3.0
Serendipity	OR	Müller-Thurgau	$$	3.0
Siskiyou	OR	Müller-Thurgau	$	3.0

MUSCAT

WINERY	STATE	WINE	PRICE	RATING
Mercer Ranch	WA	Muscat Canelli	$$	4.0
Covey Run	WA	Morio-Muskat	$	3.5
Eyrie	OR	Muscat Ottonel	$$	3.5
Latah Creek	WA	Muscat Canelli	$	3.5
Stewart	WA	Muscat Canelli	$$	3.5
Paul Thomas	WA	Muscat Canelli	$$	3.5

Appendix A

WINERY	STATE	WINE	PRICE	RATING
Arbor Crest	WA	Muscat Canelli	$$	3.0
Columbia	WA	Muscat	$	3.0
Snoqualmie	WA	Muscat Canelli	$	3.0
Tucker	WA	Muscat Canelli	$	3.0

PINOT GRIS

WINERY	STATE	WINE	PRICE	RATING
Adelsheim	OR	Pinot Gris	$$	4.0
Eyrie	OR	Pinot Gris	$$	4.0
Lange	OR	Pinot Gris	$$	4.0
Ponzi	OR	Pinot Gris	$$	4.0
Rex Hill	OR	Pinot Gris	$$	4.0
Tyee	OR	Pinot Gris	$$	3.0

PINOT NOIR

WINERY	STATE	WINE	PRICE	RATING
Adelsheim	OR	Pinot Noir, Elizabeth's Reserve (Yamhill)	$$$	5.0
Amity	OR	Pinot Noir, Reserve	$$$$	5.0
Eyrie	OR	Pinot Noir, Reserve	$$$$	5.0
Knudsen Erath	OR	Pinot Noir, Vintage Select	$$$	5.0
Ponzi	OR	Pinot Noir, Reserve	$$$	5.0
Adelsheim	OR	Pinot Noir (Polk)	$$$	4.5
Amity	OR	Pinot Noir (Estate)	$$$	4.5
Bethel Heights	OR	Pinot Noir	$$$	4.5
Bethel Heights	OR	Pinot Noir, Reserve	$$$	4.5
Cameron	OR	Pinot Noir	$$$	4.5
Cameron	OR	Pinot Noir, Reserve	$$$	4.5
Elk Cove	OR	Pinot Noir (Wind Hill)	$$$	4.5
Eyrie	OR	Pinot Noir	$$$	4.5
Rex Hill	OR	Pinot Noir (Archibald)	$$$$	4.5
Rex Hill	OR	Pinot Noir (Maresh)	$$$	4.5
Adams	OR	Pinot Noir	$$$	4.0
Adams	OR	Pinot Noir, Reserve	$$$	4.0
Broadley	OR	Pinot Noir, Reserve	$$	4.0

Appendix A

WINERY	STATE	WINE	PRICE	RATING
Oak Knoll	OR	Pinot Noir, Vintage Select	$$$	4.0
Panther Creek	OR	Pinot Noir	$$$	4.0
Rex Hill	OR	Pinot Noir (Medici)	$$$	4.0
Rex Hill	OR	Pinot Noir (Wirtz)	$$$	4.0
Sokol Blosser	OR	Pinot Noir (Hyland)	$$$	4.0
Sokol Blosser	OR	Pinot Noir (Red Hills)	$$$	4.0
Sokol Blosser	OR	Pinot Noir, Reserve (Red Hills)	$$$	4.0
Tualatin	OR	Pinot Noir, Reserve	$$$	4.0
Veritas	OR	Pinot Noir	$$$	4.0
Yamhill Valley	OR	Pinot Noir	$$$	4.0
Amity	OR	Pinot Noir	$$	3.5
Arterberry	OR	Pinot Noir, Reserve (Red Hills)	$$$	3.5
Elk Cove	OR	Pinot Noir (Estate)	$$$	3.5
Evesham Wood	OR	Pinot Noir	$$	3.5
Flynn	OR	Pinot Noir	$$	3.5
Glen Creek	OR	Pinot Noir, Whole Cluster	$	3.5
Knudsen Erath	OR	Pinot Noir (Willamette)	$$	3.5
Ponzi	OR	Pinot Noir	$$	3.5
Rex Hill	OR	Pinot Noir (Willamette)	$$$	3.5
Salishan	WA	Pinot Noir	$$	3.5
Amity	OR	Pinot Noir Nouveau	$	3.0
Broadley	OR	Pinot Noir	$$	3.0
Chateau Benoit	OR	Pinot Noir	$$	3.0
Chateau Ste. Michelle	WA	Pinot Noir	$$	3.0
Elk Cove	OR	Pinot Noir (Dundee Hills)	$$$	3.0
Eola Hills	OR	Pinot Noir	$$$	3.0
Glen Creek	OR	Pinot Noir	$$$	3.0
Oak Knoll	OR	Pinot Noir	$$	3.0
Pellier	OR	Pinot Noir	$$	3.0
Rex Hill	OR	Pinot Noir (Dundee Hills)	$$$	3.0
Serendipity	OR	Pinot Noir	$$	3.0
Shafer	OR	Pinot Noir	$$$	3.0
Staton Hills	WA	Pinot Noir (Oregon)	$$	3.0

WINERY	STATE	WINE	PRICE	RATING
Tyee	OR	Pinot Noir	$$$	3.0
Wasson Brothers	OR	Pinot Noir	$$$	3.0
Woodburne	WA	Pinot Noir	$$	3.0

RIESLING

WINERY	STATE	WINE	PRICE	RATING
Arbor Crest	WA	Riesling, Late Harvest	$$$	5.0
Covey Run	WA	Riesling Ice Wine	$$$$	5.0
Stewart	WA	Riesling, Late Harvest	$$$	5.0
Chateau Ste. Michelle	WA	Riesling, Late Harvest (Hahn Hill)	$$$	4.5
Chateau Ste. Michelle	WA	Riesling, Select Cluster	$$$	4.5
Blackwood Canyon	WA	Riesling, Late Harvest	$$	4.0
Blackwood Canyon	WA	Riesling, Ultra Late Harvest	$$$	4.0
Cameron	OR	Riesling, *Botrytis* "Eugenia"	$$$$	4.0
Covey Run	WA	Riesling, White (Mahre)	$$	4.0
Covey Run	WA	Riesling, White (Whiskey Canyon)	$$	4.0
Hogue	WA	Riesling, Late Harvest (Markin)	$$	4.0
Langguth	WA	Riesling, Select Cluster	$$$	4.0
Mount Baker	WA	Riesling, Select Cluster	$$$	4.0
Ponzi	OR	Riesling, Dry	$	4.0
Stewart	WA	Riesling, Johannisberg	$	4.0
Paul Thomas	WA	Riesling	$$	4.0
Alpine	OR	Riesling	$$	3.5
Barnard Griffin	WA	Riesling	$$	3.5
Bookwalter	WA	Riesling	$	3.5
Chateau Ste. Michelle	WA	Riesling	$	3.5
Hinzerling	WA	Riesling, Late Harvest	$$	3.5
Kiona	WA	Riesling, Dry	$	3.5
Kiona	WA	Riesling, Late Harvest	$$	3.5

WINERY	STATE	WINE	PRICE	RATING
Knudsen Erath	OR	Riesling, Vintage Select	$$	3.5
Worden's	WA	Riesling, Late Harvest	$$	3.5
Yakima River	WA	Riesling, Dry Berry Select	$$$$	3.5
Arterberry	OR	Riesling, Vintage Select	$$	3.0
Bethel Heights	OR	Riesling	$$	3.0
Bonair	WA	Riesling	$	3.0
Elk Cove	OR	Riesling, Late Harvest	$$$	3.0
French Creek	WA	Riesling Ice Wine	$$$	3.0
Girardet	OR	Riesling	$	3.0
Hillcrest	OR	Riesling	$	3.0
Hinman	OR	Riesling	$	3.0
Hogue	WA	Riesling	$	3.0
Kiona	WA	Riesling	$	3.0
Oakwood	WA	Riesling	$	3.0
Pacific Crest	WA	Riesling	$	3.0
Preston	WA	Riesling, Select Harvest	$$	3.0
Quarry Lake	WA	Riesling	$	3.0
Salishan	WA	Riesling, Dry	$$	3.0
Seven Hills	WA	Riesling	$	3.0
Snoqualmie	WA	Riesling, Late Harvest	$$	3.0
Ste. Chapelle	ID	Riesling, Late Harvest	$$	3.0
Wenatchee Valley	WA	Riesling	$	3.0
Weston	ID	Riesling	$	3.0
Worden's	WA	Riesling, Johannisberg	$	3.0

SAUVIGNON BLANC (FUMÉ BLANC)

WINERY	STATE	WINE	PRICE	RATING
Hogue	WA	Fumé Blanc	$$	4.0
Arbor Crest	WA	Sauvignon Blanc	$$	3.5
Chateau Ste. Michelle	WA	Sauvignon Blanc	$	3.5
Covey Run	WA	La Caille de Fumé	$	3.5
Paul Thomas	WA	Sauvignon Blanc	$$	3.5
Preston	WA	Fumé Blanc	$$	3.5

Appendix A

WINERY	STATE	WINE	PRICE	RATING
Barnard Griffin	WA	Fumé Blanc	$$	3.0
Cavatappi	WA	Sauvignon Blanc	$$	3.0
Chateau Benoit	OR	Sauvignon Blanc	$$	3.0
Chinook	WA	Sauvignon Blanc	$$	3.0
Hood River	OR	Sauvignon Blanc	$$	3.0
Quarry Lake	WA	Sauvignon Blanc	$	3.0
Shafer	OR	Sauvignon Blanc	$$	3.0
Snoqualmie	WA	Fumé Blanc	$$	3.0
Staton Hills	WA	Sauvignon Blanc	$$	3.0
Waterbrook	WA	Sauvignon Blanc	$$	3.0
Worden's	WA	Fumé Blanc	$$	3.0

SEMILLON

WINERY	STATE	WINE	PRICE	RATING
Blackwood Canyon	WA	Semillon	$$	4.0
Chateau Ste. Michelle	WA	Semillon	$	3.5
Columbia	WA	Semillon	$	3.5
Columbia Crest	WA	Semillon	$	3.0
Latah Creek	WA	Semillon	$	3.0
Snoqualmie	WA	Semillon	$	3.0

SPARKLING WINE

WINERY	STATE	WINE	PRICE	RATING
Hogue	WA	Brut	$$$	4.0
Newton and Newton (Whittlesey-Mark)	WA	Brut (Oregon)	$$$	4.0
Chateau Benoit	OR	Blanc de Blancs	$$$	3.5
Chateau Ste. Michelle	WA	Blanc de Noir Brut	$$$	3.5
Knudsen Erath	OR	Brut (Oregon)	$$$	3.5
Newton and Newton (Whittlesey-Mark)	WA	Rosé (Oregon)	$$$	3.5
Chateau Benoit	OR	Brut	$$$	3.0
Horizon's Edge	WA	Champagne	$$$	3.0

WINERY	STATE	WINE	PRICE	RATING
Mont Elise	WA	Blanc de Noir Brut	$$$	3.0
Ste. Chapelle	ID	Champagne, Chardonnay	$$	3.0

FRUIT AND BERRY WINE

WINERY	STATE	WINE	PRICE	RATING
Hoodsport	WA	Raspberry	$	4.0
Paul Thomas	WA	Bartlett Pear, Dry	$	4.0
Paul Thomas	WA	Raspberry	$$	4.0
Wasson Brothers	OR	Raspberry	$	4.0
Oak Knoll	OR	Raspberry	$	3.5
Shallon	OR	Peach	$$	3.5
Bainbridge Island	WA	Strawberry	$$	3.0
Bjelland	OR	Wild Blackberry	$	3.0
Hoodsport	WA	Loganberry	$	3.0
Oak Knoll	OR	Blackberry	$	3.0
Shallon	OR	Blackberry	$$	3.0
Wasson Brothers	OR	Blackberry	$	3.0

ODDS AND ENDS

WINERY	STATE	WINE	PRICE	RATING
Bainbridge Island	WA	Siegerrebe	$$$	4.0
Bethel Heights	OR	Pinot Noir Blanc	$	3.5
Girardet	OR	Vin Rouge, Reserve	$$	3.5
Mount Baker	WA	Madeline Angevine, Reserve	$$	3.5
Rex Hill	OR	Encore	?	3.5
Adams	OR	Portland's House Wine	$	3.0
Amity	OR	Oregon Blush	$	3.0
Cameron	OR	Red Table	$	3.0
Girardet	OR	Vin Rouge	$	3.0
Kiona	WA	Merlot Rosé	$	3.0
Rose Creek	ID	Pinot Rosé Vin Gris	$$	3.0
Warden's	WA	Gomay Beaujolais Rosé	$	3.0

APPENDIX B: AWARDS

The Wine Festival of the Enological Society of the Pacific Northwest, held in Seattle, is the largest Northwest-only wine competition, and the Oregon State Fair competition (open only to entries from Oregon) is the most important for that state's wines. Both include both local and outside judges. The 1988 results are included here to give the consumer a reference to award-winning wines, although the author does not agree with all the results. Only gold and silver medal winners are listed, and it should be noted that the Enological Society allows only vinifera entries.

Wine judgings are a crap shoot. A great deal depends on the makeup of the judging panel, the prejudices that each judge brings, and the interaction of the different personalities. Northwest wineries have complained consistently, and with merit, that judges from the California industry, no matter how professional, judge Northwest wines by California standards, and therefore frequently "miss the point" of a wine. In addition, some judgings are very liberal with awards (so that a bronze medal becomes almost meaningless), and others quite stingy. The idiosyncrasies of wine judgings are reflected in the widely varying results: Most wineries enter as often as they can, in hopes of hitting an occasional winner. It's a very rare wine indeed that does well in every competition.

ENOLOGICAL SOCIETY OF THE PACIFIC NORTHWEST WINE FESTIVAL, AUGUST 1988

GRAND PRIZES

Gordon Brothers Merlot 1986
Paul Thomas Chardonnay Reserve 1986

GOLD

Amity Estate Pinot Noir 1985
Gordon Brothers Merlot 1986
Hogue Reserve Chardonnay 1986
Hogue Fumé Blanc 1987
Hogue Johannisberg Riesling 1987
Knudsen Erath Vintage Select Pinot Noir 1986
Langguth Late Harvest Johannisberg Riesling 1987
Mercer Ranch Cabernet Sauvignon 1985
Rose Creek Cabernet Sauvignon 1985
Ste. Chapelle Reserve Chardonnay (Symms) 1986
Snoqualmie Late Harvest White Riesling 1987
Tagaris Johannisberg Riesling 1987
Paul Thomas Reserve Chardonnay 1986
Paul Thomas Dry Riesling 1987
Woodward Canyon Cabernet Sauvignon 1985
Worden's Chenin Blanc 1986

SILVER

Airlie Müller-Thurgau 1987
Alpine Chardonnay 1987
Alpine White Riesling 1987
Amity Dry Riesling 1987
Arbor Crest Select Late Harvest Johannisberg Riesling 1987
Arbor Crest Sauvignon Blanc 1987
Bethel Heights Pinot Noir 1986
Blackwood Canyon Chardonnay 1986
Cascade Crest Johannisberg Riesling 1987
Chateau Ste. Michelle Sauvignon Blanc 1986
Columbia Crest Merlot 1984
Covey Run Merlot 1985
Covey Run Morio-Muskat 1987
Covey Run *Botrytis* Affected White Riesling 1986
Desert Sun Semillon 1987
Elk Cove Gewürztraminer 1987
Henry *Botrytis* Affected White Riesling 1987
Hillcrest Riesling 1984
Hoodsport Gewürztraminer 1987
Hoodsport Johannisberg Riesling 1987
Kiona Chenin Blanc 1987

Mount Baker Madeline Angevine 1987
Mount Baker Müller-Thurgau 1987
Neuharth Cabernet Sauvignon 1986
Neuharth Johannisberg Riesling 1987
Oak Knoll White Riesling 1987
Pacific Crest Late Harvest Gewürztraminer 1986
Preston Fumé Blanc 1986
Quilceda Creek Cabernet Sauvignon 1984
St. Josef's Weinkeller Cabernet Sauvignon 1984
St. Josef's Weinkeller "L'Esprit" Gewürztraminer 1987
St. Josef's Weinkeller Pinot Noir 1985
Shafer Gewürztraminer 1987
Staton Hills Pinot Noir 1986
Stewart Late Harvest White Riesling 1987
Paul Thomas Chardonnay 1987
Tyee Gewürztraminer 1987
Tyee Pinot Gris 1987
Woodward Canyon Chardonnay (Columbia) 1987

OREGON STATE FAIR WINE COMPETITION, AUGUST 1988

GOLD

Henry Late Harvest White Riesling 1987 (Governor's Trophy)
Knudsen Erath Vintage Select Pinot Noir 1986
Laurel Ridge Reserve Sauvignon Blanc (Finn Hill) 1987
Wasson Brothers Chardonnay 1986
Wasson Brothers Raspberry (Governor's Trophy)

SILVER

Airlie Müller-Thurgau 1987
Bethel Heights Pinot Noir 1986
Bridgeview "Inspiration" Red Table
Bridgeview Winemaker's Reserve Pinot Noir 1986
Broadley Reserve Pinot Noir 1986
Elk Cove Commander's Cabernet (Dundee Hills) 1985
Elk Cove Pinot Noir (Wind Hill) 1986

Elk Cove Estate Reserve Pinot Noir 1986
Eola Hills Chenin Blanc 1987
Forgeron Pinot Noir 1985
Girardet Chardonnay 1987
Girardet White Riesling 1986
Henry Reserve Chardonnay 1985
Hillcrest Select Harvest White Riesling 1985
Honeywood "Twin Harvest" Peach and Riesling
Knudsen Erath Cabernet Sauvignon 1986
Lange Pinot Gris 1987
Ponzi White Riesling 1987
St. Josef's Weinkeller "L'Esprit" Gewürztraminer 1987
Serendipity Maréchal Foch 1987
Shafer Sauvignon Blanc 1985
Shafer White Riesling 1986
Sokol Blosser Reserve Chardonnay 1986
Sokol Blosser Müller-Thurgau 1987
Tyee Pinot Gris 1987
Wasson Brothers Boysenberry
Wasson Brothers Early Muscat 1987
Wasson Brothers Strawberry

INDEX

Adams, Leon, 40, 43
Adams, Peter and Carol, 139
Adams Vineyard Winery, 139
Adelsheim, David, 47, 141
Adelsheim Vineyard, 141–142
Airlie Winery, 144–145
Aligoté, 102–103
  Covey Run, 273–274
Allen, Don, 282
Allison, Victor, 43
Alpine Vineyards, 145–147
Alsace region (France), 42, 53, 54, 55, 88, 93
American Wine Growers, 42, 43, 44
Amity Vineyards, 28–30, 61, 147–149
Ankeny Vineyards Winery, 149–150
Arbor Crest, 242–244
Arterberry, Fred, Jr., 151
Arterberry Cellars, 151–152
Ashland Hills Winery, 152

Associated Vintners, *see* Columbia Winery
Autumn Wind Vineyard, 152–153
awards for wine, 376–379

Bacchus Vineyards, 44
Bainbridge Island Winery, 244–246
Balcom, Maury, 319
Barnard, Deborah, 246
Barnard Griffin Winery, 246–247
Baty, Dan, 268
Beaulieu Vineyard, 43
Beaver Gold, Ellendale, 170
Benham, Scott, 331
Bentryn, Gerard and Joan, 244
Bethel Heights Vineyard, 154–155
Big Fir Winery, 241

Index 381

Index

Index 385

Index 387

Index

Maison Joseph Drouhin, 167
Mansfield, Richard, 160
Manz, Michael, 307
Marcil, Wayne, 316
Maréchal Foch, Serendipity,
  219, 220
Marker, Jon, 194
Martin, Jamie, 356
Martin, Lester, 202
Martini, Louis M., 230
Maywine, Latah Creek, 298
Mead, Ellendale, 170–171
Meador, Doug, 249
Mercer, Don, 303–304
Mercer Ranch Vineyards, 82,
  303–304, 320
Merlot, 53, 65, 68, 72, 78,
  90–91
  Adelsheim, 142–143
  Alpine, 145–147
  Arbor Crest, 91, 243
  Chateau Ste. Michelle, 91,
    261
  Chinook, 91, 263, 264
  Columbia, 270
  Columbia Crest, 265, 266
  Columbia River Cellars,
    317
  Covey Run, 273, 275
  Facelli, 276
  food and, 120
  French Creek, 280
  Gordon Brothers, 91, 280,
    281
  Henry Estate, 185
  Hinzerling, 283
  Hogue, 91, 286
  Hoodsport, 288
  Johnson Creek, 293
  Kiona, 295
  Knudsen Erath, 195, 196
  Latah Creek, 91, 297, 298
  L'École No. 41, 299
  Leonetti, 91, 300, 301

Lost Mountain, 302
Neuharth, 310
Oakwood Cellars, 312
Salmon Bay, 326
Snoqualmie, 328
Paul Thomas, 91, 335, 336
Valley View, 91, 234
Waterbrook, 91, 341
Woodward Canyon, 91
Worden's Washington, 348
Yakima River, 349
Mirassou, Mitch, 207
Mirassou Cellars of Oregon
  (Pellier), 207–208
Mission Mountain, 290
Montalieu, Laurent, 158
Mont Elise Vineyards (Bingen
  Wine Cellars), 4, 44, 192,
  305–306
Montinore Vineyards, 200–202
Mook, Mimi, 358
Moore, James, 49
Moore, Mike, 249
Morio-Muskat, 92
  Covey Run, 273, 274, 275
Mountain Dome Winery,
  307
Mount Baker Vineyards,
  307–309
Mt. Hood Winery, 202
Mulhausen, Zane, 202
Mulhausen Vineyards, 202
Müller-Thurgau, 74, 78,
  91–92
  Airlie, 144–145
  Autumn Wind, 152–153
  Bainbridge Island, 245
  Bridgeview, 157–158
  Chateau Benoit, 163–164
  food and, 120
  Foris, 178
  Johnson Creek, 293
  Montinore, 201
  Mount Baker, 307, 309

Index

Index

Index

Index

About the Author

Corbet Clark, a native of Seattle, has spent ten years reporting on the emergence of the Northwest wine region. He writes a weekly column on Northwest wines for the Tacoma *Morning News Tribune*. He lives in Portland, Oregon.